Lecture Notes in Computer Science 8300

Commenced Publication in 1973
Founding and Former Series Editors:
Gerhard Goos, Juris Hartmanis, and Jan van Leeuwen

Lecture Notes in Computer Science 8300

Commenced Publication in 1973
Founding and Former Series Editors:
Gerhard Goos, Juris Hartmanis, and Jan van Leeuwen

Editorial Board

David Hutchison
  Lancaster University, UK
Takeo Kanade
  Carnegie Mellon University, Pittsburgh, PA, USA
Josef Kittler
  University of Surrey, Guildford, UK
Jon M. Kleinberg
  Cornell University, Ithaca, NY, USA
Alfred Kobsa
  University of California, Irvine, CA, USA
Friedemann Mattern
  ETH Zurich, Switzerland
John C. Mitchell
  Stanford University, CA, USA
Moni Naor
  Weizmann Institute of Science, Rehovot, Israel
Oscar Nierstrasz
  University of Bern, Switzerland
C. Pandu Rangan
  Indian Institute of Technology, Madras, India
Bernhard Steffen
  TU Dortmund University, Germany
Madhu Sudan
  Microsoft Research, Cambridge, MA, USA
Demetri Terzopoulos
  University of California, Los Angeles, CA, USA
Doug Tygar
  University of California, Berkeley, CA, USA
Gerhard Weikum
  Max Planck Institute for Informatics, Saarbruecken, Germany

Guojun Wang Indrakshi Ray Dengguo Feng
Muttukrishnan Rajarajan (Eds.)

Cyberspace Safety and Security

5th International Symposium, CSS 2013
Zhangjiajie, China, November 13-15, 2013
Proceedings

 Springer

Volume Editors

Guojun Wang
Central South University
School of Information Science and Engineering
Changsha, Hunan Province, P.R. China
E-mail: csgjwang@gmail.com

Indrakshi Ray
Colorado State University
Computer Science Department
Fort Collins, CO, USA
E-mail: iray@cs.colostate.edu

Dengguo Feng
Chinese Academy of Sciences
Institute of Software
Beijing, P.R. China
E-mail: fengdg@263.net

Muttukrishnan Rajarajan
City University London
Information Security Group
London, UK
E-mail: r.muttukrishnan@city.ac.uk

ISSN 0302-9743 e-ISSN 1611-3349
ISBN 978-3-319-03583-3 e-ISBN 978-3-319-03584-0
DOI 10.1007/978-3-319-03584-0
Springer Cham Heidelberg New York Dordrecht London

Library of Congress Control Number: 2013953551

CR Subject Classification (1998): K.6.5, D.4.6, C.2, K.4, K.5, E.3

LNCS Sublibrary: SL 4 – Security and Cryptology

Typesetting: Camera-ready by author, data conversion by Scientific Publishing Services, Chennai, India

Printed on acid-free paper

Springer is part of Springer Science+Business Media (www.springer.com)

Message from the CSS 2013 General Chairs

As the General Chairs and on behalf of the Organizing Committee of the 5th International Symposium on Cyberspace Safety and Security (CSS 2013), we would like to express our gratitude to all participants who attend the conference and associated symposiums/workshops in Zhangjiajie, China, during November 13–15, 2013. This famous city is the location of China's first forest park (The Zhangjiajie National Forest Park) and a World Natural Heritage site (Wulingyuan Scenic Area).

The aim of CSS 2013 was to bring together researchers and practitioners working on cyberspace safety and security areas to present and discuss emerging ideas and trends in this highly challenging research field. It attracted many high-quality research papers that highlight the foundational work that strives to push beyond the limits of existing technologies, including experimental efforts, innovative systems, and investigations that identify weaknesses in the existing safety and security services.

CSS 2013 was sponsored by the National Natural Science Foundation of China, Springer, the School of Information Science and Engineering at Central South University, the School of Software at Central South University, and Inder-Science IJCSE; it was organized by Central South University, National University of Defense Technology, Hunan University, and Ji Shou University. CSS 2013 comprised of the main conference and three international symposiums/workshops. The conference program contained 11 keynote speeches shared by the co-located IEEE HPCC 2013, IEEE/IFIP EUC 2013, and CSS 2013 conferences which highlight the latest research trends in various aspects of computer science and technology.

Many individuals contributed to the success of this high-caliber international conference. We would like to express our special appreciation to the Program Chairs Prof. Indrakshi Ray, Prof. Dengguo Feng, and Prof. Muttukrishnan Rajarajan for giving us this opportunity to hold this prestigious conference and for their guidance in the symposium organization. Thanks also to the Workshop Chairs Prof. Jemal H. Abawajy, Prof. Jin Hee Cho, Prof. Yanjiang Yang, and Prof. Yeong Deok Kim for their excellent work in organizing the attractive symposiums/workshops. We thank the Publicity Chairs Prof. Peter Mueller, Prof. Yulei Wu, and Prof. Scott Fowler for their great work on this event. We would like to give our thanks to all the members of the Organizing Committee and Program Committee for their efforts and support.

Finally, we are grateful to the authors for submitting their fine work to CSS 2013 and all the participants for their attendance. Hope you enjoy the conference proceedings!

October 2013

Guojun Wang
Vijay Varadharajan
Gregorio Martinez

Message from the CSS 2013 Program Chairs

On behalf of the Program Committee of the 5th International Symposium on Cyberspace Safety and Security (CSS 2013), we would like to welcome you to the conference proceedings.

The conference focuses on cyberspace safety and security, such as authentication, access control, availability, integrity, privacy, confidentiality, dependability, and sustainability issues of cyberspace. The aim of this conference is to provide a leading-edge forum to foster interaction between researchers and developers in cyberspace safety and security, and to give attendees an opportunity to network with experts in this area.

CSS 2013 was the next event in a series of highly successful international conferences on cyberspace safety and security (CSS), previously held as CSS 2012 (Melbourne, Australia, December 2012), CSS 2011 (Milan, Italy, September, 2011), CSS 2009 (Chengdu, China, August, 2009), and CSS 2008 (Sydney, Australia, December, 2008).

This international conference collected research papers on the above research issues from all over the world. This year we received 105 submissions in response to the call for papers. Each paper was reviewed by at least three experts in the field. After detailed online discussions with among the program chairs and the track chairs, 30 papers were finally accepted, leading to an acceptance ratio of 28.4%.

We feel very proud of the high number of submissions, and it was difficult to select the best papers from all those received, but at the end we defined an amazing conference.

We would like to offer our gratitude to the General Chairs Prof. Guojun Wang, Prof. Vijay Varadharajan, and Prof. Gregorio Martinez for their excellent support and invaluable suggestions for the success of the final program. In particular, we would like to thank all researchers and practitioners who submitted their manuscripts and the Program Committee members and additional reviewers for their tremendous efforts and timely reviews.

We hope all of you enjoy the proceedings of CSS 2013.

October 2013

Indrakshi Ray
Dengguo Feng
Muttukrishnan Rajarajan

Welcome Message from the CSS 2013 Workshop Chairs

Welcome to the proceedings of the 5th International Symposium on Cyberspace Safety and Security (CSS 2013) held in Zhangjiajie, China, during November 13–15, 2013. This year's program consisted of three symposiums/workshops that covered a wide range of research topics on cyberspace safety and security:

(1) The Third International Symposium on Security and Quantum Communications (SQC 2013)
(2) The 2013 International Workshop on Security and Reliability in Transparent Computing (SRTC 2013)
(3) The 2013 International Workshop on Trust, Security and Privacy for Big Data (TrustData 2013)

The aim of these symposiums/workshops is to provide a forum to bring together practitioners and researchers from academia and industry for discussion and presentation of the current research and future directions related to cyberspace safety and security. The themes and topics of these symposiums/workshops are a valuable complement to the overall scope of CSS 2013 and give additional value and interest. We hope that all of the selected papers will have a good impact on future research in the respective field.

We offer our sincere gratitude to the workshop organizers for their hard work in designing the call for papers, assembling the Program Committee, managing the peer-review process for the selection of papers, and planning the workshop program. We are grateful to the workshop Program Committees, external reviewers, session chairs, contributing authors, and attendees. Our special thanks go to the Organizing Committees of CSS 2013 for their strong support, and especially to the Program Chairs Prof. Indrakshi Ray, Prof. Dengguo Feng and Prof. Muttukrishnan Rajarajan for their guidance.

Finally, we hope that you will find the symposium and workshop proceedings interesting and stimulating.

October 2013

Jemal H. Abawajy
Jin-Hee Cho
Yanjiang Yang
Yeong-Deok Kim

CSS 2013 Organizing and Program Committees

General Chairs

Guojun Wang	Central South University, China
Vijay Varadharajan	Macquarie University, Australia
Gregorio Martinez	University of Murcia, Spain

Program Chairs

Indrakshi Ray	Colorado State University, USA
Dengguo Feng	Institute of Software, Chinese Academy of Sciences, China
Muttukrishnan Rajarajan	City University, UK

Workshop Chairs

Jemal H. Abawajy	Deakin University, Australia
Jin-Hee Cho	U.S. Army Research Laboratory, USA
Yanjiang Yang	Institute for Infocomm Research, Singapore
Yeong-Deok Kim	GSE hi-tech CO, Korea

Organizing Chairs

Zhigang Chen	Central South University, China
Zhiying Wang	National University of Defense Technology, China
Keqin Li	Hunan University, China
Bin Hu	Jishou University, China

Publicity Chairs

Peter Mueller	IBM Zurich Research, Switzerland
Yulei Wu	Chinese Academy of Sciences, China
Scott Fowler	Linköping University, Sweden

Publication Chairs

Wang Yang	Central South University, China
Zhe Tang	Central South University, China

Finance Chairs

Guihua Duan   Central South University, China
Jin Zheng   Central South University, China

Local Arrangements Chair

Guomin Cai   Jishou University, China

Program Committee (in alphabetical order)

1. Data and Applications Security

Chairs

Raman Adaikkalavan   Indiana University South Bend, USA
Di Ma   University of Michigan-Dearborn, USA

Members

Lynn Battern   Deakin University, Australia
Sabrina De Capitani di
  Vimercati   Università degli Studi di Milano, Italy
Clemente Galdi   University of Naples Federico II, Italy
Paolo Gasti   New York Institute of Technology, USA
Hongxin Hu   Delaware State University, USA
Ali Ismail Awad   Al Azhar University, Egypt
Sokratis Katsikas   University of Piraeus, Greece
Jihye Kim   Kookmin University, Korea
Haibing Lu   Santa Clara University, USA
Stefano Paraboschi   University of Bergamo, Italy
Kui Ren   State University of New York at Buffalo, USA
Nicolas Sklavos   Technological Educational Institute of Western
                                  Greece, Hellas, Greece
John Solis   Sandia National Labs, USA
Claudio Soriente   ETH Zürich, Switzerland
Vrizlynn Thing   Institute for Infocomm Research, Singapore
Cong Wang   City University of Hong Kong, Hong Kong,
                                  SAR China
Yongdong Wu   Institute for Infocomm Research, Singapore
Qi Xie   Hangzhou Normal University, China
Ping Yang   SUNY at Binghamton, USA
Attila Yavuz   Robert Bosch Research and Technology Center,
                                  USA
Bingsheng Zhang   State University of New York at Buffalo, USA
Yan Zhu   University of Science and Technology Beijing,
                                  China

2. Network and Communications Security

Chairs

Robin Doss	Deakin University, Australia
Yulei Wu	Chinese Academy of Sciences, China

Members

Alexandru Amaricai	Universitatea "Politehnica" din Timisoara, Romania
Manoj Balakrishnan	University of California at San Diego, USA
Saad Bani-Mohammad	Al al-Bayt University, Jordan
Carlo Blundo	University of Salerno, Italy
Roksana Boreli	NICTA, Australia
Christian Callegari	University of Pisa, Italy
Yingying Chen	Stevens Institute of Technology, USA
Robert Deng	Singapore Management University, Singapore
Zhiguo Ding	Newcastle University, UK
Xiaolei Dong	Shanghai Jiao Tong University, China
El-Sayed El-Alfy	King Fahd University of Petroleum and Minerals, Saudi Arabia
Franco Frattolillo	Università del Sannio, Italy
Steven Furnell	University of Plymouth, UK
Wei Gao	Ludong University, China
Debasis Giri	Haldia Institute of Technology, India
Xiangjian He	Univeristy of Technology, Australia
Xinyi Huang	Fujian Normal University, China
Salil Kanhere	University of New South Wales, Australia
Sokratis K. Katsikas	University of Piraeus, Greece
Constantine Katsinis	Drexel University, USA
Dong Seong Kim	University of Canterbury, New Zealand
Shinsaku Kiyomoto	KDDI R&D Laboratories Inc., Japan
Vitaly Klyuev	University of Aizu, Japan
Kenichi Kourai	Kyushu Institute of Technology, Japan
Albert Levi	Sabanci University, Turkey
Chris Mitchell	Royal Holloway, University of London, UK
Selwyn Piramuthu	University of Florida, USA
Matthew Warren	Deakin University, Australia
Yee Wei Law	University of Melbourne, Australia

3. Software and Systems Security

Chairs

Rose Gamble	University of Tulsa, USA
Jianxun Liu	Hunan University of Science and Technology, China

Members

Rafael Accorsi	University of Freiburg, Germany
Gail-Joon Ahn	Arizona State University, USA
Cheng-Kang Chu	Institute for Infocomm Research, Singapore
Chun-I Fan	National Sun Yat-sen University, Taiwan
Dieter Gollmann	Hamburg University of Technology, Germany
Jiankun Hu	UNSW@ADFA, Australia
Audun Josang	University of Oslo, Norway
Muhammad Khurram Khan	King Saud University, Saudi Arabia
Cheng-Chi Lee	Fu Jen Catholic University, Taiwan
Chun-Ta Li	Tainan University of Technology, Taiwan
Xiong Li	Hunan University of Science and Technology, China
Jay Ligatti	University of South Florida, USA
Peng Liu	Pennsylvania State University, USA
Maode Ma	Nanyang Technological University, Singapore
Fabio Martinelli	CNR, Italy
Gerardo Pelosi	Politecnico di Milano, Italy
Damien Sauveron	University of Limoges, France
Juan Tapiador	Universidad Carlos III de Madrid, Spain
Mahesh Tripunitara	University of Waterloo, Canada
Zhi Xu	Palo Alto Networks, USA
Yingjie Yang	The PLA Information Engineering University, China
Tsz Hon Yuen	University of Hong Kong, Hong Kong, SAR China
Xiangfen Zhao	Chinese Academy of Sciences, China

4. Cloud Security

Chairs

Dhiren Patel	NIT Surat, India
Hua Wang	University of Southern Queensland, Australia

Members

Claudio Ardagna	Università degli Studi di Milano, Italy
Karima Boudaoud	Laboratoire I3S - CNRS / University of Nice Sophia Antipolis, France
Marco Casassa-Mont	HP Labs, UK
David Chadwick	University of Kent, UK
Sudip Chakraborty	Valdosta State University, USA
Frederic Cuppens	Enst Bretagne, France
Xiaohong Jiang	Future University Hakodate, Japan
Siuly Kabir	University of Southern Queensland, Australia

Hiroaki Kikuchi	Tokai University, Japan
Shinsaku Kiyomoto	KDDI R&D Labs, Japan
Yi Mu	University of Wollongong, Australia
Nils Müllner	University of Oldenburg, Germany
Udaya Parampalli	University of Melbourne, Australia
Agusti Solanas	Rovira i Virgili University, Spain
Willy Susilo	University of Wollongong, Australia
Lingyu Wang	Concordia University, Canada
Weichao Wang	UNC Charlotte, USA
Yan Wang	Macquarie University, Australia
Ian Welch	Victoria University of Wellington, New Zealand
Xun Yi	Victoria University, Australia
Dana Zhang	Google, USA
Ji Zhang	The University of Southern Queensland, Australia

5. Cyberspace Safety

Chairs

Steven Furnell	Plymouth University, UK
Avinash Srinivasan	George Mason University, USA

Members

Shirley Atkinson	Plymouth University, UK
Simone Fischer-Hübner	Karlstad University, Sweden
Mark Harris	University of South Carolina, USA
Ram Herkanaidu	Kaspersky Lab, UK
Vasilis Katos	Democritus University of Thrace, Greece
Khurram Khan	King Saud University, Saudi Arabia
Costas Lambrinoudakis	University of Piraeus, Greece
Yair Levy	Nova Southeastern University, USA
Herb Mattord	Kennesaw State University, USA
Moussa Ouedraogo	Public Research Centre Henri Tudor, Luxembourg
Malcolm Pattinson	University of Adelaide, Australia
Tonia San Nicolas-Rocca	Colorado State University, USA
Kerry-Lynn Thomson	Nelson Mandela Metropolitan University, South Africa
Johan Van Niekerk	Nelson Mandela Metropolitan University, South Africa
Paul Watters	University of Ballarat, Australia
Ibrahim Zincir	Yasar University, Turkey

Secretariat

Fang Qi   Central South University, China
Tao Peng   Central South University, China

Webmaster

Biao Deng   Central South University, China

SQC 2013 Organizing and Program Committees

General Chairs

Han-Chieh Chao   National Ilan University, I-Lan, Taiwan
Guihua Zeng   Shanghai Jiao Tong University, China

Program Chairs

Howard E. Brandt   U.S. Army Research Laboratory, USA
Ying Guo   Central South University, China

Program Committee (in alphabetical order)

Muhammad Bashir Abdullahi	Federal University of Technology, Minna, Nigeria
Yuri L. Borissov	Bulgarian Academy of Sciences, Sofia, Bulgaria
Wenshan Cui	Qingdao Agricultural University, China
Ying Guo	Central South University, China
Guangqiang He	Shanghai Jiao Tong University, China
Jia Hou	Soochow University, China
Xueqin Jiang	Donghua University, China
Moon-Ho Lee	Chonbuk National University, Korea
Yuan Li	Shanghai Dianji University, China
Wenping Ma	Xidian University, China
Felix Musau	Kenyatta University, Kenya
Dongsun Park	Chonbuk National University, Korea
Jun Peng	Central South University, China
Fang Qi	Institute for Infocomm Research, Singapore
Ronghua Shi	Central South University, China
Wei Song	Liaodong University, China
Bin Wang	Central South University, China
Xiang-Gen Xia	University of Delware, USA
Yang Xiao	Beijing Jiao Tong University, China
Nanrun Zhou	Nanchang University, China
Guihua Zeng	Shanghai Jiao Tong University, China
Congxu Zhu	Central South University, China

Publicity Chairs

Houcine Hassan   Universitat Politecnica de Valencia, Spain
Fangfang Zhou   Central South University, China

Webmaster

Biao Deng   Central South University, China

SRTC 2013 Organizing and Program Committees

General Chairs

Jianer Chen   Central South University, China
Jianxin Wang   Central South University, China
Ju Lu   Intel Corporation, USA

Program Chairs

Jie Wu   Temple University, USA
Gregorio Martinez   University of Murcia, Spain
Guojun Wang   Central South University, China

Publicity Chairs

Scott Fowler   Linköping University, Sweden
Qin Liu   Central South University, China
Carlos Becker Westphall   Federal University of Santa Catarina, Brazil

Program Committee

Jiannong Cao	The Hong Kong Polytechnic University, Hong Kong, SAR China
Jianer Chen	Central South University, China
Jingde Cheng	Saitama University, Japan
Zixue Cheng	The University of Aizu, Japan
Xiangzhong Fang	Shanghai Jiao Tong University, China
Michael Greene	Intel Corporation, USA
Minyi Guo	Shanghai Jiao Tong University, China
Yanxiang He	Wuhan University, China
Imad Jawhar	United Arab Emirates University, UAE
Runhe Huang	Hosei University, Japan
Weijia Jia	City University of Hong Kong, Hong Kong, SAR China
Hai Jin	Huazhong University of Science and Technology, China
Qun Jin	Waseda University, Japan
Jie Li	University of Tsukuba, Japan
Kenli Li	Hunan University, China

Keqin Li	State University of New York at New Paltz, USA
Keqiu Li	Dalian University of Technology, China
Qin Liu	Central South University, China
Wang Liu	Central South University, China
Ju Lu	Intel Corporation, USA
Jianhua Ma	Hosei University, Japan
Gregorio Martinez	University of Murcia, Spain
Geyong Min	University of Bradford, UK
Ken Nguyen	Clayton State University, USA
Yi Pan	Georgia State University, USA
Indrakshi Ray	Colorado State University, USA
Hong Shen	The University of Adelaide, Australia
Eunjee Song	Baylor University, USA
Avinash Srinivasan	George Mason University, USA
Ivan Stojmenovic	University of Ottawa, Canada
Guojun Wang	Central South University, China
Haodong Wang	Cleveland State University, USA
Huaimin Wang	National University of Defense Technology, China
Jianxin Wang	Central South University, China
Youwei Wang	Aspire Company, China
Jie Wu	Temple University, USA
Min Wu	Central South University, China
Ming Wu	Intel Corporation, USA
Xiaofei Xing	Guangzhou University, China
Neal Xiong	Colorado Technical University, USA
Dong Xiang	Tsinghua University, China
Yang Xiang	Deakin University, Australia
Yonghua Xiong	Central South University, China
Chengzhong Xu	Wayne State University, USA
Laurence T. Yang	St. Francis Xavier University, Canada
Shuhui (Grace) Yang	Purdue University Calumet, USA
Wang Yang	Central South University, China
Yu Shui	Deakin University, Australia
Yunquan Zhang	Institute of Software, Chinese Academy of Sciences, China
Wanlei Zhou	Deakin University, Australia
Xingshe Zhou	Northwestern Polytechnical University, China
Yuezhi Zhou	Tsinghua University, China
Wei Zhong	University of South Carolina Upstate, USA

Webmaster

Biao Deng	Central South University, China

TrustData 2013 Organizing and Program Committees

General Chairs

Guojun Wang	Central South University, China
Jin-Hee Cho	U.S. Army Research Laboratory, USA
Lizhe Wang	Chinese Academy of Sciences, China

Program Chairs

Qin Liu	Central South University, China
Muhammad Bashir Abdullahi	Federal University of Technology, Minna, Nigeria
Yongming Xie	Guangzhou University, China

Program Committee (in alphabetical order)

Muhammad Bashir Abdullahi	Federal University of Technology, Minna, Nigeria
Maurizio Atzori	University of Cagliari, Italy
Fenye Bao	LinkedIn Corporation, USA
Pascal Bouvry	University of Luxembourg, Luxembourg
Kevin Chan	US Army Research Laboratory, USA
You Chen	Vanderbilt University, USA
Gulustan Dogan	City University of New York, USA
Sara Foresti	Università degli Studi di Milano, Italy
Horacio Gonzalez-Velez	National College of Ireland, Ireland
Yu Hua	Huazhong University of Science and Technology, China
Young-Sik Jeong	Dongguk University, Republic of Korea
Rajaraman Kanagasabai	Institute for Infocomm Research, Singapore
Samee Khan	NDSU, USA
Ryan Ko	University of Waikato, New Zealand
Joanna Kolodziej	Cracow University of Technology, Poland
Qin Liu	Central South University, China
Abhishek Parakh	University of Nebraska Omaha, USA
Rajiv Ranjan	CSIRO, Australia
Yacine Rebahi	Fraunhofer Fokus, Germany

.

Table of Contents

Software and Systems Security

Cloud Security and Cyberspace Safety

Workshop Papers

Security and Quantum Communications

Security and Reliability in Transparent Computing

Trust, Security and Privacy for Big Data

A Crawler Guard
for Quickly Blocking Unauthorized Web Robot

Jan-Min Chen

The Dept. of Information Management,
Yu Da University of Science and Technology, Miaoli 36143, Taiwan
ydjames@ydu.edu.tw

Abstract. Nowadays Web robots can be used to perform a number of useful navigational goals, such as statistical analysis, link check, and resource collection. On one hand, Web crawler is a particular group of users whose traverse should not make part of regular analysis. Such disturbance affects site decision making in every possible way: marketing campaigns, site re-structuring, site personalization or server balancing, just to name a few. Therefore, it is necessary to correctly detect various robots as soon as possible so as to let the robots to be used under the security policy. In this paper, we come up with a crawler guard to detect and block unauthorized robots under the security policy. It can immediately differentiate various robots based on their functions (navigational goals) to ensure that only the welcome robots which obey the security policy are allowed to view the protected Web pages. Our experiment focuses on how the crawler guard could identify precisely the viewing goal of the robots under certain limits of Web page hits. The experimental results show that the request count is smaller than 8 while the accuracy of detection is 100%.

Keywords: Web Crawler, Web Robot, Navigational Behavior.

1   Introduction

A Web robot is a program with automated browsing. It is an agent that traverses the Web's hypertext structure by retrieving a document, and recursively retrieving all documents that are referenced without any significant human involvement. Robots can be used to perform a number of useful tasks, such as statistical analysis, maintenance of the hypertext structure, implementation of Web mirroring and resource discover. Otherwise the use of robots comes at a price, especially when they are operated remotely on the Internet. Robots require considerable bandwidth and place extra demand on servers as well, so they may affect the navigation of normal customers. Moreover, unauthorized robots can severely falsify the browsing behavior analysis of the customer in many E-commerce Web sites or induce information disclosure. For example, Web robot can inflate the clicking rate on the advertisement banner to misuse a payment scheme. Some robots ignore the Robot Exclusion Protocol [20], a standard that allows Web site administrators to specify their rules of operation via the robots.txt

G. Wang et al. (Eds.): CSS 2013, LNCS 8300, pp. 1–13, 2013.
© Springer International Publishing Switzerland 2013

file, and open up privacy and security issues. Hence, in order to avoid damages and economic losses, it is important to identify Web robots. From the defense's point of view, it is necessary to detect all unauthorized Web robots and take proper measures to redirect or block them. Moreover, the safeguarded scheme should maintain the system's functionality and ease of use for normal visitors. Unfortunately, most of the common methods are not able to satisfy this requirement.

Today, the most widely used methods, such as checking the [IP address] and [user agent] fields in logfile entries, checking of requests for robots.txt and using hidden link traps (embedding of HTML code that looks like a link, but indeed is invisible for a real user), for robot detection [10-12]. Another enhanced techniques based on statistics are used to discover session attributes for characterizing Web crawler behavior [1-4, 13-15]. These enhanced methods are used to find implicate log characteristics from Web access logs for Web navigation behavior analysis and then identify some kinds of robots based on the calculated attribute values.

Our study differs and complements from the results previously published that our techniques are much simpler to implement yet effective in producing accurate detection for incoming request in real time. It has some differences from these methods in several aspects. First, the simple methods are just suitable for differentiating robot from human visits. However they can't further identify various robots, while our scheme, named crawler guard can identify various robots based on their function. Second, some other methods are too complex to distinguish robots in real time, while our work can redirect all suspected robot visits to the classifier and then differentiate them regarding the navigation characteristics of various goals. The load of data preprocessing can be deeply lowered as only suspected traffic is redirected. Thus the crawler guard can quickly distinguish various specific Web robots while the visits are still in progress. Third, various robots can be correctly differentiated so as to ensure both the functionality and ease of use of a protected Website. Instead of irrationally blocking, we can ensure that robots can be normally used according to security policy.

The main contributions of this paper are summarized below.

1. Our scheme can redirect all suspected robots' traffic to the Classifier through the ingenious filter page so speediness of detection is independent on the objects in a Web page and suitable for all Web sites.
2. Our scheme can make the load of pre-processing session deeply lower so various specific Web robots can be quickly distinguished while the crawler visit is still in progress.
3. Our robot identification algorithm can correctly differentiate various robots based on functions so we can ensure that robot can be normally used under the security policy, and both the functionality and ease of use of a protected Web site will not be affected. Thus our approach successfully strikes a balance between security functionality and ease of use for users.

The rest of the paper is organized as the following: The next section gives an overview on the related work. Section 3 describes the differences between Web robot and Web browser in navigation behavior and also shows the methods for discovering various Web robots. In Section 4, we provide a detailed overview of the crawler guard. Section 5 discusses the experimental results on the accuracy and speediness of identifying various robots. Finally, we present our conclusion in Section 6.

2   The Technologies for Web Robot Detection

Today's most widely used technologies for Web robot detection can be divided into four major categories: simple methods, traps, Web navigation behavior analysis and navigational pattern modeling [1, 4]. The simple methods to detect robots are by matching the IP address of a Web client against those of known Web robots. Sun et al. designed a BotSeer to provide an efficient tool for researchers, Webmasters and developers to study Web robot related issues and design Web sites. It can be used to assist the regulation and development of Web robots [12]. Unfortunately, these techniques are time-consuming. Often time, they only discover robots that are already well-known. Moreover the "User-Agent" HTTP request header is easily forged. On one hand, Kadakia presents many methods to detect robots such as hidden field trap and robot.txt honeypot trap [6]. The methods' function is limited because it can only tell human form robots. Park et al. developed simple yet effective algorithms to detect human users and test the effectiveness of these algorithms on live data by implementing the CoDeeN network, and robot related abuse complaints which had dropped by a factor of ten [10]. Tan et al. investigated the navigational pattern of Web robots and applied a machine learning techniques to exclude robot traces from the Web access log of a Web site [1]. They noted that the navigational pattern of the Web crawlers is different from the human users, and these patterns can be used to construct the features by a machine-learning algorithm. Maria et al. focus on the analysis of some commercial robots with the objective of characterizing their behaviors and their access patterns. The outcomes of this temporal analysis could be very useful for Web site administrators to estimate and predict the load of their sites and develop regulation policies aimed at improving site availability and performance [21]. Shinil et al. expresses the behavior of interactive users and various Web robots in terms of a sequence of request types [22]. The approach can work well on detection of many Web robots, such as image crawlers, email collectors and link checkers. However, above-mentioned algorithms are not adequate for real-time traffic analysis since they require a relatively large number of requests for accurate detection. Andoena Balla et al. present a methodology for detecting Web crawlers in real time. They use decision trees to classify requests in real time, as originating from a crawler or human, while their session is ongoing. To identify the most important features to differentiate humans from crawlers, they used machine-learning techniques. The high accuracy, with which their system detects crawler IP addresses while a session is ongoing, proves the effectiveness of our proposed methodology [23]. However the method is only capable of differentiating humans from crawlers. It cannot be used to detect various Web robots.

On the other hand, hiding the Web pages having flaws from malicious crawler is another scheme to protect Web site. Kandula et al. used CAPTCHA tests to optimize the test serving strategy to produce better good put during DDoS attacks [16]. Although CAPTCHA tests are generally regarded as a highly effective mechanism to block robots, they are impractical if we consider the user-friendly problem, since human users do not want to solve quiz every time they access a Web page. Ollmann examined techniques which are capable of defending an application against automated attack tools; providing advice on their particular strength and weakness and proposing solutions capable of stopping the next generation of automated attack tools [11]. NAKAO et al. observed network behaviors and malware behaviors from darknet and honeypots, and strictly analyze to produce a set of profiles containing malware characteristics. To this end, inter-relationship between above two types of profiles is practically discussed and studied so that frequently observed malwares behaviors can be finally identified in view of scan-malware chain [17]. KIM et al. proposed a hybrid intrusion forecasting system framework for an early warning system. The proposed system utilizes three types of forecasting methods: time-series analysis, probabilistic modeling, and data mining method. By combining these methods, it is possible to take advantage of the forecasting technique of each while overcoming their drawbacks [18]. DU et al. first proposed a traffic decomposition method, which decomposes the traffic into three components: the trend component, the autoregressive (AR) component, and the noise component. A traffic volume anomaly is detected when the AR component is outside the prediction band for multiple links simultaneously. Then, the anomaly is traced by using the projection of the detection result matrices for the observed links which are selected by a shortest-path-first algorithm [19].

3   Discovery of Web Robot

If we hope to increase security of a Web site and keep ease of use for normal visitors, we should be capable of detecting unauthorized Web robots and take proper measures to redirect or block them. To achieve the aims, at first we should analyze the navigational patterns for various types of Web robots and show that these patterns are quite different from those for human users.

There are some obstacles on the way that makes the task of blocking Web robot a lot more difficult than it already is. Some Web robots may be used to perform a number of useful tasks, such as statistical analysis, maintenance of the hypertext structure, implementation of Web mirroring and resource discover. For example some businesses run solely on search engine rankings. Blocking these robots will apparently lose their services. Furthermore, most of the Web sites are designed to let human users easily surf, and none of techniques should affect the usability of a Web site while they are used to block Web robot. Thus we need to propose an advanced proposal to accurately distinguish various robots, that is, any proposal preformed for stopping robot should be viable to accurately block some specific types of robots according to the security policy, and they must not affect original functionality and ease of use of protected Web site.

Human traverses various Web sites through a Web browser. To achieve the goal mentioned above, we try to find some features for quickly distinguishing between Web browser and robot, and further, we hope to eliminate the specific Web robot threat according to the security policy. The target can be achieved in two phases. First, we need to find a way to quickly differentiate Web browser between robots. Second, we should find clues of further differentiating various robots. Somewhat surprisingly, there were very little previous researches regarding the problem of distinguishing various Web robots. Most previous work we know about is in the context of identifying human from robots [1-4].

We suppose that the behavior of the Web browser or the robot is relevant to its functionality. The Web browser concerns itself with the look of a Web page so it must retrieve all embedded objects in a Web page. The Web robot is good at retrieving complete information on a Web site so it is a leading concern to continue to traverse all hyperlink of a Web page. Likewise we reason that the visitor having a particular functionality may have a specific behavior pattern. For verifying above assumption, we try to select and classify the visitors based on their function, and let them surf some experimental Web sites to find some helpful clues from Web access logs.

3.1   The Differences between Web Robot and Browser in Navigation Behavior

As a Web robot is a program with automated browsing to assist in speeding up resource discovery, we can assume that the navigation behavior of the Web robot may be distinct from human users. A Web robot starts from a seed page and then starts its crawling process picking a URL from the queue, downloading its associated page by sending HTTP request to the target server and analyzing it for obtaining new links which are then added to the queue, until a sufficient number of pages are identified, no URLs left in queue, a specified depth level is reached or some higher level objective is reached.

A Web robot can also treat embedded objects, such as image files and music files, according to various navigational goals in addition. For example some search engines serving as entry points to Web pages strive for coverage that is as broad as possible so they will add the URLs of these objects to the queue, and some robots implementing Web mirroring should maintain the look and feel of the page mirrored exactly so they will retrieve all embedded objects. If the navigational goal of the robot is to collect a specific kind of file, there is only this type of embedded object in all request URLs. Although these robots may have different functions, we find that the requests of the embedded objects are not sent at once for all robots when we analyze the navigational logs of these robots. Therefore we can assume that there are some successive requests for the Web page type (such as htm, asp, php, etc) in the Web access log, which exactly represents the of the navigation behavior of Web robot.

Human traverses various Web sites through a Web browser. Web browsers submit information to Web servers as well as fetch Web pages from them by using HTTP. On the other hand, the browser will parse and format the response Web page to display and interact with embedded objects such as images, videos, music and games located on a Web page. For showing complete appearance, if there are any embedded objects, the browser will automatically and successively perform HTTP requests until these objects have been retrieved. Therefore one request from the browser may generate many records in the Web access log. There is no specific arrangement of the files type in URL fields of these records because the embedded objects are placed according to appearance, and do not follow any specific rules. By analyzing Web access log, we also find that Web browsers are the most-commonly-used type of HTTP user agent.

We can also illustrate the difference between Web robot and browser from their respective function. Web robot is a software program which automatically locates and retrieves information on the Internet so it should traverse all hyperlink structures of each Web site to achieve the goal. A Web browser is another software application which enables a user to display and interact with text, images, videos, music, games and other information typically located on a Web page at a Website. In terms of the completeness of a Web site, the Web robot concern, but not in terms of the appearance of each Web page. Contrary to Web robot, the Web browser is good at presenting any kind of content that can be part of a Web page. If there are any embedded objects in a Web page, the browser will automatically and successively sent requests at once until all of them have been retrieved. On the contrary, a Web robot will treat embedded objects according to various purposes of visit so the requests of the embedded objects are not sent at once.

3.2   Quickly Telling Human from Web Robots

The observations of the navigation behavior of human user and Web robot are shown as follows. First, the visibility of human user is different from the robot. Human user, for example, must only follow visible links, whereas robot usually automatically traverses all the links in a page. Second, human user surfs Web site by a mouse or keyboard, whereas robot has no activity of mouse or keyboard. Third, human user can interact with a Web page, whereas robots can't do it. According to above descriptions, we can design a spider trap to tell human from robots.

A spider trap is a method of identifying crawlers as they browse your site and a way of determining if a crawler is good or bad by monitoring where it browses. It is a set of Web pages that may intentionally or unintentionally be used to cause a Web crawler or search robot to make an infinite number of requests or cause a poorly constructed crawler to crash [5]. The basic idea of spider trap is to take advantage of the scanners lack of ability to differentiate real links from set traps [6]. A robot renders a Web page and analyzes just code so it misses the visual output of the code. For example, a null href link (<a href="trap.php"/>) can be visited by robot but can't be seen by human. According to above-mentioned observations of the navigation about human or robots, a spider trap named hidden link has been design to tell human from robots. The trap can be embedded in front-end Web pages to snare all Web robots [8-9].

We propose an innovative scheme, which named crawler guard, for discovering all crawling traffic and differentiating it according to the different visit behaviors. The processes of the crawler guard are portioned out two phases. Phase 1 is responsible for accurately tell apart human users and Web crawler as quickly as possible. All robots will be caught in Phase 1 and then be redirect to phase 2 for classification based on their function. In Figure 1, the diagram of crawler guard's phase 1 and how it works is described in detail. In phase 1, the crawler guard comprises a trap hunter, hooks and monitors. The trap hunter can automatically plant proper hooks on front-end Web pages. The hooks are embedded in front-end Web pages via hidden link and linked to the monitor on server-side Web page. The monitor is capable of analyzing the HTTP request headers to get necessary visit information of the trapped visitors from hooks and then and finally saved to the respective logfiles in the Logger. On all occasions, the crawler guard can accurately tell apart human users and Web crawler as quickly as possible in phase 1.

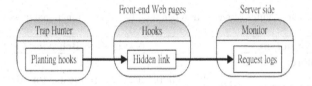

Fig. 1. The diagram of telling human from robots Pass

3.3   Quickly Differentiating Various Robots

Some robots may be used to perform a number of useful tasks, such as statistical analysis and resource discover so blocking these robots will apparently lose their services. On the other hand, some robots' navigation logs may disturb site decision making in every possible way, such as marketing campaigns, site re-structuring and server balancing. Therefore a better scheme for blocking robot will be capable of identifying the robots having respective functions, and then allow or deny them according to the real needs. Moreover it must not affect original functionality and ease of use of the protected Web site.

Robots crawl a site and operate differently depending on the task a robot is programmed to do. Therefore, robots traversing a site with the same information will exhibit similar navigational patterns. Doran et al. had proposed a novel functional classification scheme to understand and analyze Web robot traffic. The classification scheme can be used to analyze Web server access logs for providing insights into the robot traffic based on their functionality [7]. These insights could guide the separation of well-behaved robots from ill-behaved ones but it is difficult to separate them in real time because of needing to preprocess a large amount of visit traffic in the Web access log file before going on analysis. Thus the ill-behaved robot could not be immediately blocked from accessing the server. We aim not to partition the robot traffic into classes according to the functions of the robots but also to isolate unauthorized robot as quickly as possible. That is to say, we need to present a methodology for detecting Web crawlers in real time. First we need to find a most obvious feature for each functional classification. After doing some numerical of experiments for various robots, we had gotten the obvious feature for some functional classification. The result is shown in table 1. The left side shows the function of the robot and the right side presents its obvious visit behavior feature hidden in the Web access log. For example, if a robot is found to send a http request to retrieve Cascading Style Sheets (CSS) embedded in a Web page, we can reason that the robot should be capable of duplicating a Web site. If a robot is found to send a query string having parameters, the robot should be an injection attack tools.

A special Web page, named Filter page, is designed meticulously to supply various embedded objects in the Web page for differentiating robot. The robot having some specific function must retrieve theses embedded objects by sending requests to them. While the robots retrieve one object, they will be trapped to its respective Web page to analyze the visit information. And then the information is finally saved to the

Table 1. The features of navigation behavior based on   functional classification

Function	Navigation Behavior Feature
E: Explore for a site structure	There are no requests for the embedded objects in visit log.
S: Search engine	
K: Search for keywords	
M: Mirror a Web site	There is a request for Cascading Style Sheets (**CSS**) in visit log.
D: Download files	There are some requests for Web pages and some **specific embedded objects** such as image type or music type.
I: Injection attack tools	The query string **has parameters**.

respective logfiles. The processes of differentiating various robots are shown in Figure 2. Here we should emphasize that our scheme is adequate for real-time detection of the robot in comparison with the solutions had been proposed. The existing methods need to preprocess a large amount of visit traffic in the Web access log file before going on analysis so it is difficult to detect robot in real time [1-7]. In contrast, our scheme designs some traps according to the obvious feature of each type of robot to redirect all suspected robots' traffic. The work of grouping together the Web log entries into a session log according to their IP address and agent fields while date is within a threshold period is unnecessary. Therefore the scheme can be used to quickly identify various robots.

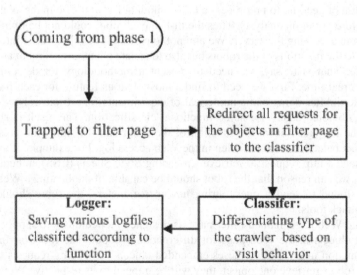

Fig. 2. The flowchart of differentiating crawler type based on visit behavior

4 System Implementation

To block unauthorized robot in real time, we design a trapped system named crawler guard. The system is viable to differentiate robots according to the obvious features of crawling traffics. The diagram of the crawler guard is shown in figure 3. The process of the crawler guard can be divided into three phases. The Phase 1 is responsible for accurately telling apart human users and Web robot. All robots can be trapped in Phase 1 and then be redirect to phase 2 to further differentiate them. In phase 2, the Filter is a particular Web page designed meticulously to supply various embedded objects to trap robots. While the robot retrieves one object, they will be trapped to its respective Web page named as Classifier_type (e.g. Classifier_M, Classifier_D, Classifier_I. The types were shown in Table 2). Table 3 summarizes the key steps of our robot identification algorithm. The first step, named sessionizing, is to combine all single requests in logfile entries into user sessions. Each HTTP-request is represented by a single line in the logfile. Each logfile entry consists of the following fields: [IP address] [date] [request] [status] [referrer] [agent]. Among them, [IP address] as client IP address, [date] as date and time of the request, [request] as HTTP-request containing the request method, the URL of the requested resource (page), and the desired HTTP-protocol, [status] as 3-digit status code returned by the server, [referrer] as URL of the referencing page and [agent] as name of the client agent (e.g., " Mozilla/4.0 + (compatible;+MSIE7.0; + windows+NT+5.1; + .NET+CLR+2.0.50727)"). For each http request, we can differentiate it according to the obvious feature of visit behavior. After phase 1 and phase 2, the result will be saved in the Logger. Finally, the Blocker can remove unauthorized robots' HTTP requests according to the security policies kept in the Policy holder in phase 3.

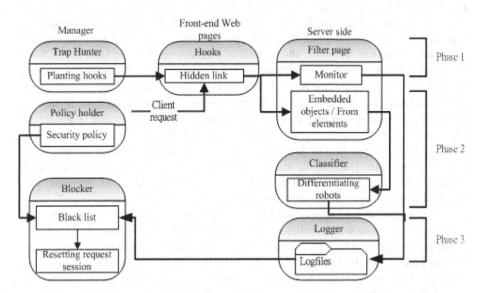

Fig. 3. The diagram of crawler guard

Table 3. The robot identification algorithm

```
    for each RequestLog Ri do
        if (containsCSS(Ri) then
            add Ri_ip to robot_M[i ]
        else if ( containsSpecificObject(Ri) then
            add Ri_ip to robot_D[i ]
        else if ( containsParameter (Ri) then
            add Ri_ip to robot_I[i ]
    end;
```

5   Experimental Evaluation

We use an experimental Web site as a case study to evaluate the accuracy of the obtained classification models and their ability for discovering various Web robots. To confirm the robots' function, we pick some robots having various functions and let them crawl on the experimental Web sites. The functions of each robot can be verified via the crawling result and summarized in table 4. The vertical columns list the robot name and the horizontal rows, the function. The functions having been previously described in table 2 are presented with a capital letter for easy identification. If a robot has one function, the intersection is marked with "*" in the field of Function in Table 4. For example, the advanced robot named BlackWindow is capable of exploring (E) and mirroring (M) a Web site on local host according to background information so the intersections of the second row and E, M columns are labeled with "*". In order to verify the accuracy and speediness of the crawler guard, we use some Web browsers and the robots having been listed in table 4 as client, and implement the crawler guard on the experimental Web site. Each client has different source IP address and launches http requests to the experimental Web site at the same time. In the logfile of the Logger, each entry consists of six fields: Phase number, Request number, IP, User agent, Visit Time and URL. Among them, the Phase number means the record comes from which phase of the crawler guard; the Request number is the line number of the session which includes all requests for the objects in the Filter page. We can compare the IP field in the Logfile with the source IP address of each client to get the information of detection. For example, if the source IP address of the BlackWindow was shown in the Logfile_M, the intersection of M column and BlackWindow row need to be labeled with "*" in the field of the Logfile in Table 4.   Thus we can compare data in the field of Logfile with the field of Function in Table 4 to verify the accuracy of detection. The results obtained from the comparison are shown in the field of Accuracy.

In the logfile of the Logger, there is a Request number field to present the line number of the session which includes all requests for the objects in the Filter page. For example, if the request for CSS object is found in fifth line of a session log, the Request number field is 5 in the Logfile_M. Thus we can reason that using only 5 requests to identify the robot. According to the experimental results, we find various robots may need different Request number because of structure of Web page or robot's program.

Table 4. The accuracy of identifying robot for crawler guard

Robot Name	Type	E	S	K	M	D	I	Accuracy (%)
Teleport Pro	Function	※	※	※	※	※		100%
	Logfile	※	※	※	※	※		
BlackWindow	Function	※			※			100%
	Logfile	※			※			
Win Web Crawler	Function	※	※			※		100%
	Logfile	※	※			※		
Visual Web Spider	Function	※	※			※		100%
	Logfile	※	※			※		
JOC Web Spider	Function	※		※	※			100%
	Logfile	※		※	※			
Gyxi's Image Spider	Function	※			※			100%
	Logfile	※			※			
DRK Spider	Function	※						100%
	Logfile	※						
Acunetix Web Vulerability Scanner	Function	※					※	100%
	Logfile	※					※	
HDSI 2005	Function	※					※	100%
	Logfile	※					※	

Therefore we use minimum Request number and average Request number to present speediness in Table 5.

All robots must be immediately trapped into the hidden link located in first line of each Web page by the Trap Hunter so they can be distinguished from all visit traffic. The prediction is verified through the first row in table 5. In addition to all of the above, others are gotten in phase 2, that is, by navigation patterns. In phase 1, the request number is dependent on the number of embedded objects in Web page so the value of request number is different to each Web site. Whereas, the request number is independent on Web page since we use the ingenious Filter page as identical Web page for visiting. The result is just dependent on robot's program in phase 2. Therefore, our

Table 5. The speediness of identifying robot for crawler guard

Type	Phase #	Min. Request #	Avg. Request #
E	1	2	5
S	2	3	3
K	2	5	7
M	2	5	6
D	2	3	3
I	2	1	1

scheme is suitable for all Web sites. Here the method was tested in real time with the help of an emulator, using only a small number of requests. In Table 5, the experimental results show that the Request count is smaller than 8 while the accuracy of detection is 100%. The results demonstrate the effectiveness and applicability of our approach.

6   Conclusions

Web robots can be used to perform a number of useful navigational goals but unauthorized robot may severely falsify the browsing behavior analysis or induce information disclosure. Therefore it is a necessary task to ensure the robots being legitimately used according to security policy. To achieve the aim, a real-time scheme to detect various robots is a critical work. In this paper, we come up with a prototype, named crawler guard, to detect and remove Web robot threats according to security policy. Crawler guard is much simpler to implement yet effective in producing accurate results for incoming request at real time. It can immediately differentiate various robots based on their navigational goals to ensure that only the authorized robots obeying security policy are allowed to visit the protected Web site. Our experimental results show that the crawler guard is really viable to remove unauthorized Web robots at once. Its speediness is better than other methods adopting log analysis and feature statistic. Moreover, our scheme is independent on specific traffic models or behavior characteristics, which may need to change with more sophisticated robots.

References

[1] Tan, P.-N., Kumar, V.: Discovery of Web robot sessions based on their navigational patterns. Data Mining and Knowledge Discovery 6(1), 9–35 (2002)
[2] Guo, W., Ju, S., Gu, Y.: Web robot Detection Techniques Based on Statistics of their Requested URL Resources. In: Proceedings of the Ninth International Conference on Computer Supported Cooperative Work in Design, vol. 1, pp. 302–306 (2005)
[3] Dikaiakos, M.D., Stassopoulou, A., Papageorgiou, L.: An Investigation of WWW Crawler behavior: Characterization and Metrics. Computer Communications 28(8), 880–897 (2005)

[4] Bomhardt, C., Gaul, W., Schmidt-Thieme, L.: Web Robot Detection - Preprocessing Web Log files for Robot detection. New Developments in Classification and Data Analysis, 113–124 (2006)

[5] Spider_trap, http://en.wikipedia.org/wiki/Spider_trap

[6] Kadakia, Y.: Automated Attack Prevention, http://www.acunetix.com/vulnerability-scanner/yashkadakia.pdf

[7] Doran, D., Gokhale, S.S.: Discovering New Trends in Web Robot Traffic Through Functional Classification. In: Seventh IEEE International Symposium Network Computing and Applications, pp. 275–278 (2008)

[8] Benedikt, M., Freire, J., Godefroid, P.: VeriWeb: Automatically Testing Dynamic Web Sites. In: Proceedings of the 11th International Conference on the World Wide Web (2002)

[9] Raghavan, S., Garcia-Molina, H.: Crawling the hidden Web. In: Proceedings of the 27th VLDB Conference, pp. 129–138 (2001)

[10] Park, K., Pai, V.S., Lee, K.W., Calo, S.B.: Securing Web Service by Automatic Robot Detection. In: Proceedings of the 2006 USENIX Annual Technical Conference (2006)

[11] Ollmann, G.: Stopping Automated Attack Tools, http://www.ngssoftware.com/papers/

[12] Sun, Y., Councill, I.G., Lee Giles, C.: BotSeer: An automated information system for analyzing Web robots. In: Proceedings of the Eighth International Conference on Web Engineering, pp. 108–114 (2008)

[13] Geens, N., Huysmans, J., Vanthienen, J.: A Probabilistic Reasoning Approach for Discovering Web Crawler Sessions. In: Advances in Data Mining 2013. LNCS, vol. 4065 (2006)

[14] Dikaiakos, M.D., Stassopoulou, A.: Web robot detection: A probabilistic reasoning approach. Computer Networks 53(3), 265–278 (2009)

[15] Dikaiakos, M.D., Stassopoulou, A., Papageorgiou, L.: Characterizing Crawler Behavior from Web Server Access Logs. In: Bauknecht, K., Tjoa, A.M., Quirchmayr, G. (eds.) EC-Web 2003. LNCS, vol. 2738, pp. 369–378. Springer, Heidelberg (2003)

[16] Kandula, S., Katabi, D., Jacob, M., Berger, A.: Botz-4-sale, Surviving organized ddos attacks that mimic flash crowds. In: Proceedings of the 2nd Symposium on Networked Systems Design and Implementation (2005)

[17] Nakao, K., Inoue, D., Eto, M., Yoshioka, K.: IEICE Transactions on Information and Systems E92-D(5), 787–798 (2009)

[18] Kim, S., Shin, S.-J., Kim, H., Kwon, K.H., Han, Y.: Hybrid Intrusion Forecasting Framework for Early Warning System. IEICE Transactions on Information and Systems E91-D(5), 1234–1241 (2008)

[19] Du, P., Abe, S., Ji, Y., Sato, S., Ishiguro, M.: A Traffic Decomposition and Prediction Method for Detecting and Tracing Network-Wide Anomalies. IEICE Transactions on Information and Systems E92-D(5), 929–936 (2009)

[20] Koster, M.: A method for Web Robots control. Network Working Group - Internet Draft (1996)

[21] Calzarossa, M.C., Massari, L.: Characterization of crawling activities of commercial Web robots. LNEE. Springer (2012)

[22] Kwon, S., Kim, Y.-G., Cha, S.: Web robot detection based on pattern-matching technique. Journal of Information Science 38(2), 118–126 (2012)

[23] Balla, A., Stassopoulou, A., Dikaiakos, M.D.: Real-time Web Crawler Detection. In: 18th International Conference on Telecommunications, pp. 428–432 (2011)

Privacy Preserving for Location-Based Services Using Location Transformation

Tao Peng, Qin Liu, and Guojun Wang*

School of Information Science and Engineering
Central South University
Changsha, Hunan Province, P.R. China, 410083

Abstract. With the increasing popularity of mobile communication devices loaded with positioning capabilities (e.g.,GPS), there is growing demand for enjoying location-based services (LBSs). An important problem in LBSs is the disclosure of a user's real location while interacting with the location service provider (LSP). To address this issue, existing solutions generally introduce a trusted *Anonymizer* between the users and the LSP. But the introduction of an Anonymizer actually transfers the security risks from the LSP to the Anonymizer. Once the Anonymizer is compromised, it may put the user information in jeopardy. In this paper, we propose an enhanced location privacy preserving (ELPP) scheme for the LBS environment. Our scheme employs an entity, termed Function Generator, to distribute the spatial transformation parameters periodically, with which the users and the LSP can performs the mutual transformation between a real location and a pseudo location. Without the transforming parameters, the Anonymizer cannot have any knowledge about a user's real location. The main merits of our scheme include (1) no fully trusted entities are required; (2) each user can obtain accurate POIs, while preserving location privacy.

Keywords: location-based service, location privacy, K-anonymity.

1 Introduction

With the proliferation of mobile communication devices loaded with positioning capabilities (e.g., GPS), location-based services (LBSs) have been gaining increasingly popularity in recent years [1] [2]. With the versatility and full-featured features, LBSs are facilitating users' daily lives, by, for instance, finding the nearest restaurant with favorite taste, gaining coupons from nearby market, and getting tourist information and route guidance in trips, etc.

However, users must provide their real locations to the location service provider (LSP) before enjoying LBSs, which poses a serious threat to their privacy. Let us consider the following scenario: a user Bob uses his GPS enabled mobile phone to issue a k-nearest neighbor (kNN) query to a LSP (e.g., Google Maps) to find the top-2 nearest hospitals. Since the LSP is potentially untrustworthy, an

---

* Corresponding author.

G. Wang et al. (Eds.): CSS 2013, LNCS 8300, pp. 14–28, 2013.
© Springer International Publishing Switzerland 2013

Fig. 1. Framework for $K - anonymity$ location privacy. kNN stands for the *k-nearest neighbor query.*

adversary who has compromised the LSP can obtain Bob's real identity, location, queries, and may deduce other sensitive information about Bob, such as his home location, health condition, and even lifestyle habit, political/religious affiliation etc. Despite the benefits provided by LBSs, the privacy threats of revealing a user's personal information through his location have become a key problem to inhibit user adoption. Ensuring location privacy, i.e., protecting user location information, is paramount to the success of LBSs. Over the past years, many promising approaches have been proposed concerning preserving location privacy. Generally, they can be classified into two main types [3]: Trusted Third Parties (TTP)-free schemes and TTP-based schemes. In TTP-free schemes, users communicate with the LSP directly. In order to protect the real location information from the untrusted LSP, users add noises to locations (e.g., enlarge user's location or generate multiple decoys at different locations), and send the "fake" ones to the LSP [4]. However, more noises in the query, more redundant results will be returned from the LSP, and a higher communication cost will be incurred on the users.

In TTP-based schemes, a trusted entity, called the *Anonymizer*, is introduced into the system [5] [6] acting as an intermediate tier between the users and the LSP. To guarantee the location privacy, most existing solutions adopt the location K-anonymity principle [7] [8]: a mobile user satisfies location K-anonymity if the location information sent to the LSP is indistinguishable from at least K-1 other users. Therefore, the fundamental idea behind K-anonymity is to replace the real location of the user by a cloaking area in which at least K users are located.

In Fig. 1, the users send their kNN queries to the Anonymizer, which is responsible for removing the user ID and constructing a cloaking area, called Anonymizing Spatial Region (ASR or K-ASR), which contains at least K users. Given the ASR, the LSP can process the query and return a set of candidate point of interests (POIs), but cannot identify any user with probability larger than $1/K$. The Anonymizer then filters candidate set, and forwards the accurate results to each user. Compared to the TTP-free solutions, the TTP-based solutions can prevent the LBS provider from knowing a user's real location with a probability higher than $1/K$, while consuming lower communication cost for the users. However, the TTP-based schemes require a trusted Anonymizer, which has the knowledge about all users' locations. Thus, the security of the whole system relies on the Anonymizer. Once the Anonymizer is attacked by an adversary, it will pose a serious threat to user privacy and may put the user information in jeopardy.

In this paper, we propose an enhanced location privacy preserving (ELPP) scheme for the LBS environment, in which location privacy is guaranteed without needing any fully trusted entities. We introduce an entity, termed Function Generator, to distribute transformation parameters periodically for users and the LSP to performs mutual transformation between a real location and a pseudo location. Without the transforming parameters, the Anonymizer cannot have any knowledge about a user's real location. However, with a set of pseudo locations, the anoymizer still has the ability to construct a correct K-ASR to achieve K-anonymity on the LSP, and to filter the false POIs for each user. Therefore, our scheme can provide enhanced security for the whole system.

Our contributions are threefold:

1. We propose a novel framework for protecting location privacy, in which we introduce a Function Generator to get rid off the need of any trusted entities. To the best of our knowledge, the ELPP scheme is the first to provide enhanced location privacy for LBS environment.
2. We utilize Hilbert Curve [9] to transform a real location to a pseudo location, with which the Anonymizer can construct the ASR and filter POIs for each user correctly without compromising the real location.
3. We thoroughly analyze the security and the performance of the ELPP scheme. Our scheme protects location privacy from the the Anonymizer, the LSP, the Function Generator, and other users.

The remainder of this paper is organized as follows: We introduce related work in Section 2 and present technical preliminaries in Section 3.We describe the scheme in Section 4 and theoretically analyze its security in Section 5. Finally, we conclude this paper in Section 6.

2   Related Work

While interacting with the LSP, user privacy can be classified into query privacy and location privacy [7]. The former is related to the disclosure of the sensitive information in the queries or the related interests about users. The latter, on the other hand, is related to the disclosure and misuse of users location information. Our work is on protecting location privacy while enjoying LBSs. The most recent work on location privacy can be classified into two main categories: Trusted Third Parties (TTP)-free approaches [4] [10] and TTP-based approaches [3] [5]

The TTP-free methods are categorized in two sub categories in [11] : obfuscation based methods and collaboration based methods. In obfuscation based schemes, users generate multiple decoys at different locations and send the fake locations to the LSP. For example, [4] proposed a scheme, named SpaceTwist, where POIs are retrieved from the LSP incrementally. This process starts with a location different from the users actual location (called anchor location), and it proceeds until an accurate query result can be reported. The main drawback

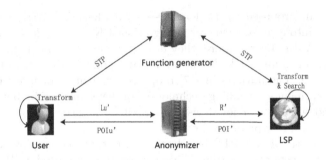

Fig. 2. Enhanced security scheme for location privacy

of this scheme is that multiple-round interaction between the users and the LSP may incur a higher communication cost.

In the collaboration based methods, each user cloaks his location by contacting his peers and collecting their location data. The first collaborative TTP-free scheme in LBS was first proposed by [12]. The user perturbs his location by adding zero-mean Gaussian noise, and then broadcasts his perturbed location to his neighbors and requests for perturbed locations from them to form a cloak. Since users only exchange perturbed locations, they do not need to trust each other for privacy. The main problem of this proposal is that the noise added to query will degrade the accuracy of the answers returned from the LSP. Therefore, the main drawback of the TTP-free methods is that the quality of the service (QoS) will degrade, due to the high communication cost incurred by the low accuracy of the answers.

In TTP-based solutions, the Anonymizer is introduced into the system, acting as an intermediate tier between the users and the LSP. the Anonymizer can behave (*i*) by deleting personal information of the users from the queries before sending to the LPS; (*ii*) by hiding or modifying the exact location of the users; (*iii*) by removing or filtering the false answers from the LSP. Existing TTP-based approaches usually require the Anonymizer to construct a K-anonymity ASR. The conception of K-anonymity was first introduced by Sweeney et al. [13] to prevent information loss and disclosure of personal data in databases. K-anonymity in LBS privacy can be viewed as a user' location is indistinguishable from K-1 other users'. So, the fundamental idea behind K-anonymity is to replace the real location of the user by cloaking areas in which at least K users are located. Inspired by their work, [8] [14] [15] [16] proposed efficient schemes to construct K-anonymity ASR. For example, Hilbert cloaking [15] [16] uses the Hilbert space filling to map 2-D space into 1-D values, and partitions the 1-D sorted list into groups of K users. In Clique Cloak [14], the Anonymizer perform spatio-temporal cloaking algorithms to search for cliques of users, and constructs a minimum bounding rectangle (MBR) of K users.

To improve the performance and QoS of the TTP-based solutions, the work in [14] enables a user to define his personal privacy requirements, e.g., the minimum level of anonymity and the maximum temporal and spatial resolutions.

In [5], Vu et al. proposed to use locality-sensitive hashing (LSH) to partition user locations into groups, each containing at least K users, before constructing K-anonymity ASRs. Furthermore, they devised an efficient algorithm based on Voronoi diagram to answer kNN queries for any point in the ASR of arbitrary polygonal shape. The authors in [17] proposed efficient in-memory processing and secondary memory pruning techniques for kNN queries in both 2D and high-dimensional spaces. They devised an auxiliary solution-based index EXO-tree to speed up any type of kNN query.

The main merit of the TTP-based schemes is that the employment of the Anonymizer protects the location privacy from the untrusted LSP, while enabling the LSB to provide better QoS. However, this kind of scheme moves users' trust from LPS to intermediate entities. The problem is that it will pose a serious threat to user privacy and may put the user information in jeopardy once the Anonymizer is compromised. Our ELPP scheme, by employing a Function Generator to the system, combines the merits of the two schemes, without fully trusted entities while providing better QoS.

3   Preliminaries

3.1   Problem Formulation

We consider this scenario: a user u sends the message {Location, ID, Query} to a LSP for kNN query. Map resources and database are stored in the potentially untrusted LSP. Upon this request, the LSP seeks the desired information in its database and returns appropriate POIs to u. The motivation of our work is to preserve location privacy for the users while enabling the LSP to provide high-quality services.

In this paper, we propose a novel enhanced location privacy preserving (ELPP) scheme that introduces an entity termed Function Generator to the TTP-based model (Fig. 2). The purpose of the Function Generator is to provide spatial transformation parameters (STPs) for users and LSP to map the 2-D space coordinate (a real location) into a 1-D space Hilbert value (a pseudo location), so that the Anonymizer without the STPs has no knowledge of a real location. The scheme works as follows: after obtaining the STP from the Function Generator, users encode their real locations to pseudo locations, denoted as Lu'. By aggregating enough pseudo locations from the users, the Anonymizer constructs a transformed ASR, denoted as R', and sends it to the LSP. On the LSP side, the transformed ASR can be decoded by the STP got from the Function Generator. The LSP then finds out the candidate POIs for the users in the decoded ASR, and transforms the real locations of POIs to pseudo locations, denoted as POI', before responding to the Anonymizer. Upon the POI's for K users, the Anonymizer accurately filters and forwards the accurate results for the querying user, denoted as POI$_u$'. The main merits of our scheme is that the ELPP scheme provides enhanced security for the whole system without needing fully trusted entities, and each user can obtain the accurate results.

3.2   Threat Model

Adversarial Capabilities. In the threat model commonly used in LBS privacy protection studies, the LSP are regarded as malicious observers, and all the other entities can be considered benign. An adversary can be the owner of an LBS entity, or is able to compromise and control of the LBS entities. In our threat model, the communication channels are assumed to be secured when queries and information are transmitted via communication networks. The existing security schemes (e.g., SSL) and conventional solutions (e.g., cryptography and hashing) can be used to protect the secrecy and integrity of the information through network. Therefore, there are three types of attackers: (i) the LSP, which knows the ASR, may be compromised by the adversary, or may leaks information for making profits. (ii) the Anonymizer, collecting all messages as an intermediate tier between the users and the LSP, may become a bigger target, and may reveal the cloaking algorithm; (iii) A small number of malicious users may want to know other users' privacy. All of these attackers are assumed to be more interested in the users' real locations than other information.

Adversarial Limitations. On the other hand, we also assume that the Anonymizer will not collude with any other entities. Collusion between the Anonymizer and other entities or malicious users could reveal privacy. This assumption has also been made in previous research by other researchers, e.g., the proxy reencryption systems [18] [19], in which the LSP performing proxy re-encryption operations is assumed to not collude with other entity to ensure system-wide security.

Our security goal is to protect location privacy for users. We consider our scheme fails if any of the following cases is true:

- The LSP knows the real location about any user with a probability larger than $1/K$.
- The Anonymizer knows any user's real location.
- The Function Generator knows any user's real location.
- The user knows real location about other users.

3.3   Hilbert Curves

The users and the LSP utilize Hilbert Curve to transform real locations to pseudo locations. A Hilbert curve is a continuous fractal space-filling curve which is first described by Hilbert [9]. Hilbert Curves pass through every point in an multi-dimensional space once and once only in some particular order according to some algorithm [20]. Given the 2-D coordinates of a point S in the lattice system, denoted as $< x_s, y_s >$, the corresponding 1-D code of S based on the Hilbert curve order, denoted as H(s), is to be determined, reversely, given the 1-D code of a point on the Hilbert curve, the corresponding lattice coordinate is to be determined, This process is defined as encoding and decoding [21].

Definition 1. The set of cells ordered by Hilbert curve is defined as:

$$H = \{C_{00}, C_{01}, C_{02}, ...C_{ij}, ..., C_{(N-1)(N-1)}\} \tag{1}$$

where C_{ij} are the $< x, y >$ coordinates of a grid and N is the number of grid cells in one dimension.

Definition 2. The Hilbert value of a point S can be defined as:

$$H(s) = \hbar(< x_s, y_s >) \tag{2}$$

where $\hbar$ is spatial transformation function, which encode the 2-D lattice coordinate into 1-D Hilbert value. Given the parameter of the function, the H-value mapping to each grid cell is assigned. The parameter refers to the curve's starting point (X_l, Y_l), curve order N, curve orientation σ, and curve scale factor Θ. We term this parameter space transformation as STP, where STP $=\{(X_l, Y_l), N, \sigma, \Theta\}$. The important property of a Hilbert curve that makes it a very suitable tool for our proposed scheme is that function $\hbar$ becomes a one-way function if the STP are not known [16]. A malicious attacker, not knowing this key, has to exhaustively check for all combinations of curve parameters to find the right curve by comparing the Hilbert values for all cells. An explicit formulas algorithm [22] by Moon et al. can be used to generate H-value ordered by $\hbar(< x, y >)$, or decode the Hilbert value inversely by $\hbar^{-1}(H)$.

Without loss of generality, we assume the user's location is a point and is identified by two values such as its latitude and longitude. We define the coordinate (x, y) refers to the spatial position of the mobile node in the two dimensional space (i.e., x-axis and y-axis). Given the STP, a point S with 2-D coordinate (x_s, y_s) can be presented by the lattice coordinates $< x_s, y_s >$.

$$< x_s, y_s >= \lfloor \frac{(x_s, y_s) - (x_0, y_0)}{U} \rfloor \tag{3}$$

U here is the unit length of each cell, which can be get from the scale of factor Θ and the number of grid cells in one dimension 2^N, and (x_0, y_0) is the real coordinate of the lower-left corner of cell $< 0, 0 >$. Note that it is possible for two or more points to have the same lattice coordinate and also the same H-value in a given curve. With high probability [22], if two points are in close proximity in the 2-D space, they will also be close in the 1-D transformation.

3.4   Voronoi Diagram

The LSP performs the k-nearest neighbor queries by using the Voronoi Diagram (VD) [23]. Consider a set of limited number of points, called *generator points*, denoted by P, in the Euclidean plane. We associate all locations in the plane to their closest generator(s). The set of locations assigned to their generator(s) forms a region called *Voronoi polygons*, denoted by $V(i)$. The nearest neighbor of any site inside a Voronoi polygon is the generator(s) of it.

The order-1 Voronoi diagram can be formally defined as: $P = p_1, ...p_n \subset \Re^2$. Assume a set of generators $P = p_1, ...p_n \subset \Re^2$, where $2 < n < \infty$ and $p_i \neq p_j$, for $i \neq j$, $i, j \in I_n = \{1, ...n\}$.

The region given by:

$$V(p_i) = \{p \,|\, d(p, p_i) \leq d(p, p_j)\} for j \neq i, j \in I_n \tag{4}$$

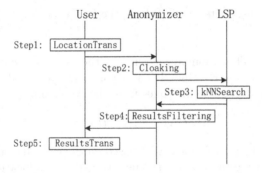

Fig. 3. Working processes of the scheme

where $d(p, p_i)$ is the Euclidean distance between two points. In order-1 VD, each polygon is associated with a point. We now extend the notion to order-N VD by considering the $V(i)$ associated with N generators, which is a subset of P, denoted by VP. That is, $V(i)$ is the locus of sites closer to all points in VP than to any other points not in VP.

4   Enhanced Location Privacy Preserving Scheme

4.1   Overview

Our basic idea is to introduce a Function Generator to transform a user's real location to a pseudo location based on Hilbert curve. As illustrated previously, the main reason for location transformation is to prevent the Anonymizer from having users' actual location information.

The system consists of the user, the Anonymizer, the Function Generator and the LSP. The ELPP scheme mainly consists of five steps, as shown in Fig. 3. We omit the interaction between the Function Generator and the users/the LSP in Fig. 3. Actually, the user/LSP should first request STPs from the Function Generator before transforming the locations. Main task of Function Generator is to construct space transformation parameter, STP=$\{(X_l, Y_l), N, \sigma, \Theta\}$, at different time point t_i (The details are provided in Section 3.3), and sends it to the user and the LSP. Since the Anonymizer does not have any knowledge of the STP, it can not deduce the real location about the users.

Step1. Location Transformation. After obtaining the STP from the Function Generator, the user runs the Alg.1 to transform his real location into a pseudo location. The messages from the user to the Anonymizer are:

$$MSG_{U2A} = \{Lu', ID, Q, t_i\} \tag{5}$$

where Lu' denotes the transformed location using Alg.1, ID is the identity of the user (e.g., IP address), Q denotes the kNN requirement, t_i refers to the time point at which the user gets the STP from the Function Generator and presents his LSBs.

Step2. Cloaking. The Anonymizer removes the user's ID and selects at least K-1 users with the same H-value. Then, it constructs a K-ASR for the K users and sends it to the LSP. The messages from the Anonymizer to the LSP are:

$$MSG_{A2L} = \{R', H(u), t_i\} \tag{6}$$

where R' denotes the transformed ASR based on the cell, $H(u)$ is the H-value of the user, t_i is the timestamp when the user transform his location and presents his LSBs.

Step3. *k*NN Search. The LSP finds out the POIs for the users in the ASR. Since the region is shifted to the cell space, it should be transformed to the real one first. The LSP will works as follows: it connects with the Function Generator to get the STP with the timestamp t_i, and then decodes the H-value to the 2-D spacial location, calculates the actual ASR from the transformed one. After that the LSP searches the candidate POIs in ASR with the VDs (details in Section 3.D) and transforms their coordinates to the corresponding cell, and finally, forwards the pseudo locations of POIs, presented by POI' to the Anonymizer. The messages from the LSP to the Anonymizer are:

$$MSG_{L2A} = \{POI's\} \tag{7}$$

where the POI' is the pseudo locations of POI.

Step4. Results Filtering. The Anonymizer gets the POI's, which may potentially be the *k*NN answers for any user within the entire ASR. Since the pseudo location of user and POIs are transformed by the same STP, the Anonymizer can exactly find out accurate kNN results for the user from the all POI's, and remove the false ones. The messages from the the Anonymizer to the user are:

$$MSG_{A2U} = \{POIu'\} \tag{8}$$

where the POIu' denotes the accurate answer for the user's *k*NN query.

Step5. Results Transformation. The user gets exact POI's from the Anonymizer, since the pseudo locations of the POIs are the offset based on the origin of coordinates of the cell, user can easily get the real POIs by transforming the offset of the cell to the real location.

4.2   Location Transformation

As described in Section 3.3, the Hilbert space filling curve imposes a linear ordering on the grid cells, assigning a single integer value to each cell. With the STP, we can map the 2-D space into 1-D Hilbert value using the function $\hbar$. The

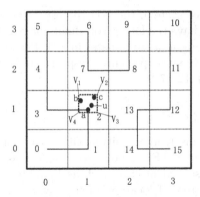

Fig. 4. Transformation based on the Hilbert space-filling curve

privacy of the solution relies on the large number of Hilbert curve parameter choices. We employ the Function Generator to distribute the STP to users and LSP. For the sake of security and efficiency, we assume the STPs are generated randomly at regular intervals (e.g.,3 minites). Getting the STP from the Function generator, user can construct a lattice system with $2^N * 2^N$ grid cells in scale Θ, the centre point of each cell is regarded as point in a space of finite granularity. If we assume the lower-left corner of each cell is the origin of coordinates in the cell space, denoted as (x_c, y_c), so the user's offset coordinate, denoted as $(x_u, y_u)'$, in corresponding grid cell $< x_u, y_u >$, can be defined as relative position between the user real location (x_u, y_u) to the origin of coordinates (x_c, y_c) by scale.

$$(x_c, y_c) = U* < x_u, y_u > +(x_0, y_0) \tag{9}$$

$$(x_u, y_u)' = (x_u, y_u) - (x_c, y_c) \tag{10}$$

Similar to the Eq. 3, U is the unit length of each cell, (x_0, y_0) is the real coordinate of the lower-left corner of cell $< 0,0 >$. The expression of location coordinate for a user u is shown in Talbe 1.

Table 1. The location coordinate of user

Real location	Lattice coordinate	Offset coordinate	Pseudo location
(x_u, y_u)	$< x_u, y_u >$	$(x_u, y_u)'$	$\{H(u), (x_u, y_u)'\}$

Therefore, with the STP, users can transform their real location (x_u, y_u) to a pseudo one, denoted as (Lu'), which is its H-value in Hilbert space and offset coordinate in corresponding cell, presented by $\{H(u), (x_u, y_u)'\}$. The process of location transformation is shown in Alg. 1.

Fig. 4 illustrates how a Hilbert curve can be used to transform a user real 2-D space location into pseudo one. In this example, starting from the centre-point of $< 0, 0 >$ in the lattice system, the 2-D Hilbert curve orderly passes $2^2 * 2^2$ grids. The users a, b, c, have the lattice coordinate of $< 1, 1 >$ in lattice system, and their offset to the origin of coordinates in $< 1, 1 >$ are (5,5)', (3,8)', (7,9)'. After transforming, they can be presented respectively by their pseudo location of $\{2, (5, 5)'\}, \{2, (3, 8)'\}, \{2, (7, 9)'\}$.

4.3   K-Anonymity Cloaking

The Anonymizer performs K-anonymity cloaking to protect the user location privacy from the untursted LSP. Upon receiving a message from a user, the Anonymizer removes users identifiers, such as IP addresses, and generates an ASR, where a given degree of location anonymity can be maintained. We assume that every cell is big enough to contain more than K users. The K-Anonymity spatial cloaking algorithm safely works as follows. Firstly, given the $MSG_{U2A} = \{Lu', ID, Q, t_i\}$, the Anonymizer removes users' identifiers, and then clusters the location of the user by their H-value. In the next step, it randomly chooses K-1 users in the same cell of the querying user. If the number of users is small than K, it can achieves the location anonymity by delaying the message until K mobile nodes have visited the same cell located by the querying user. Once the K users are determined, the cloak region can be represented by rectangles, disks or simply the set itself. In this paper, we construct a K-anonymity ASR using the *minimum bounding rectangle* (MBR) which encloses these K users (the query user and other K-1 users) in the same cell, denoted as R'. Since all the user pseudo positions are presented by their offset based on the origin of coordinates in the corresponding cell, the MBR can be also expressed by its vertexes using the offset coordinate in this cell, which are $(x_{v1}, y_{v1})' \sim (x_{v4}, y_{v4})'$. During the processing of K-anonymity cloaking, the Anonymizer does not have any real location information about users. Finally, the ASR in a corresponding cell, presented by R' and the H-value, is constructed and forwarded to the LSP. The $MSG_{A2L} = \{R', H(u), t_i\}$, where $R' = (x_{v1}, y_{v1})' \sim (x_{v4}, y_{v4})'$, $H(u)$ is the H-value of the cell, t_i is the timestamp of user presenting the LSBs.

Fig. 4 shows an example of K-ASR construction, where u is the querying user. Assume K = 4 and u selects users who have the same H-value as u. According to the K-anonymity cloaking procedure, the K-anonymity user set is [u1, a, b, c]. Since all the users are presented by their offset based on the origin of coordinates in the cell 2, the MBR enclosing these four users can be also expressed by its vertexes using offset coordinate based on the cell, which is $(x_{v1}, y_{v1})' \sim (x_{v4}, y_{v4})'$.

4.4   *k*NN Search Algorithm

Before the LSP searches the POIs for users, it needs to get decoding parameter from the Function Generator with the timestamp t_i to calculate the actual ASR from R' and H-value. With the STP, the LSP maps the H-value to the 2-D spacial location, and get the origin of coordinate of the corresponding cell, and then obtain the real location of R'. The LSP can not deduce what the users

---

Algorithm 1. LocationTrans

1: {Input STP $=\{(X_l, Y_l), N, \sigma, \Theta\}$, User location coordinate (x_u, y_u)}
   {Output $Lu' = (H(u), (x_u, y_u)')$}
2: Construct a lattice system with $2^N * 2^N$ cells in scale Θ.
3: Transform the (x_u, y_u) into lattice coordinate $< x_u, y_u >$ using Eq. 3.
4: Get the $H(u)$ by Eq. 2 //using STP.
5: Compute the the origin of coordinates of the cell (x_c, y_c) using Eq. 9.
6: Get the offset $(x_u, y_u)'$ using Eq. 10.

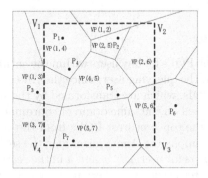

Fig. 5. Search POIs based on order-2 VD

are located exactly, since it just have the information about the K-anonymity region.

The kNN search problem can be solved efficiently with the Order-k VDs. According description in Section 3.4, the kNN answer of any site inside one polygon are its associated generator points. That means searching the POIs in ASR for all users is to identify the order-k polygons that *overlap* with the ASR, and find the union of their corresponding associated points. The term *overlap* here means the polygon intersects or lies completely inside ASR. For example, in Fig. 5, with the STP, the LSP can calculate the real coordinate of the ASR, which is $V_1 \sim V_4$. To get the results of the kNN query in this area, it can search the union of associated generator points for all the polygons which overlap with this rectangle, the results of POIs for all users in the ASR are the $p_1...p_7$. Similar to [16], due to the time-consuming process of finding the kNN query, we use a computationally efficient algorithm by considering polygons that intersect with ASR and polygons that are inside ASR separately, which takes O(logn + Kn) worstcase running time. The process of kNN Search algorithm is shown in Alg. 2. Before the LSP forwards the POIs to the Anonymizer, it should transform the location of them to the pseudo ones (POI'), which we can get from the offset based on the cell.

$$POI' = POI - (x_c, y_c) \tag{11}$$

Algorithm 2. kNN search algorithm run by LSP

1: {Input: STP $=\{(X_l, Y_l), N, \sigma, \Theta\}$, R', H-value}
   {Output: the set of POI'}
2: Construct a lattice system with $2^N * 2^N$ grid cells in scale Θ.
3: Decode the H-value using $\hbar^{-1}(H(u))$.
4: Compute the the origin of coordinates of the cell (x_c, y_c) using Eq. 9.
5: Get real coordinates of ASR from R' and the (x_c, y_c).
6: Search POIs in real ASR.
7: Get POI's using Eq. 11.

4.5 Results Filtering

The Anonymizer gets the POI's for any users within the entire ASR. It should find out the exact answer for the querying user. Since the Anonymizer has the pseudo locations of users and POIs, which are transformed by the same STP, and whose offset coordinates are based on the same origin of coordinates of the cell (x_c, y_c). It can exactly find out the top-k nearest POI's from the pseudo location of the querying user. In our example, the Anonymizer gets the set of $p'_1...p'_7$ (in Fig. 5), which are the kNN answers for user a, b, c, and u in the rectangle (in Fig. 4), only p'_4 and p'_5 are the exact results for the querying user u. So the Anonymizer will filter the false answers, and return the accurate results to u.

4.6 Results Transformation

Given the exact locations of POI's, which are the offsets based on the origin of coordinates of the cell (x_c, y_c), the user can transform the pseudo locations to the real locations of POI's by inverse operation of Eq. 11, and finally gets the accurate answer for his kNN query.

5 Security Analysis

Our analysis will focus on how the ELPP scheme can achieve the users location privacy preservation and resist the possible privacy leakage from Anonymizer and other entities in the system. In particular, the security requirements discussed in Section 3.2, note that, the collusion between the Function Generator and the Anonymizer or the malicious users are out of the scope of this paper. The security and privacy requirements are satisfied if the following four cases are true.

    Case 1: The LSP does not know the location information about user . The message between the Anonymizer and the LSP is $MSG_{A2L} = \{$R', H(u), $t_i\}$. Since ASR is a cloaking region of K users, the LSP can not know exact position of each user with probability larger than $1/K$ due to the K-anonymity principle. The POIs searched by the LSP are candidate results for all users in ASR, neither the adversary nor the LSP knows which results are returned to the honest users. So, they can not deduce the location information about user. Therefore, case 1 is true.

Case 2: The Anonymizer cannot know any user's real location. The location information from each user to the Anonymizer is an pseudo one encoded by transformation function. The parameter of the decode function is only known by the users and the LSP, without of the STP, the Anonymizer itself cannot deduce the real location. Even if the Anonymizer is compromised by the attackers, the knowledge about user on the Anonymizer will not leak any user location privacy. The security of transformation used in the scheme are proved to be strongly robust in [16]. The POIs returned from the LSP are also transformed by the Hilbert filling curve, it is hard for the Anonymizer to guess each user's interest without STP. Assume that adversary can somehow gained the knowledge for the value of the STP, the similarity of Hilbert curve he can guess to the real one is very small. Therefore, case 2 is true.

Case 3: The Function Generator can not know any user location. The main task of Function Generator is to construct the STP, and launch it to the users and LSP. The STP itself will not reveal any valuable information. Therefore, case 3 is true.

Case 4: The user will not know location information about other users. The Anonymizer can correctly returns results to each user, who can only obtains its own results, having no knowledge about others'. Even if a small number of malicious users work cooperatively, they cannot know other honest usersinterests. Therefore, case 4 is true.

6   Conclusion

In this paper, we propose a comprehensive ELPP scheme for protection of user location privacy in LBS. A key feature of the system is that we get rid off the fully trusted entities to provide enhanced security. In our future work, we will improve our scheme by deploying multiple Anonymizers to avoid the potential botteleneck between the users and the Anonymizer, and ensure the high security of the system.

Acknowledgment. This research was supported in part by NSFC grants 61272151 and 61073037, and the Ministry of Education Fund for Doctoral Disciplines in Higher Education under grant 20110162110043.

References

1. Lu, R., Lin, X., Liang, X., Shen, X.: A dynamic privacy-preserving key management scheme for location-based services in vanets. IEEE Transactions on Intelligent Transportation Systems 13(1), 127–139 (2012)
2. Shin, K.G., Ju, X., Chen, Z., Hu, X.: Privacy protection for users of location-based services. IEEE Wireless Communications 19(1), 30–39 (2012)
3. Pingley, A., Zhang, N., Fu, X., Choi, H.A., Subramaniam, S., Zhao, W.: Protection of query privacy for continuous location based services. In: Proceedings IEEE INFOCOM, pp. 1710–1718 (2011)

4. Yiu, M.L., Jensen, C.S., Huang, X., Lu, H.: Spacetwist: Managing the trade-offs among location privacy, query performance, and query accuracy in mobile services. In: Proceedings of IEEE ICDE, pp. 366–375 (2008)
5. Vu, K., Zheng, R., Gao, J.: Efficient algorithms for k-anonymous location privacy in participatory sensing. In: Proceedings IEEE INFOCOM, pp. 2399–2407 (2012)
6. Ghinita, G., Zhao, K., Papadias, D., Kalnis, P.: A reciprocal framework for spatial k-anonymity. Information Systems 35(3), 299–314 (2010)
7. Pan, X., Xu, J., Meng, X.: Protecting location privacy against location-dependent attacks in mobile services. IEEE Transactions on Knowledge and Data Engineering 24(8), 1506–1519 (2012)
8. Gruteser, M., Grunwald, D.: Anonymous usage of location-based services through spatial and temporal cloaking. In: Proceedings of ACM MobiSys, pp. 31–42 (2003)
9. Hilbert, D.: Ueber die stetige abbildung einer line auf ein flaechenstueck. Mathematische Annalen 38(3), 459–460 (1891)
10. Ghinita, G., Kalnis, P., Khoshgozaran, A., Shahabi, C., Tan, K.L.: Private queries in location based services: anonymizers are not necessary. In: Proceedings of ACM SIGMOD, pp. 121–132 (2008)
11. Solanas, A., Domingo-Ferrer, J., Martínez-Ballesté, A.: Location privacy in location-based services: Beyond ttp-based schemes. In: Proceedings of PILBA, pp. 12–23 (2008)
12. Domingo-Ferrer, J.: Microaggregation for database and location privacy. In: Etzion, O., Kuflik, T., Motro, A. (eds.) NGITS 2006. LNCS, vol. 4032, pp. 106–116. Springer, Heidelberg (2006)
13. Sweeney, L.: k-anonymity: A model for protecting privacy. International Journal of Uncertainty, Fuzziness and Knowledge-Based Systems 10(5), 557–570 (2002)
14. Gedik, B., Liu, L.: Location privacy in mobile systems: A personalized anonymization model. In: Proceedings of IEEE ICDCS, pp. 620–629 (2005)
15. Kalnis, P., Ghinita, G., Mouratidis, K., Papadias, D.: Preventing location-based identity inference in anonymous spatial queries. IEEE Transactions on Knowledge and Data Engineering 19(12), 1719–1733 (2007)
16. Khoshgozaran, A., Shahabi, C.: Blind evaluation of nearest neighbor queries using space transformation to preserve location privacy. In: Papadias, D., Zhang, D., Kollios, G. (eds.) SSTD 2007. LNCS, vol. 4605, pp. 239–257. Springer, Heidelberg (2007)
17. Hu, H., Lee, D.L.: Range nearest-neighbor query. IEEE Transactions on Knowledge and Data Engineering 18(1), 78–91 (2006)
18. Liu, Q., Tan, C.C., Wu, J., Wang, G.: Cooperative private searching in clouds. Journal of Parallel and Distributed Computing 13(1), 1019–1031 (2012)
19. Green, M., Ateniese, G.: Identity-based proxy re-encryption. In: Katz, J., Yung, M. (eds.) ACNS 2007. LNCS, vol. 4521, pp. 288–306. Springer, Heidelberg (2007)
20. Lawder, J.K.: Calculation of mappings between one and n-dimensional values using the hilbert space-filling curve. School of Computer Science and Information Systems (2000)
21. Liu, X., Schrack, G.: Encoding and decoding the hilbert order. Software: Practice and Experience 26(12), 1335–1346 (1996)
22. Moon, B., Jagadish, H.V., Faloutsos, C., Saltz, J.H.: Analysis of the clustering properties of the hilbert space-filling curve. IEEE Transactions on Knowledge and Data Engineering 13(1), 124–141 (2001)
23. Lee, D.T.: On k-nearest neighbor voronoi diagrams in the plane. IEEE Transactions on Computers 100(6), 478–487 (1982)

Design of Lightweight Web Page Tamper-Resistant Mechanism for Linux

Ang Mi, Weiping Wang, Shigeng Zhang, and Hong Song

School of Information Science and Engineering, Central South University, Changsha 410083
704097835@qq.com, {wpwang,sgzhang,songhong}@mail.csu.edu.cn

Abstract. Resisting malicious Web page tampering is critical to provide robust web services. Existing Web page tamper-resistant solutions either require extra equipments (e.g., storage equipments or content distribution systems), or suffer from significant performance degradation. In this paper, we design and implement a lightweight Web page tamper-resistant system for the Linux system. In our design, we adopt the system call interception, event-trigger mechanism, the attribute of Linux file system, and combine them together to resist tampering attempts to the Web page files. Our solution is very lightweight and does not require any additional storage equipments or content distribution systems. We implement a prototype of our mechanism on Linux with kernel version 2.6, and deploy it in a campus Web server. Experiment results show that our mechanism can effectively protect Web page files from being tampered, incurring only negligible increase in response delay and CPU utilization ratio.

Keywords: Web page tamper-resistance; system call interception; event-trigger; Linux.

1 Introduction

Nowadays, malicious tampering of pages by hackers brings serious crisis to Web services. Many methods can be used by hackers to modify Web files. The first method is uploading a web shell. The attackers often take vulnerabilities of uploading functions provided by the website to upload malicious codes. Although the web site will check the file type, such checks could be bypassed by attackers easily (e.g., via file header spoofing). As a common page, web shell runs in the Web server account, so it has the privilege to modify the other page files and could be visited or connected through HTTP. Attackers would connect their web shells with Explorer or other tools (e.g., "Chinese copper"), and run the modification command to hack the website. They could even upload Trojans by the web shell to do further attacks.

The second common method used by attackers is to get the permission to use the manager pages of Web background. Attackers may use SQL injection or password-guessing to get the weak password, and then obtain the control of the Web background. With the permission, hackers could modify the Web pages, upload some web shells, or modify some legal pages to web shell (e.g., "one-word" web shell to PHP, ASP, ASPX, JSP) to leave backdoors.

G. Wang et al. (Eds.): CSS 2013, LNCS 8300, pp. 29–39, 2013.

We can see that resisting tampering of Web pages not only protects the integrity of single page, but also perceives and denies the illegal uploading or other illegal options initiatively. Thus it is critical to protect the folder structure of the web site, and notify the administrators in time in case the Web pages are tampered.

In this paper, we design and implement a lightweight page tamper-resistant system on the Linux operating system. We combine the system-call interception in kernel space, an event triggered mechanism in the application layer, and the property of Linux file system together to protect the pages against being maliciously tampered. Compared with existing solutions, our design does not need to back up the website file or deploy any additional hardware. We implement our design on Linux with kernel version 2.6 and deploy it in a campus Web server. Experiment results show that our mechanism can effectively protect Web page files from being tampered, incurring only negligible increase in response delay and CPU utilization ratio. When there are 50 concurrent requests, the response delay increases only 2ms after our system is deployed and the CPU utilization ratio increases only one percent. When there are 100 concurrent requests, the response delay increases only 0.1s and the CPU utilization ratio increases only 3 percent.

The rest of the paper is organized as follows. Section 2 overviews related work. Section 3 describes our page tamper-resistant strategies. In Section 4 we give the details in implementing our system and analyze its security. We deploy our system and evaluate its performance in a campus Web server, and report the results in Section 5. Finally, in Section 6 we conclude this paper and point out some future research directions

2   Related Work

In recent years many tamper-resistant solutions have been proposed. We would first introduce some commonly used approaches to resisting Web page tempering attacks. Watermark detections [1,2] are often performed by combining a content distribution system (CMS) and an embedded module in the Web server. When distributing Web pages, the CMS computes watermarks of the original pages and restores a backup copy of the watermarks. When processing web requests, the embedded model locates the page files and computes the watermark of the page files. It then compares the computed watermark with corresponding backup watermark. If the two watermarks do not match, we can determine that the page is tampered. This mechanism could ensure that the tampered pages would not flow out of the server. However, there are some limitations of this mechanism. For example, the watermark computation may significantly increase the average response delay, and the website needs to equip a CMS.

Event triggered programs [3,4] need to work together with synchronous backup servers. An event trigger program will be noticed if any changes to the page files occur, and then it can use the backup server to recover changed page files. Some researchers studied optimization of this type of mechanisms [5,6]. However, the problem of this type of mechanism is that there will be a delay during the file recovery. The defense capability for continuous tampering attack is poor, and the tampered pages may flow out. Furthermore, the website server needs to deploy an additional synchronization backup server (e.g., Rsync,) to back up the original file pages.

On the Windows platform, the popular trend is to control page modification by file filters because this mechanism could save much more resources [6,7]. Another reason for programmers to use this mechanism is that the programmers could easily handle the IRP packets to control file options, by using multiple level interfaces provided by the Windows platform to intercept file operations. However, this mechanism could be used on Windows platform only. As most web sites are deployed on Linux servers nowadays, the applicability of this mechanism is severely limited.

3   Page Tamper-Resistant Strategies and System Structure

The Linux system provides two security mechanisms to resist illegal file modification. The first one is file permission control, with which users without writing privilege could not modify the file. Unfortunately, this mechanism is useless for the protection of pages, as the web shell has all the privileges of Web server account. The second mechanism is the immutable attribute, which is a feature of *EXT* file system (one of the most common file systems on Linux). When the immutable attribute for a certain file or directory is activated, the system can prevent all users from modifying the file or creating/deleting files in the folder. However, this mechanism could just provide passive protection, i.e., it could not catch and warn the illegal options initiatively. Moreover, some websites need to provide uploading function to users, in which case activating the attribute would affect the quality of web service. More than that, the attribute-flag could be cleared by the process with root privilege. Thus solely using this mechanism could not meet our demand.

In order to prevent attackers from uploading malicious codes or tampering page files, we first briefly describe the entire process of file operation on Linux system.

Figure 1 shows how file operations are handled on Linux. From Figure 1, we know that all file operations need to transform into system-call and enter into kernel space before they can be further processed, no matter these operations are started by applications (including Web servers), Shell terminals, or other methods. When conduct file operations, system calls need to visit the Inode structure that is located in the virtual file system (VFS) in the Linux kernel in order to access the files. Inode is a structure in the kernel space that is used to identify the real files or directories. It contains some important information associated with the files or directories, e.g., the attribute-flags of the file system (like immutable attribute flag), the time of latest modification. This information plays a crucial role in the processing of system calls.

From the above analysis, we can learn that in order to modify a file on Linux system, the attacker must rely on the information contained in the Inode structure of the target file or directory, and he needs to execute the system-call function successfully.

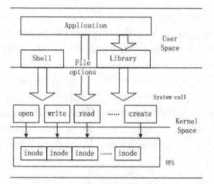

Fig. 1. File operation processing of Linux OS

Therefore, our system combines system call interception, immutable attribute of file system, and event-trigger mechanism together to resist page tampering attacks. Before entering the system call to trap into the kernel space, our system intercepts the operation, and rejects invalid ones to use the system-call functions. The illegal operations will be recorded in a log file. Meanwhile, we will set the immutable attribute flag in the corresponding Inode of the protected page files or directories to make them immune to modification. As a result, we can prevent the tampering at two control-points in the modification process. At the same time, in the application layer, our system uses the event-trigger mechanism to assist the above two mechanisms by monitoring the page files and directories, recording the monitor log in time and issuing an early warning if the monitored object is modified. As the last line of defense, it provides evidences for the administrator to determine the validity of modification.

According to the page tamper-resistant strategy presented above, the entire structure of our system design is shown in Figure 2.

As is shown in Figure 2, our system consists of three modules: a system call interception module in the kernel space, a file attribute control module, and an event-monitor module in the application layer. The working mechanism of each module is briefly introduced below.

The system call interception module is responsible for intercepting the system calls related to file modification. The module maintains a list of paths that need to be protected. When the modification options from upper layers call the related system-call function, the module will firstly check the operation's target path. If the operated object is a subdirectory or a file in the protected path, the module will return an error to the upper layer, and reject the call and record the log in time. As for operations on other paths, it will be processed by the original system call directly.

The file attribute control module is responsible for activating the immutable attribute of the protected files and directories, which makes the page files and directories immune to modification in the VFS level. As have been pointed out in previous sections, it must work with the other modules together to ensure that the page files are not maliciously tampered.

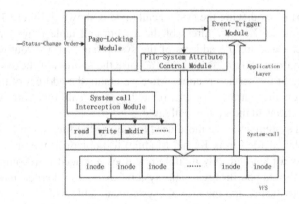

Fig. 2. Structure of our tamper-resistant system

The event-trigger module is responsible for monitoring the content of page files and the structure of folders in real time, acquiring its modifying event in time, and creating a monitor log to inform the website administrator promptly.

Then, through the mutual assistance in the layers of system-call and VFS, our system will intercept the page modification, record logs of malicious behaviors in time, and monitor the changes of the page files and directories in real time. This forms a multiple layered protection system to ensure the security of page files effectively.

For the convenience of the administrator to maintain and modify the pages, a page locking module is implemented in our system. When the administrator is doing some normal modification to a certain page or file directory, the lock will be released to permit the administrator's modification. During the rest of the time, the page locking module will lock the page files, which will reject all modifications during this period.

Taking into account that some web sites would allow users to upload some personal information files (e.g., images), our system provides another work mode. Only to those directories for user uploading, our system works in monitor mode in order to discharge the options and generate the logs. To the other import paths that store the page files or other resources, the system still work in the protection mode.

4   System Implementation and Security Analysis

4.1   System Implementation

System Calls Interception
Linux uses the system call table to save the entrance of system call functions. When a system function is invoked, the OS first searches the entrance related to the function in the system call table and then executes the function. In order to intercept the system call, we modify the system call table during the running time of our system and replace the system call entrances related to the file or directory modification operations with the address of our intercepting functions.

The flowchart of modifying the system call table is shown in Figure 3. In the Linux OS of the version 2.6.X, the address of the system call table is no longer exposed. Therefore, we can acquire the address of the system call service routine through the interrupt descriptor of INT 0x80, and then acquire the address of the system call table through the code of the service routine. After we obtain the address of the system call table, we replace the entrance of the related system call functions with the new intercepting functions in the system call table.

The involved system calls are those used to modify the file system, e.g., *create* and *write*. We use the LKM (Linux Kernel Module) to implement the above interception mechanism. It is a plug-and-play module that does not need to recompile the whole kernel. When the tampering resistant system exits, the kernel module will be uninstalled automatically and the original system call table will be recovered, so there will be no follow-up affects to the OS.

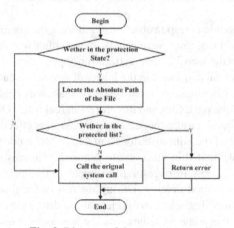

Fig. 3. Diagram of the new system call

Event-Trigger Monitor

In our system, the implementation of the event-trigger monitor utilizes the Inotify technology [8]. Inotify is a new feature added after the kernel version 2.6.14. It is a fine-grained and asynchronous monitor of file system events. By using this mechanism to register a monitor on the files or directories, we can get the events in real time. The principle of Inotify is to add a monitoring data item to the Inode structure, and send the event to the monitor located in the application layer. The monitor will insert the event into the event queue to notify the user, who will deal with it latter. Our system uses the mechanism to monitor the event such as IN_MODIFY (the monitored object is modified) and others related to the file or directory modification.

Netlink Communication

Netlink is a communication mechanism specialized on Linux. It aims to transmit data between the kernel space and the user space. It provides the program in user space with a group of standard socket interfaces to implement the full-duplex communication.

Compared with the *ioctl* and *proc* file system, netlink has many advantages. It is an asynchronous communicative method, and the interface is very convenient to use. Moreover, it is suitable for massive data and the conversation could be initiated by the kernel space.

4.2 Security Analysis

Security Analysis of the System

To analyze the security of Web pages, we first introduce the operation principle of our system. Our system applies the daemon mechanism [9]. As shown in Figure 4, the system will start the master process as a daemon, which can make process run in background and get rid of the control of terminal. The master process will insert the kernel module into the kernel space and start two child processes: the page locking monitoring process and the kernel information gathering process. The kernel module registered in the kernel space uses netlink-based socket protocols to communicate with the monitoring process in user space, so it is always in busy status and could not be uninstalled. When the system is running, the daemon will closely watch the status of the two child processes by the signal mechanism. Once the child processes exit unexpectedly, the daemon will immediately restart them. Meanwhile, the daemon itself shields the "*sigtem*" signal [8] (the signal of common kill command) to prohibit legal user's incorrect operation. The process can normally exit only after the administrator who is authorized to run the instruction of exit. Thus, by using daemon mechanism and monitoring the child processes, we could ensure the tamper-resisting functions work properly.

Taking into account that the attackers with root privilege could use the *sigkill* signal to destroy any processes by force, we use the same technology to intercept the system-call *sys_getdents* to hide our process. Thus the attacker could not see our process with the *ps* command. We provide all the option interfaces to authorized user, even though they could not see our process in the process list, they could operate our system as usual. So that attackers could not disguise as legal ones to modify our protection. Even if the hackers successfully prompt to root privilege, they could hardly notice our system as our processes don't exist in the process list. Furthermore, their attempts to tamper the pages would be recorded by our system.

Security Analysis of Page Files

As we have pointed out in previous sections, the attackers could hardly stop our system from protecting the content and directory structure of web pages. In this subsection we analyze the security of web pages under the protection.

We divide the analysis into three cases. First, for the websites that provide functions of uploading and modification to only web administrators, even after the hackers get control of the background process of the web (e.g., by using weak password or SQL-injection attacks), they still could not modify the web-pages or upload their web shells as our system locks all the page paths. All the modification and uploading options will translate into system-call like "write" and so on, and our system would reject them. Only the authenticated web administrator could unlock the paths and use background processes to perform legal modifications. When the web administrator locks the pages again, or if the duration of unlocking status exceeds a pre-defined threshold, our system would lock the paths again and reject all the modifications.

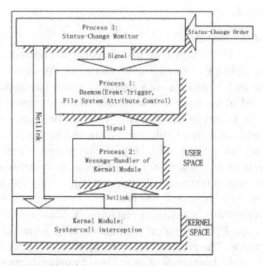

Fig. 4. Diagram of the tamper-resistant system

For the websites that provide vulnerable user-uploading services, the hackers could upload their web shells or other malicious codes successfully because our system just monitors the folder for user-uploading. However, the attackers still could not modify the Web pages because the web shell would also fail to call the system-calls to do modification on the page file paths. If the attackers get the root privilege, they could only disable the immutable attribute of the file-system, but could not notice and stop our system as analyzed before. In addition, all of their attempts would be recorded at once.

In the third case, there may be some other procedure loopholes in the website. In this case, the attackers could run the command remotely. For example, the attackers could take advantage of Structs2 loopholes to get an interactive shell and run the remote command to create web shells or modify the pages [10]. As we have pointed in Section 3, all the commands or options need translate into system-calls. Thus, as same as in the first case, our system would resist the illegal calls to protect the web pages and notice the administrators.

5   Performance Analysis and Test Results

5.1   Performance Analysis

The system call interception module that is shown in Figure 2 will process file operations first. It needs to determine whether the path of target files is a sub-file or sub-directory in the paths to be protected. This searching process can be completed with at most N comparison operations, where N is the number of path-items in the protection list. Usually the number of paths recorded in the protection list is small, so the searching process can be quickly done and will not introduce significant response delay. Meanwhile, the maximum length of a path name on Linux is 256 bytes. It takes only a few milliseconds for the common string matching algorithm to perform path name matching. Therefore, it takes just several milliseconds for system interception.

The file system features are provided by Linux file system. The time needed can almost be ignored. The event-trigger work will not affect the file operations for just monitoring. In conclusion, the time delay introduced by the tamper-resistant system is only several milliseconds, so it will not affect the normal running of the website significantly.

5.2   Test Results

In order to validate the effectiveness in protecting process of the system, we deployed our system in a Web server in our campus network and monitored the attacks to the Web server. During a half of a month monitoring, we intercept 2 uploading of web shell and 6 tampering to the pages and its directory structure. Fig. 5 shows an example record of an illegal deleting operation to the website's resources files intercepted by our system.

```
01|32|[2012-01-11 10:55:53][File Protect]-DENY_DELETE:/usr/local/apache-tomcat-6.0.2
0/webapps/WebSite/resources/images/20100312.bmp[Domain:localhost][Method:Protect]$
```

Fig. 5. Example record of an illegal deleting operation

To evaluate the efficiency, we opened an empty file and wrote data in the same size(1KB) for 10,000 times under the following four different conditions, and then observed the time difference in different conditions. The test results are shown in Table 1.

It should be noticed that under the condition of "load the protection system and provide protection", the time delay is much less than under other conditions. This is because the modification was rejected and there are no I/O operations afterward. As for the condition of "load the protection system but not to provide protection", the time delay is a little bit more than the others due to the matching of file paths in the kernel. We can learn from Table 1 that the delay is in a reasonable range.

Table 1. Efficiency of file modification

Protection Method	Average Delay (ms)
Do not load the protection system	5.8
Load the protection system and provide protection	1.2
Load the protection system but not to provide protection	8.3
Only to monitor with event-trigged mechanism	5.9

For the further performance test, we used the HP Load runner to simulate large-scale concurrent users in laboratory. The tested website used the open-resource version of Crossday Discuz! Board and we use the same testing scripts during the process. The results are shown in Table 2. We observe that when the concurrent number is 50, the average response time of the websites which loaded the page tamper-resistant system just increases 2ms, and the CPU utilization increases about 1%. But when the concurrent number is 100, the average response time increases 0.1s, and the CPU utilization increases 3%. This means that the tamper-resistant system does not consume much resource. It proved that the system reached the requirement of lightweight in resource consumption.

Table 2. Performance Test

Concurrent Number of Users Online Simultaneously	State	Average Response Time (s)	Average CPU Utilization (%)
50	Before Deployment	0.696	49.251
50	After Deployment	0.698	50.682
100	Before Deployment	1.678	80.009
100	After Deployment	1.714	83.105

6   Conclusion

The page tamper-resistant system designed in this paper is able to minimize the page file's risk of being tampered to ensure the security with lightweight resource consumption. Therefore, we need not to back up the page files in addition, which avoids the participation of reliable backup system or back servers. For the websites without CMS distribution system, there is no need to add one and modify the overall running mechanism of the Web service. We can resist the tampering to pages in a convenient and efficient way.

Acknowledgement. This work was supported by the National Natural Science Foundations of China (Grant no. 61173169, 61103203) and the Program for New Century Excellent Talents in University(Grant no. NCET-10-0798).

References

1. Long, X., Peng, H., Zhang, C., et al.: A fragile watermarking scheme for tamper-proof of Web pages. In: Proc. of IEEE WASE International Conference on Information Engineering 2009, Taiyuan, China, pp. 155–158 (2009)
2. Jin, C., Xu, H., Zhang, X.: Web pages tamper-proof method using virus-based watermarking. In: Proc. of International Conference on Audio, Language and Image Processing 2008, Shanghai, China, pp. 1012–1015 (2008)
3. Huo, J., Qu, H., Liu, L.: Design and Implementation of Automatic Defensive Websites Tamper-Resistant System. Journal of Software 7, 2379–2386 (2012)

4. Fan, J.H., Song, Y.B.: Web page Tamper-resistant Mechanism Based on File-filtering Driver and Event-triggering. Journal of Chongqing Institute of Technology (Natural Science) 12, 65–70 (2009)
5. He, Q., Zhao, B., Wang, Y., et al.: Web file protection based on the Rsync algorithm and local snapshots. Computer Engineering 39, 190–199 (2013)
6. Yao, Y.: Research and Design of page tamper system. Computer Security 6, 53–55 (2010)
7. Zhou, J., He, Q., Yao, L.: A Distributed Website Anti-tamper System Based on Filter Driver and Proxy. In: Jin, D., Lin, S. (eds.) Advances in MSEC Vol. 1. AISC, vol. 128, pp. 415–421. Springer, Heidelberg (2011)
8. Ian S.: Monitor Linux file system events with inotify, `http://www.ibm.com/developerworks/opensource/library/l-inotify/index.html`
9. Stevens, W.R., Rago, S.A.: Advanced Programming in the UNIX Environment, 2nd edn. Pearson (2005) ISBN 978-0321525949
10. Common Vulnerabilities and Exposures, `http://www.cve.mitre.org/cgi-bin/cvename.cgi?name=CVE-2013-225`

Multiple-Bank E-Cash without Random Oracles

Jiangxiao Zhang, Zhoujun Li, and Hua Guo

State Key Laboratory of Software Development Environment,
Beihang University, Beijing 100191, PRC
orange_0009200@163.com

Abstract. Multiple-bank e-cash (electronic cash) model allows users
and merchants to open their accounts at different banks. Most e-cash
systems in the literature have been proposed in the single bank model
in which clients and merchants have accounts at the same bank. In recent years, some multiple-bank e-cash systems were proposed, but they
were proven secure in the random oracle model. In this paper, based
on the Groth-Sahai proof system and Ghadafi group blind signature, we
construct a multiple-bank e-cash system which is proven secure in the
standard model. We achieve the dual privacy requirement (i.e., the user
anonymity and bank anonymity) by using the group blind signature. Our
scheme can also trace the identity of the signer. At last, some security
properties of our scheme, such as anonymity, unforgeability, identification of the double spender and exculpability, are proved in the standard
model.

Keywords: multiple-bank e-cash, group blind signature, automorphic
blind signature, Groth-Sahai proofs.

1 Introduction

Group blind signature and multiple-bank e-cash were firstly introduced by
Lysyanskaya and Ramzan [1]. Group blind signature combines the properties
of both a group signature scheme and a blind signature scheme and therefore
it maintains the anonymity of the signer as well as the message to be signed.
Multiple-bank e-cash system consists of a large group of banks which are monitored by the Central Bank, opener, users and merchants. Each bank can dispense
e-cash. The users and merchants can open their accounts in different bank. To
make e-cash systems acceptable to government, the multiple-bank e-cash system should provide the owner tracing, coin tracing, identification of the double
spender and signer tracing.

The multiple-bank e-cash system consists of Group Manager (GM), opener
(OP), multiple banks $B_1, \cdots, B_n$, the users $U_1, \cdots, U_n$ and the merchants
$M_1, \cdots, M_n$. Existing multiple-bank e-cash systems were proven secure in the
random oracle model. Some results [2,3] have shown that some schemes proven
secure in the random oracle model, are not secure in the standard model. Therefore, we propose a multiple-bank e-cash system proven secure in the standard
model. We consider the dual privacy requirement, such as the user anonymity
and bank anonymity.

G. Wang et al. (Eds.): CSS 2013, LNCS 8300, pp. 40–51, 2013.

Related Work. Much research has been performed in the area of e-cash [4,5,6,7,8,9,10,11]. The compact e-cash scheme [4] allows a user to withdraw a wallet containing 2^L coins efficiently and satisfies all the security properties mentioned above. However, the number of the coins that the user wants must be chosen in the withdrawal protocol, and be spent one by one in the spending protocol. Belenkiy, Chase, Kohlweiss and Lysyanskaya [12] proposed a compact e-cash system with non-interactive spending in the standard model. This scheme is based on P-signature [13], simulatable verifiable random functions [14] and Groth-Sahai proofs systems [15]. Izabachene and Libert proposed the first divisible e-cash scheme [11] in the standard model. They used a different method to authenticate the spending path. Unfortunately, the communication complexity of the spending scheme is proportional to the level number of the spent node. Zhang *et al.* constructed an anonymous transferable conditional e-cash [16] in the standard model.

The concept of group blind signatures was first introduced by Lysyanskaya and Zulfikar [1], where it was mainly used to design a multiple bank e-cash system in which digital coins could be issued by different banks. Based on the group blind signature [1], Jeong and Lee constructed a multi-bank e-cash system [17]. However, the system is proven secure in the random oracle model. In 2008, a multiple-bank e-cash [18] is proposed by Wang et al. However, it does not satisfy the unforgeable requirement. In order to obtain unforgeability, Chen et al. proposed an e-cash system [19] with multiple-bank. All the security of above multiple-bank e-cash are proven in the random oracle model which is known not to accurately reflect world (see [2] for instance).

Using divertible zero-knowledge proofs [21], Nguyen et al. proposed a group blind signature [20]. However, to eliminate the interaction in proof, it relies on the Fiat-Shamir transformation. Therefore, it is proven secure in the random oracle model. In 2013, Ghadafi constructed a group blind signature [22] in the standard model. He gave the formalizing definitions of the group blind signature. He also offered the dual privacy requirement, such as the user anonymity and the signer anonymity.

Our Contribution. We construct a multiple-bank e-cash system by using automorphic blind signature scheme [23] and Ghadafi group blind signature [22] in the standard model. We make the following contribution.

– We can trace the identity of the signer by the opener.
– By introducing a security tag, we can recover the identity of double spender.
– We give the security proof in the standard model. The new system satisfies anonymity, unforgeability, identification of double spenders and exculpability.

Paper Outline. The rest of the paper is organized as follows. In Section 2 we present preliminaries on the various cryptographic tools and assumptions. Definitions and the security properties of divisible e-cash are presented in Section 3. In Section 4, we present our construction and give efficiency analysis. We give the security proof in Section 5. Finally we conclude in Section 6.

2 Preliminaries

2.1 Mathematical Definitions and Assumptions

Definition 1. (Pairing). *A pairing* $\hat{e} : \mathbb{G}_1 \times \mathbb{G}_2 \to \mathbb{G}_3$ *is a bilinear mapping from two group elements to a group element [15].*

- $\mathbb{G}_1, \mathbb{G}_2$ *and* $\mathbb{G}_3$ *are cyclic groups of prime order* p*. The elements* G, H *generate* $\mathbb{G}_1$ *and* $\mathbb{G}_2$ *respectively.*
- $\hat{e} : \mathbb{G}_1 \times \mathbb{G}_2$ *is a non-degenerate bilinear map, so* $\hat{e}(G, H)$ *generates* G_3 *and for all* $a, b \in \mathbb{Z}_n$ *we have* $\hat{e}(G^a, H^b) = \hat{e}(G, H)^{ab}$*.*
- *We can efficiently compute group operations, compute the bilinear map and decide membership.*

Definition 2. (Diffie-Hellman Pair). *A pair* $(x, y) \in \mathbb{G}_1 \times \mathbb{G}_2$ *is defined as a Diffie−Hellman pair [24], if there exists* $a \leftarrow \mathbb{Z}_p$ *such that* $x = G^a, y = H^a$*, where* G, H *generate* $\mathbb{G}_1$ *and* $\mathbb{G}_2$ *respectively. We denote the set of* $\mathcal{DH}$ *pairs by* $\mathcal{DH} = \{(G^a, H^a) | a \in \mathbb{Z}_p\}$*.*

2.2 Mathematical Assumptions

The security of this scheme is based on the following existing mathematical assumptions, i.e., the Symmetric External Diffie-Hellman (SXDH) [15], AWF-CDH [26] and the asymmetric double hidden strong Diffie-Hellman assumption (q-ADH-SDH) [23].

Definition 3. (Symmetric External Diffie-Hellman). *Let* $\mathbb{G}_1, \mathbb{G}_2$ *be cyclic groups of prime order,* G_1 *and* G_2 *generate* $\mathbb{G}_1$ *and* $\mathbb{G}_2$*, and let* $\hat{e} : \mathbb{G}_1 \times \mathbb{G}_2 \to \mathbb{G}_3$ *be a bilinear map. The Symmetric External Diffie-Hellman (SXDH) Assumption states that the DDH problem is hard in both* $\mathbb{G}_1$ *and* $\mathbb{G}_2$*. For random* a, b*,* $G_1, G_1^a, G_1^b \leftarrow \mathbb{G}_1$ *and* $G_2, G_2^a, G_2^b \leftarrow \mathbb{G}_2$ *are given, it is hard to distinguish* G_1^{ab} *from a random element from* $\mathbb{G}_i$ *for* $i = 1, 2$*.*

Definition 4. (AWF-CDH). *Let* $G_1 \leftarrow \mathbb{G}_1, G_2 \leftarrow \mathbb{G}_2$ *and* $a \leftarrow \mathbb{Z}_p$ *be random. Given* $(G_1, A = G_1^a, G_2)$*, it is hard to output* $(G_1^r, G_1^{ar}, G_2^r, G_2^{ar})$ *with* $r \neq 0$*, i.e., a tuple* (R, M, S, N) *that satisfies*

$$\hat{e}(A, S) = \hat{e}(M, G_2) \qquad \hat{e}(M, G_2) = \hat{e}(G_1, N) \qquad \hat{e}R, G_2 = \hat{e}(G_1, S).$$

Definition 5. (q-ADH-SDH). *Let* $G, F, K \leftarrow \mathbb{G}_1, H \leftarrow \mathbb{G}_2$ *and* $x, c_i, v_i \leftarrow Z_p$ *be random. Given* $(G, F, K, G^x; H, Y = H^x)$ *and*

$$\left(A_i = (K \cdot G^{v_i})^{\frac{1}{x+c_i}}, B_i = F^{c_i}, D_i = H^{c_i}, V_i = G^{v_i}, W_i = H^{v_i}\right)$$

for $1 \leq i \leq q-1$*, it is hard to output a new tuple* $(A = (K \cdot G^v)^{\frac{1}{x+c}}, B = F^c, D = H^c, V = G^v, W = H^v)$ *with* $(c, v) \neq (c_i, v_i)$ *for all* i*. i.e., one that satisfies*

$$\hat{e}(A, Y \cdot D) = \hat{e}(K \cdot V, H), \hat{e}(B, H) = \hat{e}(F, D), \hat{e}(V, H) = \hat{e}(G, W).$$

2.3 Useful Tools

Groth-Sahai Proofs. Groth and Sahai [15] constructed the first NIZK proof systems. They prove a large class of statements in the context of groups with bilinear map in the standard model. In order to prove the statement, the prover firstly commits to group elements. Then the prover produces the proofs and sends the commitments and the proofs to the verifier. And last the verifier verifies the correctness of the proof.

Groth-Sahai proofs can be instantiated under different security assumptions but since as noted by [25] the most efficient Groth-Sahai proofs are those instantiated under the SXDH assumption, we will be focusing on this instantiation. Following the definitions of Ghadafi [22], the proof system consists of the algorithms $GS = (GSSetup, GSProve, GSVerify, GSExtract, GSSimSetup, GSSimProve)$. For ease of composition, we also define the algorithm $GSPOK$ $(crs, \{w_1, \ldots, w_i\}, \{\varepsilon_1 \wedge \ldots \wedge \varepsilon_j\})$ [22] which proves j multiple equations involving witness $(w_1, \ldots, w_i)$ and returns a vector of size j of Groth-Sahai proofs.

Automorphic Blind Signature. Abe et al. proposed an automorphic blind signature scheme [23] which is structure-preserving signatures on group elements. The automorphic blind signature to sign one message is done between U and signer. We define the automorphic blind signature to sign one message as $ABSign()$ and the verification of the signature as $ABSVerify()$.

In order to sign two messages, we use the definition 2 in [23] to finish a generic transformation [23] from any scheme signing two messages to one singing one message.

Group Blind Signature. Ghadafi constructed a group blind signature [22] which provides the dual privacy requirement. On the one hand, the signer (the bank) can hide his identity and parts of the signature that could identify him. On the other hand, the user can hide the message and parts of the signature which could lead to a linkage between a signature and its sign request. Ghadafi presented two example instantiations. We use the first construction and define the first construction as $GGBS()$. The CERT signature [22] is instantiated by using the above automorphic blind signature [23]. Note that when we sign one message, we use the $ABSign()$ to generate the signature. However, when we sign two messages, we use the transformation signature which transforms the signature to two messages into the signature to one message.

3 Definitions for Multiple-Bank E-Cash

Our model builds on the security models for the Ghadafi group blind signature [22] and the transferable e-cash [10]. The parties involved in a multiple-bank e-cash are: a group manager GM, an opener OP, many banks B_i and users U_i. Note that merchants M are the special users.

In the following, we first describe the algorithms for multiple-bank e-cash.

3.1   Algorithms

We represent a coin as *coin*, which its identity is *Id*. A multiple-bank e-cash system, denoted Π, is composed of the following procedures, where λ is a security parameter.

- ParamGen(1^λ) is run by some trusted third party (TTP) which takes as input 1^λ and outputs the public key *mbpk* for the multiple-bank e-cash system, the group manager's secret key sk_{GM} and the opener's extraction key (ck_{op}, ek_{op}).
- BKeyGen() is run by the banks B_i, to generate his pairs of personal secret/pulbic keys $(bssk_i, bspk_i)$ and $(bgsk_i, bgpk_i)$. The former is used in the joining protocol. The latter is used for issuing the group blind signature in the withdrawal protocol. We assume that the public key is publicly accessible.
- UKeyGen() is run by the users U_i, to generate his pair of personal secret/pulbic keys (sk_{U_i}, pk_{U_i}). Note that the merchants M are special users.
- Issue($B_i(mbpk, i, bssk_i), GM(sk_{GM}, i, bspk_i)$) is an interactive protocol between a bank B_i and the group manager GM. After a successful completion of this protocol, B_i becomes a member of the group. If successful, B_i obtains the certificate $cert_i$, and stores the second secret/public keys $(bgsk_i, bgpk_i)$ and $cert_i$ into gsk_i. GM obtains the signature sig_i on the second public key $bgpk_i$ and stores the second public key $bgpk_i$ and sig_i into reg_i.
- Withdraw($U_i(mbpk, m), B_i(gsk_i, pk_{U_i})$) is an interactive protocol between a user U_i and an anonymous bank B_i. If the protocol completes successfully, U_i obtains a blind signature π_m on the message m. B_i does not learn what the message was. U_i only knows the signature that is signed by the bank, but he does not know which bank issues the signature.
- Spend($U_i(coin, pk_M, sk_{U_i}, pk_{U_i}, ck_{op}), M(sk_M, pk_M, bgpk_i)$) is an interactive protocol between a user U_i and a merchant M. If the protocol completes successfully, U_i obtains the corresponding serves. M obtains an e-coin *coin*.
- Deposit($M(coin, sk_M, pk_M, bgpk_i), B_i(pk_M, DB)$) is an interactive protocol between a merchant M and a bank B_i. If *coin* is not valid, B_i outputs $\perp$. Else, B_i checks whether the database DB contains an e-cash $coin'$ in which the serial number is the same as the one in *coin*. If DB contains $coin'$, B_i outputs $(coin, coin')$. Else, B_i adds *coin* to DB, and credits M's account.
- Identify($coin, coin'$) is a deterministic algorithm executed by B_i. It outputs the public key pk_{U_i} and a proof τ_G.
- VerifyGuilt(pk_{U_i}, τ_G) is a deterministic algorithm that can be executed by anyone. It outputs 1 if τ_G is correct and 0 otherwise.
- Open($mbpk, ek_{op}, reg_i, m, \pi_m$) is a deterministic algorithm in which the opener uses his extraction key ek_{op} to recover the identity i of the banker and produces a proof τ_S attesting to this claim.
- VerifySigner($mbpk, i, bspk_i, m, \pi_m, \tau_S$) is a deterministic algorithm which inputs an index i and returns 1 if the signature π_m was produced by the bank B_i or 0 otherwise.

3.2 Security Properties

In this section, we give the brief description of the security properties in our scheme.

Anonymity. Anonymity includes the bank anonymity and the user anonymity. In the following, we give the formal definition of the bank anonymity and the user anonymity.

The bank anonymity guarantees that the adversary is unable to tell which bank produced a signature. We employ the same signer anonymity used by [22], where we require that the adversary is given two banks of its choice, the adversary still cannot distinguish which of the two banks produced a signature.

The user anonymity guarantees that the adversary is unable to tell which message it is signing. We employ the blindness property used by [22], where we require that the adversary is given a signature on a message m_i for $i = \{0, 1\}$ of its choice, he still cannot distinguish which of the two messages is signed.

Unforgeability. Unforgeability guarantees that no collection of users can ever spend more coins than they withdrew. Formally, we have the following definition based on the experiment given below.

Identification of Double-Spender. The identification of double-spender guarantees that no collection of users, collaborating with the merchant, can spend an e-cash twice without revealing one of their identities. Formally, we have the following experiment.

Exculpability. The exculpability guarantees that the bank, even when colluding with malicious users, cannot falsely accuse hones users of having double-spent a coin. Formally, we have the following experiment.

4 Multiple-Bank E-Cash

Multiple-bank e-cash allows users and merchants to open their accounts at different banks. It supplies the users anonymity and the banks anonymity. In the following, we give the details of this scheme.

4.1 Setup

On input 1^λ and output the public parameters of bilinear groups $bgpp = (p, \mathbb{G}_1, \mathbb{G}_2, \mathbb{G}_3, \hat{e}, G, H)$, where λ is the security parameter. We choose random elements $F, K, T \in \mathbb{G}_1$. On input $bgpp$ run the setup algorithms for Groth-Sahai proofs and return two reference strings crs_1, crs_2 and the corresponding extraction keys ek_1, ek_2. The two reference strings and the extraction keys are used for the first round and the second round of the automorphic blind signature scheme which is used for issuing the group blind signature on the e-cash. The opener's commitment key and extraction key are $(ck_{op} = crs_2, ek_{op} = ek_2)$. On choose $s_{GM} \leftarrow \mathbb{Z}_p$ and output the key pair of group manager $(sk_{GM} = s_{GM}, pk_{GM} = (S_1 = G_1^{s_{GM}}, S_2 = G_2^{s_{GM}}))$. The public key of multiple-bank e-cash is $mbpk = (bgpp, F, K, T, crs_1, crs_2, pk_{GM})$. $\mathcal{H}$ is a collision-resistant hash function.

Each bank B_i chooses $s_{B_i}, s'_{B_i} \leftarrow \mathbb{Z}_p$ and creates two key pairs $(bssk_{B_i} = s_{B_i}, bspk_{B_i} = (S_1 = G_1^{s_{B_i}}, S_2 = G_2^{s_{B_i}}))$ and $(bgsk_{B_i} = s'_{B_i}, bgpk_{B_i} = (S_1 = G_1^{s'_{B_i}}, S_2 = G_2^{s'_{B_i}}))$. The first key pair is the bank's personal key pair. The second one is used for signing the e-cash. Each user U_i chooses $s_{U_i} \leftarrow \mathbb{Z}_p$ and generates the key pair $(sk_{U_i} = s_{U_i}, pk_{U_i} = (S_1 = G_1^{s_{U_i}}, S_2 = G_2^{s_{U_i}}))$. Each merchant M_i also creates the key pair $(sk_{M_i} = s_{M_i}, pk_{M_i} = (S_1 = G_1^{s_{M_i}}, S_2 = G_2^{s_{M_i}}))$.

4.2   The Joining Protocol

The joining protocol allows the bank to obtain a certificate from the group manager. In order to issuing e-cash, each bank firstly joins into the group whose manager is GM. Then the bank B_i obtains the certificate $cert_i$. Using the certificate and the key pair $(bgsk, bgpk)$, the bank issuing the e-cash. In the following, we give the details of the protocol.

1. $(B_i \rightarrow GM)$. The bank B_i generates the signature $sig_i = ABSign(bssk_i, bgpk_i)$. Then B_i sends $sig_i, bgpk_i = (S_1^{bg} = G_1^{s_{B_i}}, S_2^{bg} = G_2^{s'_{B_i}})$ to the group manager GM.
2. $(GM \rightarrow B_i)$. GM checks whether the public key $bgpk_i$ has existed in the database DB_{pk} or verifies $\hat{e}(S_1^{bg}, G_2) \neq \hat{e}(G_1, S_2^{bg})$. If it is not, GM verifies the signature sig_i. If $ABSverify(bspk_i, bgpk_i, sig_i) = 1$, GM generates the certificate $cert_i = ABSign(sk_{GM}, bgpk_i)$. At last, GM sends $cert_i$ to B_i.
3. B_i verifies the correctness of the certificate. If $ABSverify(pk_{GM}, bgpk_i, cert_i) = 1$, B_i saves the certificate $cert_i$.

4.3   The Withdrawal Protocol

The withdrawal protocol allows U_i to withdraw an e-cash from B_i. c_m is defined as the commitment and corresponding proof to the message m. $C_m^{ck_{op}}$ is defined as the commitment to m using the commitment key ck_{op}. In the following, we give the protocol in detail.

1. $(U_i \rightarrow B_i)$. U_i chooses $s_m \leftarrow \mathbb{Z}_p$ and generates the serial number $S = (G_1^{s_m}, G_2^{s_m})$. U_i also chooses $q_1, q_2 \leftarrow \mathbb{Z}_p$ and computes $Q_1 = G_1^{q_1}, Q_2 = G_2^{q_1}, Q_3 = G_1^{q_2}, Q_4 = G_1^{q_2}$. U_i picks at random nonces $\iota_1, \iota_2 \leftarrow \mathbb{Z}_p$. To hide the serial number, U_i generates the following commitments c_S and the correct proofs π_S by using the commitment key ck_{op} of the opener. U_i also generates

the commitment $c_{pk_{U_i}}$ and the correct proof $\pi_{pk_{U_i}}$ to U_i's public key $pk_{U_i} = (S_1 = G_1^{s_{U_i}}, S_2 = G_2^{s_{U_i}})$.

$$c_S = (C_{G_1^{s_m}}^{ck_{op}}, C_{G_2^{s_m}}^{ck_{op}}, C_{Q_1}^{ck_{op}}, C_{Q_2}^{ck_{op}}, U_1 = T^{\iota_1} \cdot G_1^{s_m}),$$
$$\pi_S \leftarrow GSPOK\{crs_1, \{G_1^{s_m}, G_2^{s_m}, Q_1, Q_2\}, \hat{e}(G_1^{s_m}, G_2) = \hat{e}(G_1, G_2^{s_m}) \wedge$$
$$\hat{e}(Q_1, G_2) = \hat{e}(G_1, Q_2) \wedge \hat{e}(T, Q_2) \cdot \hat{e}(G_1^{s_m}, G_2) = \hat{e}(U_1, G_2)\},$$
$$c_{pk_{U_i}} = (C_{G_1^{s_{U_i}}}^{ck_{op}}, C_{G_2^{s_{U_i}}}^{ck_{op}}, C_{Q_3}^{ck_{op}}, C_{Q_4}^{ck_{op}}, U_2 = T^{\iota_2} \cdot G_1^{s_{U_i}}),$$
$$\pi_{pk_{U_i}} \leftarrow GSPOK\{crs_1, \{G_1^{s_{U_i}}, G_2^{s_{U_i}}, Q_3, Q_4\}, \hat{e}(G_1^{s_{U_i}}, G_2) = \hat{e}(G_1, G_2^{s_{U_i}}) \wedge$$
$$\hat{e}(Q_1, G_2) = \hat{e}(G_1, Q_2) \wedge \hat{e}(T, Q_2) \cdot \hat{e}(G_1^{s_{U_i}}, G_2) = \hat{e}(U_2, G_2)\}.$$

At last, U_i sends $\{pk_{U_i}, c_S, \pi_S, c_{pk_{U_i}}, \pi_{pk_{U_i}}\}$ to B_i.

2. $(B_i \rightarrow U_i)$. B_i verifies the public key pk_{U_i}, π_S and $\pi_{pk_{U_i}}$. If $GSVerify(crs_1, \pi_S) = 1$ and $GSVerify(crs_1, \pi pk_{U_i}) = 1$, B_i generates the group blind signature $GGBS(S, pk_{U_i})$ [22] on c_S and $c_{pk_{U_i}}$ by using the definition 2 in [23]. $GGBS(S, pk_{U_i})$ includes the signature $\sigma_{(S, pk_{U_i})}$ and the proof $\pi_{\sigma_{(S, pk_{U_i})}}$. $\pi_{\sigma_{(S, pk_{U_i})}}$ gives a proof that $\sigma_{(S, pk_{U_i})}$ is a valid signature on c_S and $c_{pk_{U_i}}$. At last, B_i sends $\pi_{\sigma_{(S, pk_{U_i})}}$ to U_i.

3. U_i verifies $\pi_{\sigma_{(S, pk_{U_i})}}$. If it is OK, to obtain the signature of the messages $(G_1^{s_m}, G_2^{s_m})$ and $(G_1^{s_{U_i}}, G_2^{s_{U_i}})$, U_i re-randomizes the proof $\pi_{\sigma_{(S, pk_{U_i})}}$ into $\pi'_{\sigma_{(S, pk_{U_i})}}$.
At last, U_i obtains the e-cash $coin = \{S, c_{pk_{U_i}}, \pi'_{\sigma_{(S, pk_{U_i})}}\}$.

4.4   The Spending Protocol

The spending protocol allows U_i to spend an e-cash to the merchant M. In order to hide U_i's identity, U_i randomizes $c_{pk_{U_i}}$ and $\pi'_{\sigma_{pk_{U_i}}}$ by $RdCom$ and $RdProve$.

1. $(M \rightarrow U_i)$. M computes $R = \mathcal{H}(pk_M||Date||r)$ and sends $\{R, pk_M, Date, r\}$ to U_i, where $r \leftarrow \mathbb{Z}_p$ is a random value.

2. $(U_i \rightarrow M)$. U_i also computes $R = \mathcal{H}(pk_M||Date||r)$. The commitment to U_i's public key is $c_{pk_{U_i}} = (C_{G_1^{s_{U_i}}}^{ck_{op}}, C_{G_2^{s_{U_i}}}^{ck_{op}}, C_{Q_3}^{ck_{op}}, C_{Q_4}^{ck_{op}}, U_1 = T^{\iota_2} \cdot G_1^{s_{U_i}})$. In order to hide U_i's public key, U_i chooses $\iota'_2, t', \mu', \nu', \rho' \leftarrow \mathbb{Z}_p$ and randomizes $c_{pk_{U_i}}$ into $c'_{pk_{U_i}}$ [24].

U_i computes $Y = G_1^{\frac{1}{s_m+1}}$ and the security tag $T = pk_{U_i} \cdot \hat{e}(Y, G_2^R)$. Meanwhile, U_i gives the following NIZK proofs π_Y, π_T. π_Y gives a proof that $Y = G_1^{\frac{1}{s_m+1}}$ and s_m in Y is equal to s_m in S. π_T gives a proof that the security tag T is correctly formed.

$$\pi_Y \leftarrow GSPOK\{crs_1, \{Y, \phi_Y, s_m\}, \hat{e}(G_1^{\frac{1}{s_m+1}}, G_2^{s_m} \cdot G_2) = 1_{\mathbb{G}_3}, \hat{e}(Y/\phi_Y, h^\theta) = 1_{\mathbb{G}_3}\},$$
$$\pi_T \leftarrow GSPOK\{crs_1, \{T, \phi_T, Y, \phi_Y\}, \{T = pk_{U_i} \cdot \hat{e}(Y, G_2^R), \hat{e}(Y/\phi_Y, h^\theta) = 1_{\mathbb{G}_3},$$
$$\hat{e}(T/\phi_T, h^\theta) = 1_{\mathbb{G}_3}\}\},$$

where $\phi_Y, \phi_T \leftarrow \mathbb{G}_1$ are auxiliary variables, and $\theta \leftarrow \mathbb{Z}_p$ is a variable [11]. At last, U_i sends the e-cash $coin' = \{S, R, c'_{pk_{U_i}}, T, \pi_{coin'} = \{\pi'_{\sigma(S, pk_{U_i})}, \pi_Y, \pi_T\}\}$ to M.

3. M verifies the proofs. If they are correct, M saves $coin'$ and supplies serves to U_i.

4.5 The Deposit Protocol

M can deposit the e-cash to any bank. We assume that M has an account in B_i. When M wants to deposit a coin $coin'$ to B_i, M just sends $coin'$ to B_i. B_i checks the validity of $\pi_{coin'}$ and the consistency with S. If $coin'$ is not a valid coin, B_i rejects the deposit. Else, B_i checks if there is already the serial number S in the database. If there is not entry in the database, then B_i accepts the deposit of the coin $coin'$, credits the M's account and adds $coin'$ in the database. Else, there is an entry $coin'' = \{S, R', c''_{pk_{U_i}}, T', \pi'_{coin'}\}$ in the database. Then, B_i checks the freshness of R in $coin'$ compared to $coin''$. If it is not fresh, M is a cheat and B_i refused the deposit. If R is fresh, B_i accepts the deposit of the $coin'$, credits the M's account and add $(coin', coin'')$ to the list of double spenders. For recovering the identity of double spender, B_i executes the **Identify** algorithm.

4.6 Identify

The Identify algorithm makes sure that when a double-spending is found, B_i recovers the identity of double spender. The description of the Identify algorithm is as follow.

B_i knows two coins $coin_1 = \{S, R_1, \{c'_{pk_{U_i}}\}_1, T_1, \pi_1\}$ and $coin_2 = \{S, R_2, \{c'_{pk_{U_i}}\}_2, T_2, \pi_2\}$. Therefore, B_i directly recovers the public key pk_{U_i} by computing $(T_1^{R_2}/T_2^{R_1})^{\frac{1}{R_2-R_1}}$.

4.7 Verify

Any one can verify the correctness of the double spenders and the signer (bank). In order to verify the correctness of the double spenders, any one executes the algorithm $VerifyGuilt$. One can parse the $coin_1$ and $coin_2$ as $(S, R_1, \{c'_{pk_{U_i}}\}_1, T_1, \pi_1)$ and $(S, R_2, \{c'_{pk_{U_i}}\}_2, T_2, \pi_2)$ and next run Identify on these values. If the algorithm Identify returns a public key, then one can check if π_1 is consistent with $(S, R_1, \{c'_{pk_{U_i}}\}_1, T_1)$ and if π_2 is consistent with $(S, R_2, \{c'_{pk_{U_i}}\}_2, T_2)$.

In order to verify the correctness of the signer (bank) who is opened by opener, any one executes the algorithm $VerifySigner$. The input of the algorithm is $(mbpk, i, bspk_i, m, \pi_m, \tau_S)$. After verifying the correctness of π_m, any one can check if the signature is signed by the bank.

4.8   Signer Tracing

Signer tracing is that the opener OP can recover the identity of the signer B_i. U_i obtains the signature $\pi_{(\sigma_S, \sigma_{pk_{U_i}})}$. Using the Open algorithm [22], OP extracts $(\sigma_{(S, pk_{U_i})}, cert_i, bgpk_i)$ from $\pi_{(\sigma_S, \sigma_{pk_{U_i}})}$. Therefore, we know which bank signs the e-cash.

4.9   Efficiency Analysis

We analyze the efficiency of our scheme, Chen's scheme [19] and Jeong's scheme [17] from the following 5 aspects, namely the efficiency of the joining protocol, the efficiency of the withdrawal protocol, the efficiency of the spending protocol, the efficiency of the deposit protocol and security model. It is somehow hard to quantify the exact cost of the spending protocol in [17] as the instantiation of the SKREP is very complex. We thus simplify the comparison by stating the total multi-exponentiations needed. The comparison is given in the following Table 1.

We assume that C_1 is the computation cost of the joining protocol. C_2 is the efficiency of the withdrawal protocol. C_3 is the efficiency of the spending protocol. C_4 is the efficiency of the deposit protocol. C_5 is the security model. ME represents the number of multi-exponentiation. ROM represents the random oracle model. SM represents the standard model.

Table 1. Efficiency comparison between related work and our scheme

		C_1		C_2		C_3		C_4	C_5
Chen's scheme [19]	B_i	$62ME$	B_i	$91ME$	M	$580ME$	B_i	$285ME$	ROM
	GM	$273ME$	U_i	$71ME$	U_i	$61ME$			
Jeong's scheme [17]	B_i	$11ME$	B_i	$10ME$	M	$12ME$	B_i	$12ME$	ROM
	GM	$12ME$	U_i	$19ME$	U_i	$11ME$			
Ours	B_i	$17ME$	B_i	$17ME$	M	$101ME$	B_i	$76ME$	SM
	GM	$17ME$	U_i	$36ME$	U_i	$26ME$			

Based on the Table 1, the number of multi-exponentiation in our scheme is less than one in Chen's scheme [19], but more than Jeong's scheme [17]. However, our scheme is proven secure in the standard model. We know that the scheme proven secure in the standard model is more securer than one proven secure in the random oracle model. Therefore, our scheme is more secure.

5   Security Analysis

Regarding the security of our construction, We have the following theorem.

Theorem 1. *Our multiple-bank e-cash system is secure under the following assumptions: unforgeability of automorphic blind signature and Ghadafi group blind signature, pseudorandomness of the Dodis-Yampolskiy PRF and soundness, witness indistinguishability and re-randomness of Groth-Sahai proofs system.*

6   Conclusion

In this paper, we present a multiple-bank e-cash which is proved secure in the standard model. We achieve the dual privacy requirement (the users anonymity and the bank anonymity) by using the Ghadafi group blind signature. To hide the identity of the user, we re-randomize the commitment to the user's public key by using the re-randomness of the Groth-Sahai proofs system. To ensure the security of the security tag, we use the pseudorandomness of the Dodis-Yampolskiy PRF. At last, we prove the security properties in the standard model.

Acknowledgments. This work was supported by the National Natural Science Foundation of China (grant number 60973105, 90718017, 61170189, 61300172), the Research Fund for the Doctoral Program of Higher Education (grant number 20111102130003, 20121102120017) and the Fund of the State Key Laboratory of Software Development Environment (grant number SKLSDE-2011ZX-03, SKLSDE-2012ZX-11).

References

1. Lysyanskaya, A., Ramzan, Z.: Group blind signature: a scalable solution to electronic cash. In: Hirschfeld, R. (ed.) FC 1998. LNCS, vol. 1465, pp. 184–197. Springer, Heidelberg (1998)
2. Canetti, R., Goldreich, O., Halevi, S.: The random oracle methodology, revisited. In: 30th AcM STOC, pp. 209–218. ACM Press (1998)
3. Bellare, M., Boldyreva, A., Palacio, A.: An uninstantiable random-oracle-model scheme for a hybrid-encryption problem. In: Cachin, C., Camenisch, J.L. (eds.) EUROCRYPT 2004. LNCS, vol. 3027, pp. 171–188. Springer, Heidelberg (2004)
4. Camenisch, J.L., Hohenberger, S., Lysyanskaya, A.: Compact E-cash. In: Cramer, R. (ed.) EUROCRYPT 2005. LNCS, vol. 3494, pp. 302–321. Springer, Heidelberg (2005)
5. Canard, S., Gouget, A.: Divisible e-cash systems can be truly anonymous. In: Naor, M. (ed.) EUROCRYPT 2007. LNCS, vol. 4515, pp. 482–497. Springer, Heidelberg (2007)
6. Au, M.H., Wu, Q., Susilo, W., Mu, Y.: Compact e-cash from bounded accumulator. In: Abe, M. (ed.) CT-RSA 2007. LNCS, vol. 4377, pp. 178–195. Springer, Heidelberg (2006)
7. Au, M.H., Susilo, W., Mu, Y.: Practical anonymous divisible e-cash from bounded accumulators. In: Tsudik, G. (ed.) FC 2008. LNCS, vol. 5143, pp. 287–301. Springer, Heidelberg (2008)
8. Belenkiy, M., Chase, M., Kohlweiss, M., Lysyanskaya, A.: Compact E-cash and simulatable VRFs revisited. In: Shacham, H., Waters, B. (eds.) Pairing 2009. LNCS, vol. 5671, pp. 114–131. Springer, Heidelberg (2009)
9. Canard, S., Gouget, A.: Multiple Denominations in E-cash with Compact Transaction Data. In: Sion, R. (ed.) FC 2010. LNCS, vol. 6052, pp. 82–97. Springer, Heidelberg (2010)
10. Blazy, O., Canard, S., Fuchsbauer, G., Gouget, A., Sibert, H., Traoré, J.: Achieving optimal anonymity in transferable e-cash with a judge. In: Nitaj, A., Pointcheval, D. (eds.) AFRICACRYPT 2011. LNCS, vol. 6737, pp. 206–223. Springer, Heidelberg (2011)

11. Izabachène, M., Libert, B.: Divisible e-cash in the standard model. In: Abdalla, M., Lange, T. (eds.) Pairing 2012. LNCS, vol. 7708, pp. 314–332. Springer, Heidelberg (2013)
12. Belenkiy, M., Chase, M., Kohlweiss, M., Lysyanskaya, A.: Compact E-Cash and Simulatable VRFs Revisited. In: Shacham, H., Waters, B. (eds.) Pairing 2009. LNCS, vol. 5671, pp. 114–131. Springer, Heidelberg (2009)
13. Belenkiy, M., Chase, M., Kohlweiss, M., Lysyanskaya, A.: P-signatures and noninteractive anonymous credentials. In: Canetti, R. (ed.) TCC 2008. LNCS, vol. 4948, pp. 356–374. Springer, Heidelberg (2008)
14. Chase, M., Lysyanskaya, A.: Simulatable vrfs with applications to multi-theorem nizk. In: Menezes, A. (ed.) CRYPTO 2007. LNCS, vol. 4622, pp. 303–322. Springer, Heidelberg (2007)
15. Goyal, V., Mohassel, P., Smith, A.: Efficient non-interactive proof systems for bilinear groups. In: Smart, N.P. (ed.) EUROCRYPT 2008. LNCS, vol. 4965, pp. 415–432. Springer, Heidelberg (2008)
16. Zhang, J., Li, Z., Guo, H.: Anonymous transferable conditional E-cash. In: Keromytis, A.D., Di Pietro, R. (eds.) SecureComm 2012. LNICST, vol. 106, pp. 45–60. Springer, Heidelberg (2013)
17. Jeong, I.R., Lee, D.-H.: Anonymity control in multi-bank E-cash system. In: Roy, B., Okamoto, E. (eds.) INDOCRYPT 2000. LNCS, vol. 1977, pp. 104–116. Springer, Heidelberg (2000)
18. Wang, S., Chen, Z., Wang, X.: A new certificateless electronic cash scheme with multiple banks based on group signatures. In: Proc. of 2008 International Symposium on Electronic Commerce and Security, pp. 362–366 (2008)
19. Chen, M., Fan, C., Juang, W., Yeh, Y.: An efficient electronic cash scheme with multiple banks using group signature. International Journal of Innovative Computing, Information and Control 8(7) (2012)
20. Nguyen, K.Q., Mu, Y., Varadharajan, V.: Divertible zero-knowledge proof of polynomial relations and blind group signature. In: Pieprzyk, J.P., Safavi-Naini, R., Seberry, J. (eds.) ACISP 1999. LNCS, vol. 1587, pp. 117–128. Springer, Heidelberg (1999)
21. Okamoto, T., Ohta, K.: Divertible zero knowledge interactive proofs and commutative random self-reducibility. In: Quisquater, J.-J., Vandewalle, J. (eds.) EUROCRYPT 1989. LNCS, vol. 434, pp. 134–149. Springer, Heidelberg (1990)
22. Ghadafi, E.: Formalizing group blind signatures and practical constructions without random oracles. In: Boyd, C., Simpson, L. (eds.) ACISP. LNCS, vol. 7959, pp. 330–346. Springer, Heidelberg (2013)
23. Abe, M., Fuchsbauer, G., Groth, J., Haralambiev, K., Ohkubo, M.: Structure-preserving signatures and commitments to group elements. In: Rabin, T. (ed.) CRYPTO 2010. LNCS, vol. 6223, pp. 209–236. Springer, Heidelberg (2010)
24. Fuchsbauer, G.: Commuting signatures and verifiable encryption. In: Paterson, K.G. (ed.) EUROCRYPT 2011. LNCS, vol. 6632, pp. 224–245. Springer, Heidelberg (2011)
25. Ghadafi, E., Smart, N.P., Warinschi, B.: Groth-Sahai proofs revisited. In: Nguyen, P.Q., Pointcheval, D. (eds.) PKC 2010. LNCS, vol. 6056, pp. 177–192. Springer, Heidelberg (2010)
26. Fuchsbauer, G.: Automorphic Signatures in Bilinear Groups and an Application to Round-Optimal Blind Signatures. In: Cryptology ePrint Archive, Report 2009/320, http://eprint.iacr.org/2009/320.pdf
27. Dodis, Y., Yampolskiy, A.: A Verifiable Random Function with Short Proofs and Keys. In: Vaudenay, S. (ed.) PKC 2005. LNCS, vol. 3386, pp. 416–431. Springer, Heidelberg (2005)

A Fast Chaos-Based Symmetric Image Cipher with a Novel Bit-Level Permutation Strategy

Chong Fu[1,*], Tao Wang[2], Zhao-yu Meng[1], Jun-xin Chen[1], and Hong-feng Ma[3]

[1] School of Information Science and Engineering, Northeastern University,
Shenyang 110004, China
fuchong@ise.neu.edu.cn
[2] Software College, Northeastern University, Shenyang 110004, China
[3] TeraRecon, 4000 East 3rd Avenue, Suite 200, Foster City, CA 94404, United States

Abstract. This paper presents a fast chaos-based confusion-diffusion type image cipher which introduces a diffusion mechanism in the confusion stage through a novel bit-level permutation. As the pixel value mixing effect is contributed by both stages, the workload of the time-consuming diffusion stage is reduced, and hence the performance of the cryptosystem is improved. Compared with those recently proposed bit-level permutation algorithms, the diffusion effect of the proposed scheme is significantly enhanced as the bits are shuffled among different bitplanes rather than within the same bitplane. Moreover, the pseudorandom locations for bits permutation are produced in a parallel manner, which further increase the performance. Lorenz system is employed as generation of keystream for diffusion. Extensive cryptanalysis has been performed on the proposed scheme, and the results demonstrate that the proposed scheme has a satisfactory security level with a low computational complexity, which renders it a good candidate for real-time secure image transmission applications.

Keywords: Image cipher, bit-level permutation, logistic map, Lorenz system, parallel iteration.

1   Introduction

With the rapid developments in multimedia and communication technologies, a great deal of concern has been raised in the security of image data transmitted over open channels. Conventional block ciphers, such as Triple-DES (Data Encryption Standard), AES (Advanced Encryption Standard) and IDEA (International Data Encryption Algorithm), are not suitable for practical image cipher due to the size of image data and increasing demand for real-time communication. To meet this challenge, a variety of encryption technologies have been proposed. Among them, chaos-based algorithms suggest an optimal trade-off between security and performance. Since the 1990's, many researchers have noticed that the intrinsic properties of chaotic dynamical systems such as extreme sensitivity to initial conditions and system parameters, ergodicity and mixing property naturally satisfy the essential design principles of a cryptosystem such

---

[*] Corresponding author.

G. Wang et al. (Eds.): CSS 2013, LNCS 8300, pp. 52–66, 2013.

as avalanche, confusion and diffusion. The fundamental architecture of chaos-based image cipher was firstly proposed by Fridrich in 1998 [1]. Under this structure, the pixels of a plain image are firstly rearranged in a secret order, so as to eliminate the strong correlations between adjacent pixels. Then in the diffusion stage, the pixel values are altered sequentially and the modification made to a particular pixel usually depends on the accumulated effect of all the previous pixel values, so as to diffuse the influence of each pixel to the whole cipher image. Following Fridrich's pioneer work, a growing number of chaos-based image cryptosystems with confusion-diffusion architecture, their cryptanalysis, and improvements have been proposed [2-25]. A brief overview of some major contributions is given below.

In [2-3, 12], the 2D chaotic cat map and baker map are generalized to 3D to enhance the effectiveness of pixel permutation. It can be seen that these two improved chaotic maps can perform the operation of shuffling the pixel positions in a more efficient manner than 2D-based methods. In [5], Xiang et al. proposed a selective image encryption scheme, which only ciphers a portion of significant bits of each pixel by the keystream generated from a one-way coupled map lattice. It is reported that an acceptable level of security can be achieved by only encrypting the higher 4 bits of each pixel, and therefore the encryption time is substantially reduced. In [7], a way of improving the security of chaos-based cryptosystem is proposed, using a hierarchy of one dimensional chaotic maps and their coupling, which can be viewed as a high dimensional dynamical system. In [8, 9], Gao et al. reported two chaos-based image encryption schemes, which employ an image total shuffling matrix to shuffle the positions of image pixels and use a hyperchaotic system to confuse the relationship between the plain image and the cipher image. In [10], Wong et al. suggested to introduce certain diffusion effect in the confusion stage by simple sequential add-and-shift operations. The purpose is to reduce the workload of the time-consuming diffusion part so that fewer overall rounds and hence a shorter encryption time is needed. To overcome the drawbacks of small key space and weak security in the widely used one-dimensional chaotic system, Sun et al. [11] proposed a spatial chaos map based image encryption scheme. The basic idea is to encrypt the image in space with spatial chaos map pixel-by-pixel, and then the pixels are confused in multiple directions of space. In [13], Rhouma et al. presented a one-way coupled map lattice (OCML) based color image encryption scheme. To enhance the cryptosystem security, a 192-bit-long external key is used to generate the initial conditions and the parameters of the OCML by making some algebraic transformations to the secret keys. In [14], Xiao et al. analyzed the cause of potential flaws in some chaos-based image ciphers and proposed the corresponding enhancement measures. In [15], Wang et al. suggested a chaos-based image encryption algorithm with variable control parameters. The control parameters used in the permutation stage and the keystream employed in the diffusion stage are generated from two chaotic maps related to the plain image. As a result, the algorithm can effectively resist all known attacks against permutation-diffusion architectures. In [16], Wong et al. proposed a more efficient diffusion mechanism using simple table lookup and swapping techniques as a light-weight replacement of the 1D chaotic map iteration. They reported that at a similar security level, the proposed cryptosystem needs about one-third the encryption time of a similar cryptosystem. In [18], Amin et al. introduced a new chaotic block cipher scheme for image cryptosystems that encrypts block of bits rather than block of pixels. The scheme employs the cryptographic primitive operations and a non-linear transformation function within encryption operation, and adopts round keys for encryption using a chaotic system. In [19], Wang et al. proposed a fast image encryption algorithm with combined permutation and diffusion. In their scheme, the image is firstly partitioned into blocks of pixels, and then, spatiotemporal chaos is employed to shuffle the blocks and, at the same time, to change the pixel values. In [23], a novel bidirectional diffusion strategy was suggested to promote the efficiency of the most widely investigated permutation-diffusion type image cipher. By using the proposed strategy, the spreading process is significantly accelerated and hence the same level of security can be achieved with fewer overall encryption rounds. In [25], Seyedzadeh et al. proposed a novel chaos-based image encryption algorithm by using a Coupled Two-dimensional Piecewise Nonlinear Chaotic Map, called CTPNCM, and a masking process. Distinct characteristics of the algorithm are high security, high sensitivity, and high speed that can be applied in encryption of color images.

Very recently, bit-level permutation algorithms were suggested by some scholars [20-22, 24]. As the permutation is performed on bitplane rather than pixel plane, the bit-level permutation has the effects of both confusion and diffusion. The workload of the time-consuming diffusion stage is reduced as the pixel value mixing effect is contributed by both stages, and hence the performance of the cryptosystem is improved. However, those proposed schemes shuffle each bitplane of an image independently. The bits distribution of a bitplane significantly affects the diffusion effect, i.e., if a bitplane contains pixels of nearly all 1s or 0s, the introduced diffusion effect will be negligible. To further enhance the diffusion effect introduced in the confusion stage, this paper proposes a novel bit-level permutation scheme which shuffles the bits among different bitplanes rather than within the same bitplane. The new method swaps each bit with another bit at a location chosen by three chaotic logistic maps that work parallelly. The architecture of the proposed image encryption scheme is shown in Fig. 1.

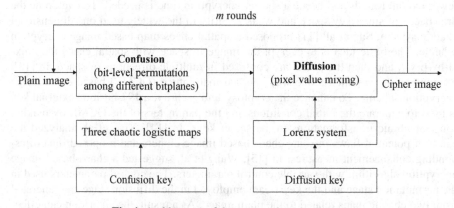

Fig. 1. Architecture of the proposed cryptosystem

In the diffusion stage, Lorenz system is employed as generation of keystream. Compared with 1D chaotic maps such as logistic map, tent map, and Chebyshev map, the Lorenz system has more complicated dynamical property and number of state variables. Consequently, cryptosystem based on Lorenz system has stronger unpredictability and larger key space, which are essential for secure ciphers. The whole confusion-diffusion operations need to be performed alternatively for m ($m > 1$) rounds according to the security requirement. Obviously, the more rounds are processed, the more secure the encryption is, but at the expense of computations and time delays.

The rest of this paper is organized as follows. Section 2 discusses the proposed bit-level permutation strategy using parallel-iterated logistic maps. Then the Lorenz system based image diffusion process is described in Section 3. In Section 4, the security of the proposed cryptosystem is analyzed in detail. Finally, Section 6 concludes the paper.

2   Bit-Level Permutation Using Parallel-Iterated Logistic Maps

As it is known, in digital imaging, a bit is the smallest unit of data. For example, each pixel in an 8-bit grayscale image can be described by

$$P(x, y) = b(7)b(6)b(5)\cdots b(0), \tag{1}$$

where $P(x, y)$ is the value of the pixel at coordinate (x, y) and the number in parentheses indicates the bit index from highest bit 7 to the lowest bit 0. Accordingly, we can decompose a L-bit image into L independent bitplanes and each bitplane is a binary image because there are only two possible intensity values (0 and 1) for each pixel.

Three parallel-iterated chaotic logistic maps are employed to implement the proposed permutation algorithm. The logistic map is described by

$$x_{n+1} = \mu x_n (1 - x_n), \ x_n \in [0, 1], \tag{2}$$

where μ and x_n are parameter and state values, respectively. When $\mu \in [3.57, 4]$, the system is chaotic. The initial value x_0 serves as the key for confusion process.

Without loss of generality, we assume the plain image is of $M \times N$ pixels with L-bit color depth. The detailed permutation procedure is described as follows.

Step 1: The L bitplanes of the plain image are extracted from highest to lowest bit, respectively.

Step 2: The three logistic maps are iterated parallelly for N_0 times to avoid the harmful effect of transitional procedure, where N_0 is a constant. Each thread is assigned with an individual initial value K_{ct} (t=1, 2, 3) as part of the confusion key.

Step 3: The logistic maps are iterated continuously. Exchange current bit with the bit at location (m, n) of the rth bit plane, where

$$\begin{cases} r = mod[\,floor(x_{1n} \times 10^{14}), L], \\ m = mod[\,floor(x_{2n} \times 10^{14}), M], \\ n = mod[\,floor(x_{3n} \times 10^{14}), N], \end{cases} \tag{3}$$

where x_{1n}, x_{2n}, are x_{3n} are current state values of the three maps, respectively, $mod(x, y)$ returns the remainder after division, and $floor(x)$ returns the value of x to the nearest integers less than or equal to x. In our scheme, all the state variables are declared as 64-bit double-precision type. According to the IEEE floating-point standard, all the variables have a 15-digit precision, and hence the decimal fractions of the variable are multiplied by 10^{14}.

Step 4: Return to ***Step 3*** until all the bits in each of the L bitplanes are swapped from left to right, top to bottom.

Step 5: Combine all the L shuffled bitplanes together and the permutated image is produced.

Let $P'(x, y)$ be the value of the pixel at coordinate (x, y) in the bit-level shuffled image, as described by

$$P'(x, y) = b'(L-1)b'(L-2)\cdots b'(0), \tag{4}$$

where $b'(i)$ ($i = 0, 1, \ldots, L-1$) are the bits swapped from other locations of different bitplanes. Obviously, the following formula holds

$$Prob\left[P(x, y) \equiv P'(x, y)\right] = \left(\frac{1}{2}\right)^{L}, \tag{5}$$

and thereby an effective diffusion mechanism is introduced.

The application of above discussed algorithm to a grayscale test image is demonstrated in Figs. 2–3. Fig. 2(i) shows the plain image of 256×256 pixels with 256 grey levels, and (a)–(h) show the 8 bitplanes of the plain image from highest bit to the lowest, respectively. The 8 shuffled bitplanes are shown in Figs. 3(a)–(h), respectively, and the resultant permutated image is shown in (i) of Fig. 3. Fig. 4 demonstrates the results of conventional bit-level permutation algorithm. As can be seen from Figs. 2 and 4, the bits in the 2nd bitplane of the plain image are not well-distributed, which significantly affect the confusion effect of the corresponding shuffled bitplanes produced by the conventional algorithm. However, the bits in all the 8 shuffled bitplanes produced by the proposed permutation algorithm are uniformly distributed, as the bits are shuffled among different bitplanes rather than within the same bitplane. As a result, the diffusion effect introduced by the proposed algorithm is superior to that of conventional algorithm. The quantitative comparison of the two algorithms will be given in Sec. 4.2.

Fig. 2. Bitplanes of plain image. (a)–(h) are the bitplanes of (i) from highest bit to the lowest, respectively.

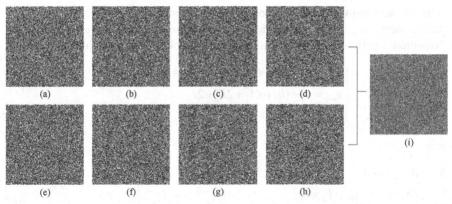

Fig. 3. The application of the proposed bit-level permutation algorithm. (a)–(h) are the 8 shuffled bitplanes, respectively, and (i) is the resultant permutated image.

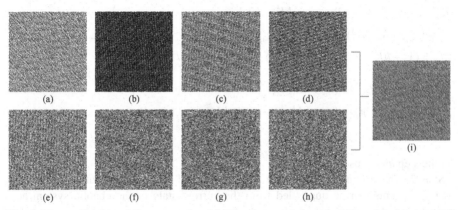

Fig. 4. The application of the conventional bit-level permutation algorithm. (a)–(h) are the 8 shuffled bitplanes, respectively, and (i) is the resultant permutated image.

3   Image Diffusion Using Lorenz System

In 1963, Edward Lorenz, an early pioneer of chaos theory, developed a simplified mathematical model for atmospheric convection. The model is a system of three ordinary differential equations now known as the Lorenz equations, as described by

$$\begin{cases} \dfrac{dx}{dt} = \sigma(y - x), \\[2mm] \dfrac{dy}{dt} = x(\rho - z) - y, \\[2mm] \dfrac{dz}{dt} = xy - \beta z, \end{cases} \tag{6}$$

where t is time and σ, ρ, β are the system parameters. When $\sigma=10$, $\rho=8/3$, $\beta=28$, the system exhibits chaotic behavior. The initial state values x_0, y_0 and z_0 serve as the diffusion key.

The detailed diffusion process is described as follows:

Step 1: Iterate Eq. (6) for N_0 times for the same purpose as explained above. To solve the equation, fourth-order Runge-Kutta method is employed, as given by

$$\begin{cases} x_{n+1} = x_n + (h/6)(K_1 + 2K_2 + 2K_3 + K_4), \\ y_{n+1} = y_n + (h/6)(L_1 + 2L_2 + 2L_3 + L_4), \\ z_{n+1} = z_n + (h/6)(M_1 + 2M_2 + 2M_3 + M_4), \end{cases} \tag{7}$$

where

$$\begin{cases} K_j = \sigma(y_n - x_n) \\ L_j = x_n(\rho - z) - y_n \quad (j = 1), \\ M_j = x_n y_n - \beta z_n \end{cases}$$

$$\begin{cases} K_j = \sigma[(y_n + hL_{j-1}/2) - (x_n + hK_{j-1}/2)] \\ L_j = (x_n + hK_{j-1}/2)(\rho - (z_n + hM_{j-1}/2)) - (y_n + hL_{j-1}/2) \quad (j = 2,3), \\ M_j = (x_n + hK_{j-1}/2)(y_n + hL_{j-1}/2) - \beta(z_n + hM_{j-1}/2) \end{cases}$$

$$\begin{cases} K_j = \sigma[(y_n + hL_{j-1}) - (x_n + hK_{j-1})] \\ L_j = (x_n + hK_{j-1})(\rho - (z_n + hM_{j-1})) - (y_n + hL_{j-1}) \quad (j = 4), \\ M_j = (x_n + hK_{j-1})(y_n + hL_{j-1}) - \beta(z_n + hM_{j-1}) \end{cases}$$

and the step h is chosen as 0.0005.

Step 2: The Lorenz system is iterated continuously. For each iteration, three key stream elements can be quantified from the current state of the chaotic system according to

$$\begin{cases} k_{xn} = mod[round((abs(x_n) - floor(abs(x_n))) \times 10^{14}), 2^L], \\ k_{yn} = mod[round((abs(y_n) - floor(abs(y_n))) \times 10^{14}), 2^L], \\ k_{zn} = mod[round((abs(z_n) - floor(abs(z_n))) \times 10^{14}), 2^L], \end{cases} \tag{8}$$

where $n = 1, 2, \ldots$ represents the nth iteration of the Lorenz system, and $round(x)$ rounds x to the nearest integers.

Step 3: Calculate the cipher-pixels value according to Eq. (9).

$$\begin{cases} c_{3 \times (n-1)+1} = k_{xn} \oplus \{[p_{3 \times (n-1)+1} + k_{xn}] \; mod \; 2^L\} \oplus c_{3 \times (n-1)}, \\ c_{3 \times (n-1)+2} = k_{yn} \oplus \{[p_{3 \times (n-1)+2} + k_{yn}] \; mod \; 2^L\} \oplus c_{3 \times (n-1)+1}, \\ c_{3 \times (n-1)+3} = k_{zn} \oplus \{[p_{3 \times (n-1)+3} + k_{zn}] \; mod \; 2^L\} \oplus c_{3 \times (n-1)+2}, \end{cases} \tag{9}$$

where $c_{3 \times (n-1)+m}$, $p_{3 \times (n-1)+m}$ ($m = 1, 2, 3$) are the output cipher-pixels and currently operated pixels, respectively, and $\oplus$ performs bit-wise exclusive OR operation. One may set the initial value c_0 as a constant, which can be regard as part of secret key.

Step 4: Return to *Step 2* until all the pixels of the permutated image are encrypted from left to right and top to bottom.

The decipher procedure is similar to that of the encipher process described above, and the inverse of Eq. (9) is given by

$$
\begin{cases}
p_{3\times(n-1)+1} = [k_{xn} \oplus c_{3\times(n-1)+1} \oplus c_{3\times(n-1)} + 2^L - k_{xn}] \ mod \ 2^L, \\
p_{3\times(n-1)+2} = [k_{yn} \oplus c_{3\times(n-1)+2} \oplus c_{3\times(n-1)+1} + 2^L - k_{yn}] \ mod \ 2^L, \\
p_{3\times(n-1)+3} = [k_{zn} \oplus c_{3\times(n-1)+3} \oplus c_{3\times(n-1)+2} + 2^L - k_{zn}] \ mod \ 2^L.
\end{cases}
\tag{10}
$$

4   Security Analysis

An effective cryptosystem should be robust against all kinds of known attacks, such as brute-force attack, known/chosen plaintext attack, statistical attack and differential attack. Detailed security analysis has been carried out in this section to demonstrate the robustness of the proposed scheme.

4.1   Key Space Analysis

The key space is the set of all possible keys that can be used in a cipher. The key space must be large enough to avoid opponents from guessing the key using a brute-force attack, but small enough for practical encryption and decryption. The key of the proposed cryptosystem is composed of two parts: confusion key Key_c and diffusion key Key_d. As mentioned above, Key_c is composed of initial conditions (K_{c1}, K_{c2}, K_{c3}) of three logistic map and Key_d is composed of initial conditions (x_0, y_0, z_0) of Lorenz system. As all the state variables are declared as 64-bit double-precision type, the total number of possible values of Key_c and Key_d are both approximately 10^{45}. The two parts of the key are independent of each other. Therefore, the total key space of the proposed cryptosystem is

$$
Key_{total} = Key_c(K_{c1}, K_{c2}, K_{c3}) \times Key_d(x_0, y_0, z_0) \approx 10^{45} \times 10^{45} \approx 2^{298},
\tag{11}
$$

which is larger than that of the well-known Triple-DES (2^{168}), IDEA (2^{128}), and AES (2^{128}, 2^{192} and 2^{256}) algorithms. Therefore, the proposed image cryptosystem is secure against brute-force attack.

4.2   Statistical Analysis

Statistical analysis is one the most common cryptanalysis techniques in use today. In this subsection, the proposed image cryptosystem has been proved to be robust against various statistical analyses by calculating the histogram, the correlation of two adjacent pixels and the information entropy.

4.2.1   Histogram
The frequency distribution of cipher-pixels is of much importance to an image cryptosystem. It should hide the redundancy of plain image and should not reveal the

relationship between plain image and cipher image. Histogram analysis is often used as a qualitative check for data distribution. An image histogram is a graphical representation showing a visual impression of the distribution of pixels by plotting the number of pixels at each grayscale level. Figs. 5(a), (c), (e), (g) show the plain image, bit-level permutated image using conventional algorithm, bit-level permutated image using proposed algorithm and the output cipher image, respectively. Their corresponding histograms are shown in (b), (d), (f) and (h) of Fig. 5, respectively.

As can be seen from Fig. 5, the histogram of the output cipher image is fairly evenly distributed and therefore does not provide any hint to employ statistical analysis. Moreover, though the histogram of the bit-level permutated image using the proposed algorithm is not distributed in a perfectly uniform, its uniformity is much better than that of the bit-level permutated image using conventional algorithm owing to the superior diffusion effect introduced in the permutation process.

4.2.2   Correlation of Adjacent Pixels

Pixels in an ordinary image are usually highly correlated with their adjacent pixels either in horizontal, vertical or diagonal direction, but the correlation of the adjacent pixels in a cipher image should be as low as possible so as to resist statistical analysis. The correlation of adjacent pixels can be graphically measured by the following procedure. First, randomly select 3000 pairs of adjacent pixels in each direction from the image. Then, plot the distribution of the adjacent pixels by using each pair as the values of the x-coordinate and y-coordinate. The correlation distribution of two horizontally adjacent pixels of the plain image, bit-level permutated image using conventional algorithm, bit-level permutated image using proposed algorithm and the output cipher image are shown in Figs. 6(a)–(d), respectively.

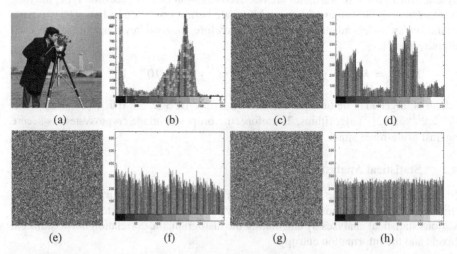

Fig. 5. Histogram analysis. (a) plain image. (b) histogram of (a). (c) bit-level permutated image using conventional algorithm. (d) histogram of (c). (e) bit-level permutated image using proposed algorithm. (f) histogram of (e). (g) output cipher image. (h) histogram of (g).

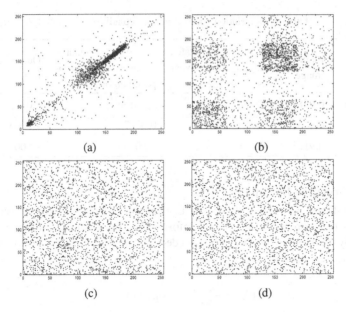

(a)

(b)

(c)

(d)

Fig. 6. (a)–(d) are correlation of horizontal adjacent two pixels of plain image, bit-level permutated image using conventional algorithm, bit-level permutated image using proposed algorithm and output cipher image, respectively.

To quantify the correlations of adjacent pixels in an image, the correlation coefficient $r_{x,y}$ is calculated by using the following three formulas:

$$r_{xy} = \frac{\frac{1}{N}\sum_{i=1}^{N}(x_i - \bar{x})(y_i - \bar{y})}{\sqrt{\left(\frac{1}{N}\sum_{i=1}^{N}(x_i - \bar{x})^2\right)\left(\frac{1}{N}\sum_{i=1}^{N}(y_i - \bar{y})^2\right)}} \tag{12}$$

$$\bar{x} = \frac{1}{N}\sum_{i=1}^{N}x_i \tag{13}$$

$$\bar{y} = \frac{1}{N}\sum_{i=1}^{N}y_i \tag{14}$$

where x_i and y_i are grayscale values of ith pair of adjacent pixels, and N denotes the total number of samples.

Table 1 lists the results of the correlation coefficients for horizontal, vertical and diagonal adjacent pixels in the four images. As can be seen from Fig. 6 and Table 1, the strong correlation between adjacent pixels in the plain image is completely eliminated in the cipher image produced by the proposed image cryptosystem. Moreover, the correlation coefficients of the bit-level permutated image using the proposed algorithm are comparable with that of the output cipher image, and evidently better than that of the bit-level permutated image using conventional algorithm.

Table 1. Correlation coefficients of two adjacent pixels

Direction	Plain image	Bit-level permutated image using conventional algorithm	Bit-level permutated image using proposed algorithm	Output cipher image
Horizontal	0.9589	0.2069	−0.0136	0.0131
Vertical	0.9435	−0.0557	0.0017	−0.0036
Diagonal	0.9162	−0.1146	−0.0249	−0.0075

4.2.3   Information Entropy

Information theory, introduced by Claude E. Shannon in 1948, is a key measure of the randomness or unpredictability of the information. Information entropy is usually expressed by the average number of bits needed to store or communicate one symbol in a message, as described by

$$H(X) = -\sum_{i=1}^{n} P(x_i) \log_2 P(x_i) \tag{15}$$

where X is a random variable with n outcomes $\{x_1, ..., x_n\}$ and $P(x_i)$ is the probability mass function of outcome x_i. Therefore, for a random image with 256 gray levels, the entropy should ideally be $H(X)=8$.

Table 2 lists the entropies for plain image, bit-level permutated image using conventional algorithm, bit-level permutated image using proposed algorithm and the output cipher image. It can be seen from Table 2 that the entropy of the output cipher image is very close to the theoretical value of 8. This means we can regard the output image as a random source. Also, the entropy for the bit-level permutated image using the proposed algorithm is close to the theoretical value and significant superior to that of the bit-level permutated image using conventional algorithm.

Table 2. Information entropy for different images

Plain image	Bit-level permutated image using conventional algorithm	Bit-level permutated image using proposed algorithm	Output cipher image
7.0097	7.6239	7.9729	7.9970

4.3   Key Sensitivity Analysis

Another essential property required by a cryptosystem is key sensitivity, which ensures that no data can be recovered from ciphertext even though there is only a minor difference between the encryption and decryption keys. To evaluate the key sensitivity property of the proposed cryptosystem, the test image (Fig. 2(i)) is firstly encrypted using a randomly selected key K_c=(0.56197972394051, 0.40110866517742, 0.14837430314112) and K_d=(3.73946235774965, 5.83069041022533, 2.8370061767-4220). Then the ciphered image is tried to be decrypted using three keys with a slight difference to the confusion key while keeps the diffusion key unchanged. The employed keys are: (i) K_c=(0.56197972394052, 0.40110866517742, 0.1483743031411 2), (ii) K_c=(0.56197972394051, 0.40110866517743, 0.14837430314112), and (iii) K_c=(0.56197972394051, 0.40110866517742, 0.14837430314113). The resultant deciphered images are shown in Figs. 7(a)-(c), respectively, from which we can see that even an almost perfect guess of the key does not reveal any information about the plain image. Similar results are obtained with a slight change in the diffusion key.

4.4   Differential Analysis

To implement differential analysis, an opponent usually makes a slight change in a plain image and then compares the two produced cipher images to find out which parts are different. With the help of other analysis methods the secret key may be obtained. However, if the slight change can be effectively diffused to the whole cipher image, then such differential analysis is infeasible. To measure the diffusion performance of a cryptosystem, two criteria *NPCR* (number of pixel change rate) and *UACI* (unified average changing intensity) are commonly used.

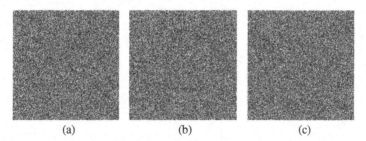

(a)   (b)   (c)

Fig. 7. Results of key sensitivity test. (a) deciphered image using key (i). (b) deciphered image using key (ii). (c) deciphered image using key (iii).

The *NPCR* is used to measure the percentage of different pixel numbers between two images. Let $P_1(i,j)$ and $P_2(i,j)$ be the (i,j)th pixel of two images P_1 and P_2, respectively, the *NPCR* is defined as:

$$NPCR = \frac{\sum_{i=1}^{W}\sum_{j=1}^{H}D(i,j)}{W \times H} \times 100\%, \qquad (16)$$

where W and H are the width and height of P_1 or P_2. $D(i,j)$ is set to 0 if $P_1(i,j) = P_2(i,j)$, and 1 otherwise.

The second criterion, *UACI* is used to measure the average intensity of differences between the two images. It is defined as

$$UACI = \frac{1}{W \times H} \left[\sum_{i=1}^{W} \sum_{j=1}^{H} \frac{|P_1(i,j) - P_2(i,j)|}{L-1} \right] \times 100\%. \tag{17}$$

The *NPCR* and *UACI* values for two truly random images, which are expected estimate for a good image cryptosystem, are 99.609% and 33.464%, respectively. To test the *NPCR* and *UACI* of the proposed cryptosystem, two plain images with only one bit difference at the lower right corner pixel are employed, as shown in Figs. 8(a) and (b). The two test images are encrypted using the same key and their corresponding cipher images are shown in Figs. 8(c) and (d), respectively. The differential image between the two cipher images can be found in Fig. 8(e). We obtain *NPCR*=99.59% and *UACI*=33.45%, which indicate that the proposed scheme is secure against differential attack.

Fig. 8. Results of diffusion performance test. (a) and (b) are two plain images with only one bit difference at the lower right corner pixel. (c) cipher image of (a). (d) cipher image of (b). (e) differential image between (c) and (d).

5   Conclusions

This paper has proposed a fast chaos-based image encryption scheme with confusion-diffusion architecture. To address the performance issues of confusion-diffusion type image cipher, the proposed scheme introduces an effective diffusion mechanism in confusion process through a lightweight bit-level shuffling algorithm. As the pixel value mixing effect is contributed by both stages, the same level of security can be achieved in a fewer number of overall rounds, and hence the performance of the cryptosystem is improved. Compared with those recently proposed bit-level permutation algorithms, the diffusion effect of the proposed scheme is significantly enhanced as the bits are shuffled among different bitplanes rather than within the same bitplane. Moreover, the three logistic maps used for producing pseudorandom locations for bits permutation are iterated in a parallel manner, which further increase the performance. We have carried out an extensive security analysis of the proposed image cryptosystem using key space analysis, statistical analysis, key sensitivity analysis and differential analysis. Based on the results of our analysis, we conclude that the proposed image encryption scheme is perfectly suitable for the real-time secure image transmission over public networks.

Acknowledgements. This work was supported by the National Natural Science Foundation of China (No. 61271350) and the Fundamental Research Funds for the Central Universities (No. N120504005).

References

1. Fridrich, J.: Symmetric ciphers based on two-dimensional chaotic maps. International Journal of Bifurcation and Chaos 8, 1259–1284 (1998)
2. Chen, G.R., Mao, Y.B., Chui, C.K.: A symmetric image encryption scheme based on 3D chaotic cat maps. Chaos Solitons & Fractals 21, 749–761 (2004)
3. Mao, Y.B., Chen, G.R., Lian, S.G.: A novel fast image encryption scheme based on 3D chaotic baker maps. International Journal of Bifurcation and Chaos 14, 3613–3624 (2004)
4. Kwok, H.S., Tang, W.K.S.: A fast image encryption system based on chaotic maps with finite precision representation. Chaos Solitons & Fractals 32, 1518–1529 (2007)
5. Xiang, T., Wong, K.W., Liao, X.F.: Selective image encryption using a spatiotemporal chaotic system. Chaos 17, 023115 (2007)
6. Behnia, S., Akhshani, A., Ahadpour, S., et al.: A fast chaotic encryption scheme based on piecewise nonlinear chaotic maps. Physics Letters A 366, 391–396 (2007)
7. Behnia, S., Akhshani, A., Mahmodi, H., et al.: A novel algorithm for image encryption based on mixture of chaotic maps. Chaos Solitons & Fractals 35, 408–419 (2008)
8. Gao, T.G., Chen, Z.Q.: A new image encryption algorithm based on hyper-chaos. Physics Letters A 372, 394–400 (2008)
9. Gao, T.G., Chen, Z.Q.: Image encryption based on a new total shuffling algorithm. Chaos Solitons & Fractals 38, 213–220 (2008)
10. Wong, K.W., Kwok, B.S.H., Law, W.S.: A fast image encryption scheme based on chaotic standard map. Physics Letters A 372, 2645–2652 (2008)
11. Sun, F.Y., Liu, S.T., Li, Z.Q., et al.: A novel image encryption scheme based on spatial chaos map. Chaos Solitons & Fractals 38, 631–640 (2008)
12. Tong, X.J., Cui, M.G.: Image encryption scheme based on 3D baker with dynamical compound chaotic sequence cipher generator. Signal Processing 89, 480–491 (2009)
13. Rhouma, R., Meherzi, S., Belghith, S.: OCML-based colour image encryption. Chaos Solitons & Fractals 40, 309–318 (2009)
14. Xiao, D., Liao, X.F., Wei, P.C.: Analysis and improvement of a chaos-based image encryption algorithm. Chaos Solitons & Fractals 40, 2191–2199 (2009)
15. Wang, Y., Wong, K.W., Liao, X.F., et al.: A chaos-based image encryption algorithm with variable control parameters. Chaos Solitons & Fractals 41, 1773–1783 (2009)
16. Wong, K.W., Kwok, B.S.H., Yuen, C.H.: An efficient diffusion approach for chaos-based image encryption. Chaos Solitons & Fractals 41, 2652–2663 (2009)

17. Mazloom, S., Eftekhari-Moghadam, A.M.: Color image encryption based on Coupled Nonlinear Chaotic Map. Chaos Solitons & Fractals 42, 1745–1754 (2009)
18. Amin, M., Faragallah, O.S., Abd El-Latif, A.A.: A chaotic block cipher algorithm for image cryptosystems. Communications in Nonlinear Science and Numerical Simulation 15, 3484–3497 (2010)
19. Wang, Y., Wong, K.W., Liao, X.F.: A new chaos-based fast image encryption algorithm. Applied Soft Computing 11, 514–522 (2011)
20. Zhu, Z.L., Zhang, W., Wong, K.W., et al.: A chaos-based symmetric image encryption scheme using a bit-level permutation. Information Sciences 181, 1171–1186 (2011)
21. Liu, H.J., Wang, X.Y.: Color image encryption using spatial bit-level permutation and high-dimension chaotic system. Optics Communications 284, 3895–3903 (2011)
22. Fu, C., Lin, B.B., Miao, Y.S., et al.: A novel chaos-based bit-level permutation scheme for digital image encryption. Optics Communications 284, 5415–5423 (2011)
23. Fu, C., Chen, J.J., Zou, H., et al.: A chaos-based digital image encryption scheme with an improved diffusion strategy. Optics Express 20, 2363–2378 (2012)
24. Zhang, G.J., Shen, Y.: A Novel Bit-level Image Encryption Method Based on Chaotic Map and Dynamic Grouping. Communications in Theoretical Physics 58, 520–524 (2012)
25. Seyedzadeh, S.M., Mirzakuchaki, S.: A fast color image encryption algorithm based on coupled two-dimensional piecewise chaotic map. Signal Processing 92, 1202–1215 (2012)

Preserving User Privacy in the Smart Grid by Hiding Appliance Load Characteristics

Baosheng Ge[1,2] and Wen-Tao Zhu[1]

[1] State Key Laboratory of Information Security (DCS Center)
Institute of Information Engineering, Chinese Academy of Sciences
87C Min Zhuang Road, Beijing 100093, China
[2] University of Chinese Academy of Sciences
19A Yu Quan Road, Beijing 100049, China
gebaosheng@126.com, wtzhu@ieee.org

Abstract. As data transmitted in the smart grid are fine-grained and private, the personal habits and behaviors of inhabitants may be revealed by data mining algorithms. In fact, nonintrusive appliance load monitoring (NALM) algorithms have substantially compromised user privacy in the smart grid. It has been a realistic threat to deduce power usage patterns of residents with NALM algorithms. In this paper, we introduce a novel algorithm using an in-residence battery to counter NALM algorithms. The main idea of our algorithm is to keep the metered load around a baseline value with tolerable deviations. Since this algorithm can utilize the rechargeable battery more efficiently and reasonably, the metered load will be maintained at stable states for a longer time period. We then implement and evaluate our algorithm under two metrics, i.e., the step changes reduction and the mutual information, respectively. The simulations show that our algorithm is effective, and exposes less information about inhabitants compared with a previously proposed algorithm.

Keywords: Smart grid, information security, privacy, utility, rechargeable battery.

1   Introduction

In recent years, electric utilities are increasingly making the transition to smart grids, which exploit large-scale smart meter deployments at power users for bi-directional realtime communications using Internet protocols [1]. For example, the US government has allocated more than 4.3 billion dollars for smart grids and similar programs are in progress in Asia and the EU [2]. A smart meter is an advanced meter that not only measures power consumption in much more detail than a conventional electricity meter, but may also potentially communicate with a number of appliances and devices. Smart meters are expected to provide accurate readings automatically at requested time intervals to the utility company, the electricity distribution network, or the wider power grid [3]. In a word, smart meters provide further information about power consumption

G. Wang et al. (Eds.): CSS 2013, LNCS 8300, pp. 67–80, 2013.
© Springer International Publishing Switzerland 2013

patterns of users, which may contribute to improved forecasts of demands in the near future, allowing for appropriate reactions on the supply side. On the other hand, county and town residents can also benefit from the deployment of smart meters in individual houses. A practical assumption is that users can shift their electricity consumption to different times according to the realtime electricity price.

Unfortunately, along with these positive effects of smart grids, some security and privacy threats are inevitable [4–6]. Since messages transmitted in the smart grid may contain sensitive data and much more personal information is delivered to the electricity supplier, the personal habits and behaviors of inhabitants will be revealed by data mining algorithms [7–9]. In fact, nonintrusive appliance load monitoring (NALM) algorithms have substantially compromised user privacy in the smart grid. It should be pointed out that such privacy concerns have already jeopardized the mandatory deployment of smart meters in some countries, leading to a deployment deadlock [10]. Thus, how to preserve user privacy in smart grids has become a hot topic of research recently. Nevertheless, power usage must always be accurately measured and reported, which means that we have to protect consumer privacy in the presence of profile-exposing smart meters.

One of the viable approaches to resolving the problem of user privacy disclosure in the smart grid is to disguise appliance load signatures using a rechargeable battery [11]. That is, a rechargeable battery and a control system are deployed between the smart meter and the circuit breaker in their houses. By mixing utility energy with energy provided or consumed by the battery to offset spikes and dips in power consumption, the load observed by the smart meter is smoothed. Then appliance load characteristics will be modified or obscured so that power usage events can be hidden. Note that this approach will not compromise the accuracy of the metered load, which means the utility provider can always establish the correct amount to charge the user.

On account of limited battery capacity, emphasis is placed on the search for an appropriate algorithm in system control, by which user privacy can be improved given feasible battery size. In this paper, we introduce a novel algorithm to transform the power usage data for the goal of hiding appliance load characteristics. The main idea of the algorithm is to keep the metered load around a baseline value with tolerable deviations. Since this algorithm can utilize the rechargeable battery more efficiently and reasonably, the metered load will be maintained at stable states for a longer period of time. The steady state means the hiding of appliance load characteristics. Therefore, the risk of privacy leakage can be reduced. We also implement and evaluate our algorithm under two metrics, i.e., the step changes reduction and the mutual information (MI), respectively, and demonstrate its validity and efficiency.

The remainder of this paper is organized as follows. The next section reviews relevant research related to user privacy in the smart grid. In Section 3, we will provide a brief background on appliance load profiles and NALM algorithms. System model and main notions are also given in Section 3. Details of the algorithm are elaborated in Section 4, followed by evaluations in terms of step changes reduction and mutual information in Section 5. Finally, conclusions are summarized in Section 6.

2 Related Work

Security and privacy issues have become a hot research topic recently in the smart grid and many efforts have been made. A good overview of the various approaches and the state of the art is given in [12]. There exist mainly two types of solutions to preserving user privacy in the smart grid. The first type relies on the encryption or the perturbation of raw metered data to protect user privacy from exposure, while the second type hides the actual power consumption by using intelligent power routers and battery buffers in individual houses.

It has been demonstrated in [13] and [14] that power consumption patterns can be extracted and tracked with the use of NALM algorithms, which made the threat of user privacy leakage realistic. The protocols proposed in [15] preserve appliance usage privacy by masking the metered load in such a way that an adversary cannot recover individual readings, while the sum of masking values across meters is set as a known value. In [16], the metered power usage data are divided into attributable data and anonymous data along with a trusted escrow service. A secure data aggregation scheme for the smart grid was presented in [17] using homomorphic encryption. The protocol proposed in [18] utilizes commitments and zero-knowledge proofs to privately derive the bill of an individual.

In [11], a pioneering approach was presented that exploits home electrical power routing through the use of rechargeable batteries, and alternates power sources to moderate the effects of load signatures. By charging and discharging the battery, an individual can manipulate the metered load to obscure some sensitive information contained in the original load. Thus, an appropriate algorithm for charging and discharging is needed to minimize information leakage. A "best effort" (BE) policy was proposed in [11], which tries to hold the metered load to its most recent value, while in [19] a stochastic policy was presented and experimentally demonstrated to be more effective in minimizing information leakage. It has been shown in [20] that BE algorithm is valid in combating data mining algorithms. In [21], another algorithm was proposed to maintain the metered load as constant as possible. Distinct from the BE policy, the metered load is pre-determined instead of being changed continually as its most recent value. A novel algorithm called stepping approach was introduced in [22], aiming at maximizing the error between the load demanded by a household and the metered load.

3 Background

3.1 Appliance Load Profiles

Distinct from conventional electromechanical residential meters deployed in the legacy power grid, smart meters play a vital role in implementing realtime monitoring and dispatch such as load management, distributed energy storage, and distributed energy generation. That is, smart meters can measure power consumption at the granularity of seconds or minutes other than months. In normal conditions, the collected fine-grained time series of electric demand by smart meters is defined as appliance load profiles, which are delivered to authorized parties (e.g., the utility provider) at or near real time for load forecasting and fraud detection. With those data in hand, NALM algorithms can be employed to extract individual appliance events. Then, along with known appliance load signatures, sensitive chronic behaviors will be revealed.

3.2 Nonintrusive Appliance Load Monitoring

NALM algorithms can extract the power consumption of individual appliances from appliance load profiles in order to deduce what electric appliances are being used [13]. They take advantage of the correspondence between power loads and appliances being turned on and off. As an appliance load profile is the aggregation of various appliances and the times during which each is operating, this technique aims to decompose the appliance load profile into individual load signatures. Besides, the approach is called "nonintrusive" because appliance load data can be gathered remotely without the knowledge of residents instead of placing sensors on each of the individual appliances. A step change is characterized by a sharp edge in the power consumed by the household. By detecting pairs of the edges with equal magnitude and opposite direction, and matching them with specific load signatures, NALM algorithms can expose individual appliance events from aggregated load profiles.

3.3 System Model and Notation

First of all, we introduce the main notions used in the sequel, which are given in Table 1. We adopt the rechargeable battery model presented in [11]. That is, in our system model, a rechargeable battery is deployed between the smart meter and household appliances, which can be discharged or charged within a metering interval Δt with power $l_b(t)$, adjusting the amount of electricity the household consumed from the power grid. Thus, the actual consumption load $l_a(t)$ will be partially disguised to reduce the information leakage from smart meter readings. A system overview is illustrated in Fig. 1.

Note that in this model, we assume $l_a(t) \geq 0$, which indicates that the home energy system cannot send electricity back to the power grid. Besides, the rechargeable battery is only used to supply electricity for appliances in the house rather than be discharged back into the power grid. In addition, we also assume our rechargeable battery model is idealized. That is, neither charging nor discharging the battery will cause additional energy loss, and the battery life is long enough.

With the moderation of the battery, the metered home load, i.e., the smart meter reading becomes $l(t) = l_a(t) + l_b(t)$. When $l_b(t) > 0$, the battery is being charged and when $l_b(t) < 0$, the battery is being discharged. Then, $l_b(t) = 0$ means that no power from the battery is mixed with the actual household

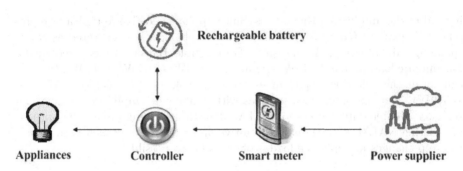

Fig. 1. A general framework of rechargeable battery system. The arrow shows the direction of power flow.

load, which does not happen frequently. We aim to moderate $l_b(t)$ in order to distort $l(t)$ in such a way that makes $l_a(t)$ undetectable. That is, $l_a(t)$ cannot be extracted with the knowledge of $l(t)$.

Table 1. Notation for TD algorithm and system parameters

t	A point in time
Δt	A metering interval
$l_a(t)$	The actual appliance load at some point
$l(t)$	The measured value of the household load by the smart meter
$l_b(t)$	The confusion value provided by the rechargeable battery
$b(t)$	The current battery level at some point
b_m	The upper bound of the battery capacity
v_b	The baseline value of $l(t)$
σ	The upper bound of the fluctuation range versus v_b

To evaluate privacy protection, it should be clear here what need to be preserved. Given a load profile $l_a(t)$, the differences between successive power measurements represent changes in the state of some appliances as they are turned on or off. These are called step changes, which are considered as private information because they can reflect user behaviors. Hence, our goal is to smooth the metered load profile $l(t)$ as much as possible to reduce step changes. Surely, if $l(t)$ is constant, then no information beyond the total power consumption is leaked. However, it is feasible only with quite large battery capacity, which is not practical. The emphasis is placed on the problem how to maximize privacy protection, given any set of appliance load $l_a(t)$ with limited battery capacity and no knowledge of the future.

4   Proposed Scheme

It should be pointed out that when employing NALM algorithms, we pay more attention to the amplitude changes from the previous sample of appliance loads instead of the amplitudes themselves. Since appliance loads are typically represented by pairs of $(time; amplitude)$, the step changes are generated as corresponding pairs of $(time; \Delta amplitude)$. For example, the smart meter recorded a four-minute load profile: t_0: 40W; t_1: 140W; t_2: 640W; t_3: 640W; t_4:140W, then we can obtain the following step changes: $(t_1; +100\text{W})$, $(t_2; +500\text{W})$, $(t_3; 0\text{W})$, $(t_4; -500\text{W})$. That is, only those samples with prominent amplitude changes can serve as valuable data sources for NALM algorithms. Therefore, for the purpose of resisting NALM algorithms, an intuitive and effective approach is to reduce the step changes in appliance load profiles as far as possible.

Algorithm 1. *TD Algorithm*

1:   $d = l_a(t) - v_b$;
2:   **if** $|d| \leq \sigma$ **then**
3:      $l(t) = l_a(t)$; {current load is in given range}
4:   **else**
5:     **if** $d > 0$ **then**
6:        (discharge the battery)
7:        **if** $b(t) \geq d$ **then**
8:           $l(t) = randchoose(v_b, (v_b + \sigma))$; {battery energy is enough}
9:           $b(t) = b(t) - (l_a(t) - l(t))$;
10:        **else**
11:           $l(t) = l_a(t) - b(t)$; {provide maximum battery energy}
12:           $b(t) = 0$;
13:        **end if**
14:     **else**
15:        (charge the battery)
16:        **if** $(b_m - b(t)) \geq |d|$ **then**
17:           $l(t) = randchoose((v_b - \sigma), v_b)$; {remaining battery capacity is enough}
18:           $b(t) = b(t) + (l(t) - l_a(t))$;
19:        **else**
20:           $l(t) = l(t) + (b_m - b(t))$; {fully charge battery}
21:           $b(t) = b_m$;
22:        **end if**
23:     **end if**
24: **end if**

A "best-effort" privacy algorithm was proposed in [11], whose idea is to maintain a constant metered load $l(t)$ if the battery capacity is kept within a safe limit. That is, when the appliance load $l_a(t)$ is larger (or smaller) than the previously metered load $l(t - \Delta t)$, the battery will be controlled by the algorithm to discharge (or charge) in order to make $l(t)$ equal $l(t - \Delta t)$. Of course, the premise is that the battery bound is not reached. While BE algorithm can obscure appliance load signatures to some extent, in [19] a finite state model was proposed to demonstrate that the stochastic battery policy is better than BE algorithm in reducing information leakage. However, we argue that this conclusion is not so precise. As in the model of [19], the battery capacity is set at 1 and will be used up with just one regulation, which does not accord with the actual situation. If the battery capacity were infinite, the metered load $l(t)$ would be constant all the time, and little information would be leaked. Hence, the main idea of BE algorithm is reliable.

Since BE algorithm is not optimal, in this paper we propose a novel algorithm called "tolerable deviation" (TD) which outperforms BE algorithm in reducing information leakage. The core idea of TD algorithm is to keep the metered load around a baseline value with tolerable deviations. More specifically, given an actual appliance load $l_a(t)$ at some point, BE algorithm tries to hold the metered load to its most recent value by setting $l(t) = l_a(t - \Delta t)$, while TD algorithm first selects an appropriate baseline value v_b along with a tolerable deviation σ, and then chooses a random value in $(v_b - \sigma, v_b + \sigma)$ as the metered load $l(t)$. That is, the transformed metered loads by TD algorithm are changing dynamically. For the same sake of maintaining a "constant" metered load $l(t)$, we make the following contributions. First of all, we replace the rigid constant $l_a(t - \Delta t)$ with a flexible choice in a tolerable range around the baseline value as $(v_b - \sigma, v_b + \sigma)$. This approach is feasible, as tiny step changes will be regarded as noise and then filtered out by NALM algorithms. Namely, samples of the amplitudes with no changes or tiny changes can be ignored for analysis. What is more crucial, TD algorithm's flexibility is conducive to utilizing limited battery capacity more efficiently due to the introduction of v_b and σ. That is, TD algorithm can maintain the metered load at approximately constant values for a longer period of time compared with BE algorithm. On the other hand, we can even intentionally introduce some fake step changes by choosing a large deviation. In this case, some amplitudes may become so large that they cannot be filtered out any longer by NALM algorithms. As the corresponding original loads remain stable, these step changes are considered fake. The outline of TD algorithm is given in Algorithm 1.

Algorithm 2. *An Extension of Step 3 in TD Algorithm*

1: $d = l_a(t) - v_b$;
2: **if** $|d| \leq \sigma$ **then**
3:     **if** $b(t)$ is below safe lower limit **then**
4:        $l(t) = v_b + \sigma$; {choose maximum metered load to charge battery}
5:        $b(t) = b(t) + (l(t) - l_a(t))$;
6:     **else if** $b(t)$ is above safe upper limit **then**
7:        $l(t) = v_b - \sigma$; {choose minimum metered load to discharge battery}
8:        $b(t) = b(t) - (l_a(t) - l(t))$;
9:     **else if** $b(t)$ is within safe limit **then**
10:      $l(t) = l_a(t)$;
11:    **end if**
12: **end if**

Note that in Step 3 of Algorithm 1, we simply set $l(t) = l_a(t)$ without any modifications because the current load is in the given range around the baseline value. In fact, TD algorithm can still take the following steps in Algorithm 2 to utilize the rechargeable battery more efficiently. That is, if the remaining capacity of battery is too small, TD algorithm will set the metered load $l(t)$ as its maximum allowed value $v_b + \sigma$ in order to charge the battery; on the contrary, if the remaining capacity is too large, TD algorithm will set the metered load $l(t)$ as the minimum allowed value $v_b - \sigma$ so that the battery can be discharged to release storage space. However, the battery may be used too frequently in this case, which should not be ignored since we must take battery life into consideration. Thus, TD algorithm can provide distinct levels of privacy protection for residents. When the current load is in the given range around the baseline value, i.e., $l_a(t) \in (v_b - \sigma, v_b + \sigma)$, if the user has strong requirements on security and privacy, more often than not Algorithm 2 will be employed. Otherwise, just setting $l(t) = l_a(t)$ can also be acceptable.

Our TD algorithm is a two-factor transformation. Both the baseline value and the deviation play a vital role in hiding appliance load characteristics. Consequently, the choice of these two parameters to a large extent determines the effectiveness of the method. Pre-selected as these two parameters are, they can be updated when required so as to keep the metered load stable as long as possible. In general, the user selects the baseline value according to her/his own realtime power consumption. To be specific, if the appliance load of an individual is heavy in a period, then a relatively large v_b is appropriate. On the contrary, the user will update v_b with a relatively small value when the appliance load is low for a while. As for the deviation, the choice of σ plays a subtle role in TD algorithm. On the one hand, a small value of σ contributes to tiny changes of output loads, so the mutual information will be reduced. Nevertheless, this strategy poses a huge strain on the battery, which signifies an increased probability of battery failure. Then more step changes will be revealed. On the other hand, a large enough value of σ results in the invalidation of TD algorithm. Because in this case, the output load profiles are exactly the same as the original load profiles. As a matter of fact, it is still a problem how to generate the optimal σ. Detailed simulation results will be given in the following section.

5   Evaluations

5.1   Datasets and Experimental Methods

In our experiments, we choose two typical datasets for detailed analysis, which are referred as D1 and D2. Both D1 and D2 are ten-minute resolution datasets, which are collected through simulating the day-to-day activities of an ordinary household and a corporate office, respectively. We optimize the model as much as possible to make the outputs consistent with the real world. Besides, we argue that the implementation costs for our work are acceptable according to [23], as the major overhead lies in the communications between the controller and the smart meter. In consequence, this approach is practical for most households equipped with rechargeable batteries.

To begin with, we operate two transformations on both datasets with the battery in the same size as 4.5kWh and the deviation fixed at 10W. The step changes from both original datasets and corresponding transformed datasets are counted to show to what extent can TD algorithm reduce step changes compared with BE algorithm. Then, D1 and D2 are transformed by BE algorithm and TD algorithm, respectively, for eleven batteries increasing in size from 0kWh to 5kWh with the same deviation as 10W. The mutual information between the original datasets and the transformed datasets is calculated for further analysis. Finally, we set the battery capacity at 4.5kWh and run our TD algorithm for D1 with an increasing sequence of deviation from 0W to 300W. We calculate the mutual information between the original dataset and the outputs from TD algorithm, and count total step changes along with fake step changes in order to find the optimal deviation. In addition, when the current load is in the given range around the baseline value, we just set $l(t) = l_a(t)$ for simplicity.

5.2   Intuitive Observation Results

An intuitive feeling of TD algorithm's effect and its comparison with BE algorithm are given by Fig. 2 and Fig. 3. We can clearly see that the behaviors of TD algorithm are in such a way that steady realtime loads with tolerable deviations comprise the majority of the TD algorithm's output profiles. That is, the controller maintains the target steady load as far as possible by charging

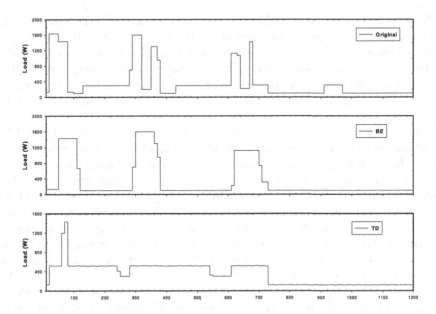

Fig. 2. Comparison between original appliance load profile and transformed load profiles in BE and TD, respectively, for dataset D1. The abscissa represents a ten-min time base for the whole day.

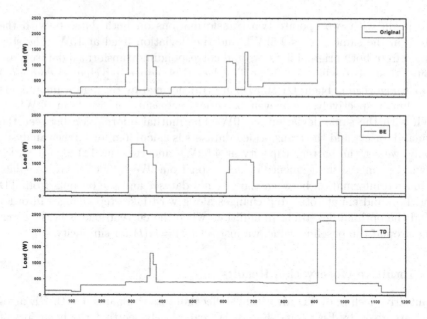

Fig. 3. Comparison between original appliance load profile and transformed load profiles in BE and TD, respectively, for dataset D2. The abscissa represents a ten-min time base for the whole day.

or discharging the battery. As the battery capacity is limited, the key point of maintaining a longer steady state lies in the choice of v_b and σ. In our experiments, to simplify the operation, we adopt just two different values of v_b, which are the means of total power consumption in day and night, respectively. We argue that the value of v_b can be updated more frequently such that the steady state will last longer. Besides, the choice of σ will be discussed in further detail below.

It cannot be neglected that a number of step changes still appear in the TD algorithm's output profiles outside of steady states. These step changes tend to appear during daylight high-demand periods instead of during night off-peak hours. If the residual battery capacity is not enough, the steady state cannot be maintained any longer and the exposure of some step changes will be inevitable. Nevertheless, while these large trends reveal some information about the resident, most notably the likelihood of human presence at home or in the office, they do not disclose the more fine-grained details such as how many occupants are or what their activities are. Compared with those in the original load profiles and the transformed outputs from BE algorithm, the step changes in the TD algorithm's output profiles show smaller amplitudes and last a shorter period, which benefits from the wiser use of the rechargeable battery. In addition, since v_b is updated continually and independent of realtime loads, the battery will become invalid at unpredictable points in time, resulting in some fake step changes in the TD algorithm's output profiles.

5.3   Quantitative Results

Next, our analysis will focus on quantifying the TD algorithm's validity in reducing individual appliance load characteristics in load profiles. We present two sorts of numerical experimental results, the step changes reduction and the mutual information, respectively.

Table 2 shows the step changes reduction of TD algorithm in our experiments. It can be seen that when the original load profiles are transformed by TD algorithm, the number of step changes drops dramatically (around 50.23%) compared with that of BE algorithm (around 29.02%). Note that step changes here include fake step changes. These fake step changes will interfere with the process of NALM algorithms to some extent. On the other hand, since the output load is randomly chosen in the given range, it will be more difficult to perform a sister matching algorithm in order to extract symmetric ON/OFF pairs from the step changes. In a word, our TD algorithm can effectively counter NALM algorithms to preserve user privacy in the smart grid.

Fig. 4 depicts the comparison of TD algorithm with BE algorithm under the mutual information metric with datasets D1 and D2. As can be clearly seen from the above figure, the mutual information is heavily dependent on the battery capacity, which is a matter of course based on the analysis in Section 4. Though TD algorithm outperforms BE algorithm in the step changes reduction, it seems that TD algorithm does not have an advantage on reducing the mutual information especially when the battery capacity is large enough. One crucial reason for this result is the introduction of σ. As the value of $l(t)$ is randomly chosen in the given range, the output load profiles of TD algorithm will contain

Table 2. Step changes reduction by BE and TD for datasets D1 and D2

Dataset	Original	BE	TD
D1	420	273	189
D2	221	182	130
Total	641	455	319

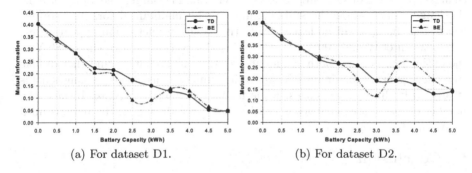

(a) For dataset D1.   (b) For dataset D2.

Fig. 4. MI between original load and transformed load with varying values of battery capacity

more various amplitudes, which contributes to the larger mutual information. Nevertheless, different from step changes, the mutual information only suggests the dependency between events in load profiles, but does not have a substantial effect on privacy disclosure. That is, the larger mutual information is not the equivalent of more step changes.

5.4   Extended Discussion of Deviation

Finally, we turn to the discussion of σ. An evaluation of TD algorithm with increasing values of σ under the mutual information metric is given in Fig. 5(a). We can see that when σ grows from 0W to 80W, the corresponding mutual information increases slowly from 0.0705 to 0.1845, which is in accord with our previous analysis. When σ is between 80W and 200W, the corresponding mutual information unexpectedly decreases slightly. Then, when σ is large enough, e.g., 300W, the corresponding mutual information nearly reaches its maximum. It can be learned from Fig. 5(a) that the mutual information does not change distinctly so long as the value of σ is not too large. Consequently, we need not pay much attention to the mutual information in search for the optimal σ.

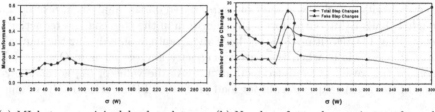

(a) MI between original load and trans-   (b) Number of step changes in transformed
formed load.   load.

Fig. 5. Effect of σ on MI and number of step changes for TD with dataset D1

Now we consider how the number of step changes changes over σ. As shown in Fig. 5(b), when σ grows from 0W to 60W, both the number of total step changes and that of fake step changes decrease. The larger the value of σ is, the longer time period the stable states can be maintained for. As a result, fewer step changes will be leaked. Note that a sharp fluctuation appears while σ is between 60W and 100W. Based on this observation, we can choose 80W as the optimal σ, because both the number of total step changes and that of fake step changes reach maximums. That is, the number of useful step changes holds steady with almost no changes, while fake step changes increase. In fact, the number of useful step changes is nearly unchanged during all the periods until the value of σ becomes too large.

6   Conclusion

We have proposed a novel algorithm called TD using an in-residence rechargeable battery to reduce information leakage in appliance load profiles. TD algorithm adopts the strategy of maintaining the metered load around a baseline value with tolerable deviations, in order to utilize the limited battery capacity more efficiently and reasonably. As a result, we can keep the metered load at stable states for a longer time period, which contributes to the hiding of appliance load characteristics and the reduced risk of privacy leakage. Intuitive observations along with quantitative results are then given by simulations. We employ two metrics for evaluations, i.e., the step changes reduction and the mutual information, respectively. The experimental results confirm the TD algorithm's validity and efficiency in preserving user privacy in the smart grid. Besides, the transformed load profiles expose less information compared with BE algorithm. Future work will focus on the choice and the update of v_b and σ to minimize private information disclosure.

Acknowledgments. The authors would like to thank all the five anonymous reviewers for their valuable comments. This work was supported by the National Natural Science Foundation of China under Grant 61272479 and the Strategic Priority Research Program of Chinese Academy of Sciences under Grant XDA06010702.

References

1. Ipakchi, A., Albuyeh, F.: Grid of the future. IEEE Power and Energy Magazine 7, 52–62 (2009)
2. Meritt, R.: Stimulus: DoE readies $4.3 billion for smart grid. EE Times (2009)
3. Wood, G., Newborough, M.: Dynamic energy-consumption indicators for domestic appliances: Environment, behaviour and design. Elsevier Energy and Buildings 35, 821–841 (2003)
4. McDaniel, P., McLaughlin, S.: Security and privacy challenges in the smart grid. IEEE Security & Privacy 7, 75–77 (2009)
5. Khurana, H., Hadley, M., Lu, N., Frincke, D.A.: Smart-grid security issues. IEEE Security & Privacy 8, 81–85 (2010)
6. Liu, Y., Ning, P., Reiter, M.K.: False data injection attacks against state estimation in electric power grids. ACM Transactions on Information and System Security 14, article no. 13 (May 2011)
7. Cavoukian, A., Polonetsky, J., Wolf, C.: Smart privacy for the smart grid: Embedding privacy into the design of electricity conservation. Springer Identity in the Information Society 3, 275–294 (2010)
8. Leo, A.: The measure of power. MIT Technology Review (2001)
9. Lisovich, M.A., Mulligan, D.K., Wicker, S.B.: Inferring personal information from demand-response systems. IEEE Security & Privacy 8, 11–20 (2010)
10. Autosense: A wireless sensor system to quantify personal exposures to psychosocial stress and addictive substances in natural environments, http://sites.google.com/site/autosenseproject
11. Kalogridis, G., Efthymiou, C., Denic, S.Z., Lewis, T.A., Cepeda, R.: Privacy for smart meters: Towards undetectable appliance load signatures. In: Proc. 1st IEEE International Conference on Smart Grid Communications (SmartGridComm 2010), pp. 232–237 (2010)

12. Skopik, F.: Security is not enough! On privacy challenges in smart grids. International Journal of Smart Grid and Clean Energy 1, 7–14 (2012)
13. Hart, G.W.: Nonintrusive appliance load monitoring. Proceedings of the IEEE 80, 1870–1891 (1992)
14. Hart, G.W.: Residential energy monitoring and computerized surveillance via utility power flows. IEEE Technology and Society Magazine 8, 12–16 (1989)
15. Kursawe, K., Danezis, G., Kohlweiss, M.: Privacy-friendly aggregation for the smart-grid. In: Fischer-Hübner, S., Hopper, N. (eds.) PETS 2011. LNCS, vol. 6794, pp. 175–191. Springer, Heidelberg (2011)
16. Efthymiou, C., Kalogridis, G.: Smart grid privacy via anonymization of smart metering data. In: Proc. 1st IEEE International Conference on Smart Grid Communications (SmartGridComm 2010), pp. 238–243 (2010)
17. Lu, R., Liang, X., Li, X., Lin, X., Shen, X.: EPPA: An efficient and privacy-preserving aggregation scheme for secure smart grid communications. IEEE Transactions on Parallel and Distributed Systems 23, 1621–1631 (2012)
18. Rial, A., Danezis, G.: Privacy-preserving smart metering. In: Proc. 10th Annual ACM Workshop on Privacy in the Electronic Society (WPES 2011), pp. 49–60 (2011)
19. Varodayan, D., Khisti, A.: Smart meter privacy using a rechargeable battery: Minimizing the rate of information leakage. In: Proc. 36th IEEE International Conference on Acoustics, Speech and Signal Processing (ICASSP 2011), pp. 1932–1935 (2011)
20. Kalogridis, G., Denic, S.Z.: Data mining and privacy of personal behaviour types in smart grid. In: Proc. 11th IEEE International Conference on Data Mining Workshops (ICDMW 2011), pp. 636–642 (2011)
21. McLaughlin, S., McDaniel, P., Aiello, W.: Protecting consumer privacy from electric load monitoring. In: Proc. 18th ACM Conference on Computer and Communications Security (CCS 2011), pp. 87–98 (2011)
22. Yang, W., Li, N., Qi, Y., Qardaji, W., McLaughlin, S., McDaniel, P.: Minimizing private data disclosures in the smart grid. In: Proc. 19th ACM Conference on Computer and Communications Security (CCS 2012), pp. 415–427 (2012)
23. Sklavos, N., Touliou, K.: Power consumption in wireless networks: Techniques and optimizations. In: Proc. 2007 IEEE International Conference on "Computer as a Tool" (EUROCON 2007), pp. 2154–2157 (2007)

Cancelable Fingerprint Templates with Delaunay Triangle-Based Local Structures

Wencheng Yang[1], Jiankun Hu[1,*], Song Wang[2], and Jucheng Yang[3]

[1] School of Engineering and Information Technology, University of New South Wales at the Australia Defence Force Academy, Canberra ACT, 2600, Australia
[2] School of Engineering and Mathematical Sciences, La Trobe University, VIC 3086, Australia
[3] College of Computer Science and Information Engineering, Tianjin University of Science and Technology, Tianjin, China
Wencheng.Yang@student.adfa.edu.au, J.Hu@adfa.edu.au,
Song.Wang@latrobe.edu.au, jcyang@tust.edu.cn

Abstract. Security of biometric templates in a fingerprint authentication system is highly critical because the number of fingers of a person is limited and the raw fingerprints cannot be reset or replaced. A cancelable template is an efficient and powerful means to provide template protection. However, in most cancelable fingerprint templates, the many-to-one based non-invertible transformation acts on each single minutia, which may greatly decrease the discriminative capability of its feature representation, and more importantly, single minutia is more sensitive than a local structure to the non-linear distortion present in a fingerprint image. In this paper, we propose a cancelable template by utilizing some nice properties of Delaunay triangle-based local structures, e.g., excellent local structural stability, to achieve satisfactory performance. The non-invertible transformation is applied to each Delaunay triangle-based local structure rather than to each individual minutia so as to mitigate the influence of non-linear distortion and retain the discriminative power of the feature data after the many-to-one mapping. Experimental results on the publicly available databases demonstrate the validity of the proposed scheme.

Keywords: Cancellable template, Delaunay triangles, fingerprint, local structure, biometrics, security.

1   Introduction

Fingerprint authentication technique is widely used in military and civil applications, e.g., banking systems, building entry systems and security systems, and occupies the most market due to the distinctiveness and stability that fingerprints can supply compared to some other biometrics, such as face, iris, trait, voice and so on [1]. Fingerprint authentication systems, which verify "Are you whom you claim to be?" to

---

*Corresponding author.

G. Wang et al. (Eds.): CSS 2013, LNCS 8300, pp. 81–91, 2013.

achieve authentication, is composed of two stages, the enrollment stage and authentication stage. In the enrollment stage, fingerprint feature data are captured and stored in the database as templates. In the authentication stage, a person who wants to pass the authentication presents his/her fingerprint, from which the query feature data are extracted and compared with the templates [2] to make a match or non-match decision. Fingerprint authentication systems provide a more efficient and secure way than traditional authentication methods, e.g., passwords and tokens, thus the problems of remembering long passwords and token loss can be avoided [3].

However, template protection for fingerprint authentication systems is a critical issue that more attention should be directed to. The storage of raw template data would cause some serious security concerns for the reason that the number of fingers of a person is limited and the raw fingerprints cannot be replaced or reset. Once they are compromised, they cannot be changed or re-issued like passwords or tokens. Furthermore, the same template is usually used in different applications, which means template loss in one application equals its loss in all other applications [4].

Cancellable biometrics and biometric cryptosystems are two major techniques that are employed to provide secure fingerprint template protection. In cancellable biometric systems, a non-invertible transformation is applied to the original template data to output transformed data in a different format during the enrolment stage. The query data, which are extracted during the authentication stage, are also transformed into a new format by utilizing the same non-invertible transformation function. The matching is conducted between the transformed template and query data instead of the original data. In this way, even though the transformed templates are compromised, the original templates are still secure and cannot be recovered because the transformation is non-invertible [5].

Ratha et al [5] first proposed the concept of the cancellable biometrics. In their research, three different transformations, Cartesian transformation, polar transformation and functional transformation, are proposed and applied to the fingerprint minutiae to generate a transformed template. A new transformed template can be re-issued just by changing the transformation key when the stored template is compromised. Subsequent to [5], several cancelable biometrics [6-13] are also proposed. Among them, [12] and [13] are two recent research works. Specifically, in [12], Ahmad et al. proposed an alignment-free pair-polar coordinate-based cancelable template to avoid fingerprint image registration that has been considered as non-trivial in poor quality and rotated images [14-16]. Meanwhile, a many-to-one mapping algorithm was applied to realize non-invertibility. Different from [12] which concentrates on the relative location between minutiae pairs in a pair-polar coordinate system, Wang and Hu [13] mainly considered the non-invertible transformation function and proposed a densely infinite-to-one mapping (DITOM) method to achieve the non-invertible property.

We observe that, in most of the existing cancelable fingerprint template design, the non-invertible transformation is loaded upon each single minutia. However, individual minutiae are more sensitive to non-linear distortion than a local structure which is composed of several neighboring minutiae. Motivated by this, in this paper we propose a local Delaunay triangle-based cancelable fingerprint template. The main contribution of our work is three-fold. First, instead of focusing on individual minutiae, the non-invertible transformation is applied to each local Delaunay triangle which is structurally more stable under distortion. Second, each local structure is composed of several Delaunay Triangles, so the feature data extracted from it are apparently more discriminative than the feature data extracted from only a single minutia or triangle. Third, the new feature, the distance from the incircle center of a triangle to the polar space center, is more insensitive to non-linear distortion than the lengths of three edges of a triangle that are used by most existing methods.

The rest of the paper is organized as follows. The proposed Delaunay triangle-based cancelable fingerprint template is presented in Section 2. In Section 3, experimental results are demonstrated and discussed. The conclusion and future work are given in Section 4.

2   Proposed Method

The employment of the Delaunay triangle-based local structure is attributed to the nice properties that such a structure can provide [17, 18]. First, each minutia in a Delaunay triangle-based local structure is likely to preserve a similar structure with its neighborhood minutiae under translation, rotation and little scale change due to nonlinear distortion. Second, missing and spurious minutiae influence the Delaunay triangulation net only locally. In other words, when some local structures are changed by some noisy minutiae, other structures would not be affected. Thus, the employment of the Delaunay triangle-based local structure in the proposed cancelable template can mitigate the negative influence of non-linear distortion present in the fingerprint images.

2.1   Delaunay Triangle-Based Local Structure

The generation of the Delaunay triangle-based local structure is based on the Delaunay triangulation net. Given a fingerprint image which contains a set of minutiae $M = \{m_i\}_{i=1}^N$, where N is the number of minutiae, as shown in Figure 1(a), a Voronoi diagram which partitions the entire fingerprint region into several small cells is generated. In each cell, a minutia m_i is located in the center and all the points in the cell around m_i are closer to m_i than to any other minutiae, as shown in Figure 1(b).

Then, by linking the centers of every cell and its neighbor cells, the Delaunay triangulation net is constructed, as shown in Figure 1(c). In this case, there is a total of ($2 \times N$-2-K) Delaunay triangles produced by the Delaunay triangulation net, where K is the number of minutiae on the convex hull of the Delaunay triangulation net. The Delaunay triangle-based local structure used in our implementation is composed of those Delaunay Triangles that share a common vertex. N Delaunay triangle-based local structures would be generated. The example of a Delaunay triangle-based local structure TS_a, which centers around vertex a, is given in Figure 1(d). We can see that the local structure TS_a is made up of seven triangles $\triangle abc$, $\triangle acd$, $\triangle ade$, $\triangle aef$, $\triangle afg$, $\triangle agh$, and $\triangle ahb$, and all these seven triangles share the common vertex a.

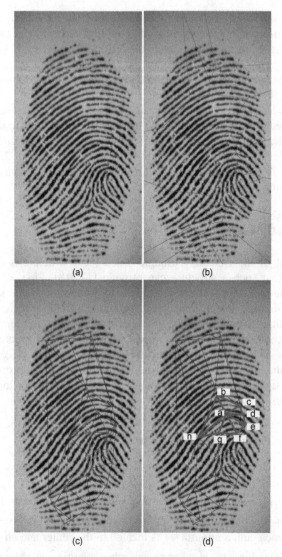

Fig. 1. (a) A set of minutiae (b) The Voronoi diagram (c) The Delaunay triangulation net (d) An example of a Delaunay triangle-based local structure TS_a

2.2   Feature Data Generation

For each Delaunay triangle-based local structure TS_i, we consider its center minutia as the origin of the coordinate system and the center minutia's orientation acts as the 0 degree axis in the polar space. Take the local structure TS_a which centers at minutia a as an example. Several features can be extracted from each of its Delaunay triangles. Below, we define some local features from the Delaunay triangle $\triangle abc$:

- l_{ao}, the length between the vertices a and o which is the incircle center of $\triangle abc$.;
- α_{cax}, the angle between the 0 degree axis (or X axis) and edge ac in the counter clock-wise direction;
- α_{bax}, the angle between the 0 degree axis (or X axis) and edge ab in the counter clock-wise direction;
- β_{bc}, the orientation difference between the orientation θ_b of vertex b and the orientation θ_c of vertex c;

Therefore, a set of feature data, e.g., $f_{abc} = (l_{ao}, \alpha_{cax}, \alpha_{bax}, \beta_{bc})$ as shown in Figure 2, can be extracted from each triangle of a Delaunay triangle-based local structure.

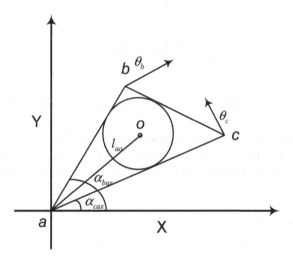

Fig. 2. Feature data $f_{abc} = (l_{ao}, \alpha_{cax}, \alpha_{bax}, \beta_{bc})$ extracted from triangle $\triangle abc$

2.3 Non-invertible Transformation of the Delaunay Triangle-Based Local Structure

In cancellable templates, a non-invertible transformation is applied to conceal the original feature data. As previously mentioned, three different transformations, Cartesian transformation, polar transformation and functional transformation, are proposed by Ratha et al [5]. Here, we employ a similar polar transformation. In contrast to [5] and [12] which apply the polar transformation to each single minutia, in our implementation the polar transformation is applied to every triangle of a local structure TS_i.

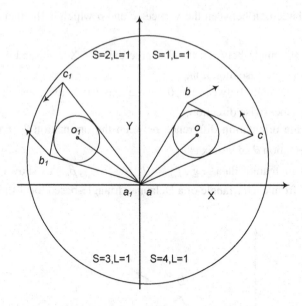

Fig. 3. The original triangle $\triangle abc$ and transformed triangle $\triangle a_1b_1c_1$

In the polar transformation, a polar space is divided into S angles and L levels. The process of the polar transformation is equivalent to the process of changing sector positions. The transformation through the matrix M_s and M_l can be expressed as,

$$T_s = S + M_s \tag{1}$$

$$T_l = L + M_l \tag{2}$$

Again we take the triangle $\triangle abc$ in the local structure TS_a which centers at minutia a as an example. We assume that the polar space, which centers at vertex a, is divided into S angles and L levels. For example, We set S=4, L=1, and define the transformation matrix M_s =[5, 7, 10, 15]. Then the transformation can be expressed as

$$
\begin{aligned}
T_s &= S + M_s \\
&= [1,2,3,4] + [5,7,10,15] \\
&= [\mathrm{mod}(6,4), \mathrm{mod}(9,4), \mathrm{mod}(13,4), \mathrm{mod}(19,4)] \\
&= [2,1,1,3]
\end{aligned}
\tag{3}
$$

This transformation is a many-to-one mapping, we can see that the points/triangles originally located in angle sectors S=2 and S=3 are both mapped to angle sector S=1. Since each triangle, e.g., $\triangle abc$, has three vertices, we choose its incircle center as the reference point for this polar transformation. As shown in Figure 3, the incircle center

o of $\triangle abc$ originally located in S=1 and L=1, together with its three vertices a, b and c, would be mapped to the sector of S=2 and L=1 to generate a new triangle $\triangle a_1 b_1 c_1$. After this non-invertible transformation, the feature data extracted from the transformed triangle $\triangle a_1 b_1 c_1$ are surely different to those extracted from the original triangle $\triangle abc$.

The union of transformation matrixes, M_s and M_l, acts as a secret key k. If the template data are compromised by the adversary, a new template could be re-issued by simply changing the transformation key k.

2.4   Fingerprint Matching

In the fingerprint matching procedure, a certain extent of deformation should be allowed to the feature data because of the elasticity of finger skin. To tolerate these feature differences between template and query images, the quantization technique is utilized to assign a same symbol to those feature values that are located in the same range. The quantization step sizes for distance, angle and orientation difference are denoted by ss_l, ss_α, ss_β, respectively. As mentioned in [19], a small quantization step size would be very sensitive to tiny distortions while a large quantization step size would result in losing the discriminative power of the feature data. So the selection of these quantization step sizes is crucial to the performance of the proposed system.

After quantization, each triangle is denoted by four quantized values. For instance, the transformed triangle $\triangle a_1 b_1 c_1$ would be expressed by $qf_{a_1 b_1 c_1} = (ql_{a_1 o_1}, q\alpha_{c_1 a_1 x}, q\alpha_{b_1 a_1 x}, q\beta_{b_1 c_1})$. If two triangles are considered as a matching pair, all their four corresponding elements should be the same.

Matching between a local structure $TS^T_{i \in [1, N_T]}$ from the template image fp^T and a local structure $TS^Q_{j \in [1, N_Q]}$ from the query image fp^Q depends on how many triangles from them are matched, where N_T and N_Q are the number of local structures in fp^T and fp^Q, respectively. Assume the number of matched triangles between $TS^T_{i \in [1, N_T]}$ and $TS^Q_{j \in [1, N_Q]}$ are N_{ij}, then the similarity between them is calculated by

$$S_{ij} = \frac{N_{ij} \times N_{ij}}{N_T \times N_Q} \tag{4}$$

If S_{ij} is equal to or larger than a pre-defined threshold t_{ij}, then these two local structures $TS^T_{i \in [1, NT]}$ and $TS^Q_{j \in [1, NQ]}$ are considered as a match, and the number of matched local structures N_{TQ} between fp^T and fp^Q would increase by one. After all the local structure matches between fp^T and fp^Q are done, if N_{TQ} is equal to or larger than a pre-defined threshold t_{TQ}, fp^T and fp^Q are judged to be matching and the authentication is passed.

3   Experimental Results

In order to evaluate the performance of the proposed scheme, we test it on two publicly available databases, namely, FVC2002 DB1 and DB2. Each database contains 800 gray-level fingerprint images collected from 100 different fingers with eight images for each finger. To extract the minutiae from fingerprint images, we adopt the software VeriFinger 6.0 from Neurotechnology [20].

Three performance indices are used in this paper to evaluate the performance of the proposed cancelable fingerprint template:

(1) False Reject Rate (FRR) - the ratio of unsuccessful genuine attempts to the total genuine attempts.
(2) False Accept Rate (FAR) - the ratio of successful impostor attempts to the total impostor attempts.
(3) Equal Error Rate (EER) - the error rate when the FRR and FAR are equal.

The matching protocol employed in this experimental is same as that in [12]. Specifically, the 1st image of each finger in the databases is set as the template and the 2nd image from the same finger is set as the query to compute FRR. And the 1st image from each finger in the database is set as the template image and compared with the 2nd image which acts as the query image from the remaining fingers in the databases to compute FAR. So there are 100 genuine matching tests and 9900 impostor matching tests over each database.

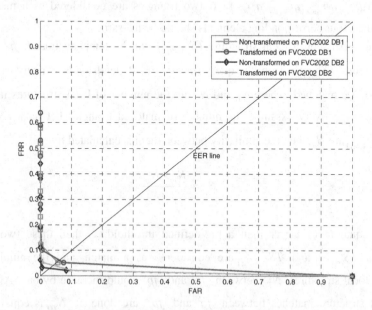

Fig. 4. Performance of the proposed method before and after transformation in terms of EER over databases FVC2002 DB1 and DB2

In the experiments, we set the quantization step sizes, $ss_l = 20$ pixels, $ss_\alpha = 5\pi/36$ and $ss_\beta = 5\pi/36$; the similarity threshold t_{ij} is set to be 0.25; the angles and levels are set to be S=8 and L=3, for both databases. Performance of the proposed scheme before and after transformation in terms of the EER is indicated in Figure 4.

From Figure 4, we can see that after the non-invertible transformation, the performance of the proposed scheme is slightly worse than that before transformation on both databases. This is because the many-to-one mapping tends to make some of the triangles from template and query images that originally match become non-matching after the non-invertible transformation. To be specific, on database FVC2002 DB1, the EER is increased from 5.41% (before transformation) to 5.93% (after transformation). But we can see that the increase of 0.52% in the EER is little. The performance on database FVC2002 DB2, before and after transformation, is EER=2.82% and EER=4%, respectively.

Table 1. Performance comparison of the proposed method with some existing methods in terms of EER(%)

Methods	FVC2002DB1	FVC2002DB2
Ahmad et al. [12]	9.0%	6.0%
Wang and Hu [13]	3.5%	4.0%
Proposed	5.93%	4.0%

In Table 1 we compare the EER of the proposed cancelable template with some existing cancelable design recently proposed. We can see that the proposed method performs better than the method in [12] on both databases FVC2002 DB1 and DB2, and performs the same as the method in [13] on database FVC2002 DB2 and slightly worse than [13] on FVC2002 DB1. However, in [13] each minutia has to be paired up with all other minutiae in the image and fingerprint matching is quite cumbersome. By contrast, the proposed method forms the Delaunay-based local structure in an efficient manner and just needs one layer of comparison in fingerprint matching.

4   Conclusion and Future Work

Cancelable fingerprint templates are an efficient and powerful means to protect biometric templates; however, the non-invertible transformation loaded on each individual minutia tends to increase the template's sensitivity to non-linear distortion and decrease the discriminative capability of the feature data since the many-to-one mapping may map multiple minutiae into one position. To address the issue, in this paper we propose a local Delaunay triangle-based cancelable fingerprint template by exploiting some nice properties of Delaunay triangles. The proposed cancelable template achieves reasonable performance after the non-invertible transformation. For future work, we will perform more extensive testing to explore the best parameter setting and further improve the performance of the proposed method.

We are also interested in investigating cancelable template design for other biometrics such as ECG [21], and keystroke dynamics [22]. Multi-modal cancelable dynamics have been least investigated which needs more attention. Existing biometrics cancelable templates are vulnerable to record multiplicity based cryptographic attacks [23]. How to design a biometric template that can resist such attacks will be a good research topic in the future.

Acknowledgement. This work was supported in part by the National Natural Science Foundation of China under Grant 61063035, ARC grants LP110100602, LP100200538, LP100100404, and LP120100595.

References

1. Xi, K., Ahmad, T., Han, F., Hu, J.: A fingerprint based bio-cryptographic security protocol designed for client/server authentication in mobile computing environment. Security and Communication Networks 4, 487–499 (2011)
2. Yang, W., Hu, J., Wang, S.: A Finger-Vein Based Cancellable Bio-cryptosystem. In: Lopez, J., Huang, X., Sandhu, R. (eds.) NSS 2013. LNCS, vol. 7873, pp. 784–790. Springer, Heidelberg (2013)
3. Yang, W., Hu, J., Wang, S.: A Delaunay Triangle-Based Fuzzy Extractor for Fingerprint Authentication. In: 2012 IEEE 11th International Conference on Trust, Security and Privacy in Computing and Communications (TrustCom), pp. 66–70. IEEE (2012)
4. Li, P., Yang, X., Qiao, H., Cao, K., Liu, E., Tian, J.: An effective biometric cryptosystem combining fingerprints with error correction codes. Expert Systems with Applications 39, 6562–6574 (2011)
5. Ratha, N.K., Chikkerur, S., Connell, J.H., Bolle, R.M.: Generating cancelable fingerprint templates. IEEE Transactions on Pattern Analysis and Machine Intelligence 29, 561–572 (2007)
6. Ahn, D., Kong, S.G., Chung, Y.-S., Moon, K.Y.: Matching with Secure Fingerprint Templates Using Non-invertible Transform. In: Congress on Image and Signal Processing, CISP 2008, pp. 29–33. IEEE (2008)
7. Teoh, A.B.J., Kuan, Y.W., Lee, S.: Cancellable biometrics and annotations on BioHash. Pattern Recognition 41, 2034–2044 (2008)
8. Jin, Z., Teoh, A., Ong, T., Tee, C.: A revocable fingerprint template for security and privacy preserving. KSII Transaction on Internet and Information System 4, 1327-1342 (2010)
9. Lee, C., Kim, J.: Cancelable fingerprint templates using minutiae-based bit-strings. Journal of Network and Computer Applications 33, 236–246 (2010)
10. Chen, H.: A novel algorithm of fingerprint encryption using minutiae-based transformation. Pattern Recognition Letters 32, 305–309 (2011)
11. Jin, Z., Jin Teoh, A.B., Ong, T.S., Tee, C.: Fingerprint template protection with minutiae-based bit-string for security and privacy preserving. Expert Systems with Applications (2011)
12. Ahmad, T., Hu, J., Wang, S.: Pair-polar coordinate-based cancelable fingerprint templates. Pattern Recognition 44, 2555–2564 (2011)
13. Wang, S., Hu, J.: Alignment-free cancellable fingerprint template design: a densely infinite-to-one mapping (DITOM) approach. Pattern Recognition 45, 4129–4137 (2012)

14. Wang, Y., Hu, J., Phillips, D.: A fingerprint orientation model based on 2D Fourier expansion (FOMFE) and its application to singular-point detection and fingerprint indexing. IEEE Transactions on Pattern Analysis and Machine Intelligence 29, 573–585 (2007)
15. Wang, Y., Hu, J.: Global ridge orientation modeling for partial fingerprint identification. IEEE Transactions on Pattern Analysis and Machine Intelligence 33, 72–87 (2011)
16. Zhang, P., Hu, J., Li, C., Bennamoun, M., Bhagavatula, V.: A pitfall in fingerprint bio-cryptographic key generation. Computers & Security 30, 311–319 (2011)
17. Abellanas, M., Hurtado, F., Ramos, P.A.: Structural tolerance and Delaunay triangulation. Information Processing Letters 71, 221–227 (1999)
18. Khanban, A.A., Edalat, A.: Computing Delaunay triangulation with imprecise input data. In: 15th Canadian Conference on Computational Geometry, pp. 94–97. Citeseer (2003)
19. Farooq, F., Bolle, R.M., Jea, T.Y., Ratha, N.: Anonymous and revocable fingerprint recognition. In: IEEE Conference on Computer Vision and Pattern Recognition, pp. 1–7. IEEE (2007)
20. VeriFinger, S.D.K.: Neuro Technology (2010)
21. Sufi, F., Han, F., Khalil, I., Hu, J.: A chaos-based encryption technique to protect ECG packets for time critical telecardiology applications. Security and Communication Networks 4, 515–524 (2011)
22. Xi, K., Tang, Y., Hu, J.: Correlation keystroke verification scheme for user access control in cloud computing environment. The Computer Journal 54, 1632–1644 (2011)
23. Li, C., Hu, J.: Attacks via record multiplicity on cancelable biometrics templates. Concurrency and Computation: Practice and Experience (2013)

Towards a Security-Enhanced Firewall Application for OpenFlow Networks

Juan Wang[1,2], Yong Wang[1], Hongxin Hu[3], Qingxin Sun[1],
He Shi[1], and Longjie Zeng[1]

[1] School of Computer, Wuhan University, Wuhan 430072, Hubei, China
[2] Key Laboratory of Aerospace Information Security and Trust Computing,
Ministry of Education, Wuhan 430072, Hubei, China
jwang@whu.edu.cn
[3] Delaware State University, Dover, DE19901, USA
hhu@desu.edu

Abstract. Software-Defined Networking (SDN), which offers programmers network-wide visibility and direct control over the underlying switches from a logically-centralized controller, not only has a huge impact on the development of current networks, but also provides a promising way for the future development of Internet. SDN, however, also brings forth many new security challenges. One of such critical challenges is how to build a robust firewall application for SDN. Due to the stateless of SDN firewall based on OpenFlow, the first standard for SDN, and the lack of audit and tracking mechanisms for SDN controllers, the existing firewall applications in SDN can be easily bypassed by rewriting the flow entries in switches. Aiming at this threat, we introduce a systematic solution for conflict detection and resolution in OpenFlow-based firewalls through checking flow space and firewall authorization space. Unlike FortNOX [1], our approach can check the conflicts between the firewall rules and flow policies based on the entire flow paths within an OpenFlow network. We also add intra-table dependency checking for flow tables and firewall rules. Finally, we discuss a proof-of-concept implementation of our approach, and our experimental results demonstrate our approach can effectively hinder the bypass threat in real OpenFlow networks.

Keywords: SDN, Firewall, Openflow, Security.

1 Introduction

Software-Defined Networking (SDN) is an innovational network framework introduced by Clean Slate [17] at Stanford University. It enables programmers to control and define the networks by software programming, which makes it be regarded as a reformation in the network field. As the core technology of SDN, OpenFlow [12] is a new network transfer model which separates the function of network controlling and network flows. This model enables users to control the operation of the packets in the networks by inserting flow entries into

G. Wang et al. (Eds.): CSS 2013, LNCS 8300, pp. 92–103, 2013.

switches. It also provides promising method to the research on designing new Internet infrastructure. Nowadays, OpenFlow has been deployed in many research institutions such as Stanford University [9], Internet2, JGN2plus, etc. Also, many network device manufacturers have produced wired and wireless devices supporting OpenFlow.

SDN separates data plane and control plane in the networks, while in a traditional network, such two planes are implemented in switches and routers. In an SDN network, the control plane controls the flow tables in the switches via OpenFlow protocol. Through this way, the control plane realizes the centralized control to the whole network. A controller will compute the shortest flow paths for specific work and control the forwarding behaviors made by the switches. The controller could be a device, a virtual computer, or a physical server [10].

Although SDN introduces many advantages in the development of networks, it also brings forth some new security challenges. One critical challenge is how to build a robust firewall application for SDN networks. A major limitation of OpenFlow is that it is almost stateless. If a host or a network device send a flow to the network, only the first packet of the flow will be checked by the controller while the subsequent packets will be directly forwarded by the switches without any exploration. Neither audit nor tracking mechanism is set towards flows in the controller. Thus, the existing firewall applications for SDN could be easily bypassed by inserting the flow entries with rewriting operations deliberately [1].

To address such a threat, we introduce a systematic approach for conflict detection and resolution in SDN firewall via checking flow space and firewall authorization space. We search the flow paths in the entire network and check them against all firewall deny rules to find out whether the flow paths conflict with the firewall rules. Then, we present different conflict resolution strategies according to different operations in the firewall rules or the flow tables. Considering that the address space of a flow path may be different from the address space of the conflicting firewall rules, we introduce a method that is to insert specific blocking flow entry into the ingress switch or the egress switch of the flow path. Through this method, the firewall application could block the packages that is in conflict with the firewall rules without disrupting other normal packages. By creating and maintaining a shifted flow graph, we establish a tracking mechanism for flows and therefore solve the bypass problem fundamentally.

The major contributions of this paper are summarized as follows:

- We address the threats and security challenges of SDN through demonstrating why SDN firewalls could be easily bypassed.
- We propose a novel policy conflict detection approach for SDN firewalls through checking shifted flow space and firewall authorization space.
- We present a flexible conflict resolution mechanism to facilitate a fine-grained conflict resolution according to different operations of flow entries and firewall rules.
- We implement an SDN firewall application in FloodLight [15] based on our proposed approach and evaluate the effectiveness and efficiency of our application.

The remainder of this paper is organized as follows. In section 2, we discuss the security challenges of OpenFlow networks. In section 3, we analyze these challenges and introduce a systematic conflict detection and resolution framework. In Section 4, we discuss the implementation of our approach and the evaluation of our firewall application. Section 5 overviews the related work and we conclude this paper in Section 6.

2   Security Challenges of OpenFlow Networks

SDN, as a new network paradigm, was just introduced a couple of years ago. Because it allows network applications to operate with switches in the networks directly, it faces a variety of security challenges [3].

First, in SDN, controller cannot ensure that there is no conflict among the various applications. Also, the firewall or other security applications can easily be bypassed by adding deliberated flow tables.

Considering a simple bypass example in Figure 1, there are four hosts, three switches and one controller in a network topology. A firewall application locates in the controller which blocks the communication between host A (IP:10.0.1.12) and host C (IP:10.0.3.32). Now, we insert three flow tables respectively into the three switches and each flow table consists of one flow entry. The first flow entry modifies the source IP address of the packet with 10.0.1.x as the source address to 10.0.4.x; the second flow entry modifies the destination IP address of the packet whose source address is 10.0.4.x to 10.0.3.x; The last flow entry forwards the packet whose source address is 10.0.4.x and destination address is 10.0.3.x. If host A sends a packet with 10.0.4.22 as the source address and 10.0.3.32 as the destination address, this packet will bypass the firewall and arrive Host C through the rewriting behavior because it doesn't match any firewall rules.

Second, the exiting approach [1] overlooks the intra-table dependency among the firewall rules or flow entries. The Security Enforcement Kernel introduced in [1] devises a conflict detecting algorithm for OpenFlow networks. However, the proposed algorithm is incapable of identifying intra-table dependency, and therefore couldn't accurately detect conflicts.

Considering the topology in Figure 1, suppose there are two rules in the firewall as shown in Figure 2. The first rule "IP:10.0.1.12->10.0.3.22 Allow" allows all the packets whose source address is 10.0.1.12 and destination address is 10.0.3.22. While, the second rule "IP:10.0.1.12,10.0.4.22->10.0.3.22 Deny" drops all packets whose source address is 10.0.1.12 or 10.0.4.22 and destination address is 10.0.3.22. Since the first rule has higher priority than the second one, the first rule overlaps the second rule partially. Therefore, when detecting the conflicts, such a rule dependency must be considered to enable precise conflict detection.

3   Our Approach

3.1   Overview of Header Space Analysis

Our conflict detection and solution algorithm is based on Header Space Analysis (HSA) [5]. A uniform and protocol-agnostic model of the network using a

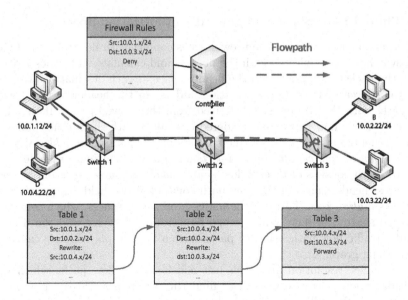

Fig. 1. Rewriting flow entries to bypass an SDN firewall

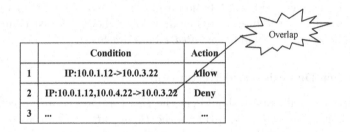

Fig. 2. Overlap of firewall rules

geometric model of packet processing is provided by HSA. A header is defined as a point in space $\{0,1\}^L$ which is called header Space (L is the length(in bit) of the packet). Network boxes are modeled using a Switch Transfer Function T, which transfers received header h in the input port to a set of packet headers on one or more output ports:

$T : (h, p) \to \{(h1, p1), (h1, p1), \ldots\}$

For example, define the transfer function T between a and b as:

$R_{a \to b} = \bigcup_{a \to bpaths} \{T_n(\Gamma(T_{n-1}(\ldots(\Gamma(T_{n-1}(h, p) \ldots)))\}$

So the paths between a and b are several transfer function groups, each like $\{T_1, T_2, T_3, \ldots, T_n\}$. The switches between a and b are:

$a \to S_1 \to \ldots \to S_{n-1} \to S_n \to b$

Using the range inverse at each step in a path, a set of headers can be found, the process is :

$h_a = T_1^{-1}(\Gamma(\ldots(T_{n-1}^{-1}(\Gamma(T_n^{-1}((h, b))\ldots)))$, using the fact that $\Gamma = \Gamma^{-1}$.

3.2 Shifted Flow Space and Denied Authorization Space

If we want to check whether the firewall rules conflict with flow tables in Open-Flow switches, we should track all the packets and calculate all the destinations which the packets can reach and the header space at each destination. We compare the source address and destination address in the header space of every flow paths with the address space derived from the firewall policy. If they have intersection, the flow rules are considered in conflict with the firewall policy.

In a general way, the firewall rule consists of 5 fields: *source address, source port, destination address, destination port*, and *protocol*. The ingress header space of a flow path consists of three fields: *source address, source port*, and *protocol*. The egress header space of the flow path consists of two fields: *destination address, destination port*. Through the ingress and egress spaces, which constructs a tracked space of a flow path, we can figure out the source and the destination of a traffic flow path. All flow paths form a flow graph, which is called the netplumbing graph [6].

Our conflict resolution approach just considers the flow paths which have rewriting actions, because we aim at hindering the bypass threats towards an SDN firewall. We call flowpaths which consists of rewriting flow entries *shifted flow paths*. Those shifted flow paths compose a graph named *Shifted Flow Path Graph*. Also, the rules in a firewall build an *Authorization Space*. When detecting the conflicts between the firewall policy and flow policies, we just compare the *Deny Authorization Space* and the *Sifted Flow Path Space*.

3.3 Conflict Detection and Resolution

Before detecting conflicts, we should get the *Deny Authorization Space* and the *Shifted Flow path Space*. For each rule in the *Deny Authorization Space* and the tracked space of each shifted flow path, we detect whether they have intersections, if so, we claim that there is a conflict between the firewall policy and the flow policies.

To resolve such conflicts, we remove the entire flow path in the network or refuse the insertion of the flow entry that could cause conflicts. We block the conflicting part of a flow path by inserting corresponding deny rules with a higher priority. For example, the flow path shown in Figure 3 has a source address $100x$ and a destination address $110x$. The firewall deny rule is "$101x \rightarrow 11xx$: DENY". Therefore, this rule is conflicting with the flow path. To resolve this conflict, a new flow rule "$1001 \rightarrow 111x$: DENY" is inserted in the ingress switch of the flow path and another new flow rule "$101x \rightarrow 1100$: DENY" is added in the egress switch to block the conflict part of the flow path.

3.3.1 Adding New Firewall Rules

Adding new rules to the firewall may cause conflicts between firewall policy and flow policies. If the new rules are with the actions other than *deny*, they will not cause bypass threats. So we just care about the deny rules. Before detecting the conflicts, we check the *Deny Authorization Space* first. We can detect the new

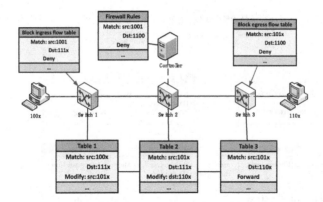

Fig. 3. Inserting rules to block conflict packets in a conflicting flow path

deny space introduced to the firewall by checking the overlapping relationships with other deny rules. Then, we get the tracked space of the *Shifted Flow Path Space* and then check the conflicts between the new *Deny Authorization Space* and the tracked space. If there are conflicts, we resolve the conflicts by adding new deny rules to the ingress switch and the egress switch of the flow path. If the new inserted firewall rule introduces new deny space, there may be conflict flow paths in network due to rewriting the content of packet header fields. Therefore, the tracked space records the source and destination of the flow path. And it is easy to detect the conflicts by comparing the tracked space with the firewall authorization space directly. If the tracked space is smaller than the firewall deny authoritarian space, this inserting request is rejected. But if the tracked space is bigger than new introduced deny space in the firewall, we should only block the conflicting part of the flow path.

As an example shown in Figure 4, when a new rule is inserted into the firewall, the firewall finds the conflicting flow path's address space bigger than the address space of new deny rule. Thus the firewall just denies the conflicting part of the flowpath at the ingress and egress switches by inserting corresponding flow entries (deny rules) with a higher priority.

3.3.2 Adding New Flow Entries

When network applications or controllers insert new flow entries to the flow tables, they may induce new conflicts with the firewall policy. Before checking the conflicts, we should update the *Shifted Flow Path Graph*, because new inserted flow entry may change current flow paths and/or create new flow paths, which may introduce new conflicts. Once the conflict are detected, different from adding new firewall rules, our conflict resolution solution only need to block the conflicting part of the flow path at its ingress switch. If the tracked space is smaller, the request of adding new flow entry will be refused directly.

As shown in figure 5, when a new flow entry is added to *Table 3*, we detect a conflict between firewall policy and the new flow entry. The address space

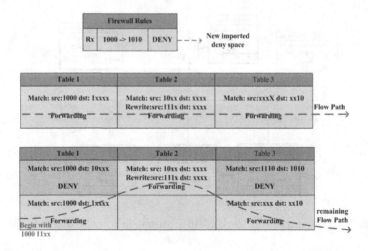

Fig. 4. Adding a deny rule to the SDN firewall

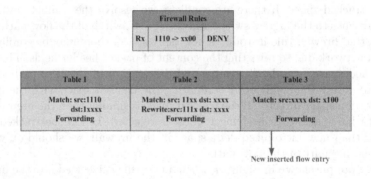

Fig. 5. Adding new flow entries to the newtowk

$(1110 \rightarrow x100)$ of flow path is smaller than the deny authorization space $(1110 \rightarrow xx00)$ of the firewall, so the request of adding this new flow entry is refused.

3.3.3 Updating Flow Entries and Firewall Rules

There are other operations to the firewall policy and flow tables: updating/deleting rules. Updating a flow entry or firewall rule may import new conflicts. Thus, these operations need to be examined for conflict detection and resolution as well.

Updating an existing rule in the firewall may change the intra-table dependency. Therefore, we need to update the D*eny Authorization Space* like adding firewall rule, and then detect and resolve the conflicts.

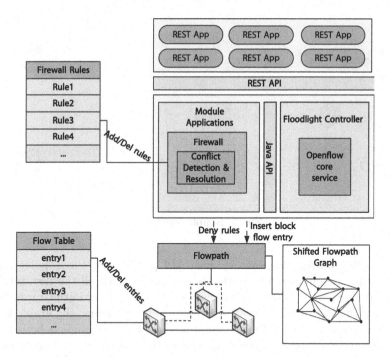

Fig. 6. Implementation framework

Updating an existing flow entry may also import conflicts. In this case, our approach first updates the *Shifted Flow Path Graph* and finds the new added flow paths. Then, the conflicts are detected and and resolved. When resolving the conflicts, the conflicting part is blocked in both ingress and egress switches.

4 Implementation and Evaluation

4.1 Implementation

Our implement is based on Ubuntu Linux operation system version 12.04 and Mininet [18] on Virtualbox. The Mininet implements our network topologies virtually. The Floodlight controller is compiled by Floodlight version 0.9.0 and hosted on an Intel 2.7GHZ core i3 CPU with 4.0G RAM. We used `Python` to implement the topology of network and `Java` to implement the enhanced modules. We deployed the *Conflict Detection and Resolution* module in the firewall application. On one hand, the detection module obtains all the firewall rules added by the administrator and all flow entries in every switch. On the other hand, the resolution module gets the blocking flow entry and inserts it to corresponding switch or rejects the insertion request. Our implementation has about 3000 lines of Java code.

As shown in Figure 6, the Detection and Resolution module are implemented as an module application in the Floodlight controller. The controller reads

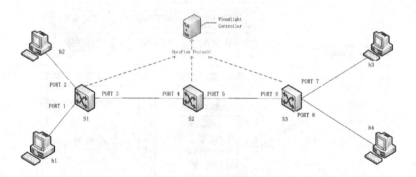

Fig. 7. Simple topology

and stores the topology message by Java API provided by the Topology Manager/Routing module service. At the same time, it reads all the flow tables in every switch by Java API function and stores them as a Flow Path Graph. When applications or controllers insert flow entries to the switches, the graph will be updated accordingly. When the detection module finds the conflicts between the flow paths and the firewall policy, it will call the resolution module to resolve these identified conflicts. All flow entries are obtained by Java API provided by the Floodlight controller platform, while all firewall rules are obtained by the function we implemented as a new Java API in the Firewall module application. To optimize the performance of our application, we convert the source and destination addresses to binary vectors. Then, our application calculates the intersection of firewall deny authorization space and flow path space by directly using their binary code for the conflict detection.

4.2   Evaluation

Figures 7 and 8 show a simple topology and a complex topology, respectively, used for our evalution. We use a remote controller installed our firewall application. The simple topology consists of three switches, S_1, S_2, S_3, and four hosts, h_1, h_2, h_3, h_4, while the complex topology consists of eight switches and sixty-four hosts. Flow tables in these switches form the flow paths. The topologies use a remote controller, Floodlight, which controls the switches based on the OpenFlow standard. If a flow entry in each switch is changed, the switch will send a Flow-Removed type message [12] to Floodlight. Thus, Floodlight could update the topology in real-time and the detection module could calculate the spaces timely.

We insert the firewall rules and flow rules to network boxes in a virtual network environment. Our conflict detection and resolution algorithms could find the shifted flow paths in the network and conflicts between the firewall policy and flow policies, and resolve the conflicts by inserting blocking entries to ingress and egress switches.

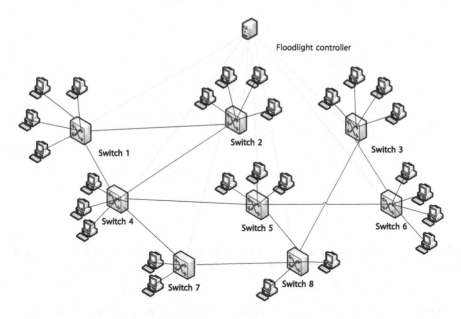

Fig. 8. Complex topology

In our experiment, our goal was to measure the delay caused by detecting the conflicts between a resident firewall policy and a number of active flow entries. To achieve the goal, we excluded the time used for getting the firewall rules and the flow entries by setting the functions to record the delay time. We pre-configured one firewall rule in the firewall module and check it against the sets of 100, 200, 300, ..., 1000 candidate flow entries. We did our evaluation in terms of both the simple topology and the complex topology. Figure 9 shows our analysis results. The results show the computing costs increase linearly along with the increasing numbers of candidate flow entries. In addition, we can observe the difference of computing costs with respect to two topologies.

5   Related Work

With the quick development of SDN techniques, the security issues in SDN have attracted more attentions recently. In [4], the researchers introduced FLOVER, a model checking system, which verifies that the aggregate of flow policies instantiated within an OpenFlow network does not violate the network's security policy. Their system detects faults leading to invalid and invisible routes, but it doesn't consider firewall policies. The key components of SDN includes OpenFlow switches and controllers. There is a few research talking about the firewall application security in the controller. In [2], the authors proposed PermOF, a fine-grained permission system, as the first line of defense to apply minimum privilege on applications. They summarized a set of 18 permissions to be enforced at the API entry of the controller. Our work is most closely related to

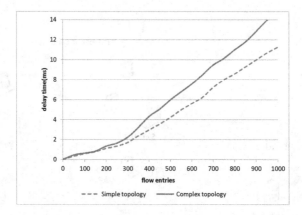

Fig. 9. These plots illustrate the performance in conducting conflict evaluation per firewall rule against 100, 200, 300, 400, 500, 600, 700, 800, 900, 1000 flow entries

FortNOX [1], which uses single IP address to identify potential bypass violations and provides a conflict detection and resolution approach. However, it detects conflicts only based on *pairwise* comparisons, while ignores ignores rule dependency in both flow tables and firewall polices. Also, it could not build an globe view of network state. In contrast, our approach is able to build an entire view of network through tracking all flow path for accurate conflict detection. In addition, our approach can check conflicts dynamically when any network state changes, such as adding, deleting and modifying firewall or flow rules.

Recently, some work could enable dynamic reachability checking and build an globe view of network state by real-time network verification [6]. Even though these approach can be applied for policy conflict detection, they could not provide effective mechanisms for policy conflict resolution. In contrast, our work provides a systematic solution for policy conflict detection and resolution in SDN.

6   Conclusion

In this paper, we addressed the challenge of building a robust SDN firewall. In our approach, the source and destination addresses of firewall rules and flow entries are first represented by binary vector. Then, conflicts between firewall rules and flow rules are checked through comparing the shifted flow space and deny firewall authorization space. During the conflict detection, the rule dependencies in both flow tables and firewall policies are considered. Furthermore, our approach provides a fine-granted conflict resolution. Finally, we implemented our security-enhanced SDN firewall application in Floodlight. Our experiment showed that our application can effectively and efficiently prevent bypass threats in OpenFlow networks.

References

1. Porras, P., Shin, S., Yegneswaran, V., Fong, M.: A Security Enforcement Kernel for OpenFlow Networks. In: Proc. of HotSDN 2012, pp. 123–125 (2012)
2. Wen, X., Chen, Y., Hu, C., Shi, C.: Towards a Secure Controller Platform for OpenFlow. In: Proc. of HotSDN 2013 (2013)
3. Kreutz, D., Ramos, F., Verissimo, P.: Towards secure and dependable software-defined networks. In: Proc. of HotSDN 2013 (2013)
4. Son, S., Shin, S., Yegneswaran, V., Porras, P.: Model Checking Invariant Security Properties in OpenFlow. In: Proc. of ICC 2013, pp. 2–6 (2013)
5. Kazemian, P., Varghese, G., McKeown, N.: Header Space Analysis: Static Checking For Networks. In: Proceedings of the Symposium on Network Systems Design and Implementation (NSDI), pp. 3–5 (2012)
6. Kazemian, P., Chang, M., Zeng, H.: Real Time Network Policy Checking using Header Space Analysis. In: Proceedings of the Symposium on Network Systems Design and Implementation (NSDI), pp. 4–6 (2013)
7. Tootoonchian, A., Gorbunov, S., Ganjali, Y., Casado, M., Sherwood, R.: On controller performance in software-defined networks. In: Proceedings of the 2nd USENIX Workshop on Hot Topics in Management of Internet, Cloud, and Enterprise Networks and Services (Hot-ICE), pp. 4–6 (2012)
8. Al-shaer, E., Marrero, W., El-atawy, A., Elbadawi, K.: Network Configuration in A Box: Towards End-to-End Verification of Network Reachability and Security. In: Proceedings of the IEEE International Conference on Network Protocols, pp. 125–127 (2009)
9. Canini, M., Venzano, D., Peresini, P., Kostic, D., Rexford, J.: A NICE Way to Test OpenFlow Applications. In: Proceedings of the Symposium on Network Systems Design and Implementation, pp. 3–5 (2012)
10. Cai, Z., Cox, A.L., Ng, T.E.: Maestro: A System for Scalable OpenFlow Control. In: Rice University Technical Report, pp.2-3 (2010)
11. Liu, A.: Formal Verification of Firewall Policies. In: Proceedings of the International Conference on Communications (ICC), pp. 1495–1497 (2008)
12. OpenFlow. OpenFlow 1.1.0 Specification,
    http://www.openflow.org/documents/openflow-spec-v1.1.0.pdf
13. OpenFlowHub. BEACON, www.openflowhub.org/display/Beacon
14. Sanfilippo, S.: HPing home page, http://www.hping.org
15. FloodLight, http://www.projectfloodlight.org/documentation/
16. Kanizo, Y., Hay, D., Keslassy, I.: Palette: Distributing Tables in Software-Defined Networks. In: Technical Report, pp. 1–3 (2012)
17. Clean Slate, http://cleanslate.stanford.edu/
18. Mininet: An Instant Virtual Network on your Laptop (or other PC),
    http://mininet.org//

Online Mining of Attack Models in IDS Alerts from Network Backbone by a Two-Stage Clustering Method

Lin-Bo Qiao, Bo-Feng Zhang, Rui-Yuan Zhao, and Jin-Shu Su

College of Computer,
National University of Defense Technology,
Changsha 410073, China
{qiao.linbo,bfzhang,zhaoruiyuan11,sjs}@nudt.edu.cn

Abstract. There is little work has been done to mine attack models online in IDS alerts from the network backbone. The contributions of this paper are three-fold. Firstly, we put forward a software-pipeline online attack models mining framework suited with alert clustering mining methods. Secondly, we propose an online alert reduction method and improve two-stage clustering method. Thirdly, we propose an approach to adjust parameters used in the framework on the fly. The experiment shows that the data feature is stable in sequence length to apply the parameters self-adjustment algorithm, and parameters self-adjustment works well under the online mining framework. The online mining attack models is efficient compare to offline mining method, and generated attack models have convincing logic relation.

Keywords: Attack model mining online, alert reduction, two-stage clustering, sequence analysis, behavior analysis, parameters adjustment.

1 Introduction

Nowadays, IDS is one of the most common security components deployed on the Internet. It provides basic information about network intrusion behaviors happening on network, but it helps network administrator little as it provides too much details for network administrator to understand them all together. Researchers in this field have proposed variety methods to generate a high-level succinct perspective of the intrusion information to tackle this problem in recent ten years. These methods help network administrator a lot to keep the network away from thoroughly compromised by some attacker and help them to discover related attack models occurred on the network. And among these methods, the clustering mining method is a promising one as it works without predefined rules or presupposition.

Through there are a lot of methods provide a succinct perspective of the intrusion behaviors, it is still a hard problem the researchers facing to nowadays to provide an online perspective of the intrusion behaviors, especially for these based on clustering methods. To provide a real-time high-level perspective of the intrusion information based on clustering method should tackle a serial challenges while the Internet

G. Wang et al. (Eds.): CSS 2013, LNCS 8300, pp. 104–116, 2013.
© Springer International Publishing Switzerland 2013

improved rapidly these years. And the methods we proposed in the paper are mainly related to the problems listed below.

How to design an online framework suits well with clustering method. It's a challenge for us to design an online mining framework working well with clustering method. As we know that the clustering is one of the data mining methods which mines knowledge from data, and generally speaking, more history data always makes a better result. It contradicts with the time criterion of online framework, so we should propose a new framework that works well with clustering method.

How to handle huge amount of IDS alerts efficiently. One of the most challenges to mine attack models online is the rapidly increase amount of the IDS alerts, which makes it difficult to realize a time critical mining method, so it is the space cost we should focus on, especially for alerts from network backbone. And the high redundancy of the alerts makes it possible to handle the huge amount of alerts, and it is necessary to propose an online redundancy reduction method to handle the huge amount of IDS alerts.

How to make parameters adjusted on the fly. The parameters are used to control the process of the software-pipeline, and even a tiny change in them may result in a big difference in result. The parameters are environment related, and they should be tuned from time to time to be suited with the changing environment. However, it's a hard problem that to evaluate the correlation process without any information of the correlation method. It's necessary to make parameters adjustment online with the information about specified correlation method.

In this paper, a software-pipeline online mining framework is proposed and works well with the two-stage clustering method. An online redundancy reduction method based on statistic measurement is proposed to reduce the redundant alert which makes the mining system successfully to handle the huge amount of IDS alerts. And we propose a parameter self-adjustment method to make sure the parameters are suited well with the ever changing environment.

The reminder of this paper is organized as follows: It is related works done in the alerts correlation and the state of the art in section 2. We address the approaches proposed in this paper in detail in section 3. In section 4 we introduce the experiment procedure, present the results of the experiment and analyze the result. And in section 5 here is conclusion of this paper and discussion about some ideas to do in future research.

2   Related Work

As it is difficult for network administrators to find out the intrusion behaviors from huge amount of low-level IDS alerts generated on the monitor network, to make a high-level network intrusion behavior alert analysis is needed and helpful. It has become a hot-point in security area. A comprehensive correlation approach is proposed by Valeur, et al. [1] , and a typical process of alert correlation is shown in Fig. 1. Lot methods have been proposed, and we put them into three classes. The first class of approaches is based on matching the attack scenario knowledge pre-defined. e.g., ADELE [2], STATL [3], LAMBDA [4] and methods which correlate alerts by matching the knowledge database. The second class of approaches is based on rebuilding the causal relationship between alerts, e.g., the JIGSAW [5] and methods which correlate alerts according to the consequences among them. The third class of approaches is based on clustering the similar alerts, e.g., the EMERALD [6] and methods which correlate alerts by clustering the alerts considering the similarities among alerts.

Fig. 1. An overview of the attack model mining

Methods proposed to reduce the alert redundancy are different from each other. Levera, et al. [7] aimed at false positive data and used a data cube and median polish method, and they did an experiment with a sound result on DARPA 1999 Intrusion Detection data set [8]. Xiao, et al. [9] reduced the redundancy alert by clustering method based on similarity among alerts. Ming Xu, et al. [10] proposed a prior restricted conditions (PRC). Considering the data feature of the alert from the network backbone and the staged followed by the reduction method. The reduction method proposed in this paper is based on statistic which is simple and effective.

Methods to correlate alerts could be put into the three classes as mentioned above. Compared to graph mining[11], a more promising classes is the clustering methods, and the clustering method has been used in the correlation procedure with different purposes. Valdes, et al. [12] use clustering method to correlate alerts based on the similarity of alerts which is measured by a set of alert attribute functions. Porras, et al. [6] used clustering method to construct accurate and complete attack sensors in a multilevel alert fusion. Siraj, et al. [13] used clustering method to strengthen the reliability of alerts fusion with a causal knowledge based inference technique. Zhang, et al. [14] used clustering method with fuzzy technique and get a reliable result on LLS DDOS2.0. Peng, et al. [15] used an improved clustering method to acquire the high level perspective of network intrusion behavior with a quantum-behaved particle swarm optimization algorithm to generate the parameters. In this paper, a two-stage clustering method with parameters self-adjustment is proposed to acquire a higher level perspective of the network intrusion behaviors through a two-phase analysis.

Online mining of attack models poses some major challenges for correlation approaches. First, the online mining method should cope with the high rate of lower-level alerts generated by the sensors on the network. Secondly, the proposed method for models extraction should develop attack models incrementally. And seldom work has been proposed on those points. Bernhard Amann, et al. [16] proposed an Input Framework to introduce the intelligence online, and they control the input data rate successfully. V.SrujanaReddy et al. [17] proposed a patterns' update algorithm, and incrementally generate the patterns. Reza Sadoddin et al. [18] proposed a framework to generate incremental frequent structure in real-time alert correlation. In this paper, we propose a novel framework suites well with clustering method and tune it to be a balanced software-pipeline.

3   Attack Models Online Mining

The attack models online mining system consists of an online mining framework with balanced software-pipeline, alert reduction method and two-stage clustering procedure with parameters' self-adjustment. The online mining framework is shown in Fig. 2. The framework is based on approaches which we proposed in our previous work [19, 20]. We apply new techniques to these offline mining methods to meet the requirement of online mining, and the key technique is a balanced software-pipeline with parameters self-adjustment. The two-stage clustering method under online mining framework re-organizes the workload of each procedure. The parameters' self-adjustment includes self-adjustment of OL-RMSR's parameter, self-adjustment of TSCA's parameter, and self-adjustment LLCS's parameter. During the self-adjustment procedure, the parameters are updated while the online mining procedures suspended. In the remaining part of this section, we will discuss the methods mentioned above in detail.

3.1   Online Mining Framework

Online mining is a time and space critical problem, and there are serials of time-related strategies to achieve a better performance. In this paper, we design our online mining framework as an adaptation of software-pipeline, and the framework is shown in Fig. 2. What we input into the system is IDS alerts, and what the system outputs is the knowledge of the attack models about intrusion behaviors took place on the network which the IDS monitors.

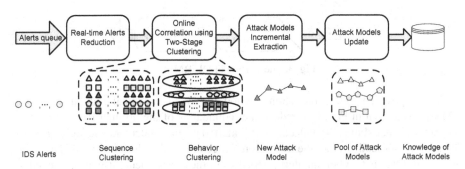

Fig. 2. The framework of attack models online mining

As shown in the framework, the pipeline consists of the following parts: real-time alerts reduction, online correlation, attack models incremental extraction, and attack models update. There is a blocking buffer between each pair-part. The system organizes the alerts from IDS sensor into a form of FIFO queue. IDS sensors push the alerts generated on the network in the front of the queue, and simultaneously the system pops the alerts at the back of the queue, the alerts in the queue are ordered by the time attribute of the alert. The alert online reduction part pops the alerts directly from the alerts queue, and then filters the redundant alert data to reduce the workload of the system to process in the following procedures. The online correlation part is made up by two sub-parts: the sequence clustering and behavior clustering. The former part rebuilds the alerts into the form of sequence and the latter part clusters the sequences into behavior-clusters. The attack models incremental extraction part extracts the attack model implicated in the clusters of behaviors. And the last part maintains the attack models and makes store the attack models into the knowledge database.

The balance of the pipeline is a hardcore problem. A bad-balanced software-pipeline will lead to a bad performance even if the architecture designed well. So it is necessary to divide the workload into stages according to the cost of each stage in software-pipeline and get a better performance.

3.2   Alert Reduction with Parameter Self-adjustment

The alert reduction ratio is a very important aspect of alert correlation method. It reflects the workload the system to handle and influences the quality of the result. However, the reduction ratio is data related. It means that an alert reduction method may have different performance on different data. So it is necessary to consider the environment produced the alert data when we propose an alert reduction method, and it is needed to modify the alert reduction method while the data's feature structure changed.

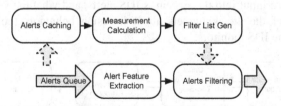

Fig. 3. The scheme of OL-RMSR

We propose an online reduction method based on statistical redundancy (OL-RMSR), as shown in Fig. 3, to reduce the redundancy of the original IDS alerts from the network backbone. It will cache the alert data and calculate the measurement features periodically. And the reduction procedure will filter the redundant alert according filter list. When an alert popped from the alerts queue, it will be cached as well as to get the alert feature. Each alert fetched from the alerts queue will have the redundant feature extracted and then make the decision whether it should be flowed to next stage or not, according to value of the redundant feature. At the same time, the alerts are cached in a buffer, a trigger is set to calculate the redundant measurement, and a filter list of alert types is generated according to the redundant measurement value.

When an alert comes into the system, it will also be cached into a buffer. The redundant list generation procedure will begin if the buffer is full. Redundant list generation mainly consists of four steps. First, it gets the statistics number of the alert flows. Alert flow consists of alerts have the same source and destination IP addresses in the time sequence. Second, it gets the statistics vector of alert types in the alert flows with an enumerative ratio over a threshold ε_{er} which used to control the percentage of the alert type should be included in statistic procedure. Then it computes the redundant value of the alert types have a ratio over a threshold ε_{atr} which is used to control the percentage of the flow to be included in redundancy ratio calculation procedure. The redundancy value of each alert type is calculated as we proposed in previous work [19]. At last, the reduction list of redundant alert types will be output after it ordered by its redundancy ratio value.

3.3   Two-Stage Clustering Alert Correlation with Parameters Self-adjustment

As shown in Fig. 4, the two-stage clustering alert correlation method consists of sequences clustering and behaviors clustering. The first stage of clustering is used for spatial and temporal analysis, and the last two procedures is the second stage clustering, which is used for behavior analysis. The parameters of clustering procedures will be updated accordingly while the clustering procedure ongoing. The details of parameters adjustment procedure will be discussed in the next section.

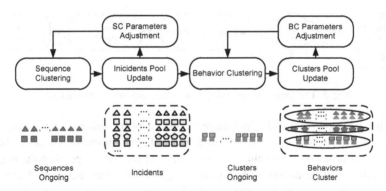

Fig. 4. The flow chart of the two-stage clustering with parameters adjustment

In the first stage of clustering, the input data is a queue of attribute vectors, the output data is a set of sequences with high-similarity alerts. The similarity of alerts determines the sequence correlation result. The similarity function is a weighted sum of the functions with attributes: the IP addresses, the time interval and the alert types. The functions are proposed in our previous work.

It is needed to pop out the sequence immediately after it finished. Once there comes an alert there will be a time-over check to see if there are some sequences have run out of the time interval, these sequences will be removed out of the sequence clustering pool into the incidents pool. And time interval may change from time to time so it's necessary to make dynamic parameters adjustment when the system is running. Considering the time cost and the memory space needed to get proper parameters set, we use a buffer here to recalculate the parameters periodically.

Sequence clustering (SC) parameters adjustment will begin when the incidents pool is full. And there is just one buffer to store the incidents generated by the first stage clustering. The adjustment procedure consists of three procedures: sequences rejoin measurement calculation and sequence clustering parameters adjustment.

As shown in Fig. 5, once the buffer of incidents is full we rejoin the sequences and rebuild the sequences into a more complete form if two or more sequences in the pool are pieces of alerts sequence related to a same malicious behavior. The sequences rejoin procedure will check each end alert and initial alert of all the sequences to find sequences may relate to same intrusion behavior. If there is one end alert and one initial alert belong to different sequence and they have a similarity over the threshold without consider the time interval ε_{td} then we will rejoin these two sequences into one. Then the alerts with same type in one sequence will be filtered out, and the measurement calculation procedure will get a proper time interval ε_{td}` for the sequence clustering. The time interval $\varepsilon_{td}$` will replace ε_{td} and be applied to the sequence clustering procedure just after the adjustment.

In the second stage clustering, we use the Edit Distance Ratio (EDR) to measure the similarity of two incidents. Compared to the Edit Distance, the EDR is much more effective especially when the sequences have a big difference in length.

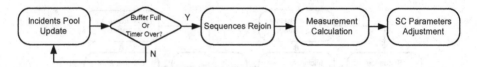

Fig. 5. The sequence clustering parameters adjustment procedure

The behavior clustering (BC) parameters adjustment procedure is almost the same as the sequence clustering parameters procedure. The measurement calculated here is the statistic information of the clusters' size ε_{csize}, and the size bigger than the majority of the clusters will be chosen to be the size ε_{csize} to trigger the action that move the clusters of behavior from the ongoing pool to the behaviors pool which will be accessed by the next stage.

3.4   Balanced Software-Pipeline

However, a bad-balanced software-pipeline will lead to a bad performance even if the architecture designed well. So it is necessary to balance the cost of each stage of software-pipeline and get a better performance. As shown in Fig. 6, it's a software pipeline with 6 stages, the input framework read alerts, the online RMSR reduces alerts redundancy, the sequences clustering with sequences clustering parameters adjustment, the behaviors clustering and the behaviors clustering parameters adjustment, the attack models extraction and the attack models output. Between the each pair of adjacent stages, a blocking buffer is set here to store the temporary data used by adjacent stages. The stages not neighboring each other could execute simultaneous.

Input (1)	Input (2)	Input (3)	Input (4)	Input (5)				
	RMSR (1)	RMSR (2)	RMSR (3)	RMSR (4)	RMSR (5)			
		SC (1)	SC (2)	SC (3)	SC (4)	SC (5)		
			BC (1)	BC (2)	BC (3)	BC (4)	BC (5)	
				LLCS (1)	LLCS (2)	LLCS (3)	LLCS (4)	LLCS (5)

Fig. 6. The stages of online mining software-pipeline

Considering the time of each part of the system cost and the function of each procedure are not equal to each other, we reorganized the stages to reach a better balanced time cost. It is a hard problem as the time cost of each stage is different from each other. After a few test on several data-set with huge amount of alerts, we obtain run time cost of each stage on these data-set. The clustering stage have a much longer time cost than the others'. To tackle this problem, we improve the clustering stage to be a parallel clustering method, both sequences clustering and behaviors clustering, we propose multithread clustering method to accelerate the clustering process as there is potential parallelism in them. The clustering level pseudo-code of the algorithm is shown in Fig. 7.

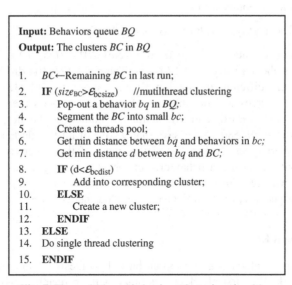

Input: Behaviors queue BQ
Output: The clusters BC in BQ

1. $BC \leftarrow$ Remaining BC in last run;
2.   **IF** ($size_{BC} > \varepsilon_{bcsize}$)   //mutilthread clustering
3.   Pop-out a behavior bq in BQ;
4.   Segment the BC into small bc;
5.   Create a threads pool;
6.   Get min distance between bq and behaviors in bc;
7.   Get min distance d between bq and BC;
8.   **IF** ($d < \varepsilon_{bcdist}$)
9.   Add into corresponding cluster;
10.   **ELSE**
11.   Create a new cluster;
12.   **ENDIF**
13.   **ELSE**
14.   Do single thread clustering
15.   **ENDIF**

Fig. 7. The multithread behaviors clustering algorithm

4   Experiment and Result Analysis

In this chapter, we report and analyze the results of experiments performed for evaluating the function of proposed methods and the performance of the proposed framework. We set up the experiment in two steps with a real world alert data-set conducted for evaluating the main components of the framework separately. A long history of real world alerts is used to test the performance of the online mining framework proposed, and also used to test the attack models reconstruction function by the two-stage clustering correlation method. The performance of the framework is evaluated through making an analysis on the size of the data processed and the time of each stage of the of the pipeline cost in multi-times running of the framework with performance log. The second purpose of the experiment performed is to test the reconstruction function by check the result of the framework generated, the result checking is mainly done in our previous work, and in the experiment performed in this paper we primarily tested the parameters adjustment function.

4.1   Experiment Setup

In order to obtain a more convincible result, we developed an input framework with speed controlling to scan more than 30G real world alerts log and input these alerts into the framework, exactly there are 126783512 raw alerts generated by IDS sensor. During the setup process, we normalized the alerts data, and each raw alert is normalized as a vector consists of the following 3 fields:

(1) *Time*: The time stamp;

(2) *Endpoints*: The endpoints with source and destination IP, port;

(3) *Alert-Type*: The alert type with PID, SID, and MSG.

The time stamp of alerts crosses from 14-Nov-2011 16:56:19 to 28-Nov-2011 09:31:07, and it's about 13 days and 17 hours. There are 4234104 different source IP addresses, 4695029 different destination IP addresses, and 2050328 IP addresses appeared both in sources and destinations. Among these alerts there are 402 alert types marked by different PID and SID pairs. The number of the alerts marked by 6 most alert types is 116985806, or it says that 92.3% of all the alerts are marked by less than 1.5% alert types. It is believed that most of these alert types have little information about the intrusion behavior. For instance, among the alert types of the real world data we used the most common alert type is about the event generated when the http_inspect preprocessor detects anomalous network traffic.

4.2   Experiment Result

Since the stability of alerts is an important basic hypothesis for the proposed online mining framework. We first check the stability both in quantity and in time. The sequence continuity is shown in Fig. 8 and Fig. 9, the sequence length varies from alert number to alert number in the same real world data, and also varies from time to time as the mining process goes on. When sequences reconstructed in quantity by the scale of million, the sequences' length varies from 5 to 11, and when sequences reconstructed in time by the scale of 24 hours, the sequences' length varies from 9 to 17. The later ones are longer than the former ones both in minimal sequence length and in maximal sequence length. It is because alerts number between each stage in the later one is larger than the alerts number of the former one, and at the same time the time interval is bigger than the duration among every million alerts.

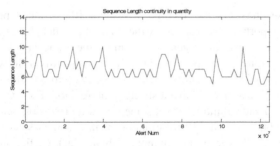

Fig. 8. Sequence length continuity in quantity

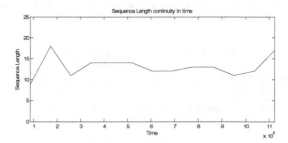

Fig. 9. Sequence length continuity in quantity

It is important to have a stable adjustment time cost for mining process scheduling, as a stable time cost will make the scheduling predictable. Using the large real world data as input alerts, we get the time cost of adjustment process. The cost of time varies from 20 seconds to 95 seconds, and the median number of them is 58.8531 seconds. The adjustment result of time interval changes from 6553.6 seconds to 52428.8 seconds according to the data window it is in.

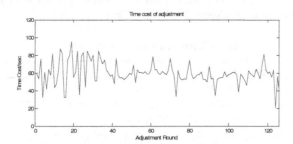

Fig. 10. Sequence length continuity in quantity

The online mining method spent much less time during the clustering procedure compared to the offline mining method, and the attack models' incremental extraction works well in the online environment. The offline mining algorithm took more than 12 hours to get the attack models. The time spent to mining attack models from alerts by the online algorithm is cross from 16:51:41 to 20:54:24, and that's 4 hours 2 minutes and 43 seconds. On the average, it's about 1037.4 alerts per second. The pipeline plays an important role, especially the stage of parallel clustering.

The online mining procedure generates almost the same attack models as the offline mining procedure we proposed in [19]. In the Appendix of it, we give a list of attack models extracted by our online method from the two day duration alert data. The steps of these attack models have a strong logic relation. For example, as shown in Table 1, there is an attack model about some kind scan intrusion behavior. The first two steps are to obtain the SNMP information of target, then scan the information about PCAnywhere, followed by an attempt to obtain Back Orifice information, and afterward scan of Amanda version is made with MISC AFS access attempt at last. In the table, an "Alert Type" is an triple marked with "SID-GID-RID", and the "Msg" is msg information in alert.

Table 1. An attack model about scan

Steps	Alert Type	Msg
1	1-1419-12	SNMP trap udp
2	1-1413-13	SNMP private access udp
3	1-566-6	POLICY PCAnywhere server response
4	105-2-1	(spo_bo) Back Orifice Client Traffic detected
5	1-634-5	SCAN Amanda client-version request
6	1-1504-8	MISC AFS access

The attack models online mining system can extract attack models without explicit IDS sensor rules information, as well as to extract attack model with instinct rules information shown in table 1. For instance, there is an attack model extracted about some kind of remote-exploitation. In this remote exploitation process, it firstly transfers shellcode to the target system, then a malformed packet with abnormal FIN number, and then downloads executable binary file and policy.

Table 2. An attack model extracted

Steps	Alert Type	Msg
1	1-1394-12	SHELLCODE x86 inc ecx NOOP
2	129-16-1	FIN number is greater than prior FIN
3	1-648-10	SHELLCODE x86 NOOP
4	1-15306-4	Portable Executable binary file transfer
5	1-16313-6	POLICY download of executable content x-header

5   Discussion

In this paper, we put forward an online attack models mining framework with a two-stage clustering method. Considering the huge amount alerts from the network backbone, we propose an online alert reduction method based on statistics with parameters online adjustment. The parameters online adjustment is built into the online mining framework and generates parameters suited the running environment from time to time. The parameters adjustment is built into the two-stage clustering method as well. The experiment shows that the data feature is stable in sequence length to apply the parameters self-adjustment algorithm, and parameters self-adjustment works well under the online mining framework. The online mining attack models is efficient compare to offline mining method, and generated attack models have convincing logic relation.

And there is still considerable work to do. The attack models mining is based on the alerts generated by the sensors deployed, and it relies heavily on the sensor's detection ability. It's impossible for the mining framework to extract an attack model without the basic alert information from sensor, especially for these unknown malicious behaviors. And it's desired that some work to improve the quality of alerts. It is still a hard problem to evaluate the quality of the attack models, further works need to be done to put the evaluation of parameters and the evaluation of attack models together.

Acknowledgments. The work was partially supported by the National Science Foundation of China (NSFC) under Grant No. 61303264, the National Science Foundation of China (NSFC) under Grant No. 61003303, Program for Changjiang Scholar and Innovative Research Team in University (PCSIRT, No. IRT1012), Aid Program for Science and Innovative Research Team in Higher Education Institutions of Hunan Province: "network technology" and Hunan Provincial Natural Science Foundation of China under Grant No. 11JJ7003.

References

1. Valeur, F., Vigna, G., Kruegel, C., Kemmerer, R.A.: Comprehensive approach to intrusion detection alert correlation. IEEE Transactions on Dependable and Secure Computing 1, 146–169 (2004)
2. Michel, C., Me, L.: ADELE: An attack description language for knowledge-based intrusion detection. In: Trusted Information: The New Decade Challenge, pp. 353–368. Kluwer Academic Publishers, Norwell (2001)
3. Steven, T.E., Giovanni, V., Richard, A.K.: STATL: an attack language for state-based intrusion detection. J. Comput. Secur. 10, 71–103 (2002)
4. Cuppens, F., Ortalo, R.: LAMBDA: A Language to Model a Database for Detection of Attacks. In: Debar, H., Mé, L., Wu, S.F. (eds.) RAID 2000. LNCS, vol. 1907, pp. 197–216. Springer, Heidelberg (2000)
5. Ning, P., Cui, Y., Reeves, D.S.: Constructing attack scenarios through correlation of intrusion alerts. In: Proceedings of the 9th ACM Conference on Computer and Communications Security, pp. 245–254. ACM, Washington (2002)
6. Porras, P.A., Fong, M.W., Valdes, A.: A Mission-Impact-Based Approach to INFOSEC Alarm Correlation. In: Wespi, A., Vigna, G., Deri, L. (eds.) RAID 2002. LNCS, vol. 2516, pp. 95–114. Springer, Heidelberg (2002)
7. Levera, J., Barán, B., Grossman, R.L.: Experimental studies using median polish procedure to reduce alarm rates in data cubes of intrusion data. In: Chen, H., Moore, R., Zeng, D.D., Leavitt, J. (eds.) ISI 2004. LNCS, vol. 3073, pp. 457–466. Springer, Heidelberg (2004)

8. Lippmann, R., Haines, J.W., Fried, D.J., Korba, J., Das, K.: Analysis and results of the 1999 DARPA off-line intrusion detection evaluation. In: Debar, H., Mé, L., Wu, S.F. (eds.) RAID 2000. LNCS, vol. 1907, pp. 162–182. Springer, Heidelberg (2000)
9. Xiao, M., Xiao, D.: Alert verification based on attack classification in collaborative intrusion detection. In: Eighth ACIS International Conference on Software Engineering, Artificial Intelligence, Networking, and Parallel/Distributed Computing, vol. 2, pp. 739–744. IEEE Computer Soc., Los Alamitos (2007)
10. Xu, M., Wu, T., Tang, J.F.: An IDS Alert Fusion Approach Based on Happened Before Relation. In: Fourth International Conference on Wireless Communications, Networking and Mobile Computing, vol. 31, pp. 12604–12607. IEEE, New York (2008)
11. Xu, J., Li, A., Zhao, H., Yin, H.: A multi-step attack pattern discovery method based on graph mining. In: 2012 2nd International Conference on Computer Science and Network Technology (ICCSNT), pp. 376–380. IEEE, Changchun (2012)
12. Valdes, A., Skinner, K.: Probabilistic Alert Correlation. In: Lee, W., Mé, L., Wespi, A. (eds.) RAID 2001. LNCS, vol. 2212, pp. 54–68. Springer, Heidelberg (2001)
13. Siraj, A., Vaughn, R.B.: Multi-level alert clustering for intrusion detection sensor data. In: 2005 Annual Meeting of the North American Fuzzy Information Processing Society, pp. 748–753. IEEE, New York (2005)
14. Zhang, Y.G., Mao, S.S., Zhuang, X., Peng, X.: Using Cluster and Correlation to Construct Attack Scenarios. In: Proceedings of the 2008 International Conference on Cyberworlds, pp. 471–476. IEEE Computer Soc., Los Alamitos (2008)
15. Zhou, C.V., Leckie, C., Karunasekera, S.: A survey of coordinated attacks and collaborative intrusion detection. Comput. Secur. 29, 124–140 (2009)
16. Amann, B., Sommer, R., Sharma, A., Hall, S.: A lone wolf no more: supporting network intrusion detection with real-time intelligence. In: Balzarotti, D., Stolfo, S.J., Cova, M. (eds.) RAID 2012. LNCS, vol. 7462, pp. 314–333. Springer, Heidelberg (2012)
17. Srujana Reddy, V., Dileep Kumar, G.: Online and Offline Intrusion Alert Aggregation. International Journal of Computer Science & Communication Networks 2, 1776–1779 (2013)
18. Sadoddin, R., Ghorbani, A.A.: An incremental frequent structure mining framework for real-time alert correlation. Comput. Secur. 28, 153–173 (2009)
19. Qiao, L., Zhang, B., Lai, Z., Su, J.: Mining of Attack Models in IDS Alerts from Network Backbone by a Two-stage Clustering Method. In: 2012 IEEE 26th International Parallel and Distributed Processing Symposium Workshops & PhD Forum (IPDPSW), pp. 1257–1263. IEEE Computer Soc., Shanghai (2012)
20. Chen, R., Qiao, L., Zhang, B., Gong, Z.: A Framework of Event-Driven Detection System for Intricate Network Threats. In: 2013 International Conference on Computer, Networks and Communication Engineering, pp. 556–560. Atlantis Press, Beijing (2013)

Detection of Covert Botnet Command and Control Channels by Causal Analysis of Traffic Flows

Pieter Burghouwt, Marcel Spruit, and Henk Sips

Parallel and Distributed Systems Group, Delft University of Technology,
Mekelweg 4, Delft 2628CD, The Netherlands
{P.Burghouwt,H.J.Sips}@tudelft.nl, M.E.M.Spruit@hhs.nl

Abstract. The Command and Control communication of a botnet is evolving into sophisticated covert communication. Techniques as encryption, steganography, and recently the use of social network websites as a proxy, impede conventional detection of botnet communication. In this paper we propose detection of covert communication by passive host-external analysis of causal relationships between traffic flows and prior traffic or user activity. Identifying the direct causes of traffic flows, allows for real-time bot detection with a low exposure to malware, and offline forensic analysis of traffic. The proposed causal analysis of traffic is experimentally evaluated by a self-developed tool called CITRIC with various types of real Command and Control traffic.

Keywords: Botnets, Network Intrusion Detection, Computer Networks.

1   Introduction

Detection of Command and Control (C&C) communication is an important step in identifying infected hosts. Much effort has been put in the identification of traffic properties that are suitable for detection of C&C communication. Common properties that are used for detection are: signatures, misuse related IP-addresses, correlation with attack traffic or other C&C traffic, and flow statistical properties[3][8][11][12][18]. The success of the presented techniques is often due to the presence of noisy attack traffic, as DDoS attacks, spam, and network scans. However, there is a growing number of botnets with sophisticated covert C&C communication that produces minimal noise. This is particularly true for espionage bots that infiltrate an enterprise network. C&C communication that uses websites of popular services and social networks as a proxy, is an effective method to hide the C&C traffic, because malicious and legitimate traffic share the same destinations and protocols. Secrecy can further be enhanced with steganography and encryption. If these techniques are applied in the right manner and not related with other observable attack behavior, detection of C&C communication can become extremely difficult [16].

In this paper, we introduce a new approach to detect covert communication by identifying direct causal relationships between network flows and prior events.

G. Wang et al. (Eds.): CSS 2013, LNCS 8300, pp. 117–131, 2013.

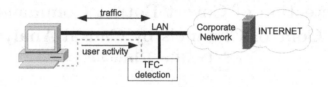

Fig. 1. Deployment of TFC-detection in a LAN

We will refer to this type of detection as *Traffic Flow Causality detection* or *TFC detection*. TFC detection can be deployed as a network IDS. It addresses the common situation of typical client computers, as PC's or mobile devices, located in a LAN of a corporate network, and protected from the Internet by a stateful firewall as shown in Figure 1. TFC detection inspects passively the network traffic per computer. User activity from the mouse and keyboard is also captured per computer by additional hardware or a software agent, and transported to the TFC detector by a separate channel. An infected computer will regularly produce traffic by "phoning home" to a malicious entity in addition to the legitimate traffic. We assume this situation throughout the paper.

The captured traffic can be organized as bidirectional flows: an aggregation of all IP-packets between two computers, on both sides identified with a unique IP-address and a Layer 4 port. A stateful firewall forces all bidirectional flows to initiate from the client computer. Traffic flows are often caused by other traffic or user activity. An example is the visit to a website: A mouse click can trigger a DNS flow, followed by a HTTP flow to the resolved IP-address. The downloaded HTML object contains URL's of other HTTP objects that can result in new HTTP flows with or without intermediate DNS flows. The flows can be organized by their causal relationships, in a tree-shaped graph, as shown in Figure 2. We will refer to this type of graph as a *Traffic Flow Causality graph* or *TFC graph*. In addition we will refer to the first flow of a tree as the *root flow* and the tree itself as a *TFC tree*. If a new flow starts, it will be either a child, connected to an existing tree, or the root flow of a new tree. The result is a forest of TFC trees, growing on the event of each new flow.

A TFC graph can be constructed by observing traffic and user activity, as mouse clicks and key strokes. An important step in the construction process is the selection of the most suitable event as the direct cause of a new flow, since there can be multiple events that qualify as potential cause of a new flow. We have developed for this selection the *Optimal Cause Selection algorithm* or *OCS-algorithm*. It evaluates the time between an event and a new traffic flow, and for some events, the presence of a reference to the destination of a new flow in the payload of prior traffic. If a root flow, initiated from a client computer, is not caused by user activity, it must be caused by an automatic process. This can be legitimate traffic, such as an automatic update of a normal application, but it can also be the C&C traffic of a bot instance. A root flow and its offspring are classified as anomalous, if the root flow is not caused by user activity. In addition, a whitelist can prevent anomaly classification of traffic that is caused

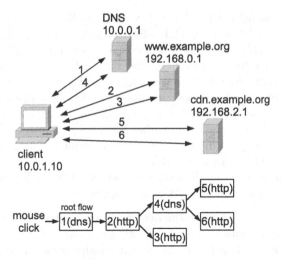

Fig. 2. Scenario of a visit to the website Example.com by a mouse click with the TFC graph of the resulting traffic flows (vertices) and their direct causes (edges)

by known legitimate automatic processes. This method allows for the detection of all types of "phone home" traffic.

Section 2 gives an overview of related work. Section 3 elaborates the construction of TFC graphs and the associated anomaly detection by the OCS algorithm. Section 4 presents CITRIC, a self-developed framework that implements TFC detection and visualization of TFC graphs. Section 5 describes experiments, conducted with CITRIC and traces of normal and botnet C&C traffic. Section 6 elaborates evasion and improvements. Section 7 and 8 summarize conclusions and future work.

2   Related Work

Our work involves anomaly detection by identifying direct causes of traffic flows, obtained from passively captured network traffic and user activity. There are many proposed and implemented anomaly detectors that analyze captured network traffic. We compare here our work with other work that involves associations between traffic flows.

Cui et al. present Binder [6], a detection approach that also measures causal relations between user events and traffic events. Zhang et al. propose a similar approach, called CR-Miner[21]. CR-Miner constructs Traffic Dependency Graphs that resembles our TFC graphs. However, both Binder and CR-Miner have fundamental differences with our approach:

- Both depend on host-internal information, as process ID's. Our TFC-detection captures passively traffic outside the observed host. Even the capture of user events can be implemented in hardware, outside the software environment of the host.

- CR-Minor constructs dependency trees by the Referer field in the HTTP header. To prevent tampering, CR-Minor signs from within the browser each HTTP header. This requires a browser that is not compromised by malware. However on an infected computer, the risk of browser compromise is significant. Another problem is that legitimate HTTP requests do not always specify the Referer field. In contrast our approach identifies direct causes by time measurements and matches between the destination of a new flow and a reference in the payload of an earlier flow. Forgery of the destination of a new flow by malware is difficult, since it will result in failed communication with the remote malicious instance.
- Our TFC graphs include all flows per host, including DNS, which allows a more complete analysis of covert communication.

Burghouwt et al. demonstrate the detection of a Twitter-based C&C channel by causally relating Twitter.com traffic with user events [4]. Our TFC detection extends this work, by identifying causal relationships between flows. In addition TFC detection does not depend on Twitter specific properties.

Karagiannis et al. present Blinc to classify traffic flows by their originating applications [15]. They use graphlets to represent flows that share L4 ports or addresses. Unlike our approach, no causal relationships are evaluated.

Iliofotou et al. introduce Traffic Dispersion Graphs that present connection patterns between different hosts [14]. Our TFC graphs are different, because they represent flows and causal relationships instead of hosts and connections.

Asai et al. map causal relations between flows in Traffic Causality Graphs to profile application traffic [2]. The resulting graphs are constructed without the use of destination references in the payload, resulting in a high uncertainty of the identified causal relationships. In addition user events are not taken into account.

3   Causal Analysis of Flows and Anomaly Detection

A bidirectional flow or dialogue is the aggregation of IP-packets, exchanged between a local and remote computer, and identified by the 5-tuple {prot, IP_{local}, IP_{remote}, $port_{local}$, $port_{remote}$ }, referring to the IP addresses and port numbers of the local and remote computer. RFC5103 [20] refers to these bidirectional flows as biflows. The direction of a bidirectional flow is defined as the direction of the first packet. Since in the remainder of this paper all traffic flows are bidirectional, the adjective "bidirectional" will be omitted. In this section we present the algorithm that identifies causal relationships between flows, and detects anomalous flows by the cause of the root flow.

3.1   The Direct Cause of a Flow

We define the direct cause of a traffic flow as the event that ultimately triggers the flow. In addition, there can be multiple indirect causes or additional preconditions that must be satisfied. If a web page shows a hyperlink and a user clicks on the link, the induced flow is directly caused by the mouse click and indirectly caused by the already open web page with the hyperlink.

Traffic events are the most common direct cause of a new traffic flows. An example is the reception of an IP-address in a DNS reply that is used immediately as destination of a new HTTP flow. Flows that are caused by traffic events contribute to the branches of trees, but can never be a root flow.

User events are certain user actions by mouse, keyboard, touch screen or another input device. Popular actions that can cause new traffic flows are the release of a mouse button and the press of the Enter key. Flows, directly caused by a user event, are always root flows.

Process events are state transitions in software processes that trigger automatically new flows, such as a software update or a check for new email. Most legitimate flows, caused by automatic processes, are well known per host and their destinations can be defined in a whitelist. Flows, directly caused by a process event, are always root flows.

Server events are new flows, initiated from external computers to the observed computer. This is only possible if incoming connections are allowed. Since this is normally blocked for clients behind a stateful firewall, we will not elaborate further on this event type.

A traffic flow is classified as anomalous if the direct cause is a process event, and the remote address or hostname is not whitelisted. Exact determination of the direct cause of a flow requires detailed analysis of the program execution of all processes inside the observed host. This is complex, platform dependent, and entails a high risk of detection and compromise by the malware. The solution for this problem is the selection of direct causes from traffic events and low level user events, both captured outside the monitored host. If no direct cause can be selected from the observed traffic and user events, and if the remote host is not whitelisted, then the flow is classified as malicious. However, the host-external approach is less accurate, because in some cases the direct cause of a new traffic flow must be selected from multiple available candidate causes. If the wrong cause is selected, a root flow can erroneously be absorbed as a branch in a tree or associated with a user event. The absorption of a malicious root flow in a tree of legitimate flows or its association with user event, results in a False Negative. On the other hand, if a direct cause is not found, a flow can erroneously be dispersed as a root flow of a new tree. This can result in a False Positive.

3.2   Optimal Selection of the Direct Cause

To select from the traffic and user events the most likely direct cause of a new flow, with minimal absorption and dispersion risk, we developed the Optimal Cause Selection Algorithm or OCS Algorithm.

For every new flow the OCS algorithm tries to find a direct cause by searching in succession through different types of events that have occurred in a defined time window before the start of the new flow. The algorithm differentiates traffic events in four different types. Combined with user events, OCS distinguishes five different types of events:

Algorithm 1 OCS Algorithm for TFC graph building and anomaly detection.

---

for *each new flow* **do**
    if $(findDNSEvent(X.IP_{remote}, T_{dns}))$ **then**
        $cause = DNSEvent;\ addToFoundTree(X);$
    else if $findURLEvent(X.name_{remote}, T_{url})$ **then**
        $cause = URLEvent;\ addToFoundTree(X);$
    else if $findUserEvent(X, T_{user})$ **then**
        $cause = USEREVENT;\ createTree(X);$
    else if $findHTTPSEvent(X, T_{https})$ **then**
        $cause = HTTPSEVENT;\ addToFoundTree(X);$
    else if $findHTTPEvent(X, T_{http})$ **then**
        $cause = HTTPEVENT;\ addToFoundTree(X);$
    else if $isWhiteListed(X)$ **then**
        $cause = WHITELIST;\ createTree(X);$
    else
        $cause = UNKNOWN;\ createTree(X);\ signalAnomaly(X);$
    end if
end for

---

1. *DNS Event*: The detector caches recently captured DNS-lookups. If a new flow X is non-DNS, the function $findDNSEvent(X.IP_{dest}, T_{dns})$ searches in its cache for a DNS translation that matches the remote address $X.IP_{remote}$. If the most recent matching DNS-record is received within the time window T_{dns} before the start of the new flow X, the event is chosen as direct cause of X. Flow X will become a child of the DNS-flow that carried the record and automatically inherits the normal or anomalous classification of the related tree.

2. *URL Event*: The detector caches the hostnames of URL's, parsed from recently captured HTTP-payloads. If a new flow X is non-DNS, the remote IP address is first translated to a hostname, $X.name_{remote}$, by the DNS-cache. If the new flow is DNS, the hostname in the DNS-request is chosen as $X.name_{remote}$. Then the function $findURLEvent(X.name_{remote}, T_{url})$ searches for a cached URL with a matching hostname. If the most recent matching URL is received within the time window T_{url} before the new flow X, the event is chosen as direct cause of X. Flow X will become a child of the HTTP-flow that carried the URL and automatically inherits the normal or anomalous classification of its tree.

3. *User Event*: Mouse clicks and specific key presses, as the Enter key are seen as events that can trigger new flows. An agent captures and sends user events from the observed computer to the detection system. Software implementation of the agent increases significantly the exposure to the malware. Malware with root privilege can suppress or mimic user events. The exposure can be reduced by the implementation of the agent in a hypervisor [13], or in hardware that reads the electrical connection of input devices [4]. The function $findUserEvent(X, T_{user})$ selects the most recent event as direct

cause of flow X if it is within T_{url}. The flow is classified as a user caused root flow.

4. *HTTPS Event*: An HTTPS event is defined as a sudden decline of the received IP packet size in a flow. This occurs typically when the last part of a requested object is received. It does not necessarily indicate the termination of the flow, because in the case of a persistent connection, as in HTTP1.1, other object requests and replies can follow within the same flow. The completion of an object downloaded, indicated by a sudden decrease of the packet size, can initiate a new flow X that depends on the received object. The function $findHTTPSEvent(X, T_{https})$ searches for the most recent HTTPS event that occurred within the time window T_{https} before the start of the new flow. If a HTTPS event is found, Flow X will become a child of the HTTPS-flow and will automatically inherit the normal or anomalous classification of the tree.

5. *HTTP Event*: Similar as HTTPS, but with packet size decrease in HTTP traffic.

If no suitable event types are found and the remote destination is not whitelisted, the flow is classified as an anomalous root flow. In practice not all URL's will be identified in the payload. Typical causes of missed URL's are: TLS-encryption of the payload, as HTTPS, client caching of a prior received HTTP messages, and complex scripts that compose URL's from received code and data. This can result in tree dissection and false positives. OCS solves the problem of missed references by searching for the more generic HTTP and HTTPS events, after an unsuccessful search for a URL event. Since this search is only based on time and not on string matching, the related expiration windows T_{https} and T_{http} must be kept as small as possible, to reduce the risk of false negatives by absorption. For simplicity OCS evaluates only traffic reference events in DNS and HTTP traffic. However, this type of cause evaluation can be extended to other less popular traffic types that carry references in the payload, such as SIP traffic that carries IP-addresses for media streams.

3.3 Detection Performance

In some cases TFC-detection can miss anomalous flows, by selecting the wrong event as direct cause. This is especially the case for the HTTP, HTTPS, and user events that are selected by merely their presence within a time window. The probability that an HTTP, HTTPS, or user event is erroneously selected as the direct cause of a malicious flow, starting at a random moment, can be approximated by $T_{window} \cdot f_{event}$ if $T_{window} << 1/f_{event}$ with f defined as the average frequency of HTTP, HTTPS, or user events. A True Positive is only possible if none of the event types is selected as a direct cause. Assuming mutual independence between all events, the True Positive Rate or detection ratio DR is estimated by Equation 1.

$$DR \approx (1 - T_{user} \cdot f_{userEvent}) \cdot (1 - T_{http} \cdot f_{httpEvent}) \cdot (1 - T_{https} \cdot f_{httpsEvent}) \quad (1)$$

Equation 1 shows that the DR benefits from small time windows. The frequency of user events can be minimized by optimal selection of only those user events that are really potential triggers of a new flow. Other solutions to improve the DR by removing the HTTP and HTTP factors are discussed in Section 6

4   CITRIC: Practical Implementation of TFC Graph Construction and Detection

TFC graph construction and detection is evaluated by our self-developed framework, called CITRIC (Causal Inspection To Recognize Illegal Communication). The main components of CITRIC are:

- *Traffic sensor*: Device that captures passively real time internet traffic in PCAP format.
- *User event sensor*: Either a hardware device that is inserted between keyboard, mouse, and the computer, or a software agent to capture and signal user events.
- *Flow aggregator*: A software object that constructs bidirectional flows of captured IP-packets. When a packet is captured and the flow already exists, flow parameters are updated. In case of a new flow, the aggregator calls the appropriate analyzers, to place the flow in a tree.
- *DNS analyzer with cache*: A software object that analyses DNS traffic and caches name-to-IP translations.
- *HTTP analyzer*: A software object that searches for potential URL events, received in HTTP traffic. In addition it searches for generic HTTP and HTTPS events by monitoring the payload size between two consecutive ingress packets of the same flow. All potential events are temporarily stored in a cache.
- *Cause Analyzer*: The central software object that constructs TFC graphs by the OCS algorithm with adjustable time windows.
- *Anomaly detection alert*: A software object that logs important events and alerts detected anomalies

All components, with the exception of the user event sensor, are implemented in C++ on a Linux computer that bridges all LAN traffic. In addition to real-time capture, CITRIC can analyze files with prerecorded traffic in PCAP format, including signaled user events.

4.1   Implementation Issues and Solutions

During development many implementation-specific issues had to be solved. The most important issues are summarized below.

1. Some operating systems use for DNS flows the same client port or a limited set of client ports. This creates a risk that different DNS queries are aggregated in the same flow. To prevent this, the DNS transaction number is added to the flow tuple, to keep the tuple unique.

2. Virtual hosting and Content Delivery Networks use IP addresses with multiple hostnames, resulting in ambiguity of the translation of an IP address to a hostname by cached DNS records. This is solved by first expanding the search for potential causal relationships to all possible names that map to the same IP of a new flow, and then choosing the most recent URL that refers to any of the hostnames.

3. In some cases scripts construct host names by combining strings. When there is no exact match between a hostname and the cached URL's, CITRIC will test a match of at least the 4 last characters of the second level domain name. In case of a well-known public suffix, such as .co in .co.uk, this partial match is expanded to the third level domain name.

4. To accomplish a fast search of matching destinations and references, hash tables are used. For the described experiments the hash is 8 bit, resulting in a 256 times smaller average seek time than in the case of a linear search. Similar hash techniques are implemented for fast DNS search by IP address and flow search by tuple.

5. Many popular websites only deliver gzipped HTTP replies. CITRIC can unzip and merge chunked HTPP replies.

6. If a DNS query fails or the answer takes too long, some DNS clients will swiftly repeat the question, resulting in multiple DNS flows that query the same name. This can lead to multiple root flows, instead of one. This is solved by combining identical queries that start within a small time window.

5   Experimental Evaluation

We have evaluated TFC detection experimentally by running CITRIC with four different traces of traffic, captured in a controlled environment.

The first trace is used for the evaluation of False Positives and contains the complete captured traffic from visits to the 30 most popular websites of the Internet. Visits to popular websites result in many additional traffic flows, caused by advertisements, mesh-ups, scripts, etc. The amount and variety of direct causes tests the TFC detection under difficult circumstances. Missed causes will result in false positives. The popular websites were derived from the rankings of Alexa [1] and Google [10]. All doubles were removed and of the remaining sites only the 30 most popular were used. Each visit started by typing the name in the browser address bar, followed by at least one typical activity, as a login on Facebook, a search in Google, etc. Traffic was captured and stored in PCAP-format by Gulp [19], a capture tool with a low probability of packet loss. The visiting computer was a laptop with a fresh installation of Windows 7 and a Firefox browser with plugins for Flash and Java. At the start of the capture both the web cache and DNS cache were emptied. A software agent, installed on the visiting host, captured mouse clicks and key strokes and transmitted every event as a special UDP-packet. Hence the events were automatically part of the captured traffic. The resulting trace, to which we will refer as Top30, contains 113505 packets, representing 4179 flows. The most popular protocols are DNS, HTTP and HTTPS. Since we assume that the captured traffic is not contaminated with malicious traffic, every detector alert is a false positive.

The other traces, intended for the evaluation of the C&C detection, are composed of the Top30 trace with injected C&C traffic. For each trace we infected a clean Windows 7 instance with real malware and manually isolated exactly one representative tree of the captured C&C traffic. The malicious tree was injected in the Top30 trace at ten different equidistant times. We developed for the injection special software that could modify packet timestamps, IP-source addresses, and colliding ephemeral L4 port numbers of the malicious traffic. The result was a consistent trace with exactly ten separated C&C trees, during the thirty legitimate website visits. We composed in this way three infected traces in PCAP format, each with a different type of C&C traffic as shown in Table 1.

Table 1. Overview of the three different traces, infected with botnet traffic

Bot	C&C type	Injected in Top30 trace
Kelihos	HTTP [7]	10 x DNS and HTTP flow
Tbot	Peer to Peer [5]	10 x TCP flow, port 9001
Twebot	Twitter as proxy [17]	10 x DNS, HTTP, and HTTPS flow

5.1 Empirical Determination of the Optimal Windows Sizes

The accuracy of a TFC graph depends on the size of the five time windows as defined in Section 3.2.

An optimal choice of the window T_{dns} depends on the maximum expected delay between the reception of a DNS-resolved IP address and its first usage in a new flow. Therefore the cumulative distribution of the delay was measured in the clean Top30 trace. Delays, during which one or more user events took place, were excluded, because in those cases it was not clear what triggered the new flow. About 90% of 726 measured delays was less than 2ms. We chose T_{dns}=500ms, resulting in only 6 flows with delays above 500ms, all related with DNS prefetches from distant websites that loaded very slowly.

In a similar way the distribution of T_{url} was determined. However this distribution was more spread out and about 10% of the 1314 measured delays was above 10s. Manual inspection also revealed that long delays were caused by missed URL's in both HTTP and HTTPS traffic. Further manual inspection revealed that undesired absorption of user-caused root flows could occur at window sizes above 10s. To prevent this, T_{url} was set to 10s. However, with this window size, URL causes with a delay of more than 10s are missed. We solved this problem by adding a second findURLEvent() test in the OCS algorithm with a window of 30s immediately after the findUserEvent() test.

To determine the optimum size of T_{https}, the OCS-algorithm was run with different values for T_{https} with T_{dns}=500ms, T_{url}=10s/30s, T_{user}=0, T_{http}=0. A larger window then 500ms resulted in the undesired absorption of user caused root flows.

Finally we ran the OCS-algorithm for different values of T_{user}. The False Positive Rate (FPR) could directly be derived from the number of detected anomalous flows, since the Top30 trace did not contain malicious flows. The expected Detection Rate (DR) for the Top30 trace was indirectly calculated by Equation 1. Figure 3 shows the influence of T_{user} on the FPR and DR in an ROC graph. In general, an ROC graph shows the effect of a parameter on the DR and FPR of a detector [9]. The ROC curves of three different setups are displayed:

- Setup 1: Detector with T_{dns}=500ms, T_{url}=10s/30s, T_{https}=500ms, T_{http}=0s. Optimum at T_{user}=100ms with FPR=0.005 and DR=0.95.
- Setup 2: Detector with T_{dns}=500ms, T_{url}=10s/30s, T_{https}=500ms, T_{http} =50ms. Optimum at T_{user}=100ms with FPR=0.0017 and DR=0.85.
- Setup 3: All windows zero except T_{user}. Unsuitable for detection

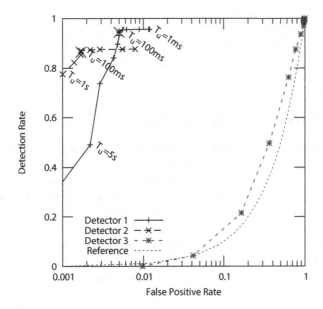

Fig. 3. ROC graph of TFC detection with different settings and a varying T_{user}

The ROC graph shows that Setup 3 is totally unusable. The reason that we tested Setup 3 is to show that a simplified algorithm, that only evaluates user events as direct causes, does not work. The ROC graph of Setups 1 or 2, shows that TFC detection can optimally detect covert channels for T_{user}=100ms. In all cases only the communication of the user event agent was whitelisted.

5.2   TFC Detection of Real C&C Traffic

The Detection Rate (DR) of Section 5.1 was indirectly estimated by the non-overlapping accumulated time of the open windows in the clean Top30 trace and was not really measured with malware. Therefore we tested TFC detection with the three malware infected traces. The applied window sizes are equal to Setup 2 of Section 5.1 with T_{user}=100ms. Table 2 shows the results. The observed DR is close to the estimated value of Section 5.1. False Negatives are caused by absorption of malicious root flows in legitimate traffic, affected by the windows T_{http} and T_{https}, and by wrong classification of root flows as user-caused, affected by T_{user}. One malicious tree of the TweBot C&C traffic was absorbed in a legitimate tree with a URL to Twitter.com. The experiments show that TFC detection performs, as predicted in Section 3 and it detects C&C traffic, including the covert traffic of social media based C&C.

Table 2. Experimental performance of TFC detection with 4 different traces

Trace	FP	TP	FPR	DR
cleanTop30	7	-	0.0017	-
Top30+Kelihos	7	8	0.0017	0.8
Top30+Tbot	7	8	0.0017	0.8
Top30+Twebot	7	7	0.0017	0.7

5.3   Visualization of the TFC Graphs

TFC graphs reveal causal relations between flows. This can be used in forensic situations to isolate a tree of related flows. We have built a tool as an extension of CITRIC to visualize each tree separately by post-analysis of the CITRIC logs. Flows are represented by the vertices, annotated with the most important properties as destination and protocol. Direct causes are represented by the edges, annotated with the event type and the delay between parent and child. The cause of the root flow is indicated as an extra annotated vertex with specification. Optionally colors can indicate the protocol. Figure 4 shows an automatically generated image of a visit to Google.com. The tree starts with a user

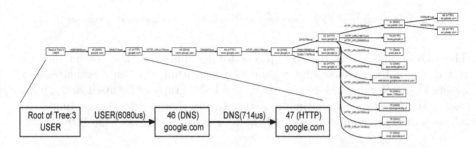

Fig. 4. Part of a TFC Graph, automatically visualized by CITRIC, of a visit to Google.com. For readability of the generated captions in this figure, the initial part of the tree is manually magnified.

event. After some DNS and HTTP redirection flows, the main page and additional objects are loaded. A large number of DNS stubs in one of the branches of the tree is caused by browser DNS prefetching.

6 Evasion and Related Improvements of TFC Detection

Discovery of TFC detection by malware is difficult, because both traffic and user activity are captured passively and can completely be implemented outside the software environment of the observed computer. If the malware is aware of TFC detection, it can adapt its communication to evade detection by hitchhiking legitimate events. The malware monitors traffic or user events and waits for a suitable moment to initiate communication. In general hitchhiking requires root privileges, to monitor network traffic or user activity. Monitoring these type of events is an anomaly that can easily be detected by a host IDS.

6.1 Solutions against Hitchhiking

Hitchhiking HTTP and HTTPS events can be prevented by removing these events from the OCS algorithm. However the evaluation of HTTPS events is necessary by the inability of the OCS-algorithm to inspect the payload of HTTPS traffic for the more selective URL events. This problem can be solved by a transparent TLS-proxy that is trusted by the observed client computers. If a client computer uses the certificate of the proxy, all communication can be decrypted in the LAN or proxy, and the more selective findURLEvent() function can find potential URL events, making the findHTTPSEvent() superfluous.

The evaluation for HTTP events is necessary, because not all potential destination references are found in the HTTP payload. Sometimes URL's are composed by the client on the fly by scripts. Improvement of the search for destination references in HTTP traffic can be achieved by feeding the received payloads to an environment that emulates the browser engine of the client, to compose references in a similar way as the browser. This would make the findHTTPEvent() superfluous.

With the removal of the HTTPS and HTTP events, it still remains possible to hitchhike user events. A possible solution is a more complete evaluation of the user input, to estimate the likelihood that a particular root flow is generated by a particular user event. An example is the search of potential host and object names in the typed input from the user, and matching these with destinations of new flows. This is not possible with mouse clicks on hyperlinks, but inspection of recent received hyperlinks and whitelisting can limit the number of possible new destinations after a click. A totally different solution is the replacement of the direct capture of user events by alternative heuristics that select the direct cause of a root flow by the likelihood that a destination reference is clicked or typed by a user.

Hitchhiking URL and DNS events is also possible, but more difficult than the other events types, because the malicious and legitimate communication must simultaneously visit the same destination. This can be the case when popular websites, as social media, are used as proxy. This type of hitchhiking can be countered by not only matching the hostname, but also the path of the URL reference. An example is the matching of Twitter.com/tlab32768 instead of Twitter.com. It is highly unlikely that both malware and legitimate processes visit the same resource on the same host within a short time interval.

7 Conclusions

By identifying the direct cause of traffic flows, it is possible to organize the traffic in tree-shaped graphs and detect C&C communication by anomalous causes. The OCS algorithm selects the optimal direct cause for each new traffic flow from passively captured traffic events and user events. Experiments with representative popular HTTP traffic and different types of malicious C&C traffic support the effectiveness of TFC detection by the OCR algorithm.

While TFC detection allows for real-time detection of all types of covert traffic, it is particularly suitable for detection of covert botnet C&C to popular websites.

Although user events need to be captured in addition to network traffic, the risk of compromise can be kept low by implementation outside the software environment of the observed computer.

Visualization of the constructed TFC graph can be used in forensic analysis.

8 Future Work

While FTC detection can successfully and feasibly detect malware, further research is needed to extend OCS to other protocols, and to develop and test the proposed improvements against hitchhiking. In particular the determination of user caused root flows by only traffic properties instead of the captured user events, will result in a detector that is easier to deploy.

References

1. Alexa.com: Alexa, the web information company (visited March 2, 2013), http://www.alexa.com/topsites
2. Asai, H., Fukuda, K., Esaki, H.: Traffic causality graphs: profiling network applications through temporal and spatial causality of flows. In: Proc. of the 23rd International Teletraffic Congress, ITCP, pp. 95–102 (2011)
3. Barford, P., Plonka, D.: Characteristics of network traffic flow anomalies. In: Proc. of the 1st ACM SIGCOMM Workshop on Internet Measurement, IMW 2001, pp. 69–73. ACM, New York (2001)
4. Burghouwt, P., Spruit, M., Sips, H.: Towards detection of botnet communication through social media by monitoring user activity. In: Jajodia, S., Mazumdar, C. (eds.) ICISS 2011. LNCS, vol. 7093, pp. 131–143. Springer, Heidelberg (2011)
5. Contagio: Skynet tor botnet / trojan.tbot samples (visited January 2013), http://contagiodump.blogspot.nl/2012/12/dec-2012-skynet-tor-botnet-trojantbot.html

6. Cui, W., Katz, R.H., Tan, W.T.: Design and implementation of an extrusion-based break-in detector for personal computers. In: 21st Annual Computer Security Applications Conference, p. 10. IEEE (2005)
7. DeependResearch: Trojan nap aka kelihos/hlux (visited February 2013), http://www.deependresearch.org/2013/02/trojan-nap-aka-kelihoshlux-feb-2013.html
8. Dietrich, C.J., Rossow, C.: Empirical research of ip blacklists. In: ISSE 2008 Securing Electronic Business Processes, pp. 163–171. Springer (2009)
9. Fawcett, T.: Roc graphs: Notes and practical considerations for data mining researchers. Tech. rep., HP Laboratories, Palo Alto CA (2004)
10. Google.com: Top 1000 sites - doubleclick ad planner (visited March 2, 2013), http://www.google.com/adplanner/static/top1000/
11. Gu, G., Perdisci, R., Zhang, J., Lee, W.: Botminer: Clustering analysis of network traffic for protocol- and structure-independent botnet detection. In: Proc. of the 17th USENIX Security Symposium SECURITY 2008. USENIX Association, Berkeley (2008)
12. Gu, G., Porras, P., Yegneswaran, V., Fong, M., Lee, W.: Bothunter: Detecting malware infection through ids-driven dialog correlation. In: Proc. of 16th USENIX Security Symposium, p. 12. USENIX Association (2007)
13. Gummadi, R., Balakrishnan, H., Maniatis, P., Ratnasamy, S.: Not-a-bot: Improving service availability in the face of botnet attacks. In: Proc. of the 6th USENIX Symposium on Networked Systems Design and Implementation NSDI 2009. USENIX Association, Berkeley (2009)
14. Iliofotou, M., Pappu, P., Faloutsos, M., Mitzenmacher, M., Singh, S., Varghese, G.: Network monitoring using traffic dispersion graphs (tdgs). In: Proc. of the 7th ACM SIGCOMM Conference on Internet Measurement, pp. 315–320. ACM (2007)
15. Karagiannis, T., Papagiannaki, K., Faloutsos, M.: Blinc: multilevel traffic classification in the dark. In: ACM SIGCOMM Computer Communication Review, pp. 229–240. ACM (2005)
16. Nagaraja, S., Houmansadr, A., Piyawongwisal, P., Singh, V., Agarwal, P., Borisov, N.: Stegobot: a covert social network botnet. In: Filler, T., Pevný, T., Craver, S., Ker, A. (eds.) IH 2011. LNCS, vol. 6958, pp. 299–313. Springer, Heidelberg (2011)
17. Nazario, J.: Twitter-based botnet command channel (visited October 2010), http://asert.arbornetworks.com/2009/08/twitter-based-botnet-command-channel/
18. Roesch, M., et al.: Snort-lightweight intrusion detection for networks. In: Proc. of the 13th USENIX Conference on System Administration, Seattle, Washington, pp. 229–238 (1999)
19. Satten, C.: Lossless gigabit remote packet capture with linux. Tech. rep., University of Washington (2008), http://staff.washington.edu/corey/gulp/
20. Trammell, B.H., Boschi, E.: Rfc5103: Bidirectional flow export using ip flow information export (ipfix). IETF (2008)
21. Zhang, H., Banick, W., Yao, D., Ramakrishnan, N.: User intention-based traffic dependence analysis for anomaly detection. In: 2012 IEEE Symposium on Security and Privacy Workshops (SPW), pp. 104–112. IEEE (2012)

Situation Calculus and Graph Based Defensive Modeling of Simultaneous Attacks

Layal Samarji[1,2], Frédéric Cuppens[2], Nora Cuppens-Boulahia[2],
Wael Kanoun[1], and Samuel Dubus[1]

[1] Bell Labs, Alcatel-Lucent
[2] Télécom Bretagne

Abstract. Recent attacks are better coordinated, difficult to discover, and inflict severe damages to networks. However, existing response systems handle the case of a single ongoing attack. This limitation is due to the lack of an appropriate model that describes coordinated attacks. In this paper, we address this limitation by presenting a new formal description of *individual, coordinated,* and *concurrent* attacks. Afterwards, we combine *Graph Theory* and our attack description in order to model attack graphs that cover the three attacks types. Finally, we show how to automatically generate these attack graphs using a logical approach based on *Situation Calculus.*

1 Introduction

Modern attack tools are rapidly evolving to become more powerful and sophisticated. Networks and information systems are frequently targeted by coordinated attacks, which can cause deterioration in system's performance and induce great damage to physical assets. Distributed large-scale attacks [1] are examples of the most dangerous coordinated attacks. Attackers can scan large numbers of hosts simultaneously to search for software vulnerabilities (e.g. stealthy scans) ; they can use self-replicating computer programs to spread their malicious code to thousands of vulnerable systems within a short time period (e.g. worms) ; and they can use thousands of compromised hosts from different network domains to overload a targeted system to disrupt its service (e.g. Distributed Denial of Service (DDOS)).

A coordinated attack is the collaboration of several attacking sources to achieve a common goal. In order to achieve their goal, attacking sources, controlled by one or several attacking entities, may cooperate by resource sharing, task allocation, synchronization, etc. As presented in [2], the great danger of coordinated attacks is that they can induce damage in the system that would not be provoked by any of the attacks if performed individually. These attacks can even mislead intrusion detection systems. Moreover, effort sharing between several attackers reduces the time needed to achieve their goal. Consequently, a security officer will have even less time to block such attack before it has caused a severe damage. Stuxnet threat [3], that targeted the Iranian nuclear control system in 2010, is a proof that coordinated attacks' damage knows no boundaries.

G. Wang et al. (Eds.): CSS 2013, LNCS 8300, pp. 132–150, 2013.

The situation can become more critical and dangerous, when different assets of a system network are threatened at the same time by collaborating groups of attackers, and several separated individual attackers. In such simultaneous attacks context, different Individual Attack (IA) actions and Coordinated Attack (CA) actions are concurrently executed.

Existing response systems proposals consider the case of a single ongoing attack [4] [5] [6]. To tackle such limitation, a model of potential simultaneous attacks must be established first. Among the numerous formal models of attack description, like LAMBDA [7], JIGSAW [8], a modified version of STRIPS [9], and so on ; we did not find a description that corresponds to a CA. Therefore, we propose in this paper a new formal description of attack actions that corresponds to both individual and coordinated attacks.

We then use the Situation Calculus (SC), a dialect of first-order logic with features to reason on changes due to action execution. SC is an adequate framework to reason on different types of attacks. It provides means to describe concurrent actions, which makes it appropriate to model simultaneous and concurrent attacks. Another major advantage of SC is that actions can easily be correlated using theorem-proving and planning capabilities. Consequently, for a set of critical assets (or services) in a system, we can derive potential sequence(s) of correlated concurrent attacks that aim at deteriorating them. Hence, based on SC planning capabilities, we propose a Simultaneous Attacks planner (SAP) that dynamically takes a snapshot of detected attackers and system's state, to generate all simultaneous attacks scenarios these attackers may potentially execute in the system. This is an original contribution of our paper that extends previous work on attack graphs restricted to individual attacks [10] to coordinated and simultaneous attacks. Attack graphs depict ways in which an adversary exploits system vulnerabilities to achieve a desired state. In a simultaneous attacks context, security administrators need to visualize, in a same graph, individual and coordinated attack scenarios that are simultaneously possible in the network. We propose in this paper, a new method that benefits from (i) a sequence of concurrent attacks generated by SAP, and (ii) *Graph Theory*, to generate online Simultaneous Attacks Graphs (SAG).

The paper is organized as follows. Section 2 presents our formal description of attacks. Section 3 formally defines SAGs. Section 4 is organized as follows: we present the basics of SC and show how it is efficient to model IA, CA and concurrent attacks; we then explain the SC planning task, and provides SAP's description. Section 5 discuss SAP's complexity and performance. Section 6 discusses related work. Section 7 concludes this paper.

2   Formal Description of Attacks

In order to formally describe all types of attacks, we model system's state in terms of predicates. And we consider three disjoint sets of predicates:

- The set Γ of system-related predicates: it includes predicates that describe the evolution of system's state. Attributes of a system-related predicate are always system assets, e.g. $is\_on(Server)$.
- Two disjoint sets A and B of attacker-related predicates: they include predicates that describe the evolution of the attacker's state. The subject of an attacker-related predicate is always an $attackerID$ which is a unique way of identifying an attacker (e.g. the IP address of a compromised machine). A is the set of predicates describing the attacker's privilege relatively to the system assets, e.g. $is\_registered(AttackerID, SIP\_Server)$. B is the set of predicates describing the knowledge gained by an attacker after exploiting a particular characteristic of the system, e.g. $knows(AttackerID, is\_on(User))$.

We model attacks by the generic definition 1 specifying: the subject(s) performing the action, the action's object(s) and six different subsets of A, B and Γ. These attack patterns are interpreted by the action *precondition* and *postcondition*. The precondition is a conjunction of one logic condition on the required number of participating subjects, and three logic conditions on the action's predicates (in A_X, B_X and Γ_X) to be satisfied in order to start executing this action. The postcondition is a conjunction of three logic conditions on the action's predicates (in A'_X, B'_X, and Γ'_X) that become true after executing it. When several subjects participate in an action, we denote them by coordinated subjects. Besides, we adopt the most pessimistic hypothesis from the defender point of view: We assume that it if there is knowledge that should be acquired by all coordinated subjects in the action's precondition, it is sufficient that one of the subjects has this knowledge, to consider that all of the others have it. Actually, we are based on the fact that knowledge can be shared between coordinated subjects. Hence, every predicate in B_X needs to be fulfilled by only one of the subjects. Similarly, for the knowledge gained after the action's execution, we consider that each coordinated subject fulfills all the predicates in B'_X.

Definition 1. $Action\_X(subject_X, objects_X)$

Attack Patterns: $subjects_X = \{s_1, s_2, ..., s_o\}$; $objects_X = \{o_1, o_2, ..., o_n\}$

$$A_X = \{\alpha_1, \alpha_2, ..., \alpha_k\} \; ; \; B_X = \{\beta_1, \beta_2, ..., \beta_l\} \; ; \; \Gamma_X = \{\gamma_1, \gamma_2, ..., \gamma_m\}$$
$$A'_X = \{\alpha'_1, \alpha'_2, ..., \alpha'_{k'}\} \; ; \; B'_X = \{\beta'_1, \beta'_2, ..., \beta'_{l'}\} \; ; \; \Gamma'_X = \{\gamma'_1, \gamma'_2, ..., \gamma'_{m'}\}$$

Precondition: $min_X < \mid subject_X \mid \leq max_X \wedge$

$$[\forall \alpha \in A_X, \exists \overrightarrow{\sigma} \in objects_X, \exists \overrightarrow{s} \in subjects_X \mid \alpha(\overrightarrow{s}, \overrightarrow{\sigma})]$$
$$\wedge \, [\forall \beta \in B_X, \exists \overrightarrow{\sigma} \in objects_X, \exists s \in subjects_X \mid \beta(s, \overrightarrow{\sigma})]$$
$$\wedge \, [\forall \gamma \in \Gamma_X, \exists \overrightarrow{\sigma} \in objects_X \mid \gamma(\overrightarrow{\sigma})]$$

Postcondition: $\left[\forall \alpha' \in A'_X, \exists \overrightarrow{\sigma} \in objects_X, \exists \overrightarrow{s} \in subjects_X \mid \alpha'(\overrightarrow{s}, \overrightarrow{\sigma})\right]$

$$\wedge \left[\forall \beta' \in B'_X, \exists \overrightarrow{\sigma} \in objects_X \mid \forall s \in subjects_X, \beta'(s, \overrightarrow{\sigma})\right]$$
$$\wedge \left[\forall \gamma' \in \Gamma'_X, \exists \overrightarrow{\sigma} \in objects_X \mid \gamma'(\overrightarrow{\sigma})\right]$$

2.1 Individual Attacks

IA is an elementary action executed by a single attacking source. The subject of an IA is an $AttackerID$. Hence, $min_{IA}=0$ and $max_{IA}=1$. For example, the attack patterns of an IA performed by the attacker $AttackerID$ and consisting in cracking the password of a system user U through an authentication server S, can be represented as follows:

$IA\_passCrack(\{AttackerID\}, \{S, U\})$
$A_{passCrack} = \{network\_access(AttackerID, S)\}$
$B_{passCrack} = \{knows(AttackerID, is\_on(S)), knows(AttackerID, user\_access(U, S))\}$
$\Gamma_{passCrack} = \{is\_on(S), user\_access(U, S)\}$
$A'_{passCrack} = \{is\_connected\_as(AttackerID, U, S)\}$
$B'_{passCrack} = \{knows(AttackerID, password(U, S))\}$
$\Gamma'_{passCrack} = \{\neg user\_access(U,S)\}$

2.2 Coordinated Attacks

CA is an action made of joint individual actions executed by several collaborating attackers. Hence, the subject is a Group of Coordinating Attackers $GCA = \{attackerID_1, ..., attackerID_o\}$. Here, we need to specify which attacker of the group fulfills which predicate of the CA subsets. Thus, we distinguish three types of CAs depending on the type of collaboration between the attackers: (a) CA with Load Accumulation ($CALA$), (b) CA with load distribution ($CALD$), and (c) CA with Role Distribution ($CARD$). The attack patterns of each type differ in, (i) the attackers' required number, (ii) the A-related conditions, and (iii) the A'-related conditions. Therefore, we will only consider these three distinguishing patterns.

2.3 Coordinated Attack with Load Accumulation (CALA)

$CALA$ is a CA that is beyond the capability of a single attacking source, and for which attackers accumulate their capacities offering a distributed and simultaneous execution of this action. Definition 2 describes the distinguishing terms of a $CALA\_X$. Although every attacker of the GCA group executes exactly the same individual action, the overlapping of all the individual effects leads to a compromised state. Consequently, each attacker fulfills all attacker-related predicates in the A_{CALA_X} set. And after a $CALA$ is executed, all attackers gain the same system privileges α'. Additionally, $CALA\_X$ needs a minimum number min_{CALA_X} of coordinating attackers to be successful. This number is striclty greater than one, and can be estimated based on the characteristics of the attack target (i.e. objects).

Definition 2. $CALA\_X(GCA_X, objects_X)$
$| GCA_X |\geq min_{CALA\_X}$
A_X-condition: $\forall \alpha \in A_X, \exists \vec{\sigma} \in objects_X | \forall attackerID \in GCA_X, \alpha(attackerID, \vec{\sigma})$
A'_X-condition: $\forall \alpha' \in A'_X, \exists \vec{\sigma} \in objects_X | \forall attackerID \in GCA_X, \alpha'(attackerID, \vec{\sigma})$

An internal DDoS attack is a $CALA$ example. Consider a group of several dozens compromised machines connected to a company's network with a limited bandwidth in sending requests to a server S. As a consequence, the flow rates of attacking sources is also limited by the compromised machines bandwidth. However, to disrupt server S, the incoming flooding traffic should exceed a certain threshold. This can be attained if coordinated attacking sources join simultaneously their flooding actions to deliver a global output rate that exceeds the server capacity. If we consider that S becomes overloaded if flooded simultaneously by ten machines, then the system is threatened by a DDoS attack. Here are the signature and the subsets of a CA corresponding to an internal DDoS attack:

$CALA\_DDoS(GCA_{DDoS}, S)$
$min_{DDoS} = 10$
$A_{DDoS} = \{network\_access(attackerID, S)\}; \ A'_{DDoS} = \{\}$
$B_{DDoS} = \{knows(attackerID, is\_on(S))\}; \ B'_{DDoS} = \{knows(attackerID, DDoS(S))\}$
$\Gamma_{DDoS} = \{is\_on(S)\}; \ \Gamma'_{DDoS} = \{DDoS(S)\}$

2.4   Coordinated Attack with Load Distribution (CALD)

$CALD$ is a shareable attack accomplished by a group of attackers. By contrast to $CALA$, $CALD$ is an action which execution can be either done sequentially by a single attacker, or partitioned into several independent parts performed simultaneously by several attackers. Consequently, a $CALD\_X$ must have the same predicates in its subsets, as those of the IA of the same attack. Hence, $A_{CALD\_X} = A_{IA\_X}$, $B_{CALD\_X} = B_{IA\_X}$, etc. Major advantages of distributing the action load are, to allow collaborating attackers to achieve their attack in shorter time, and to avoid detection. Especially considering that nowadays Intrusion Detection Systems fail to correlate actions with different subjects. Definition 3 describes the distinguishing terms of a $CALD\_X$. Here, collaborating attackers race to get a knowledge of the system. Therefore, they execute similar actions, but with different variants. The one who executes the action with the correct variant gets the knowledge first, and acquires a certain privilege, accomplishing by this the goal of the group. Consequently, each attacker of the GCA should fulfill all the attacker-related predicates of A_X set. After a $CALD$ is executed, attacker-related predicates of A'_X set are fulfilled by a single attacker (i.e. the one who tried the correct variant). Additionally, unlike other CA types, only two attackers are sufficient to do a $CALD$.

Definition 3. $CALD\_X(GCA_X, objects_X)$
$| GCA_X | \geq 2$
$A_X\text{-}condition: \forall \alpha \in A_X, \exists \vec{\sigma} \in objects_X \mid \forall attackerID \in GCA_X, \alpha(attackerID, \vec{\sigma})$
$A'_X\text{-}condition: \forall \alpha' \in A'_X, \exists \vec{\sigma} \in objects_X \mid \exists! attackerID \in GCA_X, \alpha'(attackerID, \vec{\sigma})$

A coordinated password cracking attack is a $CALD$ example. Consider a server S that handles confidential information in a company, and two internal machines compromised by two collaborating attackers. Consider also that one of the attackers discovers the identity of a legitimate user U and communicates it to his partner. In order to guess the victim's password, attackers send REGISTER messages to the authentication server with different passwords using a dictionary. By dividing the dictionary into equal parts that each coordinating attacker uses for its registration attempts, attackers are able to divide the load and time to guess U's password. The first who finds the password will be connected from U account, accomplishing the goal of the GCA. $CALD\_passCrack(GCA_{passCrack}, S, U)$ is the signature of a coordinated password cracking attack. Attacker related and system related sets corresponding to the pre/postconditions of this action are the same as those of the individual password cracking attack of section 2.1.

2.5   Coordinated Attack with Role Distribution (CARD)

$CARD$ is a multi-task action, for which attacking sources distribute the roles or the tasks to accomplish their goal and avoid detection. Contrarily to other CA types, tasks performed by each coordinating attacker are different, and should be simultaneously executed. Note that, some multi-task actions can be done by a single attacker if he/she is able to execute more than one action at the same time. Therefore, similarly to $CALD$, some $CARD$ can have the same predicates in their subsets, as those of the IA of the same attack. Moreover, as each coordinating attacker is allocated a different task, there are attacker-related predicates in A_{CARD_X} that must be fulfilled by only one attacker. Besides, the number of coordinating attackers who can participate is limited to the number of tasks max_{CARD_X} that should be simultaneously executed. Consequently, any additional attacker to a group of max_{CARD_X} attackers will not bring additional help. Definition 4 describes the distinguishing terms of a $CARD\_X$. Provided that attackers do different tasks, the A'_X-condition states that they do not necessarily gain same privileges.

Definition 4. $CARD\_X(GCA_X, objects)$
$2 \leq | GCA_X | \leq max_{CARD\_X}$
A_X-condition: $\forall \alpha \in A_X, \exists \vec{\sigma} \in objects_X \mid \exists attackerID \in GCA_X, \alpha(attackerID, \vec{\sigma})$
$\qquad\qquad\quad \wedge \; \exists \alpha \in A_X, \exists \vec{\sigma} \in objects_X \mid \exists ! attackerID \in GCA_X, \alpha(attackerID, \vec{\sigma})$
A'_X-condition: $\forall \alpha' \in A'_X, \exists \vec{\sigma} \in objects_X \mid \exists attackerID \in GCA_X, \alpha'(attackerID, \vec{\sigma})$

It is possible to consider a coordinated version of the Mitnick attack as a $CARD$ example. Two compromised attacking agents will cooperate in order to hack a machine. First, one of the agents detects a trust relationship between two hosts h_1 and h_2. Afterwards he determines the TCP sequence number of h_2. Attackers can now distribute the tasks: the first executes a SYN flooding on host h_1 as a Denial of Service attack. Meanwhile, the second spoofs the IP address of h_1 to send a SYN request to h_2. Using a correct TCP sequence number, he compromises h_2. Here are the signature and the subsets corresponding to the coordinated Mitnick attack.

$CARD\_Mitnick(GCA_{Mitnick}, h_1, h_2)$

$max_{CARD\_Mitnick} = 2$

$A_{Mitnick} = \{network\_access(attackerID, h_1), network\_access(attackerID, h_2),$
$predicted\_seq(AttackerID, h_2)\}; \ A'_{Mitnick} = \{hacked(attackerID, h_2)\}$

$B_{Mitnick} = \{knows(attackerID, trust\_relation(h_2, h_1))\}; \ B'_{Mitnick} = \{\}$

$\Gamma_{Mitnick} = \{trust\_relation(h_2, h_1)\}; \ \Gamma'_{Mitnick} = \{trust\_relation(h_2, attackerID),$
$DoS(h_1)\}$

In this section, we proposed a new formal description of IA and CA. The next section makes use of these actions to define simultaneous attacks graphs. Later on in the paper (sections 4.2, 4.3), we show how to use SC language to automatically generate these attack graphs.

3 Attack Graphs Modeling

3.1 Individual Attack Graphs (IAG)

In *Set theory*, a Strictly Totally Ordered Set $STOS$ is a set with a strict total order over its elements (i.e. any pair of its elements are comparable under $<$). In *Graph theory*, a totally ordered graph $\langle N, E, < \rangle$, where N is the set of nodes and E is the set of edges, is a graph with a strict total order over its nodes. In such graph, the parents of a node are the nodes that are joined to it and preceding it in the ordering. In other words, n is a parent of m if $(n, m) \in E$ and $n < m$. Let us define an Individual Scenario Graph (ISG) as a totally ordered graph that fulfills the following property:

$$\forall n \in N, \ \forall m \in N, \ |(n < m) \wedge (\neg \exists l \in N \mid l > n \wedge l < m) \leftrightarrow (n, m) \in E$$

An ISG is then a sequence of nodes where every node, except the first and the last nodes, has a single parent, and is itself a parent of one and only other node.

Let us define a bijective application T which, for every element in a $STOS$, matches a node in an ISG, preserving over the nodes the same strict total order relation that exists over the set elements. Accordingly, given a $STOS$, it is possible to conceive only one ISG using T. Consider now a sequence of individual attacks executed by a single attacker. If we associate with each attack the time at which it was executed, then attacks can be compared by their timestamps and the set of these attacks is a $STOS$. We then define an Individual Attack Graph as the ISG that results from applying T to the set of individual attacks.

3.2 Simultaneous Attacks Graphs (SAG)

In *Set theory*, a Strictly Partially Ordered Set $SPOS$ is a set with a strict partial order over its elements (i.e. not every pair of its elements are comparable). Consequently, every subset of a $SPOS$ having every pair of its elements comparable is then a $STOS$. A $SPOS$ can thus correspond to the union of several $STOSs$.

Consider now an offline generated sequence of individual and coordinated attacks performed by several attackers. If we associate with each attack, the time at which it was executed, and we consider that the comparable attacks are those performed by the same attacker, then the set of these attacks is a *SPOS*. Applying the bijection T, we can now generate, for every *STOS* in this *SPOS*, the *IAG* corresponding to each attacker. Finally the union of all these *IAGs* is what we call a Simultaneous Attacks Graph. Note that, if there is a coordinated action (see section 2.2) in the *SPOS*, it will be included in each *STOS* corresponding to a collaborating attacker for this action.

Here is an example of a system threatened simultaneously by three different attacking sources: *AttackerIDa*, *AttackerIDb* and *AttackerIDc*. Consider that we generated the following possible sequence of attack actions:

$SPOS = \{A1(AttackerIDa, t1),\ B1(AttackerIDb, t2),\ C1(AttackerIDc, t3), AB2$
$(\{AttackerIDa, AttackerIDb\}, t4),\ C2(AttackerIDc, t5),\ A3(AttackerIDa, t6)\}$

For each attacker, we extract the corresponding *STOS* as follows:

$STOS_{AttackerIDa} = \{A1(AttackerIDa, t1), AB2(\{AttackerIDa, AttackerIDb\}, t4),$
$\qquad\qquad\qquad A3(AttackerIDa, t6)\}$
$STOS_{AttackerIDb} = \{B1(AttackerIDb, t2), AB2(\{AttackerIDa, AttackerIDb\}, t4)\}$
$STOS_{AttackerIDc} = \{C1(AttackerIDc, t3),\ C2(AttackerIDc, t5]\}$

Figure 1 depicts the *SAG* that results from the union of the *IAGs* corresponding to these *STOSs*.

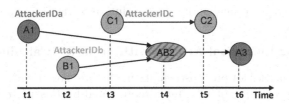

Fig. 1. Simultaneous Attacks Graph.

This section showed how to construct *SAG* given a sequence of simultaneous attacks. In section 4.5, we conceive a Situation Calculus (SC) planner for simultaneous attacks to automatically generate such sequence.

4   The Situation Calculus (SC)

4.1   Basics of the Situation Calculus

Situation Calculus [11] [12] is a dialect of first order logic, with second order-logic terms for representing dynamic change. It basically consists of:

- Situations: a situation is a first-order term denoting a sequence of actions. It represents the system's state, and the action's history (i.e. sequence) from an initial empty action sequence $S0$.

- Fluents and Predicates: the world is described in terms of static predicates and fluents. Static predicates do not change, no matter what actions are taken. Whereas fluents are predicates that can vary over time, and thus must take situations as arguments. For example, $Server(Serv)$ is a static predicate meaning that $Serv$ is a server. While, $network\_access(AttackerID, Serv, s)$ is a fluent meaning that $AttackerID$ has a network access to $Serv$ in situation s. Additionally, Fluents can be either relational, or functional. Relational fluents return boolean values, e.g. $is\_on(Serv, s)$, while functional fluents return a non boolean value, e.g. $received\_flow(Serv, s) = 500$.
- Actions: consist of a function symbol and its arguments. For example, $ip\_spoof(AttackerID, h)$ is the action of spoofing the IP address of host h by $AttackerID$. In order to reason about the effects of an action, we need to be able to refer to the situation that results from the execution of this action. This is done using the do function. $do(a, s)$ denotes the situation that results from doing action a in situation s.

SC also provides essential axioms to represent dynamic changes:

- Action precondition axioms: for each action a, there is a predicate $Poss(a, s)$ that states if it is possible for action a to be executed in situation s.
- Successor state axioms: there is one for each fluent F. It characterizes the conditions under which a fluent $F(x, do(a, s))$ changes from situation s to situation $do(a, s)$, providing by this a solution to the frame problem [13].

4.2 Modeling Individual Attacks with Situation Calculus

SC provides semantics for pre/postconditions that are not provided by other languages. The precondition of action a is represented by $Poss(do(a, s))$. Whereas the postcondition is represented by the function $do(a, s)$ which denotes the fluents that change after applying action a to situation s. SC provides an expressive framework for encoding actions whose effects are functions of the state in which they are executed. Therefore, SC was adopted in [14] to describe individual cyber attacks whose effects depend crucially on the system's state, and to represent dynamic changes which is the case for network systems exposed to attacks. Knowledge in SC [12] is represented by a fluent $knows(AttackerID, \Phi, s)$. Here is the SC modeling of the password cracking IA, formally described in 2.1.

$passCrack(AttackerID_x, Server_y, User_z)$
$\textbf{Poss}(passCrack(AttackerID_x, Server_y, User_z), s) \leftrightarrow$
$network\_access(AttackerID_x, Server_y, s) \land Knows(AttackerID_x,$
$is\_on(Server_y), s) \land knows(AttackerID_x, user\_access(User_z, Server_y), s)$
$\land is\_on(Server_y, s) \land user\_access(User_z, Server_y, s)$
$\textbf{do}(passCrack(AttackerID_x, Server_y, User_z), s) = s' \rightarrow knows(AttackerID_x,$
$password(User_z), s') \land is\_connected\_as(AttackerID_x, User_z, Server_y, s')$

4.3   Modeling Coordinated Attacks with Situation Calculus

By contrast to languages of first-order logic, SC provides second order terms through functional fluents. These fluents return situation-related values, which are essential to model CA as described in section 2.2. For instance, the number of attackers participating in a CA, $Cardinal(GCA_x, s)$ should be modeled with a functional fluent. Besides, SC affords all logical operators and quantifiers needed for CA modeling. As an example, we give a SC model of the coordinated password cracking attack.

$passCrack(GCA_x, Server_y, User_z)$
Poss$(passCrack(GCA_x, Server_y, User_z), s) \leftrightarrow Cardinal(GCA_x, s) \geq 2$
$\wedge\ \forall AttackerID_i \in GCA_x, network\_access(AttackerID_i, Server_y, s)\ \wedge$
$\exists AttackerID_k \in GCA_x, Knows(AttackerID_k, is\_on(Server_y), s)]\ \wedge$
$\exists AttackerID_j \in GCA_x, knows(AttackerID_j, user\_access(User_z, Server_y), s)]$
$\wedge\ is\_on(Server_y, s)\ \wedge\ user\_access(User_z, Server_y, s)$
do$(passCrack(GCA_x, Server_y, User_z), s) = s' \rightarrow \forall AttackerID_a \in GCA_x,$
$knows(AttackerID_a, password(User_z), s') \wedge \exists AttackerID_b \in GCA_x,$
$is\_connected\_as(AttackerID_b, User_z, Server_y, s')$

4.4   Modeling Simultaneous Attacks with Situation Calculus

In [15] and [16], SC ontology was expanded to handle concurrency. A new sort *concurrent* is added. Every *concurrent* variable c is a set of concurrent simple actions a. In our case IA and CA are simple actions. The binary function $do(c, s)$ returns a situation term that results from the application of concurrent actions c in situation s. And item $Poss(a, s)$ is extended to concurrent actions. Consequently, $Poss(c, s)$ means that concurrent actions set c is possible in situation s. Additionally, in a simultaneous actions context, some actions can not be performed concurrently. This is due to incompatibility between actions in terms of resources that each action uses. For instance, if action a_1 needs a resource for its execution, and another action a_2 needs the same resource, then the set of concurrent actions $c = \{a_1, a_2\}$ can not be executed unless this resource can be shared. As a solution, Pinto [16] proposed to add a finer level of granularity by appealing to the notion of resource: $xres(a, r)$ means that action a requires the exclusive use of the resource r, and $sres(a, r)$ means that action a requires the use of the resource r for its execution, but r can be shared. Finally, $poss(c, s)$ makes use of a precondition Interaction predicate $preInt$ to test compatibility between actions:

$$preInt(c) \leftrightarrow \exists a_1, a_2 \in c, \exists r\ |\ [(xres(a_1, r) \wedge xres(a_2, r)) \vee$$
$$(xres(a_1, r) \wedge sres(a_2, r)) \vee (sres(a_1, r) \wedge xres(a_2, r))]$$
$$Poss(c, s) \leftrightarrow [\forall a \in c, Poss(a, s)] \wedge \neg preInt(c)$$

In a simultaneous attacks context, different IA and CA are launched at the same time (i.e. in the same situation). And, it is likely that an attacking source finds itself unable to execute its action because of an incompatibility with another action executed by a non collaborating attacking source. Therefore, concurrent

SC is appropriate to model simultaneous attacks actions. For example, consider two attack entities threatening a system: (1) a group of coordinated attackers GCA_x, and (2) an individual attacker $AttackerID_y$. Consider also, that we defined in the attack model, the following predicates:

$xres(DDoS(GCA, Server), Server)$
$sres(passCrack(AttackerID, Server, User), Server)$

Unlike the case of a password cracking attack, in a $DDoS$ attack, an overflowed server can not participate or interact in any other action. To determine whether it is possible for the two entities to execute simultaneously a $DDoS$ attack, and an individual password cracking attack, we can test:

$poss(\{DDoS(GCA_x, Serv), passCrack(AttackerID_y, Serv, User)\}, s)$

In this example $poss$ returns false, because the following predicate returns false.

$preInt(DDoS(GCA_x, Serv), passCrack(AttackerID_y, Serv, User))$

Considering this feature, we can eliminate all attack scenarios where concurrent actions are incompatible. Advantageously, response systems can avoid launching unnecessary responses.

In the next section, we show how to generate all potential simultaneous scenarios and the corresponding attack graphs.

4.5 Planning Simultaneous Attacks in Situation Calculus

In [12], the author presented and implemented the world's simplest breadth-first planner ($wspbf$). $wspbf$ is a SC planner for an agent who can perform concurrent or sequential actions. It is supplied with a goal predicate $plannerGoal(s)$, and a domain dependent predicate, $badSituation(s)$. This latter is true if, based on domain specific knowledge, and depending on the goal, s is considered to be a bad situation for the planner. $badSituation$ is also a domain specific search control heuristic added to reduce in practice the theoretical complexity of the planner. Here is the Golog [17] program of the $wspbf$:

proc $wspbf(n)$
$plans(0, n)$
endProc
proc $plans(m, n)$
$m \leq n?; [actionSequence(m); plannerGoal? \mid plans(m+1, n)]$
endProc
proc $actionSequence(n)$
$n = 0? \mid$
$n > 0?; (\pi c) [concurrent\_actions(c)?; c] ; \neg badSituation?; actionSequence(n-1)$
endProc

The planner generates all sequences of concurrent actions c avoiding bad situations. It terminates with failure if it does not find a sequence, which length is smaller or equal to n, that fulfills the $plannerGoal$.

In order to construct simultaneous attacks graphs, we need to exhaustively generate all potential sequences of concurrent attacks as an input to our proposed method in section 3.2. Therefore, we propose SAP, a Simultaneous Attacks Planner, by generalizing Reiter's work to the case of several attack entities that can perform, concurrently or sequentially, a set of individual and coordinated actions. We also adopt the following hypothesizes, allowing SAP to reason in simultaneous attacks contexts:

- In a situation S, an attacker can not be a member of two independent GCAs. This hypothesis can be expressed through the following logic rule:

Hypothesis 1. $conflict(Action_X(GCA_X, Objects_X),$
$Action_Y(GCA_Y, Objects_Y), S) \leftrightarrow \exists attackerID(A) \mid A \in GCA_X, A \in GCA_Y.$

- In a situation S, an attacker does not execute the same attack that he/she has already executed successfully in an anterior situation, unless he/she changes the parameters (i.e. objects) of this attack. This hypothesis can be expressed by adding a condition to the *poss* predicate of each action, as follows:

Hypothesis 2. $poss(Action_X(Subjects_X, Objects_X), S) \leftrightarrow (A_X\text{-}condition \wedge B_X\text{-}condition \wedge \Gamma_X\text{-}condition) \wedge \neg postconditions(Action_X(Subjects_X, Objects_X), S).$

- Due to some unshareable resources, some attacks can not be executed together. Therefore, we add the *preInt* predicate described in 4.4, to SAP.
- The *badSituation* heuristic used in *wspbf* lowers the execution time of the decision procedures by avoiding paths that will not converge to the planner's goal. In our case, this heuristic limits the creativity of attackers in constructing different paths to reach their goals. In other words, by defining bad situations related to a given goal, we may eliminate some sequences that attackers can follow to reach this goal. Therefore, we avoid using such heuristic in SAP.

To define the planner's goal, an expert should first describe undesired states for critical assets. Every detected attacker has an attack goal that matches with one of these states. Hence, a solution goal for the planner would be to find a situation (i.e. a sequence of simultaneous attacks) where every attacker has reached an attack goal, either individually, or through coordinating in a GCA. Another possibility of a solution goal is to have an attacker becoming inactive at a certain level of the attack sequence. In this case, the attacker is unable to progress because he/she was accidentally blocked by another independent attacker. We formally describe SAP's goal as follows:

$plannerGoal(S) \leftrightarrow \forall attackerID(A), [\ attack\_goal(A, S) \vee$
$(\exists GCA \mid A \in GCA, attack\_goal(GCA, S)) \vee blocked(A, S)\ ].$
with
$blocked(A, S) \leftrightarrow [\ (\neg \exists\ Action_X(A, Objects_X)) \vee$
$(\neg \exists\ Action_X(GCA_X, Objects_X) \mid A \in GCA_X)\ ] \mid poss(Action_X, S).$

Here again, we notice the benefit of using SC. Contrarily to first-order logic languages, SC allows to quantify over actions in $blocked(A, S)$ description.

As a simultaneous attacks planning example, we consider a set of servers and users within a system. Here, an undesired state is reached when one of the servers gets overflowed, or when one of the users' accounts is highjacked. Hence, the *attack_goal* can be described with the following logic rule:

$attack\_goal(Attack\_Entity, S) \leftrightarrow overflowed(Attack\_Entity, Server, S) \lor$
$highjacked((Attack\_Entity, User, S).$

Attack_Entity can represent a single attacker or a GCA. Then, we describe in SC (as in sections 4.2 and 4.3) all attacks and legitimate actions that assets can execute in the system. As attack examples, we consider a DDoS, a password cracking, and a user registration highjacking that an attacker can execute once he/she finds a user's password. Consider now that we observed the following threats: ten of the enterprise's machines, $\{a1, a2, ..., a10\}$, were compromised, and one of them has discovered the presence of a server $serv_x$. Additionally, two other compromised machines, $\{a11, a12\}$ discovered the presence of a user $user_y$ which has network access to server $serv_y$. We can now run SAP to find potential simultaneous attacks scenarios. For scenarios of length 2, the results of SAP are those presented after:

1 : [$DDoS(\{a1, a2, ..., a10\}, serv_x), passCrack(\{a11, a12\}, serv_y, User_y)$],
    [$highjack(a11, user_y)$].
2 : [$DDoS(\{a1, a2, ..., a10\}, serv_x), passCrack(\{a11, a12\}, serv_y, User_y)$],
    [$highjack(a12, user_y)$].
3 : [$DDoS(\{a1, a2, ..., a10\}, serv_x), passCrack(a11, serv_y, User_y),$
    $passCrack(a12, serv_y, User_y)$], [$highjack(a11, user_y)$]
4 : [$DDoS(\{a1, a2, ..., a10\}, serv_x), passCrack(a11, serv_y, User_y),$
    $passCrack(a12, serv_y, User_y)$], [$highjack(a12, user_y)$]
5 : [$passCrack(\{a11, a12\}, serv_y, User_y)$],
    [$DDoS(\{a1, a2, ..., a10\}, serv_x), highjack(a11, user_y)$]
6 : [$passCrack(\{a11, a12\}, serv_y, User_y)$],
    [$DDoS(\{a1, a2, ..., a10\}, serv_x), highjack(a12, user_y)$]
7 : [$passCrack(a11, serv_y, User_y), passCrack(a12, serv_y, User_y)$],
    [$DDoS(\{a1, a2, ..., a10\}, serv_x), highjack(a11, user_y)$]
8 : [$passCrack(a11, serv_y, User_y), passCrack(a12, serv_y, User_y)$],
    [$DDoS(\{a1, a2, ..., a10\}, serv_x), highjack(a12, user_y)$]

We can verify that in the trivial use case of search for scenarios of length 2, SAP exhaustively generates all possibilities of two attacks steps which can be performed by the 12 considered attackers. For instance, in solutions 1 and 2, attackers $\{a1, a2, ..., a10\}$ coordinate to execute a DDoS attack, while attackers $\{a11, a12\}$ coordinate to execute a password cracking attack. In the next step one of the second group highjacks $user_y$'s account. Whereas, in solutions 3 and 4, $a11$ and $a12$ are two independent attackers, they concurrently execute password cracking attacks. In the next step, one of them highjacks $user_y$'s account, blocking by this the other attacker from reaching its goal. Solutions 5 till 8 differ from the first four solutions by having DDoS executed in the next step, concurrently with highjacking attack.

5   Complexity and Performance of SAP

By postulating the hypothesizes presented in section 4.5, we were able to reduce the theoretical complexity of the planner from $(N_{actions})^{N_{attackers} \times L_{ength}}$, for the original *wspbf*, to $(1\text{-}ConlictRatio) \times (\frac{N_{actions}}{e})^{N_{attackers} \times (L_{ength}-1)}$, for our SAP. $N_{actions}$ is the number of modeled actions, *ConflictRatio* is an estimated number of incompatible actions over the total number of actions, L_{ength} is the desired length of attacks sequences, and finally, $N_{attackers}$ is the number of attackers. This latter can reach, in the worst case, the number of machines in the system.

In order to evaluate SAP's performance, we conducted three different experiments associated with $N_{attackers}$, $N_{actions}$, and L_{ength}. The measures are collected on a machine with a Core2 Duo processor clocked at 2.26 GHz and 1.94 GB of RAM. We used SWI prolog[1] as a Situation Caluclus interpreter.

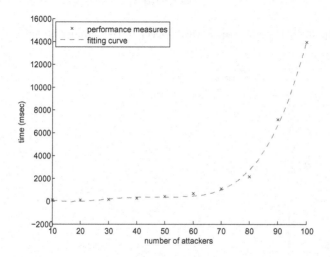

Fig. 2. SAP performance with respect to the number of attackers

In the first experiment, presented in figure 2, we generated several random attackers, and measured the time needed by SAP to fulfill the planner's goal. The measure confirms that a $o(n^3)$ complexity is achieved, and that SAP is able to generate all solution sequences for 80 attackers in less than 2 seconds. This result is very competitive for an average-size network.

In the second experiment, presented in figure 3, we added several random attacks to the model, and measured the time needed by SAP to fulfill the planner's goal. The measure confirms that a $o(n^4)$ complexity is achieved, and that SAP is able to generate all solution sequences for 15 different attacks in less than 3 seconds. This result is convenient for networks running a small number of services, where a small number of attacks are modeled. However, for multi-service

---

[1] www.swi-prolog.org

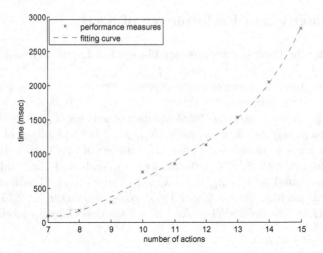

Fig. 3. SAP performance with respect to the number of actions

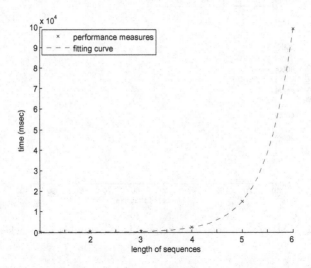

Fig. 4. SAP performance with respect to the length of sequences

systems, for which a huge number of attacks have to be modeled, SAP may take greater time to generate solutions.

In the third experiment, presented in figure 4, we measured the time needed by SAP to fulfill the planner's goal with respect to the length of solution sequences. We found that SAP's performance drops with an exponential rate $o(2^n)$. Despite this complexity, SAP is able to generate all sequences of length 5 in less than 2 seconds. As a reference, if we look at most striking attacks performed in the recent days, like the Stuxnet attack[2], we see that they can be accomplished in

---

[2] www.isssource.com/stuxnet-report-v-security-culture-needs-work/

less than 5 attack steps. Moreover, response systems are more interested to react against attackers that can reach their goals within few steps than those who need a greater number of steps to procure a considerable damage in the system.

Note that, without our added hypothesizes, the planner's performance drops with exponential rates for the three different experiments. Hence, performance results are coherent to our complexity calculus. In other words, the reduction in complexity we introduced in SAP, using the hypothesizes, is experimentally noticeable.

6   Related Work and Discussion

Attack Modeling has been an active topic, and several languages were proposed.

LAMBDA is a pre/postcondition based language [7] to model attack actions. The various steps of the attack process are associated with events, which may be combined using specific algebraic operators, generating by this the sequence of actions that the attacker has to do before reaching its goal.

The **JIGSAW** [8] language describes attack components in terms of capabilities and concepts. It provides a Requires/provides model for computer attacks. But, rather than thinking of attacks as a series of events, sees attacks as a set of capabilities that provides support for abstract attack concepts, while providing new capabilities to support other concepts.

Unfortunately, both of these languages lack concurrent actions description, which is a very important feature for modeling simultaneous attacks.

Modified STRIPS [9], formally models coordinated attacks using a modified version of a first-order logic language, STRIPS, to describe concurrent attacks. An action is described by: a subject, preconditions, other actions performed concurrently, and effects. Compatibility between actions is captured by a concurrent action list. It specifies what actions must, or must not, be executed concurrently in order to enable positive synergy. Unfortunately, this language has a limited scalability, and needs a lot of expertise. For each new added attack action, an expert should study its compatibility with all the others. Moreover, every attack should be modeled differently when the number of attackers changes. The effects of an action should be studied depending on other concurrent attackers' actions. Therefore, this language is limited to $CARD$ modeling where a maximum attackers number can be estimated. Besides, it is not mandatory for attackers' individual actions to be concurrent to perform a CA. In $CALD$, for instance, attackers may execute their actions sequentially to avoid detection.

A common limitation of these languages is the lack of functional fluents, and second-order logic terms that allow the quantification over actions as explained in 4.5. Moreover, they do not provide solutions for the frame problem.

Concerning planning with concurrent actions, a variant of modified STRIPS, POMP [18], was the preferred representation of the planning community for several years. However, being a first-order logic language, modified STRIPS language is not as much expressive as concurrent SC. Moreover, the performance of POMP is greatly affected by the ordering of agenda items / actions. Hence, heuristics were proposed through defining subgoals for each goal. However, finding subgoals in network attacks requires a high level expertise, especially when goals can be reached by several paths. This is not the case for SAP, which performance is relatively satisfactory without using heuristics.

Concerning attack graphs, a coordinated attack graph is defined in [9] as possible sequences of concurrent actions executed by all the attackers observed in the network. However, guessing whether attackers are collaborating, or simply simultaneous is not possible. Their graphs lack CA nodes. Actually, determining $GCAs$ enables response systems to select exclusive and more effective responses for those groups. For example, if in a DDoS attack, the response system knows about coordinated attacking sources, it can respond by blocking exclusively incoming requests from these sources. Otherwise, it will apply a threshold on the total received flow by the server, which may have a more penalizing effect (e.g. discarding requests of legitimate users). Moreover, approaches based on offline attack graphs generation modules has been proposed (e.g. [19]). With those approaches, an abstract attack graph covering all possible attacks paths is generated before running the system, and then attacks nodes are instantiated as corresponding attacks are observed online. Nevertheless, we think that our approach of dynamically generating instantiated SAG is more suitable for response systems: On one side, considering a SAG, when an attacker does not continue its trip to reach a critical goal, we can deduce that he is been blocked by another one. This exclusive property offers the safe possibility to avoid reacting against already blocked attackers. On the other side, when a minor change occurs in the system (e.g. adding a machine), it can be easily taken into consideration when dynamically generating instantiated attack graphs. This is not the case for offline graphs, which should be regenerated each time the system changes.

7   Conclusion

In this paper, we introduced a new formal description of attacks that models individual, coordinated and simultaneous attacks. We then chose an appropriate language, the Situation Calculus, to model these actions. Additionally, we presented a new method, based on *Set Theory* and *Graph Theory*, to generate simultaneous attacks graphs. These graphs leverage response systems means to estimate the global risk inferred by simultaneous ongoing attacks, and to reason about appropriate responses. Finally, we presented a Simultaneous Attacks Planner that generates attack scenarios, which are required for graphs construction. The complexity and performance of this planner is studied, and it turns to be competitive for an average-size system.

As future work, we intend to estimate the risk [20] inferred by simultaneous attacks on a system network. Precisely estimating this risk is crucial for response system to react intelligently against the most dangerous attacks. We will also study the applicability of SC to model a response system that is able to launch, concurrently, different reactions against simultaneous ongoing attacks.

References

1. Zhou, C.V., Leckie, C., Karunasekera, S.: A survey of coordinated attacks and collaborative intrusion detection. Computers & Security, 124–140 (2010)
2. Braynov, S.: On Future Avenues for Distributed Attacks, pp. 51–60. Management Centre International Limited (2003)
3. Falliere, N., Murchu, L.O., Chien, E.: W32. stuxnet dossier. White paper, Symantec Corp., Security Response (2011)
4. Toth, T., Kruegel, C.: Evaluating the impact of automated intrusion response mechanisms (2002)
5. Stakhanova, N., Basu, S., Wong, J.: A cost-sensitive model for preemptive intrusion response systems. In: Proceedings of the 21st International Conference on Advanced Networking and Applications, AINA 2007, pp. 428–435. IEEE Computer Society, Washington, DC (2007)
6. Kanoun, W., Cuppens-Boulahia, N., Cuppens, F., Dubus, S.: Risk-aware framework for activating and deactivating policy-based response. In: International Conference on Network and System Security, pp. 207–215 (2010)
7. Cuppens, F., Ortalo, R.: Lambda: A language to model a database for detection of attacks. In: Debar, H., Mé, L., Wu, S.F. (eds.) RAID 2000. LNCS, vol. 1907, pp. 197–216. Springer, Heidelberg (2000)
8. Templeton, S.J., Levitt, K.: A requires/provides model for computer attacks. In: Proceedings of the 2000 Workshop on New Security Paradigms, NSPW 2000, pp. 31–38. ACM, New York (2000)
9. Braynov, S., Jadliwala, M.: Representation and analysis of coordinated attacks. In: Proceedings of the 2003 ACM Workshop on Formal Methods in Security Engineering, Ser., FMSE 2003, pp. 43–51. ACM, New York (2003)
10. Sheyner, O., Haines, J., Jha, S., Lippmann, R., Wing, J.M.: Automated generation and analysis of attack graphs. In: Proceedings of the 2002 IEEE Symposium on Security and Privacy, pp. 273–284 (2002)
11. Mccarthy, J., Hayes, P.J.: Some philosophical problems from the standpoint of artificial intelligence. Machine Intelligence 4 (1969)
12. Reiter, R.: Knowledge in Action: Logical Foundations for Specifying and Implementing Dynamic Systems, illustrated edition ed. The MIT Press, Massachusetts (2001)
13. Reiter, R.: The frame problem in situation the calculus: a simple solution (sometimes) and a completeness result for goal regression. In: Lifschitz, V. (ed.) Artificial Intelligence and Mathematical Theory of Computation, pp. 359–380. Academic Press Professional, Inc., San Diego (1991)
14. Goldman, R.P.: A stochastic model for intrusions. In: Wespi, A., Vigna, G., Deri, L. (eds.) RAID 2002. LNCS, vol. 2516, pp. 199–218. Springer, Heidelberg (2002)
15. Reiter, R.: Natural actions, concurrency and continuous time in the situation calculus. In: Aiello, L.C., Doyle, J., Shapiro, S.C. (eds.) KR, pp. 2–13. Morgan Kaufmann (1996)
16. Pinto, J.A.: Temporal reasoning in the situation calculus (1994)
17. Levesque, H.J., Reiter, R., Lespérance, Y., Lin, F., Scherl, R.B.: Golog: A logic programming language for dynamic domains (1994)

18. Boutilier, C., Brafman, R.I.: Partial-order planning with concurrent interacting actions. J. Artif. Int. Res. 14(1), 105–136 (2001)
19. Autrel, F., Cuppens, F.: Crim: un module de corrélation d'alertes et de réaction aux attaques. Annales des Télécommunications 61(9-10), 1172–1192 (2006)
20. Kanoun, W., Dubus, S., Papillon, S., Cuppens-Boulahia, N., Cuppens, F.: Towards dynamic risk management: Success likelihood of ongoing attacks. Bell Labs Technical Journal 17(3), 61–78 (2012)

Geolocation and Verification of IP-Addresses with Specific Focus on IPv6

Robert Koch, Mario Golling, and Gabi Dreo Rodosek

Universität der Bundeswehr München,
Faculty of Computer Science, D-85577 Neubiberg, Germany
{robert.koch,mario.golling,gabi.dreo}@unibw.de

Abstract. Geolocation, the mapping of a network entity with its geographical position is used frequently in today's internet. New location aware applications like e-commerce, web site content and advertisements are just some examples of what has appeared since the last couple of years. Regarding network security, Geolocation also has a significant impact, since it offers possibilities for advanced network security (e.g., including sophisticated geo-based attack correlation/classification). However, determining the physical position of a network entity is challenging, as there is no inherent relationship between an IP address and its geographical location. In addition, with the introduction of IPv6, the address space is enhanced by a factor of 2^{96} making the process far more complex in comparison to IPv4. Although numerous techniques for Geolocation are existing, each strategy is subject to certain restrictions. Therefore, this publication illustrates and evaluates different approaches of Geolocation. Furthermore, strategies to obtain additional information related to the location of IP addresses are examined. After considering procedures how to verify the achieved data and following the ideas of Endo et al., we are designing an architecture for a combination of different methods for optimized Geolocation. Finally we introduce and evaluate our Proof of Concept called geolabel, a tool capable of mapping IPv4 as well as IPv6 addresses to certain geographical locations on a country level.

Keywords: IP Geolocation, IPv6, prosecution of computer fraud, attack attribution, network analysis.

1 Introduction

Within the Internet, addressing a host or an entity in general is nowadays almost exclusively done by the use of the TCP/IP protocol suite and here especially with the use of the Internet Protocol (IP) and the corresponding address (also called IP address respectively IP).

1.1 Problem Statement

The IP address space of the Internet is maintained by the Internet Assigned Numbers Authority (IANA) which in turn subdelegates its responsibility - depending on the geographical location to five so called Regional Internet Registries

G. Wang et al. (Eds.): CSS 2013, LNCS 8300, pp. 151–170, 2013.

(RIR). In return the RIRs are assigning smaller address ranges to different Local Internet Registries (LIR), National Internet Registries (NIR) as well as Internet Service Providers (ISP) [1].

Latest at the level of the ISPs, the hierarchical allocation of IP addresses becomes far less stringent. ISPs are given an high level of freedom on how they like to allocate their addresses to their customers. So, very often different methods are in place. In addition, larger organizations such as Apple or IBM have their own address block (in case of Apple the block 17.0.0.0 / 8). This can lead to the fact that, within a few square meters, completely different IP addresses resp. IP addresses of different address blocks, depending on the ISP of the user, are in place. An obligation to publish details about the geographical distribution of IP addresses however does not exist at this level.

1.2   Examples for Geolocation

Content Localization: The main application for Geolocation is content localization. An example would be someone who types the word "cars" into a search engine and only receiving results on cars in the local area [2]. Geolocation allows to present content dynamically in different languages or provide the local weather forecast. Another field of application is targeted advertising for placing ads based on the estimated geographical origin of a user.

Network Management and Routing: In the field of academic research and for ISPs, Geolocation helps to simplify network management and supports network diagnostics, for instance to detect routing anomalies. Furthermore it is a key enabler for efficient routing policies, traffic labeling and load balancing. Content Delivery Networks optimize the load balancing between their servers and provide better traffic management for downloads based on information gained through Geolocation.

Network Security: New location aware applications like e-commerce, web site content and advertisements are just some examples of what has been appeared since the last couple of years. Regarding network security, Geolocation also has a significant impact, since it offers possibilities for advanced network security (e.g., including sophisticated geo-based attack correlation/classification): Currently, due to the way the Internet works, attacks can be executed from nearly everywhere. However, for an attribution, besides knowledge of logical addresses (e.g., IPs and Ports), knowledge about geographical addresses is also very important - the origination of an attack. Thus, Geolocation is a prerequisite for criminal prosecution, especially in the context of a cyberwar, in order to be able to trace back an attacker (*ex post* investigation/forensic). As a recent study from the security company Mandiant [3] - claiming to analyze China's Cyber Espionage Units - proclaimed, "a large share of hacking activity targeting the US could be traced to an office building in Shanghai". Although the Chinese government has denied the accusations [4], the political pressure on China from the

US continues. In return, it also seems that the US government has been hacking Hong Kong and China for years [5]. Both examples show how important an attribution in cyber space is and thus the rising importance of Geolocation to support attribution. Geolocation is also a necessary condition for identifying and examining the network structure of the opponent in order to (i) counterattack (for example in a Cyber Conflict) and to (ii) finally bring down the attack. Although numerous techniques can be used to scramble the real IP address of an attacker (e.g., NAT, proxies, anonymizing networks like TOR or the use of Bots, which are under control of the attacker), here, tracing and locating the geographical position can also support subsequent activities like isolating a system.

Besides that, Geolocation can also be used very successfully to increase the security of a network during its operation mode (i.e. before an intrusion actually has taken place; *ex ante*). Based on attacks detected (e.g., by Intrusion Detection Systems such as Snort), a correlation of these attacks with new connections is possible as well. Thus as a consequence, new connections originating from a location very close to where a recent attack was launched may be inspected in more detail in comparison to normal network traffic. Analog to greylisting in emails, Geolocation allows to (i) correlate attacks detected with new connections (attack correlation) and as a consequence (ii) to classify traffic a priori as more suspicious (thus particularly allowing to inspect this traffic in more detail, for instance performing a deep packet inspection on this traffic while the regular traffic is only inspected flow-based).

1.3   Structure of the Publication

The aim of this publication is to design a method for advanced Geolocation of IP addresses with specific focus on IPv6. Following the idea of Endo et al. [6], this publications tries to overcome shortcomings of existing approaches with a combined solution of different methods.

The paper is structured as follows: A short overview of state-of-the-art Geolocation techniques and tools is presented in Section 2. Thereafter, our architecture is illustrated (Section 3) as well as the corresponding Proof of Concept (Section 4), before an evaluation is performed in Section 5. Finally, Section 6 contains a Conclusion and Outlook.

2   Related Work

This section starts with giving a brief overview of the differences of IPv4 compared to IPv6. After that, an overview of Geolocation strategies, including a brief summarization regarding signification and eligibility in respect of IPv6 is given.

2.1   IPv4 versus IPv6

The main addressing scheme in recent networks, including the global Internet, is based on the Internet Protocol. The most prevalent version IPv4 is mentioned in RFC 791 [7]. According to information from 2010 [8], about 47.3% of the IPv4-address space is allocated to the United States, followed by 39.7% for the rest of the top 15 countries of the world. This is mainly due to the historical development [9]. Hence, there is only 13% of the whole IPv4-address space left for other countries as well as for future services where more and more devices will communicate with IP [9]. Consequently, in February 2011, IANA allocated the last blocks of IPv4 addresses.

RFC 2460 [10] describes the next generation of the Internet Protocol, known as IPv6, which is an evolution of its predecessor with focus of keeping the tried and trusted, and to overcome the weaknesses of version four. Thus, scalability and flexibility is given priority to address the expansion rate of the Internet as well as the requirements of the current and future services [9]. Amongst others, main new features of IPv6 include [11]:

- Increased address space (from 2^{32} addresses to 2^{128})
- Simplifying and improving the protocol frame (header data), which relieves routers computational effort
- Stateless Address Autoconfiguration (SLAAC) of IPv6 addresses; stateful methods such as Dynamic Host Configuration Protocol (DHCP) are unnecessary when using IPv6
- Build-in support of Mobile IP and multihoming
- Implementing IPsec in IPv6 standards, which allows for encryption and verification of the authenticity of IP packets (but *not* mandatory any longer)
- Support of network technologies in terms of quality of service and multicast

2.2   Existing Methods for Geolocation

Endo et al. [12] divides *Geolocation* approaches in two main categories:

- IP address mapping based strategies (*passive*)
- Measurement based strategies (*active*)

This corresponds with other classification efforts, e.g., Dahnert [13] and Eriksson [14]. Padmanabhan et al. [15], whose work is to be considered as the first investigation on IP address Geolocation, describes three different categories which nevertheless can be classed in those mentioned above [16].

Passive IP Address Mapping Based Strategies
Usually approaches based on IP address mapping are relying on lookups against databases **without direct interactions involving the target system** [12, 17]. Relating examples are the Domain Name System (DNS), datasets maintained by the five RIRs or analysis of Border Gateway Protocol (BGP) message (see below). This can also be done by crawling websites and extracting associated Geolocation information [18].

Geolocation Databases: The use of Geolocation databases (also known as geoservices) for mapping a given IP address to a physical location is common for services relying on coarse-grained estimations only. Geoservice provider like Max-Mind [19] or Quova [20] offer their products either for free or commercial use, whereby commercial ones are more accurate [21, 22]. The location estimation is performed by looking up a given IP address in the corresponding datasets. Hence, accuracy, reliability and scope depends on the geoservice provider [21–23]. Most provider seem to use exhaustive tabulation of public as well as private data received through cooperating ISPs [15, 24]. However, due to the lack of concrete knowledge how the datasets are collected and the missing large scale ground-truth, an evaluation is difficult [23]. In addition, the algorithms and methodologies employed by the provider are proprietary; as a consequence, accuracy and credibility of such services has to be considered as questionable [22, 25, 26]. Nevertheless different empirical studies [21–23] have proven an accuracy of geo-databases from 96% up to 98% at country level.

Regional Internet Registries: Information about which RIR is currently maintaining a certain IP address block can be obtained by downloading the latest delegations. These files are also indicating, besides Autonomous System Number (ASN) and IP version, related geographic data on country level. More detailed intelligence about particular addresses respectively ranges is available by using the *Whois* protocol [27]. The client application *Whois* is named the same way and integral part of each common OS. Querying a RIR for a given IP typically results in information like relating IP range, customer respectively organization details, point of contact as well as listing country, city, zip codes and further geographic details. Several approaches using such data have been published taking advantage in terms of *Geolocation*. *NetGeo* [28] [15], which uses a database build by *Whois* records as well as ASN (to map IP addresses onto geographic locations [12]), is one example.

Domain Name System: In addition to querying the databases of the five RIRs, the *Whois* client application can also be used to extract geographic information through the Domain Name System [29], which is a worldwide hierarchical system for mapping FQDN respectively domain names to IP addresses [17]. In comparison to the RIRs, there are no central regional administrations. Since the name space is divided into categories such as "Generic top-level domain" (gTLD) or "country code top-level domain (ccTLD)" and structured in a hierarchical way, queries have to be performed along this hierarchy, resulting in location information as well as further intelligence like organization, nameserver (valuable starting point for obtaining further intelligence) or point of contact [17, 30]. Another way to benefit from DNS in terms of Geolocation is the approach published in RFC 1876 [31]. In his experimental paper "A Means for Expressing Location Information in the Domain Name System" [31] Davis proposes to add geographic data such as longitude, latitude and altitude within a new DNS resource record, called LOC record. Although this record is not widely established, it still holds information according to the location of a relating (sub)network or host. Since this may be a security risk, accuracy and reliability are depending on the responsible administration [31, 32].

GeoCluster divides the entire IP address space into blocks or clusters. The basic assumption is that all IP addresses of a cluster can be found in the same region. Thus, based on the allocation of a cluster to a geographic region, the actual location of the destination system is suggested. Consequently, in order to assign a logical address to a cluster, extensive information on the general distribution of the IP portfolio is required. This information is obtained by the evaluation of Border Gateway Protocol (BGP) routing tables/BGP address prefixes, *Whois* databases and information gathered from other sources such as ISPs or registry data from Service Providers. Due to the fact that the records of the databases are usually not checked intensely for correctness, a deliberate falsification is possible. The same applies to the *Whois* protocol. A mapping of a single IP to a precise location is also not easily possible, because usually only the address of the headquarters of the owner is deposited. This in turn brings no benefit if the corresponding autonomous system is geographically widely distributed.

Active (Measurement-Based) Strategies
In comparison to strategies based on IP address mapping, measurement-based approaches are inferring the approximate geographical location of a host, either through **active delay measurement by probing the target system**, or passive traffic analysis which does not insert additional packets [25]. To be successful, passive techniques require appropriate measurement equipment [33] as well as a traffic generating target systems. Furthermore, it is necessary that this traffic passes installed monitoring systems [17].

GeoPing: Common approaches like *GeoPing* [15] are working with well known location information of reference hosts, also called *Landmarks* or *Vantage Points* [12, 15]. *GeoPing* is a method that utilizes the correlation between latency values (such as Round Trip Time; RTT), and a geographical distance [34]. The existence of this relationship is a fundamental part of the GeoPing algorithm and at the same time represents a major challenge. In contrast to conventional opinions, that such a correlation does not exist, Ziviani et al. confirm their very existence [35]. The conclusion to the geographical position of a host is done using so-called landmarks (entities with known location). For this purpose, the minimum RTT of the client to the landmarks is measured and the results are then transferred to a map (see Figure 1). The granularity of the results depends largely on the amount and location of usable landmarks [35]. Also distortion caused by, for example, routing loops, the last mile and safety aspects represent fundamental problems in locating an IP address. The accuracy of the results provided in GeoPing is limited to a discrete solution space, which in this context means a concrete landmark and not a region. GeoPing has an important shortcoming, since it relies on a discrete set of possible geographical locations. To overcome this, techniques like *Constraint-based Geolocation* have been

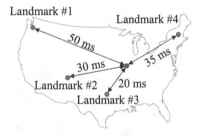

Fig. 1. Functionality of GeoPing

introduced [36], which are using multilateration and are resulting in continuous reliability areas for position estimation.

Constraint Based Geolocation (CBG) was developed to deal with the problems of a discrete solution space for the localization, using landmarks (see GeoPing) [6]. In "Constraint-based geolocation of internet hosts" [37] Gueye et al. provide an approach based on multilateration (see Figure 2), where the position of a host is also determined based on the distance to known landmarks. Here, a continuous solution space is achieved by using two values: a minimum and a maximum distance. Based on latency measurements of signals in fiber optic cables as well as the assumption that up to the last mile (respectively satellite links) almost all lines are made of fiber, the theoretical minimum distance is assumed to be $min = \frac{2}{3}c$; where c is the speed of light [38] (represented in Figure 2 by complete circles), the maximum distance is represented by $max = c$ (represented in Figure 2 with the use of dashed circles). The intersection over all discovered circular functions (minimum and maximum distance) is used to determine a geographic region whose center is assumed to be the exact position [37]. CBG deliberately makes an overestimation of the upper limit to ensure that the solution space is not empty. This, however, at the same time increases the intersection and thus the potential target area. Accuracy is influenced by the number of available landmarks [35] and their positions. A fundamental problem in this case are firewalls, proxies and Intrusion Detection Systems. Since CBG exclusively uses Ping-based methods to determine the delay, it can be assumed that many measurements are faulty.

Hybrid Approaches
Basically, hybrid approaches are combining delay measurement and IP mapping-based strategies to increase accuracy and reliability of the location estimation by overcoming the respective general limitations.

Topology Based Geolocation (TBG) is an evolved variant of CBG, also taking topological aspects into account and thus increasing the accuracy significantly. TBG is only an extended version of the CBG-algorithm and thus raises the same problems. In addition, the reduction of errors is done at the expense of performance.

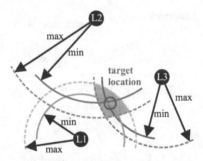

Fig. 2. Multilateration used in Constraint Based Geolocation [38, 39]

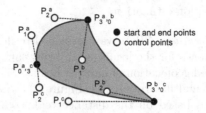

Fig. 3. Octant - Bézier Graph [40]

Octant is a modular framework for Geolocation, which uses a variety of geometric curves, known as Bézier curves, to determine the physical location of a target system, as well as positive and negative conditions [6, 40] (see Figure 3). The framework, developed by Wong et al. [40], was built on the results of TBG and extends this approach by using network nodes of the path towards the client as additional landmarks. The modular design enables Octant to formulate additional constraints that can limit a possible geographic region significantly. These constraints are based on collected demographic data, for example, and may limit the location of a possible site to inhabited areas. Other possibilities are the introduction of information from RIRs and the use of Geoservice providers such as MaxMind or Quova. Nevertheless, also Octant has the same problems TBG or CBG has.

Geolocation IPv6

In general, IP mapping-based as well as measurement-based approaches can be applied for geolocating IPv6 addresses, since the basic principles are protocol independent. Thus, the same limitations apply. Considering the enhanced address space of IPv6 by factor 2^{96} and new introduced features, certain further constraints have emerged. The larger address space itself has no direct implications from the point of *Geolocation*. However, due to Stateless Address Autoconfiguration (SLAAC) and a discontinuity of the Dynamic Host Configuration Protocol (DHCP), the distribution of IP addresses is differently in comparison to its predecessor. In combination with the abolishment of Network Address Translation (NAT), an opportunity to track a particular host is offered. Basically this is possible, since the *Interface Identifier*, a part of the IPv6 address, is partly derived from the MAC address of the corresponding network interface [9, 17]. This problem has already been addressed by randomization, although it is not common for every device and implementation [41, 42]. Considering that, according to Trostle et al. [41] an IPv6 address narrows the approximate physical location of its relating host to at least city level.

Overview of Methods and Approaches

Table 1 provides a brief overview of methods and approaches for Geolocation. Column one lists some of the previously discussed methods. The second column indicates whether the approach relies on the use of landmarks. The third column indicates whether the approach uses active/passive methods or a combination (hybrid). The fourth column provides information about the solution space. Column number five indicates whether the approach is suitable for IPv4 and/or IPv6. Finally, resources needed referring to technical (amount of devices, knowledge etc.) as well as economical aspects are listed in column six.

Table 1. Overview of Geolocation approaches

METHOD	LANDMARKS REQUIRED	PASSIVE/ ACTIVE/HYBRID	SOLUTION SPACE	IP VERSION	RESOURCES/ EFFORT
Geoservices	-	passive	discrete	4 & 6	middle
Address block based	-	passive	discrete	4 & 6	low
Whois RIR	-	passive	discrete	4 & 6	low
Analysis of FQDN	-	passive	discrete	4 & 6	middle
DNS LOC record	-	passive	discrete	4 & 6	low
Whois DNS	-	passive	discrete	4 & 6	low
GeoCluster	-	passive	discrete	4 & 6	middle
GeoTrack	-	passive	discrete	4 & 6	middle
NetGeo	-	passive	discrete	4	low
IPv6 IP-LOC	-	active/passive	discrete	6	middle
Pure delay measuring	√	active/passive	discrete/continuous	4 & 6	high
CBG	√	hybrid	continuous	4 & 6	high
TBG	√	hybrid	continuous	4 & 6	high
Octant	√	hybrid	continuous	4 & 6	high

2.3   Evaluation of Related Work

Performing an evaluation of the approaches presented is not easy (see Table 2). This is mainly due to the fact, that (i) not all of them publish information about the corresponding accurateness and (ii) the source code is not publicly available. Since NetGeo was officially discontinued in 1999 and thus is no longer developed and - as a consequence - is no longer fully available as a web-based solution, this approach is no longer considered for further considerations within this paper [43, 44]. Due to the lack of access to the information needed, GeoCluster and GeoTrack are also not considered within the architecture and the corresponding Proof of Concept (PoC) [34].

3   Overview of our Architecture

The previous section has shown that each strategy is subject to certain restrictions. E.g., the accuracy is too low, a complex infrastructure is needed for the execution of the programs or no selection of active or passive measurements is possible. Following the idea of Endo et al., we already presented a new algorithm which combines several Geolocation techniques to increase the accuracy [45]. The algorithm is able to locate IPv4 addresses with a high accuracy of 99 percent on country level, outperforming current approaches (see Table 2). Because of the (i) usage-limitation to single IP addresses and (ii) the restriction to IPv4 addresses, it was not an appropriate solution for building comprehensive datasets based on IP blocks or ranges, nor a future-oriented solution (in terms of IPv6). Therefore, we present a new algorithm for the Geolocation of IPv6 addresses and IP ranges.

Table 2. Evaluation of Related Work

METHOD	LOCALISATION LEVEL	ACCURACY
IP2GEO	Country/ISP	98%
(GeoPing,GeoCluster, GeoTrack) [46]	Region	75%
	City	63%
CBG [37]	Western Europe *(Median Error)*	below 25 km
	U.S. *(Median Error)*	below 100 km
OCTANT [47]	*Median Error*	22 miles
STRUCTON [48]	Province	93,5%
	City	87,4%
Our Approach [45]		
PARANOID MODE	Country	99,78%
	City	87,57%
REGULAR MODE	Country	99,78%
	City	90,49%

3.1   Components of the Algorithm

Our new algorithm is built from components as follows:

Geodatabases
Since geodatabases are commonly proprietary and the methodologies employed by geoservice providers (to build and maintain them) are neither clear nor publicly available, their consistency and accuracy is considered questionable [49]. But according to Poese et al. [22] such datasets are providing correct geographic locations at country level in 96% to 98% of the cases, at least in terms of IPv4. Additional other studies have revealed similar results [21, 23].

Regarding IPv6, to the best of our knowledge, no comprehensive research, except Zander [50], has been published. But even in this case, it can be assumed that at least on a country basis, those sets are providing correct location estimations depending on the geoservice provider. Although 96% to 98% (for IPv4) is quite high, we have decided to crosscheck the information with other geographic data in order to improve the results. The former PoC uses four geodatabases for a first coarse-grained location estimation and to limit the possible solution space by restricting further steps to particular countries. Therefore, it is obvious to use the same geoservice providers (MaxMind, HostIP, IP2Location and IPInfoDB) again [19, 51–53]. However, current investigations have shown that IP2Location and IPInfoDB are now under the same administration and therefore provide the same results (IPInfoDB uses the IP2Location Lite version and refers to the IP2Location Commercial version) [54]. Moreover, even the free databases are only available after a registration, which was not possible during our work, because neither a registration email nor further information could be obtained.

HostIP, a database mainly relying on voluntary information, has been evaluated as less accurate than the other ones [22, 23] and thus has the lowest influence on the location estimation within the former PoC. As, the database not available in the Internet any longer, HostIP is therefore not presenting a suitable alternative.

In comparison, MaxMind has been evaluated several times and is also the only provider which was analyzed in terms of IPv6 [50]. In addition it "is one of the pioneers in geolocation, founded in 2002, and it provides a range of databases" [55] as well as monthly updates and APIs for different programming respectively script languages like Perl and C.

Because of the lack of free and appropriate alternatives, MaxMind is now the only geoservice provider left for an adaption within the scope of the PoC. In addition, MaxMind provides different levels of accuracy, ranging from (i) country to longitude and latitude, and (ii) free to commercial sets. Although the free databases offered by MaxMind are less accurate than the commercial ones, studies have shown that this difference is slightly lower than expected [21–23, 50]. Keeping this in mind as well as the objectives of our work, the free databases - as shown in Table 3 - are used within the new PoC.

Table 3. Overview of used MaxMind databases (date: July'13). GeoLite City IPv6 is currently in beta state.

Database	Records	ASN	AS Provider	IP Blocks/ Ranges	Country
GeoLite City	1 999 247	-	-	√	√
GeoLite City IPv6	15 095	-	-	√	√
GeoLite ASN	197 447	√	√	√	-
GeoLite ASN IPv6	12 651	√	√	√	-

Databases of RIRs

As already stated, a crosscheck is used within our approach to improve the results. Therefore, after the analysis of the IP address (based on geodatabases) is performed, data of the RIRs is used for the verification of the results. Therefore, the cost-free *Whois*-service is integrated into the algorithm. Unfortunately, the different RIRs are using different query and output schemes. Because of that, it must be differentiated where the address is registered to execute a correct direct query. Pattern matching and regular expressions are used to analyze and extract the geoinformation from the result sets.

Code Databases

For the further analysis of the fully qualified domain name (FQDN), the algorithm is using code databases. Four types of such databases are available: City-, regional-, airport- and radiobeacon-codes. For the implementation, cumulated databases of the International Air Transport Association (IATA) and Very high frequency Omnidirectional Radio range (VOR) are used. In addition, beacon codes are considered, too. Here, the network entity, the primary DNS server identified by the Start of Authority (SOA) Record and the hops in the catchment area of the target address identified by route tracing are examined. Therefore, the country code of the targets (queried from one of our databases) is used to narrow down the results. Each FQDN is split into its individual segments with the help of pattern matching and regular expressions. The verification of the Geolocation based on code-databases is the last step of the process. In order to merge the output of the three components of the algorithm, different weightings are used based on the concrete usage of the algorithm (see below). In particular, three basic modes are implemented, whereof two are presented in more detail in Section 4: *create* and *verify*.

3.2   Sources of Error

Because of the heterogeneity of the different databases and information sources, different errors are possible. On the one hand, the transfer of million of records into a common format is nontrivial. On the other hand, other aspects have to be considered, e.g., failures when querying the RIR databases or errors in the `traceroute` runs. In detail, different sources of error in the weighting and verification process are:

Geodatabases

As different empirical studies have shown, geodatabases are by far not complete [56–59]. Deliberate or unwanted falsifications are possible within the data sets. As HostIP for instance is filled entirely based voluntary input, this is particularly a risk for corruption. By using multiple verification steps, as used in our algorithm, different results can be recognized and attenuated.

Databases of RIRs

The databases of the RIRs can have errors or can be manipulated as well. Also, there is no standardized query. This strongly hampers the automatic evaluation of addresses.

Code Databases

The most important problem arising by the use of code databases is the overlapping of information. Especially airport- and radiobeacon-codes can have many overlaps among each other.

Therefore, it is recommended to use the country code as the precondition before the verification process (with the code databases) is performed (as done in our PoC). This may lead to additional errors, because a preliminary containment is required.

4 Proof of Concept

Within this section, the PoC (called *geolabel*) for the Geolocation of (IPv6) addresses and IP ranges is presented.

4.1 Program Modes

Two basic program modes are available to cover the requests for assignment, namely:

- *Create:* The mode *create* is one of the three basic features. It is responsible for obtaining all required resources as well as querying the RIR according to the prefix. In addition, the responses are analyzed in terms of location information and further intelligence.
- *Verify:* The *verify* mode is executed after the *create* mode and tries to verify the extracted location information by comparing it with different other resources like for example the geodatabases provided by MaxMind. Hereby, the weighting algorithm is applied to respect the significance of the different data sources (see below).

4.2 Weighting Algorithm

With regard to *Geolocation*, the *verify* mode is quite important, since it compares different sources according to their location estimation. Here, each source has to be weighted after certain aspects: The first stage of the *verify* mode is to obtain all needed files, like the MaxMind GeoLite databases. Afterwards all sets are correlated, processed and stored. The data is then used to update missing records. Therefore an Patricia-Trie is used, which allows to compare IP ranges bit by bit. *Geolabel* provides certain parameters which can be used to define the amount of bits to be shifted. The pitfall at this point is that by shifting bits, correct IP prefix to ASN mappings can not be guaranteed. Hence this has to be included in the weighting algorithm. After the updates are done, all tables are correlated to build a dataset for each IP range (extracted in *create* mode). One set consist of an IP range, the relating address prefix and four country codes obtained by the following sources: To determine which country may be inferred for the location estimation of a certain IP range, the country code from each source is considered individually. Based on this, several variables are used to calculate an estimation value for each estimation according to the source, see Table 4. Since it has been demonstrated that geodatabases are accurate by 96% up to 98% [22], the lower bound is chosen to express this fact.

All country estimations are analyzed according to their validity or if they are equal to EU (European Union) or AP (Asian Pacific), which causes a depreciation, since both are usually only used when a specific country code has not

Table 4. Influence of different variables on the estimation value according to the source

Source	Country Code	Netmask	Bit Shifting	Rank
Whois queries	√	√	-	3
MaxMind geodatabases	√	-	√	4
Relating address prefix	√	√	√	2
Relating ASN	√	-	√	1

been designated (for instance satellite connections or the IP range is currently not assigned). For the codes obtained by *Whois* queries and address prefixes, the prefix length respectively the netmask will be taken into consideration. According to Freedman et al. [60] prefixes with short netmasks tend to be more geographically dispersed than longer ones. Considering that, a longer prefix has less influence than a shorter one. All sources which are updated or correlated by bit shifting are weighted additionally, since this may cause wrong assignment. Thus the amount of bits shifted has to be taken into consideration. To determine an overall country inference including an overall estimation value, all obtained country codes as well as the calculated estimations values are correlated. This is done according to the following cases:

1. Decision by majority
2. If two solutions are possible (parity), the decision is made by taking into account the weighting factors
3. If there is no consensus at all, the decision is made according to the rank of each source, whereby the geodatabase has the highest one and thus is chosen in the first place if a country is provided

All countries which are obtained, but not used for the overall country inference, are marked and stored as optional solutions, but without any rating. Thus the solution space is increased.

After that, the analysis of the hops can be done. If it was possible to resolve the complete path, the last two hops are examined. Otherwise, the last hop which can be resolved is examined. Finally, if a VPN connection had been used, the connection is closed down and the program run is completed.

4.3 Known Shortcomings

Different studies have shown [21–23] that geodatabases are commonly based on proprietary methodologies. Thus they are questionable in terms of reliability, scalability and maintainability. Considering that "prefixes within databases are not clearly related to IP prefixes as advertised in the routing system" [22], the datasets may be corrupted by unwanted or intentional falsifications [45]. In addition, data provided by *Whois* may be outdated, incomplete or even hijacked [17]. Thus the obtained information has to be verified. Next to incomplete sets, malformed records have also been observed. For the lack of groundtruth and concrete figures, the weighting algorithm is based on assumptions which have been deduced from research work and studies over the past few years (see also [45, 61]).

In addition, because of missing recent studies in terms of IPv6 Geolocation, the algorithm is applied for both versions in the same way.

5   Evaluation

To evaluate the accuracy of the PoC, testruns with tuples of known IP address to location mappings have been applied. Obtaining an appropriate amount of these tuples is difficult because of a missing groundtruth. Therefore, it is typically done by using personal connections to certain ISPs or other sources which are able to provide such data. Research networks are another way to obtain the needed information and thus are used as well. Two active measurement projects, Archipelago (Ark) maintained by the Cooperative Association for Internet Data Analysis (CAIDA) and RIPE Test Traffic Measurement Service (TTM) [62, 63], are publishing FQDNs as well as relating geographic positions. In addition, all monitors of the RIPE TTM project are equipped with GPS. Another source which has been identified is TOR, which provides the possibility to specify the countries where the *Exit-Node* is located.

The first step of the testing procedure is to build a basic dataset using the *create* mode for both IP versions. Afterwards the obtained information are analyzed by using the *verify* mode, which results in a dataset used in the evaluation procedure. In preparation for the evaluation per se, all testing sets have to be processed to a proper format, since the address information obtained from Ark and RIPE TTM are only provided as FQDN. Thus the IP addresses have to be queried by using the host command or dig, for instance. In addition, all verified sets are used to build a Patricia-Trie with an IP range as (primary) key and the relating country as well as optional ones as value. Next, the created Patricia-Trie was used to match all IP addresses of the evaluation set to a certain range and compared to the relating countries. If the countries are not matching in the first place, optional ones are used for further investigations, resulting in consensus or no match at all and thus no positive rating on a country level.

About 59% of the IP addresses have matched in first or second place (see Table 5). While the datasets provided by Ark and RIPE TTM are considered to be accurate, TOR is still based on assumptions. Without TOR, the matching rate raises up to about 72%. But this value has to be considered carefully, because now the set consists of 163 tuples which is not enough to prove a certain accuracy. Since the results are much lower than expected, it has to be questioned what the reasons therefore are, considering the supposed accuracy of the involved geodatabases. One reason may be that no bit shifts have been applied. There are several possibilities during the whole procedure (of creating and verifying) to adjust the amount of bits shifted and thus to increase the likelihood for a successful IP to country mapping. Another reason may be corrupt or outdated sets from MaxMind, since all tests have been conducted with the same GeoLite databases which have not been updated for over one month. Also, the reliability and accuracy of all sets based on TOR may be disputable.

As already determined, an *accurate* evaluation for IPv6 is not possible *yet* due to the lack of a comprehensive groundtruth. Table 6 shows the current results according to the available test field: Therefore, the PoC has an accuracy of about 79% on country level. Considering the enlarged address space of IPv6 as well as the fact that the results are obtained without any use of bit shifting, the matching rate may be increased by applying certain bit shifts.

Table 5. Evaluation result IPv4, $\mathcal{E}$ describes the amount of test IP addresses, loc_{ipr} describes a match in first and $locOpt_{ipr}$ second place, $\emptyset$ stands for no match at all. $\mathcal{S}$ is the amount of sets to check against, after *verify* mode has been applied

SOURCE	$\mathcal{E}$	loc_{ipr}	$locOpt_{ipr}$	$\emptyset$
ARK	77	46	1	30
RIPE TTM	86	70	0	16
TOR	3 722	2 554	78	1 090
$\sum$	3885	2670	79	1136
% (overall)	100	68.73	2.03	29.24
% (Ark & TTM only)	100	71.17	0.61	28.22

$|\mathcal{S}| = 6\ 032\ 219$

Table 6. Evaluation result IPv6

SOURCE	$\mathcal{E}$	loc_{ipr}	$locOpt_{ipr}$	$\emptyset$
ARK	23	18	0	5
RIPE TTM	36	29	0	7
$\sum$	59	47	0	12
%	100	79.66	0	20.34

$|\mathcal{S}| = 192\ 368$

6   Conclusion and Outlook

Determining the physical position of a network entity is challenging as there is no inherent relationship between an IP address and its geographical location. Thus research facilities, legal authorities as well as industry are showing an increasing interest on certain Geolocation strategies. With the introduction of IPv6, the address space is enhanced by a factor of 2^{96}, rendering this process even more complex in comparison to IPv4. Regarding IPv6 Geolocation in general, except Zander et al. [50], no comprehensive research work is available. Since the groundtruth data set obtained for an evaluation in terms of IPv6 is not sufficient, it is difficult to assess the PoC in this field. Hence, without further information (e.g., how IPv6 is applied in general for instance dispersion according to IP address blocks as well as ASN), it is difficult to evaluate the accuracy of a PoC. During the process of evaluation, some noticeable problems were observed. For example, reserved IP address ranges respectively IP addresses have been identified (192.168.0.0/16 etc.) during all tests; they have been extracted from *Route Views* datasets obtained by CAIDA. Considering that, this implies that they are announced by BGP, which may be subject to router misconfigurations. The PoC is able to map IP addresses and ranges to a specific location on country level. Despite the accuracy problem, the PoC has several advantages towards approaches which are not based on bulk data copies. One of them is that dial-up users can also be located, since at least smaller ISPs tend to assign certain address ranges regionally. The accuracy of the developed approach is currently not as high as expected. The reasons for that may be outdated sets of involved geodatabases. Considering the different results with increased accuracy by using only groundtruth from Ark and Ripe TTM, this leads also to the question if geodatabases are as accurate as they claim to be? Bit shifting may help to address the problem and lead to a significant increase of the matching rate, but this has to be analyzed in further investigations. To build further groundtruth, already existing addresses can be traced and analyzed in terms of relating nameservers. After extracting these information, the SOA as well as the last hops have to be geolocated. Since SOA and last hops tend to be geographically near to the end user [15, 64, 65], it can be inferred that they are located near to the addresses of the groundtruth set. This procedure may be applied recursively on every address which is taken into consideration.

References

1. Internet Corporation for Assigned Names and Numbers (ICANN), Number Resources (2013), https://www.iana.org/numbers
2. CSN interviews Frank Bobo, "You can really do that?" - the power of Geolocation technology, ClientSide News Magazine 10(6), 6–9 (November/December 2010)
3. Mandiant, APT1 - Exposing One of China's Cyber Espionage Units (2013), http://intelreport.mandiant.com/Mandiant_APT1_Report.pdf
4. Jie, C.: Ministry of National Defense, The People's Republic of China, China has no cyber warfare troops: spokesman (2013),
   http://eng.mod.gov.cn/Press/2013-03/01/content_4434894.htm
5. Lam, L.: South China Morning Post, Edward Snowden: US government has been hacking Hong Kong and China for years (2013), http://www.scmp.com/
   news/hong-kong/article/1259508/edward-snowden-us-government-has-been-hacking-hong-kong-and-china
6. Endo, P., Sadok, D.: Whois based geolocation: A strategy to geolocate internet hosts. In: 2010 24th IEEE International Conference on Advanced Information Networking and Applications (AINA), pp. 408–413. IEEE (2010)
7. Postel, J.: Internet Protocol, RFC 791 (1981)
8. BGPexpert.com, 2010 IPv4 Address Use Report (July 27, 2013),
   http://bgpexpert.com/addrspace2010.php
9. Hagen, S.: IPv6. Grundlagen - Funktionalität - Integration, 2nd edn. Sunny Edition (2007)
10. Deering, S., Hinden, R.: Internet Protocol, Version 6 (IPv6), RFC 2460 (1998)
11. Stockebrand, B.: IPv6 in Practice: A Unixer's Guide to the Next Generation Internet, 2007th edn. Springer (2006)
12. Endo, P.T., Sadok, D.F.H.: Whois Based Geolocation: a strategy to geolocate Internet Hosts, IEEE International Conference on Advanced Information Networking and Applications, Tech. Rep. (2010)
13. Dahnert, A.: HawkEyes: An advanced IP Geolocation approach: IP Geolocation using semantic and measurement based techniques. In: Cybersecurity Summit, Second Worldwide (WCS) (June 2011)

14. Eriksson, B., Barford, P., Maggs, B., Nowak, R.: Posit: An Adaptive Framework for Lightweight IP Geolocation, BU/CS, Tech. Rep. (July 2011)
15. Padmanabhan, V.N., Subramanian, L.: An investigation of geographic mapping techniques for internet host, ACM SIGCOMM, Tech. Rep. (2001)
16. Stiemert, L.: Geolokalisation - Verfahren und Methoden, Seminararbeit, Universität der Bundeswehr München, Institut für Technische Informatik (October 2011) (unpublished)
17. Thorvaldsen, Ø. E.: Geographical location of internet hosts using a multi-agent system, Ph.D. dissertation, Norwegian University of Science and Technology (2006)
18. Guo, C., Liu, Y., Shen, W., Wang, H.J., Yu, Q., Zhang, Y.: Mining the web and the internet for accurate ip address geolocations, INFOCOM, Tech. Rep. (2009)
19. MaxMind, Inc., MaxMind Geolocation Service (August 19, 2013), http://www.maxmind.com
20. Quova, Inc., Quova's geolocation services (August 19, 2013), http://www.quova.com/
21. Huffaker, B., Fomenkov, M., Claffy, K.: Geocompare: a comparison of public and commercial geolocation databases, Network Mapping and Measurement Conference (NMMC), Tech. Rep. (May 2011)
22. Poese, I., Kaafar, M.A., Donnet, B., Gueye, B., Uhlig, S.: IP Geolocation Databases: Unreliable? Deutsche Telekom Lab./TU Berlin, Germany, Tech. Rep. (March 2011)
23. Shavitt, Y., Zilberman, N.: A Study of Geolocation Databases, School of Electrical Engineering, Tech. Rep. (July 2010)
24. Laki, S., Mátray, P., Hága, P., Sebők, T., Csabai, I., Vattay, G.: Spotter: A Model Based Active Geolocation Service, IEEE INFOCOM, Tech. Rep. (2011)
25. Laki, S., Mátray, P., Hága, P., Csabai, I., Vattay, G.: A model based approach for improving router geolocation. Computer Networks 54, 1490–1501 (2010)
26. Siwpersad, S.S., Gueye, B., Uhlig, S.: Assessing the geographic resolution of exhaustive tabulation for geolocating internet hosts. In: Claypool, M., Uhlig, S. (eds.) PAM 2008. LNCS, vol. 4979, pp. 11–20. Springer, Heidelberg (2008)
27. Daigle, L.: WHOIS Protocol Specification, RFC 3912 (September 2004)
28. Moore, D., Periakaruppan, R., Donohoe, J., Claffy, K.: Where in the world is netgeo.caida.org? INET, Tech. Rep. (2000)
29. Mockapetris, P.: Domain Names - Concepts and Facilities, RFC 1034 (1987)
30. Internet Assigned Numbers Authority (IANA), IANA (March 1, 2013), http://www.iana.org/
31. Davis, C., Vixie, P., Goodwin, T., Dickinson, A.: A means for expressing location information in the domain name system, RFC 1876 (1996)
32. Wang, Y., Burgener, D., Flores, M., Kuzmanovic, A., Huang, C.: Towards Street-Level Client-Independent IP Geolocation, USENIX, Tech. Rep. (März 2011)
33. Coppens, J., Markatos, E.P., Novotny, J., Polychronakis, M., Smotlacha, V., Ubik, S.: SCAMPI - a scaleable monitoring platform for the Internet. In: Proceedings of the 2nd International Workshop on Inter-Domain Performance and Simulation, IPS 2004 (March 2004)
34. Padmanabhan, V., Subramanian, L.: An investigation of geographic mapping techniques for internet hosts. In: ACM SIGCOMM Computer Communication Review, vol. 31, pp. 173–185. ACM (2001)
35. Ziviani, A., Fdida, S., de Rezende, J., Duarte, O.: Improving the accuracy of measurement-based geographic location of internet hosts. Computer Networks 47(4), 503–523 (2005)
36. Gueye, M.C.B., Ziviani, A., Fdida, S.: Constraint-based geolocation of internet hosts, IEEE/ACM Transactions on Networking, Tech. Rep. (2004)

37. Gueye, B., Ziviani, A., Crovella, M., Fdida, S.: Constraint-based geolocation of internet hosts. In: Proceedings of the 4th ACM SIGCOMM Conference on Internet Measurement, pp. 288–293. ACM (2004)
38. Gueye, B., Uhlig, S., Ziviani, A., Fdida, S.: Leveraging buffering delay estimation for geolocation of internet hosts. In: Boavida, F., Plagemann, T., Stiller, B., Westphal, C., Monteiro, E. (eds.) NETWORKING 2006. LNCS, vol. 3976, pp. 319–330. Springer, Heidelberg (2006)
39. Laki, S., Mátray, P., Hága, P., Sebok, T., Csabai, I., Vattay, G.: Spotter: A model based active geolocation service. In: 2011 Proceedings of the IEEE INFOCOM, pp. 3173–3181. IEEE (2011)
40. Wong, B., Stoyanov, I., Sirer, E.: Octant: A comprehensive framework for the geolocalization of internet hosts. In: Proceedings of the NSDI, vol. 7 (2007)
41. Trostle, J., Matsuoka, H., Tariq, M.M.B., Kempf, J., Kawahara, T., Jain, R.: Cryptographically protected prefixes for location privacy in ipv6. In: Martin, D., Serjantov, A. (eds.) PET 2004. LNCS, vol. 3424, pp. 142–166. Springer, Heidelberg (2005)
42. Heuse, M.: Recent advances in IPv6 insecurities, 27th Chaos Communication Congress (27c3) (December 2010)
43. Moore, D., Periakaruppan, R., Donohoe, J., Claffy, K.: Where in the world is netgeo. caida. org. INET (2000)
44. Cooperative Association for Internet Data Analysis. NetGeo, http://www.caida.org/tools/utilities/netgeo/
45. Koch, R., Golling, M., Rodosek, G.D.: Advanced Geolocation of IP Addresses. In: International Conference on Communication and Network Security (ICCNS), pp. 1–10 (2013)
46. Jgsoft Associates. IP2Geo: Frequently Asked Questions, How accurate is IP-Country-Region-City-ISP database? (2013), http://www.ip2geo.net/ip2location/ip-country-region-city-isp-faq.html
47. Wong, B., Stoyanov, I., Sirer, E.G.: Geolocalization on the internet through constraint satisfaction. In: Proceedings of the 3rd Conference on USENIX Workshop on Real, Large Distributed Systems, p. 1 (2006)
48. Guo, C., Liu, Y., Shen, W., Wang, H.J., Yu, Q., Zhang, Y.: Mining the web and the internet for accurate ip address geolocations. In: IEEE INFOCOM 2009, pp. 2841–2845. IEEE (2009)
49. Gueye, B., Uhlig, S., Fdida, S.: Investigating the Imprecision of IP Block-Based Geolocation. In: Uhlig, S., Papagiannaki, K., Bonaventure, O. (eds.) PAM 2007. LNCS, vol. 4427, pp. 237–240. Springer, Heidelberg (2007)
50. Zander, S.: How Accurate is IP Geolocation Based on IP Allocation Data? Centre for Advanced Internet Architectures (CAIA), Tech. Rep. (May 2012)
51. HostIP, My IP Address Lookup and GeoTargeting Community Geotarget IP Project (July 29, 2013), http://www.hostip.info
52. IP2Location (July 29, 2013), http://www.ip2location.com/
53. IPInfoDB (July 28, 2013), http://ipinfodb.com/
54. IPInfoDB. IPInfoDB - Free IP Address Geolocation Tools (September 09, 2013), http://ipinfodb.com/
55. Srinivasan, K., Venkatasubramanian, K.: Geography of the web - Design and Analysis of Algorithm, CSE 450/598, Arizona State University, Tech. Rep. (2003)
56. Huffaker, B., Fomenkov, M., Claffy, K.: Geocompare: a comparison of public and commercial geolocation databases. Technical Report, network, Mapping and Measurement Conference (NMMC) (May 2011)

57. Poese, I., Kaafar, M.A., Donnet, B., Gueye, B., Uhlig, S.: Ip geolocation databases: Unreliable? Deutsche Telekom Lab./TU Berlin, Technical Report (March 2011)
58. Siwpersad, S.S., Gueye, B., Uhlig, S.: Assessing the geographic resolution of exhaustive tabulation for geolocating internet hosts. In: Claypool, M., Uhlig, S. (eds.) PAM 2008. LNCS, vol. 4979, pp. 11–20. Springer, Heidelberg (2008)
59. Shavitt, Y., Zilberman, N.: A study of geolocation databases, School of Electrical Engineering, Technical Report (July 2010)
60. Freedman, N.F.M.J., Vutukuru, M., Balakrishnan, H.: Geographic Locality of IP Prefixes, Internet Measurement Conference (IMC), Tech. Rep. (2005)
61. Stiemert, L.: Localisation and Advanced Evaluation of IP-Addresses with Focus on IPv6, Master's thesis, Institut für Technische Informatik, Universität der Bundeswehr München, Germany (2013), https://www.unibw.de/inf3/forschung/dreo/publikationen/ba-und-ma/2013_Stiemert-Geolocation.pdf
62. The Cooperative Association for Internet Data Analysis (CAIDA), Cooperative Association for Internet Data Analysis (March 01, 2013), http://www.caida.org/
63. RIPE Network Coordination Centre (RIPE NCC), Test Traffic Measurement Service (June 27, 2013), https://www.ripe.net/data-tools/stats/ttm/test-traffic-measurement-service/
64. Gummadi, K.P., Saroiu, S., Gribble, S.D.: King: Estimating Latency between Arbitrary Internet End Hosts. ACM IMW, Tech. Rep. (November 2002)
65. Leonard, D., Loguinov, D.: Turbo King: Framework for Large-Scale Internet Delay Measurements. INFOCOM, Tech. Rep. (2008)

Fast Scalar Multiplication on Elliptic Curve Cryptography in Selected Intervals Suitable for Wireless Sensor Networks

Youssou Faye[1], Herve Guyennet[1], Ibrahima Niang[2], and Yanbo Shou[1]

[1] Femto-st DISC, Franche-Comte University, France
yfaye@femto-st.fr, hguyenne@femto-st.fr, yshou@femto-st.fr
[2] Department of Mathematics and Computer Sciences, UCAD University, Senegal
iniang@ucad.sn

Abstract. In Wireless Sensor Networks (WSNs), providing a robust security mechanism with limited energy resources is very challenging because of sensor node's limited resources. Symmetric-key can fulfill the requirement, but if the number of nodes is large, asymmetric-key cryptography is the best natural method because of its scalability. Asymmetric-key cryptography is power-hungry; nevertheless, Elliptic Curve Cryptosystems (ECC) are feasible and more flexible for sensor nodes. Scalar multiplication is the most widely used operation on ECC. Various methods for fast scalar multiplication are based on the binary/ternary representation of the scalar. In this paper, we present a novel technique to make fast scalar multiplication on ECC over prime field for light-weight embedded devices like sensor nodes. Our method significantly reduces the computation of scalar multiplication by an equivalent representation of points based on point order in a given interval. Since our technique can act as a support for most existing methods, after an analytical and efficiency analysis, we implement and evaluate its performance in different scenarios.

Keywords: Elliptic Curve Cryptography, Fast Scalar Multiplication, Wireless Sensor Networks.

1 Introduction

Security in Wireless Sensor Networks has attracted more and more attention in recent years. Symmetric cryptography is the most suitable application in constrained platforms such as sensor devices. For a large number of devices, the natural method employed is the asymmetric key cryptography algorithm because of its scalability. Compared to other asymmetric cryptosystems like RSA, Elliptic Curve Cryptography is an emerging favorite due to its shorter key length requirements for the same level of security strength [1]. The mathematical hierarchy of elliptic curve involves three arithmetic levels: scalar arithmetic, point arithmetic and field arithmetic [2]. Point operations involve points addition and

G. Wang et al. (Eds.): CSS 2013, LNCS 8300, pp. 171–182, 2013.
© Springer International Publishing Switzerland 2013

doubling, tripling or quadrupling (or similar operations). Scalar multiplication denoted by kP where P represents a point on the ellipic curve and k represents a scalar. The scalar multiplication is the central and most time-consuming operation in ECC because it is used for key generation, encryption/decryption of data and signing/verification of digital signatures. To perform fast computation of scalar multiplication, which is the major computation involved in ECC, much research has been devoted to the point arithmetic level and the scalar arithmetic [3-10]. On the scalar arithmetic level, the double-and-add technique is the traditional binary algorithm which is based on points operations, namely doubling of a point and addition of points. Also, well-known algorithms, such as Non-Adjacent Form (NAF), window NAF, and sliding window [3], [9], can effectively reduce the number of point operations. Again, some other algorithms, such as double-base chains, have been developed to compute faster scalar multiplication by using binary and ternary representation[4-6]. Thus, algorithms, based on the aforementioned algorithms, optimize faster scalar multiplication[7], [8], [10].

In addition, on point arithmetic, some schemes use algebraic substitutions of the multiplication operations with squaring operations and other cheaper field operations such as addition, subtraction and multiplication or division by a small constant [10].

Recently, a new concept of using multiprocessor architectures to process several operations of scalar multiplication simultaneously has been developed. At the point arithmetic level, some algorithms parallelize ECC formulas to reduce the time complexity of scalar multiplication [11]. At the scalar arithmetic level, the algorithm in [12] parallelizes the series of doubling and addition operations of a point on the binary algorithm with two processor architectures. For other solutions, parallelization is done by partitioning the scalar into n equal-length bit substrings on multiprocessor architectures [13],[14]. In very recent research, this partitioning technique is used on the sensor nodes in [15].

In this paper, we propose a method to accelerate scalar multiplication. For a given scalar multiplication kP, we replace it with an equivalent representation dP where the scalar $d < k$. Our technique is based on point order and the negative of point. Current research shows this is the first method based on this technique. The proposed technique has the same level of security and retains all the advantages of ECC. All the above mentioned algorithms can basically use our technique to perform faster computation on scalar multiplication.

The rest of this paper is organized as follows: Section 2 describes some preliminaries about ECC over prime fields; in Section 3, we present our new scalar reduction. After outlining the context of our contribution (Section 3.1), we describe the new scalar reduction (Section 3.2), and make respectively, an analytical evaluation and efficiency analysis (Section 3.3) and (Section 3.4). In order to verify our claims we implemented a simulator in Java and analyze its performance (Section 3.5). Finally, Section 4 is related to our conclusions and perspectives.

2   Preliminaries on Elliptic Curves over Prime Fields

In this section, a brief background description about ECC over finite prime fields is given. An elliptic curve E over finite field $\mathbb{F}$ (of order n) denoted by $E(\mathbb{F})$ can be defined by the long Weierstrass equation [2]:

$$E : y^2 + a_1xy + a_3y = x^3 + a_2x^2 + a_4x + a_6 . \tag{1}$$

where a_1, a_2, a_3, a_4 *and* a_6 are elements in $\mathbb{F}$.

The field generally used in cryptography relates to the prime field denoted by $\mathbb{F}_p$ where p= q^m and q a prime number called the characteristic of $\mathbb{F}_p$. If $q^m = p$, $\mathbb{F}_p$ is called a prime field. In this paper, we work with a prime field $\mathbb{F}_p$, where $p > 3$. For prime fields, if the characteristic is more than 3, the Weierstrass equation can transform to:

$$E : y^2 = x^3 + ax + b . \tag{2}$$

where a and b $\in \mathbb{F}_p$.

To be used for cryptography, the necessary condition is the discriminant of polynomial:

$$f(x) = x^3 + ax + b, \triangle = 4a^3 + 27b^2 \neq 0. \tag{3}$$

The points (x, y), where integer coordinates x, y satisfy the above equation and the point at infinity denoted by ∞ is also a point on the curve and form an abelian group. The group law mainly consists of two basic operations: point doubling $(2P)$ and point addition $(P+Q)$ where P and Q are two different points on the curve.

Given $P = (x_p, y_p)$ and $Q = (x_q, y_q)$ two points ($\neq \infty$) which are on the elliptic curve over $\mathbb{F}_p$ denoted by $E(\mathbb{F}_p)$. The points addition $P+Q = (x_{pq}, y_{pq})$ or point doubling $2P = P+Q = (x_{pq}, y_{pq})$ if $P = Q$ can be calculated as:

$$\begin{cases} x_{pq} = \lambda^2 - x_p - x_q \\ y_{pq} = \lambda(x_p - x_{p+q}) - y_p \end{cases} \tag{4}$$

$$\begin{cases} \lambda = \dfrac{y_q - y_p}{x_q - x_p}, if P \neq Q \\ \lambda = \dfrac{3x_p^2 + a}{2y_p}, if P = Q \end{cases} \tag{5}$$

The negative of a point only involves the change of at most one of its coordinate values in the point representation. For example, the negative of a point $P = (x_p, y_p)$ is its reflection in the x-axis: the point $-P$ is $(x_p, -y_p)$. Notice that for each point P on an elliptic curve, the point $-P$ is also on the curve.

3   New Scalar Reduction Method

3.1   Context

In this section, we present a new improvement in the scalar arithmetic level. This improvement is based on specific reduction of the scalar in a selected interval.

Assume that $\mathbb{F}_p$ has a characteristic greater than 3. Let $E(\mathbb{F}_p)$ be an elliptic curve over a prime field. Let $\#E(\mathbb{F}_p)$ denotes the number of points of the elliptic curve over $E(\mathbb{F}_p)$. $\#E(\mathbb{F}_p)$ is also called the order of group of points. A well-known theorem of Hasse states that [2]: $|\#E(\mathbb{F}_p)$ - p - $1 \leq 2\sqrt{p}$ |. Let $\mathbb{G}$ be a cyclic group of $E(\mathbb{F}p)$ of order n generated by a base point P (namely generator point). The points in $\mathbb{G}$ are expressed as multiples of P: $\mathbb{G}=\langle P\rangle=\{\infty, P, 2P, \ldots,$ $(n\text{-}2)P, (n\text{-}1)P\}\subseteq E(\mathbb{F}_p)$ with $nP=\infty$. The order of point P (denoted by $\#P$) is n.

3.2   Description of Our New Scalar Reduction Method

In our approach, we replace the point, namely kP, in the main scalar multiplication operation by an equivalent representation point dP (k and d two scalars and $k > d$) in the interval $[\lfloor n/2\rfloor+1, n\text{-}1]$, where $\lfloor n/2\rfloor$ denotes the integer-part function of $n/2$. As the negative of a point is obtained freely, we use it to make fast computation. Given the point $P=(x_p, y_p)$ in affine coordinates, to compute the negative (inverse) of the point $kP=(x_{kp}, y_{kp})$, we can compute $kP=(x_{kp}, y_{kp})$ and then change the sign on the y-coordinate (y_{kp}). Notice that for each point P on an elliptic curve, the point -P is also on the curve. Thus, we can replace the point kP by an equivalent point representation dP utilizing the negative of point. For a secret scalar k (integer number), by the point kP, we get an equivalent points representation dP by following the equations, in a general case:

$$
\begin{cases}
a. & \text{If } k > n \,, kP = dP \quad \text{where } d = (k - \lfloor k/2\rfloor.n); \\
b. & \text{If } k \in \,]\lfloor n/2\rfloor, n\text{-}1], kP = dP \quad \text{where } d = (k - n); \\
c. & \text{If } k \in \,]0, \lfloor n/2\rfloor], kP = dP \quad \text{where } d = k; \\
d. & \text{If } k=n \text{ or } 0 \text{ or } -n, kP = \infty; \\
e. & \text{If } k \in [-(n\text{-}1), -\lfloor n/2\rfloor[, kP = dP \quad \text{where } d = (n + k); \\
f. & \text{If } k \in [-\lfloor n/2\rfloor, 0[, kP = dP \quad \text{where } d = k; \\
g. & \text{If } k <\text{- } n, kP=dP \quad \text{where } d=k+n.\lfloor|k|/2\rfloor.
\end{cases}
\tag{6}
$$

In Elliptic Curve Cryptography $k \in \,]0, (n\text{-}1)]$, we get an equivalent representation for point dP by equations (6.b) and (6.c) following:

$$
\begin{cases}
(b) & \text{If } k \in \,]\lfloor n/2\rfloor, n\text{-}1], kP = dP \quad \text{where } d = (k - n); \\
(c) & \text{If } k \in \,]0, \lfloor n/2\rfloor], kP = dP \quad \text{where } d = k.
\end{cases}
$$

We use an example of the above description in order to better express our reduction method.

Example: We choose the prime number $p =23$. Note that this process mainly reflects our new protocol. In real cases, the p is much bigger than this. If we consider the elliptic E over $\mathbb{F}_{23}$ defined by $E(\mathbb{F}_{23})$: $y^2=x^3+x+1$, then $\# E(\mathbb{F}_{23})=28$, $E(\mathbb{F}_{23})$ is a cyclic group. Let $P(0,1)$ be a generator point. The points in $E(\mathbb{F}_{23})$ are shown below:

$P=(0, 1)$ $2P=(6, -4)$ $3P=(3, -10)$ $4P=(-10, -7)$
$5P=(-5, 3)$ $6P=(7, 11)$ $7P=(11, -3)$ $8P=(5, -4)$
$9P=(-4, -5)$ $10P=(12, 4)$ $11P=(1, -7)$ $12P=(-6, 3)$
$13P=(9, -7)$ $14P=(4, 0)$ $15P=(9, 7)$ $16P=(-6, 3)$
$17P=(1, 7)$ $18P=(12, -4)$ $19P=(-4, 5)$ $20P=(5, 4)$
$21P=(11, -3)$ $22P=(7, -11)$ $23P=(-5, -3)$ $24P=(-10, -7)$
$25P=(3, 10)$ $26P=(6, 4)$ $27P=(0, -1)$ $28P=\infty$

For this example, the general and elliptic curve cryptography cases can be shown respectively in Figure 1 and Figure 2. On one hand, we can see the general case from Figure 1 that the points $-34P$, $-6P$, $22P$, $50P$ have the same coordinates. To process the point $-6P$ (the negative of $6P$), we compute the point $6P$ and affix the minus sign to the y-coordinate. Thus, computation of $-6P$ is free and almost equal to computing $6P$. The scalar multiplication using our method in the the general case would be computed as follows:

to calculate $50P$, we compute $-6P$ by applying formula; (6.a)
to calculate $22P$, we compute $-6P$ by applying formula; (6.b)
to calculate $-34P$, we compute $-6P$ by applying formula. (6.g)

On the other hand, for the special case of ECC, we can see from Figure 2 that computing the points from $[15P,16P,.........26P, 27P]$ can be replaced respectively by $[-13P, -12P,.........,-2P, -P]$. In this case, computing $27P$ can be replaced by $-P$ and is almost free.

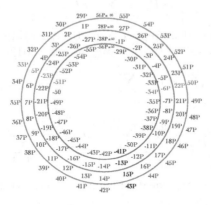

Fig. 1. General elliptic curve case

3.3 Analytical Evaluation

Since sensor nodes are in low-power energy, replacing computation kP by computation dP using formula (6.b) in $[\lfloor n/2 \rfloor+1, n-1]$ can help us deduce faster computation on scalar multiplication. Meanwhile, the scalar k can be chosen

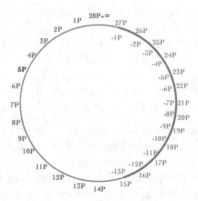

Fig. 2. Elliptic Curve Cryptography case

only in this interval for computation in WSNs. From formula (7), we can scan all scalars in a given interval:

$$\sum_{k=1}^{n-1} kP = \sum_{k=1}^{\lfloor n/2 \rfloor - 1} kP + \lfloor \frac{n}{2} \rfloor P + \sum_{k=\lfloor n/2 \rfloor + 1}^{n-1} kP \qquad (7)$$

where $\displaystyle\sum_{k=\lfloor n/2 \rfloor + 1}^{n-1} kP = \sum_{k=1}^{\lfloor n/2 \rfloor - 1} kP + 2\sum_{k=1}^{\lfloor n/2 \rfloor - 1} kP$

By using our method, if we replace respectively $[15P, 16P, \ldots\ldots 26P, 27P]$ by $[-13P, -12P, \ldots\ldots, -2P, -1P]$ in the interval $[\lfloor n/2 \rfloor + 1, n-1]$ the expression :

$\displaystyle\sum_{k=\lfloor n/2 \rfloor + 1}^{n-1} kP$ can be replaced by $\displaystyle\sum_{k=1}^{\lfloor n/2 \rfloor - 1} |k|P$, see formula (9).

$$\sum_{k=1}^{n-1} kP = 2\sum_{k=1}^{\lfloor n/2 \rfloor - 1} kP + \lfloor \frac{n}{2} \rfloor P + 2\sum_{k=1}^{\lfloor n/2 \rfloor - 1} kP \qquad (8)$$

By using our method, the equation (8) can be replaced by equation (9):

$$\sum_{k=1}^{n-1} kP = \sum_{k=1}^{\lfloor n/2 \rfloor - 1} kP + \sum_{k=1}^{\lfloor n/2 \rfloor - 1} |k|P + \lfloor \frac{n}{2} \rfloor P. \qquad (9)$$

By scanning all scalars k for computation of kP in the interval $[\lfloor n/2 \rfloor + 1, n-1]$, we can see from formulas (8)-(9), that we gain a rate of $\sum_{k=1}^{\lfloor n/2 \rfloor - 1} 2kP$. The speed-up for a given scalar kP is $2(k-(n/2))$. For example, in Figure 2, computing $kP=22P$, is equal to computing $6P$, the speed-up is $2(22-(14/2))= 16P$ since

$16P+ 6P= 22P$. In fact, the complexity of scalar multiplication is determined by the length bit of k which is equal to $\lfloor log_2(k)\rfloor +1$ or $log_2(k)$ if k=2^x, where x is an integer. In binary representation, $log_2(k)$ can be replaced in our method by:

$$log_2(k - 2(k - \frac{n}{2})) = log_2(k) + log_2(k + \frac{n - 2k}{k}) \tag{10}$$

Thus, the speed-up in length bit is:
$$|log_2(k + \frac{n - 2k}{k})| = |log_2(\frac{|d|}{k})|, \text{ where } log_2(k + \frac{n - 2k}{k}) < 0.$$
Since our reduction method is not possible for $n=1$, from Figure 3, we can see in interval $[\lfloor n/2\rfloor +1,$ n-1] the sum of all scalars. For a scalar in $[2, \lfloor n/2\rfloor]$, our method is not used since its design is only for the interval $[\lfloor n/2\rfloor +1,$ n-1]. Consequently, it is very efficient in Figure 3,in which we only consider scalars in this interval. From formula (11), we make the average computation of all scalar k in interval$[\lfloor n/2\rfloor + 1, n - 1]$, where our technique can be applied

$$\frac{1}{n - 1 - \lfloor n/2\rfloor}(\sum_{k=\lfloor n/2\rfloor +1}^{n-1} kP) = \frac{1}{n - \lfloor n/2\rfloor}(\sum_{k=1}^{\lfloor n/2\rfloor -1} kP). \tag{11}$$

The average of scalar k can be found in Figure 4, where we can also apply our technique in the interval$[\lfloor n/2\rfloor +1$, n-1]. Optimization can be done in the interval $[\lfloor n/2\rfloor +1$, n-1] by using only even numbers for order n.

If the order $n >2$ is an even number:$\sum_{k=\lfloor n/2\rfloor +1}^{n-1} kP=3\sum_{k=1}^{\lfloor n/2\rfloor -1} kP.$

If the order $n \geq 3$ is an odd number: $3\sum_{k=1}^{\lfloor n/2\rfloor -1} kP > \sum_{k=\lfloor n/2\rfloor +1}^{n-1} kP \geq 2\sum_{k=1}^{\lfloor n/2\rfloor -1} kP.$ Figure 5 shows the speed-up between even and odd numbers. We can see that if n is even, the speed-up curve is a horizontal line whose equation is y=3. But if n is odd, the line $y=3$ is a horizontal asymptote for the speed-up curve. If we work with even order, the speed is three times faster. If the order is odd, the enhancement is > 2, and < 3.

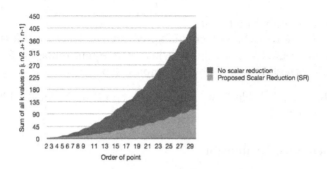

Fig. 3. Sum of all k values function of order n in $[\lfloor n/2\rfloor +1$, n-1]

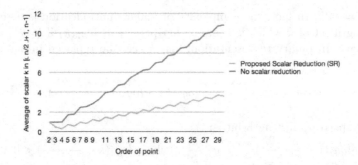

Fig. 4. Average of all k values function of order in $[\lfloor n/2 \rfloor + 1, \text{n-1}]$

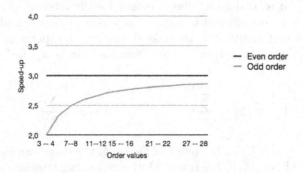

Fig. 5. Speed-up rate between even and odd order

3.4   Efficiency Analysis

The unit of this speed-up can be the length bit or the number of doubling/addition operations. For example, NAF needs $log_2(k)$ doubling and $log_2(k)/3$ addition. In the interval $[\lfloor n/2 \rfloor + 1, n - 1]$, three cases are possible for the speed-up:

- If $log_2(n)$=x, where x is an integer, our method can speed up the scalar multiplication in interval $[\lfloor n/2 \rfloor + 1, n - 1]$ by reducing the length bit of k.
- If $log_2(n)$=x, where x is not an integer, our method can speed up the scalar multiplication only in interval $[2^{\lfloor log_2 \frac{n}{2} \rfloor + 1}, n - 1]$
- If $k= (n-1)$, we reach the maximum speed-up, the length bit of the scalar k is maximum (equal to $log_2(n - 1)$), where it is equal to one bit for d. In this case, our method does not require computation.

From Table 1 and Table 2, we can see the speed-up in length bit for some values of the scalar k.

3.5   Performance Evaluation

To test the performance of our solution, we have implemented a simulator in Java. The program is then run on an Intel Core i5-2520 processor taking into

Table 1. Speed-up S for some values of k for x integer

Values of k	$\lfloor n/2 \rfloor + 1$	$>= (\lfloor n/2 \rfloor + 1)$	(n-1)
Speed-up(bits)	1	$1 < S < log_2(k)$	$log_2(k)$

Table 2. Speed-up S for some values of k for x not integer

Values of k	$2^{\lfloor log_2 \frac{n}{2} \rfloor + 1}$	$>= 2^{\lfloor log_2 \frac{n}{2} \rfloor + 1}$	(n-1)
Speed-up(bits)	1	$1 < S < log_2(k)$	$log_2(k)$

account the computing power difference between this processor and a MSP 430 MCU. During the test, we choose an elliptic curve over $\mathbb{F}_p$ using NIST-192 recommended parameters which are given in Table 3. p is the size of prime field $\mathbb{F}_p$, and a, b are coefficients of the simplified Weierstrass form of our curve. $P(x_P, y_P)$ is chosen as the generator point, and its order equals n.

Table 3. NIST-192 recommended elliptic curve parameters

Parameter	NIST-192 recommended values
p	$2^{192} - 2^{64} - 1$
a	-3
b	0x 64210519 e59c80e7 0fa7e9ab 72243049 feb8deec c146b9b1
x_P	0x 188da80e b03090f6 7cbf20eb 43a18800 f4ff0afd 82ff1012
y_P	0x 07192b95 ffc8da78 631011ed 6b24cdd5 73f977a1 1e794811
n	0x ffffffff ffffffff ffffffff 99def836 146bc9b1 b4d22831

As indicated in equation (6.b), when we need to perform a scalar multiplication kP for cryptographic purpose, we choose $k < n$ where n is the order of the generator point P, which means $nP = \infty$. In addition, theoretically our method works only when $k \in]\lfloor \frac{n}{2} \rfloor, n-1]$. To prove this property, we have chosen 6 values of 192 bits for k which are distributed uniformly in $]0, n-1]$ (see Table 4).

Table 4. Values of k chosen for performance evaluation

k	Value in hexadecimal
$n/6$	0x 2aaaaaaa aaaaaaaa aaaaaaaa 99a5295e 58bca19d 9e2306b2
$n/3$	0x 55555555 55555555 55555555 334a52bc b179433b 3c460d65
$n/2$	0x 7fffffff ffffffff ffffffff ccef7c1b 0a35e4d8 da691418
$2n/3$	0x aaaaaaaa aaaaaaaa aaaaaaaa 6694a579 62f28676 788c1aca
$5n/6$	0x d5555555 55555555 55555555 0039ced7 bbaf2814 16af217a
$n-1$	0x ffffffff ffffffff ffffffff 99def836 146bc9b1 b4d22830

Table 5. Running times (ms) using affine coordinates (SR: Scalar reduction)

NAF	SR	$n/6$	$n/3$	$n/2$	$2n/3$	$5n/6$	$n-1$
		6579	6572	7604	6555	6931	7471
√		6282	6326	5317	6239	6698	5114
	√	6578	6573	7600	6416	6600	27
√	√	6279	6325	5320	6445	6556	28

We have tested our method using both affine and jacobian coordinates, the scalars are represented respectively in binary and NAF form combined with the proposed scalar reduction method. The test results are given in Tables 5 and 6, and illustrated graphically in Figure 6 and 7.

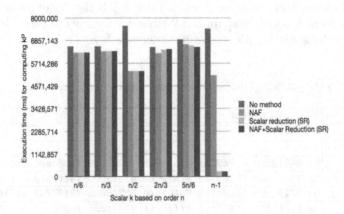

Fig. 6. Running times (ms) using affine coordinates

In both cases, we can notice that, firstly when the scalar is in NAF form, the computation is faster than the one using binary form. Secondly when $k \in]0, \frac{n}{2}]$, we cannot apply the proposed scalar reduction method. However, if $k \in]\frac{n}{2}, n-1]$, we may accelerate slightly the computation by reducing the scalar. Especially when the value of k is close to $n-1$, the computation can be done instantaneously since $(n-1)P = -P$.

Table 6. Running times (ms) using jacobian coordinates (SR: Scalar reduction)

NAF	SR	$n/6$	$n/3$	$n/2$	$2n/3$	$5n/6$	$n-1$
		3066	3102	3621	3072	3202	3520
√		3053	3074	3592	3071	3189	3541
	√	3070	3100	3622	3030	3107	9
√	√	3050	3075	3597	3194	3136	9

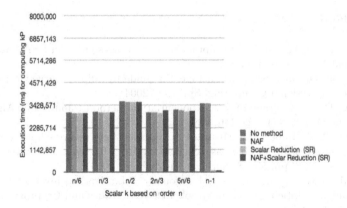

Fig. 7. Running times (ms) using jacobian coordinates

When we use jacobian coordinates, as we don't need to repeat the modular inverse (see equation (5)), the computation is obviously faster than the first case. Same as the results obtained using affine coordinates, our scalar reduction method can be used during the computation only when $k \in]\frac{n}{2}, n - 1]$. When it's applied, the scalar is reduced, and the computation can run faster.

According to the results of performance evaluation, our scalar reduction method does speed up the computation of scalar multiplication on a standard NIST-192 elliptic curve. The acceleration rate strongly depends on the value of the scalar used. The scalar k can be reduced if $k \in]\frac{n}{2}, n - 1]$, and once applied, the computation task can be simplified and carried out more quickly.

4   Conclusion

In this paper, we have proposed a novel method based on point order and the negative of point to speed up the computation of scalar multiplication on elliptic curve cryptosystems. On one hand, the proposed method will significantly reduce the computation time in the interval $[\lfloor n/2 \rfloor + 1, n\text{-}1]$. On the other hand, we show that the usage of even order is more efficient than odd order. Our method is a very suitable tool for embedded devices such as WSNs. Also, it can be easily applied to almost all existing fast scalar multiplication methods as shown in NAF. Thus, that's comparisons are nor required regarding some existing schemes. Additionally, a thorough analysis and simulation based on evaluations will show that the proposed solution does speed up the computation of scalar multiplication on a standard NIST-192 elliptic curve. Our future research plans will be oriented towards experimenting our current technique on real sensor nodes with elliptic curves over finite prime fields.

References

1. Robshaw, M.J.B., Yin, Y.L.: Elliptic Curve Cryptosystems. An RSA Laboratories Technical Note (revised June 27, 1997)
2. Hankerson, D., Menezes, A., Vanstone, S.: Guide to Elliptic Curve Cryptography. Springer Professional Computing. Springer (2004)
3. Gordon, D.M.: A survey of fast exponentiation methods. Journal of Algorithms, Academic Press 27(1), 129–146 (1998)
4. Dimitrov, V.S., Imbert, L., Mishra, P.K.: Efficient and secure elliptic curve point multiplication using double-base chains. In: Roy, B. (ed.) ASIACRYPT 2005. LNCS, vol. 3788, pp. 59–78. Springer, Heidelberg (2005)
5. Ciet, M., Joye, M., Lauter, K., Montgomery, P.L.: Trading inversions for multiplications in elliptic curve cryptography. Designs, Codes and Cryptography 39(2), 189–206 (2006)
6. Méloni, N., Hasan, M.A.: Elliptic curve scalar multiplication combining yao's algorithm and double bases. In: Clavier, C., Gaj, K. (eds.) CHES 2009. LNCS, vol. 5747, pp. 304–316. Springer, Heidelberg (2009)
7. Tian, M., Wang, J., Wang, Y., Xu, S.: An Efficient Elliptic Curve Scalar Multiplication Algorithm Suitable for Wireless Network. In: Second International Conference on Networks Security Wireless Communication and Trusted Computing (NSWCTC), vol. 1, pp. 95–98. IEEE Wuhan, Hubei (2010)
8. Suppakitpaisarn, V., Imai, H., Masato, E.: Fastest Multi-Scalar Multiplication Based on Optimal Double-Base Chains. In: World Congress on Internet Security (WorldCIS 2012), pp. 93–98. IEEE Guelph, ON (2012)
9. Rivain, M.: Fast and Regular Algorithms for Scalar Multiplication over Elliptic Curves. Cryptology ePrint Archive, Report 2011/338 (2011), http://eprint.iacr.org/2011/338.pdf
10. Bernstein, D.J., Lange, T.: Analysis and optimization of elliptic-curve single-scalar multiplication. Finite Fields and Applications, Contemporary Mathematics Series 461, 1–19 (2008)
11. Longa, P., Miri, A.: Fast and Flexible Elliptic Curve Point Arithmetic over Prime Fields. IEEE Transactions on Computers 57(3), 289–302 (2008)
12. Ansari, B., Wu, H.: Parallel Scalar Multiplication for Elliptic Curve Cryptosystems. In: International Conference on Communications, Circuits and Systems, vol. 1, pp. 71–73. IEEE Computer Society (2005)
13. Wu, K., Li, D., Li, H., Yu, C.: Partitioned Computation to Accelerate Scalar Multiplication for Elliptic Curve Crypto-systems. In: 15th International Conference on Parallel and Distributed Systems (ICPADS), pp. 551–555. IEEE, Shenzhen (2009)
14. Lim, C.H., Lee, P.J.: More flexible exponentiation with pre-computation. In: Desmedt, Y.G. (ed.) CRYPTO 1994. LNCS, vol. 839, pp. 95–107. Springer, Heidelberg (1994)
15. Shou, Y., Guyennet, H., Lehsaini, M.: Parallel Scalar Multiplication on Elliptic Curves in Wireless Sensor Networks. In: Frey, D., Raynal, M., Sarkar, S., Shyamasundar, R.K., Sinha, P. (eds.) ICDCN 2013. LNCS, vol. 7730, pp. 300–314. Springer, Heidelberg (2013)

Alert Correlation Algorithms: A Survey and Taxonomy

Seyed Ali Mirheidari[1,2], Sajjad Arshad[2], and Rasool Jalili[2,3]

[1] Computer Engineering Department, Sharif University of Technology, International Campus
[2] Data and Network Security Laboratory (DNSL), Sharif University of Technology
[3] Computer Engineering Department, Sharif University of Technology
mirheidari@kish.sharif.edu, msarshadir@gmail.com,
jalili@sharif.edu

Abstract. Alert correlation is a system which receives alerts from heterogeneous Intrusion Detection Systems and reduces false alerts, detects high level patterns of attacks, increases the meaning of occurred incidents, predicts the future states of attacks, and detects root cause of attacks. To reach these goals, many algorithms have been introduced in the world with many advantages and disadvantages. In this paper, we are trying to present a comprehensive survey on already proposed alert correlation algorithms. The approach of this survey is mainly focused on algorithms in correlation engines which can work in enterprise and practical networks. Having this aim in mind, many features related to accuracy, functionality, and computation power are introduced and all algorithm categories are assessed with these features. The result of this survey shows that each category of algorithms has its own strengths and an ideal correlation frameworks should be carried the strength feature of each category.

Keywords: Network Security, Intrusion Detection System, Alert, Alert Correlation, Attack Scenario, Similarity-based, Knowledge-based, Statistical-based.

1 Introduction

An intrusion detection system (IDS) contains a widespread set of software or hardware whose mission is to detect improper behaviors by receiving information from their network. In terms of data processing types, such systems are divided into two categories: Anomaly-based and Misuse-based IDSs. Anomaly-based IDSs detect abnormal behaviors by checking statistical information about system execution and maintains normal behavioral patterns. Misuse-based IDSs maintain suspicious or attack patterns categories. Whenever the received information is in correspondence with the IDS signature or in contradiction with normal behavioral patterns, an alert is generated. Nowadays, many networks use such systems either commercially or open source versions. However, problems such as bad parameter settings and inappropriate IDS tuning which should be dealt with in a higher level [1]. The existence of such problems makes the alert processing system necessary. Such problems are as follows:

- **Large amount of alerts:** One of the very crucial problems of using intrusion detection systems is the large number of generated alerts by these systems. The main

G. Wang et al. (Eds.): CSS 2013, LNCS 8300, pp. 183–197, 2013.
© Springer International Publishing Switzerland 2013

reasons for this large number of alerts might be imprecise incident definition, incompatibility in network, and sometimes number of real intrusions or illegal behaviors, which tend to mislead the system supervisor from the main attack or the attack goal. Anyhow, the usual number of alerts is too much to enable the system supervisor checking all of them manually. As a result, only a portion of them is checked.

- **Heterogeneous alerts:** The supervisor usually receives a wide range of alerts from different sensors and different sensors generate alerts with different formats. Hence, in order to process the alerts, it is required to normalize them.
- **False alerts and unidentified incidents:** In all types of intrusion detection systems, false in detection are made due to the lack of information describing incidents and inaccuracy of the attack pattern. Thus, a very useful activity of higher level systems is to detect mistakes made by IDSs, and correcting mistakes as much as possible. These mistakes are divided into two categories: wrong reports of illegal or unusual events which even have not occurred or their occurrence has been unsuccessful; and unreported events which must be reported.
- **Inability in connecting current alerts with the previous ones:** Nowadays, most attacks are sequential activities, which the intruders provide many phases for reaching their goals. Detecting such connections among the attack phases is sometimes very difficult, as the pattern of the first attack stage is not necessarily unique all the time and is not definitely determinable. On one hand, some attacks might not be successful due to unusual reasons or the attacker does not some parts of attack due to having direct information sources. On the other hand, the attacker might take another step of an attack in spite of the unsuccessful previous step. Being able to detect several patterns, the system supervisor would have the ability to predict the next attack step and can stop the attack before it reaches its goal.
- **Not providing the reliability level and alert priorities**: The existence of comprehensive factors for evaluating an alert importance and reliability will ease prioritizing assessments for system supervisors. But, many intrusion detection systems do not report a factor for the reliability of generated alerts, and in cases of provided criteria, the presented results are not comparable with other recourse results due to the lack of common standardization among all resources. On the other hand, the importance of an alert depends on the target importance which is not related to the IDSs. So, if a higher level system is able to assess the alert importance and priorities, it would be a valuable help to system administrators to choose alert priorities correctly.

To fulfill these requirements, Alert Correlation Systems are introduced. In the simplest manner, an alert correlation engine functions exactly as the derived meaning of the word "correlation". In fact it correlates alerts in a way that a new meaning is derived. Sometimes the number of events is so many that its manual analysis is impossible. In such cases, the correlation engine can reduce a large amount of information to a manageable rate. In addition, it can identify malicious activities from an overall and abstract view, instead of analyzing each alert separately. In other words, an alert correlation system is a system which receives incidents from various heterogeneous systems, reduces the required information for assessments, removes false alerts, and detects high level attack patterns.

Different algorithms have been introduced in alert correlation. To the best of our knowledge, some surveys have been presented. The first research [2] made a deep review on published papers and available tools with the aim of explaining some differences between them. In another research [3], presented a mapping among framework components and proposed techniques. In this survey, we aim to present taxonomy in which the weaknesses and strengths of previous proposed algorithms are explained. The emphasis of our survey is on some features which help correlation engine designer to propose a more accurate, practical, extendable, and low cost computation power. We believe that our approach gives a better understanding of this area as more literature works are presented and the blind area related to algorithms benefits will be kindled.

The remainder of this paper is outlined as follows. In Section 2, we provide a general categorization on alert correlation algorithms. Each category is completely introduced and its advantages and disadvantages are explained in Section 3, 4, and 5. In Section 6, we compare different algorithms based on various factors and we present conclusion and future work in Section 7.

2 Alert Correlation Algorithms

Alert correlation algorithms can be divided into three categories based on their characteristics: 1) Similarity-based, 2) Knowledge-based and 3) Statistical-based [4]. The similarity-based and statistical-based algorithms need less context information and they are able to correlate only based on similarities between alert features and learned information from previous steps whereas knowledge-based algorithms completely perform base on alert meanings. It has to be known that this categorization is not completely precise and some algorithms are on the edge between two categories. Thus, assigning an algorithm to a category is based on the fact that the algorithm has the most similarity to which one. Each category is introduced in the following subsections and in next sections the most important algorithms will be described.

2.1 Similarity-Based Algorithms

The basis for this category of algorithms is defining factor to compare the similarity of either two alerts or an alert with a cluster of alerts (meta-alert). If an alert or meta-alert has needed similarity, each one of them is merged with the alert or meta-alert and otherwise a new meta-alert is created. Thus, the goal of these algorithms is to cluster similar alerts in time. The most important advantage of these algorithms is that there is no need for precise definition of attack types. Moreover, the correlation can be done only with definition of similarity factors for alerts features.

Three main subcategories are assumed for these types of algorithms. The first subcategory is based on defining very simple rules for expressing relations between alerts. The second subcategory is presented with the goal of identifying basic drawbacks in the network structure. The third subdirectory includes algorithms which produce comparison factors using models based on machine learning. In the following subsections, different researches in each subcategory will be described.

2.2   Knowledge-Based Algorithms

This category is based on a knowledge base of attack definitions. Algorithms existing in this category are divided into two main subcategories: 1) Pre-requisites and Consequences and 2) Scenario. The basis of Pre-requisites and Consequences algorithms is on the definition of pre-requisites and possible occurring results. Thus, each incident is chained to other incidents by a network of conjunction and disjunction combinations and generates the possible network of attacks. Hence, this idea is placed in an higher level than correlation based on features similarities and in a lower level than combining based on pre-defined attack patterns. Although these algorithms do not require precise definition for each attack scenario like scenario-based algorithms, the previous knowledge is necessary for determining pre-requisites and all existing incident results. Scenario algorithms are based on the idea that many intrusions include various steps which must run one by one to success the attack. Thus, low level alerts can be compared with pre-defined intrusion steps and correlate a sequence of alerts related to each attack. Thus, a set of different attack scenarios definitions exist in a knowledge base in this type of algorithm. A list of current attack scenarios are maintained when the correlation system is operating, which this list includes all scenarios that at least one step of them are done recently. By the arrival of a new alert, it is compared to the current scenario and if the possibility is more than a certain threshold, it will attach to the scenario. Otherwise, if the alert is compatible with one of the possible scenario definitions inside the knowledge base, a new current scenario is generated using this alert. The main challenge for these algorithms is definition of attack scenarios even with existing automatic attack scenario learning methods. Also, these algorithms are completely deficient against new attacks.

2.3   Statistical-Based Algorithms

The basic idea of these algorithms is that relevant attacks have similar statistical attributes and a proper categorization can be found by detecting these similarities. These types of algorithms store causal relationships between different incidents and analyses their occurred frequencies in the system education period using previous data statistical analysis and then attack steps are generated. After learning these relationships and being confirmed by the supervisor, this knowledge is used for correlating different attack stages. Pure statistical algorithms do not have any prior knowledge on attack scenarios. But scientific results indicate that using these algorithms is possible only in very specific domains in which domain attributes are taken in account of designing algorithms and otherwise, high error rate exist. In addition, combining data using this algorithm is impossible if the previous sensors provide incomplete or abnormal information. This category is also divided into three subcategories. The first subcategory's goal is to detect alerts which are regularly repeated and finding their repetition pattern. The purpose of the second subcategory is estimating causal relationships between alerts, predicting next alert occurrence, and detecting attacks and the third subcategory's goal is combining reliability with completely similar alerts.

2.4   Assessment

To be able to describe the advantages and disadvantages of algorithms and assess their functionalities, we extracted several factors and explained each algorithm based on these factors. Important factors for this assessment are:

1. Algorithm Capability: Expected capabilities in algorithms are: Alert Verification, Similar Alert Clustering, Attack Sequence Detection, and Repetitive/Unimportant Alert Reduction.
2. Algorithm Accuracy: As this system is to omit incorrect alerts and combine a large number of them with the aim of expressing a summary of system states, it should have a significant exactness of errors and not to ignore any event by mistake.
3. Algorithm Computation Power: According to the high amount of calculation for correlation engine and necessity of fast and online correlation, it is necessary to assess memory usage and processing power of algorithms.
4. Required Knowledge Base: It is necessary to know the required information for each algorithm, from where this data is extracted and whether all the required data is accessible according to local presented system conditions.
5. Algorithm Extendibility and Flexibility: How much and how is the algorithm performance procedure changeable, localizable and adaptable to new conditions, by the user.

3   Similarity-Based Algorithms

3.1   Simple Rules

The main idea of this subcategory can be seen in EMERALD product [5]. The functionality of this idea is based on defining very simple rules to express relations among alert features which can be combined together. In this subcategory, algorithms try to define simple rules in order to compute similarity between attributes of alerts and find the relation.

The significant works are presented in [5], [6], [7], [8], and [9]. The major required knowledge for this style of correlation rules are rule structures and required functions for checking similarity. Thus, these algorithms do not rely so much on knowledge bases. These algorithms can be used in different hierarchical levels and alerts are correlated form various aspects. In the detecting attack sequence capability, these algorithms include limits for defining attack types and can only detect sequences specified based on attack class. If the pattern definition is in a form that partitions conditions of the domain of that alert which alerts can be combined together into separate sets, it can also allocate input data to parallel processors for each pattern based on these conditions. Thus, these algorithms have a very good parallelism capability. These algorithms require maintaining all generated meta-alerts in the current time window for each pattern. Thus, its required memory is linearly proportional to alert input rate multiplied by the time window length.

3.2   Hierarchical Rules

This subcategory includes algorithms which have formed abstraction levels hierarchically and it makes decisions about security event detections based on these abstraction levels. This set of algorithms introduces researches that express similarity factors in a hierarchical of concept generalization.

The methods presented in [10], [11] and [12] are examples of such algorithms which is designed to detect root causes in networks. These algorithms include a method for comparing alert values, with a linear calculation degree proportional to generalization hierarchy tree depths. The required memory for these algorithms is also linear and equivalent to generalization tree sizes. Previous knowledge requirement level in these algorithms is up to defining generalization trees and thus precise and deep network structure and elements knowledge is not necessary, except in case of needing definition for address values and attack classes hierarchy.

3.3   Machine Learning

The last subcategory is algorithms in which comparison factors are generated automatically. Pre-requisite for supervised algorithms is the existence of a set of clustered alerts which the learning algorithm can set the parameters of its decision making model based on them. Algorithms without such a requirement (unsupervised), give the responsibility for training how to measure similarity to the algorithm. Three branches are considered for this type of algorithms.

In the first branch, the algorithms presented in [13] and [14] cluster alerts based on decision tree learning by previous data features. This algorithm exists in single-step and multi-step clustering (detecting similar alerts and attack sequences). This algorithm requires a huge and comprehensive set of training examples for creating a decision tree about how to perform correlation and in case that this set is incomplete, there is no guarantee for the correct performance of this algorithm. In terms of the required processing resources amount, it is similar to simple comparison algorithms, because each new alert must be compared to all meta-alerts existing in the current time window and the comparison procedure must be carried out with one decision tree with linear time cost. The necessary comparison structure makes it possible to divide the algorithm to few processors for comparing meta-alerts existing in the memory. Also based on the generated decision tree, partitioning input alerts and dividing them between different processors also might exist before correlation. Flexibility, compatibility with new conditions and extendibility are very hard in this algorithm and need pre-training the decision tree with new data.

In the second branch, the algorithms presented in [15] and [16] perform alert clustering based on alert Reconstruction Error by a neural network. The application of this algorithm is in single-step clustering and decision making based on cluster statistics. The only previous knowledge used in this algorithm is a set of alerts and it does not use any knowledge base and so, not using any environmental knowledge makes it hard to rely on the detection precision of this algorithm. In terms of required processing power and comparison modularity, this algorithm is very fast and simple, because of the arriving of each alert; it calculates the reconstruction error, completely independent from existing meta-alerts in the system. In case of re-learning with new condition data sets, still there is no guarantee for algorithm behavior change, because the used training model only focuses on alert re-creation precision and previous mistakes do not help the re-learning precision and new data might not have much impact on the new generalization model.

In the last branch, the algorithms described in [17] and [18] learn and apply true and false alert patterns based on labeled data by the system supervisor. The algorithm has online training capability and very good flexibility and its decision making factors are mostly based on information related to similar alerts in time ranges close to new alert arriving. Due to dependency of decision making about each alert to a wide range of similar alert statistical features, partitioning this algorithm is only possible if limiting under observation alert features to specific clusters capable of being partitioned and it is done in each unit centralized and without parallelism. This can also be mentioned for the used memory. Each executive unit in this algorithm must whether maintain statistical information related to all clusters of its own processor in the memory which is practically impossible, or check close similar cases in the permanent storage resource for each decision making. Thus, it requires a lot of access to one of the two permanent or temporary memories.

4   Knowledge-Based Algorithms

4.1   Prerequisites/Consequences

The algorithms in this subcategory observe and control meanings of alerts and existing concepts in the network and then detect a security event. In addition, makes extracting and forming a relation between different attack stages possible, with the pre-assumption of knowing a knowledge base which describes all existing prerequisites/consequences of an alert, and a database describing the network configurations and structure.

One of the first algorithms in using the background knowledge has been proposed in [19]. Following this idea, a model with a simpler and applicable expression has been proposed in [20], [21], [22] and [23]. In these algorithms, alerts are modeled using first order logic and causal relationships are defined for backgrounds, and consequences of each event. Thus, a graph of possible alerts and relationships between them can be created and provide appropriate tools to reduce the amount of information shown to the user. To continue, some researches expanded the mentioned tools to identify attack scenarios, analyzed the attack procedure [24] [25] [26] and also detected lost components of an attack [27] [28].

In terms of the reliance amount on environmental knowledge, these algorithms have the most requirements and in contrast, generate conclusion outputs without any bias and completely based on real alert meanings. Given that these algorithms do not use any pre-assumed information in addition to default environmental knowledge, they are very flexible and extendable algorithms and the algorithms behavior changes in real time with any change in the environmental knowledge. In addition,

In cases of required processing power, unity, parallelism ability and required previous data, these algorithms are in the heaviest existing algorithms range, because on one hand with the arrival of each new alert, any kind of its relationship with all other alerts in the active time window must be checked and this task needs a huge amount of adjustments between alert types, prerequisites/consequences, and their information details like source and destination address. On the other hand, because these algorithms are performing around meanings, continuous maintaining and updating a lot of incidents for different resources can play a very important role in the algorithm precision. Algorithm presented in [19], [20], [21], [22], [24], [25], [26], [27], [28], [29] and [23] limit the user checking domain to overcome processing problems and making the resulting data usable. In [30] [31] [32] another method is introduced which solves the problem of requiring processing power by sacrificing the memory.

4.2   Scenario

The main application of this set of algorithms is detecting multi-step attacks and their reliance is on the existence scenario of these kinds of attacks. Some of these works are presented in [33], [34], [35], [36], [37], [38] and [39]. Various languages are presented for describing these scenarios but the main idea in all of them is specifying attack steps and prerequisites and its goals. Thus, in terms of required amount of environmental knowledge, this set of algorithms require a higher level of knowledge than pre-requisites and results-based algorithms, but this knowledge can have less amount and domain. So, required processing resources in this branch is based on defined rules, can be less than the pre-requisites and results-based algorithms. But due to the very wide range of possible cases, unitizing and paralleling will be difficult. In case of defining a context language for expressing scenarios, these algorithms are completely flexible and extendable, because the system behavior must change in real time according to any change or extension in rules. The required memory for detecting scenarios rises according to the number of defined scenarios and required time window.

5   Statistical-Based Algorithms

5.1   Statistical Traffic Estimation

In this subcategory of statistical-based algorithms, patterns of occurred alerts are recognized and the repetition pattern is derived and non-similarity with these patterns will be detected in the future.

The goal of algorithms presented in [40], [41] and [42] is creating a statistical network traffic model, predicting it, and removing predictable cases. An important category of this kind of alerts contains alerts which occur periodically, due to wrong network or security system adjustments. These algorithms do not need any context knowledge and all of their activities are carried out based on the statistics of each alert. According to this point that each of these filters is defined on a certain alert domain (according to choices made by the system supervisor), parallelism is easily possible in this application and before processing, and the alert processing unit can be easily specified. The processing load of this algorithm completely depends on the used statistical model, but all models presented in previous researches had linear and less processing load. The algorithm requirement of data set is determined based on the model time depth, but due to the use of only statistical information, storing or accessing real alerts is not necessary and only the relatively low and constant memory capacity is necessary. All presented statistical models in mentioned researches include online training and thus, compatibility with current conditions and flexibility based on new changes, are completely possible.

Also, the algorithms described in [43], [44] and [45] are expressed based on Association Rules for detecting alerts which normally occur together. An important application of this method is determining alert priorities based on this that which alerts have occurred together and have these accompaniments occurred on a usual procedure or a new pattern is observed, but also this algorithm can be used for creating related meta-alerts. Training is carried out offline in this algorithm and it is done in a time other than the execution time, but it can update model parameters in the run time and optimize the model according to new data. This algorithm does not need environmental knowledge and knowledge base and makes decision completely based on alert statistics. The algorithm requirement amount to memory is determined based on activity time window and windows are defined separately. In each window, statistical information about all alerts is calculated and the resulted statistics are compared to previous ones. Based on the determined domain by the user for applying this algorithm, arrived data from different units can be pre-partitioned and thus alerts related to each unit can be processed independently and only in their own processing unit, and processing in each unit is also very much parallelizable according to the need of counting different alert combinations.

5.2   Causal Relation Estimation

The purpose of this subcategory is finding alert sequence or association dominant patterns and using these patterns for detecting false cases, or proper combinations. Some of these algorithms are more proper for learning attack patterns and some for detecting false alerts or lost ones.

Several works were introduced based on analyzing causal relationships between alerts according to assessing the impact amount of using an alert in predicting other occurrence statistics of an alert [46] [47] [48]. The goal of these algorithms is creating a possible model for determining correlation relationships between alerts. Using this model, alerts can be correlated without environmental knowledge, but gaining a precise and reliable model requires a huge amount of previous data about the attacks. The algorithm acts in two separate training and functional phases. Training is performed offline and it is performable on archive data and thus its relatively huge processing load does not create any problems for practice use. In the test phase, due to the use of previous data, the model processing load is not too much and it can be decreased very much using some optimizations. Due to the high dependency of the training algorithm to huge data amount, flexing the algorithm against new conditions is not much easy, but with the direct user interference in learned relationships in the training phase, the algorithm behavior can be changed fast. Extending the algorithm is also possible using more data and wider education.

In [49], very simple algorithm for finding existing attack sequences is introduced. In this algorithm, first the possible attack graph is generated like previous algorithms and then, passed procedures in this graph are specifies in a set of previous stored alerts, and their correlation possibility is determined based on the cases that two steps of this graph have occurred in a row in real attacks [50]. In [51], an algorithm has been presented a completion of [49] idea by implementing it with Hidden Markov Model (HMM). A different feature of this algorithm is the possibility of defining the possibility of each scenario occurrence and performing each attack step based on previous steps. The knowledge of this algorithm is completely gained based on previous stored and categorized data and thus, training a strong Markov model requires a huge amount of data and correctly categorizing and specifying previous attacks. This style is focused on attacks with specified source and destinations, due to this input data are completely able of being partitioned for dividing the processing procedure into parallel processors, but the processing is relatively centered and undividable in each unit. The flexibility of this algorithm against new conditions is very slow due to high dependency to a huge amount of training data, but increasing it is possible a little by the direct interference of the system supervisor and changing Markov possibility table. For extending the algorithm, training with new labeled data is necessary.

5.3   Reliability Degree Combination

The goal of this subcategory is introducing an algorithm for combining reliability with completely similar alerts [52] [53]. In this type of algorithm, changing the reliability to alerts is proposed based on equivalent alert repetitions. The goal is changing the importance\priority of an alert, based on its approval by other resources. The presented algorithms require a huge amount of labeled previous data for generating probability models. The main idea can be simplified by removing all possible processing details and only accept the amount of an alert repetition as a factor independent from alert importance and resource history. The main algorithm acts in two training and function phases and thus the relatively huge amount of processing load does not have any impact on speed in time. Also the algorithm speed in execution time is completely proper and from the order of O (1). Due to the independency of the algorithms process for alert clusters, input data are completely able of being partitioned and due to the high simplicity of the processing inside each cluster; there is no need of parallelism. Flexibility against new conditions is slow due to the need of training with a lot of data, but the reliability to different resource opinions can change by the direct interference of the system supervisor and changing the algorithm behavior in real time. In addition, extending the algorithm requires extending learning data.

6   Comparison

In this section, we compared different algorithms from different viewpoints. In Table 1, we provided an overall comparison between three main categories of algorithms. Also, Table 2 compared all subcategories based on various factors. Considering the surveyed literature, it is obvious that in case of detection accuracy, the second category either prerequisite/consequence or scenario is high and has noticeable difference with other categories. Beside the accuracy factor, all categories have their own advantages in case of algorithm capability. We cannot ignore any of the categories because of the condition, attack and sensor type. Thus, to solve this problem, usually a hybrid approach can be used. Considering the required memory and the computation power, it should be noticed that statistical-based algorithms and the first two subcategories of similarity-based algorithms need average resources. But in the third subcategory, requirement defer according to the taken clusters. Also in the prerequisite/consequence algorithm, while there is a need for high amount of memory, there is a little need for computation power. But in contrast to prerequisite/consequence, scenario algorithms needs average resources. Another important point to be mentioned can be the weakness of statistical-based algorithm in which they have less flexibility and extendibility compared with the other categories. Also, algorithms in second category are not parallelizable because of their inner type of behavior and if partitioned, they wound have much accuracy.

Table 1. Overall comparison

Characteristic	Similarity-based	Knowledge-based	Statistical-based
Combining alerts from various sensors	Yes	Yes	No
Requiring Prior knowledge	Yes	Yes	No
Detecting false alerts	Yes	Yes	Guessing
Detecting multi-stage attacks	Hardly	Yes	Guessing
Find new attacks	Yes	No	Yes
Error rate	Average	Low	High

Table 2. Comparison based on different factors

			Accuracy	Flexibility	Extendibility	Required Memory	Computation Power	Parallelizing	Knowledge base
H		High							
A		Average							
L		Low							
AD		Require Attack Definition							
AM		Require Alert Meaning							
Similarity-based		Simple Rules	A	H	H	A	A	H	-
		Hierarchical Rules	A	H	H	A	A	H	AD
		Machine Learning (Decision Tree)	A	A	A	A	A	A	-
		Machine Learning (Re-creation)	A	A	A	L	H	H	-
		Machine Learning (Verification)	A	A	A	H	H	L	-
Knowledge-based		Prerequisites/Consequences	H	H	H	H	L	L	AM
		Scenario	H	H	H	A	A	L	H
Statistical-based		Statistical Traffic Estimation	A	H	A	L	H	H	-
		Statistical Traffic Estimation (Association Rules)	A	L	L	A	A	A	-
		Causal Relationship Estimation (Ganger Test)	A	L	L	A	A	H	-
		Causal Relationship Estimation (Markov Model)	A	L	L	A	A	A	-
		Reliability Degree Combination	A	L	L	A	A	H	-

7   Conclusion and Future Work

Regarding the analysis of many algorithms, it is necessary to take the advantages of different categories. As it is clear from the term "correlation", the more abstract the system is in networks, the better perspective the network managers have. Using more correlation measurements in this section will face great number of Events per Second (EPS). As a result, it is very important to pay attention to computation power in designing algorithms. To continue the research in future, we will take advantage of algorithms in each category to design an algorithm which has the least possible computation power consumption and can process multi thousand EPS and also has an extendable and flexible design.

References

[1] Tjhai, G.C., Papadaki, M., Furnell, S.M., Clarke, N.L.: Investigating the Problem of IDS False Alarms: An Experimental Study Using Snort. In: Proceedings of the IFIP TC 11 23rd International Information Security Conference, pp. 253–267 (2008)

[2] Pouget, F., Dacier, M.: Alert Correlation: Review of the state of the art. EURECOM, Technical Report (2003)

[3] Sadoddin, R., Ghorbani, A.: Alert correlation survey: Framework and techniques. In: Proceedings of ACM International Conference on Privacy, Security and Trust: Bridge the Gap Between PST Technologies and Business Services (2006)

[4] Al-Mamory, S.O., Zhang, H.: A survey on IDS alerts processing techniques. In: Proceeding of the 6th WSEAS International Conference on Information Security and Privacy (ISP), pp. 69–78 (2007)

[5] Valdes, A., Skinner, K.: Probabilistic alert correlation. In: Lee, W., Mé, L., Wespi, A. (eds.) RAID 2001. LNCS, vol. 2212, pp. 54–68. Springer, Heidelberg (2001)

[6] Debar, H., Wespi, A.: Aggregation and correlation of intrusion-detection alerts. In: Lee, W., Mé, L., Wespi, A. (eds.) RAID 2001. LNCS, vol. 2212, pp. 85–103. Springer, Heidelberg (2001)

[7] Cuppens, F.: Managing alerts in a multi-intrusion detection environment. In: Proceedings of the 17th Annual Computer Security Applications Conference, ACSAC (2001)

[8] Valeur, F., Vigna, G., Kruegel, C., Kemmerer, R.A.: Comprehensive approach to intrusion detection alert correlation. IEEE Transactions on Dependable and Secure Computing, 146–169 (2004)

[9] Elshoush, H.T., Osman, I.M.: Intrusion Alert Correlation Framework: An Innovative Approach. In: IAENG Transactions on Engineering Technologies, pp. 405–420 (2013)

[10] Julisch, K.: Mining alarm clusters to improve alarm handling efficiency. In: Proceedings of 17th Annual Computer Security Applications Conference (ACSAC), pp. 12–21 (2001)

[11] Julisch, K.: Clustering intrusion detection alarms to support root cause analysis. ACM Journal Name 2(3), 111–138 (2002)

[12] Al-Mamory, S.O., Zhang, H.: IDS alerts correlation using grammar-based approach. Journal of Computer Virology 5(4), 271–282 (2009)

[13] Dain, O.M., Cunningham, R.K.: Building scenarios from a heterogeneous alert stream. In: Proceedings of IEEE Workshop on Information Assurance and Security (2001)

[14] Dain, O., Cunningham, R.K.: Fusing a heterogeneous alert stream into scenarios. In: Proceedings of ACM Workshop on Data Mining for Security Applications, pp. 1–13 (2001)

[15] Smith, R., Japkowicz, N., Dondo, M., Mason, P.: Using unsupervised learning for network alert correlation. In: Advances in Artificial Intelligence, pp. 308–319 (2008)

[16] Smith, R., Japkowicz, N., Dondo, M.: Clustering using an autoassociator: A case study in network event correlation. In: Proceedings of the 17th IASTED International Conference on Parallel and Distributed Computing and Systems (2008)

[17] Pietraszek, T., Tanner, A.: Data mining and machine learning towards reducing false positives in intrusion detection. Information Security 10(3), 169–183 (2005)

[18] Pietraszek, T.: Using adaptive alert classification to reduce false positives in intrusion detection. In: Jonsson, E., Valdes, A., Almgren, M. (eds.) RAID 2004. LNCS, vol. 3224, pp. 102–124. Springer, Heidelberg (2004)

[19] Templeton, S.J., Levitt, K.: A requires/provides model for computer attacks. In: Proceedings of the Workshop on New Security Paradigms, pp. 31–38 (2001)

[20] Ning, P., Cui, Y.: An intrusion alert correlator based on pre-requisites of intrusions (2002)

[21] Ning, P., Cui, Y., Reeves, D.S.: Constructing attack scenarios through correlation of intrusion alerts. In: Proceedings of the 9th ACM on Computer and Communications Security, pp. 245–254 (2002)

[22] Ning, P., Cui, Y., Reeves, D.S., Xu, D.: Techniques and tools for analyzing intrusion alerts. ACM Transactions on Information and System Security (TISSEC) 7(2), 274–318 (2004)

[23] Cuppens, F., Autrel, F., Miege, A., Benferhat, S.: Correlation in an intrusion detection process. In: Proceedings SEcurite des Communications sur Internet (SECI), pp. 153–171 (2002)

[24] Ning, P., Xu, D.: Learning attack strategies from intrusion alerts. In: Proceedings of the 10th ACM Conference on Computer and Communications Security (CCS), pp. 200–209 (2003)

[25] Ning, P., Cui, Y., Reeves, D.S.: Analyzing intensive intrusion alerts via correlation. In: Wespi, A., Vigna, G., Deri, L. (eds.) RAID 2002. LNCS, vol. 2516, pp. 74–94. Springer, Heidelberg (2002)

[26] Ning, P., Cui, Y., Reeves, D.S., Xu, D.: Towards automating intrusion alert analysis. In: Workshop on Statistical and Machine Learning Techniques in Computer Intrusion Detection (2003)

[27] Ning, P., Xu, D.: Hypothesizing and reasoning about attacks missed by intrusion detection systems. ACM Transactions on Information and System Security (TISSEC) 7(4), 591–627 (2004)

[28] Ning, P., Xu, D., Healey, C.G., Amant, R.S.: Building attack scenarios through integration of complementary alert correlation methods. In: Proceedings of the 11th Annual Network and Distributed System Security Symposium, NDSS (2004)

[29] Zhai, Y., Ning, P., Iyer, P., Reeves, D.S.: Reasoning about complementary intrusion evidence. In: 20th Annual IEEE Computer Security Applications Conference (ACSAC), pp. 39–48 (2004)

[30] Wang, L., Liu, A., Jajodia, S.: An efficient and unified approach to correlating, hypothesizing, and predicting intrusion alerts. In: De Capitani di Vimercati, S.,Syverson, P.F., Gollmann, D. (eds.) ESORICS 2005. LNCS, vol. 3679, pp. 247–266. Springer, Heidelberg (2005)

[31] Wang, L., Liu, A., Jajodia, S.: Using attack graphs for correlating, hypothesizing, and predicting intrusion alerts. Computer Communications 29(15), 2917–2933 (2006)

[32] Zali, Z., Hashemi, M.R., Saidi, H.: Real-Time Intrusion Detection Alert Correlation and Attack Scenario Extraction Based on the Prerequisite-Consequence Approach. The ISC International Journal of Information Security 4(2) (2013)

[33] Cheung, S., Lindqvist, U., Fong, M.W.: Modelling multistep cyber-attacks for scenario recognition. In: DARPA Information Survivability Conference and Exposition, pp. 284–292 (2003)

[34] Eckmann, S.T., Vigna, G., Kemmerer, R.A.: STATL: An attack language for state-based intrusion detection. Journal of Computer Security 10(1/2), 71–104 (2002)

[35] Cuppens, F., Ortalo, R.: LAMBDA: A language to model a database for detection of attacks. In: Debar, H., Mé, L., Wu, S.F. (eds.) RAID 2000. LNCS, vol. 1907, pp. 197–216. Springer, Heidelberg (2000)

[36] Morin, B., Mé, L., Debar, H., Ducassé, M.: M2D2: A formal data model for IDS alert correlation. In: Wespi, A., Vigna, G., Deri, L. (eds.) RAID 2002. LNCS, vol. 2516, pp. 115–137. Springer, Heidelberg (2002)

[37] Morin, B., Mé, L., Debar, H., Ducassé, M.: A logic-based model to support alert correlation in intrusion detection. Information Fusion 10(4), 285–299 (2009)

[38] Al-Mamory, S.O., Zhang, H.: Intrusion detection alarms reduction using root cause Analysis and clustering. Computer Communications 32(2), 419–430 (2009)

[39] Kabiri, P., Ghorbani, A.A.: A rule-based temporal alert correlation system. International Journal of Network Security 5(1), 66–72 (2007)

[40] Viinikka, J., Debar, H.: Monitoring IDS background noise using EWMA control charts and alert information. In: Jonsson, E., Valdes, A., Almgren, M. (eds.) RAID 2004. LNCS, vol. 3224, pp. 166–187. Springer, Heidelberg (2004)

[41] Viinikka, J., Debar, H., Mé, L., Séguier, R.: Time series modelling for IDS alert management. In: Proceedings of Information, Computer and Communications Security, pp. 102–113 (2006)

[42] Viinikka, J., Debar, H., Mé, L., Lehikoinen, A., Tarvainen, M.: Processing intrusion detection alert aggregates with time series modelling. Information Fusion 10(4), 312–324 (2009)

[43] Manganaris, S., Christensen, M., Zerkle, D., Hermiz, K.: A data mining Analysis of RTID alarms. Computer Networks 34(4), 571–577 (2000)

[44] Treinen, J.J., Thurimella, R.: A framework for the application of association rule mining in large intrusion detection infrastructures. In: Zamboni, D., Kruegel, C. (eds.) RAID 2006. LNCS, vol. 4219, pp. 1–18. Springer, Heidelberg (2006)

[45] Ren, H., Stakhanova, N., Ghorbani, A.A.: An online adaptive approach to alert correlation. In: Kreibich, C., Jahnke, M. (eds.) DIMVA 2010. LNCS, vol. 6201, pp. 153–172. Springer, Heidelberg (2010)

[46] Lee, W., Qin, X.: Statistical causality Analysis of INFOSEC alert data. In: Managing Cyber Threats, pp. 101–127 (2003)

[47] Qin, X., Lee, W.: Attack plan recognition and prediction using causal networks. In: 20th Annual Computer Security Applications Conference (ACSAC), pp. 370–379 (2004)

[48] Qin, X., Lee, W.: Discovering novel attack strategies from INFOSEC alerts. In: Data Warehousing and Data Mining Techniques for Cyber Security, pp. 109–157 (2007)

[49] Geib, C.W., Goldman, R.P.: Plan recognition in intrusion detection systems. In: DARPA Information Survivability Conference and Exposition, pp. 46–55 (2001)

[50] Dorigo, M., Maniezzo, V., Colorni, A.: Ant system: Optimization by a colony of cooperating agents. IEEE Transactions on Systems, Man, and Cybernetics 26(1), 29–41 (1996)

[51] Ourston, D., Matzner, S., Stump, W., Hopkins, B.: Applications of hidden markov models to detecting multi-stage network attacks. In: Proceedings of the 36th Annual IEEE Hawaii International Conference on System Sciences (2003)

[52] Gu, G., Cardenas, A.A., Lee, W.: Principled reasoning and practical applications of alert fusion in intrusion detection systems. In: Proceedings of ACM Symposium on Information, Computer and Communications Security, pp. 136–147 (2008)

[53] Siraj, A., Vaughn, R.B.: Multi-level alert clustering for intrusion detection sensor data. In: Annual Meeting of the North American on Fuzzy Information Processing Society, pp. 748–753 (2005)

Construction and Verification of Mobile Ad Hoc Network Protocols

Natsuki Kimura and Noriaki Yoshiura

Department of Information and Computer Science, Saitama University,
255, Shimo-ookubo Urawa-ku, Saitama City, Japan

Abstract. In recent years, Mobile Ad hoc Networks (MANETs) have
been focused with the development and the spread of mobile devices.
However, MANETs have a security problem. MANETs do not have choke
points like Firewalls. It is difficult for MANETs to have choke points because each mobile device in MANETs moves and because fixed routing
does not exist. Moreover there are many kinds of attacks in MANETs
such as packet sniffing, tampering, spoofing, etc. Gang Xu et al. proposed a method for constructing secure MANETs. The method is considered to prevent attacks against MANETs because each mobile device
in MANETs uses Trusted Platform Module (TPM). TPM can become
foundation of security because Tamper-resistance of TPM is difficult to
analyze. However, Gang Xu et al. does not present the concrete protocol.
This paper constructs the concrete protocol from the proposal of Gang
Xu et al and verifies the concrete protocol by SPIN to construct secure
protocol. This paper presents the process of constructing secure protocols from ideas of protocols. As a result of constructing and verifying
the protocols, this paper concludes that the secure protocol cannot be
constructed from the proposal of Gang Xu et al without the connection
with certificate authority (CA) of public keys.

Keywords: Mobile Ad Hoc Network, Model Checking, Protocol Verification, SPIN.

1 Introduction

Recent development of mobile devices such as mobile phones, tablet PCs, note
PCs or so on enables to carry communication tools outdoors easily. Current wireless communication systems use base stations of mobile phones or access points
of wireless networks. As new wireless communication system, mobile Ad hoc networks (MANETs) have been researched[6,7,8,9,10]; MANETs do not use base
stations or access points. Each mobile device in MANETs has a function of forwarding packets such as WiFi direct. However, MANETs have several problems,
one of which is security because MANETs do not have firewalls or choke points
that can exist in current wireless networks. It is difficult to install choke points in
MANETs because mobile devices in MANETs can move and do not have fixed
routing information. Thus the methods of constructing secure MANETs without

G. Wang et al. (Eds.): CSS 2013, LNCS 8300, pp. 198–212, 2013.

choke points have been proposed[11]. Gang Xu et al. proposed the method of constructing secure MANETs by using Trusted Platform Module (TPM)[1]. The proposed method also uses Satem[2], which is software using TPM and guarantees tamper-resistance of OS kernel and software. Gang Xu et al. assert that the proposed method keeps security of MANETs[1].

Gang Xu et al. proposed the method of constructing secure MANETs[1], but do not proposed the concrete protocol; they proposed only overview of the protocols. Thus, it is uncertain whether the concrete secure protocol can be constructed from the idea of Gang Xu et al. This paper constructs the concrete secure protocol from the idea of Gang Xu et al. by using SPIN to verify the security of constructed protocols. SPIN is a software verification tool[5] and is also used as protocol verification[4]. The procedure of constructing protocols is to construct the protocol from the idea and to verify the protocol by SPIN. If the verification shows that the constructed protocol is insecure, the protocol is revised and verified again. The construction of the protocol is finished when the verification shows that the constructed protocol is secure.

After trying to construct the concrete protocol, this paper concludes that the protocols that are based on the idea of Gang Xu et al. cannot become secure. To construct secure protocols requires that all mobile devices in MANETs can communicate with certificate authority (CA) of public keys. Usually all network equipment in the Internet can connect with CA, but all MANETs do not connect with the Internet; some of MANETs are intranets. This paper constructs the concrete protocol that uses CA via the Internet and verifies that shared keys in MANETs are not known to attackers by SPIN. The result of the verification is that the concrete protocol that uses CA via the Internet is secure for the threats of impersonation attacks.

This paper is organized as follows: Section 2 explains Mobile Ad hoc Networks and Section 3 explains the MANET protocol that is proposed by Gang Xu et al. Section 4 constructs and verifies the protocol based on the idea of Gang Xu et al. Section 5 concludes this paper.

2   Mobile Ad Hoc Networks

MANETs (Mobile Ad hoc Networks) are wireless networks in which each mobile device has a function of forwarding packets. Mobile devices in MANETs are called nodes. Nodes in MANETs are connected so that each node in MANETs can access any node in MANETs by tracing the nodes between the two nodes. The nodes of MANETs are supposed to be note PCs, mobile phones and so on.

MANETs have several advantages, one of which is to construct wireless networks in wide areas without base stations or access points. This advantage enables to construct wide area wireless networks with low cost. Another advantage is that the nodes can participate in and leave MANETs easily. This advantage enables to construct urgent wireless networks under disasters, temporary simple wireless networks for events, and inter-vehicle communication networks. For example, it is difficult to construct wireless networks for vehicles in tunnels with access points, but if each vehicle works as access point, MANETs can be available in tunnels.

2.1   Overview of MANETs

Current wireless networks are based on access points or base stations. Each mobile node communicates with access points or base stations directly and nodes communicate with other nodes or the Internet via access points or base stations. MANETs do not require access points or base stations; MANETs are scalable and mobile nodes that would like to join MANETs can join MANETs by connecting one of nodes in MANETs. To keep security of MANETs requires to authenticate or authorize nodes that try to join MANETs. If some bad mobile devices join MANETs, MANETs are insecure; the bad mobile devices can be relay spoof, tap or tamper with packets between some nodes in MANETs. Thus, the protocols that are used in joining MANETs are very important. Many researches have proposed protocols that are used in joining MANETs and Gang Xu et al. provide one protocol of joining MANETs to keep security of MANETs[1].

2.2   Problems of Mobile Ad Hoc Networks

Spreading MANETs into worlds has several problems as follows:

1. Routing
   The nodes in MANETs move so often; some nodes often move outside of radio wave range of the nodes that they connect directly. In MANETs, most nodes are client nodes and relay nodes, and movement of nodes causes some troubles in communication in MANETs. Each node must construct new routing information at movement of some nodes. Many researches focus on dynamic routing or reconstructing communication path after movement of nodes[3].
2. Operating time
   Electric powers of mobile devices are usually batteries. Durations in which nodes participate in MANETs depend on the capacity of the batteries, processing protocols and software of MANETs. Thus, it is important to develop low-power protocols and software of MANETs.
3. Security
   In constructing MANETs, each node must occasionally communicate with the nodes that it does not identify. Each node does not always communicate with strange nodes directly, but it has possibilities of sending data to destination nodes via some nodes that it does not identify. Thus, MANETs always have possibilities of attacks of spoofing, tapping or tampering with packets. MANET protocol requires functions of detecting and preventing these kinds of attacks.

Regarding security, public key encryption is one of security measures. Public key encryption enables to detect and prevent several kinds of attacks, but public key encryption requires certificate authority (CA) to detect and prevent the attacks. The nodes in MANETs are mobile devices and are likely to repeat coming into and going out of the range of radio wave; the repetition changes MANET topology. If the nodes in MANETs use public key encryption in participating in MANETs to identify other nodes, they must communicate with CA and identify the nodes that they try to communicate with directly whenever they participate in MANETs. This procedure takes time and electric power. Moreover, using CA requires another network that the nodes use to communicate with CA. The mobile devices that have public key certificates of CA can identify other nodes without communicating with CA, but all mobile devices do not have public key certificates of CA. Therefore, this is an assumption of using CA when CA is used to identify nodes in MANETs. However, this assumption undermines the advantages of MANETs and this paper focuses on security issues of constructing MANETs.

3 MANET Protocol Proposed by Gang Xu et al.

This section explains the protocol that is proposed by Gang Xu et al.

3.1 TPM and Satem

Gang Xu et al. proposed the secure method of constructing MANETs. This method uses TPM and requires that all nodes in MANETs have TPM. This method also uses Satem, which is software that guarantees integrity of other software. The integrity of Satem is guaranteed by TPM. The following explains TPM and Satem[13,14].

TPM. TPM is both the name of a published specification detailing a secure cryptoprocessor that can store cryptographic keys, and implementations of that specification. TPM specification is made by Trusted Computing Group (TCG)[17]. The chips of TPM include the following functions: calculation, generating and storing key, hash calculation and so on. The chips of TPM also have tamper resistance; it is difficult to analyze the inside of the chips of TPM[1].

Satem. Satem is software that guarantees integrity of other software or data. Specifically, Satem constructs commitments that guarantee integrity of software or data. Commitments are based on TPM. If devices such as note PCs are asked to guarantee integrity of software or data by other software or other devices that are connected via networks, the devices ask Satem to generate commitments of the software or data. The integrity of Satem is guaranteed by TPM[1]. The commitments consist of hash values of OS kernel image or binaries that may be executed in the software. The devices send commitments to software or other devices that require integrity of software or data. The software or devices that receive commitments ask Satem to check the commitments. Satem compares hash values in commitments to check integrity of OS kernel or software.

Gang Xu et al. proposes the secure protocol that is used in joining MANETs. This protocol requires several commitments in joining MANETs; the method requires commitments for integrity of boot strap program, OS kernel image and applicant. The applicant is the software that applies security policies to nodes. Security policies are sets of rules that nodes must obey to keep security and fairness of MANETs. Strictly, Satem cannot guarantee the security of MANETs. Satem only guarantees that boot strap program, OS kernel image and application software are not tempered.

3.2 Realizability

The method proposed by Gang Xu et al. is realizable because many note PCs and smart phones and so on have TPMs. The widespread use of TPMs owes to reducing cost of computers and downsizing of TPMs. In the near future, mobile phones, tablet PCs and PDA (Personal Digital Assistants) will have TPMs because of downsizing of TPMs. Thus, the method proposed by Gang Xu et al. will be used in construction of MANETs with many computers and many mobile phones[1].

3.3 Communication Protocol

The method proposed by Gang Xu et al. uses two communication protocols to construct MANETs. One is JOIN protocol, which is used when a node participates MANETs and the other is MERGE protocol, which is used when two MANETs combine[1]. This paper verifies JOIN protocol. The reliability of JOIN protocol depends on TPMs. The specification of JOIN protocol is described under the assumption that TPM is not destroyed physically or tempered.

The proposed protocol gives not only a secure method of joining MANETs, but also a method of applying security policy of MANETs to the new nodes that join MANETs. The nodes in MANETs should obey security policy of MANETs. Security policies are different in MANETs; each MANET has its own security policy. Keeping security of MANETs requires security policy and all nodes in MANETs must obey security policy. If one malicious node of MANETs sends attack packets to other nodes of MANETs, other nodes of MANETs relay or receive packets and have serious security problems. Thus, it is important to check whether the nodes that would like to join MANETs are not malicious. This check is other function of the protocol that is used in joining nodes to MANETs. Thus, JOIN protocol must not only authenticate the nodes that would like to join MANETs but also check whether the nodes obey the security policy of MANETs.

3.4 JOIN Protocol

This subsection explains the JOIN protocol that is proposed in [1]. Fig. 1, which is used in [1], shows the behavior of JOIN protocol. In this figure, Node A tries to participate MANETs and Node B is a member of MANETs. Node B is an entrance of MANETs for Node A.

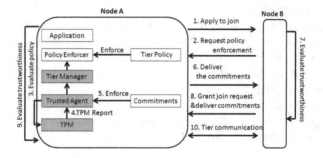

Fig. 1. Behavior of JOIN protocol[1]

1. Apply to join
   When Node A tries to participate MANETs, Node A communicates with the near node (Node B) that is a member of MANETs and sends "Apply to join" message to Node B.
2. Request policy enforcement
   After Node B receives "Apply to join" message from Node A, Node B sends "Request policy enforcement" message to Node A. This message contains the policy that Node A should obey.
3. Evaluate policy
   Node A evaluates the security policy in "Request policy enforcement" message to decide whether Node A accepts the security policy or not. If Node A decides that it does not accept the security policy, it finishes communication with Node B.
4. Guarantee of Satem
   After Node A decides to accept the policy in "Request policy enforcement" message, Node A confirms and guarantees the integrity of Satem (Trusted agent) by TPM.
5. Guarantee of software
   After the integrity of Satem is confirmed, Satem in Node A confirms the integrity of software that is used in MANETs.
6. Deliver commitments
   Node A constructs commitments that guarantee integrity of Satem and software that are used in MANETs. Node A sends the commitments and the public key of Node A to Node B.
7. Evaluate trustworthiness
   Node B confirms the commitments that are sent from Node A.
8. Grant join request and deliver commitments
   After confirming the commitments that are sent from Node A, Node B sends Node A the commitments of Satem and software of Node B. Node B also sends the shared key that is used for communication between Node A and B. The commitments and the shared key are encrypted by the public key of Node A when they are sent to Node A. The shared key is used in communication between Node A and Node B or among MANETs.

9. Evaluate trustworthiness

   By the private key of Node A, Node A decrypts the commitments and the shared key that are sent from Node B and are encrypted by the public key of Node A. Node A confirms the commitments. If the commitments do not guarantee the integrity of Satem and software of Node B, Node A stops communicating with Node B.

10. Tier communication

    Node A participates MANETs if the commitments guarantee the integrity of Satem and software of Node B.

The advantages of JOIN protocol are as follows[1].

- JOIN protocol enables to apply security policies to nodes in MANETs without choke points such as firewall or proxies.
- JOIN protocol can prevent and detect spoofing by public key encryption.

In the protocol, if attackers know shared keys, all packet are known to attackers. Thus, it is important to exchange share keys securely.

JOIN protocol has advantages, but the paper [1] only gives the overview of JOIN protocol. JOIN protocol enables to authenticate the nodes that would like to join MANETs and to apply security policies of MANETs to the nodes. However, vulnerability of JOIN protocol is not investigated much. For example, some of concrete protocols that are constructed from the overview of JOIN protocol may be vulnerable. The following sections construct secure JOIN protocol from the overview of the protocol by using SPIN.

4   Construction and Verification of Protocol

This paper uses model checker SPIN to verify the properties of protocols. In SPIN, the behaviors of protocol and attackers are described by language Promela and the properties that should hold in protocols are described in linear temporal logic (LTL). SPIN can check the properties of the protocols exhaustively. To verify the protocol, SPIN does not require to describe all possible behaviors of attackers against the protocol but to describe the behaviors of attackers nondeterministically; SPIN checks all behaviors of attackers according to the description of nondeterministic behaviors of attackers. The important point of using SPIN is that the descriptions of the behaviors of protocol and attackers must be simple so that SPIN can check the properties[15]; the complexity of checking the properties of protocol is NP-hard [12] and if the descriptions are complicated, it takes much time to check the properties.

Fig. 2 shows the overview of the procedure of checking and revising protocols. At the beginning, the concrete protocol is constructed from the overview of JOIN protocol. The next step constructs Promela code of the concrete protocol. An attacker behavior is also implemented by Promela according to the code of the concrete protocol. Next, the properties that the concrete protocols must satisfy are described in LTL. From the Promela codes and LTL formulas of the

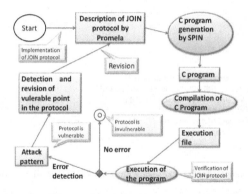

Fig. 2. Verification and revision

properties, SPIN generates C program, which verifies that the concrete protocol satisfies the properties under attackers. The next step compiles the C program and runs the execution file. If the result of the execution is "No error", the concrete protocol is invulnerable and the procedure finishes. If the result of the execution is "Error detection", the procedure revises the concrete protocol. In this case, trail files are generated by the execution of SPIN. The trail files include the protocol behavior in which properties do not satisfy; in other words, the trail files include the protocol behavior in which attacks succeed. Analyzing the trail files obtains the behavior of attackers and revising the concrete protocol requires to prevent the behavior. After revising the concrete protocol, the procedure revises the behavior of attackers according to the revised protocol and repeats the whole steps. This repetition finishes when verification programs output "no error".

4.1 Verification of Properties in JOIN Protocol

This paper verifies the property that attackers do not know shared keys that are used in MANETs. According to the procedure in Fig. 2, this paper describes the behavior of protocol in Promela and the properties in LTL and verifies the properties by SPIN. A file JOIN.pml, which is described in Promela, represents JOIN protocol, the possible behaviors of impersonation attackers and the properties that should hold in the protocol. Fig. 3 shows a part of Promela code Node A in JOIN.pml. The result of verification is that the property does not hold in the protocol and trail files are created. The trail files have information on the behavior of protocol in failure of the property. The trail file that is created by the execution of SPIN for the verification has 2389 lines. The trail file shows the successful behavior of impersonation attack (man-in-the-middle attack) to obtain a shared key in MANETs. Fig. 4 shows the part of the trail file. This part is a key point of the successful impersonation attack.

```
#define CBUF 5
#define PKnum 0
#define SKnum 1
#define CKnum 2
#define SATEMnum 3

mtype = {request,policy,commitmentA,commitmentB};
mtype = {PK1,PK2,SK1,SK2,CK, UNLOCKED, nothing, SATEM};
mtype NODE_As[ANUM], NODE_Bs[ANUM], EVILs[ANUM];
chan AtoB = [CBUF] of {mtype,mtype,mtype};
chan BtoA = [CBUF] of {mtype,mtype,mtype};
int FirstFlag = 1, RequestFlag = 0;

active proctype NODE_A()
{
  mtype stateA,messageA,keyA; int checkFlagA = 0; NODE_As[SATEMnum] = SATEM;
  do
    ::(FirstFlag == 1)||(RequestFlag == 1)->AtoB!UNLOCKED(request,nothing);
      FirstFlag = 0 ; RequestFlag = 0;

    ::(FirstFlag == 0)&&(RequestFlag == 0)->BtoA?stateA(messageA,keyA);
      if
      ::(messageA == policy)->checkFlagA = 0;
        if
          ::(stateA == UNLOCKED)||((stateA == PK1)&&(NODE_As[SKnum] == SK1))
          ||((stateA == PK2)&&(NODE_As[SKnum] == SK2))
          ||((stateA == SK1)&&(NODE_As[PKnum] == PK1))
          ||((stateA == SK2)&&(NODE_As[PKnum] == PK2))
          ||((stateA == CK)&&(NODE_As[CKnum] == CK))->checkFlagA = 1;
          ::else->skip;
        fi;
        if
          ::(checkFlagA == 1)->
            if
              ::(NODE_As[SATEMnum] == SATEM)
              ->AtoB!UNLOCKED(commitmentA,PK1);
                NODE_As[SKnum] = SK1;
              ::else->printf("SATEM lost\n"); RequestFlag = 1;
            fi
          ::else->printf("NODE_A can't decode policy\n"); RequestFlag = 1;
        fi
      ::(messageA == commitmentB)->checkFlagA = 0;
        if
          ::(stateA == UNLOCKED)||((stateA == PK1)&&(NODE_As[SKnum] == SK1))
          ||((stateA == PK2)&&(NODE_As[SKnum] == SK2))
          ||((stateA == SK1)&&(NODE_As[PKnum] == PK1))
          ||((stateA == SK2)&&(NODE_As[PKnum] == PK2))
          ||((stateA == SK2)&&(NODE_As[PKnum] == PK2))
          ||((stateA == CK)&&(NODE_As[CKnum] == CK))->checkFlagA = 1;
          ::else->skip;
        fi;
        if
          ::(checkFlagA == 1)->printf("communicable\n");
            NODE_As[CKnum] = keyA; NODE_As[PKnum] = false;
            NODE_As[SKnum] = false; NODE_As[CKnum] = false;
            NODE_As[SATEMnum] = SATEM; NODE_As[PKnum] = false;
            NODE_As[SKnum] = false; NODE_As[CKnum] = false;
            NODE_As[SATEMnum] = SATEM; RequestFlag = 1;
          ::else->printf("NODE_A can't decode reportB\n"); RequestFlag = 1;
        fi
      ::else->RequestFlag = 1;
      fi;
  od
}
```

Fig. 3. Promela code for the protocol

2304: proc 0 (NODE_A) JOIN.pml:70 (state 3)
[AtoB!UNLOCKED,request,nothing]
2318: proc 1 (NODE_B) JOIN.pml:166 (state 3)
[AtoB?stateB,messageB,keyB]
2330: proc 1 (NODE_B) JOIN.pml:186 (state 13)
[BtoA!UNLOCKED,policy,nothing]
2332: proc 0 (NODE_A) JOIN.pml:75 (state 7)
[BtoA?stateA,messageA,keyA]
2344: proc 0 (NODE_A) JOIN.pml:99 (state 18)
[AtoB!UNLOCKED,commitmentA,PK1]
2348: proc 2 (EVIL) JOIN.pml:242 (state 2)
[AtoB?stateE,messageE,keyE]
2352: proc 2 (EVIL) JOIN.pml:249 (state 4)
[AtoB!UNLOCKED,messageE,PK2]
2360: proc 1 (NODE_B) JOIN.pml:166 (state 3)
[AtoB?stateB,messageB,keyB]
2372: proc 1 (NODE_B) JOIN.pml:211 (state 29)
[BtoA!keyB,commitmentB,CK]
2374: proc 2 (EVIL) JOIN.pml:258 (state 11)
[BtoA?stateE,messageE,keyE]

Fig. 4. Behavior of successful impersonation attack

The top line (2304) in Fig. 4 represents that the process NODE_A (process ID is 0) executes [AtoB!UNLOCKED,request,nothing], which is 6th line in NODE_A in Fig. 3. This execution is 2304th step in the behavior in the trail file. AtoB is a name of communication channel in Fig. 3. In JOIN.pml, [AtoB!UNLOCKED,request,nothing] represents that the message "request and nothing" is sent to the communication channel "AtoB" without encryption. "UNLOCKED" represents "without encryption".

The second line in Fig. 4 shows that the process NODE_B (the process ID is 1) executes [AtoB?stateB,messageB,keyB], which is one line of the Promela code of Node_B in JOIN.pml [1]. This execution is 2318th step in the behavior in the trail file. After the step, the variables stateB, messageB and keyB have "UNLOCKED", "request" and "nothing" respectively. Like this, this paper analyzes the trail file and obtains the procedure of impersonation attacks. The following shows the procedure of impersonation attacks. In the procedure, EVIL represents an impersonation attacker and if EVIL knows a shared key that is used in MANETs, the impersonation attack is successful.

In 5th step in Fig. 1, Node A sends message to Node B and this message includes public key and the commitment of Node A. In the impersonation attack, the attacker receives this message and sends a fake message to Node B by replacing the public key of Node A with the public key of the attacker. Node

---

[1] This paper does not show the Promela code of Node_B for want of space of this paper.

B receives the fake message and confirms the commitment in the fake message. Node B cannot know that the message is fake because the commitment in the fake message is created by Node A and is guaranteed by Satem. Thus, Node B recognizes that the fake message is sent by Node A and uses the public key of the attacker in the fake message as the public key of Node A. By the public key of the attacker, Node B encrypts the commitment of Node B and the shared key that would be used between Node A and Node B. Node B sends the encrypted commitment and key to Node A. The attacker receives the encrypted commitment and key and decrypts the commitment and the key by the secret key of the attacker because these are encrypted by the public key of the attacker. As a result, the attacker can know the shared key that would be used between Node A and Node B.

This procedure is created from the trail file. This paper finds that an impersonation attack is successful in the protocol of MANETs.

4.2   Revision and Verification of JOIN Protocol

The result of verification shows that the protocol in MANETs is vulnerable to the threats of impersonation attacks. This section tries to revise the protocol and verify the revised protocol. This subsection revises the protocol according to the following two points.

First point

In first step in Fig. 1, Node A sends "Apply to join" message to Node B. In the revised protocol, Node A creates commitment, encrypts this commitment by a random number key and sends "Apply to join" message with the encrypted commitment. Node B receives "Apply to join" message with the encrypted commitment and keeps the encrypted commitment. Afterward, if Node A receives "Request policy enforcement" message, Node A sends the random number key that was used in encryption of the commitment, the public key of Node A and the commitment of Node A. By the random number key that is sent from Node A, Node B decrypts the encrypted commitment that is sent to Node B at "Apply to join" message. Node B compares the decrypted commitment and the commitment that is sent from Node A. If the two commitments are equal, Node B encrypts, by the public key of Node A, the shared key that is used between Node A and Node B and the commitment and sends encrypted data.

Because of this revision, an attacker must obtain the encrypted commitment of Node A that is sent from Node B in sending "Apply to join" message. This revision would enable Node A or Node B to detect impersonation attacks. However, an attacker can obtain the encrypted commitment of Node A by replay attack when Node A sends "Apply to join" message. In this protocol, an attacker can use the commitment of Node A for replay attack. If an attacker obtains the encrypted commitment, it is possible to succeed impersonation attacks. To prevent the replay attack, the paper revises the protocol as follows.

Second point

This paper introduces time stamps to messages including commitments. Without time stamps, the commitments of Node B are equal and it is easy to use the commitments in replay attack. In this revision, time of creating commitment is used as time stamp and time stamps are included in commitments. From the start to the end of one processing of "Apply to join" message, the same time stamp is used.

This revision enables to detect replay attack of commitments because the commitment that is used for connection request is different from the commitment that is used in replay attack.

4.3   Verification of Revised Protocol

Fig. 5 is a part of Promela code of Node A in the revised protocol. By SPIN, this subsection verifies that the revised protocol satisfies the property that shared keys are not known to attackers. The result of verification is that the revised protocol does not satisfy the property. In this verification, a Promela code of attackers is the same as that of the verification of the first version of the protocol. Fig. 6 is a part of a trail file in the verification of the revised protocol.

Fig. 6 can be read like Fig. 4, but the message format in the revised protocol is different from that in the first version of the protocol. In the revised protocol, the messages have six items. In the first version, the messages have three items and the first item represents whether the other items are encrypted or not. In the revised protocol, the first, third and fifth items represents whether the second, fourth and sixth items are encrypted or not. The procedure of impersonation attack is obtained from the trail file as follows.

In the revised protocol, Node A sends "Deliver commitments" message that includes the public key of Node A, a random number key and the commitment to Node B. If an attacker receives the message, the attacker sends a fake message to Node B by replacing the public key of Node A with the public key of the attacker. After Node B receives the fake message, Node B checks a commitment in the fake message; Node B recognizes that the commitment is guaranteed by Satem because the commitment is created by Node A correctly. By the random number key in the fake message, Node B decrypts the commitment that was sent with connection request because the random key in the fake message is correct. Node B thinks that the decrypted commitment is the same as the commitment that was sent with connection request and that the time stamp of the decrypted commitment is the same as that of the commitment with connection request. Therefore, Node B recognizes that the fake message would be correct and uses the public key of the attacker as the public key of Node A. Node B encrypts the commitment of Node B by the public key of the attacker and sends the encrypted commitment. If the attacker receives the encrypted commitment, it decrypts the commitment and obtains the shared key in MANETs.

```
active proctype NODE_A()
{
  mtype stateA1,stateA2,stateA3,messageA1,messageA2,messageA3;
  int n = 0;
  NODE_As[PKnum] = UNLOCKED;  NODE_As[SKnum] = UNLOCKED;
  NODE_As[CKnum] = UNLOCKED;  NODE_As[RKnum] = UNLOCKED;
  NODE_As[SATEMnum] = SATEM;  NODE_As[RKnum] = RK_A;

  do
    ::(FirstFlag == 1)||(RequestFlag == 1)->
      atomic{
      time++; commitmentA_time = time;
      AtoB!UNLOCKED,request,RK_A,commitmentA,UNLOCKED,nothing;
      FirstFlag = 0; RequestFlag = 0; printf("A send request\n");
      }
    ::(RequestFlag == 0)->BtoA?stateA1,messageA1,stateA2,messageA2,stateA3,messageA3;
      if
        ::(messageA1 == policy)->checkFlagA = 0;printf("A_get_policy\n");
        if
          ::(stateA1 == UNLOCKED) ||((stateA1 == PK_A)&&(NODE_As[SKnum] == SK_A))
            ||((stateA1 == PK_E)&&(NODE_As[SKnum] == SK_E))
            ||((stateA1 == SK_A)&&(NODE_As[PKnum] == PK_A))
            ||((stateA1 == SK_E)&&(NODE_As[PKnum] == PK_E))
            ||((stateA1 == CK)&&(NODE_As[CKnum] == CK))
            ||((stateA1 == RK_A)&&(NODE_Bs[RKnum] == RK_A))
            ||((stateA1 == RK_E)&&(NODE_Bs[RKnum] == RK_E))->checkFlagA = 1;
          ::else->skip;
        fi;
        if
          ::(checkFlagA == 1)->
            if
              ::(NODE_As[SATEMnum] == SATEM)
                ->AtoB!UNLOCKED,commitmentA,UNLOCKED,PK_A,UNLOCKED,RK_A; time++;
                NODE_As[SKnum] = SK_A; NODE_As[PKnum] = PK_A;
                printf("check_A_sent_repoetAandPK\n");
              ::else->printf("SATEM lost\n"); RequestFlag = 1; break;
            fi
          ::else->printf("NODE_A can't decode policy\n"); RequestFlag = 1; break;
        fi
        ::(messageA1 == commitmentB)->checkFlagA = 0; printf("check_A_get_commitmentB\n");
        if
          ::(stateA1 == UNLOCKED)||((stateA1 == PK_A)&&(NODE_As[SKnum] == SK_A))
            ||((stateA1 == PK_E)&&(NODE_As[SKnum] == SK_E))
            ||((stateA1 == SK_A)&&(NODE_As[PKnum] == PK_A))
            ||((stateA1 == SK_E)&&(NODE_As[PKnum] == PK_E))
            ||((stateA1 == CK)&&(NODE_As[CKnum] == CK))
            ||((stateA1 == RK_A)&&(NODE_Bs[RKnum] == RK_A))
            ||((stateA1 == RK_E)&&(NODE_Bs[RKnum] == RK_E))->checkFlagA = 1;
          ::else->skip;
        fi;
        if
          ::(checkFlagA == 1)->printf("communicable\n"); NODE_As[CKnum] = messageA2; n = 0;
            do
              ::(n<ABNUM)->NODE_As[n] = UNLOCKED; NODE_Bs[n] = UNLOCKED; n++;
              ::else->NODE_As[SATEMnum] = SATEM; NODE_Bs[SATEMnum] = SATEM; break;
            od;
            RequestFlag = 1; break;
          ::else->printf("NODE_A can't open commitmentB\n"); RequestFlag = 1; break;
        fi;
        ::else->printf("A get request\n"); RequestFlag = 1; break;
      fi;
    ::else->skip;
  od
}
```

Fig. 5. Promela code for the revised protocol

105: proc 0 (NODE_A) JOIN2.pml:133 (state 10)
      [AtoB!UNLOCKED,request,RK_A,commitmentA,UNLOCKED,nothing]
113: proc 1 (NODE_B) JOIN2.pml:259 (state 7)
      [AtoB?stateB1,messageB1,stateB2,messageB2,stateB3,messageB3]
129: proc 1 (NODE_B) JOIN2.pml:284 (state 20)
      [BtoA!UNLOCKED,policy,UNLOCKED,nothing,UNLOCKED,nothing]
137: proc 0 (NODE_A) JOIN2.pml:139 (state 16)
      [BtoA?stateA1,messageA1,stateA2,messageA2,stateA3,messageA3]
155: proc 0 (NODE_A) JOIN2.pml:163 (state 29)
      [AtoB!UNLOCKED,commitmentA,UNLOCKED,P_A,UNLOCKED,R_A]
157: proc 2 (EVIL) JOIN2.pml:432 (state 50)
      [AtoB?stateE1,messageE1,stateE2,messageE2,stateE3,messageE3]
665: proc 2 (EVIL) JOIN2.pml:465 (state 144)
      [AtoB!UNLOCKED,commitmentA,UNLOCKED,P_E,UNLOCKED,R_A]
671: proc 1 (NODE_B) JOIN2.pml:259 (state 7)
      [AtoB?stateB1,messageB1,stateB2,messageB2,stateB3,messageB3]
693: proc 1 (NODE_B) JOIN2.pml:324 (state 44)
      [BtoA!messageB2,commitmentB,messageB2,CK,UNLOCKED,nothing]
695: proc 2 (EVIL) JOIN2.pml:489 (state 166)
      [BtoA?stateE1,messageE1,stateE2,messageE2,stateE3,messageE3]

Fig. 6. Behavior of successful impersonation attack after revision

4.4 Revision again

The verification of the revised protocol does not show that revise the protocol satisfies the property. This paper tries to obtain the concrete protocol from the proposal of [1] again, but this paper cannot obtain the concrete protocol. Thus, this paper decides that all nodes in MANETs must communicate with certificate authority (CA) of public keys in the protocol proposed in [1].

This paper constructs the concrete protocol using CA via the Internet and describes Promela codes of the protocol and attackers for the concrete JOIN protocol. The result of the verification is that the concrete protocol using CA via the Internet is secure for the threats of impersonation attacks.

5 Conclusion

This paper constructs the concrete JOIN protocol in MANETs from the proposal of the protocol in MANETs in [1] because there may be several versions of protocol in [1] and because this paper does not find the concrete protocol in [1]. This paper inspects vulnerability of JOIN protocol in MANETs and finds that JOIN protocol is vulnerable to the threats of impersonation attack. This paper also revises the protocol to prevent impersonation attack and inspects vulnerability of JOIN protocol by SPIN. However, this paper cannot construct the protocol that is invulnerable to the threats of impersonation attack.

Under the assumption that all nodes in MANETs can communicate with certificate authority (CA) of public keys, this paper constructs the concrete JOIN protocol that is invulnerable to the threats of impersonation attack. The future work is to give the method of determining whether secure concrete protocols can be constructed from the overview of protocols.

References

1. Xu, G., Borcea, C., Iftode, L.: A policy Enforcing Mechanism for Trusted Ad Hoc Networks. IEEE Transactions on Dependable and Secure Computing 8(3), 321–336 (2011)
2. Xu, G., Borcea, C., Iftode, L.: Satem: A Service-Aware Attestation Method toward Trusted Service Transaction. In: Proceedings of IEEE Symposium on Reliable Distributed System (SRDS), pp. 321–336 (2006)
3. Perkins, C.E., Royer, E.M.: Ad Hoc On-Demand Distance Vector Routing. In: Proceedings of Second IEEE Workshop Mobile Computing Systems and Applications, pp. 90–100 (1999)
4. Zhou, L., Yin, X., Wang, Z.: Protocol Security Testing with SPIN and TTCN-3. In: 2011 IEEE Fourth International Conference on Software Testing, Verification and Validation Workshops (ICSTW), pp. 511–519 (2011)
5. Holzmann, G.J.: The Model Checker SPIN. IEEE Transactions on Software Engineering 23(5), 1–17 (1997)
6. Capkun, S., Hubaux, J., Buttyan, L.: Mobility Helps Security in Ad Hoc Networks. Proceedings of ACM MobiHOC, 46–56 (2003)
7. Ni, S.-Y., Tseng, Y.-C., Chen, Y.-S., Sheu, J.-P.: The Broadcast Storm Problem in a Mobile Ad Hoc Network. Proceedings of ACM/IEEE MobiCom, 151–162 (1999)
8. Xu, G., Iftode, L.: Locality Driven Key Management for Mobile Ad-Hoc Networks. In: Proceedings of First IEEE International Conference on Mobile Ad-Hoc Networks and Sensor Systems (MASS 2004), pp. 436–446 (2004)
9. Kong, J., Zerfos, P., Luo, H., Lu, S., Zhang, L.: Providing Robust and Ubiquitous Security Support for Mobile Ad-Hoc Networks. In: Proceedings of Ninth IEEE International Conference on Network Protocols (ICNP 2001), p. 251 (2001)
10. Capkun, S., Buttyan, L., Hubaux, J.P.: Self-Organized Public-Key Management for Mobile Ad Hoc Networks. IEEE Transaction on Mobile Computing 2(1), 52–64 (2003)
11. Xu, G., Borcea, C., Iftode, L.: Trusted Application-Centric Ad-Hoc Networks. In: Proceedings of Fourth IEEE International Conference on Mobile Ad-Hoc Networks and Sensor Systems, MASS 2007 (2007)
12. Rusinowitch, M., Turuani, M.: Protocol insecurity with a finite number of sessions and composed keys is NP-complete. Theoretical Computer Science 299(1-3), 451–475 (2003)
13. Trusted Computing Group: TCG 1.1b Specifications (2010), https://www.trustedcomputinggroup.org.home
14. Trusted Computing Group-Mobile Phone Working Group: Use Case Scenarios v2.7 (2005)
15. Ben-Ari, M.: Principles of the Spin Model Checker (2008)
16. SPIN website, http://spinroot.com/spin/whatispin.html
17. Trusted Computing Group, http://www.trustedcomputinggroup.org

Zero-Day Traffic Identification

Jun Zhang, Xiao Chen, Yang Xiang, and Wanlei Zhou

School of Information Technology,
Deakin University,
Melbourne, Australia, 3125
{jun.zhang,chxiao,yang.xiang,wanlei}@deakin.edu.au

Abstract. Recent research on Internet traffic classification has achieved certain success in the application of machine learning techniques into flow statistics based method. However, existing methods fail to deal with zero-day traffic which are generated by previously unknown applications in a traffic classification system. To tackle this critical problem, we propose a novel traffic classification scheme which has the capability of identifying zero-day traffic as well as accurately classifying the traffic generated by pre-defined application classes. In addition, the proposed scheme provides a new mechanism to achieve fine-grained classification of zero-day traffic through manually labeling very few traffic flows. The preliminary empirical study on a big traffic data show that the proposed scheme can address the problem of zero-day traffic effectively. When zero-day traffic present, the classification performance of the proposed scheme is significantly better than three state-of-the-art methods, random forest classifier, classification with flow correlation, and semi-supervised traffic classification.

Keywords: Traffic classification, semi-supervised learning, zero-day applications.

1 Introduction

Classification of traffic can help identify different applications and protocols that exist in a network, which is a basic tool for network management [1]. For example, most of QoS control mechanisms has a traffic classification module in order to properly prioritize different applications across the limited bandwidth. In addition, to implement appropriate security policies, it is essential for any network manager to obtain a proper understanding of the applications and protocols in the network traffic. In the last decade, traffic classification has absorbed much attention in the industry and academia.

The existing traffic classification techniques can be classified into three categories: ports-based method, payload-based method, and flow statistics based method [2]. Traditional ports-based method relies on checking the standard ports used by well-known applications. However, it is not always reliable since not all current applications use standard ports. Some applications even obfuscate themselves by using well-defined ports of other applications. The payload-based

G. Wang et al. (Eds.): CSS 2013, LNCS 8300, pp. 213–227, 2013.

method deeply inspects the application's signature in IP payload, which can avoid the problem of dynamic ports. Hence, it is most prevalent in current industry products. However, more often than not, the payload-based method fails with encrypted traffic and goes against the user privacy. In recent academic research, substantial attention has been paid on the application of machine learning techniques into the flow statistics based method. The statistical method uses only flow statistical features, such as inter-packet time, without the requirement of inspecting content of IP packets. This new method displays its potential in identifying complex traffic, but also faces big challenges.

We observe that the flow statistics based method suffers from a critical problem, namely 'zero-day traffic'. The zero-day traffic is defined as network traffic generated by previously unknown applications in a traffic classification system. Most of flow statistics based methods solve a multi-class classification problem by using supervised or unsupervised machine learning algorithms. In supervised traffic classification [3–8], a classifier is learned from the labeled training set, which classifies any traffic into the predefined known classes. By contrast, the unsupervised methods [9–11] automatically categorize a set of unlabeled training samples and apply the clustering results to construct a traffic classifier with the assistance of other tools such as deep payload inspection (DPI). Under the assumption that any traffic comes from a known class, a number of promising results have been reported in the literature. Obviously, these methods are unable to handle zero-day traffic since they do not belong to any known class. When zero-day traffic present, the performance of these methods will be influenced severely by misclassifying zero-day traffic into known classes.

This paper presents a novel scheme to address the problem of zero-day traffic. Taking zero-day traffic into account, we propose to incorporate a generic unknown class into conventional multi-class classification framework. Thus, the problem becomes how to obtain the training samples of zero-day traffic. We furthermore propose to extract zero-day traffic information from a set of unlabeled traffic which are randomly collected from the target network. The major contributions of this work are summarized as follows.

- We develop a novel traffic classification scheme with the capability of zero-day traffic identification.
- We present a new algorithm to automatically extract the samples of zero-day traffic from a set of unlabeled network traffic.
- We propose a new mechanism to achieve fine-grained classification of zero-day traffic with little human effort.
- We provide a theoretical study to confirm the effectiveness of the proposed scheme.

To evaluate the new scheme, a large number of experiments are carried out on a big traffic dataset. The results show the proposed scheme significantly outperform the state-of-the-art traffic classification methods when zero-day traffic present.

The rest of this paper is organized as follows. Section 2 states the research problem through a critical review of the flow statistics based method. In

Section 3, a novel scheme is proposed to deal with zero-day traffic. Section 4 reports the experiments and results. Finally, Section 5 concludes this paper.

2   Problem of Zero-Day Traffic

The flow statistics based method will not be practical until it meets several big challenges. In years gone by, the biggest challenge is real-time traffic classification at increasing wire speeds. But now the operators are facing another challenge - zero-day traffic, which is due to the tremendous rate of development of new applications. A traffic classification system is difficult to obtain sufficient information of all existing applications, particularly in current situation with the explosive growth in the number of web and mobile applications. This section provides an analysis on the impact of zero-day traffic by critically reviewing the state-of-the-art flow statistics based methods.

Let's start with a real-world network scenario. Suppose the traffic dataset, Ω, consists of K known classes and U unknown classes.

$$\Omega = \{\omega_1, ..., \omega_K, \overline{\omega}_1, ..., \overline{\omega}_U\}$$

A known class ω_k refers to a well-known application in the traffic classification system. In this paper, a set of labeled flow samples, ψ_k, is available for a known class, ω_k. By contrast, an unknown class is associated with a previously unknown application in the system. Therefore, no labeled flow samples are available for an unknown class. Given the labeled training samples $\{\psi_1, ..., \psi_K\}$, the traffic classification problem is how to identify the class of flows in Ω.

- A flow consists of successive IP packets with the same 5-tuple: source ip, source port, destination ip, destination port, transport protocol.

Considering the flow statistics-based method, a number of statistical features, such as number of packets, packet size, and inter-packet time, are calculated to represent a flow $\mathbf{x}$.

2.1 K-Class Classification

Conventional flow statistics based methods address a K-class classification problem without consideration of zero-day traffic [3–14]. A typical K-class classification method uses the labeled flow samples, $T = \bigcup_{i=1}^{K} \psi_i$, straightforward and employs a machine learning algorithm to construct a classifier. The classifier trained by using T will classify any testing flow into one of the predefined classes. Thus, the zero-day traffic flows in the unknown classes, $\{\overline{\omega}_1, ..., \overline{\omega}_U\}$, will be misclassified into K known classes. It is assumed that all testing flows come from the known classes, so the classification performance will be severely affected by zero-day traffic.

2.2   Semi-supervised Classification

A semi-supervised method [15] was proposed to take unknown applications into account. Firstly, some mixture of labeled and unlabeled training samples are grouped into k clusters by using traditional clustering algorithms such as k-means. Then, the traffic clusters are mapped to $\omega_1, ..., \omega_K$, or unknown according to the locations of the labeled (supervised) training samples. For traffic classification, a flow will be predicted to the class of its nearest cluster. This method demonstrates the potential of dealing with zero-day traffic generated by unknown applications. Unfortunately, the performance evaluation about zero-day traffic identification was not reported in [15]. Moreover, the semi-supervised method is heuristic in nature. A large k is necessary for generating high-purity clusters, while it will lead to many false unknown clusters. Later, the ensemble clustering technique was introduced to improve the semi-supervised method [16]. However, these semi-supervised methods have been evaluated by only using the data in known classes, which is against their basic motivation.

2.3   One-Class Classification

Some methods address a one-class classification problem for the purpose of traffic classification. Considering one-class classification, any testing flow can be determined whether it belongs to a known class. If the flow does not belong to any known class, it is identified as unknown traffic. In this way, the problem of zero-day traffic could be by passed. An early work is creating an one-class classifier using normalized threshold on statistical features [17]. This method is heuristic and not reliable since the normalized threshold is hard to tune beforehand especially without any information of zero-day traffic. A modified one-class SVM method has been proposed for traffic classification [7]. For a known class ω_k, the training samples in ψ_k are used to learn a one-class SVM and other training samples in $\bigcup_{i=1, i \neq k}^{i=K} \psi_i$ are used to adjust the decision boundary. This method has two big issues. Firstly, one-class SVM normally needs a large number of training samples and the modified method cannot outperform a traditional two-class SVM. Secondly, the decision boundary is still poor due to the lake of the information about unknown classes, $\{\overline{\omega}_1, ..., \overline{\omega}_U\}$.

2.4   Remarks

The above critical review indicates that the classifiers created by using the pre-labeled samples cannot deal with zero-day traffic. The information of unknown classes is crucial for zero-day traffic identification. Therefore, this work focus on discovering the information of unknown classes, $\{\overline{\omega}_1, ..., \overline{\omega}_U\}$. Inspired by the semi-supervised method [15], we realize that the data randomly collected from the target network contains traffic flows generated by unknown applications. Formally, we can obtain a set of unlabeled samples, $\Omega_r \subset \Omega$. Then, the key problem becomes how to extract the samples of zero-day traffic from Ω_r. Finally, the extracted zero-day traffic samples can be combined with the pre-labeled

---

noend 1. Zero-day samples extraction

Require: labeled sets $\{\psi_1, ..., \psi_K\}$, unlabeled set T_u
Ensure: zero-day sample set U
1: $T_l \leftarrow \bigcup_{i=1}^{K} \psi_i$
2: $T \leftarrow T_l \cup T_u$
3: Perform clustering on T to obtain clusters $\{C_1, ..., C_k\}$
4: $V \leftarrow \emptyset$
5: **for** $i = 1$ **to** k **do**
6:     **if** C_i does not contain any labeled flows from T_l **then**
7:         $V \leftarrow (V \cup C_i)$
8: Combine $\{\psi_1, ..., \psi_K\}$ and V to train a $(K+1)$-class classifier f_c {V is for a generic unknown class}
9: $U \leftarrow \emptyset$
10: **while** Classify all flows in T_u by f_c **do**
11:     **if** $\mathbf{x}$ is predicted to the unknown class **then**
12:         Put $\mathbf{x}$ into U

---

training set, $T = \bigcup_{i=1}^{i=K} \psi_i$, to create a super classifier with the capability of zero-day traffic identification.

3   Proposed Scheme

In this section, we present a new traffic classification scheme with zero-day traffic identification. There are three important modules in the proposed scheme: unknown discovery, compound identification, and system update. The module of unknown discovery is aimed to automatically find new samples of zero-day traffic in a set of unlabeled traffic which are randomly collected from the target network. The module of compound identification takes the pre-labeled training samples and the zero-day traffic samples as input to build up a classifier for robust traffic classification. To achieve fine-grained classification, the module of system update can intelligently analyze the zero-day traffic and construct new classes to complement the system's knowledge.

3.1   Unknown Discovery

Unknown discovery is a key point for the new scheme of zero-day traffic identification. We propose a two-step method to extract zero-day traffic samples from a set of unlabeled network traffic. The basic assumption is that the pre-labeled training set for known classes does not contain zero-day samples. However, zero-day traffic must exist in the data randomly collected from the target network.

The two-step method for unknown discovery is summarized in Algorithm 1. Given the pre-labeled training sets $\{\psi_1, \ldots, \psi_K\}$ and an unlabeled set T_u, in the first step, we roughly filter some zero-day samples out from T_u by using a semi-supervised idea. The labeled and unlabeled samples are merged to feed a clustering algorithm, k-means. The k-means clustering aims to partition the traffic flows into k clusters ($k \leq |T|$), $C = \{C_1, \ldots, C_k\}$, so as to minimize the within-cluster sum of squares:

$$\underset{C}{\arg\min} \sum_{i=1}^{k} \sum_{\mathbf{x}_j \in C_i} \|\mathbf{x}_j - \mathbf{m}_i\|, \tag{1}$$

where $\mathbf{m}_i$ denotes the centroid of C_i and it is the mean of flows in C_i. The traditional k-means algorithm uses an iterative refinement technique. Given an initial set of randomly selected k centroids $\{\mathbf{m}_1^0, \ldots, \mathbf{m}_k^0\}$, the algorithm proceeds by alternating between the assignment step and the update step [18]. In the assignment step, each flow is assigned to the cluster with the closest mean.

$$C_i^t = \{\mathbf{x}_j : \|\mathbf{x}_j - \mathbf{m}_i^t\| \leq \|\mathbf{x}_j - \mathbf{m}_l^t\| \text{ for all } l = 1, \ldots, k\} \tag{2}$$

In the update step, the new means are calculated to be the centroid of the flows in the cluster.

$$\mathbf{m}_i^{t+1} = \frac{1}{|C_i^t|} \sum_{\mathbf{x}_j \in C_i^t} \mathbf{x}_j. \tag{3}$$

By choosing a large k [10, 19], we can obtain the high-purity traffic clusters, $\{C_1, \ldots, C_k\}$. Then, the pre-labeled training samples can be used to identify zero-day traffic clusters. The rule is, if a cluster does not contain any pre-labeled samples, it is a zero-day traffic cluster.

We observe that the zero-day samples detected in this simple way is insufficient. To fix this issue, in the second step, the flow set V collected for zero-day traffic in the first step are temporally used as the training set for a generic unknown class. Thus, we have a specific classification problem which involves K known classes and 1 unknown class. The pre-labeled training sets $\{\psi_1, \ldots, \psi_K\}$ and the temporal zero-day training set V can be combined to train a multi-class classifier, f_c, such as random forest. We further apply f_c to classify the flows in T_u, so as to obtain a high-purity set of zero-day samples, U. In particular, to guarantee the purity of zero-day samples, we apply a new classification method by considering flow correlation in real-world traffic, which will be described in details in Section 3.2.

3.2 Compound Identification

For robust traffic classification, we further propose a new compound method to build up a super classifier with the capability of zero-day traffic identification. The novelty is to consider flow correlation in real-world network traffic and classify correlated flows jointly rather than single flows.

Algorithm 2 presents the proposed method of compound identification. Given the pre-labeled training sets $\{\psi_1, \ldots, \psi_K\}$ and the zero-day sample set U produced by the module of unknown discovery, we can build up a classifier, f_c, for the $(K+1)$-class classification. f_c is able to categorize zero-day traffic into the generic unknown class. Following our previous work [8], we incorporate flow correlation

---

noend 2. BoF-based traffic classification

Require: labeled sets $\{\psi_1, ..., \psi_K\}$, zero-day sample set U, testing set Ω_t
Ensure: label set L_t for testing flows
1: Combine $\{\psi_1, ..., \psi_K\}$ and U to train a $(K + 1)$-class classifier f_c {U represent a generic unknown class}
2: Construct BoFs $\mathbf{X} = \{X_i\}$ from Ω_t according to 3-tuple heuristic {consider flow correlation in traffic classification}
3: **while** $\mathbf{X} \neq \emptyset$ **do**
4:    Take a BoF X_i from $\mathbf{X}$
5:    **for** $j = 1$ **to** $|X_i|$ **do**
6:        Classify $\mathbf{x}_{ij}$ by f_c
7:    Make find decision by aggregating the predictions of flows in BoF X_i
8:    Assign the label of X_i to all flows in this BoF

---

into traffic classification process in order to significantly improve the identification accuracy. Flow correlation can be discovered by the 3-tuple heuristic [20], that is, in a short period of time, the flows sharing destination ip, destination port and transport protocol are generated by the same application/protocol. For convenience of traffic classification, we use "bag of flows" (BoF) to model flow correlation. A BoF can be described by $X = \{\mathbf{x}_1, \ldots, \mathbf{x}_g\}$, where $\mathbf{x}_i$ represents the ith flow in the BoF. Classification of a BoF can be addressed by aggregating the flow predictions produced by a conventional classifier. In this paper, the aggregated classifier $f_{bof}(X)$ can be expressed as

$$f_{bof}(X) = \Theta_{\mathbf{x} \in X}(f_c(\mathbf{x})), \tag{4}$$

where $f_c(\mathbf{x})$ denotes the random forest classifier and Θ is the majority vote method [21]. For BoF X, we have g flow predictions $y_{x1}, \ldots, y_{xg}$ which are produced by f_c. The flow predictions can be straightforwardly transformed into votes,

$$v_{ij} = \begin{cases} 1, & \text{if } y_{xj} \text{ indicates the } i\text{-th class,} \\ 0, & \text{otherwise.} \end{cases} \tag{5}$$

Then, the compound decision rule is

$$\begin{aligned} &\text{assign } X \to \omega_l \text{ if} \\ &\sum_{j=1}^{g} v_{lj} = \max_{i=1,\ldots,q} \sum_{j=1}^{g} v_{ij} \end{aligned} \tag{6}$$

Consequently, all flows in X are classified into ω_l. The BoF-based traffic classification is also used for unknown discovery in Section 3.1.

3.3 System Update

With unknown discovery and compound identification, the proposed scheme has been able to identify zero-day traffic when performing traffic classification. The

---

noend 3. New class detection

Require: zero-day traffic Z
Ensure: training samples for new classes
1: Perform clustering on Z to obtain k clusters $\{C_1, ..., C_k\}$
2: **for** $i = 1$ **to** k **do**
3:     Randomly select A flows from C_i
4:     Manually inspect these A flows {Involve a little human effort}
5:     **if** All flows are generated by the same application **then**
6:         **if** This is a new application **then**
7:             **if** It has been identified **then**
8:                 Merge C_i and its training set
9:             **else**
10:                Create a training set ψ' for this new application

---

module of system update is proposed to achieve fine-grained classification of zero-day traffic. The purpose is to learn new classes in the identified zero-day traffic and complement the system's knowledge. The capability of learning new classes makes the proposed scheme different to conventional traffic classification method.

The procedure of learning new classes is shown in Algorithm 3. Given a set of zero-day traffic, Z, which is the outcome of compound identification, we perform the k-means clustering to obtain the clusters $\{C_1, \ldots, C_k\}$. For each cluster, we randomly select several sample flows (e.g.,three) for manual inspection. To guarantee the purity of new training sets, the consensus strategy is adopted to make prediction. If all of the selected flows indicate a new application/protocol, we will create a new class and use the flows in the cluster as its training data. For a new class which has been created during the system update, the flows in the cluster will be added into the training set of that class. Once the cluster inspection is completed, the new detected classes will be added into the set of known classes and the training dataset will be extended accordingly. In this way, the classification system is able to learn new classes. The updated system can deal with more applications and achieve more fine-grained classification.

4   Performance Evaluation

This section reports the empirical study on the performance of our scheme. A large number of experiments are carried out on a complex traffic dataset to compare our scheme with the state-of-the-art traffic classification methods.

4.1   Traffic Dataset

In this paper, four Internet traffic traces are used for our experimental study. They are captured from three Internet positions located around the world, such that the sampling points are heterogeneous in terms of link type and capacity. The collection time ranges from 2006 to 2010, covering five recent years in which

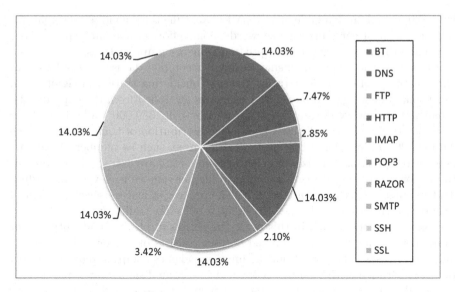

Fig. 1. Class distribution of the complex dataset

the Internet has grown and evolved rapidly. Since either partial or full packet payload is preserved in these traffic traces, we can build the ground truth (i.e. the actual classes of traffic flows) with high confidence. The keio and wide traces are provided by the public traffic data repository maintained by the MAWI working group (http://mawi.wide.ad.jp/mawi/). The keio trace is captured at a 1Gbps Ethernet link in Keio Universitys Shonan-Fujisawa campus in Japan and it is collected in August of 2006. The wide-08 and wide-09 traces are taken at a US-Japan trans-Pacific backbone line (a 150Mbps Ethernet link) that carries commodity traffic for WIDE organizations. The original traces collected as part of the 'a Day in the Life of the Internet' project last 72 hours on 2008/03/18-2008/03/20 and 96 hours on 2009/03/30-2009/04/02. For each of them, we use a 5-hour subset in our work. Forty bytes of application layer payload are kept for each packet while all IP addresses are anonymized in keio and wide traces. In addition, the isp data set is a trace we captured using a passive probe at a 100Mbps Ethernet edge link of an Internet Service Provider located in Australia. Full packet payloads are preserved in the collection without any filtering or packet loss. The trace is 7-day-long starting from November 27 of 2010.

We focus exclusively on the TCP traffic that constitutes the vast majority traffic (up to 95%) in the observed networks. In consideration of practical uses, we adopt a 900-second idle timeout for the flows terminated without a proper tear-down. To establish the ground truth in the datasets, we develop a DPI tool that matches regular expression patterns against payloads. Two distinct sets of application signatures are developed, which are based on previous experience and some well-known tools such as l7-filter (http://l7-filter.sourceforge.net) and Tstat (http://tstat.tlc.polito.it). The first set is designed to match against full flow payload (for the isp trace). For the rest traces in which only 40 bytes of payload are available in each packet, we tune the second set of signatures to match against early message keywords. Some effort of manual inspection are also made to investigate the encrypted and emerging applications.

To evaluate the proposed scheme, we create a complex dataset by random sampling in the pool of the four traffic traces. Considering statistical significance, some small classes and unrecognized traffic are excluded from the experiments. Finally, the complex dataset is constituted by over 350,000 traffic flows from 10 major traffic classes. Figure 1 shows the distribution of traffic classes in the dataset. 20 unidirectional flow statistical features, such as number of packets, number of bytes, packet size, inter-packet time, etc., are extracted to represent traffic flows. We apply feature selection to further remove irrelevant and redundant features from the feature set [22]. The process of feature selection yields 9 features for the complex dataset. To simulate zero-day traffic, we manually set a few classes to "unknown". In this work, the classes of bt, dns, and smtp are set to unknown. Therefore, the modified dataset consists of 7 known classes and 3 unknown classes. The flows from the unknown classes compose zero-day traffic. In the experiments, the dataset is divided into four disjoint parts: pre-labeled set, unlabeled set, and two testing sets. For known classes, 5% of the flows are randomly selected from the pre-labeled set to form a supervised training set. It is important to note that no any samples of unknown classes are available for the classification system. Some flows are randomly selected from the unlabeled set and used in the proposed scheme. Two testing sets are used to evaluate the proposed scheme with or without system update, respectively.

4.2   Experiments and Results

A large number of special experiments are conducted to evaluate our new scheme. We present the average performance over 100 runs.

Overall Classification Performance. When zero-day traffic present, we compare the proposed scheme with three state-of-the-art traffic classification methods: random forest, BoF-based method [8], semi-supervised method [15]. For the sake of fairness, the proposed scheme without system update is evaluated in the experiments. We take random forest as a representative of conventional supervised traffic classification methods. In our empirical study, random forest displays superior performance over other supervised algorithms, such as k-NN and support vector machine. The BoF-based method [8] is able to effectively incorporate flow correlation into supervised classification. Our previous work showed the BoF-based method outperforms conventional supervised methods. We implement the BoF-based method by employing random forest algorithm and majority vote rule. In addition, we test Erman's semi-supervised method [15] which has the capability of unknown identification. F-measure is adopted to compare the overall performance of four competing methods. In the proposed scheme and semi-supervised method, the number of k-means clusters is set to 700 and 5000 unlabelled flows are provided.

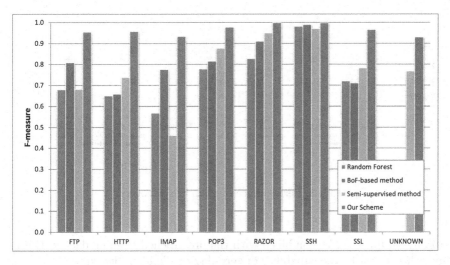

Fig. 2. Overall performance

Fig. 2 reports the F-measures of the proposed scheme and three competing methods. The results show that the proposed scheme significantly outperforms other methods in any class. For example, the proposed scheme is better than Erman's semi-supervised method over 20 percent in class http. In class ftp, the F-measure of the proposed scheme is higher than the second best method, BoF-based method, about 15 percent. The proposed scheme displays good robustness against zero-day traffic. Although the semi-supervised method is able to detect zero-day traffic, it is sensitive to different classes. For example, in class IMAP, the semi-supervised method is the worst one among four. One can see that the proposed scheme can perfectly deal with zero-day traffic as well as traffic flows of known classes. The reason is that it combines the advantages of the BoF-based method and semi-supervised method. The BoF model can effectively improve the classification performance of known classes. In Fig. 2, the BoF-based method shows higher F-measures than conventional random forest. In class ftp and class imap, the BoF-based method is even better than the semi-supervised method. The semi-supervised method has the potential to extract zero-day samples from unlabelled data. Its F-measure in class unknown can achieve 0.77, while the supervised methods cannot identify any zero-day traffic.

We observe that the superiority of the proposed scheme is due to its excellent functionality of unknown discovery. A new two-step unknown discovery is developed for our traffic classification scheme. The first step borrows the idea of the semi-supervised method to roughly detect some zero-day samples. The experimental results show the true positive rate of zero-day traffic detection in the first step is 69.1% and the false positive rate is 3.2%. The second step constructs a random forest classifier by using the outcome of the first step, which can further improve the effectiveness of zero-day sample extraction. In the experiment, the true positive rate raises to 91% and the false positive rate reduces to 0.7%. Thus,

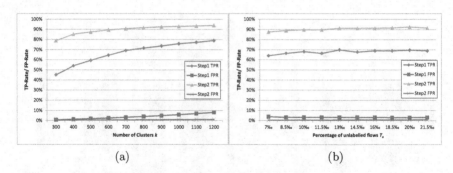

(a)   (b)

Fig. 3. Performance of unknown discovery

zero-day samples can be combined with the pre-labelled training data to train a super classifier with the capability of zero-day traffic identification.

Impact of Parameters. Generally speaking, the setting of parameters is a big challenge for a traffic classification method which applies machine learning techniques. We perform a set of experiments to test the impact of two parameters, k and T_u on classification performance of our scheme. k denotes the number of clusters produced by k-means clustering. We change it from 300 to 1,200 with an interval of 100. T_u denotes the number of unlabelled flows which feeds to unknown discovery. T_u is tested from 7‰ to 21.5‰ with an interval of 1.5‰. These two parameters could affect the classification performance, since they control the amount and purity of extracted zero-day samples. Accuracy is adopted in the experiments for performance evaluation. It is the ratio of the sum of all correctly classified flows to the sum of all testing flows. This metric can be used to measure classification performance on the whole testing data.

Totally, we have tested 100 accuracy values produced by 100 pairs of parameters. The results show that our scheme is insensitive to parameters. In particular, the classification accuracy of using any pair of parameters is between 96.5% and 97.5%. This is a beautiful characteristic, which is convenient for the system operator to choose the parameters in practice. The cause is that our scheme adopts the two-steps unknown discovery. The change of parameters could affect the outcome of the first step, while the second step can make self-adjust to extract zero-day samples effectively. The slight variations on classification accuracy are related to the unlabelled dataset which is randomly created and the randomness of k-means clustering.

We further perform a set of experiments to investigate the robustness of unknown discovery. Fig. 3 reports the true positive rate (TPR) and false positive rate (FPR) of zero-day sample detection in the two steps of unknown discovery. Fig. 3(a) shows the results with a fixed $T_u = 5,000$ and various k. One can see that, FPR produced in the first step is low, while TPR is not high. The second step can significantly improves TPR and further reduces FPR. TPR of unknown

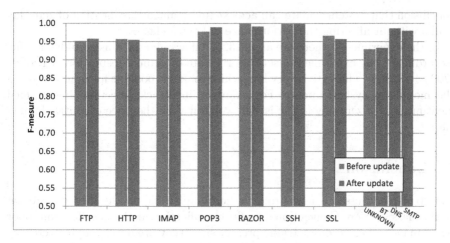

Fig. 4. Performance of system update

discovery changes from about 80% to 92% when k increase from 300 to 1,200. It is interesting to see that FPR is always close to 0. Consequently, the set of extracted zero-day samples from T_u has big size and high-purity. This leads to the classification performance is insensitive to the parameter k. By fixing k to 700 and varying T_u from 7‰ to 21.5‰, we obtain Fig. 3(b). This figure shows that increasing T_u can affect TPR and FPR slightly. Compared with the first step, the second step can dramatically improve TPR from about 68% to 90%. At the same time, FPR decreases from 3% to nearly 0. Therefore, we can obtain sufficient and high-purity zero-day traffic samples with various T_u. In summary, the proposed scheme relies on the two-step unknown discovery strategy, which is insensitive to the parameters k and T_u.

Evaluation of System Update. A set of experiments are designed to evaluate the module of system update. We test the classification performance of our scheme with and without system update. The setting of parameter is: $k = 700$ and $T_u = 5,000$ for unknown discovery. In the module system update, the identified zero-day traffic is categorized into 200 clusters and 3 flows are randomly selected from each cluster for new class construction. F-measure is used to evaluate the classification results.

Fig. 4 reports F-measures of our scheme before update and after update. The results show that the proposed scheme with system update can achieve fine-grained classification of zero-day traffic. For example, zero-day traffic can be identified with a F-measure of 93% before update. After update, the zero-day traffic can be classified into three new classes with excellent F-measures. In the known classes, the performance of our scheme changes very slightly (about 1%) after system update. For example, it changes from 93.3% to 92.8% in class imap. In class pop3, F-measure raises from 97.5% to 99%. We can draw an initial conclusion that system update can achieve fine-grained classification of zero-day traffic without affecting the performance of known classes.

In the experiments, there are about 32560 flows identified as zero-day traffic. According to the experimental setting, the rate of manual inspection is 1.8%[≈ (200 * 3)/32560]. This rate is very low, which makes it possible for practical using the module of system update. For example, in attack detection, fine-grained identification of zero-day traffic is well worth it with the price of a little human effort.

5 Conclusion

This paper addressed a new problem, zero-day traffic, in the area of Internet traffic classification. Conventional traffic classification methods suffer from poor performance when zero-day traffic present since they are misclassifying zero-day traffic into pre-defined application classes. We proposed a novel scheme which can identify zero-day traffic as well as accurately classify the traffic generated by pre-defined application classes. The proposed scheme has three important modules, unknown discovery, compound identification, and system update. A large number of well designed experiments were carried out on a complex dataset which is created from four big traffic traces. The results showed that, considering zero-day traffic, the proposed scheme without system update significantly outperforms three state-of-the-art methods, random forest classifier, classification with flow correlation, and semi-supervised traffic classification. With system update, the proposed scheme can further achieve more fine-grained classification of zero-day traffic. Moreover, a quantitative analysis on flow correlation was also provided confirm the effectiveness of the proposed scheme.

References

1. Cisco, WAN and application optimization solution guide, Cisco Systems, Inc., Tech. Rep. (2008), http://www.cisco.com/en/US/docs/nsite/enterprise/wan/wan_optimization/wan_opt_sg.html
2. Nguyen, T.T., Armitage, G.: A survey of techniques for internet traffic classification using machine learning. IEEE Commun. Surveys Tuts. 10(4), 56–76 (2008)
3. Auld, T., Moore, A.W., Gull, S.F.: Bayesian neural networks for internet traffic classification. IEEE Trans. Neural Netw. 18(1), 223–239 (2007)
4. Bernaille, L., Teixeira, R.: Early recognition of encrypted applications. In: Uhlig, S., Papagiannaki, K., Bonaventure, O. (eds.) PAM 2007. LNCS, vol. 4427, pp. 165–175. Springer, Heidelberg (2007)
5. Bonfiglio, D., Mellia, M., Meo, M., Rossi, D., Tofanelli, P.: Revealing skype traffic: when randomness plays with you. In: Proceedings of the Conference on Applications, Technologies, Architectures, and Protocols for Computer Communications, New York, NY, USA, pp. 37–48 (2007)
6. Kim, H., Claffy, K., Fomenkov, M., Barman, D., Faloutsos, M., Lee, K.: Internet traffic classification demystified: myths, caveats, and the best practices. In: Proceedings of the ACM CoNEXT Conference, New York, NY, USA, pp. 1–12 (2008)

7. Este, A., Gringoli, F., Salgarelli, L.: Support vector machines for tcp traffic classification. Computer Networks 53(14), 2476–2490 (2009)
8. Zhang, J., Xiang, Y., Wang, Y., Zhou, W., Xiang, Y., Guan, Y.: Network traffic classification using correlation information. IEEE Trans. Parallel Distrib. Syst., 1–15 (2012), doi:10.1109/TPDS.2012.98
9. Zander, S., Nguyen, T., Armitage, G.: Automated traffic classification and application identification using machine learning. In: Annual IEEE Conference on Local Computer Networks, Los Alamitos, CA, USA, pp. 250–257 (2005)
10. Erman, J., Arlitt, M., Mahanti, A.: Traffic classification using clustering algorithms. In: Proceedings of the SIGCOMM Workshop on Mining Network Data, New York, NY, USA, pp. 281–286 (2006)
11. Bernaille, L., Teixeira, R., Akodkenou, I., Soule, A., Salamatian, K.: Traffic classification on the fly. SIGCOMM Comput. Commun. Rev. 36, 23–26 (2006)
12. Glatz, E., Dimitropoulos, X.: Classifying internet one-way traffic. SIGMETRICS Perform. Eval. Rev. 40(1), 417–418 (2012)
13. Jin, Y., Duffield, N., Erman, J., Haffner, P., Sen, S., Zhang, Z.-L.: A modular machine learning system for flow-level traffic classification in large networks. ACM Trans. Knowl. Discov. Data 6(1), 4:1–4:34 (2012)
14. Nguyen, T., Armitage, G., Branch, P., Zander, S.: Timely and continuous machine-learning-based classification for interactive ip traffic. IEEE/ACM Trans. Netw., 1–15 (2012), doi:10.1109/TNET.2012.2187305
15. Erman, J., Mahanti, A., Arlitt, M., Cohen, I., Williamson, C.: Offline/realtime traffic classification using semi-supervised learning. Performance Evaluation 64(9-12), 1194–1213 (2007)
16. Casas, P., Mazel, J., Owezarski, P.: MINETRAC: Mining flows for unsupervised analysis & semi-supervised classification. In: Proceedings of the 23rd International Teletraffic Congress, pp. 87–94 (2011)
17. Crotti, M., Dusi, M., Gringoli, F., Salgarelli, L.: Traffic classification through simple statistical fingerprinting. SIGCOMM Comput. Commun. Rev. 37, 5–16 (2007)
18. MacKay, D.J.C.: Information Theory, Inference and Learning Algorithms. Cambridge University Press, Cambridge (2003)
19. Wang, Y., Xiang, Y., Zhang, J., Yu, S.-Z.: A novel semi-supervised approach for network traffic clustering. In: International Conference on Network and System Security, Milan, Italy (September 2011)
20. Ma, J., Levchenko, K., Kreibich, C., Savage, S., Voelker, G.M.: Unexpected means of protocol inference. In: Proceedings of the 6th ACM SIGCOMM Conference on Internet Measurement, New York, NY, USA, pp. 313–326 (2006)
21. Bishop, C.M.: Pattern Recognition and Machine Learning. In: Jordan, M., Kleinberg, J., Scholkopf, B. (eds.). Springer (2006)
22. Guyon, I., Elisseeff, A.: An introduction to variable and feature selection. J. Mach. Learn. Res. 3, 1157–1182 (2003)

Design and Implementation of a Testbed for the Security Assessment of MANETs

Christian Callegari, Stefano Giordano, Susanna Mannella, and Michele Pagano

CNIT & Dept. of Information Engineering, University of Pisa,
Via Caruso 16, I-56122, Italy
{c.callegari,s.giordano,s.mannella,m.pagano}@iet.unipi.it

Abstract. A MANET (Mobile Ad-hoc NETwork) is a self-configuring network of mobile devices connected by wireless links. Given its structure, a MANET has no clear line of defence, so it is accessible to both legitimate network users and malicious attackers. For this reason, MANETs are vulnerable to security attacks, mainly related to the poisoning of the routing protocols. The focus of this paper is two-folded, on one hand it presents a survey of the most significant attacks towards MANETs and on the other hand it details the design and implementation of an experimental testbed for assessing the security of a MANET, by allowing to perform the described attacks. The obtained results have shown that, in some cases, the purely theoretically described attacks presented in the literature, are in fact not realisable because of some "real world" operation details left unconsidered in the original paper.

Keywords: MANET, Security Assessment, Network Attacks.

1 Introduction

A MANET is a collection of mobile nodes that can communicate with each other without the use of pre-existing infrastructure or centralised administration [1]. Each device in a MANET is free to move independently in any direction and network topology will therefore change frequently.

Each node acts not only as a host but also as a router to forward messages for other nodes that are not within the same direct wireless transmission range [2].

Due to the lack of central administration, a node communicates with each other on the basis of mutual trust. In addition, because data are transferred wirelessly, it can easily be intercepted or interfered with. Finally, restricted energy supply and limited computational power narrow down the use of complex security mechanisms. These characteristics make MANET more vulnerable to be exploited by an attacker [3], with respect to wired networks.

More in detail, most of the security problems typical of a MANET are related to the routing protocols used in such a network. Indeed, due the previously described constraints (e.g., the need of having lightweight protocols), the main routing protocols do not present any security mechanism, meaning that the exchanged messages are neither authenticated nor encrypted.

G. Wang et al. (Eds.): CSS 2013, LNCS 8300, pp. 228–242, 2013.

Thus, malicious nodes mainly aim to disrupt the correct operations of the routing protocol, denying network services. Such nodes can use or modify sensitive routing information, as for example, the distance metrics used in conventional protocols (e.g., the number of hops). It is worth noticing that both data packets and control packets, used by the routing protocol, are vulnerable to attacks [4].

This paper is organised as follow: in Section 2 we describe the related works, while in Section 3 we provide some insights on the most used routing protocols in MANETs. Then, Section 4 describes the most important attacks and in Section 5 we detail the design and the implementation of the testbed realised in this work. Finally, Section 6 concludes the paper with some conclusive remarks.

2   Related Work

In the literature there are several works that describe single security attacks in MANETs. Apart from these work (most of them will be referred in the following sections), there are some works that provide a "general" discussion on the attacks toward MANETS. Among these in [4] we can find a qualitative analysis of the implications of using either a reactive or a proactive routing protocol on the effectiveness of a network attack, while in [9] the authors present a survey of the most prominent attacks described in the literature, in a consistent manner so as to provide a concise comparison of the different attack types.

Nonetheless, to the best of our knowledge, there is no work in the literature that provides a discussion on the aspects related to the real implementation of such attacks and on the "real" impact that the choice of the routing protocol can have on the security level of the MANET.

3   Routing Protocols

Routing protocols in MANETs can be classified into two main categories: reactive protocols and proactive protocols. Reactive routing protocols are also called "on-demand" protocols because paths are searched for when needed. Instead, in proactive routing protocols, all nodes need to maintain a consistent view of the network topology. Thus, periodical updates are exchanged among the nodes.

In the following we briefly describe the main features of the two most important protocols (one for each category), just highlighting those characteristics that are important to better understand the network attacks, while we refer the reader to the cited documents for a complete description.

3.1   Ad-Hoc on Demand Distance Vector Routing Protocol

In Ad-hoc On Demand Distance Vector (AODV) routing protocol [5], each mobile host in the network acts as a specialised router and routes are obtained as needed, thus making the network self-starting.

When a node wants to communicate it initiates a route discovery process by broadcasting a route request packet (RREQ) to its neighbours. This packet contains, among the others, a destination sequence number field that is set to a value that is either zero or the latest sequence number received in the past for any route towards the destination. The neighbours, upon reception of the RREQ, rebroadcast it to their neighbours, incrementing the Hop Count field.

RREQ travels from node to node until it reaches the destination node that generates a route reply packet (RREP) that travels back to the source along the shortest path. This packet has the destination sequence number field set to the sequence number of the destination node (that is a state variable maintained by each node) incremented by one. Hence, it is clear that the RREP destination sequence number field contains a value that is equal of greater to the value stored in the destination sequence number of the RREQ.

There is also the case in which a RREP is generated by an intermediate node on behalf of the destination node. This happens if such an intermediate node has a route entry for the desired destination with an associated destination sequence number greater than or equal to the one contained in the RREQ. Such value of the destination sequence number will be inserted in the RREP. Another field, that is important to the aim of poisoning the routing protocol is the hop count field, such a field is initialised to zero by the destination node when creating the RREP.

It is important to highlight that, if an intermediate node receives a RREP or RREQ for a destination for which it has a valid route entry, it checks for the destination sequence number field of the message. If either such a field is greater or equal and the hop count is smaller than the stored one, the node updates routing information and propagates the message; otherwise, it drops this packet [6]. This behaviour will be exploited in several attacks to "modify" the routing table of the network nodes.

In addition to such messages, the nodes also periodically broadcast local Hello messages to advertise the neighbours of its presence.

3.2   Optimized Link State Routing Protocol

Optimized Link State Routing (OLSR) protocol [7] is based on periodic exchange of topology information. The key concept of OLSR is the use of multipoint relay (MPR) to provide an efficient flooding mechanism by reducing the number of required transmissions. In OLSR, each node selects its own MPR from its neighbours. Only nodes selected as MPR nodes are responsible for advertising. Generally, two types of routing messages are used in the OLSR, namely a HELLO message and a Topology Control (TC) message.

The HELLO messages are used for neighbour sensing and MPR selection and are periodically generated by all the nodes. Such messages contain the address of the node and the list of its one-hop neighbours. HELLO messages are exchanged locally by neighbour nodes and are not forwarded further to other nodes. A TC message is used for route calculation and it is generated periodically. Only MPR nodes are responsible for forwarding TC messages. Upon receiving TC messages from all of the MPR nodes, each node can learn the partial network topology and can build a route to every node in the network. Each node selects its MPR set so as to reach all its two-hop neighbours [1].

When calculating a routing table, pure RFC-compliant OLSR simply minimises the number of hops towards each destination, even if this means that a route via a single very bad link will be preferred to a route via two excellent links, although the later would probably have been the better choice. To solve this problem, in the implementation used in this work, a Link Quality extension of OLSR (not complaint with the RFC) is applied. Hence the routing tables are computed taking into account a new metric, used to describe the quality of the links. In more detail two parameters are introduced: Link Quality (LQ) and Neighbour Link Quality (NLQ), that represent the probability that a packet sent by a neighbour of ours actually make it to us (LQ) and that a packet that we send actually makes it to our neighbour (NLQ) [8].

4   Attacks

In this section we present an overview of the most important attacks towards MANETs.

Replay Attack

Replay attack consists in retransmitting valid data: the attacker first records traffic at a given time, with the aim of later replaying it [13]. This can result in a falsely detected network topology or help to impersonate a different node identity [14].

The malicious node doesn't have to replay control packets back to the node from which it has received the packets. The only way of detecting replay attacks is to keep trace of the sequence number of all the exchanged packets, making the detection of such attacks quite hard [4].

Resource Consumption Attack

Resource Consumption Attack is actually more specific to MANETs. The aim is to consume or waste resources of other nodes. The idea behind this kind of attack is to request the services a certain node offers, over and over again, by constantly making it busy. The attacks could be in the form of unnecessary requests for routes, very frequent generation of beacon packets, or forwarding of stale packets to nodes (an example is given by the *sleep deprivation attack*) [9].

Blackhole, Grayhole and Jellyfish Attacks

These attacks all aim at intercepting the traffic flowing between two legitimate nodes. The attacks differ one from another according to the actions performed on the intercepted traffic. Blackhole, Grayhole and Jellyfish Attacks have a common first step, where the malicious node exploits the routing protocol to advertise itself as having a valid route to a destination node, even though the route is spurious, with the intention of intercepting packets.

In the second step Blackhole Attack aims to disrupt the communication between source and destination, so the attacker drops the intercepted packets without forwarding them. Grayhole attacker alternates a correct behavior with a malicious one, by dropping the intercepted packets with a given probability or behaves maliciously only for some time duration by dropping packets and switches to normal behavior later [9].

Finally, the goal of Jellyfish attack is to increment the end-to-end delay and thus degrade the performance of network services, especially for real time applications. This attack can be carried out by employing several mechanisms [10], such as *Reorder Buffer Attack* or *Delay Variance Attack*. The former consists in delivering all received packets, but in scrambled order instead of the canonical FIFO order [11], while the latter involves holding packets for a random time before processing them, so as to delay the packets unnecessarily for some amount of time, thus increasing delay variance [10].

Neighbour Attack

The goal of neighbour attack is to convince two nodes, that are not within the communication range of each other, that are neighbours. The attacker, which is necessarily located between the two victims, simply forwards routing packets without changing them (e.g., without incrementing the hop count field), so that the nodes believe that they can communicate directly. The result is that data packets are lost because two extremity of connection aren't actually linked [9].

Neighbour attack is similar to Blackhole attack in the sense that they both prevent data packets from reaching the destination. The difference is that in Blackhole attack, the attacker drops packets, while in neighbour attack, after poisoning routing, the attacker is not involved any longer [12].

Wormhole Attack

The Wormhole attacker is aimed at poisoning the routing tables, making packets to be forwarded along the wrong routes. A Wormhole attacker records packets at one location in the network and tunnels them to another colluding attacker which forwards them in its area [9]. This tunnel between two attackers is referred as a wormhole; it can be established by means of a wired link, a high quality wireless out-of-band link or a logical link via packet encapsulation [15].

The Wormhole attack in reactive protocol aims at disrupting routing and putting the attackers in a favorable condition, so that they take complete control over a link in the network and they can sniff traffic, drop packets or launch a man-in-the-middle attack [17].

Instead, in proactive protocols the two colluding attackers act in tandem to distort the perceived network topology. So false informations are propagated, the routing is disrupt and network performance is degraded [18].

Byzantine Attack

In Byzantine Attack, a compromised intermediate node works to create routing loops, forwarding packets through non-optimal paths, or selectively dropping packets, which results in disruption or degradation of the routing services.

This attack can be carried out by employing several mechanisms, some examples are:

- *Link spoofing attack*, in which the attacker announces a fake link in order to disrupt routing operations. This attack is meaningful only with proactive protocols
- *Routing loop Attack*, which is possible only in networks with reactive protocol. An attacker modifies routing messages during route discovery process with the intent of creating a loop
- *Packet dropping attack*, which consists in dropping packets (both data and routing packets). This attack can also be the result of a lack of cooperation from the internal nodes to the network operations to preserve their resources without malicious designs [19]

Sybil Attack

The Sybil attack aims at degrading network performance by "creating" a nonexistent node. In more detail, the malicious node impersonates some nonexistent node in the case when cooperation is necessary, and affects the configuration schemes and the routing services based on trust model [9]. The attacker can also steal the identity of an existing node [20], resulting able to receive routing messages destined to the victim node.

5   Testbed Implementation

For the testbed implementation we used seven general purposes personal computers with Linux operative system (Linux Ubuntu 10.04) equipped with an Intel i3 2.0 GHz, with 4GB of RAM and a TP-LINK WN722N wireless card. The mobile ad-hoc network has been configured using iw, a based CLI configuration utility for wireless devices. Moreover, given that all the computers are in the same laboratory, we have had the need of emulate different physical topologies, so that not all the nodes see the others nodes as neighbours. To this aim we have used the iptables Linux tool, which allows the node to drop packets directly at MAC layer, emulating a situation in which two nodes do not see each other directly.

To evaluate the effectiveness of the different attacks when using either a reactive protocol or a proactive protocols we have realised two different testbed settings, using either AODV or OLSR. The routing protocols used in our tests for AODV and OLSR are enabled by the latest version (at the moment of the tests) of the standard implementations of such protocols for Linux (i.e., aodv-uu-0.9.6 and olsr-0.5.6). Instead, regarding the attacks we have implemented them by using C coding and the libraries: Libnet for fake packets creation, Libpcap for packet capture, Libnet_filter_queue for queue management. Moreover, given that some attacks require the attacker to perform several operations in parallel, we have implemented these attacks using multi-thread coding.

In the following subsections, we provide some insights on the implementation of the different attacks, also discussing the effect of the single attacks when launched towards the two different routing protocols and discussing the conditions (usually at the topology level) needed for the attack to be successful.

Replay and Sleep Deprivation Attack

The Replay Attack is one of the simplest attacks and its implementation is the same when using both AODV and OLSR.

A BPF filter (Berkley Packet Filter), before Libcap capture, selects the packet the attacker wants to replay. Hence, we capture the packet by using the function pcap_next() which returns the copy of the selected packet. Then, using the Libpcap function pcap_sendpacket(), the attacker replays the packet.

Replay Attack may also be a method to implement Sleep Deprivation Attack, obtained just sending the replayed packet over and over. As an alternative method, we have considered the creation of a fake packet sent over and over. For example in AODV, the attacker builds and sends a false RREQ for inexistent destination. The nodes that receive these packets are forced to process them consuming their limited resources.

This attack does not pose any particular implementation problem and result to be successful both with AODV and OLSR.

Blackhole, Grayhole and Jellyfish Attack

In Blackhole, Grayhole and Jellyfish attacks, an attacker poison the routing protocol so as to advertise that it has the shortest path to the node whose packets it wants to intercept, even though the route is spurious. When implementing it, we have to consider that this first step is different in AODV and in OLSR.

Let us consider the topology shown in Fig.1, where node A is the attacker, nodes S and D are the victims of the attacks, being respectively the source and the destination of the target communication.

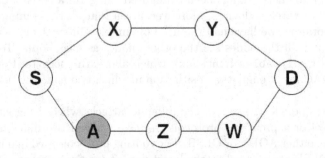

Fig. 1. Topology for Blackhole, Grayhole and Jellyfish Attack

Considering AODV, the attack is implemented as follow: A captures all UDP packets with UDP port (either source port or destination port) equal to 654, by using the Libpcap function pcap_loop. When it receives a RREQ from S to D, A creates a fake RREP (by using a opportunely defined Libnet function) claiming a route to D with a destination sequence number bigger than the one used by S (meaning that the route is "recent") and the hop count field set to one (meaning that it is a direct neighbour of D) [22]. Thus the packet is sent to S [21]. At

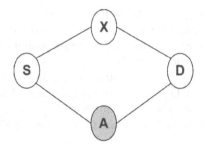

Fig. 2. Topology for Neighbour Attack

this point, S will start sending to A the packets destined to D, considering that A is at one hop from D.

When considering OLSR, the implementation is obviously different and it is based on the creation of fake HELLO messages [23]. Hence, the attacker creates HELLO messages, in which it advertises a link with non-neighbour D and announces that quality of the links A-D and A-S is good. From the implementation point of view, these Hello packets are created with a specifically defined Libnet function. For the attack to be successful the sequence number field of the packets is incremented and the fake packets have to be sent more frequently then the correct HELLO packets. Moreover, A sends fake HELLO messages to S, impersonating X and advertising that S-X is a bad quality link. In this way S thinks that the path through the attacker is the shortest and the best one.

Once the malicious node has been able to insert itself between S and D, it is able to do "whatever it wants" with the intercepted packets:

- A Blackhole attacker drops all packet, for example using iptables
- In Grayhole attack, the packets are queued and, using Libnetfilter_queue library, they are alternatively forwarded or dropped
- In Jellyfish reorder buffer, the attacker delivers all packets, yet after placing them in a reordering buffer rather than a FIFO buffer. To implement such an attack, with Libnetfilter_queue library, we can define a function that changes the packet ID that is used to indicate the order in which the packets are served, allowing us to forward them in scrambled order. An alternate method simply consists in delaying packets and it is obtained by queuing them and forwarding them after a random period of time

The implementation of such attacks has been successful in both the AODV and OLSR scenarios. Nonetheless, this kind of attacks poses some constraint on the physical topology, meaning that the attacker cannot be in any position in the network. In more detail, taking into consideration AODV that is simpler to analyse (but the same considerations can be extended to the OLSR case), the attack is always possible if A is a direct neighbour of S and, more in general, when the route S-A (incremented by one) is shortest than any route S-D. This is due to the fact that A advertises to be at one hop from D, thus the number of hops of the route S-D that passes through A will be equal to the number of hops of the route S-A (that cannot be poisoned) incremented by one. As an example, in the topology shown in Fig. 1, apart from the presented case, the attack would not be successful in any other cases. It is important to highlight that in case A and Z positions are switched, the two routes S-X-Y-D and S-Z-A-W-D (poisoned so as to appears as S-Z-A-D to S) become equivalent. The experimental tests have shown that in this case the behaviour of the network is unpredictable with the traffic flowing through the two routes for alternate periods of time.

Neighbour Attack

As in the previous case, also the implementation of the Neighbour attack is different in the AODV and OLSR scenarios. To exemplify the implementation of this attack, let us consider the network topology given in Fig. 2, where, as in the previous case, node A is the attacker and nodes S and D are the victims.

When considering the AODV scenario, the attacker, to impersonate the false neighbour, captures all the UDP packets with destination or source port equal to 654, by using the Libpcap function `pcap_loop` and when it captures a packet from either S or D, it uses the `process_packet` function, to perform the following actions:

- if the packet is a HELLO packet, A creates a copy of the packet which is then forwarded to the other victim (note that in the "normal" operation the HELLO packets are not forwarded)
- if the packet is a RREQ, A first copies the packet and sends it to the other victim and then sends a fake RREP incrementing the destination sequence number, so that the correct RREP isn't considered (appearing as "older" then the fake one). Alternatively, A could also not send a fake RREP and just copy and forward the real RREP from D (without modifying it)

In the OLSR scenario, given that the routing protocol mainly relies on the exchange of HELLO messages, A has to periodically send fake HELLO messages. Hence, first of all, A captures, by using the Libpcap library, all the UDP packet from/to S and D, with port (either source or destination port) equal to 698 and copies the value of the sequence numbers. Then, it creates the fake HELLO packets, that advertise a good quality link between S and D, with the Packet Sequence Number incremented by at least one and the Message Sequence Number incremented by at least 12 (because in the used OLSR implementation, between two consecutive HELLO messages there are 12 TC messages).

The final result, valid for both the considered scenarios, is presented in Fig. 3, where the dotted link between S and D indicates that the two nodes believe to be direct neighbour, but in fact the communication will go through node A. The proof of the success of the attack is that the victims are not able to communicate with each other because the direct link between them doesn't actually exist.

As for the previous attacks, also the neighbour attack poses some topological constraints for being successful. Indeed, in both the AODV and OLSR scenarios, the attack is only possible if A is a direct neighbour of both S and D.

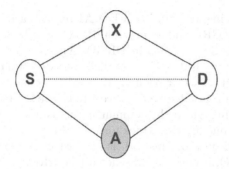

Fig. 3. Topology perceived from S and D under Neighbour Attack

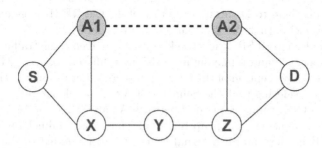

Fig. 4. Topology for Wormhole Attack

Wormhole Attack

The wormhole attack is much more complicated than the previously described ones and requires two colluding nodes to act as attacker. For the implementation of such an attack, let us refer to the topology in Fig. 4, where nodes A1 and A2 are the two colluding attacks and, as previously S and D are the victims.

Referring to the description of the wormhole attack provided in the previous section, it is important to highlight that we have not taken into account the case of the creation of an out-of-bad tunnel. Thus, we have considered the case in which the two attackers establish a GRE tunnel between them, using `iptunnel` command and adding a static route in order to only tunnel the packets from and to S and D.

Let us analyse the way of implementing the attack in the two different scenarios, starting with the AODV one.

In this case, the aim of the attack is the following: two colluding attackers work to intercept packets of a communication between S and D. In the literature, if S broadcasts a RREQ to find a route to D, A1 receives this RREQ, encapsulates and tunnels it to A2 through an existing data route, in this case A1-X-Y-Z-A2. Then A2 rebroadcasts the RREQ, which shows that it has only traveled S-A1-A2-D. In our considered topology, the alternative route is S-X-Y-Z-D; so the path via A1 and A2 is considered shorter than the alternative path [25].

In our experimental testbed we have implemented such an attack in two different ways, but none of them has resulted to be successful. Let us analyse them in details. In the first implementation, when A1 receives a RREQ, encapsulates the packet adding the GRE and an external IP headers (built with Libnet functions) and then sends it to A2 (as in OLSR). A1 also modifies some fields of RREQ in order to be "considered" by D (i.e., source/destination and sequence number). But, in AODV, when A1 and A2 want to communicate through the tunnel, they initiate a route discovery process to create the tunnel. This process takes some time, during which the communication is normally started through the alternative path, making the attack unsuccessful.

The second implementation, instead, is realised in the following way: when A1 receives the RREQ, it creates and sends a fake RREP, advertising that it is a neighbour of D (so as to avoid the delay due to the creation of the tunnel). In the meanwhile the tunnel is created and when S starts to send data packets to A1, A1 sends them to D through the tunnel. But, a RERR is generated and sent to S announcing that the destination is unreachable.

When considering OLSR, the attack consists in recording traffic from one region of the network and replaying it "as is" in a different region [24], so as to distort the correct perception of the network topology. Let us analyse the actions taken by A1, considering that the behavior of A2 is complementary.

First of all a GRE tunnel is created between A1 and A2, then A1 captures all packets from S, by using a Libpcap function. Thus, using Libnet functions, A1 creates a GRE header and an external IP header to be added to the captured packets, which are then sent to A2 through the tunnel. A1 also captures packets from tunnel interface (that are all sent by A2), decapsulates them, removing the external IP and GRE headers, and adds (with a Libnet function) a layer 2 header. Finally, it forwards the packets. It is important to highlight that it is necessary to "manually" insert the interesting packets in the tunnel, because broadcast packets are normally not tunneled. From a practical point of view all the packets exchanged between S and D are sent through a tunnel, this implies that the intermediate nodes do not modify the "original" IP header, but just the external header. Thus when the packets are de-tunneled, removing the external headers and adding an "ad-hoc" layer 2 header, they appear as directly sent from the source to the destination without any intermediate hop.

From the point of view of the topology constraints to successful realise such an attack, they are more relaxed than in the previous cases, only requiring to have A1 neighbour of S and A2 neighbour of D, but not requiring the A1 and A2 to be neighbours.

Byzantine Attack

Regarding this attack, we have implemented three distinct variants: Link Spoofing, Packet Drop and Route Loop.

Link Spoofing Attack

In AODV it is meaningless given that it relies on the idea of announcing a fake link and that in AODV there are no link advertisements. Instead in OLSR it has been implemented, but without any success. Let us analyse the reason: if an attacker announces a fake link to another node, but the other node (which should also announce it, given that the links are announced by both the edges) does not cooperate, the fake link is not considered in building the topology. Thus to be successful, the attack would require two colluding attackers, even if in the literature this case is not presented.

Packet Drop Attack
Such an attack aims at disrupting routing services or degrading network performance. This attack is very simple to be realised and can be implemented, in both the scenarios, by simply using `iptables` to drop packets.

Route Loop Attack
The route loop attack is not possible in OLSR, indeed given that all the nodes know the whole network topology, the realisation of such an attack would require to poison all the routing messages exchanged among the nodes, implying a level of cooperation among nodes that is not usually available to an attacker.

Instead it is feasible when considering the AODV scenario and, in our testbed, it has been implemented considering the topology shown in Fig. 5.

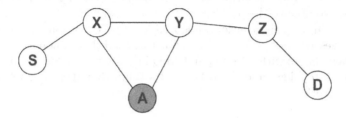

Fig. 5. Topology for Routing Loop Attack

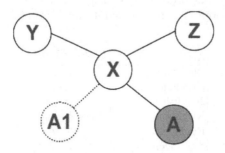

Fig. 6. Topology for Sybil Attack

First of all A creates a static route, indicating that X is the next hop to D, in this way the received packets destined to D will be forwarded to X. Then, when A receives a RREQ from S to D, it creates a fake RREP to be sent to Y. This message, that has an incremented destination sequence number (so that it is considered more recent than the one sent by any other nodes), announces an one hop route to D. In this way Y will think that the shortest route to D passes through A. Thus when S sends packet to D, it is receive by X that normally forwards it to Y. Then Y sends the packet to A (because of the route advertised by the fake RREP), which sends the packet to X (because of the static route). This effectively creates a loop and all packets are dropped when their TTLs drop to zero [26].

From the topological point of view, the constraint we have is that the attacker has to be close to the link X-Y, that means that it must be a neighbour of both X and Y (i.e. , it must be neighbor of two consecutive nodes).

Sybil Attack

In Sybil Attack, referring to Fig. 6, the malicious node A impersonates an inexistent node A1. So it basically runs all operations both with its address and with another one.

When considering AODV, A captures allthe routing packets with Libpcap. When it captures a RREQ, in addition to performing the usual operations, it also creates a fake RREP (using Libnet functions) with random parameters. For further chaos, A increments the destination sequence number and set Hop Count to 1, in order to deceive the source.

Instead, in OLSR, the attacker sends HELLO and TC messages periodically. These messages are created using Libnet functions and they announce existent or inexistent neighbours with false LQ and NLQ in order to give faulty information about network topology and the other nodes think that there is another node A1 in the network.

5.1   Results Discussion

The following Table summarises the obtained results, indicating for each performed attack and routing protocol if it has been successful ($\checkmark$), unsuccessful (NO), or not implemented because not significant for that routing protocol ($-$).

Attack	AODV	OLSR
Blackhole	$\checkmark$	$\checkmark$
Grayhole	$\checkmark$	$\checkmark$
Jellyfish	$\checkmark$	$\checkmark$
Neighbour	$\checkmark$	$\checkmark$
Replay	$\checkmark$	$\checkmark$
Sleep Deprivation	$\checkmark$	$\checkmark$
Paket Drop	$\checkmark$	$\checkmark$
Route Loop	$\checkmark$	$-$
Sybil	$\checkmark$	$\checkmark$
Wormhole	NO	$\checkmark$
Link Spoofing	$-$	NO

As it appears clearly, most of the attacks result successful in both the considered scenarios, with the following exceptions:

- route loop attack is obviously unfeasible in the OLSR scenario
- wormhole attacks is not successful, when considering AODV. This is due to the route discover process started by the tunnel creation, which is not taken into account in the literature
- Link spoofing attack is not significant in AODV and does not succeed in OLSR because it would require the cooperation of the network nodes

6   Conclusions

In this paper we have presented a survey of the most significant attacks towards MANETs, detailing for each of them the implementation in an experimental testbed. In many cases, the literature does not provide any hints on how to implement the described attacks, leading to several possible implementations, as seen in the case of the Wormhole attack. Moreover, the obtained results have shown that, in some cases, the purely theoretically attacks presented in the literature are in fact not realisable because of some "real world" operation details left unconsidered in the description.

It is important to highlight, that even if we have only considered two routing protocols, these results can be extended to all the "standard" protocols belonging to the two categories (proactive and reactive), given that the presented attacks do not exploit any particular characteristic of the protocols, but the general working principles. As a conclusion, we can say that from a security point of view the analysed protocols do not differ in a significant way.

References

1. Khokhar, R.H., Ngadi, M.A., Mandala, S.: A review of current routing attacks in mobile ad hoc networks. International Journal of Computer Science and Security (2008)
2. Vidhya, K.U., Priya, M.M.: A novel technique for defending routing attacks in OLSR MANET. In: IEEE International Conference on Computational Intelligence and Computing Research (2010)
3. Irshad Ullah Shoaib Ur Rehman. Analysis of black hole attack on MANETs using different MANET routing protocols. Master's thesis, School of Computing Blekinge Institute of Technology, Sweden (2010)
4. Yau, P.-W., Hu, S., Mitchell, C.J.: Malicious attacks on ad hoc network routing protocols. International Journal of Computer Research (2009)
5. Perkins, C., Belding-Royer, E., Das, S.: Ad hoc On-Demand Distance Vector (AODV) Routing. IETF RFC 3561 (2003)
6. Gorantala, K.: Routing protocols in mobile ad-hoc netwoks. Master's thesis, Umeå University (2006)
7. Clausen, T., Jacquet, P.: Optimized Link State Routing Protocol (OLSR). IETF RFC 3626 (2003)
8. Olsr link quality extensions,
   http://www.olsr.org/docs/README-Link-Quality.html

9. Jawandhiya, P.M., Ghonge, M.M., Ali, M.S., Deshpande, J.S.: A survey of mobile ad hoc network attacks. International Journal of Engineering Science and Technology (2010)

10. Aad, I., Hubaux, J.-P., Knightly, E.W.: Impact of denial of service attacks on ad hoc networks. IEEE/ACM Transactions on Networking (2008)

11. Seshadri Ramana, K., Chari, A.A., Kasiviswanth, N.: Review and analysis of trust based routing in MANETs. International Journal of Computer Science and Research (2010)

12. Nguyen, H.L., Nguyen, U.T.: A study of different types of attacks on multicast in mobile ad hoc networks. In: Proceedings of the International Conference on Networking (2006)

13. Lacharité, Y., Wang, M., Lamont, L.: Findings on a Semantically-Based Intrusion Detection Approach for OLSR MANET Protocol. In: 3rd OLSR Interop / Workshop (2006)

14. Goyal, P., Batra, S., Singh, A.: A literature review of security attack in mobile ad-hoc networks. International Journal of Computer Applications (2010)

15. Bensaou, B., Taleb, T.: Detecting and avoiding wormhole attacks in wireless ad hoc networks. IEEE Communications Magazine (2008)

16. Hu, Y.-C., Perrig, A.: Wormhole attacks in wireless networks. IEEE Journal on Selected Areas in Communications (2006)

17. Khalil, I., Bagchi, S., Shroff, N.B.: Liteworp: A lightweight countermeasure for the wormhole attack in multihop wireless networks. In: Proceedings of the 2005 IEEE International Conference on Dependable Systems and Networks (2005)

18. Lynch, D., Knight, S., Gorlatova, M.A., Lacharité, Y., Lamont, L., Liscano, R., Mason, P.C.: Providing effective security in mobile ad hoc networks without affecting bandwidth or interoperability. In: Proceedings of the 26th Army Science Conference (2008)

19. Razak, S.A., Furnell, S.M., Brooke, P.J.: Attacks against mobile ad hoc networks routing protocols. Proceedings of 5th Annual Postgraduate Symposium on the Convergence of Telecommunications, Networking & Broadcasting (2004)

20. Ebinger, P., Bucher, T.: Modelling and Analysis of Attacks on the MANET Routing in AODV. In: Proceedings of the 5th International Conference on Ad-Hoc, Mobile, and Wireless Networks (2006)

21. Khokhar, R.H., Ngadi, M.A., Mandala, S.: A review of current routing attacks in mobile ad hoc networks. International Journal of Computer Science and Security (2008)

22. Sharma, S., Gupta, R.: Simulation study of blackhole attack in the Mobile Ad hoc Networks. Journal of Engineering Science and Technology (2009)

23. Gerhards-Padilla, E., Aschenbruck, N., Martini, P., Jahnke, M., Tolle, J.: Detecting Black Hole Attacks in Tactical MANETs using Topology Graphs. In: 32nd IEEE Conference on Local Computer Networks (2007)

24. Adjih, C., Raffo, D., Mhlethaler, P.: Attacks Against OLSR: Distributed Key Management for Security. In: 2nd OLSR Interop/Workshop (2005)

25. Rai, A.K., Tewari, R.R., Upadhyay, S.K.: Different types of attacks on integrated MANET-internet communication. International Journal of Computer Science and Security (2010)

26. Zhang, Y., Huang, Y.A., Lee, W.: An extensible environment for evaluating secure MANET. In: International Conference on Security and Privacy for Emerging Areas on Communication Networks (2005)

A Bio-inspired Jamming Detection and Restoration for WMNs: In View of Adaptive Immunology

Qiang Liu[1], Jianping Yin[1], and Shui Yu[2]

[1] School of Computer, National University of Defense Technology,
Changsha, Hunan, P.R. China
libra6032009@gmail.com, jpyin@nudt.edu.cn
[2] School of Information Technology, Deakin University, Burwood,
Victoria 3125, Australia
shui.yu@deakin.edu.au

Abstract. The wireless mesh network is vulnerable to jamming attacks due to open share of physical medium. Since such attacks induce severe interferences resulting in denial of regular service, highly efficient detection and restoration methods are vital for a secure wireless mesh network. On the other hand, artificial immune mechanisms originated from the immunology are considerable methods to inspire design of an detection and restoration system. In this paper, we propose an immunological anti-jamming method as per the adaptive immune system of human beings to defeat the reactive jamming. The proposed method consists three function modules, i.e., the monitoring agent for monitoring the packet reception, the decision agent for detecting attacks and the recovery agent for restoring the network from the ongoing attacks. Simulation results show that the proposed method is effective to defeat the reactive jamming and to maintain considerable performance of the overall network.

Keywords: Wireless mesh network, Reactive jamming, Anti-jamming method, Adaptive immune system.

1 Introduction

The wireless mesh network (WMN), which is formed by wireless nodes communicating with each other via multiple hops, offers high-capacity and high-speed data transfer under distributed network operations. Compared to mobile terminals, mesh nodes including mesh access points, mesh routers and mesh gateways generally have stronger processing and storage capacity, higher transmission power but lower mobility to provide backhaul services. Since the WMN has advantages in flexible deployment, high reliability and multi-hop transmission, it can be applied to various scenarios, such as last-mile access, wireless metropolitan area network and emergency communications.

However, potential threats make the security of the WMN a challenge. One severe issue of wireless transmission is that wireless links are prone to passive or

G. Wang et al. (Eds.): CSS 2013, LNCS 8300, pp. 243–257, 2013.

active attacks, such as eavesdropping and jamming. It is even harder to defeat these attacks in the WMN because the network uses multi-hop relay over successive mesh nodes in order to provide connectivity for pairwise nodes. Zdarsky et al. [21] analyzed potential security threats in wireless mesh backhauls and assessed their corresponding risk. They indicated that intelligent jamming is the top one threat which has high impact and high likelihood. They also presented various styles of jamming strategies like prevention of management and control frames, hijacking of protocol messages, and degradation of link quality, which incurred topology and route flapping of a WMN. Therefore, it is vital to defeat jamming attacks in order to minimize the performance degradation. In addition, Wu et al. [19] summarized different types of jamming models on wireless networks, namely constant jamming, deceptive jamming, random jamming and reactive jamming. Although enormous methods have been proposed to detect jamming attacks [15], they are weak to defeat reactive jamming attacks. In the reactive jamming model, a reactive jammer only jams some specific types of packets. Specifically, it keeps quiet when the channel is idle, but immediately emits radio signals after sensing the transmission of those types of packets. Therefore, the reactive jamming model, compared with constant, deceptive and random jamming models, is much more intelligent. Since reactive jammers do not continuously emit radio signals or do not block all messages going through the jammed area, it is hard to detect reactive jamming attacks that target the reception of a packet.

On the other hand, many techniques originated from other disciplines have been adopted to counteract jamming attacks, e.g., game theory [10, 17], optimization [6] and bio-inspired techniques [1]. As a matter of fact, the immune system of human beings provides a considerable way to design an intrusion detection system for defeating anomalies in wireless mesh networks [11]. Therefore, we propose an immunological anti-jamming method to defeat reactive jamming attacks targeting WMNs. The proposed method consists of three function modules, namely monitoring agent, decision agent and recovery agent. Moreover, an attacking pattern database is used to store the features of known attacks. Specifically, the monitoring agent functions as the helper T cell in the adaptive immune system, and the decision and recovery agents serve as B cell and antibody, respectively. Similar to the effects of the adaptive immune system in immunology, the proposed method is able to detect and to restore the WMN from the reactive jamming. The advantages of the proposed method include fully distributed control, adaptive attack detection and quick reaction.

The rest of this paper is organized as follows: The next section reviews the related work. Section 3 presents the system model and some assumptions. Section 4 introduces the adaptive immune system of human beings and gives a detailed description of the immunological anti-jamming method. Then, Section 5 presents simulation results to justify the advantages of the proposed method. Finally, Section 6 concludes the paper.

2   Related Work

Due to open broadcasting medium of wireless networks, it is easy for an attacker to launch jamming attacks by interfering the available channels at will. As a result, a WMN with the presence of jamming attacks turns to be unstable due to topology and route flapping. Thus, the studies of jamming detection, restoration, and new jamming attacks have drawn more and more attentions. In the following, we summarize related works under two main aspects, namely jamming detection and jamming restoration.

Currently, most of studies in the area of jamming detection use the packet delivery ratio (PDR) as the indicator of jamming. However, conventional PDR-based schemes require one to monitor communications for a long time before making a decision, resulting in a delay of jamming detection. Thus, Siddhabathula et al. [15] proposed a collaborative detection scheme, which evaluated the packet delivery ratio in an area instead of pairs of nodes. Specifically, a node used observations from other nodes to speed up the jamming detection. However, the work is weak to detect the reactive jamming because it only targets the constant jamming. In [16], a novel jamming detection scheme was proposed to detect reactive jamming attacks by identifying the cause of bit-errors for individual packets based on the received signal strength during the reception of these bits. More precisely, bit-errors are detected based on either predetermined knowledge, error correcting codes, or limited node wiring in the form of wired node chains, and the detection scheme comprises three steps: error sample acquisition, interference detection, and sequential jamming test. Li et al. [8] studied the idealized case of perfect knowledge by both the jammer and the network about the strategy of each other, including knowledge about the network channel access probability, the number of neighbors of the monitor node, the jamming probability of the jammer, etc. They also studied the case where the jammer and the network lack the knowledge to solve the optimal jamming attack and defense policies. Moreover, a new detection method of jamming attack in ad hoc networks was proposed based on the measure of statistical correlation [4]. The network is alarmed about jamming attack if the correlation coefficient between the reception error time and the correct reception time is larger than that obtained based on the measured error probability. Lin and Li [9] proposed a Bayesian-based distributed detection scheme, in which multiple monitor nodes jointly detect the existence of a jammer to minimize the probability of error. They further studied optimal defense strategies with the goal of maintaining a desirable quality-of-service. In addition, Thamilarasu and Sridhar [17] proposed a game theoretic framework to detect jamming attacks in wireless ad hoc networks. They formulates jamming as a two-player, non-cooperative game to analyze the interaction between a jammer and monitoring nodes in the network. After solving the game by computing the mixed strategy Nash equilibrium, they derived optimal attack and detection strategies.

Another hot area of defeating jamming attacks is jamming restoration. Pelechrinis et al. [12] built an anti-jamming reinforcement system called ARES driven by measurements in the physical layer, which is composed of a rate module and a power control module. By tuning the parameters of rate adaptation and power control, they improved the performance in the presence of jammers. In order to mitigate Medium Access Control (MAC) layer jamming attacks, Lin and van der Schaar [10] firstly used a non-cooperative game model to characterize the interactions between regular users and a malicious user. Since they found that the Nash equilibrium of the game is either inefficient or unfair for the regular users, they introduced an intervention user to transform the original game into a new game augmented by the intervention function. By properly designing the intervention function, the intervention user can effectively mitigate the jamming attacks from the malicious user. Jamming defense strategies for the MAC layer can also be found in [7, 14, 18]. Another key technique for protecting against jamming attacks is cross-layer design. Jiang and Xue [6] investigated network restoration solutions via the joint design of traffic rerouting, channel reassignment, and scheduling over a multi-radio multi-channel WMN to recover from jamming attacks and maintain an acceptable level of service degradation. They formulated the optimal network restoration problem as a linear programming problem, then provided a greedy scheduling algorithm using dynamic channel assignment.

3   System Model and Assumptions

In this section, we give network and adversary models to be studied, and then some assumptions are made to facilitate the design of an anti-jamming method.

3.1   Network Model

We model a single-interface WMN as $G = <V, E, R_T, prop, mac, rp>$, where V is the set of stationary mesh nodes. All mesh nodes use the same radio-propagation model, MAC and routing protocol that are respectively denoted as $prop$, mac and rp. Furthermore, we assume that each node transmits with an omni-directional antenna, and the radius of transmission range is defined by R_T. A node within the transmission range of node i can correctly decode messages originated from i. An edge $e = (i, j) \in E$ denotes that node i and j are located within the transmission range of each other, i.e., their Euclidean distance satisfies $d(i, j) \leq R_T$.

3.2   Adversary Model

We consider a set of reactive jammers J in a WMN. The reactive jammer only jams wireless channels after sensing the transmission of some specific types of packets that it tends to block. Consequently, the reactive jammer degrades the overall performance of the network without wasting too much resources. Moreover, it is harder for existing detection methods to detect such attacks since reactive jammers emits radio signals on demand rather than continuously. The reactive jammer's goal is to corrupt the transmission of legitimate messages by selectively interfering wireless channels in order to degrade the receiving Signal to Interference and Noise Ratio (SINR). Consequently, the corresponding receiver nodes are blocked from receiving these data packets. The mechanism of the reactive jamming is illustrated in Fig. 1, where RSSI is the receive signal strength indicator and FCS means frame check sequence. T_{samp} denotes the time to sample the RSSI of the underlying wireless channel, T_{period} and T_{start} are the period of sampling and the time to initialize hardware and device status, respectively.

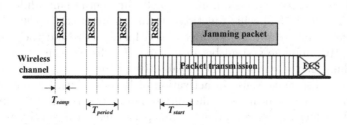

Fig. 1. The mechanism of the reactive jamming model

For the convenience of description, a reactive jammer is formally defined as $j = (ID_j, X_j, Y_j, R_j) \in J$, where ID_j denotes the identifier of the jammer. X_j and Y_j are the horizontal and vertical coordinates of the jammer, respectively. Similarly, we consider that the jammed region is a circular region with a radius R_j centered at the jammer's location.

3.3   Assumptions

Generally speaking, mesh nodes in WMNs form a mesh backbone for conventional mobile terminals. Thus, we consider that all mesh nodes are stationary and have enough processing and storage capacities. Furthermore, our proposed method is based on following assumptions:

1) The WMN is strongly connected, and the number of mesh nodes is much larger than that of reactive jammers. Thus, when jamming attacks occur, the transmission path can be switched to another route with a high probability.

2) Single path transmission is used, i.e., every source node uses one transmission path at a time to transmit packets. Multi-path transmission is out of the scope of this paper.

4   The Immunological Anti-jamming Method

Based on the system model and assumptions described above, we propose an immunological anti-jamming method as per the adaptive immune system of human beings in this section. Specifically, we first show how the adaptive immune system of human beings works to defend against diverse pathogens. Then, we present the design methodology of the proposed anti-jamming method and give detailed explanations towards some important function modules.

4.1   Adaptive Immune System

The adaptive immune system is composed of highly specialized, systemic cells and processes that eliminate or prevent pathogenic challenges [5]. It is activated by the innate response, more specifically, by dendritic phagocytes or B lymphocytes digesting their matching antigens, which are termed antigen presenting cells (APCs). There are two major types of lymphocytes taking responsibility in the system, called B cells and T cells. They are useful only if they are active. By recognizing Major Histocompatibility Complex (MHC) molecules on APCs with the help of co-receptor expression, naive T cells differentiate into different types of mature T cells with specific functions, including cytotoxic T cells, helper T cells, and $\gamma\delta$T cells. However, we focus on helper T cells and their functions in the adaptive immune system because helper T cells play an important role in establishing and maximizing the capabilities of the system [5]. In addition, helper T cells also make sense in activation of B cells. With the aid of helper T cells, naive B cells will further differentiate into active B cells (also known as plasma cells) which secrete antibodies. Some plasma cells will survive to become long-lived antigen specific memory B cells which can be called on to respond quickly if the same pathogen re-infects the host. Fig. 2 shows the typical B lymphocyte activation pathway. Antibodies binding to matching antigens undertake jobs of making them easier targets for phagocytes and triggering the complement cascade.

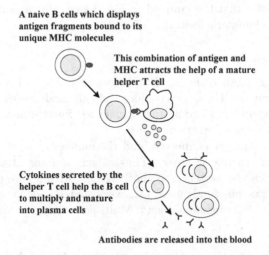

A naive B cells which displays
antigen fragments bound to its
unique MHC molecules

This combination of antigen and
MHC attracts the help of a mature
helper T cell

Cytokines secreted by the
helper T cell help the B cell
to multiply and mature
into plasma cells

Antibodies are released into the blood

Fig. 2. The B lymphocyte activation pathway

4.2   Design Methodology

In this section, we present the immunological anti-jamming method for the WMN in detail. Since mesh nodes have some unique features such as low mobility, strong processing and storage capacity, sufficient power supply, etc., we consider that mesh nodes in the WMN keep alive in a long period of time. Inspired by the the adaptive immune system, Table 1 shows the relationships between entities in the adaptive immune system and components in the immunological anti-jamming method. We consider monitoring agents as T helper cells in the immune system of human beings. T helper cells, which is a key subtype of T lymphocytes, help determine which types of immune responses the body will make to a particular pathogen. On the other hand, decision agents are considered as B cells in the immune system. After being activated by T helper cells, B cells begin to divide, and their offspring, known as plasma cells, produce antibodies, each of which recognizes a unique antigen and neutralize specific pathogens. Note that some plasma cells will survive to become long lived memory B cells. Moreover, we consider recovery agents as antibodies in the immune system. Millions of antibodies in human body circulate in blood plasma and lymph, bind to antigens and mark them for destruction. Antibodies can also neutralize pathogens directly by binding to toxins or by interfering with the receptors that viruses and bacteria use to infect regular cells.

Table 1. Relationships between the adaptive immune system and the immunological anti-jamming method

Entities in the adaptive immune system	Components in the anti-jamming method
Body	Wireless mesh network
Self cells	Regular mesh nodes
Non-self cells	Reactive jammers
Helper T cells	Monitoring agents
B cells	Decision agents
Antibodies	Recovery agents
Immunological memory	Attacking pattern database

Fig. 3 shows the framework of the proposed method, where an agent is a software module which is responsible for particular functions. A monitoring agent attached to each mesh node monitors the behaviors of its neighbors and periodically sends results to decision agents. After collecting information from monitoring agents, the decision agent detects jamming attacks based on its local jamming pattern database, which stores the features of known jamming attacks. If jamming attacks indeed occur, the decision agent activates several recovery agents to eliminate the impacts of these attacks. It is worth to mention when new jamming attacks are recognized by examining both abnormal behaviors of jammers' radio signals and packet losses, the decision agent extracts jamming patterns from these abnormal behaviors and then appends them into the jamming pattern database. Finally, recovery agents eliminate the impacts of jamming attacks through various mechanisms, such as path switching, Direct Sequence Spread Spectrum (DSSS), Frequency Hopping Spread Spectrum (FHSS), etc.

Note that decision agents could be deployed in a portion of selected mesh nodes for performance concerns. Among these three types of agents, the monitoring and the decision agent are stationary, while the recovery agent may be either stationary or mobile.

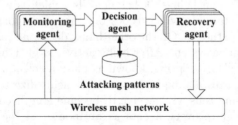

Fig. 3. Framework of the immunological anti-jamming method

4.3 Monitoring Agent

Similar to T helper cells in the adaptive immune system of human beings, monitoring agents are deployed in all mesh nodes to monitor behaviors of direct neighbors. After monitoring in a certain time period, they send results to nearby decision agents via dedicated or outband channels. Owing to sharing wireless medium, monitoring agents passively work in silence resulting in low overheads of collecting information. Besides, node behaviors can be further expressed in a compressed format to reduce the communication cost among agents. For example, Table 2 shows the mapping results of different behaviors.

Table 2. Mapping table of different behaviors

Behavior	Code
Emitting radio signals at a power exceeding the normal level	HP
Sending a RTS control packet	SR
Receiving a RTS control packet	RR
Sending a CTS control packet	SC
Receiving a CTS control packet	RC
Sending a DATA packet	SD
Receiving a DATA packet	RD

4.4 Decision Agent

We consider the decision agent as the B cell in the adaptive immune system. A decision agent is responsible for collecting monitoring results from monitoring agents, making reactions and activating recovery agents. Similarly, the decision agent detects various attacks by integrating the known attacking patterns for detecting known attacks with the specified policies for detecting unknown attacks. Note that the ability of detecting unknown attacks highly depends on the efficiency of existing specified policies towards normal behaviors of mesh nodes. Therefore, efficient anomaly based and specification based detection techniques are important to improve such ability. Similar works can be found in [2, 11, 20]. The work flow of a decision agent is illustrated in Fig. 4.

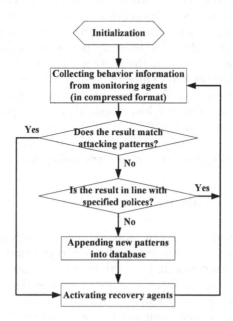

Fig. 4. Work flow of a decision agent

4.5 Recovery Agent

Recovery agents are considered as antibodies in the immune system, and their life time is controlled by a timer. The tasks of recovery agents are to eliminate the attacking impacts and to restore the WMN from the ongoing attacks. Multiple recovery agents collaboratively perform following three steps to defeat reactive jamming attacks:

Step 1. Those mesh nodes that locate at the border of the jammed area install recovery agents through two possible ways: One is activating existing recovery agents that are already installed in the nodes via some signals, e.g., the identifiers of abnormal nodes; The other is obtaining mobile recovery agents originated from decision agents via dedicated channels.

Step 2. Recovery agents perform countermeasures that are assigned by decision agents, e.g., path switching, to restore the network from potential attacks.

Step 3. When the timer expires, recovery agents turn to be inactive or are simply deleted for saving storage space.

4.6 Discussion

It is obvious that the value of the timer affects the performance of recovery agents. On the other hand, the countermeasure used in recovery process should be considered as well. Taking path switching as an example, a larger value of the timer results in a longer recovery delay but a greater probability of finding a clean transmission path that does not contain any jammer as the relay node. Therefore, we briefly discuss how to select the timer in practical usage. To minimize the recovery delay, a smaller value of the timer is required. However, we argue that the value must be no less than the discovery period of a new route. Therefore, the initial value can be assigned by the decision agent to the time period of the latest route discovery procedure. Once the decision agent fails to find a clean path before the timer expires, the value of the timer will increase in the next recovery procedure. Note that the first assumption in this paper ensures that a clean route can be always discovered when the value of the timer is large enough. Thus, a proper value of the timer can be determined to make a tradeoff between the recovery delay and the security of data transmissions.

5 Performance Evaluation

To evaluate the performance of the proposed method with the presence of reactive jamming attacks, we first establish an experimental environment that contains a square grid network and several reactive jammers. Note that the attacking strength of those jammers is adjusted by selecting different values of the following two parameters: jamming range and number of reactive jammers. Then, we present comparative results of the performance of different detection methods in terms of packet delivery ratio and network throughput.

5.1 Simulation Setup

We use network simulator ns2 (v2.33) for simulations and evaluate the performance of the proposed method in terms of Packet Delivery Ratio (PDR) and Valid Network Throughput (VNT). Omni-antenna is used as the antenna model, and Two Ray Ground model [3] is adopted as the radio-propagation model. Furthermore, since the basic 802.11 DCF MAC layer protocol is implemented in the ns2 simulator by default, the MAC protocol is selected as the IEEE 802.11b/g in the 2.4GHz Industrial, Scientific and Medical band. The underlying routing protocol is set to Ad hoc On-Demand Distance Vector (AODV) [13], a classical reactive routing protocol. For simplicity, all reactive jammers in simulations have the same jamming range.

The evaluated network in the simulations consists of a square grid of 49 evenly-spaced stationary nodes (numbered from node 0 to node 48 column by column) located in a 1350m×1350m square. Node 0 at one corner of the network serves as the source node of a data flow that start at simulation time of 20s, and node 35 that locates at the opposite corner to node 0 functions as the destination.

The source node originates User Datagram Protocol (UDP)/constant bit rate (CBR) flows with a packet size of 200 bytes and a sending rate of 96 kilobit per second (kbps) to its intended destination. Each simulations lasts 200 seconds, and each data point in the results is an average of 20 independent trials. More simulation parameters are listed as follows: Transmission range and horizontal/vertical distances between adjacent nodes are set to 250 meters and 150 meters, respectively. The locations of all reactive jammers are randomly generated in a rectangle area determined by four corner points whose coordinates are (500,400), (600,400), (500,500) and (600,500). Moreover, path switching serves as the recovery mechanism in our simulations. For the sake of comparison, we change settings of the jamming range and the number of reactive jammers to simulate different attacking scenarios.

To validate the advantages of the proposed method, we compare it with the collaborative detection scheme proposed in [15] in three cases. Firstly, we compare the two methods by adjusting the number of reactive jammers with simulation time in terms of VNT. In terms of PDR, we then compare the two methods with respect to different jamming ranges of reactive jammers. Lastly, we compare the two methods regarding different numbers of jammers to show the effectiveness of the proposed method. For the simplicity of description, we name the collaborative detection scheme [15] as the comparative method in the following simulation results. Specifically in the comparative method, wireless nodes periodically send out beacon signals, and the loss of beacon messages within each time interval is evaluated in order to detect the existence of jamming attacks.

5.2 Simulation Results

Before we present the simulation results, we define PDR and VNT as follows: the PDR of a flow is the number of data packets received by the destination divided by the number of data packets originated from the source, and the VNT, which is measured in kilobit per second (kbps), is defined as the average rate of successful packet delivery over the simulated network.

5.2.1 Performance Comparisons of the Adaptivity Towards New Reactive Jammers

In this part, we compare the proposed method with the comparative method in terms of VNT by changing the number of jammers with simulation time, where the jamming range of each reactive jammer is set to 100m. Moreover, the jammers launch attacks at simulation time of 20s. Fig. 5 illustrates the comparative results of VNT by adjusting the number of jammers with time. We see that the VNT of the comparative method dramatically decreases with the increase of the number of jammers. However, the VNT performance maintains a high level when the proposed method is used. We also observe in Fig. 5 that no matter what the number of jammers is, the VNT of the proposed method outperforms that of the comparative method. The above results stem from two reasons: Firstly, reactive jammers jam the network only if they sense the transmission of data packets whereas act normally when they sense the transmission

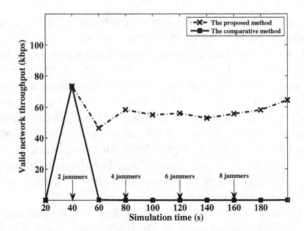

Fig. 5. Comparative results of VNT by adjusting the number of jammers with time

of control packets. Therefore, the comparative method is weak to detect such attacks because the node can not see a significant drop on the number of beacon messages received from neighbors. Secondly, the proposed method detect reactive jamming attacks by checking the number of data packets received from neighbors and investigating the abnormal behaviors of neighbors' radio signals. Then, the proposed method recover the network from jamming attacks using path switching. By appending the features of detected jamming attacks into attacking pattern database, the proposed method can quickly react known attacks in future. Thus, the proposed method is effective to protect the network from attacks launched by reactive jammers.

5.2.2 Performance Comparisons With Respect to Different Jamming Ranges

To justify the advantages of the proposed method compared to the previous one, we further carried out another group of simulations by changing the jamming range of reactive jammers, where the number of jammers was set to 2, and the total jamming time included two time intervals, i.e., [40s, 80s] and [120s, 160s]. Fig. 6 shows the comparative results of PDR of the two methods with respect to different jamming ranges. We find that no matter what the jamming range is, the proposed method outperforms the comparative one. Basically, the results are owing to similar analysis as before. As a matter of fact, the proposed method is adaptive to the changes of jammed area by monitoring via monitoring agents and restoring via recovery agents, and then guarantee the transmission of subsequent data packets.

5.2.3 Performance Comparisons Regarding Different Numbers of Reactive Jammers

In this part, we simulated different attacking scenarios using different numbers of reactive jammers, where the jamming range was 100m and the jamming time

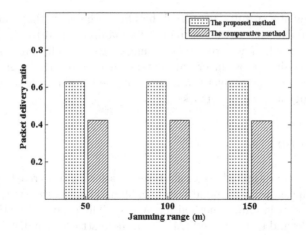

Fig. 6. Comparative results of PDR with respect to different jamming ranges

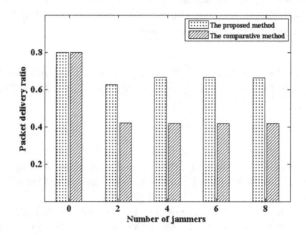

Fig. 7. Comparative results of PDR regarding different numbers of jammers

was selected as before, i.e., [40s, 80s] and [120s, 160s]. Then, we compared the proposed method with the comparative one in terms of PDR. Note that in each run of simulation, the number of jammers is fixed. Fig. 7 illustrates the comparative results of PDR regarding different numbers of jammers. From Fig. 7, we have two observations: one is that the performance of the proposed method is better than that of the comparative one with varied numbers of jammers, and the other is that compared to the previous method, our method has much smaller performance decrease when jamming attacks occur. The reason is that after detecting jamming, the proposed method reroutes the transmission path to a new available path that does not compromise nodes located in the jamming area. Therefore, ongoing jamming attacks have no influences on the subsequent data transmission.

The experimental results presented highlight the fact that the proposed method is more effective to detect the reactive jamming and to restore the network from the attack. These results also suggest that an efficient anti-jamming scheme must consider cross-layer parameters, such as received signal strength, packet bit errors, packet delivery ratio, etc., at the beginning of design in order to detect intelligent jamming attacks.

6   Conclusions

This paper have investigated a specific type of jamming, i.e., reactive jamming. According to the adaptive immune system of human beings, we have proposed an immunological anti-jamming method for WMNs. The proposed method detects jamming attacks and restores the WMN from these attacks in a distributed manner. Our results demonstrate the effectiveness and advantages of the proposed method for defeating reactive jamming attacks. Note that this work addresses detection and restoration but not countermeasures against malicious jammers, which is an interesting area for future studies.

Acknowledgments. This research was supported by the National Natural Science Foundation of China (No.61170287, No.60970034 and No.61232016).

References

1. Atakan, B., Akan, O.B., Tugcu, T.: Bio-inspired communications in wireless sensor networks. In: Guide to Wireless Sensor Networks. Computer Communications and Networks, pp. 659–685. Springer, London (2009)
2. Broustis, I., Pelechrinis, K., Syrivelis, D., Krishnamurthy, S.V., Tassiulas, L.: A software framework for alleviating the effects of mac-aware jamming attacks in wireless access networks. Wireless Networks 17(6), 1543–1560 (2011)
3. Eltahir, I.K.: The impact of different radio propagation models for mobile ad hoc networks (manet) in urban area environment. In: 2nd International Conference on Wireless Broadband and Ultra Wideband Communications, AusWireless 2007 (2007)
4. Hamieh, A., Ben-Othman, J.: Detection of jamming attacks in wireless ad hoc networks using error distribution. In: 2009 IEEE International Conference on Communications (ICC 2009), pp. 1–6 (2009)
5. Hofmeyr, S.A.: An Interpretative Introduction to the Immune System. In: Design Principles for the Immune System and Other Distributed Autonomous Systems. Oxford University Press, USA (2001)
6. Jiang, S., Xue, Y.: Providing survivability against jamming attack for multi-radio multi-channel wireless mesh networks. Journal of Network and Computer Applications 34(2), 443–454 (2011)
7. Kirachaiwanich, D., Liang, Q.: The combined-jamming model for ieee 802.11 fh/mfsk networks. European Transactions on Telecommunications 22(1), 14–24 (2011)

8. Li, M., Koutsopoulos, I., Poovendran, R.: Optimal jamming attack strategies and network defense policies in wireless sensor networks. IEEE Transactions on Mobile Computing 9(8), 1119–1133 (2010)

9. Lin, Y., Li, M.: Distributed detection of jamming and defense in wireless sensor networks. In: 43rd Annual Conference on Information Sciences and Systems (CISS 2009), pp. 829–834 (March 2009)

10. Lin, Z., van der Schaar, M.: Mac layer jamming mitigation using a game augmented by intervention. EURASIP Journal on Wireless Communications and Networking 2010, 78:1–78:14 (April 2010)

11. Liu, Q., Yin, J., Jokar, P., Hu, X.: Enhanced detection and restoration of low-rate denial-of-service in wireless multi-hop networks. In: 2013 International Conference on Computing, Networking and Communications (ICNC 2013), pp. 195–199 (2013)

12. Pelechrinis, K., Broustis, I., Krishnamurthy, S.V., Gkantsidis, C.: A measurement-driven anti-jamming system for 802.11 networks. IEEE/ACM Transactions on Networking 19(4), 1208–1222 (2011)

13. Perkins, C., Belding-Royer, E., Das, S.: Ad hoc on-demand distance vector (aodv) routing (2003)

14. Richa, A., Scheideler, C., Schmid, S., Zhang, J.: A jamming-resistant mac protocol for multi-hop wireless networks. In: Lynch, N.A., Shvartsman, A.A. (eds.) DISC 2010. LNCS, vol. 6343, pp. 179–193. Springer, Heidelberg (2010)

15. Siddhabathula, K., Dong, Q., Liu, D., Wright, M.: Fast jamming detection in sensor networks. In: IEEE International Conference on Communications (ICC 2012), pp. 934–938 (2012)

16. Strasser, M., Danev, B., Čapkun, S.: Detection of reactive jamming in sensor networks. ACM Transactions on Sensor Networks 7(2), 16:1–16:29 (2010)

17. Thamilarasu, G., Sridhar, R.: Game theoretic modeling of jamming attacks in ad hoc networks. In: 18th International Conference on Computer Communications and Networks (ICCCN 2009), pp. 1–6 (2009)

18. Wood, A.D., Stankovic, J.A., Zhou, G.: Deejam: Defeating energy-efficient jamming in ieee 802.15.4-based wireless networks. In: 4th Annual IEEE Communications Society Conference on Sensor, Mesh and Ad Hoc Communications and Networks (SECON 2007), pp. 60–69 (June 2007)

19. Xu, W., Trappe, W., Zhang, Y., Wood, T.: The feasibility of launching and detecting jamming attacks in wireless networks. In: 6th ACM International Symposium on Mobile Ad Hoc Networking and Computing (MobiHoc 2005), pp. 46–57. ACM, New York (2005)

20. Yi, P., Wu, Y., Chen, J.: Towards an artificial immune system for detecting anomalies in wireless mesh networks. China Communications 8(3), 107–117 (2011)

21. Zdarsky, F.A., Robitzsch, S., Banchs, A.: Security analysis of wireless mesh backhauls for mobile networks. Journal of Network and Computer Applications 34(2), 432–442 (2011)

Anonymous Identity-Based Broadcast Encryption with Adaptive Security

Leyou Zhang[1,3], Qing Wu[2], and Yi Mu[3]

[1] Department of Mathematics, Xidian University, Xi'an, 710126, China
xidianzhangly@126.com
[2] School of Automation, Xi'an University of Posts and Telecommunications,
Xi'an, 710121, China
xiyouwuq@126.com
[3] School of Computer Science and Software Engineering, University of Wollongong,
Wollongong, NSW, 2522 Australia
yimu@uow.edu.au

Abstract. Anonymous identity-based encryption(IBE) can be used to build Public-Key Encryption with Keyword Search. But no efficient previous works in the identity-based broadcast encryption are known. In this paper, we extend the anonymous IBE definition to the identity-based broadcast encryption. Then a new construction of anonymous identity-based broadcast encryption is proposed in the standard model. In the new construction, the ciphertexts and private keys are indistinguishable for the different receivers set. The proposed scheme has constant size ciphertexts and achieves adaptive security. In addition, the security of the proposed scheme is reduced to the static assumptions in a composite group.

Keywords: Identity-based encryption, anonymous identity-based broadcast encryption, dual system encryption, static assumptions, standard model.

1 Introduction

Broadcast Encryption (BE) was introduced by Fiat and Naor in [1]. In this scheme a broadcaster encrypts a message for some subset $S_i \subset S$ of users who are listening on a broadcast channel. Any user in Si can use his private key to decrypt the broadcast. Any user outside the privileged set Si should not be able to recover the message. Recently it has been widely used in digital rights management applications such as pay-TV, multicast communication, and DVD content protection. Since the first scheme appeared in 1994, many BE schemes have been proposed [2-5].

Identity-based encryption (IBE) was introduced by Shamir[6]. It allows for a party to encrypt a message using the recipient's identity as a public key. The ability to use identities as public keys avoids the need to distribute public key certificates. So it can simplify many applications of public key encryption (PKE) and is currently an active research area[7-12].

G. Wang et al. (Eds.): CSS 2013, LNCS 8300, pp. 258–271, 2013.

Identity-based broadcast encryption(IBBE) [13-18] is a generalization of IBE. One public key can be used to encrypt a message to any possible identity in IBE schemes. But in an IBBE scheme, one public key can be used to encrypt a message to any possible group of S identities. In [13, 15], the proposed scheme was based on random oracles. In addition, the size of the ciphertexts grows linearly with the number of the users. The well known construction of IBBE was proposed by Delerablée [14]. This construction achieved constant size private keys and constant size ciphertexts. However the security of her main scheme achieved only selective-identity security(a weak security) and relied on the random oracles. In [16, 17], two schemes with full security were proposed respectively. But they were impractical in real-life practice since their security relied on the complex assumptions which were dependent on the depth of users set and the number of queries made by an attacker. In addition, the work in [17] had the sublinear-size ciphertexts. Moreover, the authors in [17] used a sub-algorithm at the Encrypt phase to achieve full security which increased the computations cost. In [18], authors also proposed an anonymous broadcast encryption scheme. However, it is constructed based on the strong Hash function which means that the security relies on the random oracles. Recent works[19] were also impractical since the size of the ciphertexts relied on the size of receivers set.

Recently, a new technique is applied to IBE. It is called Dual Encryption Technique. In a dual system[20,21], ciphertexts and keys can take on two forms: normal or semi-functional. Semi-functional ciphertexts and keys are not used in the real system since they are only used in the security proof. A normal key can decrypt normal or semi-functional ciphertexts, and a normal ciphertext can be decrypted by normal or semi-functional keys. However, when a semi-functional key is used to decrypt a semi-functional ciphertext, decryption will fail. More specifically, the semi-functional components of the key and ciphertext will interact to mask the blinding factor by an additional random term. Waters[20] first proposed a broadcast encryption scheme based on this new technique. However, the proposed scheme is not based on identity and also inefficient since its cost of decryption is dependent on depth of users set. Based on this technique, two schemes are proposed in [21,22] respectively.

However, the existing works are not anonymous. They can not protect the privacy of the receivers in the different subsets in S. Bellare et al[24] treated firstly the notion of anonymity or key privacy for a cryptosystem. In this notion the ciphertext of an encryption may not give any information on the key that was used to perform the encryption, in addition to the privacy of the message. Combining anonymity with identity-based encryption is a logical step. Anonymous identity-based cryptosystems can be used to construct Public key Encryption with Keyword Search (PEKS) schemes, which was observed by Boneh et al.[25]. Many schemes have appeared in this area[26-28]. However, these techniques are not suit for the broadcast encryption system.

Our contributions. According to the definition of anonymous IBE, we give the definition of the anonymous identity-based broadcast encryption and the corresponding security model at first. Then based on the dual system encryption, a concrete construction is proposed. The new scheme has constant size ciphertexts and achieves the adaptive security. The security of the new scheme does not rely on the random oracles and is reduced to some static assumptions in the composite bilinear group.

2   Preliminaries

2.1   Composite Order Bilinear Groups

Composite order bilinear groups were used in [22,23]. In this paper, the output is (N= p₁p₂p₃ p₄, G , G_1 ,e), where p₁ ,p₂ ,p₃ ,p₄ are distinct primes, G and G_1 are cyclic groups of order N. A bilinear map e is a map $e: G \times G \to G_1$ with the following properties:

(i) Bilinearity: for all $u, v \in G$, a, b$\in Z_N$, we have $e(u^a, v^b) = e(u, v)^{ab}$;

(ii) Non-degeneracy: $\exists$ $g \in G$ such that $e(g, g)$ has order N in G_1 .

(iii) Computability: there is an efficient algorithm to compute $e(u, v)$ for all $u, v \in G$.

2.2   Hardness Assumptions

In this section, we give our complex assumption. These assumptions have been used in [20-23].

Assumption 1 (Subgroup decision problem for 4 primes) Given (N=p₁p₂p₃p₄, G , G_1 ,e), select randomly

$$g_1, A_1 \in G_{p_1} ,\ A_2, B_2 \in G_{p_2} ,$$

$$B_3 \in G_{p_3} , g_4 \in G_{p_4} , T_1 \in G_{p_1 p_2 p_3} ,\ T_2 \in G_{p_1 p_3}$$

and set D=(N, G , G_1 , e, g_1, g_3, g_4 , $A_1 A_2$, $B_2 B_3$). It is hard to distinguish T_1 from T_2 . The advantage of an algorithm is defined as

$$Adv_1 = |\Pr[A(D, T_1) = 1] - \Pr[A(D, T_2) = 1]|.$$

Definition 1. Assumption 1 holds if Adv_1 is negligible.

Assumption 2. Given (N=p₁p₂p₃p₄, G , G_1 ,e), select randomly $\alpha, s, r \in Z_N$,

$$g_1 \in G_{p_1} ,\ g_2, A_2, B_2 \in G_{p_2} ,\ g_3 \in G_{p_3} ,\ g_4 \in G_{p_4} ,\ T_2 \in G_1 ,$$

and set

$$T_1 = e(g_1, g_1)^{\alpha s}, D=(N,\ G, G_1, e,\ g_1, g_3, g_4 ,\ g_1^\alpha A_2 ,\ g_1^s B_2 ,\ g_2^r A_2^r).$$

It is hard to distinguish T_1 from T_2 . The advantage of an algorithm is defined as

$$Adv_2 = |\Pr[A(D, T_1) = 1] - \Pr[A(D, T_2) = 1]|.$$

Definition 2. Assumption 2 holds if Adv_2 is negligible.

Assumption 3. Given (N=p₁p₂p₃p₄, G , G_1 ,e), select randomly $s, \hat{r} \in Z_N$,

$$g_1, U_1, A_1 \in G_{p_1}, \quad g_2, A_2, B_2, D_2, F_2 \in G_{p_2},$$

$$g_3 \in G_{p_3}, \quad g_4, A_4, B_4, D_4 \in G_{p_4}, \quad T_2 \in G_{p_1 p_2 p_4}, \quad A_{24}, B_{24}, D_{24} \in G_{p_2 p_4},$$

and set

$$T_1 = A_1^s D_{24}, \text{D=(N, } G, G_1, \text{e, } g_1, g_3, g_4, \quad U, U^s A_{24}, \quad U^{\hat{r}}, \quad A_1 A_4, A_1^{\hat{r}} A_2,$$

$$g_1^{\hat{r}} B_2, g_1^s B_{24}).$$

It is hard to distinguish T_1 from T_2. The advantage of an algorithm is defined as

$$Adv_3 = | \Pr[A(D, T_1) = 1] - \Pr[A(D, T_2) = 1] |.$$

Definition 3. Assumption 3 holds if Adv_3 is negligible.

2.3   Anonymous IBBE

An identity-based broadcast encryption scheme(IBBE) with the security parameter and the maximal size m of the target set is specified as follows.

Setup. Take as input the security parameter and output a master secret key and public key.

Extract. Take as input the master secret key and a user identity *ID*. Extract generates a user private key d_{ID}.

Encrypt. Take as input the public key and a set of included identities S={ID_1,..., ID_s} with s ≤ m, and output a pair (*Hdr, K*). Then algorithm computes the encryption C_M of *M* under the symmetric key K and broadcasts (*Hdr, S, C_M*).

Decrypt. Take as input a subset S, an identity ID_i and the corresponding private key, if $ID_i \in$ S, the algorithm outputs *K* which is then used to decrypt the broadcast body C_M and recover *M*.

2.4   Security Model

Setup The challenger runs Setup to obtain a public key PK. He gives A the public key PK.

***Query phase* 1.** The adversary A adaptively issues queries q_1,..., q_{s0}, where q_i is one of the following:

• Extraction query (ID_i): The challenger runs Extract on ID_i and sends the resulting private key to the adversary.

Challenge. When A decides that phase 1 is over, A outputs two same-length messages (M_0 M_1) and two users set (S_0^*, S_1^*) on which it wishes to be challenged. The challenger picks a random b ∈ {0,1} and sets the challenge ciphertext C^* =Encrypt(params, M_b, S_b^*). The challenger returns C^* to A.

Query phase 2: The adversary continues to issue queries $q_{s0+1}, \ldots, q_t$, where q_i is one of the following:

- Extraction query (ID_i), as in phase 1 with the constraint that $ID_i \notin S_0^*, S_1^*$.

Guess Finally, the adversary A outputs a guess $b' \in \{0, 1\}$ and wins the game if $b = b'$.

Let t denote the total number of extraction queries during the game. The advantage of A in winning the game is defined as follows:

$$Adv_{IBBE}(t, m, A) = |2P(b = b') - 1|.$$

Definition 4. An anonymous identity-based broadcast encryption scheme(IBBE) is said to be (t, m,)-IND-ID-CPA secure if $Adv_{IBBE}(t, m, A)$ is negligible.

3   Our Construction

3.1   New Works

In this section, we give our construction for an anonymous IBBE scheme.

Let G be cyclic groups of order $N = p_1 p_2 p_3 p_4$ and l denote the maximum number of the set of possible users. Our scheme works as follows.

Setup. To generate the system parameters, the PKG picks randomly $g_1, h_1, u_1, \cdots, u_l \in G_{p_1}$, $g_3 \in G_{p_3}$, $g_4, h_4 \in G_{p_4}$, $\alpha \in Z_N$ and set $t = h_1 h_4$. The public parameters are defined as PK={N , $g_1, g_3, g_4, t, u_1, \cdots, u_l$, $v = e(g_1, g_1)^\alpha$ }and the master key is (h_1, α).

Extract. Given the identity $ID_i \in S(|S| = k \leq l)$, PKG selects randomly $r_i \in Z_N$ and also chooses random elements $R_{i0}, R'_{i0}, R_{i1}, \cdots, R_{i(i-1)}, R_{i(i+1)}, \cdots, R_{ik} \in G_{p_3}$. Then it computes private keys as follows:

$$d_{ID_i} = (d_0, d', d_1, \cdots, d_{i-1}, d_{i+1}, \cdots, d_k)$$

$$= (g_1^\alpha (h_1 u_i^{ID_i})^{r_i} R_{i0}, g_1^{r_i} R'_{i0}, u_1^{r_i} R_{i1}, \cdots, u_{i-1}^{r_i} R_{i(i-1)}, u_{i+1}^{r_i} R_{i(i+1)}, \cdots, u_k^{r_i} R_{ik});$$

Encrypt. Without loss of generality, let $S = (ID_1, ID_2, \cdots, ID_k)$ denote the set of users with $k \leq l$ and M be the encrypted message. A broadcaster selects a random $s \in Z_N^*$ and $Z, Z' \in G_{p_4}$, computes

$$C = (C_0, Hdr) = (C_0, C_1, C_2)$$

$$= (v^s M, (t \prod_{i=1}^k u_i^{ID_i})^s Z, g_1^s Z').$$

Decrypt. Given the ciphertexts $C = (C_0, C_1, C_2)$, any user $ID_i \in S$ uses his private keys d_{ID_i} to compute

$$M = C_0 \frac{e(C_1, d')}{e(d_0 \prod_{j=1, j\neq i}^{k} d_j^{ID_j}, C_2)}.$$

In order to show the correctness, the orthogonality property of $G_{p_i} (i = 1, \cdots, 4)$ will be used.

Lemma[19]. 1 When $h_i \in G_{p_i}, h_j \in G_{p_j}$ for $i \neq j$, $e(h_i, h_j)$ is the identity element in G_1.

Correctness:

$$\frac{e(C_1, d')}{e(d_0 \prod_{j=1, j\neq i}^{s} d_j^{ID_j}, C_2)}$$

$$= \frac{e((t \prod_{i=1}^{k} u_i^{ID_i})^s, g^{r_i} R'_{i0})}{e(g_1^\alpha (h_1 \prod_{i=1}^{k} u_i^{ID_i})^{r_i} R_{i0} (\prod_{j=1, j\neq i}^{k} R_{ij}^{ID_j}), g^s)}$$

$$= \frac{e((h_1 \prod_{i=1}^{k} u_i^{ID_i})^s, g^{r_i}) e(h_4^s, g^{r_i})}{e(g_1^\alpha, g_1^s) e((h_1 \prod_{i=1}^{k} u_i^{ID_i})^{r_i}, g^s)}$$

$$\cdot \frac{e((t \prod_{i=1}^{k} u_i^{ID_i})^s, g^{r_i}) e((t \prod_{i=1}^{k} u_i^{ID_i})^s, R'_{i0})}{e(R_{i0}, g^s) e((\prod_{j=1, j\neq i}^{k} R_{ij}^{ID_j}), g^s)}$$

$$= \frac{1}{v^s}.$$

By using lemma 1, one can obtain

$$e(R_{i0}, g^s) = e((\prod_{j=1, j\neq i}^{k} R_{ij}^{ID_j}), g^s) = e(h_4^s, g^{r_i}) = e((h \prod_{i=1}^{k} u_i^{ID_i})^s, R'_{i0}) = 1.$$

Table 1. Comparisons of Efficiency

Scheme	Hardness	PK size	pk size	Ciphertext size	Anony
[16]	TBDHE	$O(\lambda)$	$O(|S|)$	$O(1)$	NO
[17] 1st	BDHE	$O(m)$	$O(|S|)$	$O(1)$	NO
[17] 2nd	BDHE	$O(m)$	$O(1)$	$O(1)$	NO
[17] 3rd	BDHE	$O(m)$	$O(1)$	Sublinear of $|S|$	NO
[22]	Static	$O(m)$	$O(1)$	$O(1)$	NO
[23]	Static	$O(m)$	$O(|S|)$	$O(1)$	NO
Ours	Static	$O(m)$	$O(|S|)$	$O(1)$	YES

3.2   Efficiency

Our construction achieves $O(1)$-size ciphertexts. The private key of construction private key is linear in the maximal size of S. In addition, $e(g_1, g_1)^\alpha$ can be precomputed, so there is no pair computations at the phase of Encryption. The security of the proposed scheme is reduced to the static assumptions. In addition, our scheme achieves anonymous. Table 1 gives the comparisons with others.

In Table 1, PK and pk denote the public key and private key respectively. Anony is the anonymous feature. From Table 1, our scheme achieves only anonymous.

4   Security Analysis

In this section, we will prove the security of the proposed scheme. We first define semi-functional keys and semi-functional ciphertexts. Let g_2 denote a generator of G_{p_2}.

Semi-functional keys: At first, a normal key $(\bar{d}_0, \bar{d}', \bar{d}_1, \cdots, \bar{d}_{i-1}, \bar{d}_{i+1}, \cdots, \bar{d}_k)$ is obtained using the Extract algorithm. Then some random elements $\gamma_0, \gamma_0', \gamma_j$ for $j = 1, \cdots, k$ and $j \neq i$ are chosen in Z_N. The semi-functional keys are set as follows.

$$d_0 = \bar{d}_0 g_2^{\gamma_0}, d' = \bar{d}' g_2^{\gamma_0'}, d_j = \bar{d}_j g_2^{\gamma_j}, j = 1, \cdots, k, j \neq i.$$

When the semi-functional key is used to decrypt a semi-functional ciphertexts, the decryption algorithm will compute the blinding factor multiplied by the additional term $e(g_2, g_2)^{x\gamma_0(\gamma_0' - \gamma_c)}$. If $\gamma_0' = \gamma_c$, decryption still work. In this case, the key is nominally semi-functional.

Semi-functional ciphertexts: At first, a normal semi-functional ciphertext (C_0', C_1', C_2') is obtained using the Encrypt algorithm. Then two random elements λ_1, λ_2 are chosen in Z_N. The semi-functional ciphertexts are set as follows:

$$C_0 = C_0', C_1 = C_1' g_2^{\lambda_1 \lambda_2}, C_2 = C_2' g_2^{\lambda_2}.$$

We organize our proof as a sequence of games. We will show that each game is indistinguishable from the next (under three complexity assumptions). We first define the games as:

Game$_{real}$: This is a real IBBE security game.
For $0 \leq i \leq q$, the Game$_i$ is defined as follows.

Game$_i$: Let Ω denote the set of private keys which the adversary queries during the games. This game is a real IBBE security game with the two exceptions: (1) The challenge ciphertext will be a semi-functional ciphertext on the challenge set S^*. (2) The first i keys will be semi-functional private keys. The rest of keys in Ω will be normal.

Note: In $game_0$, the challenge ciphertext is semi-functional. In $game_q$, the challenge ciphertexts and all keys are semi-functional.

Game$_{final'}$: This game is same with $game_q$ except that the challenge ciphertext is a semi-functional encryption of random group element of G_1.

Game$_{final}$: This game is same with $game_{final'}$ except that the challenge ciphertext is a semi-functional encryption of random group element of $G_{p_1 p_2 p_4}$.

We will show that these games are indistinguishable in a set of Lemmas. Let Adv-$_{game}$A denote the advantage in the real game.

Lemma 1. Suppose that there exists an algorithm A such that $Adv_{game_{real}} A - Adv_{game_0} A = \varepsilon$. Then we can build an algorithm B with advantage ε in breaking Assumption 1.

Proof. Our algorithm B begins by receiving $D = (N, G, G_1, e, g_1, g_3, g_4, A_1 A_2, B_2 B_3)$. It works as follows:

Setup. B chooses random elements $\alpha, a_1, \cdots, a_l, b, c \in Z_N$ and sets

$$u_i = g^{a_i}, \ 1 \le i \le l, h_1 = g_1^b, \ h_4 = g_4^c.$$

It sends the public keys PK$=\{ N, g_1, g_3, g_4, t = h_1 h_4, u_1, \cdots, u_l, v = e(g_1, g_1)^\alpha \}$ to A. Note that B knows the master keys at this phase.

Query Phase 1. The adversary A issues a private key query for identity $ID_i \in$ S($|S| = k \le l$). B answers as follows: It selects randomly $r, t_0, t_0', t_j, 1 \le j \le k, j \ne i$ in Z_N. Then it sets

$$d_{ID_i} = (d_0, d', d_1, \cdots, d_{i-1}, d_{i+1}, \cdots, d_k)$$
$$= (g^a (h_1 u_i^{ID_i})^r X_3^{t_0}, g^r X_3^{t_0'}, u_1^r X_3^{t_1}, \cdots, u_{i-1}^r X_3^{t_{i-1}},$$
$$u_{i+1}^r X_3^{t_{i+1}}, \cdots, u_k^r X_3^{t_k}).$$

It is a valid simulation to A.

Challenge. The adversary A outputs two challenge message M_0, M_1 and the challenge sets $S_0^* = \{ ID_{01}^*, \cdots, ID_{0k}^* \}, S_1^* = \{ ID_{11}^*, \cdots, ID_{1k}^* \}$. Then the ciphertext $C = (C_0, C_1, C_2)$ is formed as

$$C_0 = M_\gamma e(T, g)^a, C_1 = T^{\sum_{i=1}^k a_i ID_{\gamma i}^* + b}, C_2 = T, \ \gamma \in \{0,1\}.$$

Query phase 2. The adversary continues to issue queries q_j, where q_i is the following:

• Extraction query (ID$_i$), as in phase 1 with the constraint that ID$_i \notin S_0^*, S_1^*$.

Guess. Finally, the adversary A outputs a guess $\gamma' \in \{0, 1\}$ and wins the game if $\gamma' = \gamma$.

If $T \in G_{p_1 p_3}$, then T can be written as $g_1^{s_1} g_3^{s_3}$ for random $s_1, s_3 \in Z_N$ and $Z = g_3^{s_3 \sum_{i=1}^{k} a_i ID_{\gamma_i}^* + b}$, $Z' = g_3^{s_3}$. In this case, $C = (C_0, C_1, C_2)$ is a normal ciphertext with $s = s_1$. If $T \in G_{p_1 p_2 p_3}$, then T can be written as $g_1^{s_1} g_2^{s_2} g_3^{s_3}$ for random $s_1, s_2, s_3 \in Z_N$ and

$$Z = g_3^{s_3 \sum_{i=1}^{k} a_i ID_{\gamma_i}^* + b}, Z' = g_3^{s_3}, \lambda_1 = s_2, \lambda_2 = \sum_{i=1}^{k} a_i ID_{\gamma_i}^* + b.$$

In this case, $C = (C_0, C_1, C_2)$ is a semi-functional ciphertext. Hence B can use A's guess to break Assumption 1 with advantage ε .

Lemma 2. Suppose that there exists an algorithm A that makes at most q queries and such that $Adv_{game_{j-1}} A - Adv_{game_j} A = \varepsilon$ for $1 \leq j \leq q$. Then we can build an algorithm B with advantage ε in breaking Assumption 1.

Proof. Our algorithm B begins by receiving D=(N, G , G_1 , e, g_1, g_3, g_4 , $A_1 A_2$, $B_2 B_3$). It works as follows:

Setup. B chooses random elements $\alpha, a_1, \cdots, a_l$, $b, c \in Z_N$ and sets $u_i = g^{a_i}$, $1 \leq i \leq l$, $h_1 = g_1^b$, $h_4 = g_4^c$. It sends the public keys

$$PK=\{ N, g_1, g_3, g_4, t = h_1 h_4, u_1, \cdots, u_l, v = e(g_1, g_1)^{\alpha} \}$$

to A. Note that B knows the master keys at this phase .

Query Phase 1. Consider a private key query for i-th identity $ID_i \in S(| S |= k \leq l)$. B answers as follows:

(1) $i < j$, B will construct a semi-functional key. It selects randomly $r, t_0, t_0', t_\kappa \in Z_N$ $1 \leq \kappa \leq k, \kappa \neq i$. Then it sets

$$d_{ID_i} = (d_0, d', d_1, \cdots, d_{i-1}, d_{i+1}, \cdots, d_s)$$
$$= (g_1^{\alpha}(h_1 u_i^{ID_i})^r (B_2 B_3)^{t_0}, g_1^r (B_2 B_3)^{t_0'}, u_1^{r_i}(B_2 B_3)^{t_1}, \cdots,$$
$$u_{i-1}^r (B_2 B_3)^{t_{i-1}}, u_{i+1}^r (B_2 B_3)^{t_{i+1}}, \cdots, u_k^r (B_2 B_3)^{t_k}).$$

It is a valid simulation.

(2) $i > j$, B runs the Extract algorithm to obtain the normal key.

(3) $i = j$, B first pick $t_0, t_j, 1 \leq \kappa \leq k, \kappa \neq i$ in Z_N at random. Then it sets

$$d_{ID_i} = (d_0, d', d_1, \cdots, d_{i-1}, d_{i+1}, \cdots, d_s) = (g_1^{\alpha} T^{a_i ID_i + b}(g_3)^{t_0}, T, T^{a_1}(g_3)^{t_1}, \cdots, T^{a_{k-1}}(g_3)^{t_{i-1}},$$
$$T^{a_{i+1}}(g_3)^{t_{i+1}}, \cdots, T^{a_k}(g_3)^{t_k}).$$

If $T \in G_{p_1 p_3}$, then T can be written as $g_1^{s_1} g_3^{s_3}$. One can verify it is a normal key. If $T \in G_{p_1 p_2 p_3}$, then T can be written as $g_1^{s_1} g_2^{s_2} g_3^{s_3}$ for random $s_1, s_2, s_3 \in Z_N$. This is a semi-functional key.

Challenge. The adversary A outputs two challenge message M_0, M_1 and the challenge sets $S_0^* = \{ ID_{01}^*, \cdots, ID_{0k}^* \}$, $S_1^* = \{ ID_{11}^*, \cdots, ID_{1k}^* \}$. Then the ciphertext $C = (C_0, C_1, C_2)$ is formed as

$$C_0 = M_\gamma e(A_1 A_2, g)^a, C_1 = (A_1 A_2)^{\sum_{i=1}^s a_i ID_{\gamma i}^* + b}, C_2 = A_1 A_2, \gamma \in \{0,1\}.$$

Query phase 2. The adversary continues to issue queries q_j, where q_i is the following:

• Extraction query (ID_i), as in phase 1 with the constraint that $ID_i \notin S_0^*, S_1^*$.

Guess. Finally, the adversary A outputs a guess $\gamma' \in \{0, 1\}$ and wins the game if $\gamma' = \gamma$.

If $T \in G_{p_1 p_3}$, then B has perfectly simulated Game$_{j-1}$. If $T \in G_{p_1 p_2 p_3}$, B has perfectly simulated Game$_j$. Hence B can use A's guess to break Assumption 1 with advantage ε.

Lemma 3. Suppose that there exists an algorithm A that makes at most q queries and such that $\text{Adv}_{game_q} A - \text{Adv}_{game_{final}} A = \varepsilon$. Then we can build an algorithm B with advantage ε in breaking Assumption 2.

Proof. Our algorithm B begins by receiving D=(N, G, G_1, e, g_1, g_3, g_4, $g_1^\alpha A_2$, $g_1^s B_2$, g_2^r, A_2^r, T), where $\alpha, s, r \in Z_N$, $g_1 \in G_{p_1}$, $g_2, A_2, B_2 \in G_{p_2}$, $g_3 \in G_{p_3}$, $g_4 \in G_{p_4}$. B will decide $T = e(g_1, g_1)^{\alpha s}$ or T is a random element of G_1. It works as follows:

Setup. B chooses random elements $a_1, \cdots, a_l$, $b, c \in Z_N$ and sets $u_i = g^{a_i}$, $1 \leq i \leq l$, $h_1 = g_1^b$, $h_4 = g_4^c$. Then it compute $v = e(g_1^\alpha A_2, g_1) = e(g_1^\alpha, g_1)$. It sends the public keys PK={ N, $g_1, g_3, g_4, t = h_1 h_4, u_1, \cdots, u_l$, $v = e(g_1^\alpha, g_1)$ } to A.

Query Phase 1. Consider a private key query for an identity $ID_i \in S(|S| = k \leq l)$. B answers as follows: B selects randomly $r_0, t_0, t_0', t_j, z_0', z_0, z_j \in Z_N, 1 \leq j \leq k, j \neq i$. Then it sets

$$d_{ID_i} = (d_0, d', d_1, \cdots, d_{i-1}, d_{i+1}, \cdots, d_k)$$
$$= (g_1^\alpha A_2 g_2^{z_0} (h_1 u_i^{ID_i})^{r_0} (g_3)^{t_0}, g_1^{r_0} g_2^{z_0'} (g_3)^{t_0'}, u_1^{r_0} g_2^{z_1} (g_3)^{t_1}, \cdots, u_{i-1}^{r_0} g_2^{z_{i-1}} (g_3)^{t_{i-1}}, u_{i+1}^{r_0} g_2^{z_{i+1}} (g_3)^{t_{i+1}},$$
$$\cdots, u_k^{r_0} g_2^{z_k} (g_3)^{t_k}).$$

This is a semi-functional key.

Challenge. The adversary A outputs two challenge message M_0, M_1 and the challenge sets $S_0^* = \{ ID_{01}^*, \cdots, ID_{0k}^* \}$, $S_1^* = \{ ID_{11}^*, \cdots, ID_{1k}^* \}$. Then the ciphertext $C = (C_0, C_1, C_2)$ is formed as

$$C_0 = M_\gamma T, C_1 = (g_1^s B_2)^{\sum_{i=1}^s a_i ID_{\gamma i}^* + b} g_4^z, C_2 = g_1^s B_2 g_4^z, \gamma \in \{0,1\}, z \in Z_N.$$

Query phase 2. The adversary continues to issue queries q_j, where q_i is the following:
• Extraction query (ID_i), as in phase 1 with the constraint that $ID_i \notin S_0^*, S_1^*$.

Guess Finally, the adversary A outputs a guess $\gamma' \in \{0, 1\}$ and wins the game if $\gamma' = \gamma$.

If $T = e(g_1, g_1)^{\alpha s}$, then $C = (C_0, C_1, C_2)$ is a valid semi-functional ciphertext. If T is a random element in G_1, $C = (C_0, C_1, C_2)$ is a valid semi-functional ciphertext for a random message. Hence B can use A's guess to break Assumption 2 with advantage ε.

Lemma 4. Suppose that there exists an algorithm A that makes at most q queries and such that $Adv_{game_{final'}} A - Adv_{game_{final}} A = \varepsilon$. Then we can build an algorithm B with advantage ε in breaking Assumption 3.

Proof. Our algorithm B begins by receiving

$$D = (N, \ G, G_1, e, \ g_1, g_3, g_4, \ U, U^s A_{24}, \ U^{\hat{r}}, \ A_1 A_4, A_1^{\hat{r}} A_2, \ g_1^{\hat{r}} B_2, g_1^s B_{24}),$$

where $s, \hat{r} \in Z_N$, $g_1, U_1, A_1 \in G_{p_1}$, $g_2, A_2, B_2, D_2, F_2 \in G_{p_2}$, $g_3 \in G_{p_3}$, $g_4, A_4, B_4, D_4 \in G_{p_4}$, $A_{24}, B_{24}, D_{24} \in G_{p_2 p_4}$, B will decide $T = A_1^s D_{24}$ or T is a random element of $G_{p_1 p_2 p_4}$.

Setup. B chooses random elements $\alpha, a_1, \cdots, a_l, \ b, c \in Z_N$ and sets $u_i = g^{a_i}$, $1 \le i \le l$, $h_1 = g_1^b$, $h_4 = g_4^c$. It sends the public keys $PK = \{N, g_1, g_3, g_4, t = h_1 h_4, u_1, \cdots, u_l, \ v = e(g_1^\alpha, g_1)\}$ to A.

Query Phase 1. Consider a private key query for an identity $ID_i \in S(|S| = k \le l)$. B answers as follows: B selects randomly $r_0, t_0, t_0', t_j, z_0', z_0, z_j \in Z_N, 1 \le j \le k, j \ne i$. Then it sets

$$d_{ID_i} = (d_0, d', d_1, \cdots, d_{i-1}, d_{i+1}, \cdots, d_k)$$
$$= (g_1^\alpha ((U^{\hat{r}})^{ID_i} (A_1^{\hat{r}} A_2))^{r_0} (g_3)^{t_0}, (U^{\hat{r}})^{r_0} g_2^{z_0'} (g_3)^{t_0'},$$
$$(U^{\hat{r}})^{r_0} g_2^{z_1} (g_3)^{t_1}, \cdots, (U^{\hat{r}})^{r_0} g_2^{z_{i-1}} (g_3)^{t_{i-1}}, (U^{\hat{r}})^{r_0} g_2^{z_{i+1}} (g_3)^{t_{i+1}}, \cdots, (U^{\hat{r}})^{r_0} g_2^{z_k} (g_3)^{t_k}).$$

This is a semi-functional key.

Challenge. The adversary A outputs two challenge message M_0, M_1 and the challenge sets $S_0^* = \{ ID_{01}^*, \cdots, ID_{0k}^* \}$, $S_1^* = \{ ID_{11}^*, \cdots, ID_{1k}^* \}$. B picks random $C_0 \in G_1$ and compute the challenge ciphertext $C = (C_0, C_1, C_2)$ as follows:

$$C_0, C_1 = (U^s A_{24})^{\sum_{i=1}^{s} a_i ID_{\gamma i}^* + b}, \quad C_2 = g_1^s B_{24}.$$

Guess. Finally, the adversary A outputs a guess $\gamma' \in \{0, 1\}$ and wins the game if $\gamma' = \gamma$.

If $T = A_1^s D_{24}$, then this is a properly distributed semi-functional ciphertext with C_0 random and for set S_γ^*. If T is a random element of $G_{p_1 p_2 p_4}$, then this is a properly distributed semi-functional ciphertext with C_0 random in G_1, C_1 and C_2 random in $G_{p_1 p_2 p_4}$. Hence B can use A's guess to break Assumption 3 with advantage ε.

Theorem 1. If Assumption 1,2 and 3 hold, then our scheme is IND-ID-CPA secure.

Proof. If Assumption 1,2 and 3 hold, by the sequence of games and Lemma from 1 to 4, the adversary's advantage in the real game must be negligible. Hence our IBBE is IND-ID-CPA secure.

5   Conclusion

In order to support the anonymity in the IBBE, in this paper, we introduce the anonymous IBBE definition and corresponding the security model. Based on the proposed model, we introduce a concrete scheme in the standard model. The scheme is constructed in a composite group. So it contains the desirable features such as short ciphertexts and achieving the adaptive security. The security of the new scheme is reduced to some general hardness assumption instead of other strong assumptions.

A drawback of the new scheme is that the private keys rely on the size of receiver set. So the future works are also to construct an anonymous IBBE system with constant size ciphertexts and private keys that is secure under a more standard assumption.

Acknowledgments. This work is supported in part by the Nature Science Foundation of China under grant (61100231, 61100165, 60970119), the National Basic Research Program of China(973) under grant 2007CB311201, the Fundamental Research Funds for the Central Universities and natural Science Basic Research Plan in Shaanxi Province of China (Program No. 2012JQ8044) and Foundation of Education Department of Shanxi Province(2013JK1096).

References

1. Fiat, A., Naor, M.: Broadcast encryption. In: Stinson, D.R. (ed.) CRYPTO 1993. LNCS, vol. 773, pp. 480–491. Springer, Heidelberg (1994)

2. Dodis, Y., Fazio, N.: Public key broadcast encryption for stateless receivers. In: Feigenbaum, J. (ed.) DRM 2002. LNCS, vol. 2696, pp. 61–80. Springer, Heidelberg (2003)

3. Dodis, Y., Fazio, N.: Public key broadcast encryption secure against adaptive chosen ciphertext attack. In: Desmedt, Y.G. (ed.) PKC 2003. LNCS, vol. 2567, pp. 100–115. Springer, Heidelberg (2003)

4. Boneh, D., Gentry, C., Waters, B.: Collusion resistant broadcast encryption with short ciphertexts and private keys. In: Shoup, V. (ed.) CRYPTO 2005. LNCS, vol. 3621, pp. 258–275. Springer, Heidelberg (2005)

5. Delerablée, C., Paillier, P., Pointcheval, D.: Fully collusion secure dynamic broadcast encryption with constant-size ciphertexts or decryption keys. In: Takagi, T., Okamoto, T., Okamoto, E., Okamoto, T. (eds.) Pairing 2007. LNCS, vol. 4575, pp. 39–59. Springer, Heidelberg (2007)

6. Shamir, A.: Identity-based Cryptosystems and Signature Schemes. In: Blakely, G.R., Chaum, D. (eds.) CRYPTO 1984. LNCS, vol. 196, pp. 47–53. Springer, Heidelberg (1985)

7. Boneh, D., Franklin, M.: Identity Based Encryption from the Weil Pairing. In: Kilian, J. (ed.) CRYPTO 2001. LNCS, vol. 2139, pp. 213–229. Springer, Heidelberg (2001)

8. Boneh, D., Boyen, X.: Efficient Selective-ID Identity Based Encryption without Random Oracles. In: Cachin, C., Camenisch, J.L. (eds.) EUROCRYPT 2004. LNCS, vol. 3027, pp. 223–238. Springer, Heidelberg (2004)

9. Boneh, D., Katz, J.: Improved Efficiency for CCA-Secure Cryptosystems Built Using Identity-Based Encryption. In: Menezes, A. (ed.) CT-RSA 2005. LNCS, vol. 3376, pp. 87–103. Springer, Heidelberg (2005)

10. Boneh, D., Boyen, X., Goh, E.-J.: Hierarchical Identity Based Encryption with Constant Size Ciphertext. In: Cramer, R. (ed.) EUROCRYPT 2005. LNCS, vol. 3494, pp. 440–456. Springer, Heidelberg (2005)

11. Boneh, D., Boyen, X.: Secure Identity Based Encryption without Random Oracles. In: Franklin, M. (ed.) CRYPTO 2004. LNCS, vol. 3152, pp. 443–459. Springer, Heidelberg (2004)

12. Gentry, C.: Practical identity-based encryption without random oracles. In: Vaudenay, S. (ed.) EUROCRYPT 2006. LNCS, vol. 4004, pp. 445–464. Springer, Heidelberg (2006)

13. Mu, Y., Susilo, W., Lin, Y.-X., Ruan, C.: Identity-Based Authentic ated Broadcast Encryption and Distributed Authenticated Encryption. In: Maher, M.J. (ed.) ASIAN 2004. LNCS, vol. 3321, pp. 169–181. Springer, Heidelberg (2004)

14. Delerablée, C.: Identity-Based Broadcast Encryption with Constant Size Cipher-texts and Private Keys. In: Kurosawa, K. (ed.) ASIACRYPT 2007. LNCS, vol. 4833, pp. 200–215. Springer, Heidelberg (2007)

15. Du, X., Wang, Y., Ge, J., et al.: An ID-Based Broadcast Encryption Scheme for Key Distribution. IEEE Transactions on Broadcasting 51(2), 264–266 (2005)

16. Ren, Y.L., Gu, D.W.: Fully CCA2 secure identity based broadcast encryption without random oracles. Information Processing Letters 109, 527–533 (2009)

17. Gentry, C., Waters, B.: Adaptive Security in Broadcast Encryption Systems. In: Joux, A. (ed.) EUROCRYPT 2009. LNCS, vol. 5479, pp. 171–188. Springer, Heidelberg (2009)

18. Krzywiecki, Ł., Kutyłowski, M.: Coalition Resistant Anonymous Broadcast Encryption Scheme Based on PUF. In: McCune, J.M., Balacheff, B., Perrig, A., Sadeghi, A.-R., Sasse, A., Beres, Y. (eds.) Trust 2011. LNCS, vol. 6740, pp. 48–62. Springer, Heidelberg (2011)

19. Libert, B., Paterson, K.G., Quaglia, E.A.: Anonymous Broadcast Encryption. Cryptology ePrint Archive Report 2011/475

20. Waters, B.: Dual system encryption: realizing fully secure ibe and hibe under simple assumptions. In: Halevi, S. (ed.) CRYPTO 2009. LNCS, vol. 5677, pp. 619–636. Springer, Heidelberg (2009)
21. Lewko, A., Waters, B.: New Techniques for Dual System Encryption and Fully Secure HIBE with Short Ciphertexts. In: Micciancio, D. (ed.) TCC 2010. LNCS, vol. 5978, pp. 455–479. Springer, Heidelberg (2010)
22. Zhang, L., Hu, Y., Wu, Q.: Adaptively Secure Identity-based Broadcast Encryption with constant size private keys and ciphertexts from the Subgroups. Mathematical and computer Modelling 55, 12–18 (2012)
23. Zhang, L., Hu, Y., Wu, Q.: Fully Secure Identity-based Broadcast Encryption in the Subgroups. China Communications 8(2), 152–158 (2011)
24. Bellare, M., Boldyreva, A., Desai, A., Pointcheval, D.: Key-privacy in public-key encryption. In: Boyd, C. (ed.) ASIACRYPT 2001. LNCS, vol. 2248, pp. 566–582. Springer, Heidelberg (2001)
25. Boneh, D., Franklin, M.: Identity Based Encryption from the Weil Pairing. In: Kilian, J. (ed.) CRYPTO 2001. LNCS, vol. 2139, pp. 213–229. Springer, Heidelberg (2001)
26. Seo, J.H., Kobayashi, T., Ohkubo, M., Suzuki, K.: Anonymous hierarchical identity-based encryption with constant size ciphertexts. In: Jarecki, S., Tsudik, G. (eds.) PKC 2009. LNCS, vol. 5443, pp. 215–234. Springer, Heidelberg (2009)
27. De Caro, A., Iovino, V., Persiano, G.: Fully Secure Anonymous HIBE and Secret-key Anonymous IBE with Short Ciphertexts. In: Joye, M., Miyaji, A., Otsuka, A. (eds.) Pairing 2010. LNCS, vol. 6487, pp. 347–366. Springer, Heidelberg (2010)
28. Zhang, L., Wu, Q., Hu, Y.: Adaptively Secure Identity-based Encryption in the Anonymous Communications. ICIC Express Letters 5(9(A)), 3209–3216 (2011)

Hierarchical Identity-Based Signature
with Short Public Keys

Qing Wu[1] and Leyou Zhang[2]

[1] School of Automation, Xi'an Institute of Posts and Telecommunications,
Xi'an, Shaanxi, 710121, China
xiyouwuq@126.com
[2] Department of Mathematics, Xidian University, Xi'an, 710071, China
xidianzhangly@126.com

Abstract. How to construct a high efficient and strong secure hierarchical identity-based signature(HIBS) with a low computation cost is the main challenge at present. A new HIBS scheme is proposed in this paper. The new scheme achieves the adaptive(full) security, constant size signatures and short size public keys. In addition, private keys size shrinks as the hierarchy depth increases. The cost of verification only requires four bilinear pairings, which are independent of hierarchy depth. Furthermore, under the CDHI assumption, the scheme is provably secure against existential forgery for adaptive chosen message and identity attack in the standard model.

Keywords: HIBS, provable security, standard model, CDHI problem.

1   Introduction

Identity-based encryption(IBE) is a public key system where user's identity is used as public parameters. IBE was introduced firstly by Shamir[1]. The ability using the recipient's identity as a public key can simplify many applications of public key encryption (PKE) and now has been an active research area [2-5]. Although the advantages of identity-based encryption are compelling: a single Private Key Generator (PKG) would complete all computations. However, it is undesirable for a large network because the single PKG becomes a bottleneck, such as the expensive computations of the private key generation, verifying proofs of identities only by PKG and establishing secure channels to transmit private keys by PKG.

Hierarchical delegation computations are issued to solve above problem. Hierarchical IBE (HIBE)[6-15] allows a root PKG to distribute the workload by delegating private key generation and identity authentication to lower-level PKGs. In a HIBE scheme, a root PKG needs only to generate private keys for domain-level PKGs, who in turn generate private keys for users in their domains in the next level. Authentication and private key transmission can be done locally. The first efficient construction for HIBE was proposed by Gentry and Silverberg [6], where security was based on the decision Bilinear Diffie-Hellman (DBDH) assumption in the random oracle model. The first construction in the standard model was due to Boneh and Boyen [8].

G. Wang et al. (Eds.): CSS 2013, LNCS 8300, pp. 272–281, 2013.

Hierarchical identity-based signature was firstly introduced by Gentry and Silverberg [6] in 2002. In [10], the first provably secure HIBS scheme was proposed. But its security was relying on the random oracle and based on the selective-identity model, which was a weak security model. Li [11] also proposed a scheme in the selective-identity model and the random oracle model. The signature size and private key size of these schemes were dependent on the number of levels, growing linearly in the hierarchical depth l. The short signature is useful for applications. Yuen and Wei[13] provided a direct construction where the size of the signature was constant and independent of the number of levels. Their scheme was constructed without random oracles. However its security was achieved under a non-standard and complex assumption, the $OrcYW$ assumption. Recently, some efficient constructions in [12, 14] were proposed in the standard model, where their schemes achieved adaptive security. But the works [15] showed that there existed security weakness in their schemes. L. Y. Zhang *etal* [16] attained an efficient scheme with adaptive security. However, the size of public parameters was too large, where it achieved $(l+1)h+t+3$. In [17], authors also proposed an efficient scheme in the standard model. But the security of the proposed scheme relies on a strong hardness assumption-SDH assumption. More recent work[18] is based on the hard problems on lattices. These schemes also have a same shortcoming where their private keys size or signature size relies on the size of users set.

In this paper, we introduce a new technique to construct HIBS scheme whose performance is better than that in the available. It has good features such as constant size signature and shrinking private keys and short size public keys. In the standard model, we also give the security proof.

2 Preliminaries

2.1 Bilinear Maps

We briefly review bilinear maps and use the following notations:

1. G and G_1 are two (multiplicative) cyclic groups of prime order p;

2. g is a generator of G.

3. e is a bilinear map $e: G \times G \to G_1$.

Let G and G_1 be two cyclic groups of prime order p of the above . A bilinear map is a map $e: G \times G \to G_1$ with the properties:

1. Bilinearity: for all $u, v \in G$, $a, b \in Z_p$, we have $e(u^a, v^b) = e(u,v)^{ab}$.

2. Non-degeneracy: $e(g,g) \neq 1$.

3. Computability: There is an efficient algorithm to compute $e(u,v)$ for all $u, v \in G$.

2.2   HIBS

An l-level HIBS scheme consists of four algorithms *Setup, Extract, Sign* and *Verify*. They are specified as follows:

Setup: On input a security parameter, *PKG* returns the system parameters together with the master key. These are publicly known while the master key is known only to the *PKG*.

Extract: On input an identity $ID = (v_1, \cdots, v_j)$, the public parameters of the *PKG* and the private key $d_{ID_{j-1}}$ corresponding to the identity $ID = (v_1, \cdots, v_{j-1})$, it returns a private key d_{ID} for *ID*. The identity *ID* is used as the public key while d_{ID} is the corresponding private key.

Sign: On input the identity *ID*, the private key and a message *M* from the message space, it outputs a signature σ corresponding to the *M* and *ID*.

Verify: On input the signature σ corresponding to the *M* and *ID*, it is accepted if *Verify*(PK, M, σ)= "*Valid*". Otherwise it is rejected.

An HIBS scheme is secure if it satisfies two requirements, *Correctness* and *Existential Unforgeability*.

2.3   Security Model for HIBS

There are mainly two definitions for the security of Identity-Based cryptography:

· Adaptive security(full security), which means that the attacker can choose adaptively the identity he wants to attack (after having seen the parameters);

· Selective-identity security, which means that the attacker must choose the identity he wants to attack at the beginning, before seeing the parameters. The Selective-identity security is thus weaker than full security.

Following [12], [14], we use the security model of HIBS based on the following game:

Setup Simulator generates system parameter *param* and gives it to the adversary.

Queries The adversary queries Extraction Oracles and Signing Oracles.

Forgery The adversary delivers a signature σ^* for signer identity ID^* and message M^* such that ID^* or its prefix have never been input to a Extraction Oracles and $(ID*, M*)$ has never been input to a Signing Oracle.

The adversary wins if he completes the Game with *Verify*($ID*, M*, \sigma^*$) = "*Valid*".

Definition. A forger A $(t, q_e, q_S, \varepsilon)$-breaks a signature scheme if A runs in time at most t, A makes at most q_e Extract queries and q_S signature queries, and the advantage of A is at least ε. A signature scheme is $(t, q_e, q_S, \varepsilon)$-existentially unforgeable under an adaptive chosen message and selective identity attack if no forger $(t, q_e, q_S, \varepsilon)$-breaks it.

2.4   Hardness Assumption

Definition. (Computational Diffie-Hellman Inversion Problem(CDHI)))[19] Given a tuple ($g, g^{\alpha}, g^{\alpha^2}, \cdots g^{\alpha^q}$), the CDHI problem in G is to output $g^{\frac{1}{\alpha}}$, where $\alpha \in Z_p$ and g is generator of G.

We say that the (t, ε)-CDHI assumption holds in G if no t-time algorithm has advantage at least ε in solving the CDHI problem in G.

3   New Constructions

3.1   Our Motivations

Our construction is motivated from the construction[9,20]. First, we give a scheme with some small modifications for the scheme of [20]. Then we will show it is transformed to an efficient scheme at last.

Let l denote maximum depth of HIBS. It works as follows.

Setup. The parameters are generated as follows: select a random generator $g \in G$ and some random elements $h_0, h_i, h_0, h_i, u_j \in G$, where $i = 1, \cdots, l$, j=0,1. Then pick randomly $\alpha, \alpha_0 \in Z_p^*$ and set $g_1 = g^{\alpha}$ where $\alpha \neq \alpha_0$. The public keys are PK=($\alpha_0, g, g_1, g_2, h_i, u_j$) where i=0, $\cdots$, l, j=0,1 , $g_2 = g^{-\alpha_0}$ and master keys are α.

Extract
(1) To generate a private for ID=(v_1), where $v_1 \in Z_p$, the algorithm picks randomly $r_k, r \in Z_p$ and outputs

$$d_{ID} = (d_0, d_{00}, d_{01}, d_1, d_2, \cdots, d_l)$$
$$= ((h_0 g^{-r_0})^{\frac{1}{\alpha - \alpha_0}} (h_1^{v_1})^r, r_0, g_1^r, g_2^r, h_2^r, \cdots, h_l^r).$$

(2) Delegation: Given the ID_{k-1} =($v_1, v_2, \ldots, v_{k-1}$) and corresponding private key
$$d_{ID_{k-1}} = (d'_0, d_{00}, d'_{01}, d'_1, d'_k, \cdots, d'_l)$$

$$= ((h_0 g^{-r_0})^{\frac{1}{\alpha - \alpha_0}} (\prod_{i=1}^{k-1} h_i^{v_i})^r, r_0, g_1^r, g_2^r, h_k^r, \cdots, h_l^r),$$

the private key of the k level identity ID_k=($v_1, v_2, \ldots, v_k$) is computing as follows:

$$d_{ID_k} = (d_0, d_{00}, d_{01}, d_1, d_k, \cdots, d_l)$$
$$= (d'_0 d_k^{'v_k} (\prod_{i=1}^{k} g^{v_i})^{r'}, d_{00}, d'_{01}(g_1)^{r'}, d'_1(g_2)^{r'}, d'_{k+1} h_{k+1}^{r'}, \cdots, d'_l h_l^{r'})$$

$$= ((h_0 g^{-r_0})^{\frac{1}{\alpha-\alpha_0}} (\prod_{i=1}^{k} h_i^{v_i})^{r'}, d_{00}, g_1^{r'}, g_2^{r'}, h_{k+1}^{r'}, \cdots, h_l^{r'}),$$

Where $\bar{r} = r + r'$ and $r' \in Z_p^*$.

Sign: A signature of M with $M \in Z_p$ under $ID=(v_1,v_2,\ldots,v_k)$ is generated as follows: let $s \in Z_p$ and compute

$$\sigma = (\sigma_0, \sigma_1, \sigma_2, \sigma_3, \sigma_4, \sigma_5)$$
$$= (d_0 (u_0 u_1^M)^s, d_{00}, d_{01}, d_1, g_1^s, g_2^s).$$

Verify: Given a signature $\sigma = (\sigma_0, \sigma_1, \sigma_2, \sigma_3, \sigma_4, \sigma_5)$ of a message M on ID, the verifier accepts it if the following equation holds:

$$e(\sigma_0, g_1 g_2)$$
$$= e(h_0 g^{-\sigma_1}, g) e(\prod_{i=1}^{k} h_i^{v_i}, \sigma_2 \sigma_3) e(u_0 u_1^M, \sigma_4 \sigma_5).$$

Correctness

If the previous signature is valid, then one can obtain the following equations holds.

$$e(\sigma_0, g_1 g_2)$$
$$= e(d_0 (u_0 u^M)^s, g_1 g_2)$$
$$= e(h_0 g^{-r_0})^{\frac{1}{\alpha-\alpha_0}} (\prod_{i=1}^{k} h_i^{v_i})^{r'} (u_0 u^M)^s, g_1 g^{-\alpha_0})$$
$$= e(h_0 g^{-r_0})^{\frac{1}{\alpha-\alpha_0}}, g_1 g^{-\alpha_0}) e((\prod_{i=1}^{k} h_i^{v_i})^{r'} (u_0 u^M)^s, g_1 g^{-\alpha_0})$$
$$= e(h_0 g^{-r_0})^{\frac{1}{\alpha-\alpha_0}}, g_1 g^{-\alpha_0}) e(\prod_{i=1}^{k} h_i^{v_i})^{r'}, g_1 g^{-\alpha_0}) e((u_0 u^M)^s, g_1 g^{-\alpha_0})$$
$$= e(h_0 g^{-\sigma_1}, g) e(\prod_{i=1}^{k} h_i^{v_i}, \sigma_2 \sigma_3) e(u_0 u^M, \sigma_4 \sigma_5).$$

Table 1. Comparison of Computation Efficiency

Scheme	PK size	pk size	S-size	Pairing	Security Model
[10]	$l+2$	$k+1$	$(k+2)|G|$	3	s-ID
[11]	$l+2$	$k+1$	$(k+2)|G|$	$k+2$	s-ID
[13]	$l+6$	$l-k+1$	$4|G|$	7	full
[14]	$2l+1$	$l-k+2$	$2|G|+p$	4	full
[16]	$(l+1)h+t+3$	$(l+1)(h-k)+2$	$3|G|$	4	full
[17]	$l+n_m+4$	$l-k+3$	$5|G|+p$	4	full
Ours	$l+7$	$l-k+3$	$5|G|+p$	4	full

3.2   Efficiency Analysis

The motivation scheme and first scheme achieve the constant size signatures. But the private keys rely on the users identity. So they can not apply to the large scale networks. Our main construction solves this limitation. The new scheme achieves constant size signatures and short size public keys which are more efficient than the existing works. In addition, there are 4 pairing computations in the verification algorithm.

4   Security Analysis

In this section, we will give the corresponding security analysis.

Theorem. The proposed scheme is (t, q_e, q_s, ε)-secure, assume that the (t', ε') q-CDH

assumption holds, where $\varepsilon' = \varepsilon \dfrac{q(q_e + q_s + 1)}{p}$, $t' = t + O((q_e k + q_s k)\rho + $

$(kq_e + q_s k)\tau)$, t is the time taken by the adversary, ρ denotes the time for a multiplication and τ is the time for an exponentiation.

Proof: Suppose there exists a (t, q_e, q_s, ε) adversary A against our scheme, then we construct an algorithm B that solves the (t', ε') *CDHI* problem. At the beginning of the game, B is given a tuple ($g, g^\alpha, \cdots g^{\alpha^q}$). The game is run as follows:

Setup. B chooses randomly a polynomial function $f(x) \in Z_q(x)$ of degree q, sets $g_1 = g^\alpha$ and $h_0 = g^{f(\alpha)}$. B selects randomly $\alpha_0, \alpha_i, \beta_1, v_0 \in Z_p$. If $\alpha = \alpha_0$, then B will solve the CDHI problem. Else it computes $h_i = g^{\alpha_i}$, $u_0 = g_1^{v_0}$, $u_1 = g_1^{\beta_1}, g_2 = g^{-\alpha_0}$, where $1 \le i \le l$. Finally it sends the public parameters

$$param = (g, g_1, g_2, h_0, h_1, \cdots, h_l, u_0, u_1, \alpha_0)$$

to A.

Queries. The adversary A will issue private key queries and signing queries and B answers these in the following way:

     • *Private key queries*: Suppose the adversary A issues a query for an identity $ID = (v_1, \cdots, v_k)$ with $k \le l$. If $\alpha = \alpha_0$, then the CDHI problem can be solved easily.

Otherwise, B constructs the q-1-degree polynomial $g(x) = \dfrac{f(x) - f(\alpha_0)}{x - \alpha_0}$ and sets

the private key as follows:

$$d_{ID} = (d_0, d_{00}, d_{01}, d_1, d_{k+1}, \cdots, d_l)$$

$$= (g^{g(\alpha)} (\prod_{i=1}^{k} h_i^{v_i})^r, f(\alpha_0), g_1^r, g_2^r, h_{k+1}^r, \cdots, h_l^r),$$

Where r is selected randomly from Z_p. In fact, let $r_0 = f(\alpha_0)$, one can obtain

$$(g^{g(\alpha)}(\prod_{i=1}^{k} h_i^{v_i})^r, f(\alpha_0), g_1^r, g_2^r, h_{k+1}^r, \cdots, h_l^r)$$

$$=(g^{\frac{f(\alpha)-f(\alpha_0)}{\alpha-\alpha_0}}(\prod_{i=1}^{k} h_i^{v_i})^r, f(\alpha_0), g_1^r, g_2^r, h_{k+1}^r, \cdots, h_l^r)$$

$$=((g^{f(\alpha)-f(\alpha_0)})^{\frac{1}{\alpha-\alpha_0}}(\prod_{i=1}^{k} h_i^{v_i})^r, f(\alpha_0), g_1^r, g_2^r, h_{k+1}^r, \cdots, h_l^r)$$

$$=((h_0 g^{-f(\alpha_0)})^{\frac{1}{\alpha-\alpha_0}}(\prod_{i=1}^{k} h_i^{v_i})^r, f(\alpha_0), g_1^r, g_2^r, h_{k+1}^r, \cdots, h_l^r)$$

$$=((h_0 g^{-r_0})^{\frac{1}{\alpha-\alpha_0}}(\prod_{i=1}^{k} h_i^{v_i})^r, r_0, g_1^r, g_2^r, h_{k+1}^r, \cdots, h_l^r).$$

Hence, d_{ID} is a valid private key.

- *Signature queries*: Consider a signature query of $M = (m_1, \cdots, m_{n_m})$ for user $ID = (v_1, \cdots, v_k)$. The adversary A makes an extraction query on ID at first using the previous manner. Then B will construct a signature in a similar way to the construction of a private key in a private key query:

$$\sigma = (\sigma_0, \sigma_1, \sigma_2, \sigma_3, \sigma_4, \sigma_5)$$

$$=(g^{g(\alpha)}(\prod_{i=1}^{k} h_i^{v_i})^r (g^{M\beta_1+v_0})^s, f(\alpha_0), g_1^r, g_2^r, g_1^s, g_2^s),$$

where s is chosen randomly from Z_p. One can verify that σ is a valid signature as:

$$(g^{g(\alpha)}(\prod_{i=1}^{k} h_i^{v_i})^r (g^{M\beta_1+v_0})^s, f(\alpha_0), g_1^r, g_2^r, g_1^s, g_2^s)$$

$$=((h_0 g^{-r_0})^{\frac{1}{\alpha-\alpha_0}}(\prod_{i=1}^{k} h_i^{v_i})^r (u_0 u_1^M)^s, f(\alpha_0), g_1^r, g_2^r, g_1^s, g_2^s).$$

Forgery. If A decides all above are over, than it outputs the challenge identity $ID^* = (v_1^*, \cdots, v_k^*)$ and message M^*. If A can forge a signature of M^* for $ID^* = (v_1^*, \cdots, v_k^*)$. Then B can solve the q-SDH problem. It is specified as:

(1) The signature is

$$\sigma^* = (\sigma_0^*, \sigma_1^*, \sigma_2^*, \sigma_3^*, \sigma_4^*, \sigma_5^*)$$

$$=((h_0 g^{-r_0^*})^{\frac{1}{\alpha-\alpha_0}}(\prod_{i=1}^{k} h_i^{v_i^*})^r (u_0 u_1^{M^*})^s, r_0^*, g_1^r, g_2^r, g_1^s, g_2^s)$$

$$=(g^{\frac{f(\alpha)-r_0^*}{\alpha-\alpha_0}} \cdot g^{r\sum_{i=1}^{k}\alpha_i v_i^*} \cdot g_1^{s(M^*\beta_1+v_0)}, r_0^*, g_1^r, g_2^r, g_1^s, g_2^s).$$

(2) Let $T(\alpha)=\dfrac{f(\alpha)-r_0^*}{\alpha-\alpha_0}$. We have $T(\alpha)=\sum_{j=1}^{q-1}k_i\alpha^i+\dfrac{k'}{\alpha-\alpha_0}$. If $k'=0$, B aborts

this game. Otherwise, it computes $k',k_0,\cdots,k_{q-1}$. Then it has

$$\frac{\sigma_1^*}{(\sigma_3^*)^{-\frac{1}{\alpha_0}\sum_{i=1}^{k}\alpha_i v_i^*}(\sigma_4^*)^{M^*\beta_1+v_0}}$$

$$=g^{\frac{f(\alpha)-r_0^*}{\alpha-v_1^*}}=g^{\sum_{j=1}^{q-1}k_i\alpha^i+\frac{k'}{\alpha-v_1^*}}.$$

Finally, B can obtain

$$\left(\frac{g^{\sum_{j=1}^{q-1}k_i\alpha^i+\frac{k}{\alpha-v_1^*}}}{g^{\sum_{j=1}^{q-1}k_i\alpha^i}}\right)^{\frac{1}{k'}}=g^{\frac{1}{\alpha-\alpha_0}}.$$

It means that B has solved the *CDHI* problem.

The probability analysis follows the proof in [3,12]. Using the similar techniques, the probability that B does not aborts is $\dfrac{q(q_e+q_s+1)}{p}$.

The time complexity of the algorithm B is dominated by the exponentiations and multiplications performed in the *Private key* and *Signing* queries. Let ρ and τ denote the time for a multiplication and an exponentiation in G. Then the time complexity is $t'=t+O((q_ek+q_sk)\rho+(kq_e+q_sk)\tau)$.

5   Conclusion

In this paper, we propose a new technique to construct HIBS scheme whose performance is better than that in the available. It has good features such as constant size signature and shrinking private keys and short size public keys. Under the CDHI problem, we also give the security proof.

Of course, the private keys size relies on the depth of the identity. How to achieve a good trade-off between the private keys and signatures is also an interesting problem.

Acknowledgment. This work was supported in part by the Nature Science Foundation of China under Grant (61100165, 61100231, 60970119) , Natural Science Foundation of Shaanxi Province (No.2012JQ8814) and Foundation of Education Department of Shanxi Province(2013JK1096).

References

1. Shamir, A.: Identity-based Cryptosystems and Signature Schemes. In: Blakely, G.R., Chaum, D. (eds.) CRYPTO 1984. LNCS, vol. 196, pp. 47–53. Springer, Heidelberg (1985)
2. Boneh, D., Franklin, M.: Identity-based encryption from the well pairing. In: Kilian, J. (ed.) CRYPTO 2001. LNCS, vol. 2139, pp. 213–229. Springer, Heidelberg (2001)
3. Gentry, C.: Practical identity-based encryption without random oracles. In: Vaudenay, S. (ed.) EUROCRYPT 2006. LNCS, vol. 4004, pp. 445–464. Springer, Heidelberg (2006)
4. Boneh, D., Katz, J.: Improved Efficiency for CCA-Secure Cryptosystems Built Using Identity-Based Encryption. In: Menezes, A. (ed.) CT-RSA 2005. LNCS, vol. 3376, pp. 87–103. Springer, Heidelberg (2005)
5. Boneh, D., Boyen, X.: Secure Identity Based Encryption without Random Oracles. In: Franklin, M. (ed.) CRYPTO 2004. LNCS, vol. 3152, pp. 443–459. Springer, Heidelberg (2004)
6. Gentry, C., Silverberg, A.: Hierarchical ID-Based Cryptography. In: Zheng, Y. (ed.) ASIACRYPT 2002. LNCS, vol. 2501, pp. 548–566. Springer, Heidelberg (2002)
7. Horwitz, J., Lynn, B.: Towards Hierarchical Identity-Based Encryption. In: Knudsen, L.R. (ed.) EUROCRYPT 2002. LNCS, vol. 2332, pp. 466–481. Springer, Heidelberg (2002)
8. Boneh, D., Boyen, X.: Efficient selective-id secure identity based encryption without random oracles. In: Cachin, C., Camenisch, J.L. (eds.) EUROCRYPT 2004. LNCS, vol. 3027, pp. 223–238. Springer, Heidelberg (2004)
9. Boneh, D., Boyen, X., Goh, E.-J.: Hierarchical Identity based encryption with con-stant ciphertext. In: Cramer, R. (ed.) EUROCRYPT 2005. LNCS, vol. 3494, pp. 440–456. Springer, Heidelberg (2005)
10. Chow, S.S.M., Hui, L.C.K., Yiu, S.M., Chow, K.P.: Secure Hierarchical Identity Based Signature and Its Application. In: López, J., Qing, S., Okamoto, E. (eds.) ICICS 2004. LNCS, vol. 3269, pp. 480–494. Springer, Heidelberg
11. Li, J., Zhang, F., Wang, Y.: A New Hierarchical ID-Based Cryptosystem and CCA-Secure PKE. In: Zhou, X., et al. (eds.) EUC Workshops 2006. LNCS, vol. 4097, pp. 362–371. Springer, Heidelberg (2006)
12. Au, M.H., Liu Joseph, K., Hon, Y.T., et al.: Practical Hierarchical Identity Based Encryption and Signature schemes Without Random Oracles. Cryptology ePrint Archive, Report 2006/308 (2006)
13. Yuen, T.H., Wei, V.K.: Constant-Size Hierarchical Identity-Based Signature / Signcryption without Random Oracles. Cryptology ePrint Archive, Report 2005/412 (2005)
14. Au, M.H., Liu Joseph, K., et al.: Efficient Hierarchical Identity Based Signa-ture in the Standard Model. Cryptology ePrint Archive, Report 2006/080 (2006)
15. Hu, X., Huang, S., Fan, X.: Practical Hierarchical Identity-based Encryption Scheme without Random Oracles. IEICE Transactions Fundamentals of Electronics Communications and Computer Sciences 92-A(6), 1494–1499 (2009)
16. Zhang, L.Y., Hu, Y.P., Wu, Q.: New Construction of Short Hierarchical ID-Based Signature in the Standard Model. Fundamenta Informaticae 90(1-2), 191–201 (2009)
17. Zhang, L.Y., Hu, Y.P., Wu, Q.: Adaptively secure Hierarchical ID-Based Signature in the Standard Model. The Journal of China Universities of Posts and Telecommunications 17(6), 95–100 (2010)

18. Rückert, M.: Strongly Unforgeable Signatures and HIBS from Lattices without Random Oracles. In: Sendrier, N. (ed.) PQCrypto 2010. LNCS, vol. 6061, pp. 182–200. Springer, Heidelberg (2010)
19. Boneh, D., Boyen, X.: Short signature without random oracles. In: Cachin, C., Camenisch, J.L. (eds.) EUROCRYPT 2004. LNCS, vol. 3027, pp. 56–73. Springer, Heidelberg (2004)
20. Zhang, L., Hu, Y., Wu, Q., Tian, X.: Secure short Hierarchical identity-based signa-ture in the standard model. In: IEEE International Conference on Network Security, Wireless Communications and Trusted Computing, vol. 1, pp. 366–369. IEEE computer society (2010)

PeerViewer: Behavioral Tracking and Classification of P2P Malware

Nizar Kheir and Xiao Han

Orange Labs, Paris

Abstract. To keep pace with the rampant malware threat, security analysts operate tools that collect and observe malicious content on the internet. Since malware is robust against static analysis, dynamic environments are being used for this purpose. They use automated platforms that execute malware and acquire knowledge about its runtime behavior. Today, malware analysis platforms are powerful in characterizing the system behavior of malware. However, little research is being done to automatically charaterize malicious code according to its network communication protocols. Yet this is becoming a real challenge as modern botnets increasingly adopt hybrid topologies that use custom P2P protocols for command and control.

This paper presents PeerViewer, a system that automatically classifies malware according to its network P2P behavior. Nowadays P2P malware either uses variants of known P2P protocols, or it builds its custom P2P protocols as for Sality and zeroAccess. PeerViewer builds classifiers for known P2P malware families. Then it builds a network footprint for malicious code running in a sandbox, and compares this footprint with those for known P2P malware families. It associates malicious code with a known botnet family where possible, or it notifies the security analysts of a new or unknown P2P malware family, so it can be considered for a deeper analysis. Our experimental results prove the ability of PeerViewer to accurately classify P2P malware, with a very low false positives rate.

1 Introduction

Over the past decade, malware has infected every corner of the internet, with no signs of it abating. So far it became the root cause for many security problems such as spam, denial of service and data theft; yet it is branching on social networks and mobile devices [3]. As long as malware is growing rampant, it ecompasses a range of threats where botnets constitute the most widespread type today. These are networks of infected nodes controled by a single attacker through a common Command and Control (C&C) network. Today, botnet trackers mostly use dynamic analysis environments where they execute malware in order to learn about its malicious techniques [2,5,13,21,22]. Whichever means they use to collect malware (e.g. traffic sampling, honeypots, monitoring phishing emails), security analysts are being overwhelmed with a huge number of malware samples daily [20]. Most of these samples are polymorphic variants of

G. Wang et al. (Eds.): CSS 2013, LNCS 8300, pp. 282–298, 2013.
© Springer International Publishing Switzerland 2013

known malware families, thus urging researchers to propose dynamic and automated malware classification models [25]. In fact variants of the same malware family share typical behavioral patterns that reflect their origin and purpose. Automated classification models thus discard samples that are variants of known malware families, creaming off new malware that would be further submitted to a deeper analysis. They observe malware runtime features such as system calls, registries and memory in order to build appropriate behavioral classifiers.

Current malware analysis tools mostly operate at the system level. They build behavioral patterns that apply to host-based malware detection and diagnosis. Yet they provide only a raw description of malware network behavior, usually limited to domain names, supported protocols and callbacks. While this level of information enables detecting and neutralizing malware that uses centralized botnet architectures, it has proven to be insufficient against hybrid and distributed botnets. With malware increasingly adopting hybrid C&C topologies, current systems are struggling with their fight against botnets [10,15]. For example, the recent switching of Zeus to a hybrid C&C topology made Zeustracker unable to produce exact C&C domain block lists [1].

Hybrid botnets have network patterns and behaviors that are clearly different from centralized botnets. They usually operate outside the DNS system, which makes domain block lists irrelevant. They use custom P2P protocols, as opposed to centralized botnets that mostly use HTTP for command and control. Hence, behavioral classification based on malware HTTP patterns is no more appropriate against P2P botnets [22]. Yet hybrid botnets use a wide range of P2P protocols, each one implementing its own set of messages such as keep-alive, route discovery, data search and broadcast. Besides, botnet P2P flows are usually encrypted and transmitted over TCP and UDP alike, which makes difficult to classify malware P2P flows based on the message types they are carrying. Therefore, the network behavior of P2P malware during dynamic analysis would be no more than a bunch of encrypted flows, with no clear evidence about their nature and remote destinations. To the best of our knowledge, *it is yet unclear how we can assign malicious code to a common P2P malware family while observing its network behavior during dynamic analysis.*

This paper presents PeerViewer, a system that automatically classifies P2P malware according to its network behavior. PeerViewer uses a learning set of known P2P malware families such as Sality, Zeus, TDSS and zero access [14,23,26]. It uses machine learning techniques in order to build a network based classifier for each family of P2P malware. It further builds a network footprint of P2P malware when executed in a dynamic analysis environment, and checks this footprint against known P2P malware classifiers. PeerViewer assigns the malicious code being analyzed to the appropriate P2P malware family where possible, or it notifies the security analysts of a new or yet unknown P2P malware family. In the latter case, the malware can be considered for a deeper analysis as it may reveal new trends in P2P botnet activity.

Through its automated and dynamic classification of P2P malware, PeerViewer offers two main contributions. First, it reduces overhead for malware

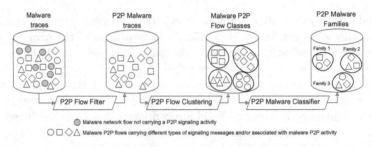

Fig. 1. Overview and workflow of PeerViewer

analysts by pinpointing only new P2P malware to be considered for further investigation. Second, it provides behavioral detection models that can be used to detect P2P bots and associate them with known or new P2P malware families. Our experimental results prove the ability of our system to accurately classify P2P malware, with only very few false positives.

This paper will be organized as follows. Section 2 presents PeerViewer and provides an overview of its architecture. Section 3 describes more in details the different modules that constitute our system. Section 4 details our experiments and results. Section 5 discusses the limitations of our system and provides future work. Section 6 presents related work, and section 7 concludes.

2   System Overview

PeerViewer builds families of P2P malware based on their network behavior when executed into a dynamic analysis environment. It aims at automatically classifying malware that uses known P2P protocols, and to cream off malware that implements new P2P protocols so it can be considered for further analysis. PeerViewer operates in two phases, the *buildup* phase and the *detection* phase. During buildup, it builds P2P classifiers using a training set of malware belonging to several P2P families. PeerViewer has a modular framework that makes possible to add new P2P classifiers when new P2P malware families are discovered. During detection, PeerViewer observes malware traffic and builds a network P2P footprint for each malware sample. It uses this footprint in order to associate malware with a known P2P family where possible. Otherwise PeerViewer notifies the security analysts about a new malware that belongs to a yet unknown P2P family.

As in figure 1, PeerViewer includes three separate modules. The P2P flow filter implements several heuristics which aim to discard malware that does not show any P2P activity during analysis. For instance, the rate of failed connection attempts is usually used as a way to detect P2P applications. Therefore, our filter discards malware whose rate of failed connection attempts does not exceed a given threshold. It also uses other heuristics such as flows initiated after successful DNS requests, number and geographical distribution of remote contacted IPs. Our experimental results prove that our filter is indeed effective in eliminating non-P2P malware, with almost no false positives.

Remaining flows for P2P malware in our dataset are used as input to the flow clustering module. It groups together malware flows that are likely to implement the same P2P functionality and that use the same P2P protocol. The flow-size distribution for P2P signaling activity shows frequent flow sizes that are associated with specific P2P message types [7,18]. Malware that implements the same P2P protocol and belongs to the same P2P botnet topology would have the same P2P signaling activity, thus resulting in similar flows when observed at the network level. PeerViewer uses unsupervised clustering in order to group together similar malware flows that are likely to implement the same P2P activity. The flow clustering process uses high-level malware traffic features such as flow size, number of packets, bits per packet, and flow duration. The output of this process is a multiple set of clusters, each one including P2P flows triggered by multiple malware samples, but carrying the same P2P signaling activity (e.g. keep-alive, route discovery, search request, push data) and protocol.

Malware of the same family has its P2P flows grouped within the same clusters because they carry the same P2P signaling activities. The malware classifier module uses P2P flow clusters in order to build families of malware that implement the same P2P protocol. In fact, PeerViewer builds a P2P footprint $\mathcal{F}_\alpha \{c_i\}_{i=1}^m$ of size m for each malware $\mathcal{M}_\alpha$ in our initial learning set, and which specifies the rate of malware P2P flows within each cluster $\{c_i\}_{i=1}^m$. In other terms, the feature $\mathcal{F}_\alpha\{c_k\}$ would be set to 0 if malware $\mathcal{M}_\alpha$ has no flows in cluster c_k, and it will be set to 1 if it has all its P2P flows in c_k. PeerViewer uses malware footprints as a training set to build P2P malware clusters, each cluster representing a new P2P malware family. Hence, malware that belongs to the same family implements the same P2P protocols and has the same P2P botnet topology.

We evaluated our behavioral P2P malware classifier against malware signatures for three anti-virus solutions. Our experiments prove that PeerViewer builds malware P2P families with a very high accuracy. It further builds a classifier for each P2P malware family, so it can be used to classify P2P malware on-the-fly. PeerViewer assigns a malware sample to the family that best fits its network footprint. Malware that matches with any of the P2P malware families in our training set belongs to an unknown family. It is thus submitted to the security analyst for a manual inquiry.

3   System Description

This section describes the architecture and workflow of PeerViewer, including the process and tools that it uses to build and classify P2P malware families.

3.1   Malware P2P Flow Filter

Malware P2P filter uses heuristics that select P2P malware and discard flows that do not carry P2P signaling activity. These heuristics characterize a distributed

P2P activity using high-level network behaviors. In fact, P2P traffic has multiple characteristics that are clearly different from other centralized network communications. For instance, P2P networks constitute unstructured topologies where P2P nodes may constantly join and leave the network. This phenomenon results in a high rate of failed connection attempts, which is a distinctive feature of P2P activity. Our filter implements the following features.

DNS Filtering is commonly used to discard non-P2P traffic. Nodes in a P2P network operate outside the DNS system [4]. They search for other peers using routing tables in the overlay network, without prior DNS requests. Although access to a central server through DNS resolution is possible at bootstrap, nodes further communicate directly using IP addresses, and access to the DNS service is usually no longer required. Therefore, PeerViewer discards malware flows initiated after a successful DNS resolution.

Failed Connection Filter processes flows not eliminated by the DNS filter. It discards non-P2P malware using the rate of failed connection attempts, which characterizes the independent arrival and departure by thousands of peers in the network. We consider as a failed connection attempt all unidirectional UDP flows, as well as failed TCP syn attempts including both no TCP response or a TCP reset. PeerViewer uses the rate of failed connection attempts within a malware trace as a way to discard non-P2P malware.

Flow size filter keeps only flows that include P2P signaling activity, and discards P2P data flows. The flow size distribution of P2P traffic usually shows discontinuities near small flow sizes, and that characterize P2P signaling activity [12]. It also includes flows with clearly higher flow sizes, usually involving data transfer. PeerViewer uses the flow size distribution in order to discard P2P data flows. It drops all flows whose size exceeds a given threshold that we empirically set based on P2P flow size distributions in [16,12].

AS-based filtering: P2P botnets constitute overlay architectures that spans multiple autonomous systems (AS). We use the rate of distinct AS numbers within a malware trace in order to discard non-P2P malware. It is defined as the number of remote AS to the total number of flows ratio in a given malware trace. We empirically set a threshold $\tau_{as} = 0.2$ for this rate, based on our malware training set. PeerViewer discards malware whose rate of distinct AS numbers does not exceed this threshold.

Although these heuristics cannot discard all non-P2P flows, they are reliable enough to characterize the network behavior of P2P applications. They describe invariants in the P2P signaling activity, and so they cannot be easily evaded without modifying the P2P protocol implementation. The output of this filter is a set of P2P signaling flows for each malware sample. We use these flows as input to the flow clustering module. It groups P2P signaling flows for malware in our training set according to protocols and message types they are carrying.

3.2   Malware P2P Flow Clustering

PeerViewer aims at classifying malicious code based on its P2P network behavior. We define the network behavior of a P2P application through its signaling activity, and which results in a different distribution of its network flows. We proceed first with a flow clustering step that groups together malware P2P flows that implement the same protocol and signaling activity. We further use clusters of P2P flows in order to define a P2P footprint for each malware sample.

We consider as a malware P2P flow both the flow triggered by a malware and its associated peer response. We represent a bidirectional flow using the following features vector: $f_\alpha =< \mathcal{M}_\alpha, proto, B_s, B_r, Pkt_s, Pkt_r, \Delta_t >$. Features of this vector are defined as follows: $\mathcal{M}_\alpha$ is a tag that associates flow f_α with malware $\mathcal{M}_\alpha$; $proto$ is a tag that designates the transport layer protocol, being either TCP or UDP; B_s and B_r are the amount of Bytes sent and received within f_α; Pkt_s and Pkt_r are the number of packets sent and received; and Δ_t is the flow duration. PeerViewer separately builds clusters for TCP and UDP flows using the $proto$ tag, as these flows clearly carry different signaling activities.

We use the unsupervised incremental K-means clustering algorithm in order to build clusters of P2P flows. It starts with an initial number of clusters, and increments clusters when the distance of a flow to all existing clusters exceeds a given threshold. We use the euclidian distance in order to compute the similarity between two separate malware P2P flows, and we set different clustering thresholds for TCP and UDP flows. In fact TCP flows have a higher offset size because of their larger TCP headers and their higher number of packets compared to UDP flows, due to TCP handshake and TCP Acks. Hence, we empirically set TCP and UDP thresholds to 100 and 20 respectively. They characterize the minimal flow size (400 and 40) to the minimal packets number (4 and 2) ratio for non-empty TCP and UDP flows.

PeerViewer builds clusters of flows by comparing P2P flows that we extracted from our malware training set. P2P flows for a malware sample $\mathcal{M}_\alpha$ may span on multiple clusters. Each cluster contains flows that have similar network features, and so they are likely to carry the same P2P signaling activity and protocol, but that are triggered by different malware samples. We further build a P2P footprint for each malware in our dataset. It specifies the rate of flows for a given malware within each P2P flow cluster provided by our system. In other terms, a malware footprint $\mathcal{F}_\alpha\{c_i\}_{i=1}^m$ is an $m - arry$ vector of size m, where m is the number of P2P flow clusters. Attribute $\mathcal{F}_\alpha\{c_k\}$ for malware $\mathcal{M}_\alpha$ corresponds to the fraction of P2P flows for $\mathcal{M}_\alpha$ within c_k, with respect to the total number of P2P flows in the network trace of $\mathcal{M}_\alpha$. Hence, attributes of a malware footprint are real values in the $[0, 1]$ interval, with $\sum \mathcal{F}_\alpha\{c_i\}_{i=1}^m = 1$.

3.3   P2P Malware Classifier

The classifier module builds clusters of malware that implement the same P2P protocol and belong to the same P2P botnet family. It groups together malware that has similar P2P footprints so they are likely to use the same P2P botnet topology. We use the unsupervised hierarchical clustering algorithm to obtain P2P malware families. It builds different families of malware according to the initial malware training set. As opposed to incremental K-means, the hierarchical clustering algorithm does not require a threshold for adding a new cluster. In fact, it is possible to set a threshold for flow clustering because of the ground truth provided by malware network traces. However, malware clustering does not have a reliable ground truth as AV solutions usually provide conflicting malware classifications (section 4 provides a detailed comparison between our system and AV signatures). Hierarchical clustering creates a dendrogram where leaf nodes are elementary P2P malware, and the root node is a set of all malware samples. We use the Davies-Bouldin index [8] to find the optimal cut in the dendrogram, and thus to obtain our set of malware P2P families. Each family includes a set of malware aggregated within a single node in the dendrogram.

Malware families provided by our system are used to classify unknown malicious code on-the-fly while executed in a dynamic analysis environment. We build a *one-class classifier* for each family of malware provided by our system [17]. It characterizes the P2P footprints for malware samples within this family. During detection, PeerViewer collects the network trace for unknown malicious code running in a sandbox. It applies P2P filtering and flow clustering, which provide clusters of P2P flows triggered by a given malware sample. These clusters constitute a network footprint that we use to associate malicious code with a known malware family. PeerViewer tests this footprint against the one-class classifiers for all malware families in the training set. It associates a malicious code with a given malware family when its P2P footprint matches the one-class classifier of this family. Yet PeerViewer is unable to classify a malicious code when its P2P footprint matches any, or more than a single malware family. It notifies the security analysit of a new or unknown P2P malware, so it can be submitted to a deeper analysis.

4   Experimentation

This section presents the malware dataset that we used in order to build and validate our system. It describes the design of our experiments, including tests and results of PeerViewer when applied to the malware dataset at our disposal.

4.1   P2P Malware Dataset

In order to validate our system, we obtained malware samples from a security company that implements its own collection and analysis platforms. Our dataset includes thirty minutes of network traffic for malware executed in a dynamic analysis environment. Malware was granted open access to its command and control infrastructure, including updates and command execution. Malware traffic was provided in separate pcap files. In fact we do not have access to malware binaries, but only to their network traces, associated each with the md5 hash for the originating malicious code. The dataset at our disposal includes network traffic for almost twenty thousand distinct malware samples collected during a three months period, between March and June 2012.

We use the virusTotal API in order to qualify P2P malware in our dataset and to validate the results of our experimens. We searched in virusTotal for md5

Table 1. Malware samples by families of malware

Malware Family	P2P protocol	Samples	Training	Evaluation	Flows	P2P flows
Sality v3 and v4	Custom	386	335	51	105178	28071
Zeus v3	Kademlia	35	27	8	8523	4227
ZeroAccess	Custom	33	24	9	14328	5676
Kelihos	Custom	41	34	7	12906	4440
TDSS	Kademlia	40	30	10	17680	4368

hashes in our dataset that match with existing P2P malware families. In order to obtain a valid ground truth for our experiments, we pick-up network traces only when their md5 labels match with more than 10 known signatures for the same P2P malware family in virusTotal. Note that AV scanners usually assign conflicting signatures for the same malware sample. For example, a same Sality malware has a `kaspersky` signature of `Virus.Win32.Sality.aa` and a `trendMicro` signature of `PE_SALITY.BU`. Therefore, we build our ground truth malware classes by matching keywords associated with known P2P malware families, as shown in table 1. We further compare in section 4.3 our malware families with signatures provided by three distinct AV scanners. Table 1 summarizes the six distinct P2P malware families that we identified within our malware dataset. Although 60% of our dataset consists of Sality (v3 and v4), it also includes significant flows for other P2P malware families. Yet we aim at experimentally validating three properties of PeerViewer using our P2P malware dataset.

First, PeerViewer identifies small malware families into a larger set of P2P malware. For instance, it accurately identifies the zeroAccess family, although it only constitutes 5% of our initial learning set. Second, PeerViewer identifies variants of the same malware family that have different implementations of P2P protocol. We validate this property using the example of Sality versions 3 and 4, that were correctly classified by our system. Third, PeerViewer separates families that use the same P2P protocol, but having different P2P signaling activity. Our system efficiently classifies samples of Zeus v3 and TDSS malware, although they are based on the same kademlia protocol.

We tested our P2P filter against the initial malware dataset, using the ground truth provided by P2P malware signatures in table 1. The DNS filter reduces up to the third the initial number of malware samples. Indeed, it cannot discard all non-P2P malware because there is multiple other reasons for malware to operate outside the DNS system, including hard coded C&C addresses, scan attempts and spam. Yet the flow size filter had little impact with only few flows being discarded, and that mostly carry malware spam activities. We believe this is mainly because of the short dynamic analysis time (30 minutes), which was not long enough for malware to trigger P2P data flows. On the other hand, the P2P filter uses two distinct thresholds, that are associated with the failed connection (τ_{fc}) and AS-based (τ_{as}) filters. We experimentally configured the values for these thresholds using our ground truth malware dataset. We were able to achieve 100% detection accuracy for values of τ_{as} in the interval $[0.1, 0.3]$

Table 2. Examples of malware P2P flow clusters detected by PeerViewer

Clstr Id	Nb of flows	Tr. proto	P2P proto	P2P activity	B_s	B_r	Pkt_s	Pkt_r
1	205	UDP	Gnutella	Query	35	130	1	1
2	937	UDP	Custom (Sality P2P)	Peer exchange	34	610	1	1
3	11944	UDP	Custom (Sality P2P)	Peer announcement	20	600	1	1
4	1674	UDP	uTorrent	find_node	450	970	3	3
5	1427	UDP	uTorrent	find_node	300	630	2	2
6	1164	UDP	Custom (Zeus P2P)	version request	200	645	2	2
7	5778	TCP	Gnutella	push	367	0	4	4
8	504	TCP	Gnutella	push	882	0	8	7

and τ_{fc} in the interval $[0.14, 0.6]$. We thus conservatively set these thresholds to the values 0.2 and 0.3 respectively, using our ground truth dataset in table 1.

We collected a total number of 541 malware samples that are classified into six distinct P2P malware families, as shown in table 1. In the remaining of this section, we validate our malware classification module using the set of P2P malware samples extracted from our dataset. We compare PeerViewer with P2P malware families provided by AV scanners. We also demonstrate its ability to efficiently classify P2P malware with high precision and recall.

4.2 Malware Classification

We split the dataset at our disposal into two separate groups. The first one includes 85% of our P2P malware learning set, and that we used to build P2P malware families. The second group includes the remaining 15% malware samples, and that we further used to test and validate our system. For the purpose of this paper, we randomly extracted the malware validation set from each P2P malware family using the ground truth families in table 1. Our validation set thus included 85 samples extracted from all six P2P malware families. We use the remaining 450 malware samples in order to build our malware classification system. The fourth column in table 1 summarizes the number of samples for each malware family that we use to build our malware classification system.

PeerViewer builds clusters of flows in order to group together malware flows that implement the same P2P protocol and signaling activity. It applies incremental k-means to the entire set of malware P2P flows, using the features vector f_α presented in section 3. The flow clustering module, applied to the 450 malware samples in our dataset, provided a total number of 28 P2P flow clusters, including 22 clusters of UDP flows and 6 clusters of TCP flows. Because of space limitations, table 2 illustrates only examples of network features for a subset of 8 P2P flow clusters identified by PeerViewer.

As shown in table 2, different signaling activities for the same P2P malware were indeed classified into different clusters. For example, clusters 2 and 3 in table 2 included two separate signaling messages (Peer exchange and Peer announcement) for the same Sality malware. As shown in table 2, Sality has different average request sizes for its two P2P signaling activities (34 vs 20), and so they

Table 3. Examples of P2P footprints for Zeus v3 and ZeroAccess families

Malware	Cltr 1	Cltr 2	Cltr 3..15	Cltr 16	Cltr 17..24	Cltr 25	Cltr 26	Cltr 27	Cltr 28
Zeus 1	0.07	0	0	0.93	0	0	0	0	0
Zeus 2	0.085	0	0	0.914	0	0	0	0	0
Zeus 3	0.03	0	0	0.97	0	0	0	0	0
Zeus 4	0.037	0	0	0.962	0	0	0	0	0
Zeus 5	0.071	0	0	0.928	0	0	0	0	0
Zeus 7	0.098	0.02	0	0.87	0	0.01	0	0	0
ZA 1	0.035	0.014	0	0	0	0.577	0.04	0.3	0
ZA 2	0.078	0.022	0	0	0	0.592	0	0.3	0.011
ZA 3	0.102	0.011	0	0	0	0.606	0.02	0.27	0
ZA 4	0.019	0.015	0	0	0	0.62	0.06	0.29	0.013

were classified into different clusters. Clusters 1, 7 and 8 provide yet another example for the Gnutella protocol. We obtained separate clusters for the query and push signaling activities of the same Gnutella P2P protocol. They respectively use UDP and TCP protocols, and they have different network features so they were classified into separate clusters. Note that we may still obtain clusters that implement the same P2P signaling activity and protocol (e.g. clusters 4 and 5 for the same uTorrent protocol). Nonetheless, these clusters show different P2P network features that characterize different implementations of the same P2P protocol by different malware families.

We use the 28 flow clusters in order to build P2P footprints for malware in our dataset. Malware footprints indicate the proportion of P2P flows for a given malware that belong to each of the 28 P2P flow clusters. Due to space limitations, table 3 illustrates examples of P2P footprints from only two P2P malware families, Zeus v3 and ZeroAccess. As shown in this table, malware of the same family has almost identical P2P footprints and so it would be grouped within the same clusters. For example, malware of the Zeus v3 family has almost all of its P2P signaling flows in cluster 16, while the few remaining flows belong to cluster 1. On the other hand, malware of the zeroAccess family has almost a third of its P2P signaling flows in cluster 27, and the remaining two thirds in cluster 25. These two malware families would be clearly separated into two clusters by the malware classifier.

The classifier module uses malware footprints in order to build families of P2P malware. We implement the hierarchical clustering algorithm using Python, and we use the Davies-Bouldin index to obtain the optimal set of clusters. The malware classifier module identified a total number of 8 clusters, associated with 8 distinct P2P malware families. We validate our P2P malware families using the ground truth classification in table 1.

Six P2P malware clusters were clearly associated with each of the six malware families in table 1. In fact all Zeus v3, ZeroAccess and Kelihos malware samples were classified into separate clusters respectively. We thus consider our clusters to characterize the P2P network footprint of these distinct malware families. On the other hand, samples of Sality malware were split into two separate clusters, including 295 and 37 samples in each cluster respectively. These clusters are likely to include malware that respectively belong to versions v3 and v4 of the Sality family. Yet we couldn't validate this assumption using our ground truth in table 1 because of the conflicting AV signatures for versions of the Sality malware. Therefore, in order to refine our ground truth, we checked the update time for AV signatures that were matching each of the malware md5 hashes associated with the Sality malware. We would expect samples for the version v4 of this malware to be more recent *in general* than samples of version v3. We admit that AV update times do not formally validate our classification because we cannot rule out the possibility of newer malware samples implementing P2P protocol for version 3 of this malware. However, signature update times still provide evidence of different version implementations for this same malware family. Yet we observed that 80% of malware in the smaller Sality P2P cluster has newer update times than all other samples in the larger P2P cluster. We believe this is a clear evidence of two families of the Sality malware, that we associate with versions 3 and 4 of this malware family. In fact, versions v3 and v4 of the Sality malware have different implementations of their P2P signaling protocols, and so AV signatures cannot correctly classify these two malware families based on their system behavior. PeerViewer thus offers a complementary approach that classifies P2P malware based on its network-level behavior, which cannot be easily characterized by host-based signatures.

Finally, we obtained two additional clusters, both including two malware samples that belong to different malware families in table 1. These are clearly outliers and so they were misclassified by our system. PeerViewer was indeed able to correctly classify 446 out of 450 malware samples in the initial training set. It clearly outperforms current AV signatures as it achieved near 0.8% misclassification rate.

4.3   Comparison with AV Signatures

This section analyzes the validity of our P2P malware families by comparing them with signatures from three AV scanners, including McAfee, kaspersky and Trend Micro. In fact, our system proposes a behavioral approach that classifies P2P malware on the fly while executing in a dynamic analysis environment. We need to verify the cohesion of our P2P malware families using a learning set of known and already qualified malware dataset. For each malware family created by our system, we collect AV signatures for all samples of this family. We compute the precision and recall of our system in order to validate the consistency of our malware classification with respect to all three AV scanners. Our experiments prove the ability of PeerViewer to accurately classify P2P malware using only network level information, with no *a-priori* knowldge about the system behavior of malware.

Table 4 compares malware families provided by our system with signatures from three AV scanners. As shown in this table, AV scanners assign different signatures for samples of the same malware families. These signatures usually constitute different aliases for the same malware family. In order to have common evaluation criteria for all three AV scanners, we used the spyware remove

Table 4. Comparison with `kaspersky`, `McAfee` and `TrendMicro` signatures

Family Id	Samples	Kaspersky	McAfee	TrendMicro
1	295	**win32.Sality: 193** **Win32.Spammy: 29** Unknown: 23	**W32/Sality: 219** Downloader-CPY: 22 Unknown: 4	**PE_SALITY: 223** WORM_KOLAB: 9 Mal_Odra-5: 2 Unknown: 11
2	27	**win32.Zbot: 25** Unknown: 2	**PWS-Zbot: 27**	**Tspy_Zbot: 27**
3	24	**Win32.Sefnit: 17** **Win32.ZAccess: 7**	**Sefnit: 24**	**Troj_Kazy: 13** Troj_Sirefef: 7 Unknown: 4
4	32	**Win32.Kelihos: 27** unknown: 5	**Win32/Kelihos: 23** GenericBackDoor.xf: 8 unknown: 1	**TROJ_FAKEAV: 29** TROJ_INJECTER: 3
5	37	**win32.Sality: 37**	**W32/Sality: 37**	**PE_SALITY: 37**
6	30	**Win32.TDSS:19** **Win32.FakeAV: 11**	**FakeAlert-JM: 26** **Trojan.Alureon:4**	**BKDR_TDSS: 30**
7	2	win32.Sality, win32.killAV	Win32/Nimnul, win32/Zbot	PE_fujacks, PE_nimnul
8	2	win32.Sality, unknown	unknown: 2	PE_fujacks, PE_down

	Kaspersky	McAfee	TrendMicro
Precision	83.16%	88.45%	86.5%
Recall	90.8%	89.31%	94.85%

	Sality v3	Sality v4	ZA	kelihos	TDSS	Zeus v3
Accuracy	99.3%	99.1%	94.2%	95%	98%	100%

Fig. 2. Precision and recall against the three AV scanners

Fig. 3. Classification accuracy by malware family

website[1] in order to associate all aliases of the same malware families. For example, the signature `win32.spammy` for the first malware family in table 4 is identified by spyware remove as a `kaspersky` alias of `spammer.sality.a`, and so we consider it as part of the sality family.

Figure 2 summarizes the classification accuracy and recall of PeerViewer against the three AV scanners. Classification accuracy is computed as the average precision rate for all six P2P malware families identified by PeerViewer. We introduce the precision rate for a P2P malware family as the ratio of malware samples that have the same predominant AV signature with respect to the total number of samples in this family. The classification recall is computed the same as for the precision rate, excluding samples that are unknown for AV scanners. As in figure 2, PeerViewer has almost stable precision and recall against all three AV scanners. It enhances by at least 11.5% the malware classification for AV scanners (in case of McAfee which provides the highest precision rate), based on our ground truth in table 1. It also differentiates samples of the same malware family that implement different variants of the same P2P protocol, as for the sality malware which is indeed represented by the same signature by all three AV scanners. Yet it replaces current AV signature aliases with a common behavioral malware classification, as in the example of the third malware family provided by PeerViewer in table 4. The latter provides a common classification for multiple aliases of the same zeroAccess malware family, including `win32.ZAccess`, `win32.sefnit`, `troj_Kazy` and `troj_Sirefef` aliases.

---

[1] http://www.spywareremove.com/

4.4 Classification and Detection

This section demonstrates the detection phase of PeerViewer, which classifies P2P malware on-the-fly during dynamic analysis. We implement the cross-validation method that consists of extracting an evaluation dataset prior to building malware classifiers, and then to use this dataset in order to test and validate our classifiers. We reiterated the cross-validation process using different evaluation sets, each time randomly extracting 15% of our malware dataset before we build our one-class classifiers. In order to guarantee the soundness of our experiments, our evaluation set had always the same malware composition, as shown in the fifth column of table 1.

We apply the P2P flow filter and we build clusters of P2P flows using the network traces for each sample in our malware validation set. Then we build a P2P footprint for each sample using its P2P flow clusters. We use malware footprints as input to the one-class classifiers for each of our six malware families. Our system achieved near 97.6% classification accuracy, based on the ground truth classification in table 1. The detailed results of our experiments for each malware family are illustrated in the table of figure 3.

Samples of Zeus v3 and TDSS malware families were accurately classified with almost no false positives. False positives in case of Sality malware were all due to mis-classifications between the different versions of this family. Note that 100% of Sality malware in our dataset was correctly classified by PeerViewer, and almost 99.2% of these samples were classified with the appropriate version of this family. In fact we couldn't formally validate our classification of Sality versions v3 and v4 because AV scanners do not constitute a reliable ground truth. Hence, we used update times for AV detection signatures in order to separate between different versions of Sality malware. On the other hand, PeerViewer has correctly classified only 94.2% of kelihos malware mostly because of the small number of samples in our learning set. Yet PeerViewer outperforms most AV scanners with an overall classification accuracy of 97.6%, while only relying on network features with no need of malware binary analysis.

5 Discussion

PeerViewer classifies malware using statistical network features such as flow size, IP distribution and traffic rate. First, it classifies flows for a given malware sample into categories where they implement the same signaling activities. Then it builds malware families using similarities in their P2P network footprints. PeerViewer would be thus unable to accurately classify P2P malware that modifies its P2P communication rounds, contacts a larger set of peers, or uses random paddings in its P2P traffic. These maneuvers modify statistical consistency in malware P2P flows and so it makes malware classification more difficult using our features. Although they are technically possible, these techniques require a malware developper to modify its P2P C&C toolkit. They also increase overhead and reduce botnet stability, which makes botnet management more difficult. Yet botnets that adopt these techniques would no longer be able to dissimulate within benign P2P flows, and so they will be exposed to other malware detection techniques.

On the other hand, PeerViewer classifies malware that uses P2P protocols only as a primary C&C channel. In fact, malware may use P2P protocols as a failover mechanism in case where it cannot access its primary C&C channel. This malware does not trigger P2P flows during analysis, and so it would not contribute to building P2P malware classifiers. Authors in [21] propose an approach that detects primary C&C channels during malware dynamic analysis. This approach dynamically intercepts primary C&C channels and forces malware to engage in a failover strategy. Using techniques such as [21] enables to trigger P2P failover strategies, and so PeerViewer will be able to take these into account during its processing of malware P2P flows. Nonetheless, these techniques apply during malware dynamic analysis and so they are out of scope in this study.

Future work will explore techniques to integrate PeerViewer into a more comprehensive malware detection system. In fact, PeerViewer classifies malware samples with a high detection accuracy. Nonetheless, it is yet unclear how PeerViewer would be a able to separate P2P flows triggered by multiple P2P applications running on the same terminal. Although it is out of scope in this paper, we experimented with PeerViewer in order to detect P2P infected nodes within live network traffic. PeerViewer efficiently *detects and characterizes* infected nodes when they do not concurrently implement other benign P2P applications. Therefore, future work will adress this issue by proposing appropriate methods that tell apart malware and benign P2P applications when they are running on the same network terminal.

6   Related Work

Several approaches detect P2P malware through behavioral analysis of network traffic, without deep packet inspection. They usually propose a binary classification of P2P nodes, that is whether being infected or benign [6,9,11,19,27,28]. Yet there is only few approaches that build families of P2P malware based on its P2P network behavior [12,24].

The first category includes solutions such as BotTrack [9], BotMiner [11] and BotGrep [19]. They correlate network flows and detect P2P bots based on their overlay C&C topologies. First, they build clusters of terminals and isolate groups of hosts that form P2P networks. Then they separate malicious P2P groups using lists of infected P2P nodes provided by sources such as honeypots. These techniques mostly rely on IDS signatures and IP blacklists to detect P2P bots. However, botnet activity is becoming stealthier and difficult to detect using IDS signatures, thus limiting the coverage of these solutions. Bilge et al. propose an alternative approach that detects botnets using large scale netflow analysis [6]. It observes traffic at large ISP networks and detects botnets through the coordinated activity for groups of infected nodes. However, this approach detects only centralized botnet architectures, and cannot accurately detect distributed P2P botnets. Another trend of research aims at detecting infected P2P bots inside a given network perimeter [27,28]. These studies propose to first discard non-P2P traffic using heuristics such as DNS traffic and failed connection attempts. They build groups of P2P nodes that have the same network behavior or that connect to a common set of remote IP addresses. Further they compute a similarity degree between network nodes in order to detect those that are likely to be part of a same botnet. However, these studies can only detect P2P bots when there is multiple infected nodes inside the same network perimeter. Yet they only provide a binary classification, without being able to identify a common malware family or a given P2P protocol.

The second category classifies P2P flows and identifies specific P2P protocols or applications [12,24]. PeerRush [24] uses features such as inter-packet delays and flow duration in order to classify P2P applications. These features achieve good detection accuracies against benign P2P applications. However, it is not clear how they will contribute to classifying P2P botnets. For exemple, inter-packet delays can be easily evaded and these are weak indicators of P2P activity. Yet PeerRush deals with all P2P signaling flows as a whole. It does not classify flows according to their embedded message types and the rate of each signaling activity. PeerViewer thus provides a better alternative as it builds specific malware P2P footprints that take it account the P2P signaling rounds and categories of message types. On the other hand, Hu et al. [12] use flow statistics to build behavior profiles for P2P applications. They experimented only with two P2P applications (PPLive and BitTorrent), and did not consider malicious P2P activity. Yet, they do not separate P2P control and data traffic. In fact data flows do not clearly characterize P2P botnet C&C activity as they depend on the content being shared. PeerViewer thus classifies P2P signaling flows and use only these as a basis for P2P botnet classification.

7   Conclusion

This paper presented PeerViewer, a system that automatically classifies P2P malware based on its P2P network behavior. It does not use system-level information, nor does it use flow content signatures during its processing of malware traffic. Indeed PeerViewer classifies P2P flows for a specific malware into categories where they implement the same P2P signaling activity. It further builds a footprint that characterizes the P2P network behavior of malware, using the different categories of signaling flows triggered by this malware. To the best of our knowledge, PeerViewer is the first to propose a fully behavioral approach that detects *and* classifies P2P malware into specific malware families. We tested our system against signatures of malware families provided by several anti-virus solutions. Experimental results prove our ability to accurately classify P2P malware with a very low false positives rate.

References

1. Zeus tracker, `https://zeustracker.abuse.ch/` (accessed at June 2013)
2. Anubis: Analyzing unknown binaries (2011), `http://anubis.iseclab.org`
3. Blue coat - exposing malnet strategies and best practices for threat protection. In: 2012 Web Security Report (2012)
4. Aberer, K., Hauswirth, M.: An overview on peer-to-peer information systems. In: Proceedings of the 4th Workshop on Distributed Data and Structures (2002)
5. Bayer, U., Comparetti, P.M., Hlauschek, C., Kruegel, C., Kirda, E.: Scalable behavior-based malware clustering. In: Proc. 19th NDSS (2009)
6. Bilge, L., Kirda, E., Kruegel, C., Balduzzi, M.: Exposure: Finding malicious domains using passive dns analysis. In: Proc. 18th NDSS (2011)
7. Bolla, R., Canini, M., Rapuzzi, R., Sciuto, M.: Characterizing the network behavior of p2p traffic. 4th International Workshop on QoS in Multiservice IP Networks (2008)
8. Davies, D.I., Bouldin, D.W.: A cluster seperation measure. In: IEEE Transactions on Pattern Analysis and Machine Intelligence (1979)
9. François, J., Wang, S., State, R., Engel, T.: Bottrack: Tracking botnets using netflow and pagerank. In: Domingo-Pascual, J., Manzoni, P., Palazzo, S., Pont, A., Scoglio, C. (eds.) NETWORKING 2011, Part I. LNCS, vol. 6640, pp. 1–14. Springer, Heidelberg (2011)
10. Grizzard, J.B., Sharma, V., Nunnery, C., Kang, B.B.: Peer-to-peer botnets: Overview and case study. In: Proceedings of USENIX HotBots (2007)
11. Gu, G., Perdisci, R., Zhang, J., Lee, W.: Botminer: Clustering analysis of network traffic for protocol and structure independent botnet detection. In: SSP (2008)
12. Hu, Y., Chiu, D.-M., Lui, J.C.S.: Profiling and identification of p2p traffic. In: Computer Networks, vol. 53, pp. 849–863 (2009)
13. Jacob, G., Hund, R., Kruegel, C., Holz, T.: Jackstraws: Picking command and control connections from bot traffic. In: 20th Usenix Security Symposium (2011)
14. Kapoor, A., Mathur, R.: Predicting the future of stealth attacks. In: Virus Bulletin (2011)
15. Karagiannis, T., Broido, A., Brownlee, N., Claffy, K., Faloutsos, M.: Is p2p dying or just hiding? In: IEEE GLOBECOM, vol. 3, pp. 1532–1538 (2004)
16. Karagiannis, T., Broido, A., Brownlee, N.: k claffy, and M. Faloutsos. File-sharing in the internet: A characterization of p2p traffic in the backbone. In: UC Riverside technical report (November 2003)
17. Khan, S.S., Madden, M.G.: A survey of recent trends in one class classification. In: Coyle, L., Freyne, J. (eds.) AICS 2009. LNCS, vol. 6206, pp. 188–197. Springer, Heidelberg (2010)
18. Lua, C.-N., Huang, C.-Y., Lina, Y.-D., Lai, Y.-C.: Session level flow classification by packet size distribution and session grouping. International Journal on Computer Networks 56, 260–272 (2012)
19. Nagaraja, S., Mittal, P., Hong, C.-Y., Caesar, M., Borisov, N.: Botgrep: Finding p2p bots with structured graph analysis. In: Proc. 19th USENIX Security (2010)
20. Neugschwandtner, M., Comparetti, P.M., Jacob, G., Kruegel, C.: Forecast: skimming off the malware cream. In: 27th Annual Computer Security Applications Conference, ACSAC (2011)
21. Neugschwandtner, M., Comparetti, P.M., Platzer, C.: Detecting malware's failover c&c strategies with squeeze. In: Proceedings of the 27th Annual Computer Security Applications Conference, ACSAC (2011)

22. Perdisci, R., Lee, W., Feamster, N.: Behavioral clustering of http-based malware and signature generation using malicious network traces. In: USENIX Symposium on Networked Systems Design and Implementation (2010)
23. Porras, P., Saidi, H., Yegneswaran, V.: Conficker c p2p protocol and implementation. Technical report, Computer Science Laboratory, SRI International (2009)
24. Rahbarinia, B., Perdisci, R., Lanzi, A., Li, K.: Peerrush: Mining for unwanted p2p traffic. In: Rieck, K., Stewin, P., Seifert, J.-P. (eds.) DIMVA 2013. LNCS, vol. 7967, pp. 62–82. Springer, Heidelberg (2013)
25. Rieck, K., Holz, T., Willems, C., Düssel, P., Laskov, P.: Learning and classification of malware behavior. In: Zamboni, D. (ed.) DIMVA 2008. LNCS, vol. 5137, pp. 108–125. Springer, Heidelberg (2008)
26. Tenebro, G.: W32.waledac threat analysis. In: Symantec Technical Report (2009)
27. Yen, T.-F., Reiter, M.K.: Are your hosts trading or plotting? telling p2p file-sharing and bots apart. In: 30th Conf. Distributed Computing Systems (2010)
28. Zhang, J., Perdisci, R., Lee, W., Sarfraz, U., Luo, X.: Detecting stealthy p2p botnet using statistical traffic fingerprints. In: Proc. 41st DSN (2011)

Selecting Features for Anomaly Intrusion Detection: A Novel Method using Fuzzy C Means and Decision Tree Classification

Jingping Song[1,2,*], Zhiliang Zhu[1], Peter Scully[2], and Chris Price[2]

[1] Software College of Northeastern University, Shenyang, Liaoning, China, 110819
[2] Department of Computer Science, Aberystwyth University, UK, SY23 3DB
{songjp,zhuzl}@swc.neu.edu.cn,
{jis17,pds7,cjp}@aber.ac.uk

Abstract. In this work, a new method for classification is proposed consisting of a combination of feature selection, normalization, fuzzy C means clustering algorithm and C4.5 decision tree algorithm. The aim of this method is to improve the performance of the classifier by using selected features. The fuzzy C means clustering method is used to partition the training instances into clusters. On each cluster, we build a decision tree using C4.5 algorithm. Experiments on the KDD CUP 99 data set shows that our proposed method in detecting intrusion achieves better performance while reducing the relevant features by more than 80%.

Keywords: Intrusion detection, Fuzzy C-Means, Feature selection, C4.5.

1 Introduction

Network intrusion detection is a very important task for network operators on the Internet [1]. There are two different approaches in the traditional network intrusion detection systems: misuse detection and anomaly detection. Misuse detection is based on signatures of previously seen attacks and is highly effective to detect the attacks which are matched to signatures. However, they could not detect a new attack. In contrast, anomaly detection uses the normal instances to build normal operation profiles, detecting anomalies as activities that deviate from them. This detection method requires training to construct a model which depends on normal instances [2].

Anomaly intrusion detection is a classification task, and machine learning theory could be valuable in this area because of the continued increase of attacks on computer networks. The classification task consists of building a predictive model which could identify attack instances. Intrusion detection can be considered as a two class problem or a multiple class problem. A two class problem regards all attack types as anomaly patterns and the other class is a

---

* Corresponding author.

G. Wang et al. (Eds.): CSS 2013, LNCS 8300, pp. 299–307, 2013.

normal pattern. A multiple problem deals with the classification based on different attacks [3].

Anomaly intrusion detection systems are complex classification domains since they have too many features or attributes which may contain false correlation. Moreover, some features may be irrelevant and some others may be redundant. For this reason, feature selection methods can be used to get rid of the irrelevant and redundant features without decreasing performance. In [3], a method consisting of a combination of discretizers, filters and classifiers is presented. The main goal of this method is to significantly reduce the number of features while maintaining the performance of the classifiers, even improving it. [4] and [5] applied feature selection in intrusion detection systems as well. [6] proposed an algorithm to use SVM and simulated annealing to find the best selected features to improve the accuracy of anomaly intrusion detection. [7] proposed mutual information-based feature selection method results in detecting intrusions with higher accuracy.

There are two categories of learning techniques: supervised and unsupervised. Supervised methods are based on classifiers, such as C4.5 [8], Bayesian [9], ID3, JRip, PART, SMO and IBK algorithms. Unsupervised methods are based on clustering method, such as Fuzzy C Means, Sub-Space Clustering (SSC) [10], Density-based Clustering [11], and Evidence Accumulation Clustering (EAC) techniques [12]. These clustering methods are able to detect unknown attacks in a completely unsupervised fashion, avoiding the need for signatures [13][14].

2   Dataset and Related Algorithms

2.1   The KDD 99 Dataset

Since 1999, KDD99 has been the most widely used data set for the evaluation of anomaly intrusion detection methods. This data set is built based on the data captured in DARPA98 IDS evaluation program. DARPA98 is about 4 gigabytes of compressed binary tcpdump data of 7 weeks of network traffic, which can be processed into about 5 million connection records, each with about 100 bytes. The two weeks of test data have around 2 million connection records [15].

A connection is a TCP data packet sequence from start to end in a certain time and data from source IP address to destination IP address in predefined protocol such as TCP or UDP. Each connection is labeled by either normal or attack. The attack type is divided into four categories of 39 types of attacks. Only 22 types of attacks are in the training dataset and the other 17 unknown types are in the test dataset. It is important to note that the test data is not from the same probability distribution as the training data, and it includes specific attack types not in the training data which make the task more realistic [16]. Some intrusion experts believe that most novel attacks are variants of known attacks and the signature of known attacks can be sufficient to catch novel variants. The KDD dataset consists of three components, which are detailed in Table 1.

The 10% KDD dataset is employed for the purpose of training. The KDD training dataset consists of approximately 4,900,000 single connection vectors

Table 1. Basic characteristics of the KDD 99 intrusion detection datasets

Dataset	Normal	DoS	U2R	R2L	Probe
10%KDD	97278	391458	52	1126	4107
Corrected KDD	60593	229853	70	16347	4166
Whole KDD	972780	3883370	52	1126	41102

each of which contains 41 features, with exactly one specific attack type or normal type. This dataset contains 22 attack types and is a more concise version of the whole KDD dataset. It contains more connections of attacks than normal connections and the attack types are not represented equally. Denial of service attacks account for the majority of the dataset [17].

On the other hand the Corrected KDD dataset (test dataset) provides a dataset with different statistical distributions than either 10% KDD or Whole KDD and contains 14 additional attacks. The list of class labels and their corresponding categories for 10% KDD are detailed in [17].

2.2 Fuzzy C Means Algorithm

Fuzzy C means (FCM) is a method of clustering which allows one piece of data to belong to two or more clusters. This method (developed by Dunn in 1973 and improved by Bezdek in 1981) is frequently used in pattern recognition. It is based on minimization of the following objective function:

$$J_m = \sum_{i=1}^{N} \sum_{j=1}^{C} u_{ij}^m ||x_i - c_j||^2 \tag{1}$$

where m is any real number greater than 1, u_{ij} is the degree of membership of x_i in the cluster j, x_i is the ith of d-dimensional measured data, c_j is the d-dimension center of the cluster, and $|| * ||$ is any norm expressing the similarity between any measured data and the center. Fuzzy partitioning is carried out through an iterative optimization of the objective function shown above, with the update of membership uij and the cluster centers c_j by:

$$u_{ij} = \frac{1}{\sum_{k=1}^{C} (\frac{||x_i - c_j||}{||x_i - c_k||})^{\frac{2}{m-1}}} \tag{2}$$

$$c_j = \frac{\sum_{i=1}^{N} u_{ij}^m \times x_i}{\sum_{i=1}^{N} u_{ij}^m} \tag{3}$$

This iteration will stop when $max_{ij}|u_{ij}^{(k+1)} - u_{ij}^{(k)}| < \epsilon$, where ϵ is a termination criterion between 0 and 1, where k are the iteration steps. This procedure converges to a local minimum or a saddle point of J_m.

2.3   C4.5 Algorithm

C4.5 is an algorithm used to generate a decision tree developed by Ross Quinlan and it is an extension of Quinlan's earlier ID3 algorithm. The decision trees generated by C4.5 can be used for classification, and for this reason, C4.5 is often referred to as a statistical classifier.

C4.5 uses the concept of information gain to make a tree of classificatory decisions with respect to a previously chosen target classification. The information gain can be described as the effective decrease in entropy resulting from making a choice as to which attribute to use and at what level. For example, if one chooses a specified attribute like the length of a phase to discriminate among cases at a given point in its rule construction process, this choice will have some effect on how well the system can tell the classes apart. By considering which of the attributes is best for discriminating among cases at a particular node in the tree, we can build up a tree of decisions that allows us to navigate from the root of the tree to a leaf node by continually examining attributes. So the order in which the attributes are considered depend on the amount of entropy correlating to a given attribute.

3   Anomaly Detection Scheme

We implemented a scheme to find anomaly instances using fuzzy C means clustering and C4.5 decision tree algorithm. We regard all the attack instances as anomaly instances and so convert a multiple class classification problem to a binary class classification. Fig.1 shows the flow chart of proposed scheme. First of all, we use feature selection methods on training data to get some selected features. But the features have different kinds of data structure. For this reason, we normalize the data so that all attribute values are between 0 and 1. Then, we use fuzzy C means method to divide the training data into two clusters and get two centres. Moreover, we calculate the membership function between each test data instance and each cluster. The test data instance is allocated to the cluster which has higher membership. Finally, in each cluster, we used C4.5 algorithm to classify the test data as an anomaly or a normal instance. Each part of the process is now described in greater detail.

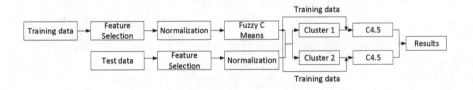

Fig. 1. Flow chart of proposed scheme

3.1   Feature Selection

Feature selection is the process of selecting a subset of relevant features for use in model construction. The central assumption when using a feature selection technique is that the data contains many redundant or irrelevant features. Redundant features are those which provide no more information than the currently selected features, and irrelevant features provide no useful information in any context. In KDD99 dataset, some features may be irrelevant and some others may be redundant since the information they add is contained in other features. These extra features can increase computation time for creating classifications, and can have an impact on the accuracy of the classifier built. For this reason, these classification domains seem to be suitable for the application of feature selection methods. These methods are centered in obtaining a subset of features that adequately describe the problem at hand without degrading performance.

Table 2 shows four feature selection tests on KDD training dataset and we select 6 to 8 features. The results show that most of the features selected by different feature selection methods are the same. Such as, all 6 features in test 3 are in the results of test 1 and six features in the result of test 4 are in test 1 results. We used the 8 features selected by test 1. They are protocol_type, service, flag, src_bytes, dst_bytes, count, diff_srv_rate, dst_host_same_src_port_rate. The evaluator in test 1 is based on Correlation-based Feature Selection (CFS), which is one of the most well-known and used filters, and ranks feature subsets according to a correlation based heuristic evaluation function.

Table 2. Results obtained by four feature selection methods over the training dataset

Test No.	Search Method	Attribute Evaluator	No. of Selected Features
1	BestFirst	CfsSubsetEval	8
2	Ranker	ConsistencySubsetEval	7
3	FCBFSearch	SymmetricalUncertAttributeSetEval	6
4	Randomsearch	AttributeSubsetEvaluator	7

One advantage of feature selection is gaining speed. Table 3 shows the time consumption comparison between C4.5 decision tree algorithm with and without feature selection methods. We can see from table 4 that the inclusion of less features greatly reduced the computation time and the time to build the decision tree model. And we also could see that the number of leaves and size of leaves significantly dropped.

3.2   Normalization

The 8 features we used have two types. The protocol_type, service, flag are symbolic and the other five features are continuous. The protocol_type has 3 values, service has 66 values, and flag has 11 values. Table 4 shows the minimum

Table 3. Computation time comparison

Algorithm	No. of attributes	No. of Leaves	Size of Tree	Computation time (s)	Time to build model (s)
C4.5	41	335	396	1104	104.21
C4.5 with FS	8	99	197	237	17.47

Table 4. Unbalanced continuous features of KDD Cup 99 dataset

Feature	Max.	Min.	Mean	StdDev	Distinct
src_bytes	693375640	0	3025.61	988218.1	3300
dst_bytes	5155468	0	868.5324	33040	10725
count	511	0	332.2857	213.1474	490
diff_srv_rate	1	0	0.020982	0.082205	78
dst_host_same_src_port_rate	1	0	0.601935	0.481309	101

and maximum value of each feature, as well as its mean, standard deviation and the number of distinct example of the five continuous features.

Normalization converts all the data in the dataset between 0 and 1. For a particular continuous data x_i, normalization follows equation (4),

$$Normalized(x_i) = (x_i - X_{min})/(X_{max} - X_{min}) \qquad (4)$$

where X_{min} is the minimum value for variable X, X_{max} is the maximum value for variable X. For a specific symbolic feature, we assigned a discrete integer to each value and then used equation (4) to normalize it.

3.3 Implemented Algorithm

In this section, we will show the algorithm of the fuzzy C means clustering and C4.5 decision tree classification methods for supervised anomaly detection. Fuzzy C means (FCM) is a method of clustering which allows one piece of data to belong to two or more clusters. Its allocation of data points to clusters is not "hard" (all-or-nothing) but "fuzzy" in the same sense as fuzzy logic. C4.5 is a well-known classification algorithm used to generate a decision tree. We use fuzzy C means algorithm to group 2 clusters and we get 2 centers. We then used C4.5 to classify in each cluster. The algorithm is shown as follows.

1. BEGIN
2. Initialization: $U = [u_{ij}] \leftarrow U^{(0)}$
3. while $||U^{(k+1)} - U^{(k)}|| \geq \epsilon$
4.   Calculate the centres C_1, C_2
5.   Update $U^{(k)}, U^{(k+1)}$
6. end While
7. for each test instance z_i
8.   Compute $u_{ij}, j = 1, 2$
9.   Find Highest Membership to z_i

10. Assign to Higher Membership cluster
11. end for
12. Classify each cluster by C4.5

4 Experimental Results

4.1 Measures of Performance Evaluation

Our proposed scheme is conducted by six measures: True Positive Rate (TPR), False Positive Rate (FPR), Precision, Recall, F-Measure. The six measures could be calculated by True Positive (TP), False Positive (FP), True Negative (TN), False Negative (FN), as follows.

True positive rate (TPR): TP/(TP+FN), also known as detection rate (DR) or sensitivity or recall.

False positive rate (FPR): FP/(TN+FP) also known as the false alarm rate.

Precision (P): TP/(TP+FP) is defined as the proportion of the true positives against all the positive results.

Total Accuracy (TA): (TP+TN)/(TP+TN+FP+FN) is the proportion of true results (both true positives and true negatives) in the population.

Recall (R): TP/(TP+FN) is defined as percentage of positive labeled instances that were predicted as positive.

F-measure: 2PR/(P+R) is the harmonic mean of precision and recall.

In our proposed scheme, we use the training dataset to construct the decision tree model and then reevaluate on the test dataset and get TP, FP, TN, FN in each cluster. After that, we calculate the four values for the test dataset. And finally, we calculate the measures for the test dataset.

4.2 Experiment Evaluation

The experiments were conducted by using KDD 99 dataset and performed on a Windows machine with Intel (R) Core (TM) i5-2400 CPU@ 3.10GHz, 3.10 GHz, 4GB of RAM, the operating system is Microsoft Windows 7 Professional. We have used an open source machine learning framework Weka 3.5.0. We have used this tool for performance comparison of our algorithm with other classification algorithms.

Table 5. Performance evaluation comparison

Algorithm	TPR	FPR	Precision	Recall	F-Measure	Class
C4.5	0.994	0.090	0.728	0.994	0.841	Normal
	0.910	0.006	0.999	0.910	0.952	Anomaly
C4.5 with FS	0.990	0.084	0.741	0.990	0.847	normal
	0.916	0.010	0.997	0.916	0.955	anomaly
Proposed Scheme	0.990	0.079	0.753	0.990	0.855	Normal
	0.921	0.010	0.998	0.921	0.958	Anomaly

Table 5 describes the performance evaluation comparison of C4.5, C4.5 with feature selection and the proposed scheme on the KDD Cup 99 test dataset. The total accuracy of these three algorithms are 0.926, 0.931, 0.935 respectively. And the comparison shows that most precision, recall and F-measure results are improved by using the proposed scheme.

5   Conclusion

This paper proposed a method based on the combination of feature selection, fuzzy C means and C4.5 algorithms that improve the performance results of classifiers while using a reduced set of features. It has been applied to the KDD Cup 99 dataset in the intrusion detection field. We used a normalization method on the KDD 99 training dataset and test dataset before applying the proposed scheme to the dataset. The method improves the performance results obtained by C4.5 while using only 19.5% of the total number of features. Performance analysis is assessed against six measures. The proposed method gives impressive detection precision accuracy and F-measure in the experiment results. An additional advantage is memory and time costs reduction for C4.5 classifier.

References

1. Tajbakhsh, A., Rahmati, M., Mirzaei, A.: Intrusion detection using fuzzy association rules. Applied Soft Computing 9(2), 462–469 (2009)
2. Casas, P., Mazel, J., Owezarski, P.: Unsupervised network intrusion detection systems: Detecting the unknown without knowledge. Computer Communications 35(7), 772–783 (2012)
3. Bolón-Canedo, V., Sánchez-Maroño, N., Alonso-Betanzos, A.: Feature selection and classification in multiple class datasets: An application to kdd cup 99 dataset. Expert Systems with Applications 38(5), 5947–5957 (2011)
4. Chebrolu, S., Abraham, A., Thomas, J.P.: Feature deduction and ensemble design of intrusion detection systems. Computers & Security 24(4), 295–307 (2005)
5. Mukkamala, S., Sung, A.H.: Feature ranking and selection for intrusion detection systems using support vector machines. In: Proceedings of the Second Digital Forensic Research Workshop. Citeseer (2002)
6. Lin, S.-W., Ying, K.-C., Lee, C.-Y., Lee, Z.-J.: An intelligent algorithm with feature selection and decision rules applied to anomaly intrusion detection. Applied Soft Computing 12(10), 3285–3290 (2012)
7. Amiri, F., Rezaei, Y., Mohammad, M., Lucas, C., Shakery, A., Yazdani, N.: Mutual information-based feature selection for intrusion detection systems. Journal of Network and Computer Applications 34(4), 1184–1199 (2011)
8. Muniyandi, A.P., Rajeswari, R., Rajaram, R.: Network anomaly detection by cascading k-means clustering and c4. 5 decision tree algorithm. Procedia Engineering 30, 174–182 (2012)
9. Altwaijry, H.: Bayesian based intrusion detection system. In: IAENG Transactions on Engineering Technologies, pp. 29–44. Springer (2013)
10. Parsons, L., Haque, E., Liu, H.: Subspace clustering for high dimensional data: a review. ACM SIGKDD Explorations Newsletter 6(1), 90–105 (2004)

11. Fred, A.L., Jain, A.K.: Combining multiple clusterings using evidence accumulation. IEEE Transactions on Pattern Analysis and Machine Intelligence 27(6), 835–850 (2005)
12. Ester, M., Kriegel, H.-P., Sander, J., Xu, X.: A density-based algorithm for discovering clusters in large spatial databases with noise. In: KDD, vol. 96, pp. 226–231 (1996)
13. Leung, K., Leckie, C.: Unsupervised anomaly detection in network intrusion detection using clusters. In: Proceedings of the Twenty-Eighth Australasian Conference on Computer Science, vol. 38, pp. 333–342. Australian Computer Society, Inc. (2005)
14. Portnoy, L., Eskin, E., Stolfo, S.: Intrusion detection with unlabeled data using clustering. In: Proceedings of ACM CSS Workshop on Data Mining Applied to Security (DMSA 2001). Citeseer (2001)
15. Kayacik, H.G., Zincir-Heywood, A.N., Heywood, M.I.: Selecting features for intrusion detection: a feature relevance analysis on kdd 99 intrusion detection datasets. In: Proceedings of the Third Annual Conference on Privacy, Security and Trust. Citeseer (2005)
16. Cho, J., Lee, C., Cho, S., Song, J.H., Lim, J., Moon, J.: A statistical model for network data analysis: Kdd cup 99data evaluation and its comparing with mit lincoln laboratory network data. Simulation Modelling Practice and Theory 18(4), 431–435 (2010)
17. Tavallaee, M., Bagheri, E., Lu, W., Ghorbani, A.-A.: A detailed analysis of the kdd cup 99 data set. In: Proceedings of the Second IEEE Symposium on Computational Intelligence for Security and Defence Applications (2009)

Detecting Stepping Stones
by Abnormal Causality Probability

Sheng Wen, Ping Li, Di Wu, Yang Xiang, and Wanlei Zhou

School of Information Technology
Deakin University
Melbourne, Australia, VIC 3125
{wsheng,pingli,wudi,yang,wanlei}@deakin.edu.au

Abstract. Locating the real source of the Internet attacks has long been an important but difficult problem to be addressed. In the real world attackers can easily hide their identities and evade punishment by relaying their attacks through a series of compromised systems or devices, called stepping stones. Currently, researchers mainly use similar features from the network traffic, such as packet timestamps and frequencies, to detect stepping stones. However, these features can be easily destroyed by attackers using evasive techniques. In addition, it is also difficult to implement an appropriate threshold of similarity which can help justify the stepping stones. In order to counter these problems, in this paper, we introduce the consistent causality probability to detect the stepping stones. We formulate the ranges of abnormal causality probabilities according to the different network conditions, and on the basis of it, we further implement two self-adaptive methods to capture stepping stones. To evaluate our proposed detection methods, we adopt theoretic analysis and empirical studies, which have demonstrated accuracy of the abnormal causality probability. Moreover, we compare of our proposed methods with previous works. The result show that our methods in this paper significantly outperform previous works in the accuracy of detection malicious stepping stones, even when evasive techniques are adopted by attackers.

Keywords: Intrusion detection, causality probability, stepping stones.

1 Introduction

Nowadays, network attacks are critical threats to the Internet. While people continue to develop different defence techniques, another important work is to identify the origins of attacks and find who is the malicious author. However, unfortunately, sophisticated attacks can adopt evasive strategies, such as stepping stones, and easily maintain their anonymity during their attacking progress [1]. Instead of using direct communication, current attacks employees a group of intermediate nodes that have been previously compromised to relay their malicious commands to the victims. The attackers can successfully construct a communication tunnel as a chain of 'stepping stones', which is actually the sequence of

G. Wang et al. (Eds.): CSS 2013, LNCS 8300, pp. 308–322, 2013.
© Springer International Publishing Switzerland 2013

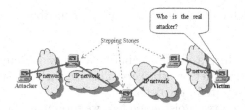

Fig. 1. Attacks using stepping stones

logins where a person login into one computer(using SSH or TelNet) and then login to another and so on. As shown in Fig. 1, if a victim is under attacks, he or she will only know the closest the intermediate node in the attack path, and the real attackers will avoid punishment. Only by disclosing the stepping stones in the network. Tracing the real attack hiding behind becomes possible. Thus, the detection the stepping stones is one of the fundamental concerns in addressing the issue of security on the Internet.

To date, there have already been some stepping stone detection systems proposed. Current stepping stone detection approaches [2–10] normally exploit traffic features to identify correlated connections. For example, IPD [11] detects stepping stones using the idea that the inter-packet delays on the correlated connections are similar. While these approaches may detect stepping stones in certain conditions, their accuracy is low and can not satisfy the detection of stepping stones in Internet environments, especially when the attackers use evasive techniques.

There are mainly two reasons for the above problem: *firstly*, those similar features which are used to detect stepping stones are easily destroyed by natural or manual disturbance from the Internet or attackers. There are packet merges, packet splits, packet losses, packet retransmissions and different packet delays during the attack commands forwarded on the Internet. The attackers may insert chaff packets into the stream, or introduce delay into the timing of the packet stream [12]. All of these can change the similar features used for detecting stepping stones. *Secondly*, it is also difficult to find an appropriate similarity threshold for the detection of stepping stones. Because of natural and man-made noise in the Internet environments, the similarity of features is not steady. While current approaches assume no packet dropped or simply use fixed parameters by experience as the threshold. The result of these methods are not accurate in the detection of stepping stones. For example, RTT(Round Trip Time) may be small in one connection, but large in another connection. Therefore, the fixed bound of RTT results in the attackers been able to avoid detection by revising by randomize the communication time.

In order to counter these problems, we introduce a normal attribute causality probability to detect stepping stones. Causality means the packet has to arrive before before it can leave a node, leading to the temporal span between any pair of packets, we presetting a certain order. The value of this attribute can not be modified by various noise and evasive techniques. On the basis of it, we can propose a robust detection method. The major contributions of this paper are list as follows:

- Firstly, we introduce a novel attribute, causality probability, which rarely changes in the Internet or attackers. This can help us significantly reduce the force positive rate in the detection.
- Secondly, based on two Poisson models, we formulate the abnormal bounds of causality probability. In addition, through the mathematical and empirical studies, we demonstrate the accuracy of the bounds of the abnormal causality probability in the evaluation.
- Moreover, we design the Abnormal Probability Detection algorithm (APD) and the Speedy Abnormal Probability Detection algorithm (SAPD) on the basis of the bounds of Abnormal Causality Probability. We compare these two methods with most current detection approaches in the experiment. The results show our proposed methods significantly outperform pervious approaches, even when evasive techniques are used.

The rest of this paper is organized as follows. In Section 2, we analyze the mathematical models of connection streams and formulas the bounds of abnormal causality probability based on two Poisson models. In Section 3, we describe the detail of two algorithms followed by the experiments in Section 4. We present related works in Section 5 and finally conclude this paper in Section 6.

2   Abnormal Causality Probability Analysis

2.1   Primer of Stepping Stone Analysis

Generally, attackers launch stepping stone attacks by constructing a chain of interactive connections on stepping stones using protocols such as Telnet or SSH. If two connections are found on the same connection chain, we consider them as a correlated connection (CC) pair. Otherwise, we consider them to be a normal connection (NC) pair. The connection which is closer to the attacker in the connection chain is called the upstream connection. The connection which is closer to the victim in the connection chain is called the downstream connection. For an interactive connections, the packets sent from an attacker (client) to a target (server) are called 'send packets', and the packets transmitted in the reverse direction are called 'echo packets'. As shown in Fig. 2, a 'send packet' arrives at the stepping stone $i - 1$, then to the stepping stone i, and continues to move until it arrives at the target. After this, the 'echo packet' is generated and sent back to the stepping stone i, and one after another until the stepping stone $i - 1$.

There is a simple causality that one packet has to arrive at a target before it leaves that node. In this paper, we define the time delay between the 'send packet' and the corresponding 'echo packet' as the Round-Trip Time (RTT) for stepping stones. To retrieve the value of RTT, we adopt the EBA algorithm [13]. This algorithm estimates the value of RTT according to previous RTTs,

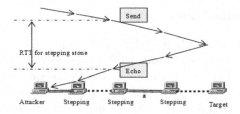

Fig. 2. Stepping stone chain between attacker and target

and then finds the 'send packet' and the corresponding 'echo packet' pair whose time-delay is the closest to the estimating value.

Definition 1 (RTT Sequence). *A RTT sequence Rtt_a is a series of RTT values in chronological order captured by the RTT retrieving algorithm on the connection a.*

Let $Rtt_a = \{Rtt_a^1(t_a^{s1}, t_a^{e1}), Rtt_a^2(t_a^{s2}, t_a^{e2}), ... Rtt_a^i(t_a^{si}, t_a^{ei})...\}$, where Rtt_a^i is the ith RTT obtained by the EBA algorithm for connection a. t_a^{si} and t_a^{ei} are the arrival epoch of the 'send packet' and the 'echo packet' of the ith RTT value on the connection a. (t_a^{si}, t_a^{ei}) is called packet pair, and $t_a^{si} = t_a^{ei} - Rtt_a^i$. For the packet pair (t_a^{si}, t_a^{ei}) on connection a, if there exists any packet pair (t_b^{sj}, t_b^{ej}) on connection b such that $(t_b^{sj}, t_b^{ej}) \subset (t_a^{si}, t_a^{ei})$ (i.e. $t_a^{si} < t_b^{sj} < t_b^{ej} < t_a^{ei}$) or $(t_a^{si}, t_a^{ei}) \subset (t_b^{sj}, t_b^{ej})$ (i.e. $t_b^{sj} < t_a^{si} < t_a^{ei} < t_b^{ej}$) , we further consider (t_a^{si}, t_a^{ei}), (t_b^{sj}, t_b^{ej}) are the causality packet pair on the connection b. In addition, for $(t_b^{sj}, t_b^{ej}) \subset (t_a^{si}, t_a^{ei})$, we have some inequalities as in

$$\begin{cases} t_a^{si} < t_b^{sj} < t_b^{sj} + Rtt_b^j < t_a^{si} + Rtt_a^i \\ t_a^{si} < t_b^{sj} < t_a^{si} + Rtt_a^i - Rtt_b^j \end{cases} \tag{1}$$

For $(t_a^{si}, t_a^{ei}) \subset (t_b^{sj}, t_b^{ej})$, we also have

$$\begin{cases} t_b^{ej} - Rtt_b^j < t_a^{ei} - Rtt_a^i < t_a^{ei} < t_b^{ej} \\ t_a^{ei} < t_b^{ej} < t_a^{ei} + (Rtt_b^j - Rtt_a^i) \end{cases} \tag{2}$$

On the basis of it, we can detive the concept of the causality probability CP_{ab} as follows,

Definition 2 (Causality Probability). *The ratio that the number of packet pairs which have causality pairs on connection b, over the number of total packet pairs of connection a.*

Actually, for the packet pair (t_a^{si}, t_a^{ei}) on connection a and the packet pair (t_b^{sj}, t_b^{ej}) on connection b, if $t_b^{s(j-1)} < t_a^{si} < t_b^{sj}(when \quad Rtt_a^{si} > Rtt_b^{sj})$ or if $t_b^{e(j-1)} < t_a^{ei} < t_b^{ej}(when \quad Rtt_a^{si} \leq Rtt_b^{sj})$, (t_b^{sj}, t_b^{ej}) will be considered as the first packet pair after (t_a^{si}, t_a^{ei}) on connection b. The causality probability for two normal connections seems random. But it is highly related to the packet frequencies and the RTT values. We will prove it in the following sections.

2.2   Modeling Connection Streams

Network streams are generally modeled as Poisson processes [14]. The famous Jackson's theorem [15], a significant development in the theory of networks of queues, assumes the packet arrivals follow the Poisson processes. To detect the stepping stones, connection streams (the packet arrivals on connections) are also presented as Poisson processes [3, 7–9]. These poisson processes used a fixed rate [3, 7–9] to generate the model. In this situation, the distribution of the packet interval follows the exponential distribution with distribution function $\lambda e^{-x\lambda}$, where λ is the expected packet arrival rate, and can be considered as $1/T$ (T is the expected packet interval, equaling the average packet interval).

In this paper, we assume every packet arrival on connection streams has a different rate $\lambda_i (i < n)$ and over time $T_i (i < n)$. On the basis of this packet interval of ith packet, we have $\lambda_i * T_i = 1$. Then, the average arrival rate is the same as the model with a fixed rate poisson distribution. The detailed process is as follows

$$\lambda = \frac{\sum_{i=1}^{n}(\lambda_i T_i)}{\sum_{i=1}^{n}(T_i)} = \frac{n}{\sum_{i=1}^{n}(T_i)} \tag{3}$$

This means the Poisson process with a fixed rate can be modeled as many Poisson distributions with varying rates, and over varying time periods [8]. As a result, connection streams can be modeled as Poisson processes with varying rates, and over varying time periods. In this situation, the distribution of every inter arrival time will follow the exponential distribution $\lambda_i e^{-x\lambda_i} (\lambda_i = 1/T_i)$.

2.3   Bounds of the Abnormal Causality Probability

Firstly, we investigate the bounds of the adnormal causality under the poisson model **with varying rate**. Let us assume normal connections a and b behave as sequences of Poisson processes. For the two RTT sequences obtained by the RTT retrieving algorithm on connection a and b during the same time duration:

$$Rtt_a = \{Rtt_a^1(t_a^{s1}, t_a^{e1}), Rtt_a^2(t_a^{s2}, t_a^{e2}), ...Rtt_a^n(t_a^{sn}, t_a^{en})\} \tag{4}$$

$$Rtt_b = \{Rtt_b^1(t_b^{s1}, t_b^{e1}), Rtt_b^2(t_b^{s2}, t_b^{e2}), ...Rtt_b^m(t_b^{sm}, t_b^{em})\} \tag{5}$$

Let the following equation exist

$$ucp(i, j) = min(\frac{1 - e^{\frac{-|Rtt_a^i - Rtt_b^j|}{bj}}}{1 - e^{\frac{-a_i}{bj}}}, 1) \tag{6}$$

wherein $(t_b^{sj}, t_b^{ej})(j < m)$ is the first packet pair on the connection b after $(t_a^{si}, t_a^{ei})(i < n)$ and $(t_b^{sj}, t_b^{ej})(j < m)$, then we can derive (proof in [16])

$$CP_{ab} \leq UVCP_{ab} = \frac{1}{n-1} \sum_{i=1}^{n-1} (ucp(i, j)) \tag{7}$$

Secondly, we examine the abnormal causality bounds under poisson model with the **fixed rate**. For the normal connections a and b, assuming they behave as Poisson processes with an equal rate of λ, then we can derive (proof in [16])

$$CP_{ab} \leq UVCP_{ab} = (1 - e^{-|\overline{Rtt_a} - \overline{Rtt_b}|\lambda})\qquad(8)$$

wherein $\overline{Rtt_a}$ and $\overline{Rtt_b}$ are the average values of RTT on the connections a and b respectively. Note that CP_{ab} should be the expected value of $P\left((t_b^{sj}, t_b^{ej}) \subset (t_a^{si}, t_a^{ei})\right)$. Since the connection a behaves as Poisson processes with rate λ, the value of a_i follows the exponential distribution.

3   Algorithm and Analysis

3.1   Abnormal Probability Detection Algorithm

According to the two causality probability bounds, we have designed two stepping stone detection algorithms. **Firstly**, based on the bounds with varied values in the poisson processes, we propose the abnormal probability detection algorithm (APD). This algorithm examines the interactive connections and can demonstrate if a connection pair is correlated within a specified monitoring duration. The duration is the time for the connection streams. In the real-time application, duration means the monitoring time for the stepping stone connections. For the same duration, the algorithm with a higher accuracy is considered to be more accurate. Larger duration means more processing and monitoring time, i.e. slow response. Therefore, for the Internet environment, this algorithm with a short duration is preferred to achieve the high rate of accuracy. When the packets arrive in a connection, APD will first calculate the value of RTT real-timely by the RTT retrieving algorithm [13]. Once a new RTT sequence Rtt_a^i is retrieved, the APD algorithm will compare with the result of each connection.

For each comparing pair, we let C_b be the connection with a larger value of RTT, and C_s be the connection with a smaller value of RTT. Since RTT of upstream is always larger than that of downstream, when RTTs in one connection are not always larger or smaller than another connection in a short duration, we consider the two connections are not a correlated connection pair. Normally, we can judge which connection is C_b or C_s by comparing the first RTT in each connection. Actually, we always look for the causality packet pair on the C_b connection. We have a variable LAST_INDEX recording the first RTT sequence index of C_b. This index appears behind the RTT sequences on C_s. When the new RTT sequence Rtt_a^i is on C_b, and if we cannot find a RTT sequence on C_s, we will set the variable LAST_INDEX with the index of the new RTT sequence. Otherwise, we will set LAST_INDEX to 0, increase the total count for the comparing connection pair, calculate $ucp(i, j)$, and check if they are the causality packet Pair. If so, we will increase the causality count. When the monitoring time expires, we calculate the CP by the ratio of causality count and total count, and the $UVCP$ by the ratio of $UVCP$ to the total count. If $CP > UVCP$, we then consider it as a correlated connection pair, otherwise it is a normal pair.

secondly, based on the bounds with fixed values in the poisson processes, we further implement the speedy abnormal probability detection algorithm. In this algorithm, the calculation of $UFCP$ deals with λ, which is the packet arrival rate for the comparing connections. It can be considered as $1/T$ (T is the expected packet inter arrival time). Since we also have the assumption that the comparing connections have the same packet arrival rate λ, how to set λ is crucial for this algorithm. In this paper, we let $\lambda = \frac{2}{(T_a + T_b)}$ (T_a and T_b is the mean packet arrival time in each comparing connections). this leads to results become more accurate.

The SAPD algorithm is similar to the APD algorithm, except that it computes the probability bound one time instead of n times (n is the number of RTT sequences on the C_b connection). Thus, the SAPD algorithm is more effective than the APD algorithm.

3.2   Analysis of the Resistance to Noise

The causality probability for correlated connections is normally high, and is rarely affected by the Internet or attackers. On the one hand, any time delay will not affect the packet arrival order on the connection chain, i.e. causality. On the other hand, the APD and SAPD algorithms are highly related to the values of RTTs obtained by the Estimation-Based (EBA) RTT retrieving algorithm [13]. This algorithm can filter imperfect internet transmission and unsymmetrical chaff packets by ignoring the packets which do not contain the corresponding 'echo or send packets'.

In fact, it is possible for attackers to evade the detection by increasing the values of UVCP and UFCP. When CP is smaller than UVCP or UFCP, a correlated connection may be categoried to a normal connection. In the previous analysis, the values of CP in correlated connection pairs are close to 1. When the values of UVCP and UFCP are close to 1, the attackers are able to evade the detection. According to the analysis in refsection2, we know that the values of UVCP and UFCP will be close to 1 when the RTT difference is larger than the packet interval. In practice, it is harder to reduce packet intervals due to the minimum packet interval time normally being controlled by OS and networks instead of attackers. It is relative easier to increase the RTT difference by adding delays. However, the delay in stepping stone attacks is usually bounded [7]. In the real world, the long time delay may cause the packets to be dropped. Furthermore, in interactive connections, there is usually a specific order according to which packets should arrive to the victim. Thus, the delay caused by earlier packets will lead to all the subsequent packets being delayed.

4   Evaluation of Our Method

4.1   Data source

Private Dataset: in this paper, we use a genuine stepping stone dataset captured from two self-built connection chains on the Internet. The connection

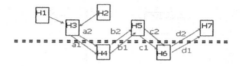

Fig. 3. Experiment topology

chains are built by SSH from host H1 and host H2, with both passing through host H3, then to hosts H4, H5, H6, and finally connecting to host H7. H4 and H6 are in the same network segment, as shown in Fig. 3. The other hosts were located in a different area of Melbourne, Australia. We started to capture the packets at host H4 when all the connection chains were built, and quickly entered the commands at the terminal of H1 and H2 concurrently for about three minutes. After that, we stopped capturing packets. This dataset includes two connection chains which are composed of four connections respectively, with every connection lasting three minutes. This dataset can be considered as the ideal data for testing stepping stone detection approaches.

Public Dataset: To prove and reinforce the experimental results by private dataset, we extracted one of the longest SSH connections respectively from four different Auckland-VIX traces [17] captured in 2008. In this dataset, every extracted connection lasts for about 30 minutes. Since the correlated connections must occur during the same time period, we altered the start packet arrival time for every extracted connection to zero. We also changed the arrival time on this connection to the time delay of the start packet of the connection.

4.2   Authenticating Abnormal Causality Probability Bounds

We already proved UVCP and UFCP are the bounds of abnormal causality probability in Theorem 1 and Theorem 2 by theory. Next we will answer the questions below related to their application in experiments.

- Is CP really smaller than UVCP or UFCP for normal connection pairs in APD and SAPD?
- Is CP really bigger than UVCP or UFCP for correlated connection pairs in APD and SAPD?
- When will the UVCP or UFCP be invalid in APD and SAPD?
- Is there any difference between APD and SAPD?
- Why use UVCP or UFCP, instead of the fixed bound parameter?

Firstly, we ran the APD and SAPD algorithm by the original private dataset with a different duration. The results of true positive and true negative are shown in Fig. 4. The true positive is the rate that correlated connection pairs are judged to be correlated connection pairs, i.e. the rate that CP is bigger than UVCP or UFCP for correlated connection pairs. The true negative is the rate that normal connection pairs are judged to be normal connection pairs, i.e. the rate that CP is smaller than UVCP or UFCP for normal connection pairs. We found that the

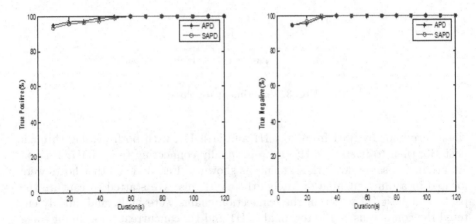

Fig. 4. True Positive and True Negative for APD and SAPD

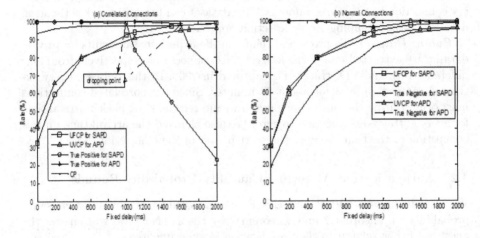

Fig. 5. The impact by different fixed delay

true positive and true negative increased with the duration time rising, in that the computing of probability is based on a large amount of data, and both the true positive and true negative for APD and SAPD can reach 100% accuracy when the duration is equal to or bigger than 60s.

From the previous analysis, we know UVCP and UFCP may be altered by increasing the RTT difference. To get a bigger RTT difference, we added fixed delay to the echo packets of the original private dataset, then ran the APD and SAPD algorithm on the dataset with the different fixed delay adding. We set the duration time to 120 seconds. The results of true positive and true negative for APD and SAPD are shown in (a) and (b) of Fig. 5 respectively. Meanwhile, we randomly selected one correlated connection pair and one connection pair. The results of CP, UVCP and UFCP for this correlated connection pair are shown in

(a) of Fig. 5, and the results of CP, UVCP and UFCP for this normal connection pais are shown in (b) of Fig. 5.

From (a) of Fig. 5, we found the CP for correlated connection pairs remained very high (more than 90%), but the UVCP and UFCP increased and was near to CP with the fixed delay (i.e. RTT difference) rising. Most importantly we found the true positive dropped significantly when the fixed delay was bigger than a certain value, which we called the dropping point. For APD, this value was around 1600ms. In addition, we found that the RTT difference on this dropping point was around 1700ms, and the mean packet intervals on the bigger RTT connection of a connection pair was around 1500ms in the dropping point. So the RTT difference was close to the mean packet interval at the dropping point for APD. For SAPD, the dropping point value was around 1000ms which was smaller than that of APD. This is because the UFCP is affected by the packet interval time on bi-directional connections. We found the mean packet interval for both connections was about 1000ms. Thus, APD and SAPD can obtain high true positive if the RTT difference is smaller than the packet interval time.

From (b) of Fig. 5, we found that the results of CP, UVCP and UFCP for normal connection pair are almost the same. UVCP or UFCP is always slightly higher than CP. Only by dynamically computing UVCP and UFCP according to the real network situation, can abnormal connections be detected with maximum likelihood. This cannot be obtained by fixed value.

From both (a) and (b) of Fig. 5, we can see that UFCP rises slightly quicker than UVCP especially when delay is large. In (a) of Fig. 5, it shows that SAPD has a smaller dropping point than APD, therefore APD is more suited to a situation where there are relative bigger delays. When a delay is small or normal, (b) of Fig. 5 shows UFCP is closer to CP for normal connection pairs. Therefore, SAPD is suited to the normal internet stream or when there are small delays.

From the above results and analysis, we can conclude that:

- CP can be 100% smaller than UVCP or UFCP for normal connection pairs in APD or SAPD when the duration is long enough.
- CP can be 100% bigger than UVCP or UFCP for correlated connection pairs in APD or SAPD when the duration is long enough.
- When the mean of the RTT difference is larger than the mean of the packet interval, the UVCP or UFCP will be invalid in APD and SAPD. Thus, it is difficult to obtain a larger mean of the RTT difference.
- SAPD is more suitable for the normal internet stream or the environment where there are small delays. APD is more suitable for the environment where there are larger delays.
- Abnormal connections can be detected by dynamically computing UVCP and UFCP according to the real network status.

4.3   Comparison with Previous Approaches

To further reinforce our approach, we implemented most of the network-based passive stepping stone detection approaches, including ON/OFF[4], IPD[6],

Table 1. Parameters of stepping stone detection approaches

Approach	Parameter	Public dataset	Private dataset
ON/OFF	T_{idle}	700ms	700ms
	δ	120ms	120ms
	γ	0.5	0.4
IPD	Window size	10	10
	δ_{cp}	0.8	0.8
	δ	0.7	0.7
DA/DMV	p_δ	3	3
DM	Δ	300ms	6s
S-III	Δ	300ms	3s
Sketching	L_{TS}	3000ms	1500ms
	ϵ	200	70
APD/SAPD	No	No	No

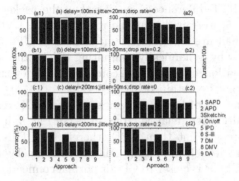

Fig. 6. Accuracy by public dataset with different durations

DA[8], DMV[10], DM[9], S-III[3], sketching[2], APD and SAPD. We will answer the below questions by comparing them with two different data sources in various scenarios.

- Which approaches can detect stepping stones with ideal stepping stone data?
- Which approaches can detect stepping stones in Internet environments?
- Which approaches can detect stepping stones in Internet environments, even if there is some disturbance of chaffs or jitters?

Since most of the approaches don't indicate the length of connection streams or how many packets they needed for detecting stepping stones, we added a duration parameter for every algorithm during the implementation. During the experiments, we found the results were affected by the value of parameters from every approach. To be fair, we attempted to use many values for every parameter, with the best results used in the following experiments. The values of parameters for every approach in our experiments are listed in Table 5.

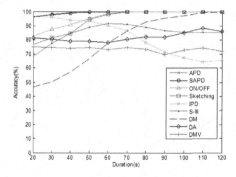

Fig. 7. Accuracy by private dataset with different durations

Firstly, we ran every approach by 4 groups of public datasets with a long duration (600s) and short duration (100s) respectively. The results of accuracy are shown in Fig. 6. From (a1), and for a longer duration, if the connection streams are perfect, i.e. the delays and jitters are small, and there is no packet drop, nearly all of them can reach 100% accuracy except for IPD, because some of the inter-packet delay of the public dataset is in the order of 1s to 10s, which may make IPD fail achieve some of thresh points. However with delays, jitters and the drop rate rising, only SAPD and APD maintain nearly 100% accuracy.

By comparing results between group a and b, group c and d, we found ON/OFF approaches are only minutely affected by packet drops. But the accuracy of S-III, DM, DMV and DA drops significantly when there are packet drops, since these approaches assume no packet having been dropped.

Through the comparison of results between group a and c, and group b and d, we found ON/OFF approaches were affected significantly by delay and jitters. Since δ parameter of ON/OFF was affected by jitters, when we used a bigger value for this parameter, we found ON/OFF still achieved high accuracy. Although in practice, the magnitude of jitters for different streams may be different, it's impossible to select and foresee the appropriate value. Meanwhile, we found S-III and DM was hardly affected by delay. This is accordance with the results from experiments conducted in [3].

From Fig. 6, we can also see when the duration is long, with the sketching approach reaching high accuracy, even if there are some delays, jitters and drops. But when the duration is short, the accuracy becomes low. This is because the succinct sketches inevitably hide some information of the packet streams when the duration is short.

Then we ran every approach using a private dataset with a different duration and achieved an accuracy as shown in Fig. 7. We can see the APD and SAPD maintains more than 95% accuracy when the duration is bigger than 20s. Sketching and ON/OFF can reach 95% accuracy when duration is bigger than 60s. S-I also can reach 95% accuracy when duration is bigger than 110s, but this is based on an abnormally big value of a max delay parameter which loses the meaning of its definitions. In practice, it's unlikely to select such a big value.

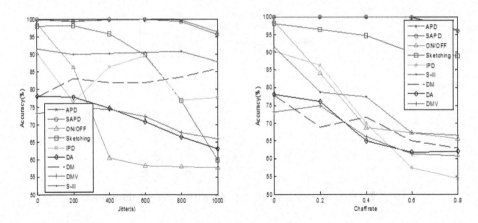

Fig. 8. Accuracy by private dataset with different chaff rates and jitters

Other approaches maintain lower or much lower accuracy than 90%. These results are nearly consistent with the result from the public dataset. In the public dataset, the sketching needs a long duration to achieve high accuracy.

Finally we ran every approach using the private dataset with 60s duration and a different chaff rate and jitters. The results of accuracy are shown in Fig. 8. From (a) of Fig. 8, we can see APD and SAPD are hardly affected by chaffs, and sketching is only slightly affected by chaffs, while others are affected a lot by chaffs. By using the public dataset results, we know ON/OFF is hardly affected by packet drops, but our results show ON/OFF is significantly affected by chaffs. This is due to the difference of packet drops and chaffs. Besides, the experimental results in [3] show that DM and S-III can resist chaffs, which is contrary to our results. In [3], they only added chaffs downstream. In our experiments, chaffs were added to both the upstream and the downstream. We can assume no packet dropped by adding chaffs downstream. This means DM and S-III [3] still maintain a high accuracy with chaffs.

(b) of Fig. 8 shows APD, SAPD, DM and S-III are rarely affected by jitters, which is consistent with the results from the public dataset.

From the above results and analysis, we can conclude that:
- Nearly all the of approaches can reach 100% accuracy for detecting stepping stones with ideal stepping stone data if the duration is long enough.
- APD, SAPD, sketching and ON/OFF can almost reach 100% accuracy in normal Internet environments if the data lasts long enough.
- APD and SAPD can have more than 95% accuracy in short duration even if there is some disturbance of chaffs or jitters.

5   Related Works

Current stepping stone detection methods can be classified into active methods [18, 19] and passive methods [11, 20–22]. *Firstly*, Staniford-Chen and Heberlein [1] first identified the problem of stepping stones and proposed an approach to detect stepping stone using similarity of packet contents on correlated connections. However it cannot be used to detect encrypted connections. *Secondly*, The "ON/OFF" approach proposed by Zhang and Paxson [4] is the first method based on similarity of timing, which can trace stepping stones even if traffic is encrypted. This approach comes from the observation that two connections are in the same connection chain if their OFF periods coincide. This approach is simple and effective, but it contains many fixed parameters to maintain the similarity. *Thirdly*, the deviation approach proposed by Yoda and Etoh [5] relies on packets flowing through a connection. If two connections belong to the same connection chain, the total size of transferred bytes should grow at a similar rate. Noticeably, this approach only works if the packet sizes are not modified at the stepping stones. *Fourthly*, based on the observation that Inter-Packet Delays (IPD) are preserved across many router hops and stepping stones, Wang et al. [6] proposed the "IPD" approach. However, this feature is hard to keep consistent in the Internet. *Finally*, the multi-scale approach proposed by Donoho et al. [7] uses the similarity of character count to detect stepping stones. This method has a high packet loss rate.

6   Conclusion

In this paper, we introduced a new attribute, causality probability, to detect stepping stones. We also examine the bounds of abnormal causality probability. Both of the theoretic proof and the experiments demonstrate that the proposed bounds are accurate. On the basis of it, we compared our algorithms with previous methods. The results show that our algorithms outperform previous methods in detecting stepping stones, even when evasion techniques were used.

References

1. Staniford-Chen, S., Heberlein, L.: Holding intruders accountable on the internet. In: Proceedings of the IEEE Symposium on Security and Privacy, pp. 39–49 (1995)
2. Coskun, B., Memon, N.: Online sketching of network flows for real-time stepping-stone detection. In: Annual Computer Security Applications Conference, ACSAC 2009, pp. 473–483 (2009)
3. Zhang, L., Persaud, A., Johnson, A., Guan, Y.: Stepping-stone attack attribution in non-cooperative ip networks. In: The 25th IEEE International Performance Computing and Conference (2006)
4. Zhang, Y., Paxson, V.: Detecting stepping stones. In: Proceedings of the 9th Conference on USENIX Security Symposium, Berkeley, CA, USA, vol. 9, p. 13 (2000)
5. Yoda, K., Etoh, H.: Finding a connection chain for tracing intruders. In: Cuppens, F., Deswarte, Y., Gollmann, D., Waidner, M. (eds.) ESORICS 2000. LNCS, vol. 1895, pp. 191–205. Springer, Heidelberg (2000)
6. Wang, X., Reeves, D.S., Wu, S.F.: Inter-packet delay based correlation for tracing encrypted connections through stepping stones. In: Gollmann, D., Karjoth, G., Waidner, M. (eds.) ESORICS 2002. LNCS, vol. 2502, pp. 244–263. Springer, Heidelberg (2002)

7. Donoho, D.L., Flesia, A.G., Shankar, U., Paxson, V., Coit, J., Staniford, S.: Multiscale stepping-stone detection: Detecting pairs of jittered interactive streams by exploiting maximum tolerable delay. In: Wespi, A., Vigna, G., Deri, L. (eds.) RAID 2002. LNCS, vol. 2516, pp. 17–35. Springer, Heidelberg (2002)
8. Blum, A., Song, D., Venkataraman, S.: Detection of interactive stepping stones: Algorithms and confidence bounds. In: Jonsson, E., Valdes, A., Almgren, M. (eds.) RAID 2004. LNCS, vol. 3224, pp. 258–277. Springer, Heidelberg (2004)
9. He, T., Tong, L.: A signal processing perspective to stepping-stone detection. In: 40th Annual Conference on Information Sciences and Systems 2006, pp. 687–692 (2006)
10. He, T., Member, S., Tong, L.: Detecting encrypted stepping-stone connections. IEEE Trans. on Signal Processing 55, 1612–1623 (2007)
11. Wang, X., Reeves, D.S.: Robust correlation of encrypted attack traffic through stepping stones by manipulation of interpacket delays. In: Proceedings of the 10th ACM Conference on Computer and Communications Security, CCS 2003, New York, USA, pp. 20–29 (2003)
12. Padhye, J.D., Wright, M.: Stepping-stone network attack kit (sneak) for evading timing-based detection methods under the cloak of constant rate multimedia streams. Master's thesis, Faculty of the Graduate School, The University of Texas at Arlington (2008)
13. Li, P., Zhou, W., Wang, Y.: Getting the real-time precise round-trip time for stepping stone detection. In: 2010 4th International Conference on Network and System Security (NSS), pp. 377–382 (2010)
14. Wikipedia: Queueing theory. Technical report, Wikipedia (2013)
15. Wikipedia: Jackson network. Technical report, Wikipedia (2013)
16. Li, P.: Detect Stepping Stones in Internet Environments. PhD thesis, School of Information Technology, Deakin University (2011)
17. WAND Network Research Group, Wits: Auckland ix trace file. Technical report, WAND (2008)
18. Tae, H., Kim, H.L., Seo, Y.M., Choe, G., Min, S.L., Kim, C.S.: Caller identification system in the internet environment. In: Proceedings of 4th USENIX Security Symposium, pp. 69–78 (1993)
19. Snapp, S.R., Brentano, J., Dias, G.V., Goan, T.L., Heberlein, L.T., Lin Ho, C., Levitt, K.N., Mukherjee, B., Smaha, S.E., Grance, T., Teal, D.M., Mansur, D.: Dids (distributed intrusion detection system) - motivation, architecture, and an early prototype. In: Proceedings of the 14th National Computer Security Conference, pp. 167–176 (1991)
20. Peng, P., Ning, P., Reeves, D.: On the secrecy of timing-based active watermarking trace-back techniques. In: 2006 IEEE Symposium on Security and Privacy, pp. 334–349 (2006)
21. Peng, P., Ning, P., Reeves, D.S., Wang, X.: Active timing-based correlation of perturbed traffic flows with chaff packets. In: Proceedings of the Second International Workshop on Security in Distributed Computing Systems (SDCS) (ICDCSW 2005), Washington, DC, USA, vol. 2, pp. 107–113 (2005)
22. Wang, X., Wang, X., Reeves, D.S., Reeves, D.S., Wu, S.F., Wu, S.F., Yuill, J., Yuill, J.: Sleepy watermark tracing: An active network-based intrusion response framework. In: Proc. of the 16th International Information Security Conference, pp. 369–384 (2001)

Algebra-Based Behavior Identification of Trojan Horse

Aihua Peng[1], Lansheng Han[1,*], Yanan Yu[1], Nan Du[1], and Mingquan Li[2]

[1] Lab of Information Security, Department of Computer Science and Technology,
Huazhong University of Science and Technology, Wuhan, 430074, China
[2] Academy of Satellite Application, Beijing, 100086, China

Abstract. Compared with the rapidly developing technology of Trojan hiding, hooking, stealing and anti-removing, the detection and recognition technology grows relatively slowly. Signature code detecting technology requiring mass storage and unable to predict new Trojan, heuristic scanning with high misreporting rate and false rate, this article is proposing algebra to describe and detect the behavior of the Trojan. Specifically, let the node of the lattice denote the status of the Trojan, and the operations in the lattice denote the combination of the behavior of Trojans. Thus, the lattice model supplies a quantitative way to identify the Trojan. Boolean Algebra (BA) and Concept Lattice (CL) are two models that are extended on model construction, identification method, and application. Finally, we present theoretical support and sample implementation process to test the theory and the test result is positive so far.

Keywords: Trojan behavior definition, Action danger, Boolean algebra, Concept lattice.

1 Introduction

Considering Trojan's diversity and quantity, Trojan detection technology is developing relatively slowly. The most popular identification method- signature detection- obviously has shortcomings: (1) only recognizes known Trojans; (2) relies on a huge signature database [1]. Facing such a dilemma, security experts come up with integrity detection, heuristic scanning and semantics and behavior detecting technique [2,3]. However, limited by ambiguity of the objects characteristics and evidences, the fault rate and fail rate performance is not good.

Trojan executes invasive code to finish some designed tasks. For instance, some common attacking tasks are trapping, hooking, remote thread injecting and running exploit, etc. [4,5]. However, those code segments can also be found in many normal programs [6] so that one-dimensional API sequence is not reliable as judgmental evidence. It's necessary to expose the specificity of Trojan.

Fortunately, task relation and dependency can present this specificity. At the same time, sensitivities of each task is also valuable for us to concern and make

---

* Corresponding author.

G. Wang et al. (Eds.): CSS 2013, LNCS 8300, pp. 323–337, 2013.
© Springer International Publishing Switzerland 2013

use of [7]. Therefore, Firstly, we define every individual task as Action Point, a set of tasks as Action Point Set and the sensitivity of Action Point Set as Dangerous Level. Then we use algebra model to draw their relationship and compute how dangerous a certain program is. The Dangerous Level, finally computed out, is what we rely on to judge a program's illegality [8].

Boolean Algebra (BA), a normative algebraic system, describes relationship of nodes. The calculable relationship among elements is a good way to present actual relations of tasks in a program. Besides, since Boolean Algebra has a strictly logical hierarchy, simple and clear algorithms can be given. Thus, mapping theory ensures the correspondence between program tasks and its dangerousness, and the boundary of Trojan becomes clear.

Nevertheless, the strictness of Boolean Algebra reduces its practicability. As a result, we can take advantage of Concept Lattice (CL) with Formal Concept Analysis (FCA) to make up this shortfall [10]. Different from things mentioned in BA, the mathematical sensitivity is Danger Level Vector (DLV). Each point in this model is a formal concept set and the underlying entrance is a single-atom set. A running program in the system is moving upward from the entrance, and apparently along its paths. The accessible paths can describe the current state. The discriminant algorithm makes use of programs paths and heights to compute their DLV by Compound Interest Method (CIM). Finally the compassion between DLV and Dangerous Threshold (DT) will distinguish Trojan from normal programs accurately.

We consider such a system as a Trojan Behavior Definition System (TBDS) which contains both modeling and discriminant. When introducing the system of Concept Lattice, an example named TBDS[N7] is given to assist readers in observing and understanding modeling processes. Following the normalized and detailed procedures, designers can build their own TBDS.

Further, The same theoretical framework support both BA model and CL model, but FCA provides a reliable flexibility and effectiveness, and 'user-customizable' as well. In other words, CL model is the developed version of BA. Relationship and difference between model BA and CL are studied particularly in a later section, comparing at a macro level.

2   Trojan Behavior Model Based on Boolean Algebra

Since the boundary of Trojan is still unknown, mathematic modeling is a potential solution to define and normalize the behavior of Trojan. Meanwhile, detail examples will be presented to support modeling method.

We here choose Boolean Algebra as the model foundation, which simplifies the implementing process and minimizes computer resource expense.

2.1   Trojan Behavior Abstraction

Compared with popular malwares, Trojan is the one with a unique code which shows its distinctive characteristics- orderly modifying particular files. From invasion, hiding, execution to successful stealing, Trojan finishes attacking by sequencing and validating some necessary actions which have exact risk levels.

Definition 1 (Monitor Camera) *is a basic monitoring program, monitoring a certain type of resource and whether a related task is finished. Each monitor camera has three statuses:*
    White: 'close';
    Green: 'normal';
    Red: 'alarming'.
'Close' status means that this Monitor Camera is not assigned to any resources yet. Whenever a Monitor Camera turns red, the program must have finished its task.

Definition 2 (Monitor) *has one or several Monitor Cameras. Every Monitor has 4 statuses: 'safe', 'normal', 'dangerous' and 'invalid'. Firstly, only when its Monitor Cameras turn red, the Monitor turns to 'dangerous'. On the contrary, if all cameras are running normally, the monitor is deemed 'safe'. Moreover, while all cameras are closed or there is no camera at all, we regard the Monitor 'invalid'.*

Definition 3 (Monitor Set) *is a set of Monitors, necessarily amounted up to 2^n.*

Definition 4 (Staff Monitor) *has only one Monitor Camera which directly calls the detecting function to catch skeptical behaviors.*

Definition 5 (Manager Monitor) *monitors Staff Monitors or other Manager Monitors.*

Definition 6 (Action) *is a description of a programs task. Whenever a Monitor Camera turns red, its corresponding Action happens.*

Definition 7 (Action Set (AS)) *is a set of Actions. Every program has an AS (as a label) which is initialized to null at the very beginning and updates dynamically over the program's running. Once a Monitor Camera turns red, the related Action will be added into AS and the Monitor will become 'dangerous'.*

Staff Monitor's AS is defined as Single-element Action Set while Manager Monitor's AS is called Multi-element Action Set.

Property 1 (Expandability) *With increasing need of a Monitor's maximum camera number, from n to $n + 1$, the element number of Monitor Set would update from 2^n to 2^{n+1} which covers both old and new behaviors.*

2.2 Modeling Method

As tasks vary in sensitivity, Actions differ in risk level. Obtained by Monitor Cameras, dynamic data measures the complexity of a program's AS. The system is vigilant to Multi-element Action Set. Once its size reaches a threshold, the program is considered to be a Trojan.

Property 2 (Partition of Action Set) *If the number of Monitor Cameras is limited, there exists a partition π of the Action Set. The number of partitions is noted as α and each block an atom (the same concept in Boolean Algebra).*

Explanation 1 *The property above lays emphasis on task independency. This property's sufficiency is apparent while its necessity must be detailed from a practical standpoint.*

No system is capable of setting a completed Monitor Set that sweeps up all possible Actions, under the circumstance that old Trojans are mutating while new Trojans are being borned. In this case, expansibility is absolutely necessary.

A modeling procedure and an example are shown as below:

Procedure 1 (Constructing Boolean Algebra Model)
- *Form an infinite maximum AS -$\overline{AS\langle MAX \rangle}$- to describe all Trojans, in which Actions are equidistant with API.*
- *Remove unknown and unnecessary parts.*
- *Divide $AS\langle MAX \rangle$ with the symbol '|' and rename each block.*
- *Consider every block as an atom of Boolean Algebra, summed to α. The total number of Boolean Algebra elements is 2^n.*

Example 1 $\overline{AS\langle MAX \rangle} = \{modify\ startup\ items,\ hijack\ startup\ files,\ intercept\ users\ information,\ sniffing\ the\ network\ packets...\}$.

$AS\langle MAX \rangle = \{modify\ startup\ files,\ hijack\ startup\ files\ |hide\ files|\ improperly\ use\ ports,\ over\ transmit\ data\ |\ intercept\ user\ information\}$.

$\pi = \{Auto\ start,\ hide,\ communicate\ in\ danger,\ steal\}$.

Set $a = Auto\ start$, $b = hide$, $c = communicate\ in\ danger$, $d = steal$, so the 2^4-element Boolean Algebra is established as below.

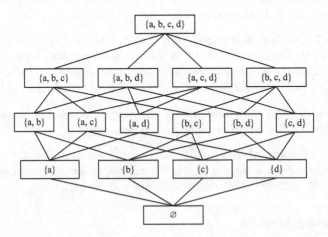

Fig. 1. 4-atom Boolean Algebra

In summary, Boolean Algebra helps us abstract all Trojans' possible behaviors into AS, providing a framework for distinguishing Trojans from the other programs.

3   The Trojan Discrimination Based on Boolean Algebra

Definition 8 (Dangerous Level (DL)) *is an attribute of Action Set. The integers in* $[1, \alpha]$ *define DL according to an* α-*atom Boolean Algebra, which equals to the total number of Actions in the Action Set.*

Definition 9 (Dangerous Threshold (DT)) *is used to be compared with DL. DT in an* α-*atom Boolean Algebra is denoted by* $\sqrt{\alpha}$.

The definition above is simple and intuitive in order to dumb down the understanding difficulty of this system. In fact, users can add some parameters and utilize complex algorithms as required. As a result, a sophisticated model structure would be introduced in next section.

Example 2 *Following last example,* $\sqrt{\alpha} = \sqrt{4} = 2$. *A certain program starts with the initial Action Set* -$\{c\}$. *When the Action Set expands to* $\{a, c, d\}$, *its Danger Level grows to 3 which surpass* $\sqrt{\alpha}$. *So the program is judged a Trojan.*

In section 2 and 3, the simplified Boolean Algebra model and discriminant algorithm help easily implement a system. However, there are three problem involved:

- There is no supplemental method to deal with a naturally small-scale problem as property 2 lowers scale.
- The setting of Danger Level is too simple.
- The setting of $\sqrt{\alpha}$ as Danger Threshold is to be improved.

Therefore, to deal with the uncertainty, we need to find another model even though storage requirement and computing time increase.

4   Trojan Behavior Model Based on Concept Lattice

Boolean Algebra model provides us an access to judge the Trojan boundary while in this section, we will construct a new model based on Formal Concept Analysis and Concept Lattice. Here we name this system as Trojan Behavior Definition System (TBDS). Example TBDS [6] is valid to embody the model.

4.1   Trojan Behavior Abstraction

Tasks will be assigned to each Monitor Camera by designer and here we call this property 'user-customizable'. Some new concepts are presented below.

Definition 10 (Action Point (AP)) *is synonymous with Action.*

Definition 11 (Action Point Set (APS)) *is a set of APs.*

Definition 12 (Behavior Point (BP)) *is APs' highest ancestor in a block of APS, which is applicable to multi-parent-child relationship. It can be generated* *through procedure retry of modeling Boolean Algebra. With the property of 'user-customizable', users can design BPs and parent-child relationships of APs themselves, obeying principle that all BPs are equidistant with API.*

Definition 13 (Child Behavior Point (CBP)) *intermediates between AP and BP which is an inheritance of AP or CBP. The minimum CBP is to be an AP.*

Definition 14 (Behavior Point Set (BPS)) *is a set of BPs which labels dynamic update of the system, substituting for APS in Boolean Algebra model. Besides, the maximum BPS lays the groundwork for modeling.*

Example 3 $APS\langle MAX \rangle = \{$ *Modify startup items, Modify startup shells, Register system services, intercept keyboard input* $\}$. *Teasing out parent-child relationships, it can be generated that* $BPS\langle MAX \rangle = \{$ *Auto start, Hide, Prepare before entering into force* $\}$.

Apparently, *'Modify startup items'* and *'Modify startup shells'* are sons of *'Auto startup'* while *'Register system services'* roots in *'Hide'* and *'Intercept keyboard input'* roots in *'Prepare before entering into force'*.

Definition 15 (Dangerous Level (DL)) *is a property of AP valued by integer in $[1, \beta]$ while the upper bound β is 'user-customizable'.*

Definition 16 (Dangerous Level Vector (DLV)) *is a property of BP which has a dimensionality β with Boolean type vectors. When vector i and $i + 1$ are both valued true, DL of vector $i + 1$ exceeds DL of vector i.*

4.2   Part 1 of TBDS [N7]

Procedure 2 (Generating Parent-Child Relation)
- *Choose α tasks and distribute a Monitor Camera to each task. All these α tasks belong to $APS\langle MAX \rangle$.*
- *Determine each element's Dangerous Level in $APS\langle MAX \rangle$.*
- *Transfer APS to BPS through Property 2, which is also applicable to transfer $APS\langle MAX \rangle$ to $BPS\langle MAX \rangle$*

Example 4 (TBDS [N7]-I.)
a) *TBDS [N7] concerns 17 tasks. $APS\langle MAX \rangle = \{$ Modify startup items, Modify startup shells, Hijack images, Register systems services, Auto execute root directories, Hijack DLL (Dynamic Link Library), Inject remote threads, Insert Trojan processes into system directories, Hide Trojan files, Reuse ports, Recall ports, Over transmit data, Connect upper level protocols, Auto screen shot, Intercept keyboard input, Search files, Sniffing network data $\}$.*
b) *TBDS [N7] determines each AP's DL by the table 1, based on project experience.*
c) *Transfer $APS\langle MAX \rangle$ to $BPS\langle MAX \rangle$ by a two-tier parent-child relation. $BPS\langle MAX \rangle = \{$ Auto start, Hide, Prepare for entering into force, Communicate in danger $\}$.*

Table 1. AP-DL Correspondence

Modify startup items	2
Modify startup shells	3
Hijack images	5
Register systems services	1
Auto execute root directories	4
Hijack DLL	6
Inject remote threads	5
Insert Trojan processes into system directories	4
Hide Trojan files	3
Reuse ports	9
Recall ports	8
Over transmit data	6
Connect upper level protocols	4
Auto screen shot	8
Intercept keyboard input	7
Search files	3
Sniffing network data	6

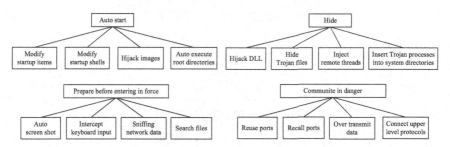

Fig. 2. Hierarchical Structure.

4.3 Formal Concept Analysis and Concept Lattice

Formal Concept Analysis (FCA) described by Rudolf Wille is continued to use in this section where concept is formalized as a two-tuples of an object set and an attribute set.

Definition 17 (Formal Context) *is such a triple* (G, M, I) *where **Object Set (OS)** G is a set of objects, **Attribution Set (AS)** M is a set of all objects' properties and **Relation** $I = \{(a, b) \mid object\ a\ has\ property\ b, a \in G, b \in M\}$. I is Boolean.*

Example 5
$$G = \{a, b, c, d\}, M = \{1, 2, 3, 4, 5\}$$

Definition 18 (Common Object Set (COS)) $\forall B \subseteq M, B' = \{g \in G | (g, m) \in I, \forall m \in B\}$ *and we consider* B' *as a COS.*

Definition 19 (Common Attribution Set (CAS)) $\forall A \subseteq G, A' = \{m \in M | (g, m) \in I, \forall g \in A\}$ *and we consider* A' *as a CAS.*

Table 2. A Formal Context Case

	1	2	3	4	5	6	7	8	9
a	1	1	1	1	0	0	0	0	0
b	1	0	1	1	1	0	0	0	0
c	0	1	0	0	1	0	1	1	0
d	0	0	0	0	0	1	1	0	1

Definition 20 (Formal Concept (FC)) *is a two-tuples (A, B) while $A \in G$, $B \in M, A' = B, B' = A, (A, B) \in I$.*

Definition 21 (Order) *Given two Formal Concepts (A, B) and (C, D) in Formal Context (G, M, I) and the Order relationship described by $\leq$:*

$$(A, B) \leq (C, D) \Leftrightarrow A \subseteq C \text{ or } B \subseteq D \tag{1}$$

Definition 22 (Concept Lattice (CL)) *$(G \times M, \leq)$, is similar to Lattice. Its binary operation can be instantiated:*

$$(A, B) \wedge (C, D) = (A \cap C, (B \cap D)'') \tag{2}$$

$$(A, B) \vee (C, D) = ((A \cap C)'', B \cap D) \tag{3}$$

Example 6

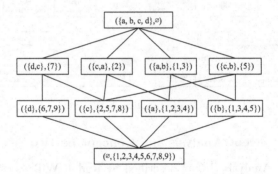

Fig. 3. Concept Lattice of Table 2.

4.4   Generating Formal Context and TBDS [N7]-II

Procedure 3 (Generating Formal Context)
- *Set Object Set $G = BPS\langle MAX \rangle$.*
- *Set the largest Dangerous Level- $DL\langle MAX \rangle = n$ and the dimension of Danger Level Vector $\beta = n$. Attribution Set $M = \{1, 2 \ldots \beta\} = \{1, 2, 3 \ldots n\}$.*
- *Based on Algorithm 1 detailed below, transmit AP's DL upward to generate BP's DLV.*

```
Algorithm 1 Computing DLV of BP
```
{Assuming $BPS\langle MAX \rangle = \{bp_1 \ldots bp_s \ldots bp_\beta\}$, $APS\langle MAX \rangle = \{ap_1, ap_2 \ldots ap_i \ldots ap_\alpha\}$, Noting DLV of bp_s as $D^{bp_s} = (d_1^{bp_s}, d_2^{bp_s} \ldots, d_9^{bp_s})$, DL of ap_i as d^{ap_i}};

```
var s : 1..β; t : 1..9;
begin
    s := 1;
    repeat
      value = d^{ap_i};
      t := 1
      repeat
        if (d_t^{bp_s} has been valued) d_t^{bp_s} = false, d_{t+1}^{bp_s} = true;
        else d_{Value}^{bp_s} = true;
      until t = 9
    until s = β
end.
```

return each $I_{st} = d_t^{bp_s}$; // I is a Concept Context

Example 7 (TBDS [N7]-II)

d) Set $G = BPS\langle MAX\rangle = \{$Auto start, Hide, Prepare before entering in force, Communicate in danger$\}$

e) $DL\langle MAX\rangle = 9, \beta = n$ and $M = \{1, 2 \ldots \beta\} = \{1, 2, 3 \ldots 9\}$.

f) Formal Context is obtained as shown in Table 3.

Table 3. Formal Context of TBDS [N7]

	1	2	3	4	5	6	7	8	9
Auto start	1	1	1	1	1	0	0	0	0
Hide	0	0	1	1	1	1	0	0	0
Prepare	0	0	1	0	0	1	1	1	0
Communicate	0	0	0	1	0	1	0	1	1

Table 3 tells that 'Communicate in danger' is more dangerous than 'Auto start' by true components' positions of Dangerous Level Vector. Moreover, it's obviously reasonable that Algorithm 1 transfers two Aps to one AP by right shift.

Thus far, all preparation work for establishing Concept Lattice is finished. Table 3 can directly construct Concept Lattice of TBDS [N7] as diagram 6 shows.

5   Trojan Behavior Discriminant Based on Concept Lattice

Supported by the largest APS and BPS, model in last chapter defines a framework of Trojan behavior. However, each BPS in a program is only a subset of the largest BPS. Hence, how dangerous a program is depends on its Dangerous Level Vector which illustrates how high the program stands in this model.

Definition 23 (Dangerous Value (DV).) is an attribution of BPS which is transformed from DLV. The method of computing DLV is based on Compound Internet Method (CIM) which will be detailed later on.

Definition 24 (Dangerous Threshold (DT).) *is the maximum tolerance of DV in a system.*

Algorithm 2 Obtaining DV by Compound Interest Method

{Assuming $BPS = \{bp_1, bp_2 \ldots bp_x\}$, $|DLV| = n$. the ith component of Sum is $Sum.i$};

var flag, DL : Int ;// flag is for marking right shift overflow of Sum;

  Sum : Vector;

Begin

  $Sum = \{0, 0 \ldots 0\}$; DL=0; Flag=0;

  i := 1;

  repeat

    Read(DLV of bp_i); $Sum = Sum \oplus DLV$;

    if($Sum.n = 1$) then flag++;

    $Sum.0 = 0$; $Sum.(i+1) = Sum.i$; i++;

  until i := x

  j := 1;

  repeat

    if $Sum.j = 1$, then DL+=j

  until j = n

End

Procedure 4 (Discriminant)

- *Obtain BPS of a program that is being tested from Procedure 2 and Procedure 3.*
- *Use the same dimension of DLV form the DLV in TBDS [N7].*
- *Set DT.*
- *Use Algorithm 2 to transform DLV to DV, and then compare it with DT.*

Example 8 (TBDS [N7]-III) *Program p_x is being tested. Its APS = {Modify startup shells, Hijack DLL, Inject remote threads, Intercept keyboard input} and BPS = {Auto start, Hide, Prepare before entering in force} are obtained. Then DLV of each BPS can be computed out step by step as below.*

$$D^{bp_1} = (0, 0, 1, 0, 0, 0, 0, 0, 0)$$
$$D^{bp_2} = (0, 0, 0, 0, 1, 1, 0, 0, 0)$$
$$D^{bp_3} = (0, 0, 0, 0, 0, 0, 0, 1, 0, 0)$$

Then transform DLV of example TBDS [N7] into DV following procedures listed below.

  $Sum_1 = D^{bp_1} = (0, 0, 1, 0, 0, 0, 0, 0, 0)$, right shift to $Sum_1' = (0, 0, 0, 1, 0, 0, 0, 0, 0)$

  $Sum_2 = Sum_1 + D^{bp_2} = (0, 0, 0, 1, 1, 1, 0, 0, 0)$, right shift to $Sum_2' = (0, 0, 0, 0, 1, 1, 1, 0, 0)$

  $Sum_3 = Sum_2' + D^{bp_3} = (0, 0, 0, 0, 1, 1, 0, 1, 0)$, right shift to $Sum_3' = (0, 0, 0, 0, 0, 1, 1, 0, 1)$

In Sum_3' we can see that position 6, 7 and 9 are valued true. Add them up and obtain DV = 6+ 7+ 9= 22.

DT in TBDS [N7] is 20, less than DV.

Through the comparison of DV and DT, we can easily judge program p_x to be a Trojan.

As long as the model has been established, processes for testing and identifying would be executed automatically by TBDS. The only job for a designer is to customize DT.

6   Equivalence, Expandability and Illustration of Models

6.1   From Boolean Algebra to Lattice

Similar characteristics in BA and CL (such as Action and Action Point and Behavior Set and Partition) show that transformation from BA to CL is achievable by inserting or deleting elements. Algorithm for this transformation, here called Algorithm BA-CL, can be constructed at the preset that we consider the normative Boolean Algebra as a formally higher structure.

Algorithm 3 Model Transformation

```
{Assuming C is a Concept Lattice, and it has n levels and m
elements in each level}
var i: 1...n; j: 1..m;
begin
  i := 1;
  repeat
    j := 1;
      repeat
        If (Action Set Element i, Element j doesn't exist in the
        next layer)
        {
          Add it to the next layer;
          Add corresponded father-child relationship to the next
          layer;
        }
      until j := m
    until i := n
  end
```

6.2   Equivalence

The equivalence between Concept Lattice model and Boolean Algebra model can be tested through Algorithm BA-CL.

Definition 25 (Pseudo-equivalence.) *Boolean Algebra Model and BA model and CL model are of pseudo-equivalence when and only when they can be transformed through Algorithm 3, meaning that:*

The two models are equivalent in BP level and element numbers in both BPSs are equal.

The two models are not equivalent in AP level even though their Action Point Sets are of the same size. Algorithm 3 is unable to reach AP and parent-child relationship. In other words, AP and BP are superficially the same but essentially different.

Real-equivalence. Boolean Algebra Model and Concept Lattice Model are of real-equivalence when and only when they are equivalent in terms of both BP and AP.

Real-equivalence reveals the inner relationship between BA model and CL model and illustrates why the two models have same framework.

In data structure, non-sparse Concept Lattices are more likely to choose Boolean Algebra in structure storage (with several points invalid) and traverse.

6.3 'User-Customizable'

'User-customizable' mentioned before can be concluded into 3 parts. We here focus on Concept Lattice model to illustrate.

a) Monitor Camera and Action Point lay on the bottom of the model, but how low they actual are is up to system designer. Monitor Camera can be customed as posets monitoring APIs or be distributed to monitor abstract resources.

   Example 9 *Designer can define an AP as a successful call of function Windows. Screen, Print().*

b) Father-child relationship between AS and BS is 'user-customizable'. Once this relationship is designed, foundations of the whole model are constructed.

   Example 10 *A father-child relationship which is nearer to API than it in TBDS [N7] is shown in Diagram 7 below.*

Fl_FindNextFile is a file Monitor Camera, monitoring the call of function *FindNextFile()*, whose Boolean value is decided by whether the program executes the kind of function like *FindNextFile()*. Similarly, Sl_CapCrtScrn is a screen Monitor Camera, detecting whether the program calls functions like *CaptureCurrentScreen()* or of the same type. Pl_SendPortNum is responsible for programs' action of sending port number as a port Monitor Chip, monitoring the call of functions like *SendPortNum()* or of the same type.

Every CBP of FL_SearchFile sums up many monitoring methods including F1_FindNextFile and F1_FindFileById shown in Diagram 7 above. And SearchFile concludes CBPs which are not in Monitor FL.

CBPs of SearchFile, along with those CBPs related to Trojan's entering in force, can be concluded upward to BP of 'Prepare before entering in force'.

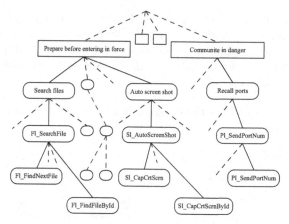

Fig. 4. Multiple Father-child Relationships

c) AP's DL and system's DT are 'user-customizable' and this property is up to the system's objectives.
Here are 2 suggestions for defining AP's DL.
  • Collect thousands of Trojans and analyze all possible APs. Then value them in ordered integer from 1 to n while the order is produced upon the Trojans' popularity and importance. For example, if Action 'Recall ports' is labeled by 'dangerous', the specific Monitor Camera will be used to monitor these Trojan samples and calculate the rate of Monitor Camera's alarming. After the rate data are obtained, those corresponded Actions will be ranked in descending order.
  • Determine the scale (n) of maximum ABS. Set n to DL of the admittedly most dangerous AP as a standard and compare all other APs to it and then all APs can be valued in the dangerous range of Trojan behaviors.
d) Although users can custom other algorithms themselves, for instance by using overlap ratio of program's vector to measure danger, as a replacement of Algorithm DV-CIM, DV-CIM's position is immovable as it provides a standard interface when working with Concept Lattice model in this text.

6.4 Illustration

In order to prove the theoretical model, 150 typical Trojans are sampled in which 47 with source code are chosen to do further study. As for the left 103 Trojans, we surmise their tasks and establish their APSs. A part of conclusion is shown below.

Table 4. Result of Detecting Trojan Behaviors

average rate of behavior matching	47%	75%	85%
with/without source code	103/37	87/25	78/23
amount of other applications	15	15	15
false negative rate	0.031	0.045	0.081
detection rate	0.57/0.84	0.68/0.85	0.75/0.88

Explanation 2 *We use Linux 2.0 and Windows operating system, preferably xp and 2003. Analyzing tool is IceSword. With antivirus software off and 70 processes on, samples and normal applications including QQ, office, Firefox and czzOA run one by one. Average RAM cost is 67KB and average time expense of each process testing is 0.13s.*

The running process flows the diagram below, besides which it describes the signature detection.

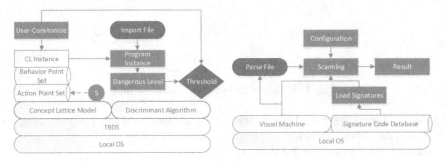

Fig. 5. Trojan Behavior Definition System   **Fig. 6.** Signature Code Detection

The 'S' with dash means that source codes support the model to be more reliable and comprehensive. It's optional but suggested to implement, otherwise BPS will only rely on customization which might not be accurate enough. But on the other hand, user's customization provides significant flexibility. Comparing the scale of Signature Code Database (Meta Bytes) with that of BPS and APS (Kilo Bytes) and the time expense of matching thousands of hundreds of signature (seconds) with that of generating DL(less than 1 second), we feel delightful that our method is more feasible and effective. From beginning to the end we hold the view that 'better modelling' means 'easier computing'.

The difficulty of matching without source code increases in step with average rate of behavior matching increases. In other words, source code makes matching easier. On the other hand, after successful matching increases, both detection rate and false negative rate would go up. This is truly above other detection methods. We predict that a clearer boundary is hidden, which is long for further study.

7   Conclusion and Further Work

Boolean Algebra and Concept Lattice are innovatively selected to describe Trojan behavior by models and algorithms. Compared with the traditional Trojan identification, we consider tasks and resources as entrance for detection and compute programs DL to clarify the boundary between Trojans and normal programs. Standing at a system designer's view, we can see that modeling procedures, discriminant algorithms, and examples are provided when all related concepts, definitions, properties are explained. We have already carried out discriminant experiments on the basis of more than one hundred Trojans. After analyzing all results of these experiments, algebraic model and its discriminant are effective.

In addition, 2 problems need to be solved in future:

1. Problem of the 'bottom' of models.

   How to set AP which is the cornerstone of modeling? We just come up with some simple methods here. Hence, looking for the optimally largest APS by using statistics, psychology and predictive analytics is waiting for further study.

2. Problem of the 'top' of models.

   If problem 1 is solved, it's necessary to adopt a more accurate algorithm to reduce the fault and fail rate. Following specifications of modeling and discriminant structure in this article, larger Concept Lattice and higher-dimension Dangerous Level Vector will work better.

References

1. Thimbleby, H., Anderson, S., Cairns, P.: A Framework for Modelling Trojans and Computer Virus Infection. Computer Journal 41(7), 444–458 (1998)
2. Zhuge, J., Holze, T., Song, C., et al.: Studying Malicoius Websites and the Underground Economy on the Chinese Web. In: The 7th Workshop on the Economics of Information Security (WEIS 2008), Hanover, New Hampshire, USA, June 25-28, pp. 123–125 (2008)
3. Haldar, V., Franz, M.: Symmetric Behavior-Based Trust: A New Paradigm for Internet Computing. In: Proceedings of the 2004 New Security Paradigms Workshop, pp. 79–84. ACM Press, Nova Scotia (2004)
4. Hofmeyr, S.A., Forrest, S., Somayaji, A.: Intrusion Detection using Sequences of System Calls. Journal of Computer Security, 23–30 (1998)
5. Kirda, E., Kruegel, C., Banks, G., et al.: Behavior-based Spyware Detection. In: 15th USENIX Security Symposium, pp. 273–288. USENIX, Vancouver (2006)
6. Chakraborty, R.S., Wolff, F., Paul, S., Papachristou, C., Bhunia, S.: MERO: A Statistical Approach for Hardware Trojan Detection. In: Clavier, C., Gaj, K. (eds.) CHES 2009. LNCS, vol. 5747, pp. 396–410. Springer, Heidelberg (2009)
7. Jin, Y., Makris, Y.: Hardware Trojan Detection Using Path Delay Fingerprint. Hardware-Oriented Security and Trust, 51–57 (June 2008)
8. Wei, S., Potkonjak, M.: Scalable Consistency-based Hardware Trojan Detection and Diagnosis. In: The 5th International Conference on Network and System Security, pp. 176–183 (September 2011)
9. Dahn, B.I.: Robbins Algebras are Boolean: A Revision of McCune's Computer-Generated Solution of the Robbins Problem. Journal of Algebra 208, 526–532 (1998) ISSN 0021-8693
10. Davey, B.A., Priestley, H.A.: Introduction to Lattices and Order. Cambridge University Press (2002)

Cryptanalysis and Improvement of an ECC-Based Password Authentication Scheme Using Smart Cards

Cheng-Chi Lee[1,2], Chun-Ta Li[3,*], Chi-Yao Weng[4], Jian-Jhong Jheng[3], Xiao-Qian Zhang[3], and Yi-Rui Zhu[3]

[1] Department of Library and Information Science, Fu Jen Catholic University
510 Jhongjheng Road, New Taipei City 24205, Taiwan (R.O.C.)
cclee@mail.fju.edu.tw
[2] Department of Photonics and Communication Engineering, Asia University
500 Lioufeng Road, Taichung City 41354, Taiwan (R.O.C.)
[3] Department of Information Management, Tainan University of Technology
529 Zhongzheng Road, Tainan City 71002, Taiwan (R.O.C.)
th0040@mail.tut.edu.tw
[4] Department of Computer Science, National Tsing Hua University
101 Kuang-Fu Road, Hsinchu City 30013, TAIWAN (R.O.C.)
cyweng@is.cs.nthu.edu.tw

Abstract. Remote password authentication has been widely used in network systems and it aims to provide secure remote access control. In 2013, Li proposed a novel password authentication scheme based on elliptic curve cryptography and smart card [17]. However, we found that Li's authentication scheme has a serious security problem in that all registered users' sensitive passwords can be easily derived by the privileged-insider of remote server. Therefore, in this paper, we propose a slight modification on Li's scheme to prevent the shortcomings. Our improved scheme not only inherits the advantages of Li's password authentication scheme but also remedies the serious security weakness of not being able to withstand insider attack.

Keywords: Cryptanalysis, Elliptic curve cryptography (ECC), Password authentication, Insider attack, Smart card.

1 Introduction

With the rapid development of network technologies and Internet users, more and more remote services such as online transactions, online games and online electronic contents etc. are supported through Internet, which provides conveniences to Internet users. However, with the increase of network attacks such as message eavesdropping, participant masquerading and secret guessing, network security and information privacy become an important research issue in networking environments. Remote user authentication is crucial to prevent unregistered

---

* Corresponding author.

G. Wang et al. (Eds.): CSS 2013, LNCS 8300, pp. 338–348, 2013.
© Springer International Publishing Switzerland 2013

users from accessing remote service systems and password authentication with smart card is one of the most popular mechanisms to verify the validity of login user.

Recently, many smart card based password authentication schemes for remote login systems have been proposed [1–3, 5–16, 18–24, 26]. Particularly, in 2013, Islam and Biswas proposed an ECC-based password authentication and key agreement scheme using smart card [4] in remote login environments. Unfortunately, in the same year, Li [17] pointed out that Islam and Biswas's scheme cannot resist off-line password guessing attack, stolen-verifier attack and insider attack. Li also proposed a slightly modified version of Islam and Biswas's authentication scheme so as to remedy the identified deficiencies. However, in this paper, we find that both original and improved schemes [4, 17] are vulnerable to the insider attack. The spotted security flaw may allow a privileged-insider of remote server to derive the passwords of all login users registered with the remote server. In order to resist security flaw, we would like to propose an improved scheme that also inherits the advantages of Li's password authentication scheme and resistance to the insider attack.

The remainder of the paper is organized as follows. Section 2 is a brief review of Li's ECC-based password authentication scheme and a cryptanalysis of Li's scheme is given in Section 3. Our improved scheme against insider attack is proposed in Section 4. Security analysis of our improved scheme is presented in Section 5 and Section 6 concludes this paper.

2   A Review of Li's Password Authentication Scheme

In this section, we review Li's password-based remote authentication scheme [17] and Li's scheme is composed of five phases, registration, password authentication, password change, session key distribution and user eviction. For convenience of description, terminology and notations used in the paper are summarized as follows:

- (ID_A, pw_A): The identity and password of the client A.
- S: The remote server.
- d_s: The secret key, which is kept secret and only known by S.
- U_S: The public key of S, where $U_S = d_s \cdot G$
- U_A: Password-verifier of the client A, where $U_A = pw_a \cdot G$.
- G: Bases point of the elliptic curve group of order n such that $n \cdot G = O$, where n is a large prime number.
- K_x: Secret key computed either using $K = pw_A \cdot U_S = (K_x, K_y)$ or $K = d_s \cdot U_A = (K_x, K_y)$.
- $H(\cdot)$: A collision free one-way hash function.
- $E_{K_x}(.)/D_{K_x}(.)$: The symmetric encryption/decryption function with key K_x.
- r_i: A random number chosen by the entity i from $[1, n-1]$.
- $+/-$: Elliptic curve point addition/subtraction.

2.1   Registration Phase

Step 1. $A \longrightarrow S$: ID_A, U_A

Client A computes $U_A = pw_A \cdot r_A \cdot G$ and sends it with ID_A to S through a secure channel, where r_A is a random number which is kept secret and only known by A.

Step 2. $S \longrightarrow A$: **SMART CARD**

S stores A's ID_A, U_A and a $status - bit$ in a write protected file as depicted in Table 1. Moreover, S writes $\{G, U_S, H(\cdot), E_K(.)/D_K(.)\}$ into a personal smart card and issues it to A through a secure channel.

Step 3. A writes r_A into the smart card. Finally, the smart card includes $\{r_A, G, U_S, H(\cdot), E_K(.)/D_K(.)\}$.

Table 1. The verifier table of S after finishing the registration phase [17]

Identity	Password-verifier	$Status - bit$
$\vdots$	$\vdots$	$\vdots$
ID_A	$U_A = pw_A \cdot r_A \cdot G$	0/1
$\vdots$	$\vdots$	$\vdots$

2.2   Password Authentication Phase

Client A inserts the personal smart card into the card reader and keys ID_A and pw_A. Then the smart card will perform the following operations:

Step 1. $A \longrightarrow S$: $ID_A, E_{K_x}(ID_A, R_A, W_A, U'_A)$

The smart card retrieves r_A, generates a random number r'_A, computes $R_A = r_A \cdot U_S = r_A \cdot d_S \cdot G$, $W_A = r_A \cdot r_A \cdot pw_A \cdot G$, $U'_A = pw_A \cdot r'_A \cdot G$ and $E_{K_x}(ID_A, R_A, W_A, U'_A)$ and sends $E_{K_x}(ID_A, R_A, W_A, U'_A)$ with ID_A to S, where the encryption key K_x is the x coordinate of $K = pw_A \cdot r_A \cdot U_S = pw_A \cdot r_A \cdot d_S \cdot G = (K_x, K_y)$.

Step 2. $S \longrightarrow A$: $(W_A + W_S), H(W_S, U'_A)$

Upon receiving the login message, S computes the decryption key $K = d_S \cdot U_A = pw_A \cdot r_A \cdot d_S \cdot G = (K_x, K_y)$ and decrypts $E_{K_x}(ID_A, R_A, W_A, U'_A)$ to reveal (ID_A, R_A, W_A, U'_A). S verifies the decrypted ID_A with received ID_A and $\hat{e}(R_A, U_A)$ with $\hat{e}(W_A, U_S)$. If they hold, S sends $\{(W_A + W_S), H(W_S, U'_A)\}$ to A, where r_S is a random number which is generated by S and $W_S = r_S \cdot U_S$. A bilinear pairing is used to assure the correctness of the scheme and is given below:

$$\hat{e}(R_A, U_A) = \hat{e}(r_A \cdot d_S \cdot G, r_A \cdot pw_A \cdot G)$$
$$= \hat{e}(G, G)^{r_A \cdot r_A \cdot pw_A \cdot d_S}$$
$$= \hat{e}(r_A \cdot r_A \cdot pw_A \cdot G, d_S \cdot G)$$
$$= \hat{e}(W_A, U_S).$$

Step 3. $A \longrightarrow S$: $ID_A, H(W_A, W_S, U'_A)$

A retrieves W_S by subtracting W_A from $(W_A + W_S)$ and compares whether the hashed result of (W_S, U'_A) is equal to the received $H(W_S, U'_A)$. If it holds, A computes $H(W_A, W_S, U'_A)$ and sends it to S.

Step 4. $S \longrightarrow A$: **Access Granted/Denied**

S uses its own W_S and (W_A, U'_A) which is received from A in Step 1 to compute $H(W_A, W_S, U'_A)$ and verifies whether the hashed result of (W_A, W_S, U'_A) is equal to the received $H(W_A, W_S, U'_A)$. If so, S granted A's login request and replaced original $U_A = pw_A \cdot r_A \cdot G$ with new $U'_A = pw_A \cdot r'_A \cdot G$. Otherwise, S rejects A's login request. Finally, A's smart card replaces old r_A with new r'_A if all of the conditions are satisfied.

2.3 Password Change Phase

When the client A wants to update his/her current password pw_A to a new password pw'_A, A notifies S to replace current password-verifier $U_A = pw_A \cdot r_A \cdot G$ with new password-verifier $U'_A = pw'_A \cdot r'_A \cdot G$.

Step 1. $A \longrightarrow S$: $ID_A, E_{K_x}(ID_A, R_A, W_A, U'_A)$
Step 2. $S \longrightarrow A$: $W_A + W_S, H(W_S, U'_A)$
Step 3. $A \longrightarrow S$: $ID_A, H(W_A, W_S, U'_A), H(W_S + W_A + U'_A)$
Step 4. $S \longrightarrow A$: **Password Change Granted/Denied**

In Step 3, if the authentication token $H(W_A, W_S, U'_A)$ and $H(W_S + W_A + U'_A)$ are valid, A's smart card replaces r_A with r'_A and the password-verifier U_A has been changed with the new password-verifier U'_A.

2.4 Session Key Distribution Phase

Step 1. $A \longrightarrow S$: $ID_A, E_{K_x}(ID_A, R_A, W_A, U'_A)$
Step 2. $S \longrightarrow A$: $W_A + W_S, H(W_S, U'_A, SK)$
Step 3. $A \longrightarrow S$: $ID_A, H(W_A, W_S, U'_A, SK)$
Step 4. $S \longrightarrow A$: **Key distribution Granted/Denied**

In this phase, A and S compute the symmetric session key $SK = (r_A \cdot r_A \cdot pw_A) \cdot W_S = r_A \cdot r_A \cdot pw_A \cdot r_S \cdot d_S \cdot G = (r_S \cdot d_S) \cdot W_A = r_S \cdot d_S \cdot pw_A \cdot r_A \cdot r_A \cdot G$, where two random numbers r_A and r_S are chosen by A and S from $[1, n-1]$, respectively. After Step 1, 2, 3 and 4 are finished, S replaced U_A with U'_A and A's smart card replaces r_A with r'_A.

2.5 User Eviction Phase

In case of a client A is evicted by S, A cannot use (ID_A, U_A) to login S because S can delete (ID_A, U_A) from its verifier table and ID_A cannot be found in the verifier table in Step 2 of the password authentication phase.

3   Insider Attack on Li's Scheme

In this section, we show insider attack on Li's password authentication scheme. Let us consider the following scenarios. If a privileged-insider of S can find an opportunity to derive client A's real password pw_A, he/she may use A's password pw_A to impersonate A to login other servers.

After finishing the registration phase, the privileged-insider knows A's password-verifier $U_A = pw_A \cdot r_A \cdot G$. In addition, during the password authentication phase, client A sends a login request $\{ID_A, E_{K_x}(ID_A, R_A, W_A, U'_A)\}$ to S. Then the privileged-insider reveals (ID_A, R_A, W_A, U'_A) by using its secret key. Finally, the privileged-insider can derive client A's real password pw_A in off-line manner by using the following three steps:

Step 1. Select a guessed password pw_A^*.
Step 2. Compute $pw_A^* \cdot G$.
Step 3. Compare $\hat{e}(R_A, pw_A^* \cdot G)$ to $\hat{e}(U_S, U_A)$.

A match in Step 3 above indicates the correct guess of client A's password. The privileged-insider verifies the equation $\hat{e}(R_A, pw_A^* \cdot G)$ to $\hat{e}(U_S, U_A)$ holds or not as follows:

$$\begin{aligned}
\hat{e}(R_A, pw_A^* \cdot G) &= \hat{e}(r_A \cdot U_S, pw_A^* \cdot G) \\
&= \hat{e}(r_A \cdot d_S \cdot G, pw_A^* \cdot G) \\
&= \hat{e}(d_S \cdot G, r_A \cdot pw_A^* \cdot G) \\
&= \hat{e}(U_S, U_A).
\end{aligned}$$

As a result, the privileged-insider succeeds to guess the low-entropy password pw_A and Li's password authentication scheme is vulnerable to insider attack.

4   The Improved Scheme

In this section, we propose some slight modifications to Li's password authentication scheme, such as registration phase, password authentication phase and password change phase of Li's scheme. The other part of Li's password authentication scheme, such as session key distribution phase and user eviction phase are the same as Li's scheme. Figure 1 shows the entire flowchart of our improved scheme.

4.1   Registration Phase

Step 1. $A \longrightarrow S$: ID_A, U_A
   When a client A wants to access the remote server S, A must register to S. A computes $v_A = H(ID_A \| pw_A \| r_A)$ and $U_A = v_A \cdot r_A \cdot G$ and sends it with ID_A to S through a secure channel, where r_A is a random number which is kept secret and only known by A.

Client A	Server S

Registration Phase:

Select ID_A, pw_A, r_A

$v_A = H(ID_A||pw_A||r_A)$

$U_A = v_A \cdot r_A \cdot G$

$$\{ID_A, U_A\} \longrightarrow$$

Store $\{G, U_S, H(\cdot), E_K(\cdot)/D_K(\cdot)\}$

SMART CARD $\longleftarrow$

Store r_A into **SMART CARD**

Password Authentication Phase:

Enter ID_A, pw_A

Retrieve r_A from **SMART CARD**

Generate r'_A

$v_A = H(ID_A||pw_A||r_A)$

$v'_A = H(ID_A||pw_A||r'_A)$

$R_A = r_A \cdot U_S$

$W_A = r_A \cdot r_A \cdot v_A \cdot G$

$U'_A = v'_A \cdot r'_A \cdot G$

$E_{K_x}(ID_A, R_A, W_A, U'_A)$

$$\{ID_A, E_{K_x}(ID_A, R_A, W_A, U'_A)\} \longrightarrow$$

Decrypt $E_{K_x}(ID_A, R_A, W_A, U'_A)$

Verify $\hat{e}(R_A, U_A) \overset{?}{=} \hat{e}(W_A, U_S)$

$W_S = r_S \cdot U_S$

$$\longleftarrow \{(W_A + W_S), H(W_S, U'_A)\}$$

Retrieve W_S from $(W_A + W_S)$

Verify $H(W_S, U'_A)$

$$\{ID_A, H(W_A, W_S, U'_A)\} \longrightarrow$$

Verify $H(W_A, W_S, U'_A)$

Replace U_A with U'_A

Access Granted/Denied $\longleftarrow$

Replace r_A with r'_A

Password Change Phase:

Enter $ID_A, pw_A, pw_A^{new}, r_A"$

$v_A" = H(ID_A||pw_A^{new}||r_A")$

$U_A" = v_A" \cdot r_A" \cdot G$

$$\{ID_A, E_{K_x}(ID_A, R_A, W_A, U_A")\} \longrightarrow$$

$$\longleftarrow \{(W_A + W_S), H(W_S, U_A")\}$$

$$\{ID_A, H(W_A, W_S, U_A"), H(W_S + W_A + U_A")\} \longrightarrow$$

Replace U_A with $U_A"$

Password Change Granted/Denied $\longleftarrow$

Replace r_A with $r_A"$

Fig. 1. The improved scheme

Step 2. $S \longrightarrow A$: **SMART CARD**

After receiving A's registration request, S stores A's identity ID_A, password-verifier U_A and a $status - bit$ in a write protected file as depicted in Table 2. Finally, S writes $\{G, U_S, H(\cdot), E_K(.)/D_K(.)\}$ into a personal smart card and issues it to A through a secure channel.

Step 3. After receiving the smart card from S, A writes r_A into the smart card and the smart card includes $\{r_A, G, U_S, H(\cdot), E_K(.)/D_K(.)\}$. Note that the client A does not need to remember r_A after finishing the phase.

Table 2. The verifier table of S after finishing the registration phase in our improved scheme

Identity	Password-verifier	$Status - bit$
$\vdots$	$\vdots$	$\vdots$
ID_A	$U_A = v_A \cdot r_A \cdot G$	$0/1$
$\vdots$	$\vdots$	$\vdots$

4.2 Password Authentication Phase

When a client A wants to access the server S, the client A inserts his/her personal smart card into card reader and keys the identity ID_A and the password pw_A. The following steps are performed during the password authentication phase.

Step 1. $A \longrightarrow S$: $ID_A, E_{K_x}(ID_A, R_A, W_A, U'_A)$

The smart card retrieves r_A, generates a new random number r'_A, computes $v_A = H(ID_A||pw_A||r_A)$, $v'_A = H(ID_A||pw_A||r'_A)$, $R_A = r_A \cdot U_S = r_A \cdot d_S \cdot G$, $W_A = r_A \cdot r_A \cdot v_A \cdot G$, $U'_A = v'_A \cdot r'_A \cdot G$ and $E_{K_x}(ID_A, R_A, W_A, U'_A)$ and sends $E_{K_x}(ID_A, R_A, W_A, U'_A)$ with ID_A to S, where the encryption key K_x is the x coordinate of $K = v_A \cdot r_A \cdot U_S = H(ID_A||pw_A||r_A) \cdot r_A \cdot d_S \cdot G = (K_x, K_y)$.

Step 2. $S \longrightarrow A$: $(W_A + W_S), H(W_S, U'_A)$

Upon receiving the login message, S computes the decryption key K_x by computing $K = d_S \cdot U_A = v_A \cdot r_A \cdot d_S \cdot G = (K_x, K_y)$ and decrypts $E_{K_x}(ID_A, R_A, W_A, U'_A)$ to reveal (ID_A, R_A, W_A, U'_A). S verifies the decrypted ID_A with received ID_A and $\hat{e}(R_A, U_A)$ with $\hat{e}(W_A, U_S)$. If they hold, S sends $\{(W_A + W_S), H(W_S, U'_A)\}$ to A, where r_S is a random number which is generated by S and $W_S = r_S \cdot U_S$. We can proof that the verification $\hat{e}(R_A, U_A) = \hat{e}(W_A, U_S)$ is correct and the remote server can confirm that A is a legal client. A bilinear pairing is used to assure the correctness of the scheme and is given below:

$$\hat{e}(R_A, U_A) = \hat{e}(r_A \cdot d_S \cdot G, r_A \cdot v_A \cdot G)$$
$$= \hat{e}(G, G)^{r_A \cdot r_A \cdot v_A \cdot d_S}$$
$$= \hat{e}(r_A \cdot r_A \cdot v_A \cdot G, d_S \cdot G)$$
$$= \hat{e}(W_A, U_S).$$

Step 3. $A \longrightarrow S$: $ID_A, H(W_A, W_S, U'_A)$

A retrieves W_S by subtracting W_A from $(W_A + W_S)$ and compares whether the hashed result of (W_S, U'_A) is equal to the received $H(W_S, U'_A)$. If it holds, A computes $H(W_A, W_S, U'_A)$ and sends it to S.

Step 4. $S \longrightarrow A$: **Access Granted/Denied**

S uses its own W_S and (W_A, U'_A) which is received from A in Step 1 to compute $H(W_A, W_S, U'_A)$ and verifies whether the hashed result of (W_A, W_S, U'_A) is equal to the received $H(W_A, W_S, U'_A)$. If so, S granted A's login request and replaced original $U_A = v_A \cdot r_A \cdot G$ with new $U'_A = v'_A \cdot r'_A \cdot G$. Otherwise, S rejects A's login request. Finally, A's smart card replaces old r_A with new r'_A if all of the conditions are satisfied.

After finishing the password authentication phase, the verifier table of S is updated and the content of the verifier table is shown in Table 3.

Table 3. The verifier table of S after finishing the password authentication phase in our improved scheme

Identity	Password-verifier	$Status - bit$
$\vdots$	$\vdots$	$\vdots$
ID_A	$U'_A = v'_A \cdot r'_A \cdot G$	$0/1$
$\vdots$	$\vdots$	$\vdots$

4.3   Password Change Phase

When the client A wants to change his/her current password pw_A to a new password pw_A^{new}, A generates a new random number r_A" and notifies S to replace current password-verifier $U_A = v_A \cdot r_A \cdot G$ with new password-verifier U_A" $= v_A$" $\cdot r_A$" $\cdot G$, where v_A" $= H(ID_A \| pw_A^{new} \| r_A$").

Step 1. $A \longrightarrow S$: $ID_A, E_{K_x}(ID_A, R_A, W_A, U_A")$

Step 2. $S \longrightarrow A$: $W_A + W_S, H(W_S, U_A")$

Step 3. $A \longrightarrow S$: $ID_A, H(W_A, W_S, U_A"), H(W_S + W_A + U_A")$

Step 4. $S \longrightarrow A$: **Password Change Granted/Denied**

In Step 3, if the authentication token $H(W_A, W_S, U_A")$ and $H(W_S + W_A + U_A")$ are valid, A's smart card replaces r_A with r_A" and the password-verifier U_A has been changed with the new password-verifier U_A". After finishing the password change phase, the verifier table of S is updated and the content of the verifier table is shown in Table 4.

5   Security Analysis of the Proposed Scheme

The improved authentication scheme benefits from the protection of registration user to prevent the sensitive password for a privileged-insider to steal and guess

Table 4. The verifier table of S after finishing the password change phase in our improved scheme

Identity	Password-verifier	$Status - bit$
$\vdots$	$\vdots$	$\vdots$
ID_A	$U_A" = v_A" \cdot r_A" \cdot G$	$0/1$
$\vdots$	$\vdots$	$\vdots$

the real password stored in the verifier table or in the exchange of authentication messages. In the following propositions, we give an in-depth analysis of the proposed scheme in terms of security properties.

Since we add only two one-way hashing operations to replace $U_A = pw_A \cdot r_A \cdot G$ with $U_A = v_A \cdot r_A \cdot G$ during registration phase, where $v_A = H(ID_A \| pw_A \| r_A)$. Therefore, using the above mentioned attack in Section 3, a privileged-insider of S who does not know client A's random number r_A tries to derive client A's real password pw_A as follows:

$$v_A^* = H(ID_A \| pw_A^* \| r_A^*)$$
$$U_A^* = v_A^* \cdot r_A^* \cdot G,$$

where pw_A^* is a guessed password and r_A^* is a guessed random number. Note that the random number r_A does not reveal to the privileged-insider of S and the bit length of $|r_A|$ is large enough. As a result, due to the intractability under the protection of $H(\cdot)$, a privileged-insider of S is unable to derive client A's pw_A without knowing r_A and client A's password pw_A will not be revealed by the privileged-insider.

On the other hand, if SHA-256 [25] is used in the proposed scheme, the privileged-insider of S may attempt to derive $v_A = H(ID_A \| pw_A \| r_A)$ and r_A due to the bit-length of v_A and r_A are 256 bits and 160 bits, respectively. Therefore, the probability to guess correct v_A and r_A at the same time are $\frac{1}{2^{256+160}}$. In addition, U_A must guess a correct password pw_A at the same time and the probability to guess a correct n characters pw_A approximated to $\frac{1}{2^{6n}}$. Therefore, it is computationally infeasible for the privileged-insider of S to guess correct $H(ID_A \| pw_A \| r_A)$, r_A and pw_A at the same time because the probability approximated to $\frac{1}{2^{6n+256+160}}$ and the privileged-insider of S will not be able to perform this attack.

6   Conclusions

In this paper, we have shown that a recently proposed ECC-based password authentication scheme in remote networking environment is insecure against insider attack and should not be implemented in real applications. To remedy the security problem, we have proposed security improvements which not only repair the weak features of Li's authentication scheme but also inherit the merits of Li's scheme.

Acknowledgements. This research was partially supported by the National Science Council, Taiwan, R.O.C., under contract no.: NSC 101-2221-E-165-002 and NSC 102-2221-E-030-003.

References

1. Chang, C.C., Lee, C.Y.: A smart card-based authentication scheme uing user identify cryptography. International Journal of Network Security 15(2), 139–147 (2013)
2. Das, A.K.: Improving identity-based random key establishment scheme for large-scale hierarchical wireless sensor networks. International Journal of Network Security 14(1), 1–21 (2012)
3. He, D., Zhao, W., Wu, S.: Security analysis of a dynamic ID-based authentication scheme for multi-server environment using smart cards. International Journal of Network Security 15(5), 350–356 (2013)
4. Islam, S.H., Biswas, G.P.: Design of improved password authentication and update scheme based on elliptic curve cryptography. Mathematical and Computer Modelling 57(11-12), 2703–2717 (2013)
5. Kar, J.: ID-based deniable authentication protocol based on Diffie-Hellman problem on elliptic curve. International Journal of Network Security 15(5), 357–364 (2013)
6. Kim, S.K., Chung, M.G.: More secure remote user authentication scheme. Computer Communications 32(6), 1018–1021 (2009)
7. Lamport, L.: Password authentication with insecure communication. Communications of the ACM 24(11), 770–772 (1981)
8. Lee, C.C., Chen, C.L., Wu, C.Y., Huang, S.Y.: An extended chaotic maps-based key agreement protocol with user anonymity. Nonlinear Dynamics 69(1-2), 79–87 (2012)
9. Lee, C.C., Hsu, C.W.: A secure biometric-based remote user authentication with key agreement protocol using extended chaotic maps. Nonlinear Dynamics 71(1-2), 201–211 (2013)
10. Lee, C.C., Li, C.T., Hsu, C.W.: A three-party password-based authenticated key exchange protocol with user anonymity using extended chaotic maps. Nonlinear Dynamics 73(1-2), 125–132 (2013)
11. Lee, C.C., Chen, C.T., Li, C.T., Wu, P.H.: A practical RFID authentication mechanism for digital television. Telecommunication Systems (article in press, 2013)
12. Li, C.T., Hwang, M.S.: An efficient biometrics-based remote user authentication scheme using smart cards. Journal of Network and Computer Applications 33(1), 1–5 (2010)
13. Li, C.T., Hwang, M.S.: An online biometrics-based secret sharing scheme for multiparty cryptosystem using smart cards. International Journal of Innovative Computing, Information and Control 6(5), 2181–2188 (2010)
14. Li, C.T.: Secure smart card based password authentication scheme with user anonymity. Information Technology and Control 40(2), 157–162 (2011)
15. Li, C.T., Lee, C.C.: A robust remote user authentication scheme using smart card. Information Technology and Control 40(3), 236–245 (2011)
16. Li, C.T., Lee, C.C.: A novel user authentication and privacy preserving scheme with smart cards for wireless communications. Mathematical and Computer Modelling 55(1-2), 35–44 (2012)

17. Li, C.T.: A new password authentication and user anonymity scheme Based on elliptic curve cryptography and smart card. IET Information Security 7(1), 3–10 (2013)
18. Li, C.T., Lee, C.C., Weng, C.Y., Fan, C.I.: An extended multi-server-based user authentication and key agreement scheme with user anonymity. KSII Transactions on Internet and Information Systems 7(1), 119–131 (2013)
19. Li, C.T., Weng, C.Y., Lee, C.C.: An advanced temporal credential-based security scheme with mutual authentication and key agreement for wireless sensor networks. Sensors 13(8), 9589–9603 (2013)
20. Li, C.T., Lee, C.C., Weng, C.Y.: An extended chaotic maps based user authentication and privacy preserving scheme against DoS attacks in pervasive and ubiquitous computing environments. Nonlinear Dynamics (article in press, 2013)
21. Liao, I.E., Lee, C.C., Hwang, M.S.: A password authentication scheme over insecure networks. Journal of Computer and System Sciences 72(4), 727–740 (2006)
22. Naveed, M., Habib, W., Masud, U., Ullah, U., Ahmad, G.: Reliable and low cost RFID based authentication system for large scale deployment. International Journal of Network Security 14(3), 173–179 (2012)
23. Kumar, M.: A new secure remote user authentication scheme with smart cards. International Journal of Network Security 11(2), 88–93 (2010)
24. Ramasamy, R., Muniyandi, A.P.: An efficient password authentication scheme for smart card. International Journal of Network Security 14(3), 180–186 (2012)
25. National Institute of Standards and Technology, US department of commerce, secure hash standard. US Federal Information Processing Standard Publication, 180–182 (2002)
26. Yang, L., Ma, J.F., Jiang, Q.: Mutual authentication scheme with smart cards and password under trusted computing. International Journal of Network Security 14(3), 156–163 (2012)

The Hot-Spots Problem in Windows 8
Graphical Password Scheme

Haichang Gao, Wei Jia, Ning Liu, and Kaisheng Li

Institute of Software Engineering, Xidian University
Xi'an, Shaanxi 710071, P.R. China
hchgao@xidian.edu.cn

Abstract. Various graphical passwords have been proposed as an alternative to traditional alphanumeric passwords and Microsoft has applied a graphical scheme in the operating system Windows 8. As a new type of password scheme, potential security problems such as hot-spots may exist. In this paper, we study user choice in Windows 8 graphical password scheme by both lab and field studies and analyze the hot-spots caused by user choice. Our analysis shows that there are many significant hot-spots in the background image when users set their passwords using Microsoft's guidance. Then, based on the data of field study, we conducted a simulated human-seeded attack to prove our conclusion. The success rate of 66.69% and 54.46% also provide strong proof of the hot-spots in Windows 8 graphical password scheme. Finally, we designed a simulated automated attack and obtained a success rate of 42.86%.

Keywords: graphical password, hot-spots, Windows 8, security.

1 Introduction

Nowadays, authentication technology is the main measure to guarantee information security, and the most comprehensive authentication method currently used is alphanumeric passwords. However, it is difficult for users to remember long complicated passwords, while short simple passwords are susceptible to attack and are therefore a security risk [1,5]. Recently, graphical password schemes have been proposed as alternatives to alphanumeric passwords by using images as passwords rather than alphanumeric numbers and biological characteristics. Graphical passwords are motivated particularly by the fact that it is generally easier for users to remember and recall images than words [2], [3], and [4], and it is conceivable that graphical passwords would be able to provide better security than alphanumeric passwords.

The existing graphical password techniques can be divided into three general categories: recall-based, recognition-based and cued-recall. The typical scheme in each category is DAS, PassFaces and PassPoints. With the Windows 8 release, Microsoft introduced a new graphical password scheme as a complement to the alphanumeric password scheme. The three types of gestures offered include tap, straight line and circles. Any combination of those gestures can be used as a password. Therefore, a person reproduces the graphical password to become a legal

G. Wang et al. (Eds.): CSS 2013, LNCS 8300, pp. 349–362, 2013.

user. Click-based graphical password schemes require a user to login by clicking a sequence of points on a single background image. The important remaining question for such schemes is hot-spots – areas of an image that are more probable than others for users to click. Windows 8 graphical password scheme also requires a user to login by doing a sequence of gestures on a single background image, so we analyze hot-spots in it. In this paper, we study user choice in Windows 8 graphical password scheme by both lab and field studies and analyze the hot-spots caused by user choice. Then, based on the data of filed study, we conducted a simulated attack to prove our conclusion.

The remainder of this paper is organized as follows: Section 2 introduces several general categories of graphical passwords and their corresponding representative schemes, also advantages and disadvantages. In Section 3, some preliminary lab studies and analysis are provided. In Section 4, we conducted a field study and simulated human-seeded attacks based on the data of field study, and then made an automated attack. Finally, concluding remarks are made and future work is discussed in Section 5.

2   Related Work

From 1996, numerous graphical password schemes have been proposed, motivated by the promise of improving password memorability and usability. According to the memory task, the graphical passwords can be divided into three general categories: recall-based systems, cued-recall systems and recognition-based systems [6] and [7]. Draw-A-Secret (DAS) [8], typical of the recall-based graphical password schemes, asked users draw their password on a 2D grid using a stylus or mouse (shown in Fig.1). To login in, users repeat the same path through the grid cells. PassPoints [9], representative of the click-based graphical password schemes, required users select a sequence of an $n = 5$ user-selected points on a system-assigned image (shown in Fig. 1). During login, users must re-enter the chosen selected points within a system-specified tolerance and also in the correct order. The image acts as a clue to help users remember their password click-points.

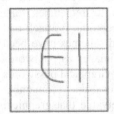

Fig. 1. DAS, PassPoints, and Windows 8 graphical password scheme

In the new operating system Windows 8, Microsoft introduced a new graphical password scheme which was a clever combination of DAS and PassPoints (shown in Fig. 1) [10]. First users can choose any image they like as their password image and then draw a set of gestures of in the image. The three types of offered gestures include: circles, straight lines, and taps. Any combination of those gestures can be used as a password.

There have been several analyses of DAS and PassPoints in terms of user choices. According to a survey conducted by Nali [11], users tend to set predictable passwords which are vulnerable to dictionary attack. The survey showed that about 86% of passwords were centered or approximately centered and 45% of passwords were totally symmetric, thereby drastically reducing the effective password space. Thorpe et al.'s study for PassPoints showed that all of the secret images had hot-spots in varying degrees and that some images had significantly more hot-spots than others [12]. They even implement and evaluate two types of attack for PassPoints: human-seeded and purely automated. Their experimental results showed that a human-seeded attack is quite effective against PassPoints: it correctly guessed 36% of user passwords within 2^{31} guesses (or 12% within 2^{16} guesses) on one image, and 20% within 2^{33} guesses (or 10% within 2^{18} guesses) on a second image.

The graphical password scheme in Windows 8 is considered as the safest graphical password schemes because of its huge theoretical password space and operational mode [10]. The designers' experiments show that using a limited set of gestures was on average more than three times as fast as the freeform method, and that people using the gesture set were consistently able to complete the task in four seconds, with repeated use. Designers point out that the password space of this scheme is very large. For sample gesture and combination gestures, they give the theoretical password space respectively, shown in table 1.

Table 1. Theoretical password space

# of tap	Password space	# of circle	Password space
1	270	1	335
2	23,535	2	34,001
3	2,743,206	3	4,509,567
4	178,832,265	4	381,311,037
5	15,344,276,658	5	44,084,945,533
6	1,380,314,975,183	6	5,968,261,724,338
7	130,146,054,200,734	7	907,853,751,427,866
8	13,168,374,201,327,200	--	--

# of line	Password space	# of multi-gesture	Password space
1	1,949	1	2,554
2	846,183	2	1,581,773
3	412,096,718	3	1,155,509,083
4	156,687,051,477	4	612,157,353,732
5	70,441,983,603,740	5	398,046,621,309,172

However, questions remain regarding the security of the scheme. First, this scheme cannot prevent shoulder surfing attack; second, it remains the threat of smudges attack; last but not the end, the user password may follow some certain patterns due to the hot-spots in the password images. To date, no theoretical study has analyzed the security of this scheme. Therefore, it is necessary to test its security. Deduction and hypothesis provided the inspiration in analyzing user choices in the Windows 8 graphical password scheme for hot-spots.

3   Lab Study and Clusters

We conducted a lab study, detailed in this section, of the Windows 8 graphical password scheme. The purpose of the study was to determine user choices for passwords. There were 71 participants in our lab study, 36 males and 35 females. All the participants belong to a university community, including staff, students, and faculty. They ranged in age between 20 and 30, and none of them were familiar with Windows 8 graphical password scheme prior to the study. In our study, we simulated a PC-based version of Windows 8 graphical password scheme for users to collect the data. We chose a PC with a 19-inch screen and 1280×1024 screen resolution as the experiment equipment because of its popularity and convenience in collecting experimental data.

The study's methodology, results and analysis are respectively provided in section 3.2, 3.3 and 3.4.

3.1   Review of Windows 8 Graphical Password Scheme

The core of Windows 8 graphical password scheme is comprised of two complimentary parts which is a picture from the user's picture collection and a set of gestures that the user draws upon it. The user can choose the picture himself/herself instead of picking from a canned set of Microsoft images, because the designers believed that choosing images by user can increase both the security and the memorability of the password. The graphical password feature is designed to highlight the parts of an image that were important to users with a set of gestures. The three types of gestures offered include tap, straight line and circles. Any combination of those gestures can be used for a password. So, someone trying to reproduce the user's graphical password needs to not only know the parts of the image the user highlighted and the order he did it in, but also the direction and the start and end points the circles and lines that he drew.

Once a user has selected a password image, the scheme divides the image into a grid. The longer dimension of the image is divided into 100 segments, while the shorter dimension is then divided on that scale to create the grid upon which the user draws gestures. To set up the graphical password, users need to draw a set of gestures on the field that the scheme creates. Individual points are defined by their coordinate (x, y) position on the grid. For the straight line, the scheme records the starting and ending coordinates, as well as the order in which they occur. It uses the ordering information to determine the direction the line was drawn (shown in Fig. 2). For the circle, the scheme records a center point coordinate, the radius, and the directionality of the circle. For the tap, the scheme records the coordinate of the touch point.

When a user attempts to login the system with graphical password, the scheme evaluates the gestures the user provides, and compares them to the set of gestures the user drew in the registration period. It analyses the difference between each gesture and decides whether to authenticate the user based on the amount of error in the set. If a gesture type is wrong – for example, it should be a circle, but instead it is a line – the authentication will always fail. When the types, ordering, and directionality are all

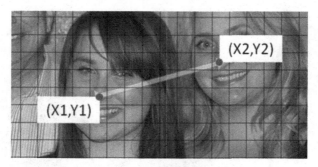

Fig. 2. Grids of the scheme

correct, the scheme will compare how far off each gesture was from the ones the user sets before, and decide if it is close enough to authenticate the user.

3.2   Methodology

In our experiment, each user was asked to create a graphical password on each 3 different images. In order to effectively collect data and study the user choice, the experiment provided three background images for users to select. The experiment asked the user to set one password in each of the three background images. Before the experiment, an experimental instruction and requirement was provided for each user. The detailed experiment steps for each image were as follows:

(1) Create: Users created a password in accordance with the requirements of the scheme. The length of each password is three.
(2) Confirm: Users confirmed their password by re-entering their gesture. If they made a mistake, they had the options of re-trying as many times as they wished, resetting their password (returning to step1), or skipping this trial.
(3) Questionnaire: Users answered two questions pertaining to their newly created password, providing their perception of how easy this password would be to remember in a week and how easy it was to create the password.
(4) Distraction task: As established in psychology studies users spent at least 30s completing a 3D mental rotation tasks to simulate a longer passage of time and to clear visual working memory.
(5) Login: Users re-entered their password. They could retry if they made mistakes, reset their password (return to step1), or skip the trial if they were unable to remember their password.

3.3   Results

Fig. 3 shows the raw data including circles, line segments and taps of lab study. The circles and line segments are presented without directions, and we will separately analyze circles, line segments and taps and divide user choice into some clusters for analysis in the following section.

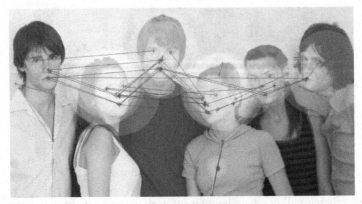

(a)   Background image 1

(b)   Background image 2   (c)   Background image 3

Fig. 3. Result of lab study

3.4   Analysis of Results

Analysis Preparation. We collected the data from the lab study as described in section 3.1, and used the K-means clustering algorithm to determine a set F of clusters and their sizes.

To calculate the clusters based on the user data set of lab study, we assigned all of the observed user operations to clusters as follows: Let R be the raw user data set of click points, T a list of temporary clusters and F the final result set of clusters. T and F are initially empty. The K-means clustering algorithm we applied as followed:

(1) For each $c_k \in R$, let C_k be a temporary cluster containing click-point c_k. Temporarily assign all user click-points in R within c_k's -region to C_k. Add C_k to T. Each $c_k \in R$ can be temporarily assigned to multiple clusters C_k.

(2) Sort all clusters in T by size, in decreasing order.

(3) Make permanent assignments of click-points to clusters as follows. Let C_l to be the largest cluster in T. Permanently assign each click-point $c_k \in B_l$ to C_l, and then delete each $c_k \in B_l$ from all other clusters in T. Delete C_l from T and add C_l to F. Repeat until T is empty.

A set F of clusters graphical password and their sizes is determined after this process.

In Windows 8 graphical password scheme, users can choose circle or line segment as parts of their passwords, and both of them contain a direction. In the first part of this section, we discuss the possibility of processing circles and line segments in the form of clusters of points.

Line segment contains a starting point and a terminal point, and we can determine the unique line segment if two points were given. Cluster algorithm can be applied to determine the clusters of starting points and terminal points. The starting points and terminal points are usually distributed to different clusters and we ignore the condition if they are in the same cluster, thus we can calculate the number of all potential line segments based on the clusters and their size. Assuming the clusters of starting points and terminal points are marked as $c_1, c_2 \cdots$ and c_n, and the size of each cluster is $a_1, a_2 \cdots$ and a_n. Let F be the set of the clusters of starting points and terminal points, and then we can calculate the amount of all line segments with direction by the following formula.

$$N = \sum a_i \left(\sum a_j \right) \; (i = 1, \cdots, n; j = 1, \cdots, n; j \neq i) \qquad (1)$$

If we draw a line segment based on the clusters in set F, the probability of getting the line segment that we drew is theoretically $1/N$ and we can get it using finite trials. Considering the effect of error tolerance, the probability may be higher than the theoretical value.

A circle can be determined by radius and a point. Given a point without radius, the number of circles we can draw in the background picture is M, and M equals the maximum radius. The radius is increased by pixel integers. Without considering the error tolerance, the probability of drawing the exact circle is $1/M$. If an error tolerance is set appropriately, which make the circle with radius r_1 to r_2 $(r_2 > r_1)$ considered as the same circle, we can get the circle that we expected in fewer trials. Assuming the clusters of the center of circles marked as $c_1, c_2 \cdots$ and c_n, the size of each cluster is $a_1, a_2 \cdots$ and a_n, and the clusters are independent from each other, we consider the circles that are determined by the points in each cluster have a similar maximum radius. For each cluster, the calculation number is approximately $a_i * r_i$, and r_i means the maximum radius in cluster c_i. The probability to get the circle in cluster c_i is $1/(a_i * r_i)$ without error tolerance. Based on the above analysis, the number of circles we can draw in all clusters is $\sum a_i * r_i (i = 1, 2, 3, \cdots, n)$. In the Windows 8 graphical password scheme, both the circle and line segment contain two directions, and users will have 5^3 choices in the register procedure. The choices in the register procedure and the combination of circles, line segments and taps in each choice are finite, thus brute force attack will be a threat to the scheme.

Analysis. Based on the above analysis, we will analyze circles and line segments in the form of tap clusters.

Fig. 4 to 6 show the clusters of the data set. According to the clusters in F, we calculated the observed "probability" p_j (based on our lab study data set) of the cluster j being clicked, as cluster size divided by total clicks observed.

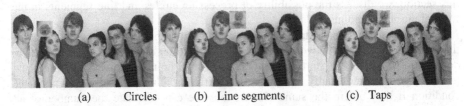

(a)   Circles   (b) Line segments   (c) Taps

Fig. 4. Separate clusters of circles, taps and line segments in background image 1

(b)   Circles   (b) Line segments   (c) Taps

Fig. 5. Separate clusters of circles, taps and line segments in background image 2

Fig. 4 to 6 show the clusters of the circle center, the starting points and terminal points of line segments and clicked taps. For each figure, we attach a partial enlarged view of the top five clusters. For circles, users select a center with a certain radius and draw a circle in any direction as the password. For line segments, users choose one starting point and terminal point, and draw a line between the two points as the password. For taps, users click any points of the password image as the password.

(c)   Circles   (b) Line segments   (c) Taps

Fig. 6. Separate clusters of circles, taps and line segments in background image 3

The probability p_j of the cluster j being clicked can be calculated, if the cluster size is given. The probability p_j indicates the probability of a cluster being clicked for a single click. When the probability p_j of a cluster is sufficiently high, we can determine a confidence interval by using the following formula, which provides the $100(1-\alpha)\%$ confidence interval for a population proportion [13].

$$p \pm z_{\alpha/2} \sqrt{\frac{pq}{m}} \tag{2}$$

Here m is the total number of clicks (i.e., five times the number of users), p takes the role of p_j, $q = 1 - p$, and $z_{\alpha/2}$ is from a z-table.

Table 2 to 4 show the selected probability and 95% confidence intervals of the top 5 clusters for the three images of the circles, line segments and taps.

According to the confidence intervals in Tables 2 to 4, we can predict that the similar population parts would be chosen by most of users with 95% confidence $(\alpha = 0.05)$. For example, the confidence interval of circles in table 3, the first row shows the highest frequency clusters, we calculated that approximately 27.5% users would choose the center of circles in this part as their passwords. Based on the formula 2, approximately 13.7% and 41.3% users are expected to choose in this cluster with 95% confidence.

From the analyses provided in this section, we can draw a preliminary conclusion that in the Windows 8 graphical password scheme, users tended to choose the parts that have obvious characters and these parts cluster in form of hot-spots. In the background image 3 of our experiment, the hot-spots clusters are dispersed, and it will take a longer time to attack by a brute force attack. Image choice has significant impact on the security [14], considering the existence of hot-spots, we can use pictures with dispersed hot-spot clusters to reduce the threat to security.

Table 2. The selected probability and 95% confidence intervals of background image 1

	Circles (40)			Line segments (92)			Taps (127)	
Size	P_j	95% CI (P_j)	Size	P_j	95% CI (P_j)	Size	P_j	95% CI (P_j)
11	0.275	(0.137; 0.413)	8	0.087	(0.029; 0.145)	11	0.087	(0.038; 0.136)
7	0.175	(0.057; 0.292)	7	0.076	(0.022; 0.130)	10	0.079	(0.032; 0.125)
6	0.15	(0.039; 0.261)	6	0.065	(0.015; 0.115)	9	0.071	(0.026; 0.116)
4	0.1	(0.007; 0.193)	5	0.054	(0.008; 0.100)	8	0.063	(0.021; 0.105)
4	0.1	(0.007; 0.193)	5	0.054	(0.008; 0.100)	8	0.063	(0.021; 0.105)

Table 3. The selected probability and 95% confidence intervals of background image 2

	Circles (36)			Line segments (98)			Taps (129)	
Size	P_j	95% CI (P_j)	Size	P_j	95% CI (P_j)	Size	P_j	95% CI (P_j)
6	0.167	(0.045; 0.289)	9	0.091	(0.034; 0.148)	9	0.069	(0.025; 0.113)
5	0.139	(0.026; 0.252)	7	0.071	(0.020; 0.122)	8	0.062	(0.021; 0.103)
4	0.111	(0.008; 0.214)	7	0.071	(0.020; 0.122)	8	0.062	(0.021; 0.103)
4	0.111	(0.008; 0.214)	5	0.051	(0.007; 0.095)	7	0.054	(0.015; 0.093)
4	0.111	(0.008; 0.214)	4	0.041	(0.002; 0.080)	6	0.046	(0.010; 0.082)

Table 4. The selected probability and 95% confidence intervals of background image 3

Circles (38)			Line segments (84)			Taps (133)		
Size	P_j	95% CI (P_j)	Size	P_j	95% CI (P_j)	Size	P_j	95% CI (P_j)
7	0.179	(0.059; 0.299)	5	0.057	(0.009; 0.105)	5	0.057	(0.009; 0.105)
6	0.154	(0.041; 0.267)	5	0.057	(0.009; 0.105)	5	0.057	(0.009; 0.105)
4	0.103	(0.008; 0.198)	5	0.057	(0.009; 0.105)	5	0.057	(0.009; 0.105)
4	0.103	(0.008; 0.198)	5	0.057	(0.009; 0.105)	5	0.057	(0.009; 0.105)
4	0.103	(0.008; 0.198)	4	0.045	(0.002; 0.088)	4	0.045	(0.002; 0.088)

4   Field Study and Attacks

4.1   Field Study and Relation to Lab Study Results

After lab study, we conducted a field study on the first background image to verify the results of lab study. The experimental conditions are the same as the lab study except for the number of participants.

Here we present the clustering results from the field study, and compare these results to those from the lab study. Fig. 7 shows that the hot clusters in field study are

(a)   Circles

(b)   Line segments   (c)   Taps

Fig. 7. Separate clusters of circles, taps and line segments of field study in background image 1

almost the same as the lab study, but other clusters also began to emerge. Table 5 shows that the selected probability of top 5 clusters all reduce to different extent. Using the top 5 clusters of circles as an example, we can see that the selected probability of the top 1 cluster reduces from 27.5% to 10.9%, and that the total selected probability of top 5 clusters reduces from 80.0% to 45.6%. The reason for this result is the user-selected area is more random with the increase of experimental data. By comparing Fig. 7 and Fig. 4, this reason is confirmed.

The field study results (and their close relationship to the lab study's results) indicate that users' choice from the lab study would provide a reasonably close approximation of their choice in the field.

Table 5. The selected probability and 95% confidence intervals in field study

Circles (311)			Line segments (468)			Taps (262)		
Size	P_j	95% CI (P_j)	Size	P_j	95% CI (P_j)	Size	P_j	95% CI (P_j)
34	0.109	(0.074; 0.144)	30	0.064	(0.042; 0.086)	15	0.057	(0.029; 0.085)
33	0.106	(0.072; 0.140)	25	0.053	(0.033; 0.073)	15	0.057	(0.029; 0.085)
28	0.090	(0.058; 0.122)	25	0.053	(0.033; 0.073)	14	0.053	(0.026; 0.080)
24	0.077	(0.047; 0.107)	23	0.049	(0.029; 0.069)	12	0.046	(0.021; 0.071)
23	0.074	(0.045; 0.103)	22	0.047	(0.028; 0.066)	11	0.042	(0.018; 0.066)

4.2   Human-Seeded Attack

Because of the clusters existing in this scheme, human-seeded attacks based on data harvest from users might prove a successful attack strategy against the Windows 8 graphical password scheme. Here we describe our method of human-seeded attack, and then our results are presented.

Method. Based on the clusters obtained by field study, we carried out a simulated attack. If a cluster includes more than 3 points, it is considered as a valid cluster. The number of valid clusters is shown in Table 6.

Attack experiments were divided into two groups. Group I used all valid clusters as a seed and group II used the top 15 valid clusters as a seed. In our experiments, each user drew three gestures as his/her password. According to the password set by users, we conducted our simulated attack. If the three gestures that the user drew were all contained in the default seed, we consider that the attack is a success, if not, a failure.

Result and Analysis. Experimental results from two groups are shown in Table 7. As we see in Table 7, the success rate of group I was 66.96% and that of group II was 54.46%. Compared with the result of group I, with the clusters reduced by nearly half, the success rate of group II reduced only 12.5%. The result shows that the top 15 valid clusters already contain the most popular areas users choose, and that further demonstrates this scheme contains serious hot-spots and is vulnerable to dictionary attacks.

Table 6. Cluster number of each gesture

	Circle	Line Segments	Taps
Cluster number	25	28	27

4.3   Automated Attack

Human-seeded attacks obtain a good success rate, but require numerous experiments for each picture. Therefore, we designed a common approach to crack this scheme. Here we describe the automated attack method, and then present the experimental results.

Method. We used the model that proposed by Dirik A E et al. to identify the most likely regions for users to choose in order to create graphical passwords and supposed that users often selected the centers of the objects in an image as password [15]. In this model, a color-based mean-shift segmentation algorithm is applied to the image in order to predict the possible choice positions. After segmentation, the centroid of each segmented which is mapped to the choice position region is calculated. Finally, we conducted a series of screening on these centroids and get the predicted selected position. The detailed processing method was shown in [15].

Based on the predicted selected position (shown in Fig. 8) obtained by the above model, we carried out a simulated attack for background image 1. In our experiment, we use the predicted selected position as a dictionary. Each user drew three gestures as his/her password. If the three gestures the user drew were all contained in the predicted selected position, we consider that the attack is success.

Fig. 8. Predicted selected points in background image 1

Result and Analysis. Experimental results of automated attack are shown in Table 7. As we see in Table 7, the success rate of the automated attack was 42.86%, demonstrating that we can discover 42.86% of 112 user passwords by searching the dictionary. Compared with the result of the human-seeded attack, the success rate decreased significantly, but it still causes a serious potential security for users.

The results of the experiment are directly related to background images. If background images contain enough complex content, the success rate will relatively low, and vice versa.

Table 7. Success rate of two groups

Attack method		# of password	# of success attack	success rate
Human-Seeded	Group I	112	75	66.96%
attack	Group II	112	61	54.46%
Automated attack		112	48	42.86%

5   Concluding Remarks and Future Work

In this paper, we conducted a series of experiments to research the potential security problems of Windows 8 graphical password scheme. In our lab study, we choose three pictures as background images to reduce the effect of image choice, which may cause a significant impact on the security. Based on the data in lab experiments, we presented the results in the form of clusters. Numerous significant hot-spots were found in the background images when users set their passwords using the guidance offered by Microsoft. After the lab study, we conducted a field study on background image 1 to verify the results of the lab study, and from the results of the field study, we also reached the same conclusion. Based on the data from the field study, we conducted an attack to prove our conclusion. The success rates of 66.69% and 54.46% obtained also strong prove the hot-spots in the Windows 8 graphical password scheme. Finally, we designed an automated method to attack this scheme, and our simulated automated attack obtained a success rate of 42.86%. In future work, we will try to improve the scheme, based on the obtained experimental results, to reduce the hot-spots threat.

Acknowledgements. The authors would like to thank the reviewers for their careful reading of this paper. This project is supported by the National Natural Science Foundation of China (60903198) and the Fundamental Research Funds for the Central Universities.

References

1. Yan, J., Blackwell, A., Anderson, R., Grant, A.: Password memorability and security: Empirical results. IEEE Security & Privacy 2(5), 25–31 (2004)
2. Paivio, A., Rogers, T.B., Smythe, P.C.: Why are pictures easier to recall than words? Psychonomic Science (1968)
3. Shepard, R.N.: Recognition memory for words, sentences, and pictures. Journal of Verbal Learning and Verbal Behavior 6(1), 156–163 (1967)
4. Bower, G.H., Karlin, M.B., Dueck, A.: Comprehension and memory for pictures. Memory & Cognition 3(2), 216–220 (1975)
5. Blonder, G.: Graphical password, US Patent No. 5.559.961 (1996)

6. Biddle, R., Chiasson, S., Van Oorschot, P.C.: Graphical passwords: Learning from the first generation. Technical Report TR-09-09, School of Computer Science, Carleton University (2009)
7. Suo, X., Zhu, Y., Owen, G.S.: Graphical passwords: A survey. In: 21st Annual on Computer Security Applications Conference, p. 10. IEEE (2005)
8. Jermyn, I., Mayer, A., Monrose, F., Reiter, M.K., Rubin, A.D.: The design and analysis of graphical passwords. In: Proceedings of the 8th USENIX Security Symposium, pp. 1–14 (1999)
9. Wiedenbeck, S., Waters, J., Birget, J.C., Brodskiy, A., Memon, N.: PassPoints: Design and longitudinal evaluation of a graphical password system. International Journal of Human-Computer Studies 63(1), 102–127 (2005)
10. Signing in with a picture password, in Building Windows 8 in the MSDN Blogs, http://blogs.msdn.com/b/b8/archive/2011/12/16/signing-in-with-a-picture-password.aspx
11. Nali, D., Thorpe, J.: Analyzing user choice in graphical passwords. School of Computer Science, Carleton University, Tech. Rep. TR-04-01 (2004)
12. Thorpe, J., van Oorschot, P.C.: Human-seeded attacks and exploiting hot-spots in graphical passwords. In: 16th USENIX Security Symposium, pp. 103–118 (2007)
13. Devore, J.L.: Probability and Statistics for Engineering and the Sciences, 4th edn. Brooks/Col, Pacific Grove (1995)
14. van Oorschot, P.C., Thorpe, J.: Exploiting predictability in click-based graphical passwords. Journal of Computer Security 19(4), 669–702 (2011)
15. Dirik, A.E., Memon, N., Birget, J.C.: Modeling user choice in the PassPoints graphical password scheme. In: Proceedings of the 3rd Symposium on Usable Privacy and Security, pp. 20–28. ACM (2007)

Static Detection of Dangerous Behaviors in Android Apps

Shaoyin Cheng[1], Shengmei Luo[2,3], Zifeng Li[1], Wei Wang[2],
Yan Wu[2], and Fan Jiang[1]

[1] Information Technology Security Evaluation Center,
University of Science and Technology of China, Hefei, 230027, P.R. China
[2] ZTE Corporation, Nanjing, 210012, P.R. China
[3] Department of Computer Science, Tsinghua University, Beijing, 100084, P.R. China
{sycheng,fjiang}@ustc.edu.cn, lzf75@mail.ustc.edu.cn,
{luo.shengmei,wang.wei8,wu.yan2}@zte.com.cn

Abstract. This paper presents a scheme to detect dangerous behaviors in Android apps. In order to identify different kinds of dangerous behaviors, we designed two analysis engines. On the one hand, taint analysis engine mainly detects privacy leak by tracking how user's sensitive data is used by an app; On the other hand, constant analysis engine focuses on the constant information in an app to identify other dangerous behaviors such as SP services ordering, phone bill consuming, and so on. We have implemented these two engines in a system called ApkRiskAnalyzer which identifies the dangerous behaviors by simulating the running process of an Android app statically. Furthermore, we analyzed 1260 malicious apps and found out dangerous behaviors in 1246 (98.9%) apps. Then we downloaded 630 normal apps from Google Play and identified dangerous behaviors in 575(91.3%) apps. These results demonstrate the effectiveness of ApkRiskAnalyzer.

Keywords: Android security, malware detection, dangerous behavior, static analysis.

1 Introduction

With the increasing popularity of smartphones, security of Android apps has attracted global attention. The distribution channels of Android apps are complex and lack of effective management mechanism, so security problems are more and more prominent. During the first half of 2012, NetQin [1] detected 17,676 mobile malware, which infect nearly 13 million phones in the world. 78% of the detected malware targeted smartphones running Android [2]. According to TrustGo [3], 23 of the top 500 Google Play [4] apps are considered high-risk. More than 175 million downloads of 'High Risk' apps were found [5]. Although Android provides a permission mechanism to try to limit the behavior of an app, the user tends to be less concerned about the permissions required by the app before installing it. Moreover, the permission mechanism cannot guarantee that the app is in the normal use of these privileges. Stotaway [6] detects 940 Android apps, and the results show that about 1/3 of the apps request a few extra privileges. Therefore, the analysis to the security of Android apps is urgently required.

G. Wang et al. (Eds.): CSS 2013, LNCS 8300, pp. 363–376, 2013.
© Springer International Publishing Switzerland 2013

Currently mobile anti-virus software detects malware by signatures extracted from known malware samples. Xuxian Jiang [7] used behavioral footprints generated from 10 known Android malware families to detect known Android malware, and used two additional heuristics to capture suspicious dynamic code loading behaviors. However, this method is limited to these footprints and cannot be used to detect unknown malware. TaintDroid [8] took dynamic analysis method to detect privacy leak by tracing how apps employ the private data. This method works only when the malicious behavior is triggered, and it cannot prevent malicious behavior in advance. For apps whose trigger logic is complex, such as triggered on a certain day of a certain month, this method shows some disadvantages.

In this paper, we propose a practical scheme to detect potential security risk in Android apps by simulating the running process of an Android app statically without relying on the malware signatures as the anti-virus software does. Our goals are to detect different types of dangerous behaviors such as privacy leak, SP (Service Provider) services ordering, phone bill consuming and so on. Dangerous behaviors are the behaviors which may trigger a potential security risk, including the malicious behavior carefully constructed by an attacker and the user behavior that perhaps triggers a security risk. Sometimes, the dangerous user behavior may be in accordance with user's real purpose, for example, sending all contacts out. However, no detecting tool can completely understand the user's real intention. The tool can only specify the dangerous behaviors, and then security analysts can distinguish the real malicious behavior and the user-wanted normal behavior by hand. To detect dangerous behaviors, we first present a taint analysis engine to track how user's sensitive data, such as contacts, SMS messages, call history, location, device ID, is used by Android apps. We also propose a constant analysis engine to track how an Android app uses certain useful constant values such as constant URL, phone number, SMS content, and so on.

We have implemented the scheme in a system called ApkRiskAnalyzer. In order to verify the effectiveness of ApkRiskAnalyzer, we analyzed 1260 malicious Android apps downloaded from Android Malware Genome Project [9]. The results show that dangerous behaviors are detected in 98% of the apps among which 85 percent apps are high-risk. Then we analyzed 630 normal apps downloaded from Google Play, including top 320 free apps and top 310 free new apps. Dangerous behaviors were detected in 582 (92%) of them. The SP services ordering behavior was detected in 7 apps and 462(73.3%) apps were found to collect user's privacy.

In summary, the main contributions of our paper can be listed as follows.

- To the best of our knowledge, ApkRiskAnalyzer is the first whole-program simulator in bytecode level. It can simulate the implicit invocations which are very common and troublesome in Android apps.
- To detect as many kinds of dangerous behaviors as possible, we propose two engines: taint analysis engine and constant analysis engine. These two engines can detect most security problems in Android apps.
- We have implemented a dangerous behavior detection system called ApkRiskAnalyzer. Extensive experiments were conducted and our system was demonstrated effective.

The rest of this paper is organized as follows. Section 2 provides a high-level overview of ApkRiskAnalyzer. Section 3 shows the specific design and implementation of ApkRiskAnalyzer. Then evaluation is presented in Section 4 and the limitations of our prototype system are discussed in Section 5. Finally, Section 6 describes related work, and Section 7 makes conclusions.

2   Approach Overview

We intend to design a dangerous behavior detection system that can detect whether an app is dangerous or not before installing. Dangerous behavior analysis on Android apps may encounter the following challenges:

- **No source code.** Android apps are mostly closed sources, in other words, source code is unavailable. We need to analyze the bytecode directly.
- **Resource constrained.** Compared with computer, smartphones may be limited in computing, storage, power, etc. These limitations should be overcome if we want to detect dangerous behaviors on smartphones.
- **Implicit invocations.** There are a number of invocations in Android system, such as interface, multiple threads, reflection, and callbacks. It is difficult for static analysis to accurately find the actual called functions.

To overcome these challenges, we apply the following approaches:

- We directly analyze the Dalvik [10] bytecode and do not need to get the source code, nor decompile the Dalvik bytecode to Java source code. Compared with x86 binary code, Dalvik bytecode has a richer semantic information. Dalvik bytecode, for example, has the specialized instruction to operate on the object data. Therefore, more accurate simulation execution analysis is available in byte code level.
- We do not run the apps and instead we complete the dangerous behaviors detection directly on the computer. With the help of the powerful computing capability of computer, we can carry out the batch concurrent detection of dangerous apps, which greatly improves the efficiency of the analysis.
- Three methods are proposed to solve the implicit invocations. The inter-procedural type information is employed to solve the problem of interface calls. A mapping table is used to solve the problem of callbacks and multiple threads. The inter-procedural constant value is propagated to deal with the reflection problem.

The overall architecture of ApkRiskAnalyzer is shown in Figure 1. Before detection, we need to unpack the APK (AndroidPackage) and extract the bytecode (.dex) file. Then we use IDA pro [11] to disassemble the bytecode and employ IDAPython [12] plug to collect the required information to the database. IDA pro [11] is a powerful commercial disassemble software and it starts to support Dalvik bytecode from v6.1. We saved the disassembly information to the MySQL database, so it does not require re-disassemble when we want to re-analyze an app. The step above is called pretreatment.

After the pretreatment, ApkRiskAnalyzer reads bytecode information from the database, and simulates the execution process of an app. The simulation execution includes two phases: intra-procedural analysis and inter-procedural analysis. In intra-procedural analysis, the execution sequence of instructions is calculated according to the control flow graph (CFG for short), and each instruction should be simulated based on its semantic. In inter-procedural analysis, function call process is simulated based on the call graph. The taint and constant analysis engines are implemented on the basis of simulation execution to trace the data flow. Then based on the results of the two analysis engines and detection rules defined in the rule base, we detect dangerous behaviors at the call point of sensitive functions, and the results are shown to users finally.

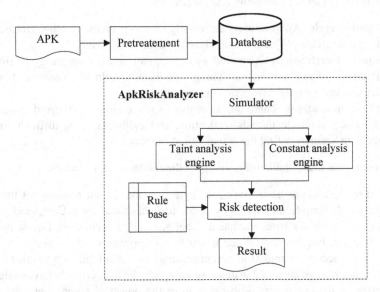

Fig. 1. The overall architecture of ApkRiskAnalyzer

3   Design and Implementation

This section analyzes the design and implementation of ApkRiskAnalyzer.

3.1   Simulator

Simulator does not need to run the app, but simulates the running process statically. Starting from an entry function, simulator traverses each instruction of a function in turn on the basis of CFG, and calls the corresponding function at each call point.

Entry Functions. Entry functions,are the functions that have no caller functions, and the entrances of static analysis. In general, there are more than one entry functions for each Android app. There are two ways to get the possible entry functions. On one hand, we can extract the possible entry functions from the file *AndroidManifest.xml*. The response function for each activity, receiver, provider and service can be regarded as entry function. On the other hand, we can search functions without caller from call graph as the entry functions. In Android apps there are a number of implicit invocations that are invoked by Android system. These implicit invocations should also be treated as the entry functions in order to ensure code coverage.

Intra-procedural Analysis. The execution process of a function is simulated in intra-procedural analysis phase, which is shown in Algorithm 1. First, for a function, the execution sequence of the basic blocks in the function should be calculated according to the CFG. Each basic block corresponds to a state. For the current basic block, if there is a parent block, all the states of its parent blocks will be merged as its initial state. Then, each instruction will be simulated according to the instruction sequence in a basic block and updates the state of current basic block until all basic blocks have been analyzed. Instructions can be divided into different categories according to the semantics [8], and simulated by the category.

```
Algorithm 1 : Intraprocedural analysis
//Input:  C is the control flow graph of a function
//Output: state of the return value and parameter
Simulate (C)
1:  currentState = ∅; //empty set
2:  blocks = calcBlockSequence(C);
3:  foreach (block in blocks)
4:    if(hasParentBlock(block))
5:      states = getParentState(block);
6:    foreach(state in states)
7:      currentState = mergeState(currentState, state);
8:      instructions = getInstructionSequence(block);
9:      foreach(ins in instructions)
10:        simulateIns(ins);
11:      updateState(currentState);
12: return currentState;
```

Inter-procedural Analysis. The call process of a function is simulated in the inter-procedural analysis phase. The inter-procedural analysis involves two phases: constructing the call condition for each invocation and resolving callee's return state. Considering a function may be called multiple times, and if all the instructions of the callee are analyzed at each invocation, the system overhead will be increased undoubtedly. To solve this problem, we build a summary for each function that has been analyzed [13]. Before a function is analyzed, the return state can be resolved directly if the summary has been built. However, summaries are not perfect, and they may reduce the accuracy of static analysis for the lack of type information and calling context. For example, when an interface function is called and the *this* object is a parameter passed in from outside, the accurate type of the object may not be determined, so we may not know which function should be called. The inheritance relationships are established to solve this problem to some extent. When in this condition, we look up all the subclasses of this interface class and invoke all the possible functions in turn.

Implicit Invocations. There are a number of implicit invocations in Android system, and the accuracy of analysis will be greatly reduced if the actual invoked functions are not found. We propose three methods to handle these implicit invocations [14]. The inter-procedural type information is employed to solve the problem of interface calls. A mapping table is used to solve the problem of callbacks and multiple threads. The inter-procedural constant value is propagated to solve the reflection problem.

3.2   Taint Analysis

A large number of user privacy information, including contacts, SMS, call history, photos, location, and device information, is stored on the smartphone. If this information can be improperly used, users will suffer too much. Taint analysis engine detects potentially dangerous behaviors by monitoring the incorrect use of sensitive data in the Android apps. In taint analysis, user's sensitive data was imported into the app by system library functions, and the relevant variable will be labeled a *Taint* tag. Then taint analysis tracks how tainted data impacts other data. Some dangerous behaviors may happen, when tainted data is propagated to a dangerous function calling point, or called taint sink.

Existing taint analysis approaches focus on the taint state, but not the value of a variable. Forexample, the database query function *ContentResolver.query(...)* will determine the queried content by the value of the first parameter. If the value of the first parameter is *ContactsContract.Contacts.CONTENT_URI*, the function will read the contracts. And if the value is *Calendars.CONTENT_URI*, the content of calendars will be read. Therefore, when analyzing the taint source methods, we should know the values of the key parameters as well. Thanks to the constant analysis engine, these constant values can be detected conveniently.

We will take the privacy leak as an example to introduce the taint analysis process. There are usually three steps to leak a user's privacy. First, user's sensitive data will be read into the app by some system methods (generally Android APIs). These methods are called taint source. The next step is the propagation of the tainted data. Finally, the tainted data are sent out though the network, SMS, etc, called taint sink.

Taint Source. The user's sensitive information is usually collected through the system library functions, which are also called taint source functions. For example, the user's device ID will be read by function *TelephonyManager.getDeviceId()*, whose return value is the device ID. So the return value is labeled with a taint flag. In order to accurately understand the sensitive data collected by the app, we refer to the Android APIs, and collect all these kinds of system functions into a rule base. A rule in the rule base includes the information of a taint source function, such as the function name, the class name that the function belongs to, the number of parameters, the type of each parameter, the category which the sensitive data belongs to, the variable that tainted by the sensitive data, and so on.

Taint Propagation. We propagate the taint tag by the semantics of Dalvik instructions, which can be divided into different categories according to the semantics [8], and each category corresponds to an analysis function. With regards to the system library functions, we should not go inside to analyze the instructions, which may actually affect the propagation of tainted data. Therefore certain special strategies are needed to follow for these system library functions [14].

Taint Sink. Privacy leak behavior happens when user's sensitive data are propagated to some dangerous functions that send the sensitive data to the outside of the app. For example, the function *SmsManager.sendTextMessage(...)* could send the sensitive data to a certain number through SMS service. These dangerous functions are also called sink functions. We collect all the sink functions from Android APIs and build a rule base that is used for dangerous behaviors detection. The detail information about the rule base is introduced in section 3.4.

3.3   Constant Analysis

The constant analysis refers to tracing how the constant values (such as constant strings and immediate value) are used by the app. In Android apps there are a lot of constant values such as phone numbers, text messages, URLs. They are meaningful and useful for us to understand the app's behavior. For some malicious apps, the text messages with constant content are sent to some constant numbers to order SP services. This kind of malicious behavior cannot be detected by taint analysis engine as there is no taint data in sink functions. Experiments of the apps on Google Play show that 70.6% of the apps open fixed URLs and 1.1% of the apps send text messages to constant SP number.

Constant Marking. Generally there are two kinds of constant value, immediate and constant strings. In Dalvik bytecode, the constant value is defined by const instructions. As an example, the instruction *const-string va, "abc"* defines a variable *va*, and the value of *va* is a constant string *"abc"*. In order to track the use of constant value, a const label is used to mark the constant value and the value of a constant variable is also saved. In the const instruction above, *va* will be marked by const label and its value will be set to *"abc"*.

Constant Propagation. Constant propagation, similar to the taint propagation, propagates the const label according to the semantics of Dalvik instructions. For the instruction *move v1, v2*, if *v2* is constant, *v1* will be set to constant. There is another example, for the instruction *add v1, v2, v3*, how to set *v1* if *v2* is constant and *v3* is not? In order to maintain as much information as possible during the constant analysis, we set *v1* to a *const* label.

3.4   Risk Detection

The dangerous behaviors are realized by invoking dangerous Android APIs. Dangerous functions are the system library functions that might be harmful to user or the Android system. The malware makers could take advantage of these dangerous functions to complete malicious goals. For example, the sending SMS functions are used to order SP services. However, these risk functions may bring different hazards depending on the context information. Take sending SMS functions for example, if the destiny number is a SP number, the app is likely to order SP services; but if the destiny number is a normal phone number, the app may gather the user's phone number and confirm which phone has installed the app.

To accurately identify different types of malicious behavior, we construct a detection rule base in which all dangerous functions information extracted from Android APIs are saved. In the detection rule base, we set a risk type according to the dangerous function's parameter. For example, the function *SmsManager.sendTextMessage (...)* has five parameters, the first is the destination number and the third is the content of the text message. If the value of the first parameter, namely destination number, is started with "*106*", it may be a SP services ordering behavior. But if the destination number is a normal phone number and the value of the third parameter is sensitive data (normally tainted), it may be a privacy leak behavior. The dangerous behaviors are classified into five types, namely SP services ordering, privacy leak, charges consumption, native code loading and constant URL connection.

In addition to distinguishing different types of dangerous behaviors, the risk level is also needed to assess. For privacy leak behavior, the risk is very different for the leakage of address book or a log file. Sending privacy over network or via SMS is also not the same, and the latter will bring charges consumption.

In order to measure the degree of harm, dangerous behaviors are divided into three categories. *High-risk* behavior is the behavior that has great threat to user's money and privacy, such as SP services ordering, gathering address book or device ID, and so on. We set *middle-risk* for the behavior that we did not find sufficient evidences, but there are higher potential security risks. For example, we identified the sending SMS behavior but the destination number is unknown. The behavior will be set to *low-risk* which brings no direct damage for user's money and data but will indirectly affect system security or generate network traffic consumption, such as advertising connection.

4   Evaluation

We have implemented the above scheme in a prototype system ApkRiskAnalyzer. The pretreatment module is mainly implemented in Python and the rest analysis modules are mainly written in Java. In total, there are 25k LOC (Lines of Code) in Java and 1.7k LOC in Python. In order to evaluate the effectiveness of the method, we downloaded 1260 malicious apps from Android Malware Genome Project [9] in October 2012, and 630 normal apps from Google Play in November 2012, including top 320 free apps and top 310 new free apps.

A risk level is attached to each app. The app is *high-risk* if an app contains high dangerous behavior. If an app does not contain high dangerous behavior but contains middle dangerous behavior, the app is *middle-risk*. If an app only contains low dangerous behavior, the app is *low-risk*. The app is no-risk if no dangerous behavior is contained.

4.1   Detect Malicious Android Apps

To analyze these 1260 malicious apps, we first calculate the MD5 of each Dex file extracted from the apps and find that only 876 apps have different bytecode file. Then we analyze the 876 distinct apps using ApkRiskAnalyzer. The result is shown in Table 1. Among the 876 distinct apps, ApkRiskAnalyzer successfully uncovers 863(or 98.9%) risk apps. High-risk behaviors are discovered in 741 apps, 115 apps contain middle-risk behaviors and 10 apps contain low-risk behaviors. There are remaining 10 apps without any dangerous behavior for the reason that ApkRiskAnalyzer is only concerned about 5 types of dangerous behaviors. Besides, if we take all 1260 malicious apps into account, ApkRiskAnalyzer finds dangerous behaviors in 1246 (98.9%) apps.

Malicious behaviors are divided into five categories. Table 2 shows the statistical information classified by the types of dangerous behaviors about the 866 distinct dangerous apps. 45 (or 5.2%) of them contain SP services ordering behavior, 781(90.2%) of them contain privacy leak behavior, 557(64.3%) of them contain charges consumption behavior, 727(83.9%) of them contain native code, and 611(70.6%) contain opening constant URL connection behavior.

Table 1. Statistics of dangerous behaviors in malicious apps

Risk level	High	Middle	Low	No
No. of apps	741	115	10	10
Percentage	84.6%	13.1%	1.1%	1.1%

Table 2. Type statistics of dangerous behaviors

Type	No. of apps	Percentage
SP services ordering	45	5.2%
Privacy leak	781	90.2%
Charges consumption	557	64.3%
Native code	727	83.9%
Constant URL connection	611	70.6%

Table 3. Category statistics of no dangerous behaviors

Malware category	No. of apps
FakeNetflix	1
gone60	9

The apps in which no dangerous behavior is detected are classified in accordance with the malware category as shown in Table 3. *FakeNetflix* [15] is a fishing app which counterfeits normal Netflix and displays the login screen. The entered username and password will be sent to a specific server. Since just sending the user's login information, the dangerous behaviors cannot be detected during our static analysis.

Gone60 [16] is a kind of malicious software that will automatically get the phone contacts, text messages, phone records, and upload them to a specified URL. The reading privacy behavior (taint source) is detected in the static analysis but the potential execution path to security risk (taint sink) is not found.

4.2   Detect Normal Android Apps

After analyzing the malicious Android apps, we analyze 630 apps from Google Play. The results are shown in Table 4. The results are beyond our imagination. In total, dangerous behaviors are detected in 575(91.3%) of them, and only 55(8.7%) apps contain no dangerous behavior. But compared with Table 1, only 17.6% of the apps are high-risk in Table 4, far less than 84.6% in Table 1.

Table 4. Statistics of dangerous behaviors in Google Play

Dangerous level	High risk	Middle risk	Low risk	No risk
No. of apps	111	337	127	55
Percentage	17.6%	53.5%	20.2%	8.7%

Table 5. Category statistics of the identified dangerous behaviors

Type	No. of apps	Percentage
SP services ordering	7	1.1%
Privacy leak	462	73.3%
Charges consumption	322	51.1%
Native code	423	67.1%
Constant URL connection	476	75.6%

The apps containing dangerous behaviors are classified in accordance with the type of the dangerous behaviors, and the results are shown in Table 5. Potential SP services ordering behavior is detected in 7 apps. The app *cn.com.fetion-20120830* sends "*KTFX*" to the SP number *10086* to order *Fetion* [17] service, which is a free service and not malicious. The app *com.anguanjia.safe-113* sends "*0000*" to *10086* to query the subscribed SP services. The app *com.blovestorm-70* sends text message to *106575555113126*. The app *com.snda.ciku-27, com.snda.cloudary-46, com.snda.youni-87* are the products of the same company [18], and send text message to some SP numbers such as *1065502180988, 10690882, 106575160882, 1065902188828.* The app *com.gamebean.Stoneage1-13* sends text message to the SP number *1065889915.*

Users' privacy data is collected by 73.3% of the apps. Further analysis of this kind of malicious behavior is shown in Table 6. Among of these apps, 21.4% of them collect user location, 3.2% of them collect user's address book, 11.3% of them read user's text message (SMS), and 37.4% of them read the device ID. The other apps read the photos, call history, log files, and other privacy data. For example, the app

Table 6. Statistics of privacy data type

Type of privacy	No. of apps	Percentage
Location	99	21.4%
Address book	15	3.2%
Text Message	52	11.3%
Device ID	173	37.4%

com.rovio.angrybirdsseasons-3010 is a very popular game [19], but it collects user's location and *IMSI* number. The app *InternetRadio.all-48* is a radio app, but it collects user's phone number, *IMEI* and *IMSI*.

51.1% of the apps will consume user's charges, such as sending text message. 67.1% of the apps contain native code, including dynamic link library (.so file) and executing system commands.

75.6% of the apps contain constant URL, including advertising links, website links, downloading app links, etc. For example, in the app *com.when.android.calendar365-29*, an app is downloaded from a constant URL "*http://when.365rili.com/dl/android*". The app *com.ijinshan.mguard-3040201* downloads an app from "*http://dl.sj.ijinshan.com/kBatteryDoctor_10010004.apk*".

4.3 Summary of Evaluation

Overall, ApkRiskAnalyzer is effective and successfully identifies most (98.9%) of the malicious apps. Then we analyzed the normal apps in Google Play using ApkRiskAnalyzer, and found that 91.3% of the apps contain dangerous behaviors. The evaluation results show that ApkRiskAnalyzer is practical and effective.

5   Discussion

Although our tool is powerful and effective to detect dangerous behaviors, there are still some limitations.

Determination of Malicious Apps. Although it is possible for ApkRiskAnalyzer to detect the dangerous behaviors of an app, we cannot accurately determine whether an app is malicious or not, even for known malware due to the limitations of the static method. For example, the app *com.anguanjia.safe-113* is a secure app and will send text message to a SP server to query the subscribed services. When the subscribed services are changed by some malicious apps, the user will receive a notification. We think this is a safe app in this case. Otherwise, it may be unsafe asthis violates our privacy.

Implicit Invocations. There are a number of implicit invocations in Android apps, including virtual functions, interfaces, multithread, reflection, and so on. In addition, callbacks are also largely used in Android apps. Although we have proposed some methods to find the actual callee function, but this does not always work. For example, in multithread functions, if a subclass of the Thread class is passed as an argument to the callee function, we can't know the real run function when a start function is invoked in the callee function.

Security of the Native Code. Native code, generally written in C/C++ and compiled into a dynamic link library (.so file), has a very different binary format from Dalvik bytecode. Our ApkRiskAnalyzer tool has not yet supported the malicious behavior detection in native code. Considering that some kind of malicious apps use native code to obtain superuser privileges, we take the native code invocation as a kind of dangerous behavior. Meanwhile, many apps use native code to improve efficiency or realize security. Therefore we set a low dangerous level for this behavior to cause the vigilance of users and to prevent too many false positives.

False Positive. There are more false positives in static analysis compared with dynamic analysis. For instance, we cannot build the structure of the system object, and we will adopt object-level analysis when analyzing the system object, which will bring a certain degree of false positives. So does the system functions.

6   Related Work

Static Analysis for Android Security. Stowaway [6] statically analyzes how the apps use the Android APIs to detect whether an app requests over privileges. Stowaway uses flow-sensitive, intra-procedural analysis and inter-procedural analysis to a depth of 1 method call to solve the reflection problem. However, the execution process of the app is not simulated. Ded [20] is a decompiler which can recover the source code from Dalvik bytecode. Static analysis is used to find evidence of malware or exploitable vulnerabilities. DroidRanger [7] extracts behavioral footprints from 10 known Android malware families to detect new samples of these malware. In order to identify unknown malicious apps, two additional heuristics are proposed to capture dynamic code loading behavior. RiskRanker [21] divides the potential risks in Android apps into three categories: high-risk, medium-risk and low-risk. And the potential risks are detected in two-order risk analysis. In the first-order risk analysis, the high-risk apps are identified that obtain superuser privileges by exploit system vulnerabilities, and the medium-risk apps are identified that cost user's money or upload user's privacy. In the second-order risk analysis, encrypted native code execution and dynamic loading Dalvik code behavior are detected.

Dynamic Analysis for Android security. Paranoid Android [22] implements an attack detection framework based on recording and replaying. Android emulator is modified to apply dynamic taint analysis for attack detection. When tainted data is executed or taken as a parameter of a function, warnings are happens. So there may be lots of false positives. And the more detail information is unavailable. TaintDroid [8] is a system-level, dynamic and real-time information-flow tracking system which tracks the flow of privacy sensitive data in Dalvik bytecode level. Dalvik stack format is modified to use dynamic taint analysis. This method relies on the Android emulator and cannot be carried out in the real environment of the mobile phone. And the detection result is heavily dependent on the trigger conditions. How to design the test examples to meet the trigger conditions is also a problem. AppInspector [23] can automatically generate input and log during program execution, and can detect the privacy leak behavior by the analysis of log information.

Other Android Security Studies. Apex [24], MockDroid [25], TISSA [26] and App-Fence [27] expand the current Android framework to better provide fine-grained controls of the sensitive system resources accessed by third-party apps. Apex [24] is the extension of the Android security framework, and allows more fine-grained permissions restrictions. It can limit the use of the app running on permission, refuse some permission to allow others, and can also limit the number of times that the permission is used. Woodpecker [28] analyzes the system pre-loaded apps using data flow analysis. The result shows that eight phone mirrors do not execute permissions model correctly, 11 of the 13 privileges are leaked to delete user's data and send text messages without applying for any permission. Comdroid [29] analyzes the application communication vulnerabilities in Android apps and finds a number of exploitable vulnerabilities. David Barrera et al. [30] analyzed the distribution of Android permission used by apps.

7   Conclusion

This paper proposes a static analysis method that the execution process of an Android app is simulated to detect dangerous behaviors.   The method includes two analysis engine, i.e., taint analysis engine and constant analysis engine. We have implemented both engines in ApkRiskAnalyzer.   The effectiveness of our tool is demonstrated by detecting 1260 malicious apps and 630 normal apps.

Acknowledgments. This research was supported in part by the Fundamental Research Funds for the Central Universities of China (WK2101020004, WK0110000007), the Specialized Research Fund for the Doctoral Program of Higher Education of China (20113402120026), the Natural Science Foundation of Anhui Province of China (1208085QF112), the Foundation for Young Talents in College of Anhui Province of China (2012SQRL001ZD) and the Research Fund of ZTE Corporation.

References

1. NetQin, http://www.netqin.com
2. Mobile malware cases nearly triple in first half of 2012, says NetQin, http://www.computerworld.com/s/article/9229802/Mobile_malware_cases_nearly_triple_in_first_half_of_2012_says_NetQin
3. TrustGo, http://www.trustgo.com
4. Google Play, https://play.google.com/store
5. Android Authority: 23 of the top 500 Google Play Apps considered to be malware; malware up 580% this year (Infographic), http://www.trustgo.com/en/media-coverage
6. Felt, A.P., Chin, E., et al.: Android Permissions Demystified. In: The 18th ACM Conference on Computer and Communications Security (CCS 2011), Chicago, USA (October 2011)
7. Zhou, Y., Wang, Z., et al.: Hey, You, Get off of My Market: Detecting Malicious Apps in Official and Alternative Android Markets. In: Proceedings of the 19th Network and Distributed System Security Symposium (NDSS 2012), San Diego, CA (February 2012)
8. Enck, W., Gilbert, P., et al.: TaintDroid: an information-flow tracking system for realtime privacy monitoring on smartphones. In: The 9th USENIX Symposium on Operating System Design and Implementation (OSDI 2010), Vancouver, BC, Canada (October 2010)
9. Android Malware Genome Project, http://www.malgenomeproject.org/

10. Dalvik bytecode, http://source.android.com/tech/dalvik/dalvik-bytecode.html
11. IDA pro, http://www.hex-rays.com/products/ida
12. IDAPython, http://code.google.com/p/idapython/
13. Cheng, S., Yang, J., et al.: LoongChecker: Practical summary-based semi-simulation to detect vulnerability in binary code. In: The 10th IEEE International Conference on Trust, Security and Privacy in Computing and Communications (TrustCom 2011), Changsha, China (November 2011)
14. Li, Z., Cheng, S., Wu, J.: Inter-procedural static analysis of Android apps, Technical report (December 2012)
15. FakeNetflix, http://www.pcmag.com/article2/0,2817,2394621,00.asp
16. Gone60, http://contagiominidump.blogspot.com/2011/09/gone-in-60-seconds-android-spyware.html
17. Fetion, http://www.fetion.com/
18. Snda, http://www.snda.com/cn/fstpage.html
19. Angrybirds, http://www.angrybirds.com/
20. Enck, W., Octeau, D., McDaniel, P., Chaudhuri, S.: A study of Android app security. In: The 20th USENIX Security Symposium (2011)
21. Grace, M., Zhou, Y., Zhang, Q., et al.: RiskRanker: Scalable and Accurate Zero-day Android Malware Detection. In: Proceedings of the 10th International Conference on Mobile Systems, Apps and Services (MobiSys 2012), Lake District, UK (June 2012)
22. Portokalidis, G., Homburg, P., Anagnostakis, K., Bos, H.: Paranoid Android: Versatile protection for smartphones. In: The 26th Annual Computer Security Applications Conference (ACSAC 2010), Austin, Texas, USA (December 2010)
23. Gilbert, P., Chun, B.G., Cox, L.P., Jung, J.: Vision: Automated Security Validation of Mobile Apps at App Markets. In: Proceedings of the International Workshop on Mobile Cloud Computing and Services (MCS 2011), New York, USA (2011)
24. Nauman, M., Khan, S., Zhang, X.: Apex: Extending Android Permission Model and Enforcement with User-Defined Runtime Constraints. In: Proceedings of the 5th ACM Symposium on Information, Computer and Communications Security (ASIACCS 2010), Beijing, China (April 2010)
25. Beresford, A.R., Rice, A., et al.: MockDroid: Trading Privacy for Application Functionality on Smartphones. In: Proceedings of the 12th International Workshop on Mobile Computing System and Applications (HotMobile 2011), Phoenix, USA (March 2011)
26. Zhou, Y., Zhang, X., Jiang, X., Freeh, V.W.: Taming Information-Stealing Smartphone Applications (on Android). In: McCune, J.M., Balacheff, B., Perrig, A., Sadeghi, A.-R., Sasse, A., Beres, Y. (eds.) Trust 2011. LNCS, vol. 6740, pp. 93–107. Springer, Heidelberg (2011)
27. Grace, M., Zhou, Y., Wang, Z., Jiang, X.: Systematic Detection of Capability Leaks in Stock Android Smartphones. In: Proceedings of the 19th Annual Symposium on Network and Distributed System Security (NDSS 2012), San Diego, USA (February 2012)
28. Hornyack, P., Han, S., Jung, J., Schechter, S., Wetherall, D.: These Aren't the Droids You're Looking For: Retrofitting Android to Protect Data from Imperious Applications. In: Proceedings of the 18th ACM Conference on Computer and Communications Security (CCS 2011), Chicago, USA (October 2011)
29. Chin, E., Felt, A.P., Greenwood, K., Wagner, D.: Analyzing Inter-Application Communication in Android. In: Proceedings of the 9th Annual Symposium on Network and Distributed System Security (MobiSys 2011), Washington, DC, USA (July 2011)
30. Barrera, D., Kayacik, H.G., Oorschot, P., Somayaji, A.: A methodology for empirical analysis of permission-based security models and its app to Android. In: Proceedings of the 17th ACM Conference on Computer and Communications Security (CCS 2010), Chicago, USA (October 2010)

A Ciphertext-Policy Attribute-Based Encryption Scheme Supporting Keyword Search Function

Changji Wang[1,2], Wentao Li[1], Yuan Li[1], and Xilei Xu[1]

[1] School of Information Science and Technology,
Sun Yat-sen University, Guangzhou 510006, China
[2] Research Center of Software Technology for Information Service
South China Normal University, Guangzhou 501631, China

Abstract. With the advent of cloud computing, more and more individuals and companies are motivated to outsource their data and services to clouds. As for the privacy and security reasons, sensitive data should be encrypted prior to outsourcing. However, encrypted data will hamper efficient query processing and fined-grained data sharing. In this paper, we propose a new cryptographic primitive called ciphertext-policy attribute-based encryption scheme with keyword search function (KSF-CP-ABE) to simultaneously solve above issues. When a data owner wants to outsource sensitive data in the public cloud, he/she encrypts the sensitive data under an access policy and also build a secure index for the set of keywords. Only authorized users whose credentials satisfy the access policy can retrieve this encrypted data through keyword search and decrypt the ciphertext. We also present a concrete KSF-CP-ABE construction from bilinear pairings and proved that the proposed KSF-CP-ABE scheme is secure against both outer attacks and inner attacks. What's more, cloud service provider can perform partial decryption task delegated by data user.

Keywords: cloud computing, ciphertext-policy attribute-based encryption, public key encryption with keyword search, bilinear pairings.

1 Introduction

Cloud computing is a revolutionary computing paradigm which enables ubiquitous, convenient, on-demand network access to a shared pool of configurable computing resources (e.g., networks, servers, storage, applications and services) that can be rapidly provisioned and released with minimal management effort or service provider interaction [1].

Cloud computing attracts considerable attention from both academia and industry. Gartner forecasts the public cloud services market will grow 18.5% in 2013 to total $131 billion worldwide [2]. But there can be potential risks when relying on a third party to provide infrastructure, platform, or software as a service. The risks of data security and privacy remain significant barriers to cloud adoption for many enterprises.

G. Wang et al. (Eds.): CSS 2013, LNCS 8300, pp. 377–386, 2013.
© Springer International Publishing Switzerland 2013

To protect data security and privacy, encryption technology seems like an obvious solution. However, encryption functionality alone is not sufficient as data owners often have also to enforce fine-grained access control on the sensitive data for sharing. Traditional server-based access control methods are no longer suitable for cloud computing scenario because cloud server cannot be fully trusted by data owners.

To address the problem of secure and fine-grained data sharing and decentralized access control, Sahai and Waters [3] first introduced the concept of attribute-based encryption (ABE) by extending identity-based encryption [4]. Compared with identity-based encryption, ABE has significant advantage as it achieves flexible one-to-many encryption instead of one-to-one. ABE have drawn extensive attention from both academia and industry, many ABE schemes have been proposed [5,7,6,8,9,10,11,12] and several cloud-based secure systems using ABE schemes have been developed [13,14,15].

There are two types of ABE depending on which of private keys or ciphertexts that access policies are associated with. In KP-ABE system, ciphertexts are labeled by the sender with a set of descriptive attributes, while users' private key are issued by the trusted attribute authority captures an policy that specifies which type of ciphertexts the key can decrypt. In CP-ABE system, when a sender encrypts a message, they specify a specific access policy in terms of access structure over attributes in the ciphertext, stating what kind of receivers will be able to decrypt the ciphertext. Users possess sets of attributes and obtain corresponding secret attribute keys from the attribute authority. Such a user can decrypt a ciphertext if his/her attributes satisfy the access policy associated with the ciphertext. Thus, CP-ABE mechanism is conceptually closer to traditional role-based access control method.

Traditional data utilization services based on plaintext keyword search will become difficult because the data are encrypted. Boneh et al. [16] proposed the concept of Public key Encryption with Keyword Search (PEKS) to to address the problem of searching on encrypted data. Although PEKS schemes provide some approaches to search over the encrypted data by keyword, they cannot support flexible access control policies on encrypted data.

In this paper, we organically integrate PEKS with CP-ABE and propose a new cryptographic primitive called ciphertext-policy attribute-based encryption scheme with keyword search function (KSF-CP-ABE). When a data owner wants to outsource his/her sensitive data in the public cloud, he/she encrypts the sensitive data under an access policy and builds a corresponding secure index for keywords. Only authorized users whose credentials satisfy the access policy can retrieve this encrypted data through keyword search and decrypt the ciphertext. We also present a concrete KSF-CP-ABE construction from bilinear pairings, which can ensure the security with fine-grained access control on shared sensitive data, and provide keyword search service for data users without leaking their privacy of queries and breaking confidentiality of data contents. Moreover, cloud service provider can perform partial decryption task delegated by query users.

The rest of this paper is organized as follows. Some necessary preliminary works are introduced in Section 2. The syntax and security notions of KSF-CP-ABE scheme are given in Section 3. A concrete KSF-CP-ABE construction and analysis are described in Section 4. We conclude our work in Section 5.

2 Preliminary Works

We first introduce some notations. If $\mathbf{S}$ is a set, then $x \in_R \mathbf{S}$ denotes the operation of picking an element x uniformly at random from $\mathbf{S}$. Let $\Omega = \{attr_1, \ldots, attr_n\}$ be the universe of possible attributes, where each $attr_i$ denotes an attribute and n is the total number of attributes. Let $\Lambda = \{kw_1, \ldots, kw_l\}$ be the universe of possible keywords, where each kw_i denotes a keyword and l is the total number of keywords.

2.1 Bilinear Pairings

Let $\mathbf{G}_1$ and $\mathbf{G}_2$ be two cyclic groups of prime order p. Let g be a generator of $\mathbf{G}_1$. A bilinear pairing $\hat{e} : \mathbf{G}_1 \times \mathbf{G}_1 \to \mathbf{G}_2$ satisfies the following properties:

- Bilinearity: For $a, b \in_R \mathbf{Z}_p$, we have $\hat{e}(g^a, g^b) = e(g, g)^{ab}$.
- Non-degeneracy: $\hat{e}(g, g) \neq 1$, where 1 is the identity element of $\mathbf{G}_2$.
- Computability: There is an efficient algorithm to compute $\hat{e}(u, v)$ for $u \in_R \mathbf{G}_1$ and $v \in_R \mathbf{G}_1$.

Decision q-parallel Bilinear Diffie-Hellman Exponent Assumption. Let $(p, \mathbf{G}_1, \mathbf{G}_2, g, \hat{e})$ be a description of the bilinear group of prime order p. The decision q-parallel bilinear Diffie-Hellman exponent assumption is that if the challenge values $R \in \mathbf{G}_2$ and

$$\boldsymbol{y} = g, g^s, g^a, \ldots, g^{(a^q)}, g^{(a^{q+2})}, \ldots, g^{(a^{2q})}$$

$$g^{s \cdot b_j}, g^{a/b_j}, \ldots, g^{(a^q/b_j)}, g^{(a^{q+2}/b_j)}, \ldots, g^{(a^{2q}/b_j)}, \forall 1 \leq j \leq q$$

$$g^{a \cdot s \cdot b_k/b_j}, \ldots, g^{(a^q \cdot s \cdot b_k/b_j)}, \forall 1 \leq j \neq k \leq q,$$

are given for unknown $a, s, b_1, \ldots, b_q \in_R \mathbf{Z}_p$, there is no polynomial time algorithm $\mathcal{A}$ can decide whether $\hat{e}(g, g)^{a^{q+1}s} = R$ with more than a negligible advantage [9].

2.2 Access Structure and Linear Secret Sharing Scheme

Let $\mathbf{P} = \{P_1, P_2, \ldots, P_n\}$ be a set of parties and let $2^{\mathbf{P}}$ denote its power set. A collection $\mathbb{A} \subseteq 2^{\mathbf{P}}$ is monotone if for every $\mathbf{B}$ and $\mathbf{C}$, if $\mathbf{B} \in \mathbb{A}$ and $\mathbf{B} \subseteq \mathbf{C}$ then $\mathbf{C} \in \mathbb{A}$. An access structure (respectively, monotone access structure) is a collection (respectively, monotone collection) $\mathbb{A}$ of non-empty subsets of $\mathbf{P}$, i.e. $\mathbf{P} \setminus \emptyset$. The sets in $\mathbb{A}$ are called the authorized sets, and the sets not in $\mathbb{A}$ are called the unauthorized sets.

Let $M_{\ell \times k}$ be a $\ell \times k$ matrix and $\rho : \{1, 2, \ldots, \ell\} \to \mathbf{P}$ be a function that maps a row to a party for labeling. A secret sharing scheme Π for access structure $\mathbb{A}$ over a set of parties $\mathbf{P}$ is a linear secret sharing scheme (LSSS) in $\mathbf{Z}_p$ and is represented by $(M_{\ell \times k}, \rho)$ if it consists of two efficient algorithms:

- Share$((M_{\ell \times k}, \rho), s)$: The share algorithm takes as input $s \in \mathbf{Z}_p$ which is to be shared. The dealer randomly chooses $\beta_2, \ldots, \beta_k \in_R \mathbf{Z}_p$, and defines $\boldsymbol{\beta} = (s, \beta_2, \ldots, \beta_k)$. It outputs $M_{\ell \times k} \cdot \boldsymbol{\beta}$ as the vectors of ℓ shares. The share $\lambda_i = \langle \boldsymbol{M}_i, \boldsymbol{\beta} \rangle$ belongs to party $\rho(i)$, where $\boldsymbol{M}_i$ is the i-th row of $M_{\ell \times k}$.
- Recon$((M_{\ell \times k}, \rho), \mathbf{S})$: The reconstruction algorithm takes as input an access set $\mathbf{S} \in \mathbb{A}$. Let $\mathbf{I} = \{i \mid \rho(i) \in \mathbf{S}\}$. It outputs a set of constants $\{\mu_i\}_{i \in \mathbf{I}}$ such that $\sum_{i \in \mathbf{I}} \mu_i \cdot \lambda_i = s$.

In our context, the role of the parties is taken by the attributes. Thus, the access structure $\mathbb{A}$ will contain the authorized sets of attributes. As in most relevant literatures [5,7,6], we will restrict ourselves to monotone access structures.

3   Definitions for KSF-CP-ABE Scheme

We consider a multi-user cryptographic cloud storage system supporting both fine-grained access control and keyword search on encrypted data. The system architecture is illustrated as Figure 1, which involves four participants.

Trusted Authority (TA). This is the key generation center, which is fully trusted by all other participants in the system. The responsibility of TA is to initialize system parameters, to generate attribute private keys and to generate keyword search keys for users.

Cloud Services Provider (CSP). This is an entity that provides data storage and retrieval service, and auxiliary decryption function for subscribing users. It stores the data content outsourced by the data owner. This content is searchable and downloadable to intended receivers who have sufficient credentials. We assume that the CSP is semi-trusted, which means that it follows the protocol specified in the system. However, it is assumed that it seeks to learn the information in the encrypted content during the query and response processes as much as possible with malicious intent.

Data Owner (DO). This is the cloud storage subscriber who wants to upload its data content anonymously to the cloud storage system after encryption. The encrypted content can be shared with intended receivers who have sufficient credentials as specified by the data owner. The responsibility of data owner is to create encrypted data, and to choose keywords to build secure index.

Data User (DU). This is another cloud storage subscriber which queries the CSP for encrypted data in the cloud storage system. Only retrievers who have legal rights satisfying the access policy specified by the data owner can access the encrypted content and restore the original message from it. The responsibility of data users is to choose keywords to create trapdoor for search, to initiate search requests, and to decrypt data.

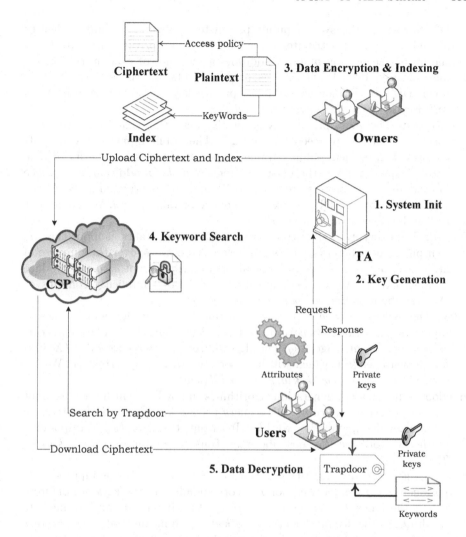

Fig. 1. System architecture and workflow

In our setting, a user will be identified by a pair $(id, \boldsymbol{w})$, where id denotes the user's identity and $\boldsymbol{w} \subseteq \Omega$ is a set of attributes. A KSF-CP-ABE scheme consists of five polynomial-time algorithms described as follows.

Setup. The setup algorithm is run by TA, which takes a security parameter κ. It outputs the master key msk and some public system parameters $params$ which include the description of attribute universe and keyword universe. TA publishes $params$ and keeps msk secret. We describe it as $\mathsf{Setup}(1^\kappa) \to (params, msk)$.

ABE-KeyGen. The attribute private key generation algorithm is an interactive protocol implemented between DU and TA. The public input to TA and

DU consists of the system public parameters $params$, the user's identity id and a set w of attributes owned by DU. The private input to TA is the master secret key msk. In addition, a sequence of random coin tosses may be used by TA and DU as private inputs. At the end of the protocol, DU can extract an attribute private key $d_{id,w}$. We describe it as ABE-KeyGen($params, msk, id, w$) → $d_{id,w}$.

KSF-KeyGen. The query private key generation algorithm is an interactive protocol implemented between DU and TA. The public input to TA and DU consists of the system public parameters $params$, the user's identity id. The private input to TA is the master secret key msk. In addition, a sequence of random coin tosses may be used by TA and DU as private inputs. At the end of the protocol, DU can extract a query private key q_{id}. We describe it as KSF-KeyGen($params, msk, id$) → q_{id}.

Encrypt. The encryption algorithm is run by DO, which takes as input the system public parameters $params$, an access structure $\mathbb{A}$ over the universe of attributes and a message msg. The algorithm will encrypt msg and produce a ciphertext ct. We will assume that the ciphertext implicitly contains $\mathbb{A}$. We describe it as Encrypt($params, \mathbb{A}, msg$) → ct

Index. The encrypted index creation algorithm is run by DO, which takes as input system parameters $params$ and a set $kw = \{kw_i\}_{i=1}^{l}$ of keywords corresponding to a message msg. The algorithm outputs a secure index $IX(kw)$ for keyword set kw, which will be associated with a ciphertext ct. We describe it as Index($params, kw, msg$) → $IX(kw)$.

Trapdoor. The trapdoor generation algorithm is run by DU, which takes as input system parameters $params$, DU's query private key q_{id} and DU's attribute private key $d_{id,w}$, and a keyword kw. It outputs trapdoor T_{kw} corresponding to the keyword kw. We describe it as Trapdoor($params, q_{id}, d_{id,w}, kw$) → T_{kw}.

Test. The keyword test algorithm is run by CSP, which takes as input system parameters $params$, a trapdoor T_{kw} corresponding to the keyword kw from a DU, the index $IX(kw)$ for keyword set kw. It outputs an intermediate result Q_{ct} of the decipherment if $kw \in kw$, which means that the ciphertext ct contains the keyword kw in the trapdoor T_{kw}. Otherwise, it outputs 0. We describe it as Test($params, T_{kw}, IX(kw)$) → Q_{ct} or 0.

Decrypt. The decryption algorithm is run by DU. The algorithm takes as input system parameters $params$, the searched ciphertext ct with corresponding intermediate decryption data Q_{ct}, and DU's attribute private key $d_{id,w}$. It outputs plaintext msg if the set w of attributes in the attribute private key $d_{id,w}$ satisfies the access policy associated with the ciphertext. Otherwise, it outputs $\perp$. We describe it as Decrypt($params, ct, Q_{ct}, d_{id,w}$) → msg or $\perp$.

We have a basic consistency requirement that for any $w \subseteq \Omega$, $kw \in \Lambda$, $msg \in \{0,1\}^*$, $(params, msk) \leftarrow$ Setup(1^κ), $IX(kw) \leftarrow$ Index($params, kw, msg$), $d_{id,w} \leftarrow$ ABE-KeyGen($params, msk, id, w$), $q_{id} \leftarrow$ KSF-KeyGen($params, msk, id$), $T_{kw} \leftarrow$ Trapdoor($params, q_{id}, d_{id,w}, kw$) and $ct \leftarrow$ Encrypt($params, \mathbb{A}, msg$), where w satisfies $\mathbb{A}$ and $kw \in kw$, we have $Q_{ct} \leftarrow$ Test($params, T_{kw}, IX(kw)$)

and $msg \leftarrow$ Decrypt$(params, ct, Q_{ct}, d_{id,w})$ with probability 1 over the randomness of all the algorithms.

We can obtain security definitions for KSF-CP-ABE similar to security model for CP-ABE [9] and security model for PEKS [16]. Due to space limitations, we omit the description of security definitions for KSF-CP-ABE here, and we will explain them in detail in the extended version.

4   A KSF-CP-ABE Construction

The proposed KSF-CP-ABE construction from bilinear pairings is described as follows.

Setup. TA chooses $(a, \alpha) \in_R \mathbb{Z}_p^{*2}$, a cryptographic secure hash function H and message authentication code function F, respectively. TA publishes system parameters $params$ as $(\Omega, \Lambda, \mathbf{G}_1, \mathbf{G}_2, \hat{e}, g, g^a, \hat{e}(g, g)^\alpha, F, H)$, while keeps the master secret key $msk = (g^\alpha, a)$ secret.

ABE-KeyGen. To generate attribute private keys for a DU with $(id, \boldsymbol{w})$, the following protocol will be executed between DU and TA.
  - DU sends a request for attribute private key along with credentials corresponding to the set $\boldsymbol{w}$ of attributes to TA.
  - TA first validates the credentials presented by DU, outputs $\perp$ if fails. Otherwise, TA chooses $t \in_R \mathbf{Z}_p^*$, generates the attribute private keys for DU corresponding to the set $\boldsymbol{w}$ of attributes as $d_{id,w} = (K = g^\alpha g^{at}, L = g^t, \{(K_x = H(x)^t\}_{x\in\boldsymbol{w}})$.
  - TA adds an entry (id, g^{at}) in the user list.
  - Finally, TA securely distributes the attribute private keys $d_{id,w}$ to DU.

KSF-KeyGen. To generate a query private key for a DU with identity id, the following protocol will be executed between DU and TA.
  - DU sends a request for query private key along with his identity id to TA.
  - TA checks whether the identity id in the user list exists or not. If the identity id does not exist, outputs $\perp$. Otherwise, TA sends a response accepting the request back to DU.
  - DU chooses $u \in_R \mathbf{Z}_p^*$, and provides a commitment $q_u = g^u$ with an interactive witness indistinguishable proof of knowledge of the u to TA. In addition, DU retains u.
  - TA verifies the proof of knowledge, outputs $\perp$ if fails. Otherwise, TA retrieves g^{at} according to id, generates a query private key $q_{id} = g^{at}q_u^\alpha$ for the user.
  - Finally, TA securely distributes the query private key q_{id} to DU.

Encrypt. To encrypt a message msg under an access policy described by (M, ρ), DO first chooses a vector $\boldsymbol{v} = (s, y_2, \ldots, y_n) \in_R \mathbf{Z}_p^n$ and $r_1, r_2, \ldots, r_\ell \in_R \mathbf{Z}_p$, where s represents the secret exponent to be shared. DO then calculates $\lambda_i = \langle \boldsymbol{M}_i, \boldsymbol{v} \rangle$ for $i = 1$ to ℓ and outputs the ciphertext $ct = (C = msg \cdot \hat{e}(g, g)^{\alpha s}, C' = g^s, \{C_i, D_i\}_{i=1}^\ell)$ along with a description of (M, ρ), where $C_i = g^{a\lambda_i} H(\rho(i))^{-r_i}$ and $D_i = g^{r_i}$.

Index. To generate a secure index for a set $\boldsymbol{kw}$ of keywords, DO fist chooses a random bit strings t_i for each keyword $kw_i \in \boldsymbol{kw}$, computes the key k_i used for the message authentication code corresponding to keyword kw_i as $k_i = \hat{e}(g,g)^{\alpha s} \cdot \hat{e}(g, H(kw_i))^s$. DO then outputs the secure index as $IX(\boldsymbol{kw}) = \{(t_i, F(k_i, t_i))\}_{kw_i \in \boldsymbol{kw}}$. Finally, DO uploads the ciphertext ct along with the index $IX(\boldsymbol{kw})$ to CSP for sharing.

Trapdoor. To generate a trapdoor for a keyword kw, DU first computes $T_q(kw) = H(kw)q_{id}^{1/u}$, $L' = L^{1/u}$, and $K'_x = K_x^{1/u}$ for all $x \in \boldsymbol{w}$. DU then set trapdoor for the keyword kw as $T_{kw} = (T_q(kw), L', \{K'_x\}_{x \in \boldsymbol{w}})$.

Test. To perform keyword test, the following protocol will be executed between DU and CSP.
- DU initiates a keyword search request by sending the trapdoor T_{kw} for the keyword kw along with the description of the set $\boldsymbol{w}$ of attributes related to DU's attribute private keys to CSP.
- CSP searches for the correspondence ciphertext ct with the desired keyword kw against each tuple $(ct, IX(\boldsymbol{kw}))$ in the storage. CSP verifies whether the submitted $\boldsymbol{w}$ satisfies the access policy (M, ρ) embedded in a ciphertext ct.
- Suppose that $\boldsymbol{w}$ satisfies (M, ρ). Let $\{\mu_i\}_{i \in I}$ be a set of constants defined in Section 2.2. CSP computes $Q_{ct} = \prod_{i \in I}[\hat{e}(C_i, L') \cdot \hat{e}(D_i, K'_{\rho(i)})]^{\mu_i}$, and $k_{kw} = \hat{e}(C', T_q(kw))/Q_{ct}$.
- CSP checks each index $IX(\boldsymbol{kw})$ related to the ciphertext ct in the scope satisfying $F(t_i, k_{kw}) = F(t_i, k_i)$. Finally, CSP sends the search result that include ciphertext ct and partial decryption data Q_{ct} to DU.

Decrypt. DU can recover the plaintext by computing $msg = C \cdot Q_{ct}^u / \hat{e}(C', K)$.

Theorem 1. *The proposed KSF-CP-ABE construction is correct.*

Proof. The correctness can be verified as follows.

$$Q_{ct} = \prod_{i \in I}[\hat{e}(C_i, L') \cdot \hat{e}(D_i, K'_{\rho(i)})]^{\mu_i} = \prod_{i \in I}[\hat{e}(C_i, L^{1/u}) \cdot \hat{e}(D_i, K_{\rho(i)}^{1/u})]^{\mu_i}$$

$$= \prod_{i \in I}[\hat{e}(C_i, L) \cdot \hat{e}(D_i, K_{\rho(i)})]^{\mu_i/u} = \prod_{i \in I} \cdot \hat{e}(g,g)^{at\lambda_i\mu_i/u} = \hat{e}(g,g)^{ats/u}$$

$$k_{kw} = \frac{\hat{e}(C', T_q(kw))}{Q_{ct}} = \frac{\hat{e}(g^s, g^\alpha g^{at/u}H(kw))}{\hat{e}(g,g)^{ats/u}} = \hat{e}(g,g)^{\alpha s} \cdot \hat{e}(g, H(kw))^s$$

$$\frac{C \cdot Q_{ct}^u}{\hat{e}(C', K)} = \frac{msg \cdot \hat{e}(g,g)^{\alpha s} \cdot [\hat{e}(g,g)^{ats/u}]^u}{\hat{e}(g^s, g^\alpha g^{at})} = msg$$

Theorem 2. *Suppose the decisional q-parallel decisional bilinear Diffie-Hellman exponent assumption holds, then there is no polynomial time adversary can selectively break the proposed KSF-CP-ABE construction with a challenge matrix of size $\ell^* \times n^*$, where $\ell^*, n^* \leq q$.*

Proof. The security proof is similar to that of Waters CP-ABE scheme [9], we omit here due to space limits, we will give the detailed security proof in the extended version.

In the proposed KSF-CP-ABE construction, keyword search scope is restricted to DUs' decryptable data group. CSP will determine whether the DU has permission to decrypt the ciphertext first, and then perform keyword search. The search process automatically excludes the ciphertext that the user can not decrypt to reduce unnecessary keyword search computation.

The Decrypt algorithm just require one bilinear pairing operations for each ciphertext. The Test algorithm seems to require a non-constant $2|\mathbf{I}| + 1$ bilinear pairing operations for each trapdoor, it only needs 3 bilinear pairing operations in fact by observing that

$$Q_{ct} = \prod_{i \in \mathbf{I}} [\hat{e}(C_i, L') \cdot \hat{e}(D_i, K'_{\rho(i)})]^{\mu_i} = \hat{e}(\prod_{i \in \mathbf{I}} C_i^{\mu_i}, L') \cdot \hat{e}(\prod_{i \in \mathbf{I}} D_i^{\mu_i}, \prod_{i \in \mathbf{I}} (K'_{\rho(i)})^{\mu_i})$$

5   Conclusions

In this paper, we propose a new cryptographic primitive called ciphertext-policy attribute-based encryption scheme with keyword search function, and present a concrete construction from bilinear pairings. The proposed KSF-CP-ABE construction is very efficient, cloud service provider only need to perform three bilinear pairing operations for each keyword search and partial decryption, and the data user only need to perform one bilinear pairing operation for each decryption. We will further study CP-ABE scheme supporting conjunctive keyword searchable, which enables one to search encrypted documents by using more than one keyword.

Acknowledgments. This work was supported by National Natural Science Foundation of China (Grant No. 61173189) and Guangdong Province Information Security Key Laboratory Project.

References

1. Mell, P., Grance, T.: The NIST Definition of Cloud. NIST Special Publication 800-145 (2011)
2. Gartner report: Forecast: Public Cloud Services, Worldwide and Regions, Industry Sectors. Report 2009–2014, http://www.gartner.com/resId=1378513
3. Sahai, A., Waters, B.: Fuzzy Identity Based Encryption. In: Cramer, R. (ed.) EUROCRYPT 2005. LNCS, vol. 3494, pp. 457–473. Springer, Heidelberg (2005)
4. Boneh, D., Franklin, M.: Identity-based encryption from the Weil pairing. In: Kilian, J. (ed.) CRYPTO 2001. LNCS, vol. 2139, pp. 213–229. Springer, Heidelberg (2001)
5. Goyal, V., Pandey, O., Sahai, A., Waters, B.: Attribute Based Encryption for Fine-Grained Access Conrol of Encrypted Data. In: ACM Conference on Computer and Communications Security, pp. 89–98 (2006)
6. Bethencourt, J., Sahai, A., Waters, B.: Ciphertext-policy attribute-based encryption. In: IEEE Symposium on Security & Privacy, pp. 321–334 (2007)

7. Ostrovsky, R., Sahai, A., Waters, B.: Attribute-Based Encryption with Non-Monotonic Access Structures. In: ACM Conference on Computer and Communications Security, pp. 195–203 (2007)
8. Cheung, L., Newport, C.: Provably Secure Ciphertext Policy ABE. In: ACM Conference on Computer and Communications Security, pp. 456–465 (2007)
9. Waters, B.: Ciphertext-Policy Attribute-Based Encryption: An Expressive, Efficient, and Provably Secure Realization. In: Catalano, D., Fazio, N., Gennaro, R., Nicolosi, A. (eds.) PKC 2011. LNCS, vol. 6571, pp. 53–70. Springer, Heidelberg (2011)
10. Lewko, A., Okamoto, T., Sahai, A., Takashima, K., Waters, B.: Fully Secure Functional Encryption: Attribute-Based Encryption and (Hierarchical) Inner Product Encryption. In: Gilbert, H. (ed.) EUROCRYPT 2010. LNCS, vol. 6110, pp. 62–91. Springer, Heidelberg (2010)
11. Lewko, A., Waters, B.: Decentralizing attribute-based encryption. In: Paterson, K.G. (ed.) EUROCRYPT 2011. LNCS, vol. 6632, pp. 568–588. Springer, Heidelberg (2011)
12. Wang, C.J., Luo, J.F.: An Efficient Key-Policy Attribute-Based Encryption Scheme with Constant Ciphertext Length. Mathematical Problems in Engineering 2013 Article ID 810969, 7 (2013)
13. Pirretti, M., Traynor, P., McDaniel, P., Waters, B.: Secure attribute-based systems. Journal of Computer Security (18), 799–837 (2010)
14. Wang, C.J., Liu, X., Li, W.T.: Implementing a Personal Health Record Cloud Platform Using Ciphertext-Policy Attribute-Based Encryption. In: Fourth International Conference on Intelligent Networking and Collaborative Systems, pp. 8–14 (2012)
15. Li, M., Yu, S.C., Zheng, Y., Ren, K., Lou, W.J.: Scalable and Secure Sharing of Personal Health Records in Cloud Computing using Attribute-based Encryption. IEEE Transactions on Parallel and Distributed Systems 24(1), 131–143 (2013)
16. Boneh, D., Di Crescenzo, G., Ostrovsky, R., Persiano, G.: Public key encryption with keyword search. In: Cachin, C., Camenisch, J.L. (eds.) EUROCRYPT 2004. LNCS, vol. 3027, pp. 506–522. Springer, Heidelberg (2004)

A Trust Model Using Implicit Call Behavioral Graph for Mobile Cloud Computing

Shuhong Chen[1], Guojun Wang[1], and Weijia Jia[2]

[1] School of Information Science and Engineering, Central South University,
Changsha 410083, China
{shchenannabell,csgjwang}@csu.edu.cn
[2] Department of Computer Science,
City University of Hong Kong 83 Tat Chee Avenue, Kowloon, Hong Kong
wei.jia@cityu.edu.hk

Abstract. Behavior patterns of users in mobile social cloud are always based on real world relationships and can be used to infer a level of trust between users. In this paper, we describe the *implicit call behavioral graph* which is formed by users' interactions with call. We rate these relationships to form a dynamic local cloud trust, which enables users to evaluate the trust values between users within the context of a mobile social cloud network. We, then, calculate local trust values according to users' behavioral attributes, such as call frequency, relevance, call moment, and satisfaction. Due to the unique nature of the social cloud, we discuss the propagation and aggregation of local trust values for global social cloud network. Finally, we evaluate the performance of our trust model through simulations, and show simulation results that demonstrate the importance of interaction-based behavioural relationships in recommendation system.

Keywords: Trust relationships, Mobile social cloud, Call behavioral graph, Trust entropy.

1   Introduction

The mobile social cloud is essentially a dynamic virtual network with trust relationships between users. With the emergence of a new generation of powerful mobile devices, novel mobile cloud computing paradigms are possible: various kinds of information and data produced through diverse mobile applications. A smart phone's cloud environment with trustworthiness is a representative scenario of trust in mobile cloud computing [1]. Compared to traditional social networks, a smart phone's cloud environment allows for data collecting with user experience, thus a method to measure trustworthiness of user is necessary [2]. In smart phone's network environment, many people communicate mainly with their friends (such as family, and coworkers) through social network services. In fact, users are more likely to trust their friends, that is based on the physical world relationship, rather than a purely online digital relationship. Mobile users

G. Wang et al. (Eds.): CSS 2013, LNCS 8300, pp. 387–402, 2013.

share their roles within their cloud via interactive behaviors, thereby increasing the overall trustworthiness of the relationship between the users being carried out. However, online social relationships always depend on physical world relationships. Hence, we can infer a level of users' trust relationships that underpins the online community where they exist according to some attributes of real world [3].

In mobile social networks, a call detail log (CDL) contains various details pertaining to each call, such as who called whom, when was it made, etc. Based on these information, one can construct a *call behavioral graph* with customer mobile numbers as nodes and the calls as edges. The weight of an edge captures the strength of the relationship between two nodes. An edge with a high weight signifies a strong tie, while an edge with a low weight represents a weak one. Consequently, one can view the call behavioral graph as a social network consisting of n users (nodes) and a relationship $R_{i,j}$ measured on each ordered pair of users $i, j = 1, \cdots, n$. We consider the call behavioral graph obtained from CDL data.

In this paper, hence, we propose a global social trust model building system by seamlessly integrating the one-dimensional trust relationship values based on interactions between users in mobile social computing environment. We suggest a method to quantify a trusting relation based on the analysis of telephone CDL from mobile devices. The quantified social trust model supports inter-user trust relationship and integration. In other words, the proposed approach not only helps decide communicating path of trustworthy users in mobile cloud environment but also helps address security issues with increased trustworthiness of user behaviors by ranking trustworthy relationships between users. By doing so, a communicating path for trustworthy users under cloud environment is suggested. With the enhanced trustworthiness, the issue of security also can be addressed. Furthermore, the implicit trust along with the application of socially corrective mechanisms inherent in social networks can also be applied to other domains. In fact, social networking platforms already provide a multitude of integrated applications that deliver particular functionality to users, and more significantly, social network credentials provide authentication in many diverse domains, for example, many sites support Facebook Connect as a trusted authentication mechanism [4].

The rest of the paper is organized as follows. Some related work are addressed in Section 2. Section 3 provides the system model and some important definitions. Section 4 and Section 5 discuss how to calculate the local trust values and global trust values, respectively. We analyze some performances of our trust model by simulation in Section 6. Finally, we conclude in Section 7.

2   Related Work

If without trust relationships between users in a mobile social cloud environment, the reliability of the total network would drop. Hence, many works have attempted to discover relationships between communication entities with social trust models. Kuada et al. [6] propose the provisioning and management approach based on collaborative strategy with social relationships in cloud computing services. Jennifer Golbeck et al. [7] and Kim et al. [8] propose a method to quantitatively infer trust between users for a recommendation system in a Web-based social network. To support mobile phones in mobile cloud to plan, schedule, and reflect on group activities, Kikin-Gil [9] and Counts [10] propose to create privately shared group spaces on mobile devices where each group is able to communicate and collaborate. In order to enhance trustworthiness on the social network, Pezzi [11] defines a social cloud as a means of cultivating collective intelligence and facilitating the development of self-organizing communities. According to Pezzi et al., the social network and its services are provided by network nodes owned by members of the network rather than by centralized servers owned by the social network. Traditionally, social cloud platforms provide only marginal functionality for enhanced communication on mobile devices [12]. However, a truly mobile social cloud will offer functionality to improve communication service by considering users' mobile behavior patterns. To support mobile awareness and collaboration, Oulasvirta et al. [13] design a named *ContextContact* approach. S. Farnham and P. Keyani. [14] provide smart convergence through mobile group text messaging, i.e., *Swarm*. However, *ContextContact* and *Swarm* are designed to enhance communication within a large group including all of a user's contacts. Kim et al. [15,16] propose a trust model that is appropriate for online communities using the user profiles. Interest in analysis and utilization of data obtained from smartphones have increased as smartphones have spread widely. In [17], the authors propose a method to filter out voice spam calls on the IP telephony system that recognizes relationships between users by analyzing sustained phone-calling behavioral pattern (i.e. duration, frequency, recent history etc.) extracted from smartphone CDL. Ankolekar et al. [18] extract the behavioral pattern of each user according to the contact lists and the phone call histories of smartphone users. It is helpful to make a decision by a recommended user list for a user. In [19], Roth et al. describe the implicit social graph which is formed by users' interactions with contacts and groups of contacts, and which is distinct from explicit social graphs in which users explicitly add other individuals as their "friends". Then, the authors describe a novel friend suggestion algorithm that uses a user's implicit social graph to generate a friend group, given a small seed set of contacts which the user has already labeled as friends. However, Roth et al do not consider the relative importance of different interaction types in determining the social relationships between users. In this paper, hence, we propose a trust model for mobile cloud computing using implicit call behavioral graph by considering these issues.

3   System Model and Definitions

3.1   System Model

In a mobile social cloud, users are more likely to trust information from a "friend" if the digital relationship between the two is based on a real world relationship (such as family, colleague, etc.) rather than a purely online relationship [4]. In a social context formal, individuals are socially motivated and subject to personal repercussions outside the functional scope of the social cloud, and Service Level Agreements (SLAs) are not as critical. Therefore, we use social incentives and the underlying real world relationships as a substitute foundation for trust. We consider a mobil social cloud computing system shown in Fig. 1.

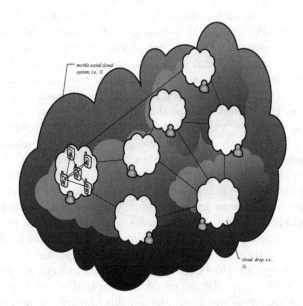

Fig. 1. System model

Let a graph $G = G(V, E)$ denote a mobil social cloud system, where the set V of vertices represents users (nodes), and the set E of edges denotes friendships between these users. If user i trusts user j, there exists a directional edge from user i to user j, and vice versa. In this paper, we ignore the direction of edge, and each edge means a bidirectional edge. We assume the graph G can be divided into multiple sub-graph, and each sub-graph G_k consists of a user k of interest and his/her direct neighbors, as shown in Fig. 2. We assume that there are N_k nodes in G_k. Each edge in G_k is formed by the sending and receiving of call. We call each G_k as *implicit call behavioral graph*, even though it may consist of a single node. A *implicit call behavioral graph* is a subset of vertices of a mobile social network that is highly connected. Edges in the *implicit call behavioral graph* have both direction and weight. The direction of an edge is determined by whether it was formed by an outgoing call sent by the user, or an incoming call received by the user. The weight of an edge is determined by the call behavioural patterns between users. An individual is added into G_k as a "friend", and it implies that at least, the user k has some degree of knowledge about the individual being added. Such connectivity between individuals can be used to infer that a trust relationship exists between them. However, it does not describe the level of trust or the context of the relationship. Therefore, it is important to provide a quantitative method to describe the trust relationship.

In our approach, the social trust relationship between users in mobile social cloud environments is inferred by users' call behaviors without external enforcement. This kind of trust with one-dimensional perspective is called *local trust*. However, it is not easy to facilitate the expansion of information using the social network in explicit or implicit relationship. Therefore, it is very important to establish a global trust social network using each user's *local trust* in the process of inferring information using social network integrations. We, next, introduce some basic definitions.

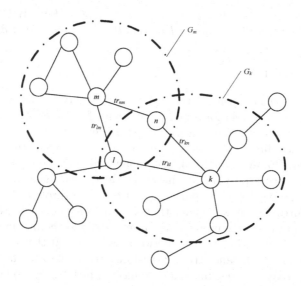

Fig. 2. Cloud drops and their trust relationships

3.2   Basic Definitions

Let $\mathbf{U}$ be the universe set of discourse, f and g are random functions with a stable tendency $f : \mathbf{U} \to [0,1]$ and $g : \mathbf{U} \to [0,1]$, respectively. To capture the intimacy degree of trust relationships, we denote ρ as an weighted value of intimacy. For the convenience of discussion, we define the relationship model between user i and user j, R, as a tuple of $\langle f, g, \rho \rangle$.

Definition 1. *For any two users i and j in mobile social cloud G, the trust relationship between them, R, indicate the trust degree and the trust value of user j for user i, and can be defined as:*

$$tr_{ij} \triangleq R\langle Ex_{ij}, WEn_{ij}, \rho_{ij} \rangle \tag{1}$$

where Ex_{ij} is the expected trust value, WEn_{ij} is a weighted entropy, and ρ_{ij} is a utility weighted value.

In this paper, tr_{ij} is the basic elements of trust space, we call it *cloud-drop*. According to Definition 1, Ex_{ij} indicates the basic trust degree of j for i. WEn_{ij} reflects the importance of the trust relationship between users i and j for user i. ρ_{ij} reflects the intimacy level of user i and user j, and we show how to determine it in Section 4.4.

Definition 2. *For user i and any other user j in G_i, the local trust model indicates the trust relationships between user i and others, and can be defined as a tuple of:*

$$loc\_cloud_i \triangleq \langle \hat{tr}_{ij}, HEn_i \rangle \qquad (2)$$

where $\hat{tr}_{ij}$ is the normalized value of tr_{ij}, i.e., $\hat{tr}_{ij} \triangleq R\langle \hat{Ex}_{ij}, \hat{WEn}_{ij}, \hat{\rho}_{ij} \rangle$ and HEn_i is the trust hybrid entropy and reflects the density of cloud drop.

3.3   Trust Transitivity

In our model, we also consider trust relationships between users: each user i keeps track of a trust relationship tr_{ij} to each of its neighbour nodes j. In social network, we assume trust relationships only exist between neighbours and users that are not directly connected cannot possibly have a trust relationship with each other. However, two such users may indirectly be connected to each other through a trust path in the network. Hence, we make the assumption that trust may propagate with appropriate discounting through the relationship path [23,24]. Furthermore, we assume that the trust distance indicates the length of the path from the source user to the target user, and the distance is denoted as the number of nodes in the path between two users. If the number of users equals to γ, we call γ-Distance trust. γ-Distance trust refers to the trust that is given to a user that is γ-Distance path connected to the user node in the path from the current user to the target user. In Fig. 3, there is a 2-distance trust between user i to target user j. If $\gamma = 0$, i.e., 0-Distance, we say there is a direct connection relationship from the user to the target user, and the trust is direct connection trust, correspondingly. In the paper, the direct connection trust can be denoted as 0-Distance trust, and all neighbor nodes have 0-Distance trust each other. On the other hand, we define the trust between unreachable nodes as ∞-Distance trust. For example, in Fig 3, the trust relationships of between user m and user j, user k and user l are ∞-Distance trust and 0-Distance trust, respectively.

In this paper, we compute the trust value along a relationships path as the product of the trust values of the links on that path. There may be more than one path between two indirect neighbour users, and each path has its own trust value. In other words, we take the position that "if i trusts j, and j trusts k, then i should have a somewhat more positive view of k based on this knowledge" [23]. For instance, there are two trust path between user k and user m in Fig. 2, i.e., $tr_{kl} : tr_{lm}$ and $tr_{kn} : tr_{nm}$, both are 1-Distance trust. In our model, trust discounting takes place by multiplying trust values along trust paths. We address this case in Section 5.

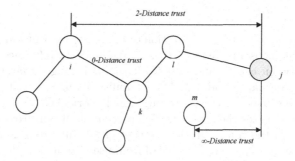

Fig. 3. γ-Distance trust

4   Computing Local Trust Value

Broadly speaking, trust means an act of faith, confidence and reliance in something that is expected to behave or deliver as promised [5,20]. Its a belief in the competence and expertise of others, such that you feel you can reasonably rely on them to care for your valuable assets [21]. Grandison and Sloman [22] have surveyed several existing trust models and they have defined the trust as "the firm belief in the capability of an entity to act consistently, securely and reliably within a specified context". They also claim that the trust is the composition of multiple attributes such as reliability, honesty, truthfulness, dependability, security, competence, timeliness, Quality of Service (QoS) and Return on Investment (ROI) in the context of an environment.

As mentioned above, we compute trust from user's connections. We consider the behavioral attributes such as call frequency, relevance, call moment, and satisfaction to compute local trust value, i.e., 0-Distance trust.

4.1   Call Frequency

Call frequency indicates the level of connections and the inter-user relationships among the users that directly connected. In other words, they are belonged to the same *cloud drop*, i.e., G_i. If the call frequency between user i and user j is greater than that between i and h, it indicates that user i trusts j more than h. For example, a user may trust his friend to whom he talks on the phone every day more than his colleagues at work to whom he talks on the phone for a significant time but with less frequency. We denote call frequency between users i and j as $Call_{freq}(i,j)$, and can calculate $Call_{freq}(i,j)$ as follows:

$$Call_{freq}(i,j) = \frac{Call_{num}(i,j)}{\sum_{k=1}^{N_i} Call_{num}(i,k)} \tag{3}$$

where $Call_{num}(i,j)$ denotes the number of call between users i and j, and any user k belongs to G_i.

4.2   Relevance

The relevance represents the the duration of inter-user relationship, i.e., the duration of call, among users. We let $Call_{rele}(i,j)$ denote the relevance degree of the relationship between users i and j. If $Call_{rele}(i,j)$ is longer than $Call_{rele}(i,k)$, we say a higher relevance and a higher reliability for users i and j. In this paper, we infer the value of relevance through the historical CDL. We assume that $DOWN_{rele}(i,j)$ denotes the total duration percent of all calls from user i to user j, and $UP_{rele}(i,j)$ the total duration percent of all calls from user j to user i. Let $Last(i,j)$ be the duration of each call from user i to user j. We, then, calculate $DOWN_{rele}(i,j)$ and $UP_{rele}(i,j)$ as shown in formula (4) and formula (5), respectively.

$$DOWN_{rele}(i,j) = \frac{\sum_{i,j \in G_i} Last(i,j)}{\sum_{\forall k \in G_i}(Last(i,k) + Last(k,i))} \tag{4}$$

$$UP_{rele}(i,j) = \frac{\sum_{i,j \in G_i} Last(j,i)}{\sum_{\forall k \in G_i}(Last(i,k) + Last(k,i))} \tag{5}$$

Obviously, the trust value between users i and j is various for different call patterns (i.e., user i send initiatively, or receive passively). To denote different relevances for different call patterns, we define a coefficient α ($0 \leq \alpha \leq 1$), which indicates the different importance for call relevance. And then, we obtain:

$$Call_{rele}(i,j) = \alpha UP_{rele}(i,j) + (1 - \alpha)DOWN_{rele}(i,j) \tag{6}$$

4.3   Satisfaction

In a distributed social cloud environment, users may still rate each other after each communication. For example, each time user i communicates with user j, he may evaluate the call as positive ($= 1$) or negative ($= -1$). User i may rate a call as negative, for example, if the call is failed or interrupted. We define rat_{ij} as the sum of the ratings of the individual calls that user i has communicated with user j. Let $sat(i,j)$ and $unsat(i,j)$ be the satisfactory calls set and the unsatisfactory calls set, respectively. User i stores the rating value (i.e., 1) of satisfactory calls it has had with user j, $sat(i,j)$ and the rating value (i.e., -1) of unsatisfactory calls it has had with user j, $unsat(i,j)$. Then, rat_{ij} can be calculated:

$$rat_{ij} = \|sat(i,j)\| - \|unsat(i,j)\| \tag{7}$$

where $\|sat(i,j)\|$ and $\|unsat(i,j)\|$ are the absolute values of the sums of all elements in $sat(i,j)$ and $unsat(i,j)$, respectively. We define a local satisfaction value, ls_{ij}, as follows:

$$ls_{ij} = \begin{cases} \frac{max(rat_{ij},0)}{\sum_k max(rat_{ik},0)} & if \quad \sum_k max(rat_{ik},0) \neq 0; \\ 0 & if \quad \sum_k max(rat_{ik},0) = 0 \ \& \ |Neigh[i]| = 0; \\ p_i & if \quad \sum_k max(rat_{ik},0) = 0 \ \& \ |Neigh[i]| \neq 0; \end{cases} \tag{8}$$

where $p_i = 1/|Neigh[i]|$ and $|Neigh[i]|$ is the user number of direct neighbors of user i.

4.4   Call Moment

Call moment refers to the occurring time of the relationship among users and a different call moment implies a different trust relationship among users. In this paper, call moment is divided into *public time*, and *private time*. The trust value of call occurring in *private time* is higher than that of call occurring in *public time*. Generally, we define the work hours is the public time, otherwise, private time. We let $D_{public}(i,j)$ and $D_{private}(i,j)$ denote the call duration in *public time* and *private time* between users i and j, respectively. We can obtain $D_{public}(i,j)$ and $D_{private}(i,j)$ from the recent CDL. Let $Intimacy(i,j)$ denote the intimacy of users i and j, and we calculate $Intimacy(i,j)$ according to formula (9):

$$Intimacy(i,j) = \frac{D_{private}(i,j)}{D_{private}(i,j) + D_{public}(i,j)} \tag{9}$$

where $i,j \in G_i$.

To determine the different trust value according to $Intimacy(i,j)$, in this study, we divide $Intimacy(i,j)$ into four ranks. Generally, the rank of $Intimacy(i,j)$ is higher than that of $Intimacy(i,k)$ means a higher reliability and trust. To capture the nature, hence, we define the weighted value of call between users i and j, i.e., ρ_{ij}, and ρ_{ij} is determined depending on the scope of $Intimacy(i,j)$ as shown in Eq. (10).

$$\begin{cases} \rho_{ij} = 3 \cdot Intimacy(i,j) & if \ Intimacy(i,j) > 0.75; \\ \rho_{ij} = 2 \cdot Intimacy(i,j) - 1 \ if \ 0.5 < Intimacy(i,j) \le 0.75; \\ \rho_{ij} = 1 & if \ 0.25 \le Intimacy(i,j) < 0.5; \\ \rho_{ij} = 1 - 2 \cdot Intimacy(i,j) & if \ Intimacy(i,j) < 0.25 \end{cases} \tag{10}$$

4.5   Computing Local Trust Value

As discussed above, local trust value is 0-Distance trust value, and we compute the value of 0-Distance trust according to formula (11).

$$Ex_{ij} = \rho_{ij}(w_1 \cdot Call_{freq}(i,j) + w_2 \cdot Call_{rele}(i,j) + w_3 \cdot ls_{ij}) \tag{11}$$

where w_1, w_2, and w_3 are nonnegative weight coefficients of the trust parameters such that $w_1 + w_2 + w_3 = 1$.

According to Definition 1, we normalize the value of Ex_{ij} as follows:

$$\hat{Ex}_{ij} = \frac{Ex_{ij}}{\sum_{k=1}^{N_i} Ex_{ik}} \tag{12}$$

We calculate $\hat{\rho}_{ij}$ and WEn_{ij} according to formulae (13) and (14), respectively:

$$\hat{\rho}_{ij} = \frac{\rho_{ij}}{\sum_{k=1}^{N_i} \rho_{ik}} \tag{13}$$

$$WEn_{ij} = -\hat{\rho}_{ij}\hat{Ex}_{ij}\log(\hat{Ex}_{ij}) \tag{14}$$

Assume non-influence for all users, we can obtain HEn from formula (15):

$$HEn_i = \sum_{k=1}^{N_i} WEn_{ik} \tag{15}$$

Hence, we obtain the local cloud model: $loc\_cloud_i \triangleq \langle \hat{tr}_{ij}, HEn_i \rangle$.

5   Propagation and Aggregation of Local Trust Values

5.1   Propagating Local Trust Values

In mobile cloud computing environment, users always can not obtain trust recommendation of strangers from their trusted neighbors directly. Hence, we need to propagate local trust values for indirect neighbor nodes.

This is a useful way to have each user gain a view of the network that is wider than his/her own experience. However, the trust values stored by user i still reflect only the experience of user i and his/her acquaintances. In order to get a wider view, user i may wish to ask his/her friends' friends. Furthermore, he/she can have a complete view of the network if he/she continues in this manner. Assume that local trust values are propagated through $n-2$ users from source to target users, i.e., $user_1$(source), $user_2$, $user_2$, $\cdots$, $user_n$(target), and the trust value from $user_i$ to $user_{i+1}$ is $tr_{i(i+1)}$. Hence, we compute the $(n-2)$-Distance trust value from $user_1$ to $user_n$ as follows:

$$tr_{1n})(Ex_{1n}, WEn_{1n}, \rho_{in}) = tr_{12} \bigotimes \cdots \bigotimes tr_{(n-1)n}$$

$$= \prod_{i=1}^{n-1} (Ex_{i(i+1)}, WEni(i+1), \rho_{i(i+1)}) \tag{16}$$

where $\bigotimes$ is a logic multiplicative operator, and $Ex_{1n} = \prod_{i=1}^{n-1} Ex_{i(i+1)}$, $WEn_{1n} = min(\sqrt{\sum_{i=1}^{n-1} En_{i(i+1)}^2}, 1)$, and $\rho_{1n} = min(\rho_{12}, \rho_{23}, \cdots, \rho_{(n-1)n})$.

5.2   Aggregating Local Trust Values

In a distributed environment, more than one trust cloud of a stranger user can be considered in many cases. Therefore, we need to aggregate the normalized local trust values.

Assume that local trust values are aggregated in n local clouds, i.e., loc_cloud_1, loc_cloud_2, $\cdots$, loc_cloud_n, and the n trust cloud can be combined into one trust cloud as follows:

$$loc\_cloud(\bar{tr}, \bar{HEn}) = loc\_cloud_1 \bigoplus \cdots \bigoplus loc\_cloud_n$$

$$= \sum_{i=1}^{n} loc\_cloud_i(\hat{tr}_i, HEn_i) \tag{17}$$

where $\bigoplus$ is a logic additive operator, $\bar{tr} = \frac{1}{n} \sum_{i=1}^{n} \hat{tr}_i$ and $HEn = \frac{1}{n} \sum_{i=1}^{n} HEn_i$.

We can obtain the global trust value by propagating and aggregating the local trust values.

6   Performance Evaluation

In order to measure the performance of our trust model, we build the framework of Fig. 1 based on users' CDL and personal information in a smartphone environment. Our simulation framework is constructed by two parts: local social network is implemented in client, and collection of personal information for global social network is processed in the server. The server computes the caller's trust value using our trust model and decide whether the call would be accepted by comparing the evaluating trust value with the predefined threshold value $Val_{threshold}$. In the paper, we define a node j is a "good" user for user i if $tr_{ij} \geq Val_{threshold}$. Otherwise, it is a "bad" user. In simulation, we apply our trust model into an agent-based recommendation system, where each user is denoted as an agent. User call records are extracted against agents. We assume that there are 1000 users and a total of 28,868 calls are extracted from all users. The extracted call information are used to construct local social network for each user and reflect call frequency, relevance, satisfaction, and call moment that are addressed in Section 4. During the simulations, agents interacted with each other for specific times. In each interact, the simulation system chose two nodes randomly, and the first is client and the other is server. To measure the intimacy value, we define the time interval [AM 8:00, PM 19:00] as *public time*, and the other is *private time*. The main simulation parameters are shown in Table 1.

Table 1. The numerical values of the main parameters

Parameter	Value
Number of user	1000
CDL	28,868
$Val_{threshold}$	0.5
α	0.7
Number of initial friend	20
w_1	0.4
w_2, w_3	0.3

We measure the performance of our trust model as compared to the profile-based trust approach [25] (P-Model for abbreviation), and the random approach (R-Model for abbreviation). To quantitatively measure the trust level of our model, we define expected trust density (ETD) as follows:

$$ETD = \frac{\sum_{i,j \in G} tr_{ij}}{Num_{link}} \tag{18}$$

where Num_{link} is a given total number of links of G.

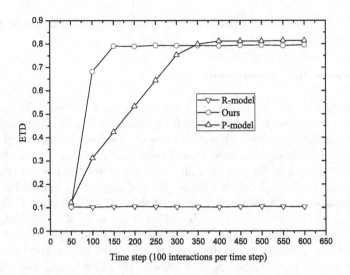

Fig. 4. ETD performance

The ETD characterizes the overall trust level of a mobile cloud environment, and a low ETD indicates the society formed by such mobile cloud environment is fragile and easy to collapse. Generally, the faster the ETD curve become horizontal, the better a trust model convergence is. Fig. 4 compare ETD performance of P-Model, R-Model, and our model with $Num_{link} = 35000$. From Fig. 4, we can find P-Model and our model are very similar and much higher than R-Model on ETD. The reason is due to R-model randomly choices node without trust, and lead to an equal distribution of "good" and "bad" nodes. Therefore, the performance on ETD of R-model is almost 0 on average. On the other hand, our model becomes horizontal faster than P-model, which means our model is easier to converge.

To measure the cooperative performance of our model, we analyze the probability of call request permission. A call request may be permitted or denied. A permissive global call depends on a cooperative social network environment. Therefore, we define the permissive probability, $Prob_{permission}$, to show the cooperative level of a mobile social cloud network. The greater the $Prob_{permission}$ is, the more cooperation a trust model is. Let Num_{call} and $Num_{permission}$ be the number of total call and the permissive call, respectively. We can calculate $Prob_{permission}$ as follows:

$$Prob_{permission} = \frac{Num_{permission}}{Num_{call}} \times 100\% \qquad (19)$$

We obtain the simulation results shown in Fig. 5 by changing the number of links, Num_{link}, from 0 to 50000 with step 100. From Fig. 5, we can find that our model has a better cooperative performance than the other approaches.

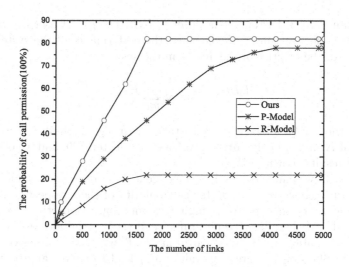

Fig. 5. Cooperative performance

Next, we analyze the difference of our trust model of the selecting recommendations as compared to P-Model, and R-Model. To evaluate the performance of our model, similarly to [25], we define an instantaneous utility function for an agent i following a recommendation from agent j on γ-Distance trust user k at time t as follows:

$$Utility(i,j,t) = \hat{E}x_{ij} \qquad (20)$$

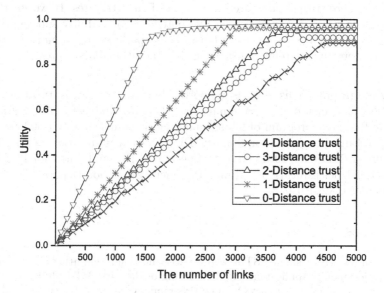

Fig. 6. Utility vs Num_{link}

For instance, for 0-Distance trust user k, $Utility(i, j, t)$ of user i is the $\hat{Ex}_{ij}$ of neighbor node j at time t. We consider the performance of the system to be the average of the utilities of the agents in the system:

$$Utility(t) = \frac{1}{N} \sum_{i \in G} \hat{Ex}_{ij} \tag{21}$$

where N is the number of agents in γ-Distance trust region. Similarity, we change the value of Num_{link} in the interval $[0, 50000]$ with step 100, and we obtain the simulating results shown in Fig. 6.

From Fig. 6, we can observe that each agent develops a trust value towards its neighboring nodes which reflects the similarity of their respective rating at begin. After some time, paths of high trust develop, connecting agents with similar profiles. As a result, the performance of the system, increases over time and reaches a stationary value as shown in Fig. 6, where the curves correspond to different values of γ. Increasing values of γ lead to curves approaching the stationary slower.

7   Conclusion

We have explained how local trust value is calculated based on user call behavioral attributes such as call frequency, relevance, satisfaction and call moment. We have proposed a novel quantitative trust management model. Furthermore, we have discussed the propagation and aggregation of local trust values for global trust model. We have demonstrated that our trust model performs better than the conventional R-Model and similar trust models such as P-Model through simulations. Here trust is measured in terms of four attributes. However, there are some more attributes such as honesty, context, accountability and auditability of social information to measure trust. These parameters are not discussed here. It is interesting to refine trust using these additional attributes.

Acknowledgment. This work is supported by the National Natural Science Foundation of China under grant numbers 61272151 and 61073037, National 973 Basic Research Program of China under grant number 2011CB302800, the Ministry of Education Fund for Doctoral Disciplines in Higher Education under grant number 20110162110043, and the Specialized Research Fund for Doctoral Program in Higher Education of Hunan Provincial Education Department under grant number CX2010B075.

References

1. Christensen, J.H.: Using RESTful web-services and cloud computing to create next generation mobile applications. In: Proceeding of the 24th ACM SIGPLAN Conference Companion on Object-Oriented Programming Systems Languages and Applications, Orlando, FL, USA, pp. 627–634 (2009)

2. Takabi, H.: Security and privacy challenges in cloud computing environments. IEEE Secur. Priv. 8(6), 24–31 (2010)
3. Heurta-Canepa, G., Lee, D.: A virtual cloud computing provider for mobile devices. In: Proceedings of the 1st ACM Workshop on Mobile Cloud Computing & Services, vol. (6) (2010)
4. Chard, K., Bubendorfer, K., Caton, S., Rana, O.F.: Social Cloud Computing: A Vision for Socially Motivated Resource Sharing. IEEE Transactions on Services Computing 5(4), 551–563 (2012)
5. Costa, C., Bijlsma-Frankema, K.: Trust and Control Interrelations. Group and Organization Management 32(4), 392–406 (2007)
6. Kuada, E., Olesen, H.: A social network approach to provisioning and management of cloud computing services for enterprises. In: Proc. of Cloud Computing, pp. 98–104 (2011)
7. Golbeck, J., Hendler, J.: Film Trust: Movie recommendations using Trust in Web-based social network. In: CCNC 2006, pp. 1314–1315. IEEE 3rd Publication (2006)
8. Kim, S., Han, S.: The method of inferring trust in Web-based social network using fuzzy logic. In: Proc. of the International Workshop on Machine Intelligence Research, pp. 140–144 (2009)
9. Kikin-Gil, R.: Affective is effective: how information appliances can mediate relationships within communities and increase one's social effectiveness. Personal and Ubiquitous Computing 10(2-3), 77–83 (2006)
10. Counts, S.: Group-based mobile messaging in support of the social side of leisure. Computer Supported Cooperative Work 16(1-2), 75–97 (2007)
11. Pezzi, R.: Information Technology Tools for a Transition Economy (September 2009), http://www.socialcloud.net/papers/ITtools.pdf
12. Grob, R., Kuhn, M., Wattenhofer, R., Wirz, M.: Cluestr: Mobile Social Networking for Enhanced Group Communication. In: Proc. of GROUP 2009, USA, pp. 81–90 (2009)
13. Oulasvirta, A., Raento, M., Tiitta, S.: ContextContacts: redesigning SmartPhone's contact book to support mobile awareness and collaboration. In: Mobile HCI, pp. 167–174 (2005)
14. Farnham, S., Keyani, P.: Swarm: Hyper awareness, micro coordination, and smart convergence through mobile group text messaging. In: HICSS, vol. 3, pp. 1–10 (2006)
15. Kim, M., Seo, J., Noh, S., Han, S.: Identity management-based social trust model for mediating information sharing and privacy enhancement. Secur. Commun. Netw. 5(8), 887–897 (2012)
16. Kim, M., Park, S.: Group affinity based social trust model for an intelligent movie recommender system. Multimed. Tools Appl. 64(2), 505–516 (2013)
17. Balasubramaniyan, V.A., Ahamad, M., Park, H.: CallRank: combating SPIT using call duration, social networks and global reputation. In: Proceedings of Fourth Conference on Email and Anti-Spam, pp. 18–24 (2007)
18. Ankolekar, A., Szabo, G., Luon, Y., Huberman, B.A., Wilkinson, D., Wu, F.: Friendlee: a mobile application for your social life. In: Proceedings of the 11st International Conference on Human-Computer Interaction with Mobile Devices and Services, vol. (27) (2009), doi:10.1145/1613858.1613893
19. Roth, M., Ben-David, A., Deutscher, D., Flysher, G., Horn, I., Leichtberg, A., Leiser, N., Matias, Y., Merom, R.: Suggesting Friends Using the Implicit Social Graph. In: KDD 2010, pp. 233–241 (2010)
20. Lund, M., Solhaug, B.: Evolution in Relation to Risk and Trust Management. Computer, 49–55 (May 2010)

21. Gambetta, D.: Can We Trust Trust? Trust: Making and Breaking Cooperative Relations, pp. 213–237. Basil Blackwell (1988)
22. Grandison, T., Sloman, M.: A survey of trust in Internet applications. IEEE Communications Survey and Tutorials, 2–16 (2000)
23. Guha, R., Kumar, R., Raghavan, P., Tomkins, A.: Propagation of trust and distrust. In: WWW 2004: Proceedings of the 13th International Conference on the World Wide Web, pp. 403–412. ACM Press (2004)
24. Gray, E., Seigneur, J.-M., Chen, Y., Jensen, C.: Trust propagation in small worlds. In: Nixon, P., Terzis, S. (eds.) iTrust 2003. LNCS, vol. 2692, pp. 239–254. Springer, Heidelberg (2003)
25. Walter, F.E., Battiston, S., Schweitzer, F.: A model of a trust-based recommendation system on a social network. Auton Agent Multi-Agent Syst. 16, 57–74 (2008)

NetSecRadar: A Visualization System for Network Security Situational Awareness

Fangfang Zhou, Ronghua Shi, Ying Zhao[*], Yezi Huang, and Xing Liang

School of Information Science and Engineering, Central South University,
Changsha, China
{zff,shirh,zhaoying, huangyezide,liangxing}@csu.edu.cn

Abstract. Situational awareness is defined as the ability to effectively determine an overall computer network status based on relationships between security events in multiple dimensions. Unfortunately, as the lack of tools to synthetically analyze the security logs generated by kinds of network security products, such as NetFlow, Firewall and Host Security, it is difficult to monitor and perceive network security situational awareness. Information visualization allows users discover and analyze large amounts of information through visual exploration and interaction efficiently. Even with the aid of visualization, identifying the attack patterns from big multi-source data and recognizing the abnormal from visual clutter are still challenges. In this paper, a novel visualization system, NetSecRadar, is proposed for network security situational awareness based on multi-source logs, which can monitor the network and perceive the overall view of the security situation by using radial graph. NetSecRadar utilizes a hierarchical force-directed graph layout for arrangement of thousands of hosts to better use the available screen space, and provides the method to quantify the dangerous levels of the security events, and finds the correlations of security events generated by multi-source logs and perceives the patterns of abnormal in situational awareness, and synthesizes interactions, filtering and drill-down to understand the detail information. To demonstrate the system's capabilities, we utilize the VAST Challenge 2013 as case study.

Keywords: Network Security, Situational Awareness, Information Visualization, Radial graph.

1   Introduction

With the size and complexity of networks continuously increasing, network security analysts face mounting challenges of securing and monitoring their network infrastructure for attacks. This task is generally aided by kinds of network security products, such as NetFlow, firewall and Host security system. As the number of security incidents continues to increase, this task will become ever more insurmountable, and perhaps the main reason that the task of network security monitoring is so difficult is

---

[*] Corresponding author.

G. Wang et al. (Eds.): CSS 2013, LNCS 8300, pp. 403–416, 2013.
© Springer International Publishing Switzerland 2013

the lack of tools to provide a sense of network security situational awareness that defined by the Department of Homeland Security as "the ability to effectively determine an overall computer network status based on relationships between security events in multiple dimensions."[1]

The fields of statistics, pattern recognition, machine learning, and data mining have been applied to the fields of network security situational awareness [2]. Although new systems, protocols and algorithms have been developed and adopted to prevent and detect network intruders automatically. Even with these advances, the central feature of Stoll's story has not changed: humans are still crucial in the computer security process [3]. Administrators must be willing to patiently observe and collect data on potential intruders. They need to think quickly and creatively.

Unlike the traditional methods of analyzing network security textual log data, information visualization approach has been proven that it can increase the efficiency and effectiveness of network intrusion detection significantly by the reduction of human cognition process [4]. Information visualization cannot only help analysts to deal with the large volume of analytical data by taking the advantage of computer graphics, but also help network administrators to detect anomalies through visual pattern recognition. It can even be used for discovering new types of attacks and forecasting the trend of unexpected events. Current research in cyber security visualization has been growing and many visual design methods have been explored. Some of the developed systems are IDGraphs [5], IP Matrix [6], Visual Firewall [7] and many others.

Even with the aid of information visualization, there are still complex issues that network security situational awareness is difficult to describe, because the security events are hard to quantify, the terminology and concepts become too obscure to understand, and large number and scope of the available security multi-source data become a great challenge to the security analysts.

In this paper, a novel visualization system, NetSecRadar, is proposed which can real-time monitor the network and perceive the overall view of security situation and find the correlation of dangerous events in logs generated by multi-source network security products using radial graph that is aesthetically pleasing and has a compact layout for user interaction. The system utilizes multi-source data to analyze the irregular behavioral patterns to identify and monitor the situational awareness, and synthesizes interactions, filtering and drill-down to detect the potential information.

The rest of this paper is organized as follows. Related work is discussed in Section 2 and the design of the visualization system is presented in Section 3. In Section 4, two examples are analyzed by using our system. Finally conclusion and the future work are shown in Section 5.

2   Related Work

As the development of network application and technology, network security events like illegal access, DDoS attack and worm spread etc become more and more serious. A mass of security equipments, like firewall, IDS and anti-virus, are widely used in monitoring networked systems, and numerous approaches, like statistics, machine learning and data mining, are deeply focused to identify anomalies [2]. However, when network security analysts face large quantities of networks events, the most difficulty question they have to answer is "How can I get an effective assessment of the global network security condition based on those events?" Bass [8] introduced situation awareness into the field of network security. After that, Network Security Situation Awareness (NSSA) became a new research field which determined the current status of all network assets based on tremendous network events in support to the further operations.

Network security visualization is a growing community of network security research in recent years. More and more visualization tools are designed to help analysts cope with huge amount of network security data. Hence the demand of visualization techniques has stretched into each step of situation awareness research like situation perception, situation comprehension and even situation prediction. NVisionIP [9] and VisFlowConnect [10] take the lead in introducing visualization technology into NSSA, NVisionIP uses multi-level matrix graphs in status analysis of a class-B network by using NetFlow logs, and VisFlowConnect is a visualization design based on parallel axis technology to enhance the ability of an administrator to detect and investigate anomalous traffic between a local network and external domains. The Intrusion Detection System (IDS) is the most popular application that reports a variety of network events taken for the important input data of NSSA, IDS RainStorm [11], SnortView [12] and Avisa [13] are typical visual analysis tools that help administrators to recognize false positives, detect real abnormal events such as worm propagations and Botnet activities and make a better situation assessment. However, those visual systems based on a single kind of logs such as NetFlow log or IDS log are obviously insufficient. To achieve situational awareness BANKSAFE [14], a scalable and web-based visualization system, analyzes health monitoring logs, Firewall logs and IDS logs in the same time, and Horn [15] uses visual analytics to support the modeling of the computer network defense from kinds of raw data sources to decision goals.

Radial visualization is an increasingly popular metaphor in information visualization research because of its aesthetic appeal, its compact layout, and its interaction ability. LiuHe [16] presents a radial visualization system to reveal the characteristics of trip or road taken by taxi drivers, and Contingency-Wheel [17] is a visual analytics system which discovers and analyzes nontrivial patterns and associations in large categorical data by using the metaphor of wheel. In the field of network security visualization, there are many tools using radial graph such as Radial-Traffic-Analyzer [18], Avisa [13], and FloVis [19] etc. VisAlert [20][21] is a radial paradigm for visual correlation of network alerts and situation awareness from disparate logs. It's very good at dealing with three attributes of network security event, namely: What, When, and Where, and this paradigm facilitates and promotes situational awareness in complex network environments by visual analytics of events correlation. IDSRadar [22] presents a novel radial visualization framework to analyze source IPs, destination IPs, alert types and time of IDS alerts. Moreover, it utilizes five categories of entropy functions to quantitatively analyze irregular behavioral patterns. There are two problems in VisAlert and IDSRadar. One is the lack of host automatic layout based on network topology to deal with the change of the host number and the growing network. Another one is visual clutter issue raised by too much straight lines appearing in the same time. To address those problems and provide a better visual tool for network events analysis and security situation assessment, the following describes our approach carefully.

3   NetSecRadar Visualization System

3.1   Information to Be Visualized

The users of our visualization system for network security situational awareness are network security analysts or administrators, who use network security products to observe network status, detect any abnormal behavior, analyze the reasons behind it and report the dangerous as soon as possible. The following fundamental questions are needed to be addressed by themselves,

- "Is anything bad occurring in the network?" (using of automated tools to distinguish suspicious behavior requiring further investigation),
- "Where is something bad occurring in the network?" (spatial assessment of macro/micro assets),
- "When did bad events first occur in the network?" (temporal assessment of activity),
- "How is something bad occurring in the network?" (mechanism of attack).

It is difficult for network security analysts to answer the questions because the mass amount of the log data generated by kinds of network security products, about a few GB a day, makes them boring; a large percent of false positive, more than 90%, makes them confused; the lack of correlation analysis among the network security products makes them low efficiency. In this paper, the data source of our visualization system comes from multiple sources, such as NetFlow, Firewall and Host security log. The following information of the logs is essential for our visualization system.

- **NetFlow:** A network flow is an abstraction of a sequence of packets between two end points. A Cisco NetFlow is defined as an unidirectional NetFlow that is identified by the following unique keys: timestamps, source IP address, destination IP address, source port, destination port, protocol type, TOS (type of service), and the amount of traffic, etc.
- **Firewall:** A firewall is used by a network security system to control the incoming and outgoing network traffic by analyzing the data packets and determining whether they should be allowed to go through or not, based on a rule set. A firewall establishes a barrier between a trusted, secure internal network and another network. The firewall logs includes properties, such as timestamp, syslog priority (information or warning), operation (Built, Teardown or Deny), protocol(TCP or UDP), source IP address, destination IP address, source port and destination port, Direction(inbound or outbound).

- **Host Health Status Log:** The security log records events such as valid and invalid logon attempts, as well as events related to resource use, such as creating, opening, or deleting files. Multiple entries may be recorded if a particular action creates multiple security events. The host security logs include properties, Timestamp; Data field entry contains the name of the type of data present and the value of the data. Typical values will include the username, the domain name, the IP address, the workstation name, or the port name.

The network security logs are saved as different file format and the same content of the logs, such as IP address, is recorded in different format and every record in the logs are sampled at different sampling time. So it is necessary for us to register the logs in sampling time and format before implementing our visualization system and MySQL database is utilized to save data from our registered multi-source logs for its quick and powerful queries.

3.2 Visual and Interaction Design

The visualization system for network security situational awareness has been developed by using radial visualization. Figure1 illustrates the design of our system, which is composed of two areas, the radial visualization area and the interactive control panel. The radial visualization area includes four parts, servers and workstations, network security events, histogram of event counts and events correlation. The interactive control panel provides the network security analysts with the function of parameter setting and selecting. The following are details of the design.

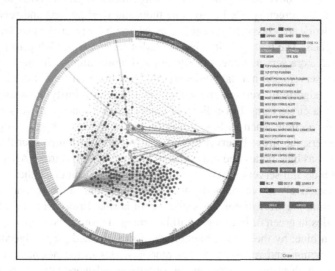

Fig. 1. Design of our visualization system

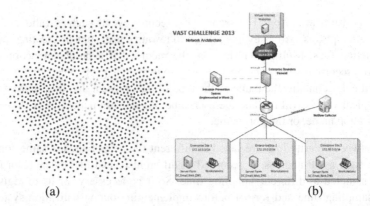

Fig. 2. (a) Servers and workstations arranged by hierarchical force-directed layout algorithm; (b) A network topology in the VAST challenge 2013

Servers and Workstations

In the center part of the radial graph, shown in figure 2 (a), the colored nodes arranged by force-directed layout algorithm are servers and workstations of a corresponding corporate network, shown in figure 2 (b), which is composed of more than one thousand workstations and about ten servers, routers and switches. The force-directed algorithm is an undirected graph layout calculated by all attraction and repulsion forces contained within the structure of graph itself, rather than relying on domain-specific knowledge. Graphs drawn with these algorithms tend to be esthetically pleasing, exhibit symmetries, and produce crossing-free layouts for planar graphs.

In this paper, we developed a hierarchical force-directed graph layout to better exploit the available screen space. Firstly, one thousand workstations and servers in the corporate network are classified into two classes, the high priority class and the normal priority class. The high priority class includes servers with high priority, such as firewall server, core server, routers of servers and workstations; the normal class includes normal servers and normal workstations. Then in a first step of our hierarchical force-directed algorithm, servers and routers in the high priority class are arranged constrained in a circle using force-directed algorithm, the routers of workstations are constrained on a circle, such as blue nodes on circle shown in figure 2 (a), and the routers of servers, the firewall server and core server are distributed near the center of the circle, such as blue nodes and red nodes in the center of the circle. After the nodes of routers in blue and servers in red get balanced, the user can close the force among them and interactively move the nodes to a better position. In the second step of our layout algorithm, the workstations or servers with normal priority in the sub-intranet, which are nodes in green or in orange, will be arranged around their routers which are other nodes in blue, by the second hierarchical force-directed graph algorithm considering all attraction and repulsion forces among nodes in the normal priority class rather than the high priority class. Finally, one thousand workstations are symmetrically distributed around the circle like petals, and severs are near the center like stamen. Our hierarchical force-directed layout algorithm and flexible interaction can help get a compact and beautiful effect of layout.

Network Security Events

The colored arcs of the ring, shown in figure3, are known as the network security event types, such as firewall deny connection ring in orange, host CPU states alert ring in blue and TCP flows flooding in green. The security event types can be any dangerous behavior in firewall, NetFlow and host security logs and are set by network security analysts and are listed on the control panel. The event types will be drawn uniformly on the ring when they are selected according to the interest of the analysts, because there is limited area on the ring and are too many event types. The width of arc for every event type on the ring, L_e, can be calculated by:

$$L_e = L_r / N_e \tag{1}$$

L_r is the perimeter of the ring, N_e is the number of selected event types.

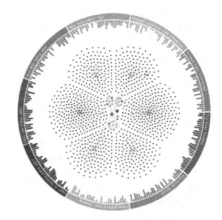

Fig. 3. The ring of event types and histogram of event counts

Three primary colors are used to visually distinguish the security events generated by different data sources, such as firewall in orange or NetFlow in green or host security logs in blue, and the intensity and saturation are used to differentiate the events from the same source, for example the color of Firewall Deny Connection is darker than that of Firewall Suspicious Built Connection. The color of every event type is set by users in advance, and the name of event type will be shown on the arc of the ring if there is enough space to better recognize event types.

Histogram of Event Counts

The histogram inside the event types is drawn clockwise along the arc of the ring. The bars of the histogram have the same color with that of the event types, and the height of the bar of histogram of the particular color arc represents the amount of this event type happened or observed in a sampling time which can be minutes or hours tuned by the security analysts. The whole time span of the arc can be also tuned by the security analysts. Our system will calculate the number and width of bars of the histogram, N_{bar} and W_{bar}, on arc according to the sampling time, t, the whole time span, T, and the width of the arc of event type, L_e .

$$N_{bar} = T / t;$$ (2)

$$W_{bar} = L_e / N_{bar}$$ (3)

The higher the bar is, the more dangerous the network security status is, and especially when several bars of event types are high at the same time. So the security analysts of network security can understand and analyze synthetically the network security trends according to events from the firewall, NetFlow and host security logs.

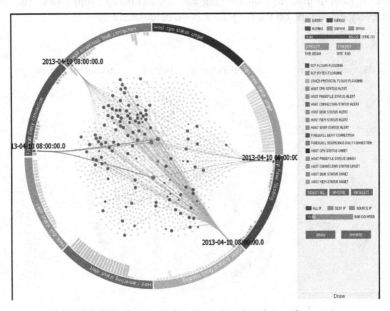

Fig. 4. Event correlation in a same time interval

Events Correlation

A network security event includes timestamp, source address and destination address. When the dangerous status was found from the histogram, the security analysts would like to know the details of the dangerous information. So we draw a curve, which connects the top of the bar of the histogram where the event happened and the source address or destination address of the topology diagram in the center of the ring, shown in figure 4. The color of the line is the same with the color of the event type. The width of the curve is related to the dangerous level which is set by network security analysts in advance. Dangerous level of an event type is related to the hosts, for example when the number of Firewall Deny Connection to a server or workstation is more than a threshold, the server or workstation is a dangerous host and would be connected by a thicker curve, and the node which represents the host is also bigger. The IP address of the host will be drawn when the dangerous node was clicked. The event correlation can help the network security analysts understand which nodes are dangerous attackers or victims. Moreover, to address visual clutter issue raised by too much straight lines appearing in the same time, we use curves to replace straight lines and implement the bundling effect

Interaction
Our visualization system provides the network security analysts with interactively setting parameters, such as the whole visiting time span, T, and the sampling time, t, and also allows the security analysts to filter by simply clicking on any of the hosts, servers, event types and bars of histograms. If the analysts, for example, want to see the attacks of an event type in a time interval, it just needs to click on the bar of event type, as shown in figure5. If a workstation is clicked, the attacks related to it will be shown. When the analyst points to a highlighted node in an event, the detail information about the host, such as host name and IP address, will be drawn. If you want to compare the attacks in this interval, multi-selection is provided with. These pointing and clicking features allow users for a smooth, thorough analysis. Another advantage of our visualization system is its use of animation to display the system transitions from one state to another in the whole time span, such as the distinct changes of event types and the amount of events to perceive the dangerous behavior pattern.

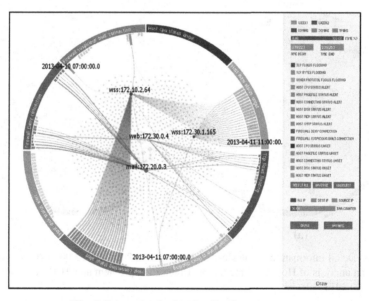

Fig. 5. Interaction in the visualization system

4   Results and Analysis

The visualization system, NetSecRadar, is implemented by Processing in windows 7 on a PC with a 1.87GHz Intel Pentium(R) 4 CPU, 4 gigabytes of memory, a Ge-Force 8800 GTX graphics card. In this section, our visualization system is used to analyze mini-challenges of IEEE VAST challenge 2013. The challenge provides multiple network security data sources, NetFlow, Firewall logs and Host Health Status logs, in

2 weeks, from 2013-4-1 7:00 to 2014-4-15 7:00, and NetFlow and Firewall has 70 million and 16 million records respectively, and Host Health Status logs generated by BigBrother software has 55 million thousand records.

In the first case study, we selected five event types, TCP Connection Flooding alert in NetFlow log, and Host Disk alert, Host CPU alert, Host Connection problem and Host Memory alert in BigBrother log, from 2013-4-1 12:00 to 2013-4-4 6:00, sampled by one hour.

Firstly, we found two events with obvious features, shown in figure 6(a), in this time span. One is the Host Disk alert detected by BigBrother which has kept reporting from Web server 172.10.0.4 and Admin server 172.10.0.40 every hour, and we further found that both disks of the servers have been occupied over 90% in log file. Another is the Host Memory alert that has never been observed in this time span.

Then a sign of the first abnormal behavior in the Intranet was found in 15:00 2013-4-1. We found a few Host CPU alerts generated by Web and Mail Servers as well as many Host Connection problems caused by subnets 172.30.2.* and 172.20.2.*, at the same time, some TCP Connection Flooding from Web Sever 172.10.0.4, Mail Server 172.10.0.3and workstation 172.10.1.251, shown in figure 6(b).

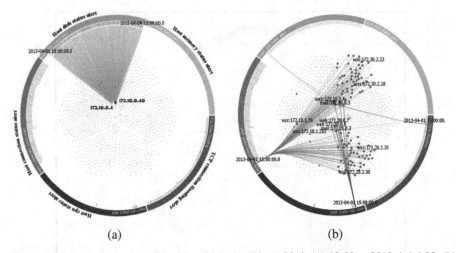

(a)   (b)

Fig. 6. (a) Detail information of the Host Disk alerts from 2013-4-1 12:00 to 2013-4-4 6:00; (b) Correlation analysis of Host CPU alert, Host Connection problem and TCP Connection Flooding in 15:00 2013-4-1

In the morning of the following day, 2013-4-2, continuous warning of TCP Flooding alerts was generated by several servers, as shown in figure 7(a). From checking the NetFlow log, a DDoS attack was found. At 5:00 April 2nd, through over 60,000 source ports, ten external hosts like 10.6.6.14, 10.6.6.6, 10.6.6.13, 10.7.7.10 started the DDoS attack to port 80 of internal Web servers, and lasted to 14:00 April 2nd. The connection alert kept emerging in the Big Brother logs, and the number of the connection alert had a significant growth after the DDoS attack on April 2nd, so we can determine the DDoS attack that brought a great harm to the Intranet.

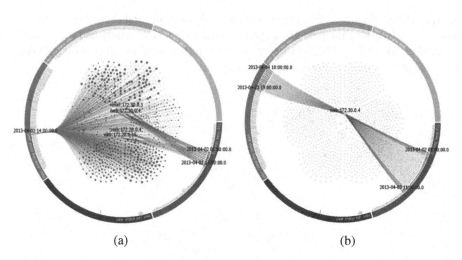

(a)   (b)

Fig. 7. (a) The network security situation under a DDoS attack on 2013-4-2; (b) Detail information about the most serious victim, server 172.30.0.4

The most serious victim is server 172.30.0.4, as shown in figure 7(b), because it generated TCP Flooding alerts continuously from 2013-4-2   5:00 to 2013-4-3 11:00. Especially it suffered more serious attacks from 5:00 to 7:00 on 2013-4-2 and from 11:00 to 12:00 on 2013-4-3 for the thicker of the green curves. We also found that the server, 172.30.0.4 seemed to go down for the constant Host connection alarm since 2013-4-3 19:00.

We select another set of log data from 2013-4-12 13:00 to 2013-4-14 20:00, 4 event types are Denied Connection alert from Firewall logs, TCP Connection Flooding in NetFlow log, Host Disk problem and Host Connection problem from Host Health Status logs.

We could first find one server, 172.0.0.4, kept sending the Host Disk alert almost every hour, shown in figure 8(a). It seems that 172.10.0.4 kept reporting alert for two weeks while 172.10.0.40 got well in the second week.

From 5:00 to 22:00 on April 13, Web servers 172.10.0.4 and 172.10.0.8 raised lots of TCP Connection Flooding alerts and Firewall Denied Connection alert. At 15:00 on April 14, more web servers, such as 172.20.0.4 and 172.20.0.15 raised TCP Connection Flooding alerts, but no firewall warning was found on those web servers at the same time, shown in figure 8(a). From 2013-4-13 5:00 to 4-13 22:00, Only a few workstations have Host Connection problem in BigBrother logs , shown in figure 8(b), but the number of the connection alert had a significant growth at 15:00 on April 14, shown in figure 8(c). Through further analysis of the log, over twenty external hosts IPs tried to attack web servers, and a massive number of TCP Flag exception packet sending from external IPs were denied by firewall, however, firewall failed to resist the attack by noon on April 14.

When observing all Firewall Deny alerts, eight internal hosts were suspicious. Not only a great number of Firewall Deny Connection events but also massive TCP Connection Flooding alerts were raised by them, shown in figure 8(d). After examining logs for further diagnosis, beginning from 8:28 April 12th, and these eight internal hosts started accessing the port 22 of external host 10.0.3.77 regularly and the accessing number to 10.0.0.4~10.0.0.14 is much larger than that to other workstations. Hence these eight internal hosts are noteworthy.

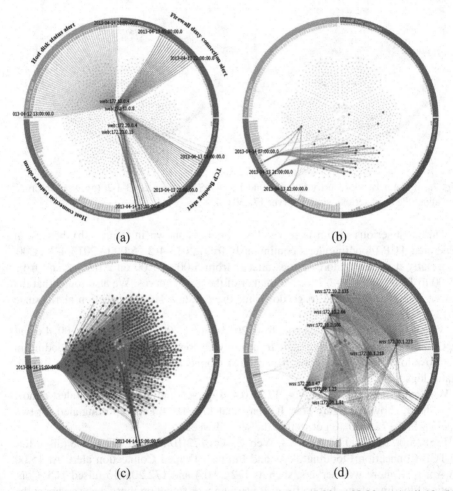

(a)   (b)

(c)   (d)

Fig. 8. (a) Detail information of workstations and servers from 5:00 to 22:00 on April 13; (b) Host Connection problem from 4-13 12:00 to 4-14 7:00; (c) Host Connection problem in 2013-4-14 15:00; (d) The workstations suffered Denny Connection and TCP Flooding

5   Conclusion and Future Work

In this paper a network security visualization system, NetSecRadar, is proposed to assist in monitoring and identifying abnormal pattern behavior based on multi-source logs in network security situational awareness by using radial graph. A hierarchical force-directed graph layout for arrangement of thousands of servers and workstations is proposed to better use the available screen space in the center of the radial graph, and a method of quantifying the dangerous levels of the security events is developed, and the correlations of security events generated by multi-source logs can be found by our graph design, and the interactions, filtering and drill-down, can help users understand the detail information of the events. We have evaluated the visualization system with attacks provided by VAST Challenge and have shown how our framework can be used to illustrate the attacks and visually correlate the events. In the future, we would like to extend the single view of radial graph to multiple views to show more details of servers and workstations. And further pattern analysis on individual host computer and individual risk will be performed.

Acknowledgments. The authors wish to thank the anonymous reviewers for their comments. The authors would also like to thank the data providers, IEEE VAST Challenge. This work is supported by the National Natural Science Foundation of China under Grant Nos. 61103108, Hunan Provincial Science and Technology Program under Grant Nos. 2012RS4049, Hunan Provincial Natural Science Foundation under Grant Nos. 12JJ3062 and Postdoc Research Funding in Central South University.

References

1. United States Department of Homeland Security. Team Coordination Training, Student Guide (May 2004)
2. Li, B., Springer, J., Bebis, G., et al.: A survey of network flow applications. Journal of Network and Computer Applications 36(2), 567–581 (2013)
3. Li, X., Wang, Q., Yang, L., et al.: The Research on Network Security Visualization Key Technology. In: 2012 Fourth International Conference on Multimedia Information Networking and Security (MINES), pp. 983–988. IEEE (2012)
4. Hadi, S., Ali, S., Ali, A.G.: A Survey of Visualization Systems for Network Security. IEEE Transactions on Visualization and Computer Graphics 18(8), 1313–1329 (2012)
5. Pin, R., Yan, G., Zhichun, L., Yan, C.: IDGraphs: intrusion detection and analysis using histographs. In: IEEE Workshop on Visualization for Computer Security, VizSEC 2005, Minneapolis, Minnesota, USA, October 26, pp. 39–46. IEEE Computer Society (2005)
6. Hideki, K., Kazuhiro, O., Kanba, K.: Visualizing Cyber Attacks using IP matrix. In: IEEE Workshop on Visualization for Computer Security, VizSEC 2005, Minneapolis, Minnesota, USA, October 26, pp. 91–98. IEEE Computer Society (2005)
7. Chris, P.L., Jason, T., Nicholas, G., Raheem, B., John, A.C.: Visual firewall: real-time network security monitor. In: IEEE Workshop on Visualization for Computer Security, VizSEC 2005, Minneapolis, Minnesota, USA, October 26, pp. 129–136. IEEE Computer Society (2005)
8. Bass, T.: Intrusion detection systems and multisensor data fusion. Communications of the ACM 43(4), 99–105 (2000)
9. Lakkaraju, K., Yurcik, W., Lee, A.J.: NVisionIP: netflow visualizations of system state for security situational awareness. In: Proceedings of the 2004 ACM Workshop on Visualization and Data Mining for Computer Security, pp. 65–72. ACM (2004)
10. Yin, X., Yurcik, W., Treaster, M., et al.: VisFlowConnect: netflow visualizations of link relationships for security situational awareness. In: Proceedings of the 2004 ACM Workshop on Visualization and Data Mining for Computer Security, pp. 26–34. ACM (2004)

11. Kulsoom, A., Chris, L., Gregory, C., John, A.C., John, S.: IDS RainStorm: visualizing IDS alarms. In: IEEE Workshop on Visualization for Computer Security, VizSEC 2005, Minneapolis, Minnesota, October 26, pp. 1–10. IEEE Computer Society (2005)

12. Hideki, K., Kazuhiro, O.: SnortView: visualization system of snort logs. In: The 2004 ACM Workshop on Visualization and Data Mining for Computer Security, VizSEC/DMSEC 2004, Washington, DC, USA, October 25-29, pp. 143–147. IEEE Computer Society (2004)

13. Shiravi, H., Shiravi, A., Ghorbani, A.A.: IDS alert visualization and monitoring through heuristic host selection. In: Soriano, M., Qing, S., López, J. (eds.) ICICS 2010. LNCS, vol. 6476, pp. 445–458. Springer, Heidelberg (2010)

14. Fuchs, J., Keim, D.A., Mansmann, F., et al.: BANKSAFE: A visual situational awareness tool for large-scale computer networks: VAST 2012 challenge award: Outstanding comprehensive submission, including multiple vizes. In: Proceedings of the 2012 IEEE Conference on Visual Analytics Science and Technology (VAST), pp. 257–258. IEEE Computer Society (2012)

15. Horn, C., D'Amico, A.: Visual analysis of goal-directed network defense decisions. In: Proceedings of the 8th International Symposium on Visualization for Cyber Security, p. 5. ACM (2011)

16. Liu, H., Gao, Y., Lu, L., et al.: Visual analysis of route diversity. In: 2011 IEEE Conference on Visual Analytics Science and Technology (VAST), pp. 171–180. IEEE (2011)

17. Alsallakh, B., Aigner, W., Miksch, S., et al.: Reinventing the contingency wheel: scalable visual analytics of large categorical data. IEEE Transactions on Visualization and Computer Graphics 18(12), 2849–2858 (2012)

18. Keim, D.A., Mansmann, F., Schneidewind, J., et al.: Monitoring network traffic with radial traffic analyzer. In: 2006 IEEE Symposium on Visual Analytics Science and Technology, pp. 123–128. IEEE (2006)

19. Taylor, T., Paterson, D., Glanfield, J., et al.: Flovis: Flow visualization system. In: Cybersecurity Applications & Technology Conference for Homeland Security, CATCH 2009, pp. 186–198. IEEE (2009)

20. Livnat, Y., Agutter, J., Moon, S., et al.: A visualization paradigm for network intrusion detection. In: Proceedings from the Sixth Annual IEEE SMC Information Assurance Workshop, IAW 2005, pp. 92–99. IEEE (2005)

21. Yarden, L., Jim, A., Shaun, M., Stefano, F.: Visual correlation for situational awareness. In: IEEE Symposium on Information Visualization, INFOVIS 2005, Minneapolis, Minnesota, USA, October 23-25, pp. 95–102. IEEE Computer Society (2005)

22. Zhao, Y., Zhou, F.F., Fan, X.P., et al.: IDSRadar: a real-time visualization framework for IDS alerts. Science China Information Sciences, 1–12 (2013)

Quantum Secret Sharing Based on Chinese Remainder Theorem in Hyperchaotic System

Ronghua Shi, Ye Kang, and Zhaoyuan Zhang

School of Information Science and Engineering,
Central South University.
Changsha,410083, China
{shirh,kangye}@csu.edu.cn,zhangzhaoyuan1024@gmail.com

Abstract. An novel quantum secret sharing (QSS) scheme is proposed based on Chinese Remainder Theory (CRT) with hyperchaotic encryption algorithm. The usage of hyperchaotic encryption strengthens the security of the quantum message. In addition, this scheme has high source capacity and convenience due to the utilization of GHZ measurement and high-dimension quantum channel. The analysis shows the presented protocol can resist the attacks from both outside eavesdroppers and inside dishonest participants.

Keywords: quantum secret sharing, hyperchaotic encryption algorithm, Chinese Remainder Theory, high-dimension GHZ state.

1   Introduction

The QSS plays a more and more significant role in the secret protection of quantum cryptography. Since 1999, Hillery et al.[1] applied three-particle and four-particle GHZ states to implement an initial QSS scheme. From then on, a lot of improved protocols and schemes have been proposed. Almost all these QSS protocols can be attributed to two types according to their goals. One is used to distribute a private key among some parties [1–5]; the other is used for sharing a secret including a classical one [6–12] or a quantum one [13–15].

Generally, the QSS scheme is known as a threshold scheme[16]. Suppose a message is divided into n sharers so that any k of n pieces could recover the message, but any set of $k − 1$ or fewer sharers fail to, which is called a (k, n)-threshold scheme. In this way, people can forbid some dishonest participants(at most $k − 1$in this threshold scheme) from knowing the whole message without the assistances of the honest ones.

With the unprecedented developments of the QSS, a myriad of the improved protocols and schemes have been proposed. For instance, cooperated with quantum secure direct communication (QSDC), Zhang presented a novel QSS [17], known as QSS-SDC, then he made use of swapping quantum entanglement of the Bell states to propose a multiparty QSS protocol based on the classical-message (QSS-CM)[18]. Moreover, an (n, n)-threshold scheme based on the quantum teleportation with the GHZ states was proposed by Wang et al. [19]. After that Han

G. Wang et al. (Eds.): CSS 2013, LNCS 8300, pp. 417–428, 2013.

et al.[20] illustrated a multiparty QSS-SDC scheme with random phase shift operations. Furthermore, an experimental QSS was reported by Bogdanski et al.[21] in the telecommunication fiber with the single-qubit protocol. Then Markham and Sanders [22] illustrated the graph states for the QSS. Recently, Sarvepalli et al. [23] proposed an approach for sharing the secret by using quantum error-correction code, which converts the Calderbank-Shor-Steane (CSS) code to a perfect QSS scheme. After that the experimental generation and characterization of a six-photon Dicke state was demonstrated by Prevedel et al.[24], then they showed the applications in multiparty quantum networking protocols such as the QSS, open-destination teleportation, and telecloning. It implies that the QSS is no long a theoretical imagery since they can be experimentally implemented by using single photons. This work has been devoted to the QSS design based on the GHZ measurements that emerges technological solutions leading to practical quantum networks[25–27].

CRT plays an significant roles in classical secret sharing, protocol and algorithms[28]. At the same time, the greatest advantage of quantum cryptography is its purely effects to provide unconditionally secure information communication. So in the reference [29], they combine them together for forming an novel QSS. But the shared secret is classical message. So in this article, it can be evolved into sharing quantum message.

It is essential to adopt a secure and reliable quantum channel for secret distribution and recovery. The scheme of quantum secure communication by using GHZ state in High-Dimension Hilbert Space proposed by Gao in the Ref.[30], is used for transmitting secret key in this paper. In order to prevent eavesdropping and save quantum entanglement resource, the scheme invites a trick: inserting particles into the particle sequence of rearrange orders. Different from the scheme, a rearranging sequence is used to rearrange orders.

In this article, quantum message $|P\rangle$ is encrypted by a hyperchaotic key K generated from hyperchaotic system. Then the key K can be split into 2 shares K1 and K2 according to the CRT equations showed in Eq.(7) or the Table1 generated from CRT. Next, using GHZ states in different dimensions to distribute $K1$ and $K2$ to remote party respectively. Only to exchange their shares, both of them can recovery the key and decrypt the quantum message.

This paper is organized as follows. In Sec.2 , 3 presents the details about quantum hyperchaotic encryption algorithm and distribution of encryption key, including hyperchaotic system and CRT. In Sec.4 the $(2, 2)$-threshold QSS scheme is exhibited.Then the analysis of the security of the scheme and some individual attack strategies are analyzed in Sec.5.

Table 1. The results of splitting encryption key according to CRT

X	0	1	2	3	4	5
$m_1 = 2$	0	1	0	1	0	1
$m_2 = 3$	0	1	2	0	1	2

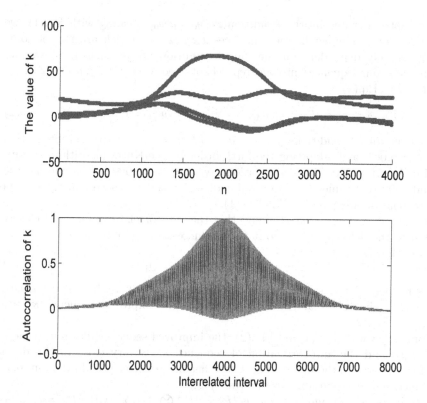

Fig. 1. The behavior of the original hyperchaotic sequence κ, the upper one shows the distribution of κ with the length of 4000 values; the under one exhibits the autocorrelation of κ

2   Quantum Hyperchaotic Encryption Algorithm

In this part, the hyperchaotic system will be introduced at first. In order to get more suitable sequence, then the hyprchaotic sequence needs to be modified, at last the encryption algorithm is depicted clearly.

In the proposed QSS scheme, an hyperchaotic system is used in the encryption progress, which is modeled by

$$\begin{cases} \dot{x} = a(y - x) + w, \\ \dot{y} = dx - xz + cy, \\ \dot{z} = xy - bz, \\ \dot{w} = xz + rw. \end{cases} \tag{1}$$

Where a, b, c, d and r are control parameters. When $a = 36; b = 3; c = 20; d = -0.5$;and $r = 0.8$, the Lyapunov exponets of system (1)are $\lambda_1 = 0.591, \lambda_2 = 0.136$, $\lambda_3 = 0, \lambda_4 = -26.109$. It is abvious that the system showed in Eq.(1) is hyperchaotic. For one intitial condition(x_0, y_0, z_0, w_0), dealing with Eq.(1), we can generate four hyperchaotic sequences x_i, y_i, z_i, w_i, which are non-periodic and sensitively dependent on the initial condition (x_0, y_0, z_0, w_0). So we can merge these four sequences into one hyperchaotic sequnece $\kappa = k_n, n = 1, 2, \ldots, L$ according to Eq.(2).

$$\kappa_{4i-3} = x_i, \kappa_{4i-2} = y_i, \kappa_{4i-1} = z_i, \kappa_{4i} = w_i, i = 1, 2, \ldots, L/4. \qquad (2)$$

Setting the initial conditions $(x_0 = 5, y_0 = 10, z_0 = 5, w_0 = 10)$ and integration step $h = 0.001$, and adoptting the forth order Runge-Kutta algorithm to solve the Eq.(1). After 2000 times integrations, we drop first 1000 results and use the second 1000 real values to obtain one-pad secret key κ, whose real values and autocorrelation are exhibited in Figs.(1).

From the Fig.(1), it is easy to know that the autocorrelation of κ is not closely related to the delta function. So it is quite necessary to make an improvement to κ as follows:

$$\kappa_n^* = k_n \times 10^m - round(k_n \times 10^m), \qquad (3)$$

where m=0,1,2,3,4.κ_n^* stands for the improved sequence κ, and $\kappa^* \in (-0.5, 0.5)$. When m=2,the values and autocorrelation of the improved sequence κ^* are showed in Fig.(2).

Comparing with Fig.(1)and Fig.(2), the improved sequence distributes more uniformly, and the autocorrelation of sequence κ^* is very close to the delta function. Therefore the modified sequence has much better pseudo-random performance and more suitable for one-time pad.

Let $|P\rangle$ be a quantum message as $|P\rangle = |P_1\rangle \otimes \cdots |P_L\rangle$ with $|P_i\rangle = \alpha_i|0\rangle + \beta_i|1\rangle, \forall i \in 1, 2, \cdots, L$. In this work, an operator $U(k, n) = e^{-\frac{2k\pi}{n}}$ is introduced, which is a special operator. When n is fixed, $U(k)$ has a period n, which means $U(k + n) = U(k)$. At the same time, it is obviously to find $U(k) \times U(-k) = 1$. According to these particular characters, U is appropriate to encrypt quantum message $|P\rangle$ as follows:

$$E_K(|P\rangle) = U(K)|P\rangle = \bigotimes_{i=1}^{L} e^{-\frac{2K_i\pi}{n}}|P_i\rangle. \qquad (4)$$

Where K is generated from hyperchaotic sequence κ^* with the same length of quantum message $|P\rangle$, the details is show in Eq.(5):

$$K_i = mod(|fix(\kappa_i^* \times 10^{14})|, n), i = 1, 2, \ldots, L. \qquad (5)$$

After encryption, the quantum message $|P\rangle$ becomes $|P'\rangle$, for each qubit, $|P_i'\rangle = \alpha_i'|1\rangle + \beta_i'|0\rangle$. Based on the characters of operator U,the decryption algorithm is given by

$$D_K(|P'\rangle) = \bigotimes_{i=1}^{L} e^{\frac{2K_i\pi}{n}}|P_i'\rangle. \qquad (6)$$

In this paper, a hyperchaotic sequence also can generate a rearrange sequence for disturbing sequence. If the hyperchaotic sequence,which can be obtained

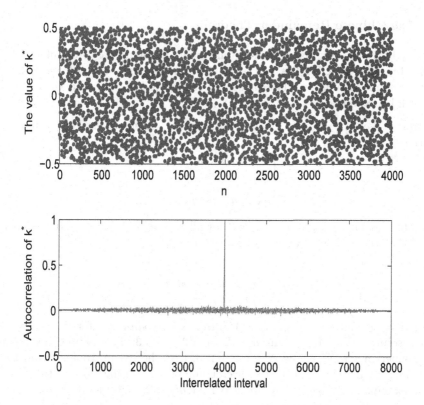

Fig. 2. The behavior of the improved hyperchaotic sequence κ^* , the upper one depicts the distribution of κ^* with the length of 4000 values; the under one paints the autocorrelation of κ^*

from Eq.(1), is H with length L, the rearrange sequence R has the following properties: 1. R has the same length L with H ; 2. The values of R sequence are all different integers between 1 and L; 3. If rank H from small to large, R_i presents the place of $H_i, i \in \{1, 2, \ldots, L\}$. Thus, R is available to rearrange a sequence S with length L, the way is described as: S_i is mapping to the place R_i , $i \in \{1, 2, \ldots, L\}$.

3   Distribution of Encryption Key

The description above shows the generation of secret key K from hyperchaotic system, and the process of encryption and decryption . In this section, the Chinese Remainder Theorem is applied to split K into m parts, which is detailedly described in "Quantum Secret Sharing Based on Chinese Remainder Theorem" by Shi et al in Refs.[29]. Following, it will be simply described:

3.1   The Chinese Remainder Theorem

Early in 1247, the original Chinese Remainder Theorem was brought out by SunZi. Resently, the CRT has lots of applications in classic cryptology, such as RSA algorithm calculation, classical secret sharing and so on. Later, the general CRT will be exhibited.

Lemma 1. Let $n \geq 2, m_1, \ldots, m_n \geq 2$, and $a_1, \ldots, a_n \in \mathbb{Z}$. The system of equations

$$\begin{cases} X \equiv a_1 \bmod m_1, \\ \vdots \\ X \equiv a_n \bmod m_n. \end{cases} \tag{7}$$

have solutions in $\mathbb{Z}$, if $gcd(m_i, m_j) = 1$, for all $1 \leq i \leq n, 1 \leq j \leq n$. It has been proved that this solution can be gotten, when

$$X = \sum_{i=1}^{n} T_i M_i a_i \bmod M, \tag{8}$$

where $M = m_1 \times m_2 \times \cdots \times m_n$, $M_i = M/m_i$, $T_i \times M_i \bmod m_i = 1$, for all $1 \leq i \leq n$, and the solution $X < M$. Setting $n = 2, m_1 = 2, m_2 = 3$, the system can present any number in set X, where $X \in \{0, 1, 2, 3, 4, 5\}$ showed in Table.(1). So the dealer maps a number $\in X$ to two secret numbers according to the Table.(1). For an example, number 5 is mapped to 1 for $m_1 = 2$, and 2 for $m_2 = 3$.

3.2   Distribution of the Secret Share

The high-dimension GHZ state is utilized in this quantum secure communication (QSC)[30]. In d-dimension Hilbert space, the maximal GHZ states are

$$|\psi_{nm}^k\rangle = \frac{1}{\sqrt{d}} \sum_{j=0}^{d-1} exp(\frac{2\pi ijk}{d})|j\rangle \bigotimes |j + n \bmod d\rangle \bigotimes |j + m \bmod d\rangle. \tag{9}$$

There are two sets of measuring basis(MB) in d-dimension Hilbert space: the Z-MB are

$$|Z_1\rangle = |0\rangle, |Z_2\rangle = |1\rangle, \cdots |Z_{d-1}\rangle = |d-1\rangle. \tag{10}$$

the X-MB are

$$\begin{cases} |X_1\rangle = \frac{1}{\sqrt{d}}(|0\rangle + |1\rangle) + \cdots + |d-1\rangle, & ; \\ |X_2\rangle = \frac{1}{\sqrt{d}}(|0\rangle + exp(\frac{2\pi i}{d})|1\rangle) + \cdots + exp(\frac{(d-1)2\pi i}{d})|d-1\rangle, & ; \\ \vdots, & ; \\ |X_{d-1}\rangle = \frac{1}{\sqrt{d}}(|0\rangle + exp(\frac{2(d-1)\pi i}{d})|1\rangle) + \cdots + exp(\frac{(d-1)\times 2(d-1)\pi i}{d})|d-1\rangle. \end{cases} \tag{11}$$

Let d=3 for an example, the 27 kinds of GHZ states are

$$
\begin{cases}
|\psi_{00}^0\rangle = \frac{1}{\sqrt{3}}(|000\rangle + |111\rangle + |222\rangle), \\
\quad\vdots \\
|\psi_{nm}^k\rangle = \frac{1}{\sqrt{3}}\sum_{j=0}^{2} exp(\frac{2\pi ijk}{3})|j\rangle \otimes |j + n mod3\rangle \otimes |j + m mod3\rangle \\
\quad\vdots \\
|\psi_{22}^2\rangle = \frac{1}{\sqrt{3}}(|022\rangle + exp(\frac{4\pi i}{3})|100\rangle + exp(\frac{8\pi i}{3})|211\rangle).
\end{cases}
\tag{12}
$$

the Z-MB are

$$|Z_1\rangle = |0\rangle, |Z_2\rangle = |1\rangle, |Z_3\rangle = |2\rangle. \tag{13}$$

and the X-MB are

$$
\begin{aligned}
|X_1\rangle &= \frac{1}{\sqrt{3}}(|0\rangle + |1\rangle + |2\rangle), \\
|X_2\rangle &= \frac{1}{\sqrt{3}}(|0\rangle + exp(\frac{2\pi i}{3})|1\rangle + exp(\frac{-2\pi i}{3})|2\rangle), \\
|X_3\rangle &= \frac{1}{\sqrt{3}}(|0\rangle + exp(\frac{-2\pi i}{3})|1\rangle + exp(\frac{2\pi i}{3})|2\rangle).
\end{aligned}
\tag{14}
$$

Thus in the communication process, the states of GHZ are used to transmit secret share, and the two sets of measure basis are utilized to check the existence of eavesdropper.

4   Scheme Descriptions

The details of QSS scheme of (2,2) is showed as follow. Suppose the dealer wants to share a quantum message $|P\rangle$, which is composed of L ($L \in \mathbb{Z}, and n mod3 = 0$)qubits with Alice and Bob.

Step1 Modulus negotiation, channel-dimension and hyperchaotic system initialization. Suppose Alice and Bob choose 2 and 3 as their moduli respectively for quantum communication. Assume the control parameters of hyperchaotic Ref.(1) and initial values are $a = 36, b = 3, c = 20, d = -0.5, r = 0.8; x_0 = 5, y_0 = 10, z_0 = 5, w_0 = 10; l = 1000, m = 2$. The parameter $l=1000$ means abandon the first 1000 iterations. Using the hyperchaotic system Ref.(1), the hyperchaotic sequence κ^* is acquired, which is utilized to generate secret key K by Eq.(5), with $n = 6$. K has the same length L with quantum message $|P\rangle$. Using the same way, we can obtain another two hyperchaotic sequences, and generating two rearrange sequences $R1$ and $R2$.

Step2 Encrypting quantum message $|P\rangle$ to $|P^*\rangle$ with K using Eq.(4) and mapping the key K to two subkey$K1 \in \{0,1\}^L$ for Alice and K2 $K1 \in \{0,1,2\}^L$ for Bob according to the CRT as Table.(1), i.e.,

$$K1_i = K_i mod2. \tag{15}$$

$$K2_i = K_i mod3. \tag{16}$$

Step3 Secret key distribution using high-dimension GHZ states.

According to the subkeys of Alice and Bob,the dealer prepares the GHZ states which are defined as $|\psi_{nm}^k\rangle$ in Eq.(9), letting

$$n = Ki_{3j-2}, m = Ki_{3j-1}, k = Ki_{3j},\qquad(17)$$

where $i \in 1, 2, j \in 1, 2, \ldots, L/3$. Then denote the prepared GHZ states sequences as Q and S respectively to Alice and Bob. Take Alice for an example: Q is described as $[Q_1^1, Q_1^2, Q_1^3, Q_2^1, Q_2^2, Q_2^3, \cdots, Q_{L/3}^1, Q_{L/3}^2, Q_{L/3}^3]$. Here Q_i^j represent the $j - th$ particle in the $i - th$ GHZ state. And then the dealer using rearrange sequence R_1 to disturb the order of the particles in Q, and obtain a new sequence Q'. Only the dealer knows R_1 for recovering the disturbed GHZ states.

For security, the dealer inserts some decoy phones named as D particle, selected randomly from $Z_0, Z_1, X_0 and X_1$, which is defined in Eq.(10,11). and writes down the positions of D particles. Then he sends the Q' sequence with D particles to Alice.

After confirming Alice has received the whole the Q' sequence with D particles, the dealer tells Alice the position and status of D particles publicly. According to this message, Alice picks out the D particles, measures them with the right MB, and then she can get the error rate of the sequence transmission. If the rate larger than the threshold,gives up the process. Otherwise, Alice will rearrange the P' sequence under the instruction of the dealer, so as to recover the P sequence. At last, Alice performs GHZ-state measurement on each three particles and obtains $K1$ according to the Eq.(17).

Similarly, the dealer have the same communication with Bob replacing $K1, Q$ and $R1$ with $K2, S$ and $R2$ for and Bob get the secret share $K2$.

Step4 Quantum message recovery. When Alice and Bob want to recover the secret message, they exchange their secret share $K1$ and $K2$, using the way as step 3. Alice sends $K1$ to Bob in 3-dimension channel,and Bob sends Alice $K2$ in 2-dimension channel. For preventing one participant refusing to sends oneself's share, after receiving the other share. They exchange their rearrange sequence $R1'$ and $R2'$ block by block. Or invite an impartial third-party, i.e., the dealer, to assist them. By another method, we can cut down the range of X showed in Table.(1)to $\{0, 1, 2, 3\}$, so numbers 4 and 5 are used as trap for authenticating participant. If the conditions of $(K1_i = 0, K2_i = 1)$ and $(K1_i = 1, K2_i = 2)$ happened, the recovery progress should be stop.

5   Security Analysis

Due to the insecure channels, we are always challenged by eavesdropping. What's worse, the dishonest member or more may cheat others to obtain the secret. So next the security of the proposed scheme will be analyzed in following possible cases:

(1) intercept-resend attack

The eavesdroppers intercept the quantum message , measure them or replace them with some new photons, then resend them to the channel. But they don't

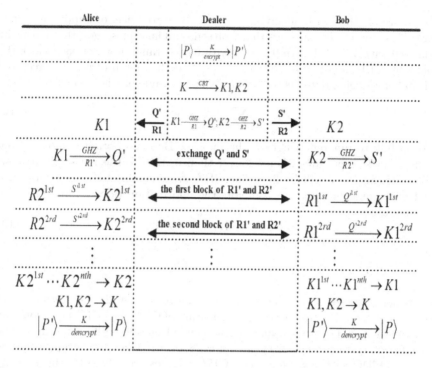

Fig. 3. The process of the QSS proposed in this paper. Here the D particle is without considering.

know the dimension , the right order of the sequence and the places and states of these D particles. Therefore, it is no gain , no matter how many particles Eve gets. The only way Eve can gets information is guess. What's worse, before the dealer broadcasting R-the order of the GHZ sequence, he will be detected with the probability $1 - (\frac{1}{m})^n$, where m is the dimension of GHZ or the kinds of D particles; n is the number of D particles inserted. So, it is easier to detect the exsitence of Eve with higher dimension or longer key.

(2) Trojan horse attack and EPR-pair attack

From references [31–33], the way to defeat these two attacks is inserting several sample photons randomly into P' sequence, which is done in this QSS scheme.

(3) Dishonest participants attack

When Alice and Bob receive their own shares, the both can guess the original key K,which is composed of L numbers, $K_i \in \{0, 1, 2, 3, 4, 5\}, i \in [1, L]$. Accoring to the Table1,it is easy to see that the probability for Alice is$(\frac{1}{3})^L$ and for Bob it is $(\frac{1}{2})^L$, to obtain the whole information of K. So, in the progress of quantum message recovery, the message is exchanged block by block, and adding two traps. Suppose the length of block is l, Bob is dishonest, he wants to get the other share of Alice without giving his own share to Alice, or supplying a fake share. This paper only considers that Bob sends all false messages, that means he replaces 0 with 1 or 2; 1 with 0 or 2; 2 with 0 or 1, randomly. For each block the probability of Bob not to be found is $p = (\frac{1}{2})^l$. If the length of message received by Bob before being detected is ℓ. The Expected value of ℓ is $E(\ell)$ calculated as

$$E(\ell) = \sum_{s=1}^{L} s \cdot l \cdot p^{s-1}. \tag{18}$$

According to different length l, the message Bob can obtain is mostly from the first block, especially when l longer than 6. Due to the message carrier is GHZ state, So $l = 6$ will be fine. The GHZ states sended by Alice stand for 0 and 1 with equal probability. Therefore the information Bob can abtain before being found is

$$H = E(\ell) * H(0.5) = E(\ell). \tag{19}$$

6   Conclusion

This paper proposes a new and simple scheme to realize $(2, 2)$ quantum secret sharing, which applies the secret sharing feature of CRT. The CRT equations can conveniently cut the secret sequence into several ones for different shares. The hyperchaotic system is used to generate random secret key to encrypt quantum message. QSDC with high-dimension GHZ provides great help for this security and large-capability quantum information channel. To recover the secert, the participants should collaborate with each other, exchange their shares, and do some caculation according to computation of the solution for CRT, or the table. Meanwhile a trap is suggested in the secret recovery phase for avoiding dishonest participants. The scheme is also available for more participants.

References

1. Hillery, M., Buzek, V., Berthiaume, A.: Quantum secret sharing. Phys. Rev. A 59(1829) (1999)
2. Karlsson, A., Koashi, M., Imoto, N.: Quantum entanglement for secret sharing and secret splitting. Phys. Rev. A 59, 162 (1999)
3. Deng, F.G., Long, G.L., Zhou, H.Y.: An effcient quantum secret sharing scheme with Einstein-Podolsky-Rosen Pairs. Phys. Lett. A 340, 43 (2005)
4. Yan, F.L., Gao, T.: Quantum secret sharing between multiparty and multiparty without entanglement. Phys. Rev. A 72, 012304 (2005)
5. Yang, C.P., Gea-Banacloche, J.: Teleportation of rotations and receiver-encoded secret sharing. J. Opt. B: Quantum Semiclass. Opt. 3, 407 (2001)
6. Zhang, Z.J., Man, Z.X.: Multiparty quantum secret sharing of classical messages based on entanglement swapping. Phys. Rev. A 72, 022303 (2005)
7. Gottesman, D.: Theory of quantum secret sharing. Phys. Rev. A 61, 042311 (2000)
8. Cleve, R., Gottesman, D., Lo, H.K.: How to share a quantum secret. Phys. Rev. Lett. 83, 648 (1999)

9. Zhang, Z.J.: Multiparty quantum secret sharing of secure direct communication. Phys. Lett. A 342, 60 (2005)
10. Bandyopadhyay, S.: Teleportation and Secret Sharing with Pure Entangled States. Phys. Rev. A 62, 012308 (2000)
11. Karimipour, V., Bahraminasab, A., Bagherinezhad, S.: Entanglement swapping of generalized cat states and secret sharing. Phys. Rev. A 65, 042320 (2002)
12. Zhang, Z.J., Li, Y., Man, Z.X.: Multiparty quantum secret sharing. Phys. Rev. A 71, 044301 (2005)
13. Li, Y.M., Zhang, K.S., Peng, K.C.: Multiparty secret sharing of quantum information based on entanglement swapping. Phys. Lett. A 324, 420 (2004)
14. Deng, F.G., Li, X.H., Li, C.Y., Zhou, P., Zhou, H.Y.: Multiparty quantum-state sharing of an arbitrary two-particle state with Einstein-Podolsky-Rosen pairs. Phys. Rev. A 72, 044301 (2005)
15. Deng, F.G., Li, C.Y., Li, Y.S., Zhou, H.Y., Wang, Y.: Symmetric multiparty-controlled teleportation of an arbitrary two-particle entanglement. Phys. Rev. A 72, 022338 (2005)
16. Cleve, R., Gottesman, D., Lo, H.K.: How to share a quantum secret. Phys. Rev. Lett. 83, 648 (1999)
17. Zhang, Z.J.: Controlled teleportation of an arbitrary n -qubit quantum information using quantum secret sharing of classical message. Phys. Lett. A 342, 60 (2005)
18. Zhang, Z.J., Man, Z.X.: Multiparty quantum secret sharing of classical messages based on entanglement swapping. Phys. Rev. A 72, 022303 (2005)
19. Wang, J., Zhang, Q., Tang, C.J.: Multiparty quantum secret sharing of secure direct communication using teleportation. Commun. Theor. Phys. 47, 454 (2007)
20. Han, L.F., Liu, Y.M., Liu, J., Zhang, Z.J.: Multiparty quantum secret sharing of secure direct communication using single photons. Opt. Commun. 281, 2690 (2008)
21. Bogdanski, J., Rafiei, N., Bourennane, M.: Experimental quantum secret sharing using telecommunication fiber. Phys. Rev. A 78, 062307 (2008)
22. Markham, D., Sanders, C.: Graph states for quantum secret sharing. Phys. Rev. A 78, 042309 (2008)
23. Sarvepalli, P.K., Klappenecker, A.: Sharing classical secrets with Calderbank-Shor-Steane codes. Phys. Rev. A 80, 022321 (2009)
24. Prevedel, R., Cronenberg, G., Tame, M.S., Paternostro, M., Walther, P., Kim, M.S., Zeilinger, A.: Experimental realization of Dicke states of up to six qubits for multiparty quantum networking. Phys. Rev. Lett 103, 020503 (2009)
25. Guo, Y., Zeng, G.H.: Encryption-based networking quantum teleportation with triplet Greenberger-Horne-Zeilinger States. Int. J. Quant. Infor. 8(5), 765 (2010)
26. Cuquet, M., Calsamiglia, J.: Limited-path-length entanglement percolation in quantum complex networks. Phys. Rev. A 83, 032319 (2011)
27. Pemberton-Ross, P.J., Kay, A.: Perfect quantum routing in regular spin networks. Phys. Rev. Lett. 106, 020503 (2011)
28. Asmuth, C., Bloom, J.: A modular approach to key safeguarding. IEEE Trans. Informat. Theory 29, 208 (1983)
29. Shi, R.H., Sun, Q., Guo, Y., Lee, M.H.: Quantum Secret Sharing Based on Chienese Remainder Theorem. Commun. Theor. Phys. 55, 573–578 (2011)
30. Gao, G.: Quantum Secret Communication by Using GHZ State in High-Dimensional Hilbert Space. Commun. Theor. Phys. 50, 368–370 (2008)

31. Cai, Q.Y.: Eavesdropping on the two-way quantum communication protocols with invisible photons. Phys. Lett. A 351, 23 (2006)
32. Deng, F.G., Li, X.H., Zhou, H.Y., Zhang, Z.J.: Improving the security of multiparty quantum secret sharing against Trojan horse attack. Phys. Rev. A 72, 044302 (2005)
33. Qin, S.J., Gao, F., Wen, Q.Y., Zhu, F.C.: Improving the security of multiparty quantum secret sharing against an attack with a fake signal. Phys. Lett. A 357, 101 (2006)

Restraining and Characterization of Virus Propagation in Large-Scale Wireless LAN

Cai Fu[1], Deliang Xu[2,*], Lansheng Han[1], Jingfang Xu[1], and Zhicun Fang[1]

[1] Computer School, Huazhong University of Science and Technology,Wuhan, China,430074
fucai@hust.edu.cn
[2] Department of Science and Technology Development,
China Shipbuilding Industry Corporation, No. 722 Institute, Wuhan, China, 430075
xudeliang2013@126.com

Abstract. Wireless communication experiences a worldwide blooming in recent decades. Virus defense becomes a key issue, receiving much attention in the academic and industrial com-munity since traditional virus defense technologies designed for wired communications have many limitations in wireless environ-ment. In this paper, by analyzing large-scale trace files of a campus wireless network and proper modeling of the propagation process, we identify several factors that affect the spreading of a virus. We then propose a new mechanism to prevent virus spreading in large-scale wireless network environment.

Keywords: Virus Spreading, WLAN, Virus Protection, Propagation Model.

1 Introduction

Recent years wireless communication infrastructures and portable computing equip-ments have widely deployed(such as lap-top computers, smart phones and PDAs). Wireless communication is deeply integrated and embedded in people's daily life, since many wireless devices are equipped with GPS devices or other advanced loca-tion technologies. A thorough understanding of user's contact patterns is bound to help the design, operation, maintenance and security of wireless communication net-works. The analysis method in wireless network nowadays is changing from early statistical method to human-behavior analyzing. Following this trend, we study virus spreading patterns in wireless network environment by analyzing large-scale trace files of a campus wireless network.

In this paper, some public campus network datasets are chosen as our research samples. Campus-wide trace dataset is easier to obtain and can serve as a good realis-tic simulation of virus spreading. First, it provides a comparative integrated and loca-lized testing sample because most people study and live within the campus, so that outside users can be reasonably ignored. Second, there are typical user groups in a campus, such as students, teachers and workmen, resulting in the structural regularity

---

[*] Corresponding author.

G. Wang et al. (Eds.): CSS 2013, LNCS 8300, pp. 429–440, 2013.

of the trace files. Many contact-based viruses propagate when two users are physically near. Thus, analyzing network traces is the first step towards virus defense.

In this work, we identify that human's behavior patterns provide unique and novel approach to understand virus spreading. First, in the social aspect, wireless networks are deeply integrated and embedded in people's daily life. Users' network behaviors reflect their social relation and activities, e.g., users with similar interests or attributes will group together, and their wireless devices may connect to the same access point. This social behavior could be identified by mining the network traces. Secondly, for virus defense, the social behavior of wireless users exert great influence on the virus propagation, so understanding the social characteristics can provide new methodology for virus protection. Furthermore, with the one-to-one mapping between network devices and users, this methodology may be some help for defending human virus, since those two kinds of virus considered in the context are both contact-based.

The main contribution of this paper is two-fold. First, by analyzing a set of network traces, we identify the behavioral patterns of network users and propose a new method for virus protection in wireless network. Second, we study how various factors affect virus spreading in wireless networks.

The paper is organized as follows. In Section 2, we introduce related work and our research problem. In section 3, different factors are analyzed by simulation for virus spreading in wireless network. In section 4, we analyzes our experimental data and presents results. We conclude this paper in Section 5.

2   Related Work and Problem Statement

The research about virus spreading in computer networks introduce lots of interesting ideas from biological virus study, because the model of biological viruses and computer viruses are closely related. Authors in [1-2] used the propagation model of biological viruses to simulate the propagation of computer viruses. However, this traditional virus propagation model (i.e. SI model) does not take into account the features of wireless networks. In this model, a virus propagates from one infected devices to those susceptible devices, which in turn become infected and continue to spread viruses to other susceptible devices. There are two assumptions in this tradition model: the number of users is constant, and each susceptible device has the same opportunity to be infected. However, in wireless networks, users may be online or offline at any time, such that susceptible devices have different opportunity to be infected with the constantly changing of the wireless network infrastructure. Based on these differences, studying virus propagation with dynamic user behaviors and network infrastructure in large wireless LAN becomes very challenging.

Mickens and Noble introduced a way of probabilistic queue, which is used to study the spread of viruses among mobile phones [3]. In this work, multiple queues were created, each of which represents a separate propagation of viruses. Zheng et al introduces a virus transmission model in mobile phone network ,which is based on radius, moving speed, and distribution density [4]. By studying network protocol to observe the propagation of viruses, De et al. obtains the propagation speed by simulating [5].

Tan and Munro proposed an adaptive probabilistic transmission protocol in an urban environment, which adapts network topology gradually [6]. Tang and Mark propose a SIR-M model to imitate viruses from a node spreading to the entire network [7]. Tang proposed an improved SI model to show the network's ability against anti-virus[8]. Wang et al. studies the mobile phone network and describes the characteristics of viruses' breaking out in such environment [9].

There are very few papers taking traces of WLAN into account when studying virus propagation. In this paper, we analyze the characteristic of WLAN with traces to show a different view about virus spreading.

3   Virus Propagation in Large Wireless LAN

We analyze the virus spreading process from three aspects. That is, the total online time of a user, the total number of unique Access Points (short for APs) that a user has visited, and the times that a user changes from one AP to another. In this section we first introduce how to use trace files to simulate virus spreading. Then we explain why we use these three factors and present our experiment results.

Our data is from Dartmouth College during spring of 2004 (04/05/0406/04/04), the data covers 586 APs in 161 buildings spread over about 200 acres, with registratio n patterns from 6202 users. The APs provide 11 Mbps coverage to entire campus duri ng this period; since the campus is compact, the interior APs tend to cover most outdoor spaces.

The APs transmit a "syslog" message every time a WiFi client card associates, re-associates, or dis-associaties with the AP; the message contains the unique MAC address of client card. A user's trace refers to the record of a single user's registration related events, including the OFF state, which represents user's departure from network (by turning off the device or leaving the ranges of all APs) [10].

3.1   Simulation of Viruses Propagation

Formula (1) shows the record format of a user:

$$\{(t_1, p_1), (t_2, p_2), \cdots, (t_n, p_n)\} \tag{1}$$

Where (t_i, p_i) is the record at time instant i, n is the total time stamps for observation, p_i represents the location and t_i represents time point when the use arrives at p_i. In favor of analysis, we will proceed the sampling every two minutes from original record. We choose the sample time as two minutes because if the sample time is too long, the virus can't spread; and if the sample time is too short, the speed of spread is too fast and it is not realistic. Figure 1 shows the process of the sampling.

Formula (2) shows the record after sampling, where p_{t_i} represents the online:

$$\{p_{t1}, p_{t2}, \cdots, p_{tn}\} \tag{2}$$

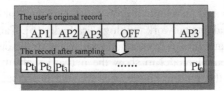

Fig. 1. The progress of data sample

Using the sampled data, we can determine whether an infected user can infect other susceptible users. For example, user A is infected and user B is susceptible, represented respectively as { pa1,pa2,...,pan } and { pb1,pb2,...,pbn } ,. If pai=pbi, then user A and user B are online at the same place and at the same time, so user A transmits viruses to user B with possibility of ε.

In order to analyze how different factors affect virus spreading in WLAN, and figure out the characteristics of viruses' breaking-out, we perform simulation experiments from the following three aspects: the total online period of users, the total number of APs, and the frequency of a user changing from one AP to another.

3.2   Total Online Period of Users

The total online period is the sum of a user's online time. Naturally, if a person has longer online time period, he has a higher probability to spread viruses or be infected by viruses.

Table 1. Algorithm 1

Preprocessing data and obtaining total online time
PreTreatmentTime   UsersData(datamatrix)
(1) while i>0
(2) read data from datamatrix, data=datamatrix[i]
(3) for each record from data
(4) record=data[j];
(5) time+=record.time;
(6) repeat 3
(7) datamatrix[i]=time; i--;
(8) repeat 1
(9) return datamatrix;

In order to analyze the impact of this parameter on virus propagation, we first find the user who has the longest online time and denote the time as t_{max}. Next, we immunize those users whose online time longer than $\alpha * t_{max}$, where α ($0<\alpha\leq1$) is a coefficient. In this experiment we increase α constantly to find the relationship between the total online time of users and the virus propagation. Algorithm 1(in Table1) and Algorithm 2(in Table2) are used to describe this process.

In Algorithm 1,Datamatrix stand for the data set of all users, data represents a user's record set, record present a record of a data, time is the total online time of a user, i represents the total number of data set, and j represents the total number of the record set.

In Algorithm 2,datamatrix stand for all users' the data set, data represents a user's record set, record present a record of a data, getvirus maens a user infected, i represents the total number of data set, j represents the total number of the record set,k represents the total number of users with viruses.

Table 2. Algorithm 2

Processing data and observing the influence of three factors above (The total online time of user/the total number of AP of user /the times of a user changing from one AP to another) on the virus spreading.

TimeEffect   TimeData(datamatrix)
(1) while j>0
(2) while k>0
(3)   read data from getvirus, data=getvirus[k];
(4)   while i>0
(5)   data_susceptible=datamatrix[i]
(6)   if(data[j]==data_susceptible[j])
(7)   i have ε chance to add to getvirus
(8)   repeat4
(9)   repeat 2
(10) repeat 1
(11) return getvirus

Table 3. Algorithm 3

Preprocessing data and getting the total number of Ap of all users

PreTreatmentWide   UsersData(datamatrix)
(1) while i>0
(2) read data from datamatrix, data=datamatrix[i]
(3) for each record from data
(4) reacord=data[j];
(5) wide[record.pos]=1;
(6) repeat 3
(7) count wide[] number to var number
(8) datamatrix[i]=number; i--;
(9) repeat 1
(10) return datamatrix;

3.3   Total Number of APs

The total number of APs of a user is the number of APs that a user connects, where a larger number means the user visits more places within the campus.

In order to analyze the impact of this factor on virus spreading, we first add up the total number of all APs of a user and record it as a vector. In order to find the relationship between these factors and virus propagation, we introduce a parameter β as immunized rate and to observe the result. The progress is described by Algorithm 2(in Table2) and Algorithm 3(in Table3).

In Algorithm 3, datamatrix stand for all users' the data set, data represents a user's record set, record present a record of a data, wide is a vector which presents the number of of Ap of all user, i represents the total number of data set , j represents the total number of the record set.

3.4   Frequency of a User Changing

If a user changes between APs back and forth, then the node may also be a key node. In order to analyze the impact of this factor on virus propagation, we first count the maximum number of AP changes of all users and let λ_{max} equals to this number. Next we immunize users, whose number of AP changes bigger than $\gamma * \lambda_{max}$,which γ is a coefficient.

Table 4. Algorithm 4

Preprocessing data and getting the data the total online time of all users
PreTreatmentFrequence   UsersData(datamatrix)
(1) while i>0
(2) read data from datamatrix, data=datamatrix[i]
(3) for each record from data
(4) reacord=data[j];
(5) if(record.time>2min)
(6) fre[i]++;
(7) repeat 3
(8) datamatrix[i]=fre[i]; i--;
(9) repeat 1
(10)return datamatrix;

We then constantly adjust γ to observe its impact on the virus propagation process. This can be described by Algorithm 2(in Table2) and Algorithm 4(in Table 4).

In Algorithm 4, datamatrix stands for all users' the data set, data represents a user's record set, record say a record of a data, fre is a vector which presents the number of all users' Ap changes, i represents the total number of data set, j represents the total number of the record set.

4   Experiment and Analysis

In this chapter, we will analysis the experimental data, and put forward conclusion. The following three diagrams are the three experimental results above section, respectively are the influence of online time on virus propagation(in Figure2); the influence of APs' number on virus propagation(in Figure3); the influence of AP changes on virus propagation (in Figure4).

In these figures, the series represent the value of α which means the proportion of un-infected nodes in all nodes. We take α as 0.01, 0.02, 0.03, 0.04, 0.05, 0.06, 0.07, 0.08, 0.09 and 0.1.

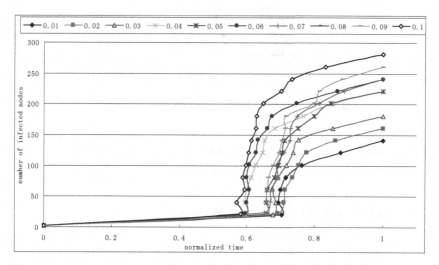

Fig. 2. The influence of online time on virus propagation

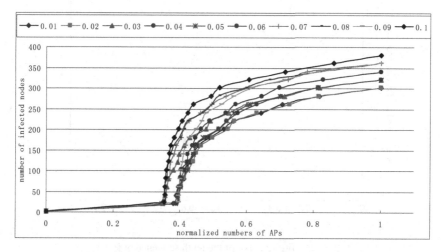

Fig. 3. The influence of APs' number on virus propagation

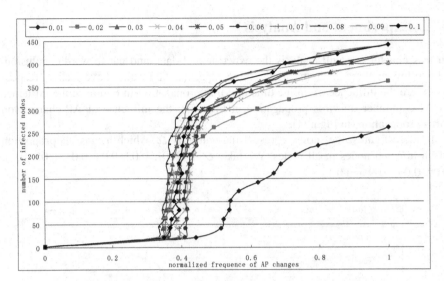

Fig. 4. The influence of AP changes on virus propagation

According to the figures above, we can find that virus propagation in wireless network satisfies logistics curve, as equation (3):

$$f(X) = \frac{A}{1 + B * e^{-cX}} \qquad (3)$$

That is, they also meet logistic regression curves.

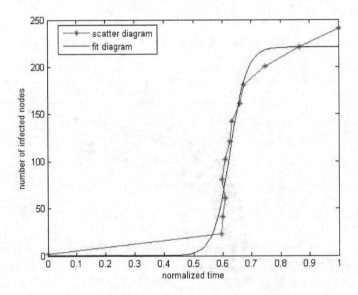

Fig. 5. The fitting curve of the tenth sequence of Fig 3

We take out the tenth sequence in Figure 2 for analyzing and use Matlab to fit curve with parameters, and obtain A = 221.01, B =2.33, C =34.44 as Figure6.

We take out the tenth sequence in Figure 3 for analyzing and use Matlab to fit curve with parameters, and obtain A=317.30, B= 2.52, C=25.73 as Figure7.

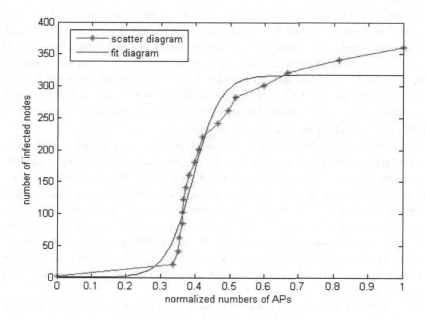

Fig. 6. The fitting curve of the tenth sequence of Fig 4

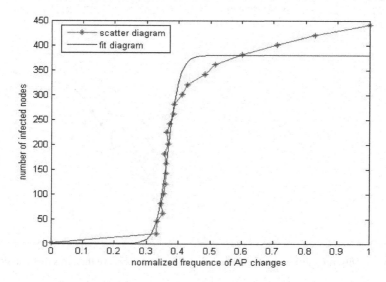

Fig. 7. The fitting curve of the ninth sequence of Fig 5

We take out the ninth sequence in picture 6 for analyzing and use Matlab to fit curve with parameters, and obtain A=379.67, B=6.06, C=55.07 as figure7.

Therefore we can consider that the virus spreading in wireless network meets the law described in Equation (3). From Equation (3), we can know the following three conclusions:

First, the three factors we discussed in Section 3 have significant effect on virus propagation in network. From the above three figures, we notice that the network viruses can not break out when $\alpha \leq 0.03$, which means viruses cannot break out if the long time users are immunized. In figure3, when $\alpha \geq 0.06$, we can see obviously that the network viruses start to grow rapidly after a critical point. From the figure4, the viruses cannot break out when $\alpha \leq 0.03$, while when $\alpha \geq 0.04$, it will break out after a critical point. the network viruses spread slowly when $\alpha \leq 0.03$, but when $\alpha \geq 0.04$, they spread rapidly after a critical point.

Based on the first conclusion above, we believe that the virus spreading in wireless network is affected by these three factors: the online time, the total number of APs, and the times for a user changing from one AP to another. The virus will not break out under the situation where users who have spend long time online and have a wide range of Ap are immunized, but when the number of infected users comes to a criti-cal point , viruses will break out rapidly. In order to prove this, we increase the num-ber of initial infection sources to observe the situation of the spread of viruses and get the following figure. From the figure8, we can see that the number of infection sources can only influence the position of critical point and can not affect whether it breaks out or not.

From Figure 9, we can see that when the number of viruses comes to 1.5% of the total number of network users, viruses will growth rapidly. So we set 1.5% of users

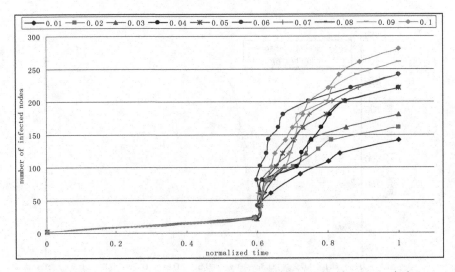

Fig. 8. Different initial number of the infected nodes to observe the virus transmission

are infected at the beginning of time. It can be seen from figure below the network viruses increase rapidly without delay.

We then can draw the second conclusion: the initial number of infected users does little contribution to breaking-out of viruses; even small number of infected users will lead to break out.

Based on the second conclusion, we get the third conclusion: in initial stage of a virus breaking-out, the path between users must be cut off completely. From the second conclusion we can see that a small number of infected users can lead to break out. Therefore, all viruses should be cleaned but this may be impossible. However from figure 3,4and 5 we found a strategy: we can immunize high risk users and this can protect all users. These three figures show that if we dislodge those users (spend long time online, have wide range of the APs, and change frequently between APs) the virus will not break out. These users are the most important nodes in protecting other users from infection.

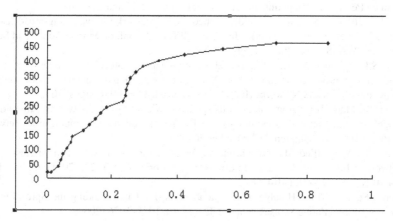

Fig. 9. 1.5% of total number of the infected nodes to observe the transmission of the virus

5   Conclusion and Future Work

In this paper we analyze the virus spreading in large-scale wireless LAN, and we get three conclusions. First, we analyze the human characteristics affecting virus spread in WLAN, and confirm that human behavior has great effect on virus spreading. Secondly, according to trace files, we propose the strategy to defend virus spread in large wireless network, which can also be used to against biological viruses. At last , but not least, through the analysis of three different factors (the frequency of changing APs, total time spending in network, and the total number of APs who has visited in), we develop a mathematical model for virus spread and find some new features, and give out the exact parameters of the model.

In our future work, we will propose a specific implementation plan which can use proposed characteristics in this paper to prevent viruses breaking out. Furthermore, with these characteristics, we can conclude a new immune program which is very cost-effective in time and bandwidth.

Acknowledgment. The paper is supported by China NSF(61272405, 60903175, 61272033,61272451, 61100221) and University Innovation   Foundation(2013TS102, 2013TS106).

References

1. Pastor-Satorras, R., Vespignani, A.: Epidemic spreading in scale-free networks. Physical Review Letters 86, 3200–3203 (2001)
2. Newman, M.E.J.: Spread of epidemic disease on networks. Physical Review E 66, 1–11 (2002)
3. Mickens, J.W., Noble, B.D.: Modeling epidemic spreading in mobile environments. In: Proc. 4th ACM Workshop on Wireless Security (WiSe 2005), Cologne, Germany, pp. 77–86 (2005)
4. Zheng, H., Li, D., Gao, Z.: An epidemic model of mobile phone virus. In: 1st Int'l Symposium on Pervasive Computing and Applications, pp. 1–5 (August 2006)
5. De, P., Liu, Y., Das, S.K.: An epidemic theoretic framework for evaluating broadcast protocols in wireless sensor networks. In: Proc. IEEE Int'l Conf. on Mobile Adhoc and Sensor Systems (MASS), Pisa, Italy (October 2007)
6. Tan, S.K., Munro, A.: Adaptive probabilistic epidemic protocol for wireless sensor networks in an urban environment. In: Proc. 16th International Conference on Computer Communications and Networks (ICCCN 2007), pp. 1105–1110 (August 2007)
7. Tang, S., Mark, B.L.: Analysis of virus spread in wireless sensor networks: An epidemic model. In: International Workshop on the Design of Reliable Communication Networks (DRCN 2009), Washington, DC (October 2009)
8. Tang, S.: A modified SI epidemic model for combating virus spread in wireless sensor networks. Int. J. of Wireless Information Networks (April 22, 2011) Online First, doi:10.1007/s10776-011-0147-z
9. González, P.W.M.C., Hidalgo, C.A., Barabási, A.-L.: Understanding the Spreading Patterns of Mobile Phone Viruses. Science 324(5930), 1071–1076 (2009)
10. Kotz, D., Essien, K.: Analysis of a campus-wide wireless network. In: Proceedings of MobiCom, pp. 789–796 (September 2002)

An Improved Differential Fault Analysis Attack to AES Using Reduced Searching Space

Zemin Cai[1], Yi Wang[1,2], and Renfa Li[1,2]

[1] Embedded Systems & Networking Laboratory, Hunan University
[2] Hunan Provincial Key Laboratory of Network and Information Security, Hunan University,
Changsha, China
estelle.ywang@gmail.com

Abstract. Differential Power Analysis against AES proved to be effective, with use mask techniques, we can truncate the relevance and defense DPA attacks successfully. In this paper, we introduce a new mean called DFA (Differential Fault Attack), DFA has been shown successfully to attack AES algorithm with masking. We inject a fault to the intermediate results and other general form to obtain the ciphertext with faults, using the ciphertext we can recover the keys. Firstly, we construct the Sbox / InvSbox distribution tables to make the results sets space is less than 2^8 with two correct/fault ciphertexts pairs, even, in most cases, the set space are strict in 2^2. Secondly, we also demonstrated that the model of DFA we constructed can ignore the masking techniques and propose some methods to recover the keys with less time consuming and reduced searching space. Lastly, we make the module into an application and prove the module is effective.

Keywords: DFA, Boolean Masking, Distribution Table, AES.

1 Introduction

DPA has been used to decipher AES [1] cryptographic algorithm successfully, however, using a masking technique , the AES cryptographic algorithm can defense against DPA, With further research Differential Fault attack (DFA) proposed by researchers. DPA attack is able to recover secret information by comparing the differences between the sample power trace and the correct key power trace. Örs et al [2] and Mangard et al [3] successfully broke the AES by using DPA attack. Higher-Order differential power attack (HODPA) is a more powerful attack that exploits joint leakage information of several intermediate values to "crack" the secret information. Joye et al [4] and Proutff et al [5] analyzed 2ODPA attack in theory respectively. Waddle et al. proposed several different 2ODPA attacks to overcome the masked cryptographic algorithm [6]. The masked AES can resist against the DPA, but it still cannot resist against Differential Fault Analysis (DFA) attack.

Fault attack first introduced by D. Boneh et.al, in 1996[7]. They showed that an induced fault in a smart-card device running RSA could reveal the entire secret key. Subsequently, Biham and Shamir proposed more lethal form of the attack [8] on DES

G. Wang et al. (Eds.): CSS 2013, LNCS 8300, pp. 441–449, 2013.

cryptosystem which known as Differential Fault Analysis. In 2001, NIST accepted Rijndael as the Advanced Encryption Standard (AES) following the attack on AES more and more.

Currently the DFA attacks on AES can mainly divided into two categories, 1) attacking the key strategies, 2) attacking the intermediate state. Dusart et.al [9] injected an error into the intermediate values before the 9th round of shiftRow Transformation; it requires 40 ciphertextes as additional information to reveal the all keys and the explore space is about 2^{24}. Gilles and Quisquater [10] make some improvements base on [9] and it injected one error into the states between mixColumns transformation located at the penultimate round and the third last round, this method need only two errors to recover the keys, but the explore space is large, it is about 2^{32}. Amir et al[11] proposed two models ,the one is inject some errors before the 9th round with six pairs of correct/fault ciphertext they recover all keys, the other use 1500 pairs correct/fault ciphertext to recover the keys, the second way need more information but have a smaller guess keys set space about 2^{16}. Tunstall et al [15] use two steps to get keys, the first step own a statistical expectation of reducing the possible key hypotheses to 2^{32}, and the second step to a mere 2^{8}. The methods above are based on the attacks at the intermediate state, the following about the attacks on key strategies. Kim and Quisquater [12] injected four faults into the 9th subkeys, it needs 12 pairs correct/fault ciphertext to recover the keys and the guess keys set space is much big. Kim [13] proposed a method inject four faults into the 8th subkey, but it needs 7 pairs ciphertext which is less than [12], but the derivation is more complicated and its explore space is more than 2^{16}.

In this paper we constructed a model base on attacking on the intermediate state, withing use this method, we need two errors and two pairs correct/fault ciphertexts, with a explore space of 2^{8}, even in most cases is 2^{2} to recover an byte of the 10th subkeys, other, we give a more flexible model which constructed base on the this model. The models we proposed are sample but efficient, they have small explore space and the time complexity to recover all key bytes are about 2^{6}--2^{14} which are smaller and lower than the exsiting methods.

2   Preliminary

2.1   AES

AES is a symmetric encryption algorithm. It supports block size of 128-bits and key sizes of 128, 192 and 256 bits. The encryption process starts with the first key addition, followed by a number of round functions, which depends on the key size. In the encryption, the round function is composed of four transformations, ShiftRows cyclically shifts to left the bytes in the last three rows of the state, with different offsets; SubBytes is the non-linear byte substitution and operates independently on each byte of the state; the MixColumns that multiplies modulo x^4+1 the columns of the state by the polynomial $\{03\}x^3+\{01\}x^2+\{01\}x+\{02\}$; and finally the AddRoundKey add a

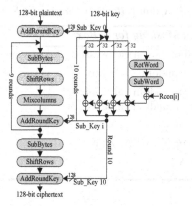

Fig. 1. Encryption process of AES

round key to the state. All the needed round keys are generated by a key schedule takes the secret key and expands it as specified in the standard.

2.2 Bollean Masking for AES

We use six independent 8-bit masking values m0, m0', m1, m2, m3 and m4, m0 is the input mask and m0' is the output mask of the modified SubBytes operation.To simplify the calculation, we define m0=m0' The remaining four masks m1, m2, m3 and m4 are the input masks of the MixColumns operation, m1 is the mask in the first row, m2 is the mask in the second row, m3 is the mask in the third row, and m4 is the mask in the fourth row. We defined the four input masks of the MixColumns as m= {m1, m2, m3, m4}, and m'= {m1', m2', m3', m4'}, which are the resulting masks of Mix-Columns.

The effect of the mask is to eliminate the correlation between the intermediate results and power depletion, so the attacker cannot use the power trace to obtain the keys for Crptographic algorithms.

At the beginning, we use m'={m1', m2', m3', m4'} to mask the plaintext p and use mkey={mk1, mk2, mk3,mk4}={m1'⊕m0, m2'⊕m0, m3'⊕m0, m4'⊕m0}to mask the SubKey k. In this way, after the MixColumns operation, all the intermediate values are masked with m0. Then, the modified SubBytes operation changes the input mask m0 into the output mask m0'. Because all bytes of the state are masked with the same mask m, the ShiftRows operation does not affect the masking. Before MixColumns, we mask the intermediate values again with mmix={mm1, mm2, mm3, mm4}={m0'⊕m1, m0'⊕m2, m0'⊕m3, m0'⊕m4}, which change the input masks into m1, m2, m3, m4 in the first, second, third and fourth row separately. We can get the output masks m'= {m1', m2', m3', m4'} of Mixcolumn which is same with the mask in the beginning. Because Sbox is nonlinear, it has special requirements differ from the other operators. Algorithm 1 shows the Boolean mask for S-box.

Algorithm 1. *Boolean Masking for S-Box*

Boolean Masking for S-Box

Input: Sbox S of n elements, each less than 2^8 in AES

Output: Randomized S-box S_u^v.

generate a random value $u < n$
generate a random value $v < 256$

   for i from 0 to n

      $S_u^v(i) \leftarrow Sbox(i \oplus u) \oplus v$

   return S_u^v

---

3   DFA Attack to Masked AES

In this subsection we discuss the reason why DFA which using the model will introduce in the section V can ignore the mask AES have been used. We inject an error into the intermediate results before the 10th Sbox operation, in the next section we will loosen this restriction into a generalized situation. With the AES which use the Boolean mask to protect against the attack, for example DPA. We can get the equation (1).

$$C = (S_u^v(S) \oplus (key \oplus w) \oplus v) \oplus w , S = s \oplus u \tag{1}$$

In equation (1), s represents the intermediate results before the Sbox of the 10th round operation. In order to get the results we choose two pair correct/fault ciphertexts, so we can get equations (2) (3) as the u, v, w are random. We use $C2'$ to replace $C1'$, the $C1$ represents the ciphertext with error free, and $C2'$ represents the ciphertext which injected a error to the intermediate results before the 10th Sbox operation.

$$C1 = (S_{u1}^{v1}(S1) \oplus (key \oplus w1) \oplus v1) \oplus w1 \tag{2}$$

$$C2' = (S_{u2}^{v2}(S2 \oplus e_j) \oplus (key \oplus w2) \oplus v2) \oplus w2 \tag{3}$$

To look up the Sbox Boolean Masking Algorithm, from (1)(2)(3) we can obtain (4).

$$\begin{aligned} C1 \oplus C2' &= (S_{u1}^{v1}(S1) \oplus (key \oplus w1) \oplus v1) \oplus w1 \\ &\oplus (S_{u2}^{v2}(S2 \oplus e_j) \oplus (key \oplus w2) \oplus v2) \oplus w2 \\ &= Sbox(s) \oplus Sbox(s \oplus e_j) \end{aligned} \tag{4}$$

According to the equation (4), we find that the equation is unrelated with the random generated values, and it degenerated into the condition with no mask. So we can use the same ways which will introduce in the next section to look for the answers. In this subsection we understand that the AES with Boolean Mask is invalid to DFA, so when we going on a DFA, the masking should be ignored.

4   Proposed Fault Module to Break AES

In this subsection, our goal is to construct a deduction model to attack the masked 128bits-AES. The most important is how to build up a fault generation modules, which can inject the faults to the proper position of the design.

First we create the AES "InvSbox Distribution Table" which is very important to reduce the search space for keys .

$$InvSbox: Input \rightarrow Output;   \text{// the InvSbox distritution}$$

$$C \oplus C' = Input$$
$$InvSbox(C) \oplus InvSbox(C') = Output$$

We can obtain the InvSbox distribution and get the possible guess values C from the map relationships.

Table 1. Examples of InvSbox Distribution

Distribution $0x1a \rightarrow 0x01$	Distribution $0x4b \rightarrow 0x04$
(94,8e),(8e,94)	(55,1e),(1e,55)
(8e,94),(94,8e)	(1e,55),(55,1e)

As discussed above in Section 2, the AES's 10th round has no the MixColunms operation the ShiftRows do not change the values of intermediate results. Therefore, when we explore the 10th round operation, we can only think of the Sbox (InvSbox) and AddRoundKey operations, we inject a known error e_j into the intermediate results before the 10th round Sbox operate, so, we can obtain the equations as follows. To simplify, we use the unprotected 128-bits AES as an example, the masked 128-bits AES can also be attacked as discussed in Section 4.

$$C = Sbox(S) \oplus key \tag{5}$$

$$C' = Sbox(S \oplus e_j) \oplus key \tag{6}$$

S represents the intermediate result before 10th Sbox. We can obtain equation (7) from Equations (5) and (6).

$$InvSbox(C \oplus key) \oplus InvSbox(C' \oplus key) = S \oplus S \oplus e_j = e_j \tag{7}$$

And (7) is equivalent to the following equation(8),

$$InvSbox: C \oplus key \oplus C' \oplus key \rightarrow e_j$$
$$=>$$
$$InvSbox: C \oplus C' \rightarrow e_j \tag{8}$$

Therefore, we can achieve the possible guessed values of $C \oplus key$, and the possible guessed keys. Alternatively, we can pick the C1 and C1' (with an inject error e_i) in the condition that the keys used for C and C1 must be the same. So we can use two pairs of correct/fault ciphertext to generate two sets of guessed key and the intersection of sets are the correct key. Using this model, we should use two faults, two pairs of the correct/fault ciphertexts to retrieve one key byte, and repeated 16 times to obtain a full private keys.

Because the faults do not affect the round keys, it only affect the intermediate states, we can reconstruct the model which was discussed before, if a fault have been injected before the 8th round, as one byte fault can expand to 4 fault bytes, then expand to 16 bytes [14] through the MixColumns Transformation, Fig.2 shows this process, we can obtain ciphertexts whose bytes are all wrong. Then we assumed that all the faults induced into the states before the Sbox operation in the 10th round of AES, no matter which round it was really. We can use the same way discuss above to recover the keys. The difference between the method discuss first and this method is whether the error ej is known or unknown which increase the flexibility for the attacker. After successfully injects a random error, we develop a program to perform an exhaustive search in the space of 2^8 to determine the errors. Then we can use it recover the all bytes of the 10th subkeys. By using this method, we only need two random faults and two pairs correct/fault ciphertexts to obtain the all bytes of keys.

In this Subsection, we introduce two methods about the DFA. The first way need 2 known faults, and 2 pairs ciphertexts to obtain one byte key, so it should do 16 times to obtain the full keys. The second way needs two random faults and 2 pairs of ciphertexts to obtain the full keys for only once. The time complexity (the number of operations to get the full keys included the time to explore the guess keys space) are 2^6 and 2^{14} which are far less than the existing methods that have been introduced in section 1.

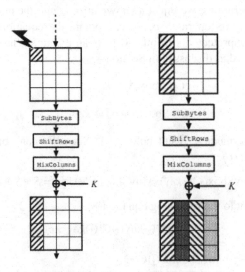

Fig. 2. The Process of Faults Expand

5   Experimental Results

As discussed before, in order to make our reduce models sample, we choose the method introduced in section 4 to prove it is effective. In order to get the right results and make the DFA successfully we should get at least two pairs of correct/faulty ciphertexts in our reduce modules. We randomly picked up two plaintexts, which defined as

$$P_1=0x328831e0435a3137f6309807a88da234$$
$$P_2= 0xec4a721e562335446ba263ee2b6372ac$$

We define the initial key are.

$$Key =0x2b7e151628aed2a6abf7158809cf4f3c$$

So the 10th keys are

$$key_{10}=0xd014f9a8c9ee2589e13f0cc8b6630ca6$$

And the map ciphertexts are

$$C1=0x3925841d02dc09fbdc118597196a0b32$$
$$C2=0x69189b1b31683c90bbdbf1ecadb909f3$$

Note here, we targeted at the last byte of key_{10} as an example to illustration DFA attack, e_j represent the one bit error in the design where j is the position of the bit flipping. If we successfully injected one bit error (e_0) to the intermediate results before Sbox, we could get the first faulty ciphertext as

$$C1'=0x3925841d02dc09fbdc118597196a0b28$$
$$
\begin{aligned}
C1 \oplus C1' \\
&=0x3925841d02dc09fbdc118597196a0b32 \\
&\quad \oplus 0x3925841d02dc09fbdc118597196a0b28 \\
&=0x1a \\
&=Sbox(s1) \oplus Sbox(s1 \oplus e_0)
\end{aligned}
$$

Our attack object is the last byte, so the last byte of $C1$ and $C1'$ are 0x32,0x28 which is regarded as the two inputs of Distribution Table for InvSbox, the input XOR is 0x1a, and the output XOR is equaling to e_0(0x01),from Distribution Table, 0x1a→0x01 entry has value 2, and only two pairs satisfy this entry, combined with the input values, we could easily retrieve the possible guess keys for $C1$ and $C1'$.

Table 2. Possible keys for 0x1a->0x01 with inputs 0x32 and 0x28

InvSbox input	possible guess keys
0x94,0x8e	0xa6,0xbc
0x8e,0x94	0xbc,0xa6

Similarly, we inject the bit error e_2 (0x04) to the intermediate results before Sbox for $C2$, and we could obtain $C2'$,

$$C2'=0x69189b1b31683c90bbdbf1ecadb909b8$$
$$C2 \oplus C2'$$
$$=0x69189b1b31683c90bbdbf1ecadb909f3$$
$$\oplus 0x69189b1b31683c90bbdbf1ecadb909b8$$
$$=0x4b$$
$$=Sbox(s2) \oplus Sbox(s2 \oplus e_2)$$

The last byte of $C2$ and $C2'$are 0xf3, 0xb8 regarded as two inputs of distribution table for InvSbox, the output is e_2=0x04, from table Distribution ,0x4b$\rightarrow$0x04(e_2) entry has value 2, and only two pairs satisfy this entry the same as Table 2,we can get our Table 3.

Table 3. Possible keys for 0x4b->0x04 with inputs 0xf3 and 0xb8

InvSbox input	possible guess keys
0x55,0x1e	0xa6,0xed
0x1e,0x55	0xed,0xa6

From table 2 and 3, the common guessed key is only 0xa6 which is the last byte of the 10th keys of AES. By selecting different ciphertext and injecting error, we could easily recover the 10th keys. We know masked design is almost the same as in the unprotected one. Therefore, it is obvious that the DFA methods we proposed could efficiently recover the keys of AES, even with masking. In our example the error we choose is bit error(s), in fact we can choose every value less than 2^8 as the error(s) injected to the intermediate results.

According to the feature of InvSbox distribution table, for each key we can restrict the explore space in the 2^8, and in most conditions the explore space is 2^2.

6   Conclusion

In this paper, we inject a error into the intermediate state before the 10th round's Sbox operation for the 128-bits AES and an other general form which is more flexible, using any one we can obtain the right/fault ciphertext pairs, with the help of InvSbox distribution table we can make the space of keys guess sets strict into 2^8, even, in most cases, the space is 2^2, and the time complexity are 2^6 and 2^{14} which are far less than the existing methods that have been introduced in section I. We also proved that the Boolean masking using in the AES can be ignored. We make the module into an application and proved the module is effective.

Our model is built on the basis of the 128 bits-AES, so facing versions for 192 and 256 bits AES the effective the model can made is limited, and they are our next works.

References

[1] National Institute of Standards and Technology. Advanced Encryption Standard (AES), FIPS-197 (2001)

[2] Örs, S.B., Gürkaynak, F., Oswald, E., Preneel, B.: Power-Analysis Attack on an ASIC AES Implementation. In: ITCC 2004, pp. 546–566. IEEE Press (April 2004)

[3] Mangard, S., Pramstaller, N., Oswald, E.: Successfully Attacking AES Hardware Implementations. In: Rao, J.R., Sunar, B. (eds.) CHES 2005. LNCS, vol. 3659, pp. 157–171. Springer, Heidelberg (2005)

[4] Joye, M., Paillier, P., Schoenmakers, B.: On Second-Order Differential Power Analysis. In: Rao, J.R., Sunar, B. (eds.) CHES 2005. LNCS, vol. 3659, pp. 293–308. Springer, Heidelberg (2005)

[5] Prouff, E., Rivain, M., Bevan, R.: Statistical Analysis of Second Order Differential Power Analysis. IEEE Transactions on Computers 58, 799–811 (2009)

[6] Waddle, J., Wagner, D.: Towards Efficient Second-Order Power Analysis. In: Joye, M., Quisquater, J.-J. (eds.) CHES 2004. LNCS, vol. 3156, pp. 1–15. Springer, Heidelberg (2004)

[7] Boneh, D., DeMillo, R.A., Lipton, R.J.: On the Importance of Checking Cryptographic Protocols for Faults (Extended Abstract). In: Fumy, W. (ed.) EUROCRYPT 1997. LNCS, vol. 1233, pp. 37–51. Springer, Heidelberg (1997)

[8] Biham, E., Shamir, A.: Differential Fault Analysis of Secret Key Cryptosystems. In: Kaliski Jr., B.S. (ed.) CRYPTO 1997. LNCS, vol. 1294, pp. 513–525. Springer, Heidelberg (1997)

[9] Dusart, P., Letourneux, G., Vivolo, O.: Differential Fault Analysis on AES. In: Zhou, J., Yung, M., Han, Y. (eds.) ACNS 2003. LNCS, vol. 2846, pp. 293–306. Springer, Heidelberg (2003)

[10] Piret, G., Quisquater, J.-J.: A Differential Fault Attack Technique against SPN Structures, with Application to AES and KHAZAD. In: Walter, C.D., Koç, Ç.K., Paar, C. (eds.) CHES 2003. LNCS, vol. 2779, pp. 77–88. Springer, Heidelberg (2003)

[11] Moradi, A., Shalmani, M.T.M., Salmasizadeh, M.: A Generalized Method of Differential Fault Attack against AES Cryptosystem. In: Goubin, L., Matsui, M. (eds.) CHES 2006. LNCS, vol. 4249, pp. 91–100. Springer, Heidelberg (2006)

[12] Kim, C.H., Quisquater, J.-J.: New Differential Fault Analysis on AES Key Schedule: Two faults are enough. In: Grimaud, G., Standaert, F.-X. (eds.) CARDIS 2008. LNCS, vol. 5189, pp. 48–60. Springer, Heidelberg (2008)

[13] Kim, C.H.: Improved Differential Fault Analysis on AES Key Schedule. IEEE Transaction on Information Forensics and Security 7(1) (February 2012)

[14] Takahashi, J., Fukunaga, T.: Differential Fault Analysis on the AES Key Schedule, IACR, eprint archive, pp. 471–480 (2007)

[15] Tunstall, M., Mukhopadhyay, D., Ali, S.: Differential Fault Analysis of the Advanced Encryption Standard Using a Single Fault. In: Ardagna, C.A., Zhou, J. (eds.) WISTP 2011. LNCS, vol. 6633, pp. 224–233. Springer, Heidelberg (2011)

An Out-of-the-Box Dynamic Binary Analysis Tool for ARM-Based Linux

Zhenyu Wang[1], Yanqiu Ye[2], and Ruimin Wang[2]

[1] Zhengzhou Institute of Information Science and Technology, Zhengzhou, China
wzyzw2008@aliyun.com
[2] State Key Laboratory of Mathematical Engineering and Advanced Computing,
Zhengzhou, China
{yyq19881203,wangruimin}@hotmail.com

Abstract. Dynamic binary analysis has demonstrated its strength in solving a wide-spectrum of computer security problems. However, existing DBA tools don't support ARM-based OS. The latest version of Valgrind can support ARM executable, but it can't perform the whole-system analysis. The other DBA/DBI frameworks, such as TEMU, PIN and DynamoRIO, do not support ARM architecture. This paper presents a dynamic analysis tool that can extract the whole-system view and analyze the behaviors in ARM-based OS in a whole-system out-of-the-box way. An exploitation analysis module is given to demonstrate how to develop an application module based on this DBA tools. The application example shows this DBA tool has the features of good feasibility and scalability.

Keywords: Dynamic Binary Analysis, ARM, Embedded OS, Exploitation Analysis.

1 Introduction

ARM processors are widely used in the embedded devices, such as routers, switches, mobile phones, printers and industrial systems. ARM-based devices are also popular in the critical communication and network infrastructure. So attacks to ARM-based embedded OS will get more and more attention from the attackers and the attacks will also be more advance. For example, though, on many new ARM-based platforms the stacks are non-executable, thus attempting to exploit them is more difficult than in the past. However, making the stack non-executable is not enough. There are possibilities to exploit the ARM when the stack is not executable [1]. The features, such as "No eXecute(NX)" and ASLR, are introduced to defend against stack/heap over-flows in ARM-based devices. But the smart attackers have found ways to exploit stack/heap overflows even though XN/ASLR protection features are enabled [2].

Dynamic binary analysis has demonstrated its strength in solving a wide-spectrum of computer security problems, such as malware analysis, protocol reverse engineering, vulnerability detection, exploitation diagnosis and software testing, etc. An extensible platform for dynamic binary analysis provides a foundation for solving these

G. Wang et al. (Eds.): CSS 2013, LNCS 8300, pp. 450–457, 2013.

problems. What's more, the out-of-the-box approach that performs analysis completely outside the execution environment can provide excellent isolation and good transparency. It makes it more difficult for malware to detect the presence of the analysis environment and interfere with analysis results.

However, existing famous DBA tools have limitations to perform out-of-the-box analysis to ARM-based Linux. For example, Pin [3] is a very famous and powerful tool for the instrumentation of programs. It supports Linux and Windows executables for IA-32, Intel64, and IA-64 architectures. What's more, it can only provide a local view (i.e. a view of a single user-mode process). Valgrind [4] is a GPL licensed system for debugging and profiling Linux programs. Valgrind supports many platforms, including x86, AMD64, ARM, PPC32/64, MIPS and etc. However, it can also provide a local view only. TEMU [5] is the dynamic analysis component of BitBlaze (a binary analysis platform) that provides whole-system emulation and dynamic binary instrumentation including taint analysis. TEMU currently supports x86-based windows and Linux, but it does not support ARM-based OS. DynamoRIO [6] is another DBI framework that allows custom instrumentation code to be integrated in the form of dynamic libraries. DynamoRIO provides efficient, transparent, and comprehensive manipu-lation of unmodified applications running on stock operating systems (Windows or Linux) and commodity IA-32 and AMD64 hardware. It has no future plan to support ARM architecture.

So there is a pressing need to develop an extensible dynamic binary analysis tool that supports ARM architecture. We have developed a proof-of-concept DBA tool based on a whole-system emulator QEMU [7]. It uses whole-system out-of-the-box approach to analyze the kernel and application processes in the ARM-based embedded OS.

2   Design and Implementation

The overview of the prototype can be found in Fig. 1. The guest operation system is running on QEMU who's an efficient CPU emulator that uses dynamic binary translation. The analysis is completely performed from outside and the target ARM-based Linux OS can remain unchanged.

2.1   Guest OS View Extraction Module Template

The OS-level view is essential for analyzing the target OS. This module extracts the necessary information for implementing useful security applications including the process list, module list, system memory, storage, hardware events, and network traffic.

We take advantage of the technique named virtual machine introspection (VMI), which was first proposed for host intrusion detection [8], to obtain the processes and modules information. According to the design of Linux kernel, every process is described by a kernel struct named task_struct, and the init_task that points to a list of active tasks maintained in a task_struct list. Firstly, we get the offsets of those import fields in the vital struct(such as the offsets of pid and mm in task_struct, the offsets of vm_start and vm_end in vm_area_struct and etc). And then we use these offsets and the global variable init_task to extract the processes and modules information. To make this information readily available for analysis, we also maintain a shadow task list with selected information about each task. We also update our shadow list whenever the base information changes. We do this by monitoring several system calls, such as do_fork and do_exec, and update the shadow task list when they return.

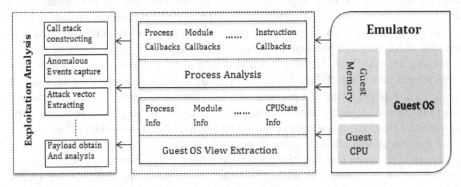

Fig. 1. Architecture overview

2.2 Process Analysis Module

We provide multi-level callbacks at runtime and registration functions for analysis application to register their callback functions for different events in the process analysis module. At native level, one can register callbacks for instruction start/end, basic block start/end, memory read/write, and register read/write. We also provide the capabilities to read and write the memory and register content of the guest OS.

To implement the callbacks, we need to instrument the translated code blocks and callback to the analysis applications in certain execution points. As the normal execution flow in QEMU is as follows: (1) a basic block of guest instructions is disassembled and translated into and intermediate representation called TCG; (2) the TCG code block is then compiled down to a block of host instructions and stored in a code cache; and (3) control jumps into the translated code block and the guest execution begins. More specifically, we insert extra TCG instructions during the code translation phase, such that this extra analysis code is executed in the execution phase. For example, the instruction level callback is implemented by inserting several TCG instructions in the arm/thumb instruction disassemble phase and the block level callbacks is implemented by inserting helper function with several TCG instructions whenever a branch occurs while disassembling.

2.3 Application Module

A flexible and comprehensive DBA tool is critical to the acceptance of its techniques by allowing these techniques to be accessible to any programmer through a set of convenient APIs that provides a useful interface for security software.

An analysis application can be developed easily based on the capabilities provided by the above module. For example, we can use the find_pid_by_name() function provided in the guest OS view extraction module to get the pid from the process name. Thus we can restrict our analysis effort to the process we are interested, and the uncorrelated process won't be analyzed. Instruction callback provide us the ability to implement instruction tracing and analysis, such as we can use QEUST_register_callback (QEUST_INSN_BEGIN_CB) function to make the control flow goes back to the callback function at the beginning of an instruction to implement instruction analysis. Using the instruction tracing and analysis we can trace the execution flow of the process and construct the call stack during the execution. Combine all the abilities, we can design and implement our exploitation analysis application and integrate the function into the monitor commands of QEMU.

To demonstrate how to develop an application module based on this DBA tools, the next section will present the implementation of an exploitation analysis module to detect stack based buffer overflow in ARM based Linux OS.

3   Application Example

Buffer overflow is one of the most common means of attack taken advantage by attackers. We constructed an exploitation sample that uses stack-based buffer overflow vulnerability to print a string on the command line. The sample is written in C, compiled by GCC and executed in Debian squeeze which runs on ARM architecture emulated by QEMU. While our analysis application runs as a plugin out of the emulated Debian squeeze and can be loaded/unloaded dynamically.

3.1   Call Stack Constructing

According to the standard ARM calling convention (APCS), when a function is called, the first step of the function is to store the "R11" and "LR" registers (R11 register is referred as the Frame Pointer, just like the EBP of x86 architecture; while the LR register is used for holding the return address when a subroutine is called) into the stack. Then the stack space for this function is specified. When the function finishes its work, the stack space for this function will be released and the values of R11 and LR registers will be restored. And the callee goes back to the caller via LR register.

We use the instruction callback to analyze every instruction in the execution. Of course, we use the process callback to attach our analysis to the process we're interested first. When the opcode is disassembled to be a "push" instruction related with LR register, such as "PUSH {R11, LR}", we extract the value of LR register and store it in a one-way circular linked list. Accordingly, when the opcode is disassembled to be "pop" instruction related with LR register, we take out the value in LR register from CPU and compare it with the value right after the head in link list. If they don't match, we regard it as an anomalous event. Then the analysis tool print the stack layout at this time and the stack layout at the time the function enter for comparing.

3.2   Potential Exploitation Report

As shown in Fig. 2, the link list is NULL in the initial state. The first "push" instruction in the "main" function (at the address 0x00008584) pushes the value of the LR register (0x4004f538) to the link list (as the step in the right column in Fig. 2). When the process enters "vuln" function, another "push" instruction at the address 0x00008554 turns up. Current value (which is 0x00008620) in LR register at this point is added into the link list, too (the step in the right column in Fig. 2). As the process goes, here comes a "pop" instruction (at the address 0x0000857c in "Vuln" function). The current value in the LR register is taken out from the CPU (the value of LR is 0x00008538) and compared with the value taken out from right after the head in link list (0x00008620, the step in the right column in Fig. 2). Apparently, the two values don't match with each other, so an anomalous event (a potential exploitation) will be reported.

source code	assemble code		call stack construction
	0x00008554 <vuln+0> : push {r11, lr}		②"push" insn detected
	0x00008558 <vuln+4> : add r11, sp, #4		
	0x0000855c <vuln+8> : sub sp, sp, #24		NULL head
Void vuln(char *arg)	0x00008560 <vuln+12> : str r0, [r11, #-24]		0x00008620 LR at 0x00008554
{	0x00008564 <vuln+16> : ldr r3, [r11, #-24]		0x4004f538 LR at 0x00008584
Char buf[10];	0x00008568 <vuln+20> : sub r2, r11, #16		
Strcpy(buf, arg);	0x0000856c <vuln+24>: mov r0, r2		
}	0x00008570 <vuln+28>: mov r1, r3		③"pop" insn detected, compare LR
	0x00008574 <vuln+32>: bl 0x8444<strcpy>		at 0x0000857c with 0x00008620
	0x00008578 <vuln+36> : sub sp, r11, #4		NULL head
	0x0000857c <vuln+40>: pop {r11, lr}		0x4004f538 LR at 0x00008584
	0x00008580 <vuln+44>: bx lr		
Int main()	0x00008584 <main+0>: push {r11,lr}		①"push" insn detected
{	0x00008588 <main+4>: add r11, sp, #4		NULL head
FILE* fp;	0x0000858c <main+8>: sub sp, sp, #48		0x4004f538 LR at 0x00008584
	0x000085a8 <main+36>: mov r0, r2		
	0x000085ac <main+40>: mov r1, r3		
Vlun(temp);	0x000085b0 <main+44>: bl 0x842c<fopen>		
Return 0;	0x0000862c <main+168>: pop {r11, lr}		finish, clear the link list and report an anomalous event in this example.
}			

Fig. 2. Exploitation detection sample

3.3   Vulnerability and Attack Vector Extraction

To dig out the vulnerability and the attack vector, we choose to construct a shadow stack layout for every function and save the initial state of the shadow stack layout as well. The shadow stack layout is referred as a shadow memory from the address of SP to R11+4 of the memory in essence. When an anomalous event reported, we get the shadow stack layout just before the stack reclaimed and compare it with the stored initial state of the shadow stack layout. The Fig. 3 shows the comparison of our example, the left side is the initial state of stack layout (in this example, the initial state of stack layout is the stack layout just after the "sub" instruction finished at the address 0x0000855c) and the right side is the layout (in this example, the stack layout here is the stack layout just before the "pop" instruction is executed at the address 0x0000857c) when the anomalous event reports.

As shown in Fig. 2, when the "vuln" function is called by the "main" function, the initial stack size is claimed to be 24 bytes (the size can be calculated by using the stored value in SP register minus the stored value in r11 register, the two values are both in the stored initial state of stack layout, and size can be also verified from the assemble code in Fig. 2). From the right side of Fig. 3, we can see, the temporary variable is stored from 16 bytes upper away from the R11. But the length of data copied to the stack is longer than 16 bytes,   so the saved frame pointer address and return address are overwritten   (the data copied to the stack is 30 bytes as shown in the assemble code in Fig. 2, here the stack layout only shows the values in the stack space of "vlun" function). So, we can infer the attack to be a buffer overflow attack and figure out where it wants the control flow of the process goes (in this example, go to the address 0x00008538).

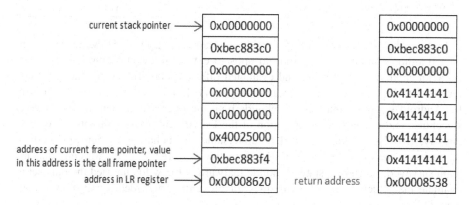

Fig. 3. Call stack layout

3.4   Payload Extraction

Based on the above two steps, we can get the address where the control flow will go when the anomalous event happens. This address value hints where the payload locates. The Payload can actually be anything the attacker wants, such as a piece of shellcode. We can dissect and comprehend the payload in further analysis.

4   Related Work

PIN, Valgrind, TEMU and DynamoRIO are the popular DBA/DBI frameworks. We can see the differences between our tool and the other distinguished dynamic analysis tools in Table 1. PIN, Valgrind and DynamoRIO are not based on the whole-system emulator, so they can only provide a local view of the target process. Pin and DynamoRIO can both supports Linux and Windows executable for IA-32, Intel64, and IA-64 architectures while Valgrind can only support Linux executable. However, Valgrind can also support ARM architecture. TEMU is a dynamic binary analysis tool that is based on whole-system emulator, it can provide a global view of the target system but it can only support x86 architecture. As far as we currently know, there're no other whole-system out-of-the-box dynamic binary analysis tools for ARM-based OS. And there're not much researches on the ARM-based embedded OS exploitation behavior analysis.

Table 1. Comparison between our tool and other DBA tool

	Pin	Valgrind	DynamoRIO	TEMU	Our Tool
Windows Executable	Yes	no	Yes	yes	Extensible
Linux Executable	Yes	Yes	Yes	Yes	Yes
ARM Support	No	Yes	No	No	Yes
Whole-system Emulation	no	No	No	Yes	Yes

State-of-the-art analyzers mostly reside in Android [9]. DroidAPIMiner [10] conducted a thorough analysis of Android apps to extract relevant features to malware behavior captured at API level, and evaluated different classifiers using the generated feature set. Lok and Yin present DroidScope [11], a virtualization based platform for Android malware analysis. It rebuilds both the operating system and Java level semantics, and enables instrumentation of the Dalvik and native instructions. Consequently, Droidscope can be used to understand the behavior of malware both at the native code level as well as at the interaction with the system. Adrienne and his team surveyed the current state of mobile malware in the wild and used the data set to evaluate the effectiveness of techniques for preventing and identifying mobile malware [12].

Exploitation diagnosis and mitigation has attracted research efforts [13, 14, 15] in the past. More recently, in PointerScope [16], a novel solution was proposed to use type inference on binary execution to detect the pointer misuses included by an exploit based on the observation that the key steps in memory corruption exploits often involve pointer misuses. T   otal-CFI [17] is an efficient and practical tool built on a software emulator can capable of exploit detection by enforcing system-wide Control Flow Integrity (CFI). Furthermore, Total-CFI enforces a CFI policy – a combination of whitelist based and shadow call stack based approaches to monitor indirect control flows and detect exploits. But these researches are not specifically on ARM-based OS.

5   Conclusion

In this paper, we presented a proof-of-concept implementation of a prototype that can extract the OS view and provide exploitation analysis to ARM-based Linux operation system in a whole-system out-of-the-box way. Though, our tool is just a prototype, it fills in gaps in whole-system out-of-the-box DBA on ARM-based Linux OS. It can also be extended to other architectures, such as PPC and MIPS.

References

1. Avraham, (Zuk) I.: Non-Executable Stack ARM Exploitation Research Paper. Blackhat (2011)
2. Ridley, S.A.: ARM exploitation and Hardware Hacking convergence memoirs. NoSuchCon 2013, Paris (2013)
3. Luk, C.-K., et al.: Pin: building customized program analysis tools with dynamic instrumentation. ACM Sigplan Notices 40(6) (2005)
4. Nethercote, N., Seward, J.: Valgrind: a framework for heavyweight dynamic binary instrumentation. ACM Sigplan Notices 42(6), 89–100 (2007)
5. Yin, H., Song, D.: Temu: Binary code analysis via whole-system layered annotative execution. Submitted to VEE 10 (2010)
6. DynamoRIO: Dynamic Instrumentation Tool Platform, http://dynamorio.org/
7. Bellard, F.: QEMU, A Fast and Portable Dynamic Translator. In: USENIX Annual Technical Conference, FREENIX Track (2005)
8. Garfinkel, T., Rosenblum, M.: A Virtual Machine Introspection Based Architecture for Intrusion Detection. In: NDSS (2003)
9. Liu, L., et al.: Exploitation and threat analysis of open mobile devices. In: Proceedings of the 5th ACM/IEEE Symposium on Architectures for Networking and Communications Systems. ACM (2009)
10. Aafer, Y., Du, W., Yin, H.: DroidAPIMiner: Mining API-Level Features for Robust Malware Detection in Android. In: SecureComm 2013 (in press, September 2013)
11. Yan, L.K., Yin, H.: Droidscope: seamlessly reconstructing the os and dalvik semantic views for dynamic android malware analysis. In: Proceedings of the 21st USENIX Security Symposium (2012)
12. Felt, A.P., et al.: A survey of mobile malware in the wild. In: Proceedings of the 1st ACM Workshop on Security and Privacy in Smartphones and Mobile Devices, ACM (2011)
13. Newsome, J., Song, D.: Dynamic taint analysis for automatic detection, analysis, and signature generation of exploits on commodity software. In: Proceedings of the 12th Annual Network and Distributed System Security Symposium, NDSS 2005 (2005)
14. Chen, S., et al.: Defeating memory corruption attacks via pointer taintedness detection. In: Proceedings of the International Conference on Dependable Systems and Networks, DSN 2005. IEEE (2005)
15. Yin, H., Song, D., Manuel, E., Kruegel, C., Kirda, E.: Panorama: capturing system-wide information flow for malware detection and analysis. In: Proceedings of the 14th ACM Conference on Computer and Communications Security. ACM (2007)
16. Zhang, M., Prakash, A., Li, X., Liang, Z., Yin, H.: Identifying and analyzing pointer misuses for sophisticated memory-corruption exploit diagnosis. In: Proceedings of 19th Annual Network & Distributed System Security Symposium (2012)
17. Prakash, A., Yin, H., Liang, Z.: Enforcing system-wide control flow integrity for exploit detection and diagnosis. In: Proceedings of the 8th ACM SIGSAC Symposium on Information, Computer and Communications Security. ACM (2013)

Towards an Open Framework Leveraging a Trusted Execution Environment

Javier González[1] and Philippe Bonnet[1,2]

[1] IT University of Copenhagen, Denmark
{jgon,phbo}@itu.dk
[2] INRIA Paris Rocquencourt, France

Abstract. Sensor data is a core component of big data. The abundance of sensor data combined with advances in data integration and data mining entails a great opportunity to develop innovative applications. However, data about our movements, our energy consumption or our biometry are personal data that we should have full control over. Likewise, companies face a trade-off as the benefits of innovative services must be weighted against the risk of exposing data that reveal core internal processes. How to design a data platform that enables innovative data services and yet enforce access and usage control? The solutions proposed in the literature to this trade-off all involve some form of trusted execution environment, where data and processing is trusted and safe from corruption by users or attackers. The hardware that could support such trusted execution environments is however closed to the research community: OEMs disable security extensions from their development boards and the software handling these security extensions is not open. In this paper we present a framework that combines commercially available hardware and open source software. It can be used today by the research community as a trusted execution environment to investigate future big data platforms.

1 Introduction

The decrease in size, price and power consumption of large classes of sensors equipped with computation and communication capabilities is making sensor data a crucial component of big data systems [4]. The sheer availability of data about energy consumption in an office raises obvious questions: does constant employee monitoring improve productivity? Does it improve the quality of facility management? Does it improve energy efficiency? What if this data is in the possession of a direct competitor: can it be misused? The trading of personal data, maintained outside our control, for innovative data services is recognized as a significant problem by analysts and even by European legal organizations [4,6]. The problem is as similar for companies that are in a position to trade sensitive internal data for innovative services.

To address this increasing information security problem, the consensual solution is to develop a data platform that enables innovative data services (relying

G. Wang et al. (Eds.): CSS 2013, LNCS 8300, pp. 458–467, 2013.

on modern data integration, mining or clustering techniques) while allowing users to retain some form of control over who access this data (access control) and how (usage control). Put differently, we need a trusted data platform to support innovative services based on sensor data. In [8], solutions involving a trusted middleware layer are described. In [1], we proposed the vision of trusted cells, a decentralized data platform based on trusted execution environments embedded on personal data devices (set top boxes, smart phones or smart meters) at the edges of the Internet. These visions are based on the premise that trusted execution environments are actually available and can be programmed to enforce access and usage control policies. However, the hardware that could support such trusted execution environments has so far been unavailable to the research community: OEMs disable security extensions from their development boards and the software handling these security extensions is neither open nor widely available. Our experience is that it requires first hand information to know which security extensions (if any) are enabled in a given board, making it impossible for most developers to determine which are the security capabilities of the processors powering their own boards.

In this paper, we describe an open framework that combines hardware and open source software, and provides a trusted execution environment that is (i) readily available to the research and open source communities, (ii) fits well into well-known programming frameworks such as Linux and Android, and (iii) is rich enough to support the design of future big data platforms. We call this framework the Arm-Xilinx/OpenVirtualization framework as it combines secure hardware from Xilinx, based on a chip equipped with the TrustZone system from ARM, with the open source, secure operating system OpenVirtualization from Sierraware.

In the rest of the paper, we discuss the requirements for supporting usage control in big data platforms (Section 2), we then discuss what kind of framework is needed to support our vision of trusted cells(Section 3). Finally, we describe the ARM-Xilinx hardware platform and the OpenVirtualization software that constitute a very promising framework in this context (Section 4). We finally draw our conclusions in Section 5.

2   Enforcing a Usage Control Model

Once a user give away some data, she loses any form of control over it. The decision of sharing data is, so far, a discrete operation: either all or none of the data is shared. When dealing with sensitive data, mid points are sometimes achieved by means of external legal agreements, such as Nondisclosure Agreements (NDAs), licenses, and other terms of usage. A user might for example give her consent to some terms of usage when she gives away personal data for a given service (e.g., giving away location for a smart phone app or giving away energy consumption data for a social game aiming at improving energy efficiency). Legal actions are then possible if a non permitted data access or distribution is perpetrated. These legal actions are complex and possibly costly. But most importantly, they are taken once the damage is already done. Furthermore, no legal agreement can prevent malicious attacks from being perpetrated against the devices storing sensitive data. Ideally, the data sharing process would enable two (or more) parties to negotiate a contract, which we call a usage model, defining who can access the shared data and how this data is used, while the underlying data platform ensures that the contract is met by all parties at all time. Put differently, the data platform enforces the usage model by preventing contract breaches either from the contract parties or from third parties. Now, we are faced with two core questions: (1) How does a usage control model looks like? and (2) what does it take to enforce it?

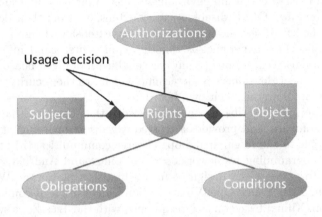

Fig. 1. $UCON_{ABC}$ model: the reference monitor enforces usage decisions (can a given subject apply a right on a given (set of) object(s)?) based on subject and object attributes, as well as authorizations, obligations and conditions.

Usage control models usually refer to $UCON_{ABC}$ [7]. In the $UCON_{ABC}$ model, subjects provide or consume data objects. Objects might contain secrets about identified subjects (the data producer, the data consumer, or possibly a third party). A subject accesses objects via a set of usage functions referred to as rights. A reference monitor is responsible for taking usage decisions based on the subject and object attributes as well as Authorization, oBligations and Conditions ABC. Authorizations are predicates that define whether a subject is authorized to hold a right; obligations are predicates that define the actions that a subject must take before or while it holds a rights; and conditions define predicates that must hold true about the environment in which the subject requires a given right.

What does it take to enforce a $UCON_{ABC}$ model? The data platform should implement a reference monitor and guarantee that there will be no access to data objects unless appropriate usage decisions (i.e., decisions that respect the contract negotiated by all parties) are taken. The basic idea is that the reference monitor is a software component that relies on hardware security features separating a secure world (where objects, attributes, as well as rights, authorizations and conditions are securely stored, while usage decisions are securely executed) and a non secure world (where the rest of the processing takes place). There is today, to the best of our knowledge, no implementation of any $UCON_{ABC}$ model. In fact, there has not been, so far, any easily accessible framework that distinguishes secure and non secure worlds. We expect that the form of hardware security and rich operating system integration that we describe below will be a breakthrough for the research community and that it will enable experimentations with various forms of usage control models.

3   Implementing Trusted Cells

In [1], we proposed a model, called Trusted Cells, where a client side reference monitor is embedded on smart devices (including set top boxes, smart phones or smart sensors) at the edges of the Internet. With trusted cells, the infrastructure (communication, computing and storage) is untrusted, while the personal devices that data owners and consumers use to provide or access data are trusted. In the rest of the paper, we focus on Trusted Cells as a data platform implementing a $UCON_{ABC}$ model. We hereby encourage the community to define alternative data platforms.

The vision of the trusted cells is based on the separation of a trusted and a rich environment maintaining a high throughput between them[1]. How to separate a non trusted and a trusted environment? There are three options. The first one (O1), is to opt for a software solution, without hardware support. The second solution (O2) is to fully separate a secure device (where software and hardware are trusted), e.g., a secure token, and a non secure device, e.g., a PC in which the secure token is plugged. The third option (O3) is to consider a processor that propose a secure mode of execution and a non secure mode of execution.

Before we review these three options, we need to precise the types of attacks that trusted cells might be submitted to [9]. First, **Hack Attacks**, which are limited to software. Examples of hack attacks include viruses or malware. These attacks are normally triggered by an user approving the installation of a piece of software that then executes the attack. Second, **Shack Attacks**, which are low-budget hardware attacks. Attackers have physical access to the device, but they lack the knowledge or equipment to carry out an attack at an integrated circuit level (e.g., scanning I/Os, forcing pins, reprogramming memory devices). Third, **Lab Attacks**, which are comprehensive and invasive hardware attacks. Attackers have access to laboratory equipment and the knowledge to perform unlimited reverse engineering of a given device (e.g., reverse engineering a design, performing cryptographic key analysis). The assumption should be that a device can always be bypassed by a lab attack given enough time and budget.

---

[1] Note that a rich non secure world and a high throughput between secure and non secure worlds, will enable innovative applications and that there is always a trade-off between how rich the secure world can be and how easy it is to guarantee that the secure operations are indeed secure. Exploring this trade-off is a topic for future work

Now, who might be a third party attacker (in addition to the Subject and Object)? We adopt the taxonomy proposed by IBM [3], which distinguish between three classes of attackers. First, **intelligent outsiders**, i.e., remote attackers, who lack specific knowledge on the system. They might have access to moderately sophisticated equipment. These attackers try to reproduce software or simple hardware attacks published in the Internet by a technical expert, rather than attempt to create new ones. Second, **trained insiders**, that are technical experts, highly educated, with experience and access to sophisticated tools. They are considered trusted, possibly employed by the company developing the device subject of the attacks. Their knowledge of the system varies, but it can be assumed that they have access to the information describing it (e.g., secret information, detailed designs). They seek discovering an sharing new class attacks. Third, **funded organizations** that represent organizationally founded teams of trained attackers. They are capable of carrying out sophisticated attacks by means of advanced analysis tools. They are capable of designing new and innovative attacks exploiting the most insignificant weaknesses.

So, what kind of attacks do we envisage? The most probable attackers are (i) data owners that might want to alter their own data (e.g., customers could try to lower their energy consumption bill by altering the measurements stored in their own smart meters), (ii) subjects that access unauthorized objects (voluntarily or not), and (iii) third parties that intentionally extract (large volumes of) data objects (e.g., organized crime that plans to sell industrial information to a competitor or organize burglaries in a neighborhood at a time when all houses are likely to be empty, inferring this information from electricity usage).

The first solution (O1), only based on software is thus not appropriate. Note that today, all popular data platforms, are only based on software solutions. Note also, that the number of large scale break-ins and leaks are getting greater by the day [2] and their effects are beginning to get noticed by the population (e.g., in Denmark[3].

The second option (O2) relies on dedicated, tamper resistant processors extended with security and cryptographic features that take care of sensitive operations. For example, a dedicated processor can be used to perform cryptographic operations associated with the management of DRM digital certificates. The main characteristic of this approach is that security is provided by physical isolation. The dedicated processors are difficult to access physically, and their design and size makes it difficult for a sophisticated lab attack to succeed. Depending on the impediments to perform a lab attack, and the response of the platform to a potential successful attack, the platform can be described in terms of its level of tamper resistance. These processors can be used in combination with certified toolkits to heighten up the overall security of the platform (e.g., a Chip-and-PIN terminal). The main downside of this approach is that their level of security is sustained by a detriment in performance and functionality,

---

[2] http://www.indefenseofdata.com/data-breach-trends-stats/
[3] http://cphpost.dk/news/national/nation-œincreasingly-
vulnerable-cyber-attack

making dedicated processors not eligible for the applications we are used to see in our phones or laptops. Examples of these dedicated, tamper-resistant processors are IBM CryptoCards[4]and ARM SecurCore Processors[5]. This class of solution might be appropriate for trusted cells, if the protection against lab attack is paramount.

The third solution (O3), where hardware is not tamper-resistant, still provides some level of hardware security together with a rich environment. For example, TrustZone is ARM's approach to bringing security and high performance together. It is tightly integrated into Cortex-A processors, making use of the AMBA AXI bus and specific TrustZone Intellectual Property (IP) blocks to extend throughout the system. This allows to secure peripherals such as memory, crypto blocks, keyboards or screen in runtime, impeding malicious software to intercept or alter communications and operations involving sensitive data. Even though ARM does not provide an implementation for TrustZone, they have worked together with Global Platform in defining a standard specification for trusted environments. The result is the Global Platform Trusted Execution Environment (TEE). From an architectural perspective, TrustZone can be conceived as a set of security extensions that enables a TEE running in parallel to a Rich Execution Environment (REE). High performance tasks are executed in the REE, while tasks that require an extra level of security are executed in the TEE. What is interesting about the REE - TEE separation is that it does not require a dedicated processor for the TEE. Each physical processor core provides two virtual cores, one considered Non-secure (Normal World) and the other Secure (Secure World), and a mechanism to context switch between them, known as the monitor mode. The implementation of the monitor mode relies on the so-called NS bit that is added to the bus transactions and to cache tags in the system. The NS bit is an addition to the AMBA3 AXI Advanced Peripheral Bus (APS), a peripheral bus that is attached to the system bus using an AXI-to-APB-bridge [2]. It is indirectly derived from the identity of the virtual core that performs a given instruction or memory access. Since the monitor is the most sensitive component of TrustZone, it is always handled by the Secure World. Also, since context switching is done by hardware, the overhead is minimal.

The main advantage we see in TrustZone is that it intrinsically supports security in high performance tasks involving sensitive data. Also, TrustZone being implemented in Cortex-A9 and Cortex-A15, which are the most popular processors for mobile platforms at the moment (e.g., Samsung Exynos and Nvidia Tegra series), gives us the advantage of developing for an already known and extensively deployed platform; not to mention the announced partnership between AMD and ARM that promises the incorporation of TrustZone-based processors in AMD chips[6] to be included in smartphones, set-top boxes and laptops.

---

[4] http://www-03.ibm.com/security/cryptocards/

[5] http://www.arm.com/products/processors/securcore/

[6] http://www.amd.com/us/press-releases/Pages/
amd-strengthens-security-2012jun13.aspx

Finally, since TrustZone does not require a dedicated processor, it saves components, making it a cheap alternative to secure tokens.

TrustZone is not tamper-resistant, however. Lab attacks are out of the scope of the hardware protection provided by the TrustZone IP blocks and the AMBA AXI peripheral bus. This is not much of a problem for trusted cells, which constitute a decentralized data platform. Much more problematic is the secrecy surrounding it. TrustZone technology was first introduced in 2003 [5] and was officially presented in a press release by ARM in 2004[7]. Surprisingly though, 10 years later, TrustZone's market is still almost exclusive to Trusted Logic, Gemalto and Giesecke&Devrient (MobiCore), and it is difficult to find it mentioned in any research work besides the one by the Graz University of Technology[8]. All three world leading security companies monopolize the TrustZone market, driven by financial stakeholders such as Visa and MasterCard, by impeding 3rd parties - specially research oriented institutions - to make use of it by opposing to open implementations. The level of security provided by TrustZone is therefore virtually increased through obscurity: A lock unknown to locksmiths is world's most secure lock.

The lack of open APIs and libraries, in combination with Original Equipment Manufactures (OEM) such as Samsung or Nvidia, disabling the TrustZone security extensions for their development boards is a big impediment for the research community to get hold of the technology. At the time of this paper the only boards fully supporting the TrustZone technology are: Xilinx Zynq-7000 AP SoC ZC702, Nvidia Kayla DevKit (Tegra 3) and ARM Versatile Express. Our experience is that they are all subject to nondisclosure agreements (NDA), if TrustZone use is intended. Overcoming the closeness of TrustZone requires implementing, supporting and promoting standards, as well as making them available to an active, diverse community. This is the main contribution of this work. We are actively pushing for the expansion and distribution of an open source implementation of a TEE for the TrustZone security extensions. This involves bringing the parts together, dealing with licensing limitations and making source code and documentation accessible.

While this third option, based on TrustZone is attractive on paper, the secrecy surrounding it and the lack of open APIs and libraries is a huge barrier to its utilization in the context of trusted cells (or any other innovative data platform). We are working together with Xilinx and Sierraware to remove this barrier.

4   The ARM-Xilinx/OpenVirtualization Framework

Sierraware[9], an embedded virtualization company, developed Open Virtualization[10], which is the first open source alternative that leverages the security extensions present in ARM TrustZone. It is composed by (i) SierraVisor, a hypervisor

---

[7] http://www.arm.com/about/newsroom/5688.php

[8] http://www.iaik.tugraz.at

[9] http://www.sierraware.com

[10] http://www.openvirtualization.org

for ARM-based systems, and (ii) SierraTEE, a TEE for ARM TrustZone hardware security extensions. While the hypervisor is an interesting contribution, it is the TEE open source implementation that changes the game, since it opens the door for developers and researchers to using TrustZone. Open Virtualization's TEE implementation is compatible with Global Platform's TEE specification.

Open Virtualization was first released between 2011 and 2012. Since then, Sierraware has maintained an open source distribution of it. However, their focus has been in their commercial distribution. The main issue with this approach is the risk of contaminating one of the versions with the other. This is specially significant when it comes to IP blocks and other licensed software. As a consequence, releasing code for the open source version requires the overhead of it having to be audited by the different vendors, making the process tough and slow, and preventing code distribution via repositories. Also, maintaining a commercial product implies inevitably that publicly available documentation is limited and incomplete.

We are working together with Xilinx[11] and Sierraware to improve this situation. Our main contributions here are (i) facilitating the distribution of Open Virtualization by structuring it and making it available through a public service code repository, (ii) increasing the public knowledge of TrustZone by working with Xilinx in documenting the support of Open Virtualization for the Xilinx SoC ZC702, and as a consequence of this (iii) helping expanding the reach of TrustZone and Open Virtualization to the research community. The git repository containing Open Virtualization is available and can be used directly for the Xilinx ZC702 board[12]. We are at the moment working with Xilinx to create a wiki to complement the repository with documentation on both TrustZone and Open Virtualization. Our intention is to continue supporting this project and improve those components of Open Virtualization that are relevant to our research. Ideally, this would be the beginning of a community around Open Virtualization, where researchers and developers could contribute and build knowledge. We are also working towards making this git repository Sierraware's main vehicle for their open source distribution.

Let us take an example of how the ARM-Xilinx/OpenVirtualization framework could support Trusted Cells. Consider Servfos, a fictive company, that provides energy services based on data obtained from the smart sensors it is world renowned for. Their clients supply Servfos with data coming from the sensing infrastructures deployed in their buildings, and Servfos uses these data to give their clients all sorts of statistics and other information on their energy usage efficiency. This allows Servfos' clients to detect energy leakages and reduce their monthly expenses. Also, Servfos works with the local municipality in a contest for "The Greenest Firm in the Block". Those business that wish to participate agree on Servfos providing the municipality with a set of spatio-temporal aggregates on their energy consumption, which are then used for the contest and for some energy awareness games in different social networks. Finally, Servfos gives

---

[11] http://www.xilinx.com
[12] https://github.com/javigon/OpenVirtualization

their clients the possibility to participate in an European project that promotes energy efficiency in office buildings. While the concrete businesses the data is coming from is not relevant, it is required to access all data points from one random office in each participant's building for a whole month. For each service they provide, Servfos has a different contract with each of their clients, where all parties agree on who will access which data, and how it is going to be used. Servfos' clients are willing to participate in green initiatives, but they are concern about potential uncontrolled accesses to their sensitive data.

In order to support all the services that Servfos offers to their clients two things are needed: a policy model that is flexible enough as to allow the definition of complex access and usage policies (the contract), and an engine that enforces this contract. Derived from this, our specific challenges are: (i) defining an usage control model for sensor data in terms of UCON authorizations, obligations and conditions, (ii) identifying which components of a database system should be placed in a secure environment in order to enforce this usage control model, and finally (iii) providing an implementation for it. The ultimately goal is to have a framework (iv) that allows companies like Servfos to provide valuable services on top of sensor data belonging to individuals or organizations, in such a way that data owners can count on the access and usage control policies they define to be enforced. Such framework represents the data platform we have described in this paper and an implementation of the trusted cells.

Data flows between the trusted cell located in the client side and the one in the Servfos side. The trusted cells control the access to the sensor data according to the $UCON_{ABC}$ model. They guarantee that sensitive data is stored in secure memory and processed by a secure processor (TEE). High performance processes take place in a REE. To do so they make use of the TrustZone security extensions of the ARM Cortex-A9 processor powering the trusted cell. The software enabling the use of TrustZone is Open Virtualization: an open source implementation of Global Platform TEE's specification developed by Sierraware. The communication between the cells is secured by cryptographic keys that are stored in the Secure World.

5   Conclusion

In the process of designing and implementing a data platform for sensor data that allows data owners to share their data while retaining a form of access and usage control over it, we have encountered a challenge in finding suitable hardware to support it. The secrecy surrounding commercially available hardware platforms that leverage secure processing, and the lack of open implementations for them, limit their use, specially inside the research community. What is more, the industrial monopoly created around secure platforms such as TrustZone virtually increases their level of security through obscurity, representing a benefit for attackers that are smart enough to find unreported loopholes.

In this paper we present our efforts for changing this situation. We have worked together with Xilinx in bringing to the research community Open Virtualization: an open source implementation of a TrustZone TEE environment developed by Sierraware. The goal is that our efforts result in the establishment of a community around Open Virtualization and TrustZone, where researchers and developers can contribute and build knowledge. In the process of discussing the suitability of TrustZone for our research purposes, we have also given an overview of commercially available hardware platforms for trusted big data platforms.

Finally we have presented the roadmap for a data platform that supports the manipulation, analysis and sharing of large volumes of sensor data, while addressing the information security problem that this introduces. This data platform is the materialization of a trusted cell. It is the combination of a formal usage control model ($UCON_{ABC}$), a commercially available, extensively deployed hardware technology that leverages security at a low price (ARM TrustZone), and an open source implementation of Global Platform's TEE standard (Open Virtualization). This is a first step towards a decentralized data platform based on a TEE at the edges of the Internet that supports innovative services on sensor data.

References

1. Ancieaux, N., Bonnet, P., Bouganim, L., Nguyen, B., Popa, L.S., Pucheral, P.: Trusted cells: A sea change for personal data services. In: CIDR (2013)
2. Amba®, A.: axitm and acetm protocol specification. Technical report, ARM (2013)
3. Abrahan, D.G., Dolan, G.M., Double, G.P., Stevens, J.V.: Transaction security system. IBM Systems Journal 30(2), 206–229 (1991)
4. Gantz, J., Reinsel, D., Lee, R.: The digital universe in 2020: Big data, bigger digital shadows, and biggest growth in the far east. In: IDC (February 2013)
5. ImObersteg, G.: Arm trustzone extension delivers hardware security for next generation, opensystem, armpowered solutions. Intelligence 2, 6–12 (2003)
6. Katzenbeisser, S., Kursawe, K., Preneel, B., Sadeghi, A.-R.: Privacy and security in smart energy grids (dagstuhl seminar 11511). Dagstuhl Reports 1(12), 62–68 (2011)
7. Park, J., Sandhu, R.: The uconabc usage control model. ACM Trans. Inf. Syst. Secur. 7(1), 128–174 (2004)
8. IEEE Computer Society. Data engineering. Bulleting of the Technical Committee on Data Engineering 35(4) (2012)
9. ARM Security Technology. Buiding a secure system using trustzone technology. Technical report, ARM (2009)

Secure Re-publication of Dynamic Big Data

Kok-Seng Wong and Myung Ho Kim

School of Computer Science and Engineering,
Soongsil University, Information Science Building,
Sangdo-Dong Dongjak-Gu, Seoul, South Korea 156-743
{kswong,kmh}@ssu.ac.kr

Abstract. Dynamic data re-publication is now an emerging issue in data publishing due to the awareness of privacy disclosure in data sharing. Existing models such as k-anonymity and l-diversity only aim to provide data protection for single release. In practical, new data arrive continuously and up-to-date dataset should be released from time to time. The release of multiple anonymized datasets (microdata) allows the attackers to learn extra knowledge by cross examines the releases within a targeted timeframe. In this paper, we study the data re-publication of dynamic big data based on the m-invariance model. In particular, we reconstruct the existing model to support re-publication for big data. We consider re-publication with insertion, deletion and update of the existing records. Counterfeit records will be used to maintain the update pattern of all the releases and to increase the false information in the knowledge learned by the attacker from the released microdata.

Keywords: privacy-preserving data publishing, dynamic data re-publication, big data privacy, m-invariance.

1 Introduction

In today's Information and Communications Technology (ICT) era, many organizations, government agencies and corporations are collecting large amount of data (big data) every day. Big data can be used to improve the development of products and services. For instance, insurance companies are using data obtained from hospitals or healthcare providers to create coverage for services such as new insurance policies. Also, the use of big data is now becoming a key basis of competition in many industries.

The sharing of big data during collaborative works involves the publication of personal information. When personal data of an individual is released for research or analysis purposes, sensitive information such as disease and salary should be protected. In other words, sensitive information must be released to improve the data utility while the privacy of the data owner should not be compromised. Hence, data privacy has been a growing concern and global issue in the era of big data. Hereafter in this section, we use the term dataset to refer to big data.

G. Wang et al. (Eds.): CSS 2013, LNCS 8300, pp. 468–477, 2013.

Several major privacy breaches have occurred in the past few years. In 2002, Sweeney shows that 87% of the United States population can be uniquely identified by matching information such as zip code, gender, and date of birth with the voter registration list (external information) [1]. In 2006, an Internet services and media company (AOL) released around 20 million of search records of 650,000 of its customers. Two reporters of the New York Times newspaper were able to identify AOL customer no. 4417749 as Thelma Arnold, a 62 years old widow living in Lilburn [2]. A recent paper published in Nature Scientific Reports showed that four points of data about each individual are enough to uniquely re-identify an individual with 95% of accuracy [3]. With only two data points, more than 50% of the individuals could be re-identified. All the cases highlight the importance of privacy preserving technology to prevent any privacy leak during the data publishing.

1.1 Motivating Scenario

Let consider a scenario where a central hospital wish to publish some patient records to a research institute for data analysis. The original medical dataset is shown in Table 1. For the sake of simplicity, we assume that each patient has only one record.

Table 1. Original medical dataset

Patient	Gender	Age	Zip	Disease
Bob	Male	15	27892	Flu
Sam	Male	13	27895	Asthma
Yuki	Female	48	27885	Cancer
Jane	Female	50	27875	Diabetes
Ellen	Female	59	27886	Heart Disease

In general, all explicit personal identity information (PII) such as name and social security number (SSN) should be removed from the original dataset before it is published. However, removing PII from the original dataset does not preserve privacy. As illustrates by Sweeney in [1], quasi-identifier QID (a set of attributes such as gender and zip code) can be used to identify an individual after linking with publicly available resources such as voter registration list. In order to address this linking attack [1], Sweeney and Samarati proposed k-anonymity model [4] to ensure that each released data be indistinguishable from at least $(k-1)$ others (i.e., by grouping k individual data based on the QID). In the k-anonymity model, individual re-identifying risk is maintained under an acceptable probability (i.e., $1/k$). However, k-anonymity is found vulnerable against background knowledge attacks by Machanavajjhala et al [5]. When the adversary has additional information about the target, there is a relatively high probability that the target will be identified.

Another privacy model called l-diversity model was proposed in [5] to complement the k-anonymity model. This model requires the representation of sensitive attributes in the released dataset with at least l "well-represented" values. In other words, the l-diversity model ensures the risk of attribute disclosure is maintained under $1/l$. Table 2 is an example of 2-diverse generalization of Table 1. In the first release M_1, all records from Table 1 are partitioned into two equivalence classes, EC_1 and EC_2 and each equivalence class consists of at least two records. Also, the sensitive attribute has at least two diseases. Note that the patient's name in Table 2 will not be released and they are included for illustration purpose only.

Table 2. A 2-diverse microdata release at t_1

EC_i	Gender	Age	Zip	Disease	Patient
1	Male	[13-15]	278*	Flu	Bob
	Male	[13-15]	278*	Asthma	Sam
2	Female	[48-50]	278*	Cancer	Yuki
	Female	[48-50]	278*	Diabetes	Jane
	Female	[48-50]	278*	Heart Disease	Ellen

The microdata in Table 2 can prevent the attacker from inferring more than $1/2$ confidence on any particular patient. However, this protection is only possible for static release. If the original dataset is updated with insertions of new data or deletions of exiting records, the attacker can cross-examine the sequence of releases to infer the sensitive data of the target.

Assuming that the data publisher needs to update the release at t_1 due to the insertion of Alice's record [Female, 19, 27835, gastritis] and the deletion of Jane's record [Female, 50, 27875, cancer]. The data publisher inserts Alice into EC_1 and removes Jane from EC_2. As shown in Table 3, the second release M_2 at t_2 is still adhere to 2-diversity. Also, the gender attribute in the EC_1 has been generalized in order to prevent the attacker from knowing Alice's record (the only female in the EC_1).

Table 3. A 2-diverse microdata release at t_2

EC_i	Gender	Age	Zip	Disease	Patient
1	Teenager	[13-19]	278*	Flu	Bob
	Teenager	[13-19]	278*	Asthma	Sam
	Teenager	[13-19]	278*	Gastritis	Alice
2	Female	[48-50]	278*	Cancer	Yuki
	Female	[48-50]	278*	Heart Disease	Ellen

Now, assuming that the attacker has access to both releases (M_1 and M_2) at t_1 and t_2 and the QID of a target. The attacker is able to infer a particular patient by cross-examine the sequence of releases. For instance, if the adversary knows that Alice, a youth adult was admitted to the hospital at t_2. After referring to M_1 and M_2, the attacker can conclude with high probability that Alice has gastritis.

1.2   Our Contributions

This paper presents a secure algorithm to facilitate the re-publication of dynamic big data. In particular, we aim to remove inference channels from the sequence of releases in data re-publication. The attacker should not be able to infer the sensitive value of any data owner with high probability. We use counterfeit records in our algorithm to hide the update patterns of two or more sequence of releases. Also, we propose to utilize counterfeit records to increase the false information in the knowledge learned by the attacker from the released microdata.

2   Preliminary Definitions

We denote T_i as the original dataset at time t_i and T_i^* as the microdata (generalization of T_i) released by the data publisher. The microdata T_i^* consists of d quasi-identifier $QID = \{QI_1, QI_2, \dots QI_d\}$ and a sensitive attribute S. We assume that the quasi-identifier can be either categorical or continuous data while the sensitive attribute is a categorical data from its domain (e.g., disease).

Defining privacy can be a daunting task. The difficulty in defining the privacy is due to the unknown background knowledge of an attacker. Recent works have shown the necessity of considering the attacker's background knowledge when reasoning about data privacy in data publishing [6]. However, in practice, it is hard for the data publisher to know what background knowledge the attacker possesses. In this paper, we assume the attacker knows the existence and the exact QID of his target in the released microdata. Also, the attacker has the access to external resources such as voter registration list.

Definition 1 (inference channel). Let T_i^* and T_{i+1}^* be two sequences of microdata released by the data publisher at time t_1 and t_{i+1}. We say that there is an inference channel between T_i^* and T_{i+1}^* if the attacker is able to infer any data owner with high probability (after cross-examine both releases).

Definition 2 (privacy breach). A privacy breach occurs when an attacker learns the sensitive attribute of any data owner with probability more than ½. We assume that the attacker has access to all the released microdata and already had the background knowledge about the target (i.e., exact QID of the data owner).

Definition 3 (data utility). The content of the released microdata T_i^* must be maintained as rich as the original dataset T_i. In particular, the analysis of T_i^* will provide accurate results as compared to the results obtained from T_i.

Definition 4 (false information). We say that the attacker learns false information if the sensitive value he discovered is wrong or not accurate.

3   Related Works

In the literature, many proposed schemes are aimed at enforcing anonymity and diversity in order to prevent the background knowledge attacks. However, k-anonymity

and l-diversity are insufficient when the adversary has sequential background knowledge. Thereafter, other attacks were discovered in the literature that lead to new
models such as (k, e)-anonymity[7], (X, Y)-anonymity[8], (α, k)-anonymity[9] and
t-closeness[10]. Most of the existing works only consider single-release and static
anonymization. A survey of recent attack models and privacy models in data publishing can be found in [11].

The first study for dynamic data re-publication was investigated in [12]. This work
preserves a weak form of l-diversity to release multiple microdata of the same table.
However, it supports only insertion of new records. Another incremental update method for continuous data publishing was proposed in [13]. These pioneering works
play an important role in dynamic data re-publication but they are not practical for
real life applications. In some applications, the deletion of records is essential (critical
absence problem [14]) and cannot be avoided. Hence, several methods have been
proposed to support both insertions and deletions of records in dynamic re-publication
[14-16].

3.1 m-Invariance

A privacy notion called m-invariance is the first study to address both data insertions
and deletions in dynamic data re-publication [14]. In particular, m-invariance aimed
to prevent the association attack when the attacker cross-examine the new release
with the previously released microdata. The m-invariance model ensures that each
record is assigned to a signature which has the same set of sensitive values (at least m
values). In other words, a record will have the same signature in all the released microdata. Therefore, the attacker is not able to associate an individual with less than m
sensitive values.

In order to achieve m-invariance, counterfeit records are added into some equivalence classes. The size of the counterfeit records in each equivalence class will be
released as auxiliary information to improve the accuracy of the data analysis. Note
that the attacker is not able to distinguish the counterfeit records from the genuine
records in the released microdata. However, the inclusion of counterfeit records may
cause false information in certain cases [17]. For instance, the counterfeit records with
negative reactions will give wrong analysis result to study such as patient's reaction to
certain drugs.

As discussed in [16], m-invariance model is vulnerable to a new attack called value equivalence attack where the sensitive value of an individual can reveal the sensitive value of other individuals. A graph-based anonymization algorithm is proposed in
[16] to address the value equivalence attack.

4   Our Algorithm

The main goal of our algorithm is to prevent any inference channel in the data re-
publication. Similar to approach in [14], we utilize the counterfeit records in our algorithm to ensure that each equivalence class (EC_i) is adhere to l-diverse requirement
and no inference cases can be determined by the attacker. Also, we aim to maintain

the data utility of the released microdata. We will discuss the details of our re-publication algorithm in the following sections.

4.1   Counterfeit Records Generation

The sensitive value of the counterfeit record in the released microdata is chosen from the domain of the sensitive attribute (e.g., disease). The counterfeit records are used to hide the update patterns of two or more sequences of microdata. However, the number of counterfeit records in each release should be controlled and minimized.

In this paper, we consider the release of big data which consists of large amounts of datasets. Therefore, the inclusion of counterfeit records will not degrade the utility of the released microdata in the data analysis. We will illustrate the usage of the counterfeit records in the following sessions.

4.2   Initial Release

At the initial release time t_1, the data publisher partitions all records in T_1 (Table 1) into n equivalence classes $EC = \{EC_1, EC_2, .., EC_n\}$ that comply with the l-diversity requirement (i.e., at least l different values on sensitive attribute). After the partition, the size of each group maybe different due to the number of records in T_1 and the constraints used to meet the l-diversity. Next, a counterfeit record will be added into each EC_i. For instance, records in Table 1 are partitioned into Table 4 where each EC_i consists of a counterfeit record c_{ij}. We denote c_{ij} as the j-th counterfeit record in the equivalence class i (i.e., c_{21} is the 1st counterfeit record in EC_2).

The sensitive values of the counterfeit records can be used to change the l-diversity of the initial microdata. For example, Table 4 is a 3-diverse microdata (after the inclusion of counterfeit records) as compared to 2-diverse in Table 2. However, we can set the counterfeit records to maintain the diversity of the microdata.

Table 4. Dataset partition with counterfeit records.

EC_i	Disease	Patient
	Flu	Bob
1	Asthma	Sam
	Fever (c_{11})	*
	Diabetes	Helen
2	Cancer	Jane
	Heart Disease	Ellen
	Diabetes (c_{21})	*

4.3   Re-publication

After the initial release at t_1, the data publisher needs to update the current release M_i when new records arrive or modification of the existing records is required. The modification is referred to the deletions or changes of the existing records.

Table 5. Anonymized release with insertion

EC_i	Disease	Patient
	Flu	Bob
1	Asthma	Sam
	Gastritis	Alice
	Bronchitis (c_{11})	*
	Diabetes	Helen
2	Cancer	Jane
	Heart Disease	Ellen
	Diabetes (c_{21})	*

Table 6. Anonymized release with deletion

EC_i	Disease	Patient
	Flu	Bob
1	Asthma	Sam
	Gastritis	Alice
	Bronchitis (c_{11})	*
	Diabetes	Helen
2	Cancer (c_{22})	*
	Heart Disease	Ellen
	Diabetes (c_{21})	*

Insertion of New Records. When a new record r_{new} arrives, the data publisher first identifies the EC in the current release M_i which can accommodate r_{new}. If the EC for r_{new} does not exist, a new group will be created. Otherwise, r_{new} will be assigned into the existing EC. For instance, when Alice's record [Female, 19, 27835, gastritis] arrives, we can insert it into EC_1 of Table 4. In order to protect the newly added record, we can change the value of c_{11} to bronchitis. By doing this, the attacker only learns that the new record being added is either gastritis or bronchitis. The second release M_2 at t_2 is shown in Table 5.

Deletion of the Existing Records. When we want to remove any existing record r_{old} from the current release M_i, the deleted record will be maintained in the new release with a counterfeit record. For instance, if we intend to remove Jane's record from Table 5, a new counterfeit record c_{22} will be used to replace Jane's record. By doing this, the attacker will not be able to detect the changes in the two releases.

Update of the Existing Records. When the existing record needs to be updated (i.e., a patient is recovering from a disease, but at the same time he/she was infected with a new disease), direct modification of the existing record allows the attacker to learn which record has been modified after examine a series of published microdata. In view of this, any changes of the existing records should be covered by the counterfeit records. Since we have at least one counterfeit record in each equivalence class, the modification of an existing record will be covered in the subsequence release.

4.4   Manipulation of the Equivalence Classes

After several updates, the number of counterfeit records in any equivalence class will be increased. For each new record arrives, the data publisher first selects one of the available counterfeit records $(j-1)$ in EC to replace the record. For example, if a new record in EC_2 arrives, either c_{12} or c_{22} can be used to place the new record. After the insertion of the new record (i.e, by replacing the counterfeit record c_{12}), the modification in the new release must not give a big different with other releases. The remaining counterfeit record c_{22} in EC_2 will be used to maintain the similarity pattern between the releases. Note that we have to maintain at least one counterfeit record in each equivalence class.

In some cases, the new records cannot be assigned into the existing EC while the existing records need to be deleted from the EC. When the number of counterfeit records increases, we can split the existing EC into two or more classes. As shown in Table 6, there are two counterfeit records in EC_2. After splitting EC_2, we have two new equivalence classes and each of them accommodates one counterfeit record.

Also, we can combine two or more equivalence classes after several releases in order to reduce the number of counterfeit records used in the microdata. The data publisher examines and tests if the newly generated microdata can be used together with other releases to compromise the privacy of any data owner. If it is free from the attacks, the data publisher publishes it as the next available microdata.

5   Analysis and Discussion

In our algorithm, the counterfeit records are used to anonymized the microdata when insertion, deletion, and updates are required. The number of counterfeit records inserted into the microdata plays an important role in preventing the data leakage. First, we can use them to prevent the attacker from knowing which record has been added into the new release by comparing it with other releases. Secondly, counterfeit records can be used to temporary *freeze* the update patterns of several releases. Since we have at least one counterfeit record in each equivalence class, it is easy for the data publisher to maintain the same set of sensitive values in two or more sequences of microdata. However, we need to ensure that the data quality of the new release is maintained and can be used for analysis.

Generally, we can assume that the big data collected are not commonly removed in a big volume. Also, the number of counterfeit records in the released microdata is relatively small. Therefore, our solution can ensure that the data utility of the anonymized microdata can be maintained at an acceptable rate.

5.1   Generating False Information

In [14], $n - 1$ counterfeit records are used to reduce the false information rate. We note that the number of counterfeit records in each equivalence class will be reduced when new records arrive. The number of counterfeit records will increase if there are many records need to be deleted. However, we aim to maintain a number of counterfeit records in each equivalence class in order to increase the rate of false information learned by the attacker.

5.2   Comparison with the Existing Work

The idea of our solution is motivated by the approach in [14]. Similarly, we utilize the counterfeit records in our algorithm to ensure that the attacker will not be able to infer the sensitive information of any data owner. Unlike solution in [14], we do not publish the auxiliary information to the data recipient. Instead, the number of counterfeit records used is kept private and only known to the data publisher. Interestingly, this can increase the rate of false information learned by the attacker. For an example, when a new record arrives, one or more counterfeit records can be set to a disease that is different (or same) from the one arrived. The attacker will see several changes of the disease but it is hard to determine the genuine one from the mixture. Hence, with high probability, the attacker will learn false information about the sensitive attribute.

6   Conclusion and Future Work

In the real world environment, the update operations of microdata such as insertion of new records, deletion and updates of the existing records are commonly happen. In this paper, we study the re-publication of dynamic sensitive data in a privacy preserving environment. The usage of counterfeit records allows the data publisher to hide the modification patterns of two or more sequences of microdata. The attacker with background knowledge about an individual is not able to learn the exact record of his target. Therefore, our solution is secure for dynamic data re-publication.

Most of the existing solutions in the literature applied the same level of privacy protection to all the data owners without considering the actual concern of each data owner. However, to enforce the same level of privacy protection to every data owner is not necessary. For example, a patient who suffers from flu may not think the symptoms are sensitive as compared with diseases such as HIV or genetic disorder. In the future work, we aim to study the user-defined privacy protection in data re-publication.

References

1. Sweeney, L.: k-anonymity: a model for protecting privacy. Int. J. Uncertain. Fuzziness Knowl.-Based Syst. 10, 557–570 (2002)
2. Barbaro, M., Zeller, T.: A Face Is Exposed for AOL Searcher No. 4417749. The New York Times (2006)
3. de Montjoye, Y.-A., Hidalgo, C.A., Verleysen, M., Blondel, V.D.: Unique in the Crowd: The privacy bounds of human mobility. Nature Scientific Reports 3 (2013)
4. Samarati, P., Sweeney, L.: Generalizing data to provide anonymity when disclosing information (abstract). In: Proceedings of the Seventeenth ACM SIGACT-SIGMOD-SIGART Symposium on Principles of Database Systems, p. 188. ACM, Seattle (1998)
5. Machanavajjhala, A., Kifer, D., Gehrke, J., Venkitasubramaniam, M.: l-diversity: Privacy beyond k-anonymity. ACM Trans. Knowl. Discov. Data 1, 3 (2007)
6. Martin, D.J., Kifer, D., Machanavajjhala, A., Gehrke, J., Halpern, J.Y.: Worst-Case Background Knowledge for Privacy-Preserving Data Publishing. In: 23rd IEEE International Conference on Data Engineering (ICDE), pp. 126–135 (2007)
7. Zhang, Q., Koudas, N., Srivastava, D., Yu, T.: Aggregate Query Answering on Anonymized Table. In: IEEE 23rd International Conference on Data Engineering, Istanbul, Turkey, pp. 116–125 (2007)

8. Wang, K., Fung, B.C.M.: Anonymizing sequential releases. In: Proceedings of the 12th ACM SIGKDD International Conference on Knowledge Discovery and Data Mining, pp. 414–423. ACM, Philadelphia (2006)
9. Wong, R.C.-W., Li, J., Fu, A.W.-C., Wang, K. (alpha, k)-anonymity: an enhanced k-anonymity model for privacy preserving data publishing. In: Proceedings of the 12th ACM SIGKDD International Conference on Knowledge Discovery and Data Mining, pp. 754–759. ACM, Philadelphia (2006)
10. Li, N., Li, T., Venkatasubramanian, S.: t-Closeness: Privacy Beyond k-Anonymity and l-Diversity. In: International Conference on Data Engineering (ICDE), Istanbul, Turkey, pp. 106–115 (2007)
11. Fung, B.C.M., Wang, K., Chen, R., Yu, P.S.: Privacy-preserving data publishing: A survey of recent developments. ACM Comput. Surv. 42, 1–53 (2010)
12. Byun, J.-W., Sohn, Y., Bertino, E., Li, N.: Secure anonymization for incremental datasets. In: Jonker, W., Petković, M. (eds.) SDM 2006. LNCS, vol. 4165, pp. 48–63. Springer, Heidelberg (2006)
13. Pei, J., Xu, J., Wang, Z., Wang, W., Wang, K.: Maintaining K-Anonymity against Incremental Updates. In: Proceedings of the 19th International Conference on Scientific and Statistical Database Management, p. 5. IEEE Computer Society (2007)
14. Xiao, X., Tao, Y.: m-Invariance: Towards Privacy Preserving Re-publication of Dynamic Datasets. In: ACM SIGMOD International Conference on Management of Data, Beijing, China, pp. 689–700 (2007)
15. Bu, Y., Fu, A.W.C., Wong, R.C.W., Chen, L., Li, J.: Privacy preserving serial data publishing by role composition. Proc. VLDB Endow. 1, 845–856 (2008)
16. He, Y., Barman, S., Naughton, J.F.: Preventing equivalence attacks in updated, anonymized data. In: Proceedings of the 2011 IEEE 27th International Conference on Data Engineering, pp. 529–540. IEEE Computer Society (2011)
17. Fung, B.C.M., Wang, K., Fu, A.W.-C., Pei, J.: Anonymity for continuous data publishing. In: Proceedings of the 11th International Conference on Extending Database Technology: Advances in Database Technology, pp. 264–275. ACM, Nantes (2008)

Author Index